No. 3047
$34.95

80386 ASSEMBLY LANGUAGE

A Complete Tutorial and Subroutine Library

Penn Brumm and Don Brumm

TAB Professional and Reference Books

Division of TAB BOOKS Inc.
Blue Ridge Summit, PA

FIRST EDITION
FIRST PRINTING

Library of Congress Cataloging in Publication Data

Brumm, Penn.
80386 assembly language : a complete tutorial and subroutine library / by Penn Brumm and Don Brumm.
p. cm.
Bibliography: p.
Includes index.
ISBN 0-8306-9047-6 ISBN 0-8306-9347-5 (pbk.)
1. Intel 80386 (Microprocessor)—Programming. 2. Assembler language (Computer program language) I. Brumm, Don. II. Title. III. Title: Eighty thousand three hundred eighty-six assembly language.

QA76.8.I2928B78 1988 88-17070
005.265—dc 19 CIP

TAB BOOKS Inc. offers software for sale. For information and a catalog, please contact TAB Software Department, Blue Ridge Summit, PA 17294-0850.

Questions regarding the content of this book should be addressed to:

Reader Inquiry Branch
TAB BOOKS Inc.
Blue Ridge Summit, PA 17294-0214

Cover photograph courtesy of Intel Corporation.

Contents

Introduction

Software needs are increasing dramatically, but the number of people available to supply that demand is increasing at a *much* slower rate. The U.S. Department of Defense figures show that qualified software personnel increases at a 4 percent annual rate, while their average productivity increases at about the same rate. Demand—that number of jobs that could be filled—is increasing at 12 percent per year. This is where you come in.

In addition to a relative dearth of people to do the work, the percentage of total system life-cycle costs attributable to software has risen steadily over the past 30 years. Software costs were less than 20 percent of total life-cycle costs in 1955. By 1985, software costs exceeded 80 percent. It's estimated that the total costs for software will double between 1985 and 1990.

Intended Audience

This book is designed to help you get to where you want to be, when you're trying to write code to solve a problem. Don and I included some topics that are background, in case you're experienced in one area and not another. We don't expect you to be expert in everything. In case you don't have time to key in all the routines, you can get a disk which contains them from the publisher.

The information in the book assumes that you have done some assembly language programming using MS-DOS (a recent version or a look-alike). It also assumes that you generally understand how assembly language works. If you code some clever routines, Don and I would like to hear from you. Write to us in care of TAB. Also write to us if you find an error, since they can creep into the best of code.

There are many operating systems for the IBM Personal Computer (and clones). This book concentrates on Microsoft's MS-DOS, at level 3.1 and higher. The programs, procedures, and shorter routines were written on an 80386-based computer (a specially-built-for-us clone), with MS-DOS 3.1, using the Microsoft Macro Assembler, level 5.0.

Don and I have a combined 45 years in the technical side of data processing: Don from the early 1960s and me (Penn) from the late 1960s. We both got started with IBM mainframe systems, only discovering the fascinating world of owning our own microcomputers in the mid-1970s. We've been part of a team that programmed an IBM mainframe operating system from scratch, written compilers, done network programming, and been systems engineers. Don stayed in systems software programming and I finally opted for management (Product Support, Quality Assurance, and Software Development). We now own (and use extensively) five microcomputers, two of which (an 80286-based and an 80386-based) were used for this book; the 80286 was used for the word processing, while the 80386 was used for coding. We have four printers, from a dot-matrix, to a daisy wheel, to a brand-new laser printer (that works at a speedy 8 pages of camera-ready output per minute). Don has a college degree in mathematics and I have an MBA. To us, data processing is the only industry in which to work.

Book Contents

Chapter 1 gives you a background on systems design, going into structured design, database design, program coding, testing, maintenance, and debugging.

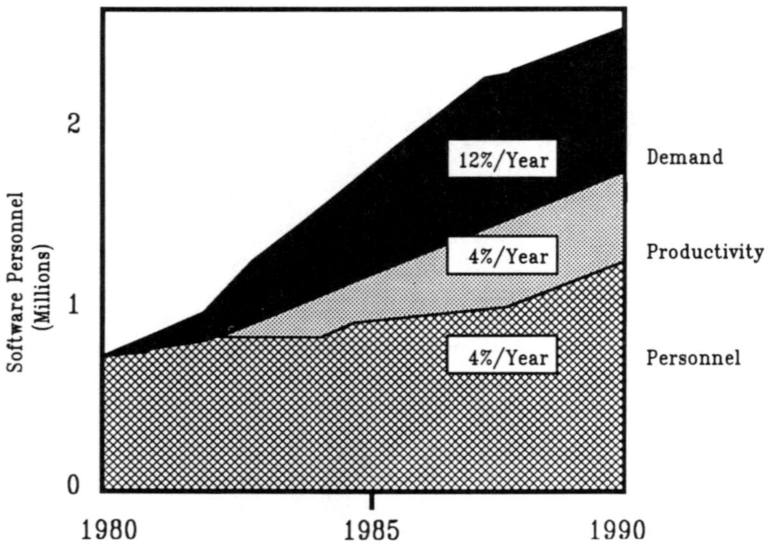

Growth of programmer demand, productivity, and personnel.

Chapter 2 is set aside to discuss general programming tips and ways to make MS-DOS work for you. Both Don and I like to get productive as soon as possible and we think you're the same, so we included a working program skeleton. You can use the skeleton to try out some of the things you find in this book. Simply insert the code in the right places in the skeleton, then assemble, link, and run. Included also in Chapter 2 are tips on how to assemble and link your code. You'll be introduced to functions and MS-DOS interrupts that make your programming life a *lot* easier.

Chapter 3 addresses the 80386 for the first time, with programming notes and tips that we found when we first began to program with Intel's new processor. We talk about "traps" you can fall into when you work with memory, descriptors, registers, tasks, privilege, protection, and test and debug.

Starting with Chapter 4, we provide background and toolkit programs, a mix of complete programs and working procedures and pieces which you can add as integral parts of whatever programs you write. Chapter 5 talks about masked and unmasked exceptions, 80386 processor interrupts, with toolkit programs.

Chapter 6 goes on to talk about bit and string manipulation and shifts. We show you how to convert uppercase to lower and vice versa and also how to allocate from a bitmap. The string operations are the standard, general ones you need for programs, such as finding one string within another.

Chapter 7 goes into 16- and 32-bit code conversion, with background information about the 80386 data handling. The toolkit programs convert hex to binary, binary to hex, ASCII to EBCDIC, EBCDIC to ASCII, BCD to ASCII and back. It goes on to show how to go from single to double precision and back. In case you're an IBM EBCDIC-based person, we included a procedure, FLIPS, that changes the System/370 data storage method to an Intel data storage method (which, by the way, are logically incompatible and confusing the first time you run into the differences).

Chapter 8 discusses input/output. It begins with background on the 80386 I/O. The toolkit programs show you how to handle input editing, reading input character by character, writing output character by character, and reading and writing from files. Toolkit procedures show you how to create a file, close one, and perform EOF handling. Also shown is how to check for existing and nonexisting files, and to count characters in files.

Algorithms are covered in Chapter 9 along with background information on the various subjects. The toolkit programs include binary search, two different sorts, buffer handling, and encrypting/decrypting. Chapter 10 starts you on graphics, with bit shifting, and the design of a character set. Elementary graphics are demonstrated with screen clearing, cursor positioning, line smoothing, point plotting, line drawing, and filling a rectangular area. Of interest, one of the programs shows how to get into graphics mode and do direct I/O to a graphics controller chip.

There are eight appendices. Appendix A covers an overview of the 80386 architecture. Appendix B describes 80386 registers in detail, showing the various flags and bits you'll use once you get familiar with what the 80386 offers. Included is the EFLAGS (the System Flags Register), the Control Register (CR0), Test Registers TR6 and TR7, Selector flags, segment descriptor flags, an alphabetic

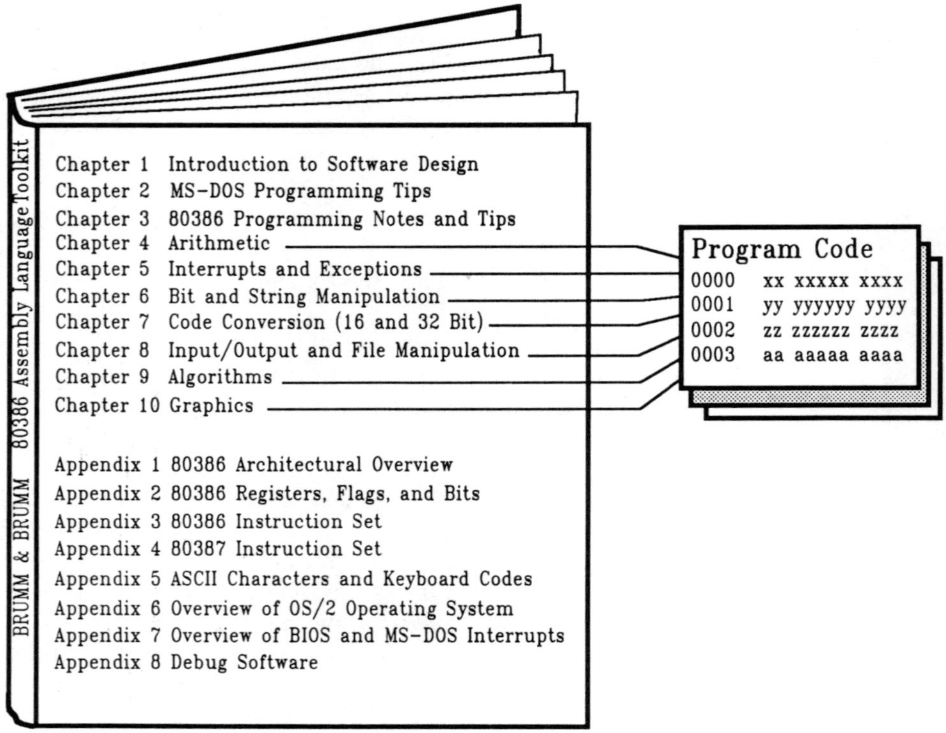

Location of toolkit code.

listing of 80386 registers, flags, and bits. Appendix C gives you an overview on the 80386 full instruction set. If you want a more complete discussion on either the architecture or the instruction set, read TAB's *80386: A Programming and Design Handbook*, which we wrote using an 80386 processor loaned to us by Intel (a *very* helpful group of people), and which is available with updated information.

Appendix D gives you the complete instruction set for the 80387 numeric coprocessor—very useful if you have one of these in your system. Appendix E shows you an ASCII to decimal to hex to binary translation, with an illustration of the "box graphics." Appendix F gives you an introduction to Microsoft's new operating system, OS/2. The subject is too broad for this type of book, but we thought you'd like to know something about OS/2 and its differences from MS-DOS. Appendix G gives a thorough overview of the BIOS and MS-DOS interrupts, one of the most thorough that appears anywhere. Appendix H walks you through a debug package (SYMDEB) to give you an example of what debug software packages offer in case you're looking to purchase one. At the back of the book, you'll find a complete glossary, in case you find a word or phrase whose meaning eludes you.

Assembly Language

For some of the procedures included in this book to be useful, they must be combined with other routines to form complete programs. This can be done by including them when you link edit, or by copying the code into your main-line program. We recommend that you divide your code into procedures, and assemble and link each (to check for assembly errors) before you combine them into one larger program. You cut down on the number of hard-to-find bugs this way.

When you get to the debug process, you might want to take a look at Appendix H. We show you a debugger, SYMDEB, and many of the more useful SYMDEB commands. Using debug software is a time-saver in even the short-run time frame.

Assembly language is the fastest and most powerful language for programming, giving you the same kind of control a stick-shift transmission does compared to an automatic transmission. Even for experienced people, however, assembly language can be time-consuming, especially when you have to write routines to perform specific tasks that you do over and over. You keep thinking you'll build a library of routines, but you're busy and that task stays on a back burner. The aim of this book is to make it easy for you to incorporate fast, efficient 80386 assembly language routines into your programs. And to not have to worry about building a library. It's here for you.

1

Introduction to Software Design

Programmers act as the link between a problem (or process to be computerized) and its successful solution on a computer. As programmers, you share in the definition and specification of the problem itself, as well as the design and coding of algorithms to be used in its solution.

After being assigned the problem, you have several actions to complete: define the scope of the problem, design the detail structure of the implementation, select the most suitable programming language, write and debug the necessary programs, and provide clear and complete documentation for both the user and other programmers who later may need to modify your program(s). To do this in the best way possible, you learn to structure programs, to make them efficient, to make them usable, to document them, and to test them for errors.

Structured Design

Structured design means the design of both the components of a system and the interrelationship between those components in the best possible way. Structured design has a significant effect on programming and program maintainability: a structured program's elements and their interdependences can be graphed on a structure chart and quickly understood. The quicker the grasp, the shorter the start-up time for new programmers.

Well-structured programs have five traits. First, the total program easily divides into modules arranged in a structure that defines their logical relationships.

That is, A links to B, which links to C, and so on. Second, execution flows from module to module in easy-to-understand schemes, where control always enters the module at one unique point and always exits at another unique point. After each subroutine call, control always returns to the calling module or program.

The third property of a structured program is that each program variable serves only one purpose, and the scope and limit of the variable is controlled and clear. For example, a variable called "Index" might be used as a step value in a loop and is not also used as a condition flag. Fourth, error processing follows normal program control (except in the case of unrecoverable errors). And finally, each module is documented to explain its function, data requirements, how it is invoked, and what it invokes.

Figure 1-1 gives an overview of structured design. Now let's look at each aspect in more detail.

- ☐ Divide each program into independent pieces, called *modules.* A module is a self-contained unit whose code is physically and logically separate from the code of any other module in the program.
- ☐ Limit independent program pieces to less than 100 instructions. This number isn't "set in concrete" but is used to help you concentrate on keeping modules small enough to handle.
- ☐ Relate the modules to one another in a hierarchical manner. That is, each lower level in the structure represents a more detailed function.
- ☐ Begin each module with a common block that explains its function, the values passed to it, the values returned, what modules call this one, and what modules this one calls. See the programs included in this book for examples of this point.
- ☐ Avoid unnecessary labels. Also, don't use labels as comments.

In Structured Design:

- **Keep module size small**
- **Design top-down**
- **Document Internally**
- **Use labels sparingly**
- **Make variable names meaningful**
- **Limit branches to within modules**
- **Keep code simple & straightforward**

Fig. 1-1. Structured design overview.

- ☐ Make all variable and module names meaningful. The names should suggest the function they perform and their purpose in the program.
- ☐ Begin variable names, ones that belong to the same table or to the same module, with the same prefix.
- ☐ Limit the scope of a branch statement to the module in which it occurs.
- ☐ Avoid obscure (tricky) code.

Structured techniques also provide some basic project management assistance. Project status information can be attached to the graphic descriptions (the basic blocks in the graphic chart). Managers can then see the status for use in status reporting. If you're managing your own job, at any point in the development cycle you can tell, at a glance, just how far into the job you are.

Efficiency

Once you have the basic structuring concepts in mind, then tackle simple efficiency techniques. Efficiency is the extent to which a program performs its intended function without wasting machine resources such as memory, storage, channel capacity, and execution time.

Efficiency is important—but not when taken to extremes. Some programmers spend so much time being certain that they use the fewest possible lines of code that they lose sight of the fact that the program should be easy to use and maintain. Some things to keep in mind are:

- ☐ Modularize the program into logical pieces, e.g., keep I/O in one section, error handling in another, and so on.
- ☐ Use only a small subset of the program's pages at any point during execution, which aids in the efficient use of memory.
- ☐ Eliminate all unused labels and expressions, to take full advantage of compiler and assembler optimizations. If it's not used, don't put it in.
- ☐ Isolate exception routines and error-handling routines in separate modules. Since errors are out of the mainstream of processing, don't clutter the main line of code with their presence.
- ☐ Process outside a loop all code which does not *need* to be processed within the loop.
- ☐ Use integer arithmetic whenever possible, instead of floating-point.
- ☐ Avoid mixed data types in arithmetic or logical operations whenever possible to eliminate unnecessary data conversions.

- ☐ Align program variables in storage.
- ☐ Avoid nonstandard subroutine and/or function calls.
- ☐ In a complex logical condition, test the most likely True condition first.
- ☐ Use the most efficient data type for subscripts.

Program Usability

Usability is difficult to define and to measure in quantitative fashion. End users see usability in ways that depend on their experience, how frequently they use a system, their ideas of human factoring, how critical the system is to getting a task done, and exactly how the software interacts with them. Programmers define usability as the ease of maintenance/enhancement/bug-fixing. Program managers often see it as how many lines of correct code can be written within a time limit. No matter what criteria are used, making programs more usable is very effective, even if the programmer is the intended final user.

Generally speaking, a usable program minimizes confusion, is easy to operate/run, and is tolerant of user errors and changing needs. Usability, simply, is the extent to which a program is convenient, practical, and easy to use. The following is a usability checklist with which to measure your programs.

- ☐ Is there a HELP feature for every function and available on request?
- ☐ Is a correct, complete explanation of each command and/or operating mode available on request?
- ☐ Can the user learn the program without human assistance?
- ☐ Does the program allow interruption of a task and is it able to restart or resume at logical points?
- ☐ Does the program allow the user to cancel it, without harmful side effects?
- ☐ Does the program have detailed, understandable prompting for input and processes, such as starting a printer?
- ☐ Are the error messages understandable? Are there suggestions as *how* to correct the errors?
- ☐ Are all input formats, requirements, and restrictions clearly explained?
- ☐ Does the program do the "housekeeping" such as deleting temporary files?
- ☐ Can the program handle typing errors?

- ☐ Can the program accept reduced input when actions are to be repeated?
- ☐ Can commands be abbreviated?
- ☐ Does the program edit/validate input data?
- ☐ Does the program allow the user to extend the commands?
- ☐ Does the program allow an experienced user to work with a faster version, such as abbreviated commands, default values, and so on?
- ☐ Are there audit trails so that users and programmers can figure out what went wrong?

If a program is used over a long period of time, it's best to make it easy to use. Human memory is tricky—people forget just that tiny detail that makes a program work correctly instead of incorrectly.

Documentation

Well-documented programs are easier to work with than undocumented programs. The key is that a program should be its own documentation. This section describes "documentation" as that needed by programmers. Not addressed is user documentation, external manuals, and operations documentation.

Program documentation describes the program components and data, what the program does, plus why and how the program works as it does. There are two types of documentation, internal and external.

External documentation is the *written* assumptions you make before you write code, the hard-copy program listings, and the typed description of inputs, outputs, and the processes of the program(s). This external documentation is separate from source code. If the program is well-structured, often the programmer allows external documentation to lapse behind the internal.

Internal documentation is those "remarks" that appear in the actual program source code, the well-defined variables, and the module headers. This is the documentation that doesn't get lost when you need it most. And it is the most accurate documentation about the program. Take a look at the internal documentation on each of the toolkit programs included in this book. No matter if you type in the code or copy it from the available diskette, the comments ensure that you'll know what the code does, and how it does it.

Creating Databases

After deciding the major structure of your program(s), next define any databases you'll need. A database is an integrated source of data that is accessed and controlled by a database management system. Figure 1-2 shows an overview of a database system. Databases are used to store information that users need for future processing, so design and structure your databases just as carefully as you do your programs. Before you design a *new* database, however, find out if the user already has something that can be used: Can part of an existing one and part of another be used? If not, then design a new one.

First, determine what files are needed in the database, by finding out what information the user needs. Ensure that each file contains the key fields needed for the end-user output(s). Define where data should be stored, e.g., floppy or hard disk, and determine how often it will be updated.

Finally, decide what software and database backup plans should be set in place. For instance, will the user back it up each time it is used, or once a week, or when?

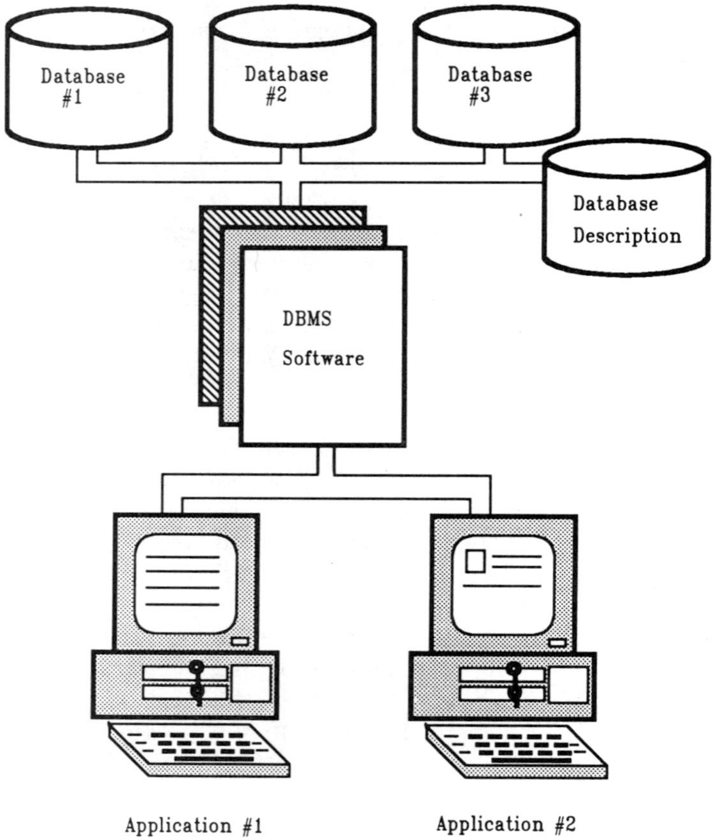

Fig. 1-2. Overview of a database management system.

Then, after the basic design, you begin your detail design:

- ☐ First, cluster the fields into groups (records), each of which forms the basis for detailed handling. Decide if new records will be created from the ones the user puts in. Are there edit or other controls that each input record must be compared to?
- ☐ Second, check each input field. Can it be simplified in its handling and storage? Be sure that each field has a specific name, specific use, and specific storage. Are there dependencies among fields? Or among different records? For instance, in a check balancing and recording system, should space be left for checks that have not yet returned, or should the program only capture those that have returned?
- ☐ Third, should space be left for future growth? If so, how much—20 percent, 50 percent? Does the user have any idea how the data has historically increased and/or decreased? Are there calendar year-ends or fiscal year-ends that will create data which must be stored for the remainder of the year?

At this point, sketch a quick chart (such as Fig. 1-3) that lists the fields of the various databases, flagging the key field of each database which ties that series of records to all other databases.

Interrupt Handling: Transfers, Subroutines, and Macros

After you've defined the program structure and the databases, you next decide how the pieces interact. They do this by the main procedure allowing interrupts, calling subroutines, or invoking macros.

When activated, most modules begin execution at the beginning, at the first executable statement. Once the interrupt occurs, processor control transfers to the process that asked for the interrupt. A jump is made out of the current executing sequence with the condition that control eventually be returned to the execution sequence from which the jump was made. The jump can be either conditional or unconditional.

A conditional transfer always refers to a target location *explicitly* (by name, address, or other identifier). Once the interrupt has been handled, control returns to the original module. A *return* always transfers to the location of an instruction in the sequence associated with the most recently conditioned transfer for which a return has not yet been made. In this way, the pattern of conditional transfers and returns always defines a fully nested set of activations. Figure 1-4 shows how the logic appears in a block diagram of transfers and returns. This system is hierarchical, since the conditioned transfer sets up its origin as a sequence having control over the target sequence.

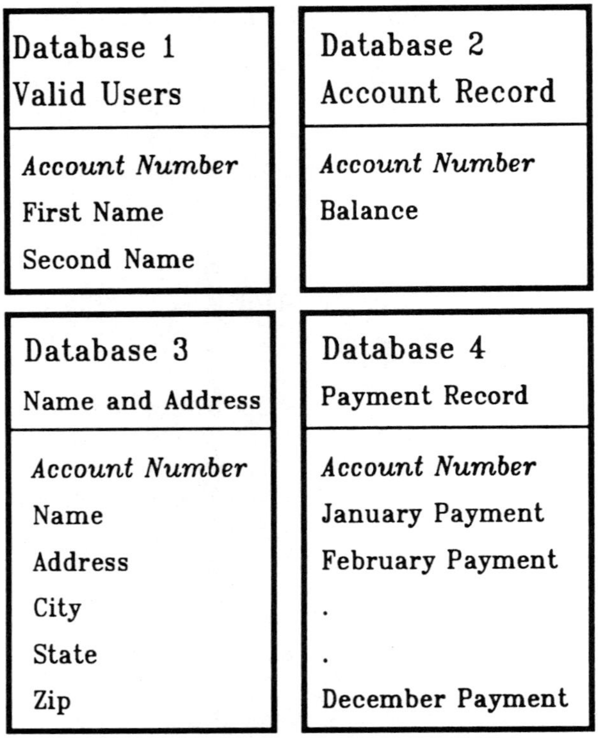

Fig. 1-3. Data dependencies. Here four databases are tied together with one field, the Account Number. Four different programs can update the databases, or any number at the convenience/design of the programmer.

The unconditional transfer carries no tacit condition of return. This transfer sets up a new control stream, activating the module as a parallel or coordination process.

A *subroutine* is a module activated at execution time by a conditioned transfer. Subroutines, as a general rule, can accept arguments and cannot be executed by themselves as standalone code. Historically, subroutines were called "closed routines" or "off-line subroutines" to differentiate them from a separate process called a *macro*.

A macro is a module whose body is effectively copied in-line during translation (for example, compilation or assembly) as the result of being invoked by name. The process of copying in-line is called *expansion.* A macro is expanded as a result of being invoked. Translation of the macro into the target may happen before, during, or after expansion, although the current trend prefers translation after expansion.

```
Line 1 – Program Initialization
Line 2
Line 3 – Calls Subroutine 1
        Subroutine 1 – Entry Point
        Subroutine Process
        Subroutine 1 – Exit (to Line 4)
Line 4
Line 5 – Calls Subroutine 2
        Subroutine 2 – Entry Point
        Subroutine – Calls Subroutine 3
              Subroutine 3 – Entry Point
              Subroutine Process
              Subroutine 3 – Exit (to Subroutine 2 Process)
        Subroutine Process
        Subroutine 2 – Exit (to Line 6)
Line 6
Line 7 – Program Termination
```

Fig. 1-4. A nested set of jumps/activities.

Termination Processing

We've seen how interrupts can transfer control to a second set of code, call a subroutine, or invoke a macro. Once the program has finished its required work, it's time to terminate. When terminating, the software should "clean up" before exiting, in either a normal exit or an unexpected exit which causes (or should cause) a dump. This clean-up includes closing of files, elimination of temporary files, and doing final input/output (I/O) to clear all buffers.

Writing a Program

Concept Framework Definition

Now that you have the design concepts in mind, it's time to specify the handling of individual programs. The first step is to define the basic assumptions. For instance, you'll write the program on (and for) a microcomputer that has a certain number of diskette drives, a hard disk, and perhaps a tape backup. That computer has a set number of bytes of memory for the program and can display to a screen and write out to a printer. List those assumptions.

For example, your target system may have: (1) an 80386 processor with an 80387 numeric coprocessor; (2) 640 kilobytes of memory; (3) two floppy disk drives (double density with about 360,000 bytes storage each); (4) Epson FX-85 parallel printer; (5) Microsoft MS-DOS 3.1; (6) a monochrome monitor with 24 lines, each of 80 characters; and (7) the *Microsoft Macro Assembler*, level 5.0.

Your software assumptions may be: (1) data will be in standard character strings (A–Z, a–z), numbers (0–9), and certain special characters (period or decimal point, comma, and dollar sign); (2) no number will be larger than can be stored in a double word; and (3) the instruction set is the 80386.

The second step is to list the specific objectives, remembering that most problems arise from a design that's too limited or one that's incomplete. Good system design avoids excessive complexity—so don't be afraid to simplify, simplify, simplify. The objective here is to decide on the pieces that fit together into a complete software program which solves the current needs, while staying flexible for future requirements. Most programs evolve in a natural process as changes come along; that's part of software life.

For now, decide what inputs will come in, what outputs will be needed, and how the inputs will get to the outputs. For instance, in a checkbook balancing program, the user may type in a series of numeric digits (their bank check numbers), and a dollar amount. The program reads from the keyboard, stores the check numbers into an array, keeps a running total of the dollar amounts, and prints a single-line item to the printer. There may be constants to include in the program, such as a bank charge if the balance falls below a certain amount. At the end of the program, the user may wish a printed balance. That balance should be saved, so the program needs to write the check numbers and the running balance to permanent storage.

The third step in the overall design is to divide those objectives into blocks that flow in a sequential manner. The result is an overall flowchart as shown in Fig. 1-5.

Fourth, define what algorithms may be needed. That is, are there certain routines that will be used again and again, such as date verification? An algorithm is a finite series of steps that performs a single task. A result is reached with relatively few instructions; often a single algorithm is a subroutine (or handled as one).

When the main program calls the subroutine, control passes temporarily to that subroutine and should be passed back when the subroutine ends. Data can be handed to the subroutine by passing parameters, or the subroutine can be written so that it "knows" where the data will be. This last design decision is how most of the procedures in this book are written.

The technique where data is transferred to a subroutine and the subroutine computation results are transferred back to the main routine are called *calling sequence* and *exit sequence.* The main routine has a calling sequence that stores data in registers or specific memory locations before the call to the subroutine. At the

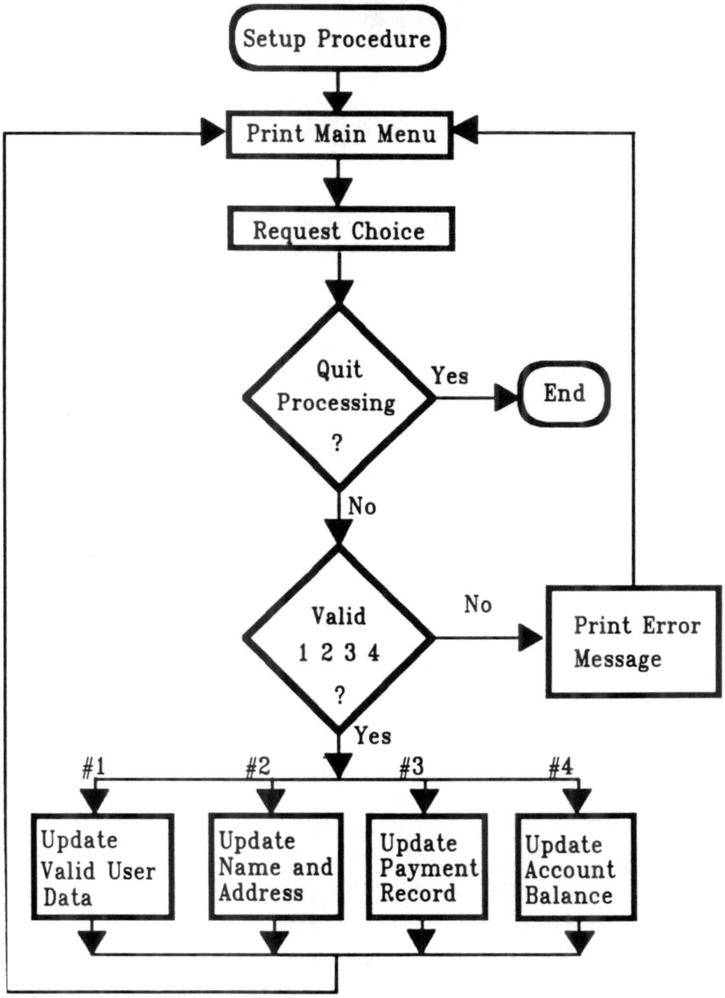

Fig. 1-5. Overview flowchart.

end of the subroutine, data is also stored in registers or specific memory locations before returning to the main program or the calling routine.

Once to this step, review the toolkit programs that are included in this book. There will be a lot of already written code that can be simply "plugged in" to your program, before you have to write any new code. This plug-in shortens your development time because you don't have to reinvent what's already invented and tested. Once you write the final program, you must test it.

Program Testing

Testability is defined as the ease with which program correctness can be demonstrated. Testability is an important program property when building high-quality software packages. In many software shops, the test process consumes approximately half of the developmemt budget. And rightfully so, when the test dollars are spent in prevention rather than "fix it after release."

The cost of correcting errors in the analysis and design phases of development is only a small fraction of the costs incurred by later correction. In fact, the cost of error correction at the actual-use phase can be 100 times more than the cost of correction during system analysis. Testing reduces these costs.

Testing a program involves selecting a set of test cases and executing the program with each case. Selecting those test cases is guided by the following:

- ☐ Each program instruction and each path should be executed at least once.
- ☐ The more heavily used paths should be tested much more thoroughly.
- ☐ All modules should be tested individually before they are combined. Then the paths between the modules should be tested.
- ☐ Test the program(s)/system as a whole, as the parts may add up to something other than what was originally designed.
- ☐ Testing should proceed from the most simple case to the most complex.
- ☐ Tests should include normal processing cases, extreme cases, and all error conditions.

Most errors that occur in software are attributable to the earliest phases: analysis and design. A study done in 1980 by TRW showed that 64 percent of software errors arose from the analysis and design phase, as shown in Fig. 1-6. Only 30 percent of those errors were being detected before the software was delivered for acceptance testing. On the other hand, 75 percent of coding (36 percent of total errors) were detected before delivery, which illustrates the importance of testing during early development stages.

Reliability is a measure of the absence of errors. What we're talking about here is a measure of your ability to *demonstrate* the absence of those errors. The simpler the program, the easier it is to demonstrate its correctness. Simplicity in this case means that the program is modular and well-structured.

Software Maintenance

Modifying existing programs is the most basic maintenance function and perhaps the most challenging of all programming activities. Not only must you make

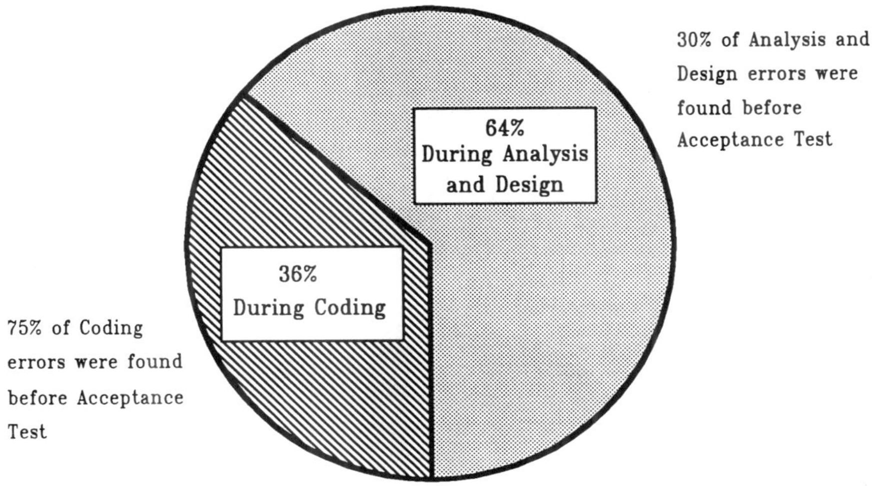

Fig. 1-6. Errors found in software.

certain that the new logic is correct, but also that the program continues to perform its functions correctly. Undesired "side effects" can result from even the most innocent-seeming program changes. These side effects cause loss of development time (until the causes are isolated and fixed), so careful consideration is the first criterion of maintenance. A common quote is, "Think before you act."

Maintenance programmers fix bugs in existing programs and add new functions to those programs. If your task is to correct an error, first locate the error and then determine how to change the program. If your task is to enhance the program, you'll develop new logic and write new code.

Use a top-down approach for designing and making program changes. First, review the program and check the interfaces, variables, and the database. Second, isolate the areas that need to be changed. Third, study the change areas carefully and then check the logic on how the changes will be inserted. Finally, desk-check all pathways to see that old procedures continue to work correctly and new ones perform as designed. Only then do you actually begin to code the changes.

Some maintenance guidelines that have evolved over thirty years of programming are:

- ☐ Always make a backup copy before beginning any changes, any whatsoever.
- ☐ Read the code to be sure of the overall flow before making even one-line changes.
- ☐ Change only what is necessary. Getting carried away (to make it prettier, sharper, more compact) may open Pandora's box. Don't "fix" what isn't broken.

- ☐ Do not attempt to share program variables that already exist, if you're not *absolutely* sure how each one is used, each time it's used.
- ☐ Write in some error-checking around the changes. That is, put in some debugging code (perhaps print lines) and do some testing before considering the change final. Remove the error checking once the change is proven correct.
- ☐ Consider what effect the change has on the overall processing of the program. Does the sort *really* have to be here? Or could it wait until later, so that the user doesn't have to sit and wait between input screens.
- ☐ Update the program documentation. Each time a change is made, type in (in the remarks area) what the change actually does.
- ☐ Use structured concepts. If a new subroutine is needed, be sure that the subroutine fits with the rest of the code in both format, idea, and physical placement.

Debugging

Once the program is written, it's time to debug it. As discussed under testing above, finding errors before they get to Acceptance Testing (whether formal or informal) significantly reduces software cost.

Debugging means finding errors. Those errors come from the programmer either incorrectly understanding the original design or, more often, from a human error in remembering flags, semaphores, logic flow, or using incorrect code statements.

How well programmers find errors depends on the individuals. Often, programmers have difficulty because they make invalid assumptions and their conjectures become prematurely fixed, which blinds them to other possibilities. Programmers often use the following as debugging aids:

- ☐ Source code listing.
- ☐ Output listing (assembly or compiler output listing).
- ☐ Statement trace.
- ☐ Debug software which "steps through" programs with debug traps or displays.
- ☐ Clues from compilers or assemblers, such as error messages.

Program errors are more likely to occur in larger, highly complex programs. A systematic approach allows programmers to find those errors more quickly. The following is a guideline for quick debugging.

- ☐ First, exclude the most unlikely sources of the error. In the search for errors, go from the most likely to the least likely.
- ☐ Isolate one error at a time and stick to that error until it is located and fixed. Only then move on to the next. If a second error is located during the search for the first, note its location and return there once the first one is fixed.
- ☐ Study *actual* output and compare it to samples of *expected* output.
- ☐ Check the data handled by the program. Often the input data is either incorrect (and not discovered during input editing) or was not included in the original design as potential data.
- ☐ Keep track of where the errors occur in the program as errors tend to "clump." This can aid in predicting where future errors will occur.

When searching for an error, don't dismiss the possibility that its cause may be a machine error or an error in the original design.

Software Aids

There are catastrophic errors from which it is difficult to recover. Sooner or later in your software design cycle, you're going to run into them. They generally group in the area of "human error while under pressure," such as erasing a file when you didn't mean to. There exists software to help you with this and one software designer, Peter Norton, deserves the reputation he's earned.

The *Norton Utilities* are a set of programs that supplement the MS-DOS operating system and help you use your computer more effectively. Norton realized that people become involved in what they're doing (programming) and often make a mistake that sets them back hours if not days.

If your computer is one of the IBM family, or closely compatible, the *Norton Utilities* will work just fine. To use the programs, you must be running with a version of MS-DOS at 2.0 or higher. Finally, to get the best use of the programs, you need to be familiar with DOS. Chapter 2 helps with that.

2

MS-DOS Programming Tips

There are many operating systems for the IBM Personal Computer (and look-alike clones). This book concentrates on MS-DOS at level 3.1 and higher. We wrote the software in this book on an 80386-based IBM-compatible clone, with MS-DOS 3.1 and the *Microsoft Macro Assembler*, version 5.0.

This chapter gives you general MS-DOS programming tips, discusses a few of the more useful MS-DOS interrupts, and gives you some easy MS-DOS bypasses for problems you'll run into. We thought you might want to get your show on the road as soon as possible, so we included a skeleton assembly language program in which you can insert code you want to write and test.

OS/2 uses system CALLs instead of INTs. Just as with MS-DOS, you move function numbers into registers; instead of issuing an INT *n* (where *n* is the hex function number), however, you do a CALL to LOC__50h. For an example, Fig. 2-1 which shows how to get the time with each type of call. The MS-DOS interrupt and function number used in the example is described later in this chapter and more fully in Appendix G.

Throughout the examples, you'll see how to code the routines using MS-DOS. Occasionally, we'll remind you about OS/2 and give you an OS/2 overview in Appendix F. Also, note that the numbers used throughout this book are in hexadecimal, unless specifically stated that they are in decimal; for example, Interrupt 21 hex is shown as INT 21, not INT 21h (only in the book—in the program listings, they're shown with the "h" because MASM defaults to decimal representation).

```
For MS-DOS
        MOV     AH,2CH        ; 2C is the Get Time function
        INT     21h           ; Issue the Interrupt

For OS/2
        MOV     AH,2CH        ; 2C is the Get Time function
        CALL    LOC_50h
```

Fig. 2-1. Get_Time program.

Definitions

Let's look at some basic MS-DOS and system terms and concepts you'll run into when you program on an IBM system or look-alike clone.

BIOS—The Basic I/O System, or BIOS, is the (usually) ROM-based code that interfaces with MS-DOS to process I/O inside your computer. BIOS is overviewed below. BIOS interrupts are detailed in Appendix G.

DEBUG—In capital letters, this is the DEBUG.COM program that usually comes with your MS-DOS disk. It's a utility program that allows you to troubleshoot your programs. With DEBUG, you can load files and sectors, edit to change them, and write changes to memory or register locations.

File Handle—Starting with MS-DOS 2.0, file handles were introduced to manipulate files, instead of using the more cumbersome File Control Blocks (FCBs). To keep track of a file, all you need is its handle, a 16-bit word that you move from register to register as required. A keyboard and a printer are considered files for purposes of using handles. If you want to refer to a file, move its handle into whatever register INT 21 requires. File handles 0-4 are predefined, as shown in Fig. 2-2, so use 5 or above for your programs.

MASM—The *Microsoft Macro Assembler* (MASM) is a software package that translates a copy of your source files into .OBJ files (for input to a linker) and .LST files (so you can scan and/or print the result of the assembly).

Microcode—A list of small program steps, and also a set of control functions performed by the instruction decoding and executing logic

Handle	Assigned Meaning
0	Standard Input Device (Usually a keyboard)
1	Standard Output Device (Usually a screen)
2	Standard Error Output Device
3	Standard Auxiliary Device (AUX)
4	Standard Printer Device (PRN)

Fig. 2-2. Preassigned file handles.

of a computer system. It's code that is "below" the level of assembly language; that is, closer to the machine.

Pseudo-OP—Pseudo-ops are commands coded with source code and are for the assembler only. There are many pseudo-ops available; among them are ASSUME, in which you tell the assembler how registers will be set; ENDS, which tells where the segment ends; and the PROC and ENDP pair, which tells where procedures start and end.

SYMDEB—A symbolic debugger which is a product of Microsoft Corporation. See Appendix H for an overview of SYMDEB and its more useful commands. With SYMDEB, you can step through a program (tracing register and flag changes), unassemble code, and modify memory and register contents.

System Overview

MS-DOS consists of three components: a *Boot* (system initialization) *record,* a *BIOS interface,* and the MS-DOS program itself (generally stored as COMMAND.COM). The boot record is read into memory when you do either a power-on or a system reset (Ctrl-Alt-Del). Boot is read into memory and given control. It checks the directory to assure that the first records are your MS-DOS controls. Then it reads initialization code which determines equipment status, resets the system, initializes the attached devices, and sets the low-numbered interrupt vectors. This initialization code is overlaid later by data areas and the command processor.

Next, Boot initializes its internal working tables, determines the correct memory locations for file allocation tables (FATs), the directory, and the data buffers. It initializes interrupt vectors (for interrupts 20 through 27) and loads COMMAND.COM. Finally, it passes control to COMMAND.COM.

COMMAND.COM consists of three separate parts. One portion contains the code to process certain critical interrupts, with overlay areas to handle others. A

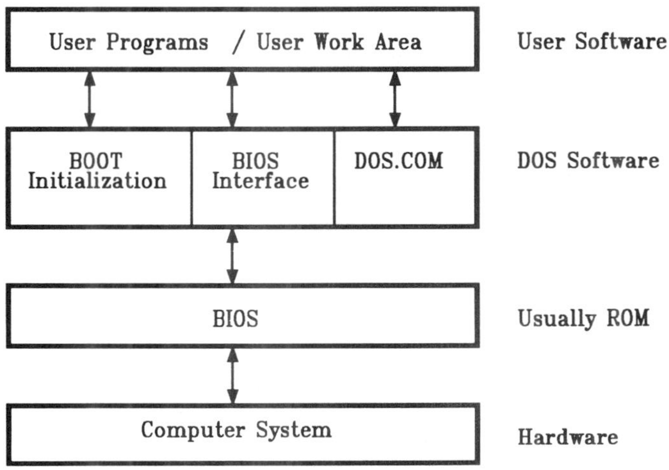

Fig. 2-3. System overview.

second portion controls startup and also contains the AUTOEXEC.BAT file processor setup routine. The third part is a command processor; one duty of this processor is to provide the prompt, e.g., C>.

MS-DOS provides a number of functions to user programs, available through the issuance of a set of interrupt codes and function calls: interrupts 20 through 27, each with subfunctions. These interrupts access BIOS entry point interrupts. BIOS and MS-DOS interrupts are discussed in two separate sections below and more fully in Appendix G.

A Skeleton Program

Assembly language instructions divide into four fields:

[*label*:] *mnemonic* [*operand*] [; *comment*]

Of these, you only *must* include the mnemonic. The brackets indicate that the other fields are optional. For mnemonics which require operands, of course, those operands are *not* optional. You enter the fields anywhere on a line (separated by a space or a tab), but it makes program reading easier if you use some standard spacing throughout your programs. Many of the programmer-helpful edit packages (such as Borland's *Turbo Editor*) insert spaces for you.

The skeleton program shown in Fig. 2-4 gives you the "must-haves" to assemble source programs correctly. The first line (PAGE) tells the assembler how many lines you want to appear on a page and how wide those lines are. The second line (.386) tells the assembler that you are including 80386 instructions and requests

```
                PAGE      55,132
                .386
STACK           SEGMENT   'STACK' STACK
                DW        100 DUP(?)
STACK           ENDS
CODE            SEGMENT   PARA 'CODE' PUBLIC USE16
                ASSUME    CS:CODE, DS:CODE, SS:CODE
; Purpose:      [Here you enter your overall documentation]
;                  [Note that each comment begins with a ";"]
;
; Inputs:
;
; Process:
;
; Outputs:
;
NAME:           MOV       AX,CS
                MOV       DS,AX
                JMP       BEGINHERE
[Define your variables and constants here]
BEGINHERE:
                   [Enter your code here]
ENDHERE:
                MOV       AH,4Ch          ; Standard Ending
                INT       21h
CODE            ENDS
                END       NAME
```

Fig. 2-4. Skeleton program.

the assembler to build 80386 displacements. For example, the assembler generates 2-byte displacements for jump instructions, instead of single-byte displacements for the 80286 and 8086/8088.

The instruction set for each successive member of the Intel 8086–80386 family contains the preceding set(s). This means that the 80386 full set includes all the instructions developed for the 8086, 80186, and 80286. See Appendix C for the 80386 instruction set descriptions, and Appendix D for the 80387 instruction set.

The next three lines of the skeleton program set up a stack segment with 100 bytes. You need this area for working space. The next line (CODE) shows where the actual code begins, with parameters making the code public and instructing the assembler to use 16-bit registers (which MS-DOS and OS/2 require). The ASSUME line initializes three segment-pointer registers for use within the program.

The next block section generally is left out of lazy programmers' work. And they regret it only a few months later when they have to debug their own work. We've included extensive internal documentation in all the programs, procedures, and modules in this book.

The NAME is where you put the name of your program, each with a unique name. The two MOV lines set data into your segment-pointer registers and initializes them. The jump (JMP) gets the working program around the variable definition that is done during assembly. Define your variables and/or initialize storage. DB defines one or more bytes. DW defines two-byte words and DD defines four-byte words ("doublewords").

The BEGINHERE: line is the start of your working code. You can use any unique label for this. Then insert your code. The ENDHERE: label is simply an easy place to remember that you are terminating your program. We used the INT 21 Function 4C exit that terminates and turns control back to the parent process (usually MS-DOS) with an optional, one-byte return code. The standard functions are defined below and more fully in Appendix G. You need two final lines: CODE ENDS and END *name,* where *name* is the same as your program NAME that you chose at the beginning.

You'll see this skeleton around most of the working programs in this book. It's easy to test the BIOS and MS-DOS functions and interrupts by inserting them in this skeleton program code, assembling, and then linking them. Once you get handy with that, you can try things out within minutes.

Assembling Programs

For this tip, it's assumed that you have your editors, assemblers, and linkers on Drive C, in a directory called ASM. Your assembly language program also is assumed to be on drive C, in the same directory. Two commas and a semicolon at the end of the command says that you want to use the same base name (in this case Program_Name) for both your .OBJ and .LST files.

After a clean assembly (See Fig. 2-5 for the command format), you get a file called Program_Name.OBJ and one called Program_Name.LST. You now need to link the object file(s) before you can run Program_Name. To do this, at the system MS-DOS prompt enter LINK and Program_Name (See Fig. 2-6). Answer

```
C: MASM Program_Name,,;
```

Fig. 2-5. Macro assembling command, where Program_Name *is the name of your program.*

```
C:> LINK Program_Name
```

Fig. 2-6. Link edit command, where Program_Name *is the ".OBJ" file you wish to link.*

with a carriage return (Enter) to all the link prompts or enter a semicolon (;) after Program_Name to tell the linker that you want to default to all the standard entries.

The linker looks for Program_Name.OBJ in your default directory. Your output will be Program_Name.EXE. Your program can now be run by entering Program_Name, as shown in Fig. 2-7. In the assembly or the link steps, you can allow the assembler and linker to prompt you for output file names. If you want to direct the output to other directories or rename the .OBJ, .EXE, or .LST files, you can enter the path names and/or different file names at the prompts.

Library Management

It's best, in the long run, if you keep your working routines in subdirectories as modules that you can assemble and link with new code. If you don't have a hard disk, divide your disk on drive B into subdirectories. We suggest putting your source code in one library, your object in another, and your executable code in a third. Be sure to back these libraries up on a regular basis.

You'll have enough to think about when you're programming; here at the start, divide your working modules logically. For instance, keep all your arithmetic modules in a directory called, for instance, \MATH\. Keep your graphics in one called \GRAPHICS\. And so on.

Routines and variables that are in one module and called/used from/in another must be declared PUBLIC within their own assembly language module. Also, they must be defined as EXTRN (external) in the file that contains the code that calls them. If you don't declare them this way, you'll get a list of errors when you try to assemble your main-line program—the assembler assumes you forgot to write them as part of your main program.

```
C:> Program_Name
```

Fig. 2-7. Program execution command, where Program_Name *is the ".EXE" program you want to run.*

```
C> TYPE FILENAME.TXT|MORE
```

Fig. 2-8. Viewing ASCII files, where FILENAME.TXT *is the file you want to view.*

Each external reference gives the name of the routine that isn't physically present in your main code. It also assigns a "type" to it. The 80386 needs this type to determine the proper machine code for referencing the external routine. Since your routines will probably be in their own separate code segments, they'll be called "far" and require "far" CALLs in machine language.

Common MS-DOS Operations

Viewing ASCII Files in DOS

For this tip, let's assume you are at the MS-DOS prompt (usually C> with a hard disk and A> with bootable diskettes) and you want to use the MS-DOS command TYPE to view a file. The file scrolls too fast for you to read easily. You can use Ctrl-S to stop the scrolling momentarily. Also you can use the MORE.COM filter. First, load the MORE.COM file into the same directory as the file you want to view (or you can use the PATH command to point to the directory where MORE.COM is). Then type the command in as shown in Fig. 2-8.

The TYPE command filters through MORE.COM and will display the text file one page at a time. The message "—MORE—" displays at the bottom of your screen. Press any key to advance the display to the next page.

Merging Files

Current versions of MS-DOS don't include a MERGE, but it is possible to combine multiple files by using the MS-DOS COPY command. For instance, assume you have two files, named FILE1 and FILE2. You can append the second to the first, as shown in Fig. 2-9.

If you don't name a target file (in the example, NEWFILE), the first file in the list (in the example, FILE1) will be replaced by a new file that contains both.

Printing Files without Saving Them

You can type documentation, a memo, or a letter at the MS-DOS prompt and print it out by using the COPY command. At the C> prompt (or A> if you're using bootable diskettes), type the entry as shown in Fig. 2-10.

```
C> COPY FILE1+FILE2  NEWFILE
```

Fig. 2-9. Merging files in MS-DOS, where NEWFILE *is the target file for the combined* FILE1 *and* FILE2.

```
C> COPY CON PRN
```

Fig. 2-10. Printing a file without having to save it, where CON is your console and PRN is your printer.

The PRN after COPY CON directs all the information you type to the printer. The file will not be printed until you finish typing and end the file by entering Ctrl-Z. You'll get a response on the screen of "1 file(s) copied." Neither the COPY CON PRN command nor Ctrl-Z (it appears as ^Z on your screen) prints on your printer. Also, since MS-DOS is not a word processor, it doesn't have word wrap. So type your information exactly as you want it to appear on the final output.

Printing the Screen

When you're working with MS-DOS interactively, you can hold down the shift key and press the PrtSc key (with some systems, you only have to press PrtSc). The information on the screen is sent to the printer. MS-DOS uses Interrupt 5 for this purpose, so you can use the PrtSc operation from within a program by issuing the command INT 5. You can prevent a user from doing a PrtSc by pointing INT 5 to a return instruction. Program INTHNDLR in Chapter 5 shows how to intercept BIOS or MS-DOS interrupts.

BIOS Interrupts

The ROM-resident Basic I/O System (BIOS) provides device-level control of the major I/O devices in the system unit. BIOS routines allow you to perform block-level (diskette and cassette) or character-level (keyboard, printer, and video communications) I/O operations without concern for device addresses and operating characteristics. BIOS also insulates you from the hardware, which allows new devices to be added to the system unit while retaining the BIOS level interface to the device. In this way, your programs are transparent to hardware modifications and enhancements.

Access to BIOS is through interrupts. Each BIOS entry point has its own interrupt vector (address), summarized in Fig. 2-11 and detailed in Appendix G. Most BIOS interrupts require parameters, although some do not (for instance, the memory-size BIOS interrupt INT 12 does not) and all parameters passed to and from BIOS go through registers. When BIOS has several possible operations, the AH register is used on input to indicate your desired operation. As a general rule, BIOS preserves all registers except AX and various flags. Other registers are modified on return only if they return a value or error condition to your program.

ROM BIOS uses the memory region from 400 to 4FF hex (See Fig. 2-12), which includes the addresses for serial and parallel ports, the equipment list (devices and internal equipment installed on your computer at the time of the last power-up or reset), and the size of working memory.

You can't alter ROM BIOS, but you may want to alter what happens when interrupts are issued. For instance, you may wish to interchange two keyboard keys. You do this by changing the interrupt vector for keyboard servicing. Then you

Interrupt Number (in Hex)	Function Name
5	Print Screen
8	Time of Day
9	Keyboard Scan Code
10	Video
11	Equipment Check
12	Memory Size
13	DIskette Service
14	Communications (Serial Transfer)
15	Cassette and TopView
16	Keyboard character
17	Printer
18	Cassette BASIC /ROM BASIC
19	Bootstrap
1A	Time of Day
1B	Keyboard Break
1C	Timer Tick

Fig. 2-11. BIOS interrupt vectors.

Starting Address	
00000	BIOS Interrupt Vectors
00080	Available Interrupt Vectors
00400	BIOS Data Area
00500	User Read/Write Memory
A0000	Reserved for Devices
F4000	User Read Only Memory
F6000	On PCs, BASIC Interpreter
FE000	BIOS Program Area

Fig. 2-12. BIOS memory map.

check each input key to see if it is one you want to change. If so, then branch to the regular ROM BIOS keyboard routine to complete the operation.

If you want to disable an interrupt, change the vector so that it points to a Return statement in the ROM BIOS. BIOS Interrupt 10 (Video Services) and its various subfunctions are explained in detail in Chapter 10, which deals with graphics.

Let's use one of the BIOS interrupts to show how this works. In the example in Fig. 2-13, we want to find out what mode the screen is in.

The function requests call MS-DOS routines to manage system resources. When MS-DOS takes control after a function call, it switches to an internal stack. Registers not used to return information (except AX) are preserved. The calling program's stack must be large enough to accommodate the interrupt system—at least 128 bytes in addition to other needs.

One final note on BIOS. It's not certain at this time just how BIOS will be integrated in the 80386 version of OS/2. The notes about BIOS here are valid for most systems up to this time. You'll want to retest your code when (and if) you move to a PS/2 80386 system and use OS/2. Appendix F gives an overview of OS/2 and has a section that discusses a few of the MS-DOS and OS/2 differences.

```
@SCREEN_MODE        MACRO
        ; This Macro determines the screen mode
        ;
        ; Register AH holds the function of 0F hex.
        ;   The mode number is returned in AL.
        ;
            MOV    AH,0Fh      ; Read the mode
            INT    10h
            ENDM
```

Fig. 2-13. SCREEN_MODE macro.

MS-DOS Interrupts

You can use MS-DOS interrupts (20 through 27) to gain entry to useful operations which MS-DOS reserves for its own use. MS-DOS maintains the table of interrupt routine vectors (addresses) in locations 80–FC; most of the interrupts have been superseded by function requests in Interrupt 21. Figure 2-14 lists the MS-DOS reserved interrupts, which are detailed in Appendix G.

Interrupt 20: Program Termination

To terminate your COM-format programs, use this interrupt and control is returned to MS-DOS, or the parent process. All open files are closed, the disk cache

Interrupt Vector (in Hex)	Function
20	Program Terminate
21	General DOS Functions
22	Terminate Address
23	CONTROL-BREAK Exit
24	Fatal Error Vector
25	Absolute Disk Read
26	Absolute Disk Write
27	Program Terminate, fix in storage

Fig. 2-14. MS-DOS reserved interrupts.

is cleaned, and all file buffers are flushed to disk. The CS register must contain the segment address of the Program Segment Prefix before you call this interrupt.

It is important to close all files that have changed in length before issuing this interrupt. The file's new length is not recorded correctly in the directory if you do not close it first. *(Tip: The most useful way to automatically close all files and finish "cleanly" is to load AH with 4C and issue INT 21 or CALL LOC_50.)*

Interrupt 21: General MS-DOS Functions

Interrupt 21 has several useful functions that are summarized in Fig. 2-15. To use this interrupt, place the appropriate function number in register AH, then issue INT 21.

Description	Function (in Hex)	Description	Function (in Hex)
Allocate Memory	48	Display String	09
Auxiliary Input	03	Duplicate a File Handle	45
Auxiliary Output	04	File Size	23
Buffered Keyboard Input	0A	Find Match File	4E
Change Attributes	43	Flush Buffer, Read Keyboard	0C
Change Current Directory	3B	Force A Duplicate of a Handle	46
Check Keyboard Status	0B	Free Allocated Memory	49
Close a File Handle	3	Get Date	2A
Close a File	10	Get Disk Free Space	36
CONTROL-C Check	33	Get Disk Transfer Address	2F
Create A File	3C	Get MS-DOS Version Number	30
Create File	16	Get Interrupt Vector	35
Create New Program Segment	26	Get Time	2C
Create Sub-Directory	39	Get/Set Date/Time of File	57
Current Disk	19	I/O Control for Devices	44
Delete a Directory Entry	41	Keep Process	31
Delete File	13	Load and Execute a Program	4B
Direct Console Input	07	Modify Allocated Memory Blocks	4A
Direct Console I/O	06	Move a Directory Entry	56
Display Character	02	Move a File Pointer	42

Fig. 2-15. Interrupt 21 functions.

Eleven of the functions are described below. They'll give you an idea of how useful Interrupt 21 is. For more detail and the remainder of the Interrupt 21 functions, see Appendix G.

Function 1: Read/Display Keyboard Character. If you want your program to halt until a key is pressed, use this function. See Fig. 2-16 for an example. Set the AH register to 1 and execute INT 21. The input character returns in register AL, if it is ASCII. If the character is extended ASCII, AL contains a value of zero. That means that this function must be repeated to get the extended code.

If the second value is less than 84, it represents the scan code of the pressed key. For example, the user may press the F1 key. The value you'll receive is a

Description	Function (in Hex)	Description	Function (in Hex)
Reserved	18	Reset Disk	0D
Reserved	1B-20	Return Country-Dependent Info	38
Reserved	32	Return Current Setting of Verify	54
Reserved	34	Return Text of Current Directory	47
Reserved	37	Return the Return Code of a Child	4D
Reserved	50-53	Search for First Entry	11
Reserved	55	Search for Next Entry	12
Open a File	3D	Select Disk	0E
Open File	0F	Sequential Read	14
Parse File Name	29	Sequential Write	15
Print Character	05	Set Date	2B
Random Block Read	27	Set Disk Transfer Address	1A
Random Block Write	28	Set Relative Record	24
Random Read	21	Set Time	2D
Random Write	22	Set Vector	25
Read from File/Device	3F	Set/Reset Verify Flag	2E
Read Keyboard	08	Step Through Directory, Matching Files	4F
Read Keyboard and Echo	01	Terminate A Process	4C
Remove a Directory Entry	3A	Terminate Program	00
Rename File	17	Write to File or Device	40

(Fig. 2-15 ends).

```
STNDINE     PROC
            MOV    AH,1     ; Standard Input with Echo
            INT    21h      ; Issue Interrupt
            RET             ; Code ends, return
STNDINE     ENDP
CODE        ENDS
            END
```

Fig. 2-16. Standard input with echo.

3B, since the scan code for F1 is 3B. See Appendix E for ASCII characters and the IBM PC keyboard scan codes.

Function 2: Write Character to Video Screen. This function is useful for writing one or two characters to the screen, especially special characters. It gets the characters from the DL register. (Function 9 writes longer character strings but it cannot write a special character—the dollar sign $—since it uses $ as the delimiter to terminate strings.)

Use Function 2 in conjunction with Function 8, which reads characters from the keyboard but does not display them. See an example of Function 2 in Fig. 2-17. We used Function 2 to display the contents of a memory input buffer in the program BUFFER (see Chapter 9).

```
@DISPL_CHAR    MACRO   PCHAR?
        ; Display input character on screen
        ; You can use this macro to:
        ;   @DISPL_CHAR 'x'   to display a character on the screen
        ;                          where x is that character
        ;   @DISPL_CHAR AL    to display contents of AL register
        ;   @DISPL_CHAR       to display a value in DL
        ;
           IFNB    <PCHAR?>
           PUSH    DX
           MOV     DL,PCHAR?
           ENDIF
           MOV     AH,2
           INT     21H
           IFNB    <PCHAR?>
           POP     DX
           ENDIF
           ENDM
```

Fig. 2-17. Displaying a single character.

If you read in the backspace key, you will move the cursor to the left but will not erase the character from the screen.

The macro in Fig. 2-17 loads into DX the location of a buffer already allocated in memory. The dummy parameter, *PCHAR?*, indicates that there is input expected. If no parameter is input to the macro, it will display whatever contents are already in register DL. You can ask it to print whatever is in AL, by using "AL" as an input parameter. The macro sets up a call to INT 21 Function 2.

Function 3: Read from Serial Port. Function 3 reads a byte from the standard auxiliary input, AUX or COM1. Store a 3 in the AH register and issue Interrupt 21. The character read is returned in AL. See examples in Fig. 2-16 and Fig. 2-17 on how to use this.

Function 4: Write to Serial Port. This function sends whatever byte is in register DL to the auxiliary port, AUX or COM1. Store a 4 in register AH and issue INT 21. See examples of function use in Fig. 2-16 and Fig. 2-17.

Function 5: Write to Printer Port. This function sends the character in register DL to the standard printer port, PRN or LPT1. Store a 5 in the AH register and issue INT 21. See examples of function use in Fig. 2-16 and Fig. 2-17 on how functions work.

Function 6: Direct Keyboard Input and Video Output. This function does both input and output. The AL register receives the input and the DL register contains the output character. Ask for input by storing FF in the DL register. Store a 6 in register AH and issue INT 21. On return from the function, the zero flag is set (ZF = 1) if no character is ready. If ZF = 0, then a character was read into AL. If DL contains any other value but FF, that character is sent to the standard output device.

This function does not wait for an input character. Also, the character is not automatically displayed on the screen. See examples of function use in Fig. 2-16 and Fig. 2-17.

Function 7: Read Keyboard Character without Echo or Break Detection. Function 7 waits for a keyboard character. If an ASCII character (number, letter, or control character) was entered, the ASCII value returns in AL. This function does not display the character and Ctrl-Break does not terminate it. (Compare this function with Function 8.)

IBM graphic-style characters can be entered by holding down the Alt key and typing the decimal value with the keypad numbers. The number is in AL. If an extended character such as a function key or Alt combination is entered, a zero is stored in AL, and Function 7 must be called a second time to find out what other character was entered. See Appendix E for the extended ASCII characters. See examples in Fig. 2-16 and Fig. 2-17 on how to use functions.

Function 8: Read Keyboard Character without Echo but with Break Detection. Function 8 is like Function 1; it waits for a character to be keyed in and terminates when Ctrl-Break is pressed. The input character is not displayed and the Tab is not expanded. To use Function 8, store an 8 in the AH register and issue Int 21.

Function 9: Display a String of Characters. To use Function 9, store a string of characters in memory somewhere and terminate it with the dollar sign ($). This means that the dollar sign cannot be part of the string. The function does not automatically send the cursor to the start of the next line after the string is printed. To do this, append "0Dh" (carriage return) and "0Ah" (line feed) to the line, just before the dollar sign. There are many programs in this book which do this. For example, see CAP_IT in Chapter 6. (If you need to print a dollar sign, use Function 2 to print that character.) Store the address of the string in the DS:DX register. Store 9 in AH and issue INT 21, as shown in Fig. 2-18.

Function 0A: Buffered Keyboard Input. Before you can use this function, you need to set up a buffer in memory. Add two auxiliary bytes at the beginning of the buffer. Set the first to the maximum length of text that can be stored in the buffer; the second holds the number of characters your user enters. Store the value of the first byte. MS-DOS stores the second after the input has been read, but does *not* include the carriage return in the count of input characters. So set the buffer size three bytes higher than you'll need. For an example of setting up a buffer and storing the bytes, see Program STRSRCH in Chapter 6, also BUFFER in Chapter 9. If you have debug software, run STRSRCH through it and watch how the buffer contents change.

All the characters typed by the user are entered into this buffer and the control keys are available for use, such as Insert, Delete, and the cursor control keys. When the user presses the carriage return (Enter) key, the entire line goes from the keyboard buffer to the input buffer.

```
Program

;    Note that a carriage return is 0Dh, and a line feed
;    is 0Ah.  The two hex characters are placed at the
;    beginning of the string to print.
;    They could also be placed at the end, such as in the
;    EXAMPLE below.
  •
  •
EXAMPLE     DB   ' This is another example.',0Ah,0Dh,'$'
PRINT—STR   DB   0Dh,0Ah,'This is the string to print.$'
  •
  •
            LEA  DX,PRINT—STR    ; Point to String
            MOV  AH,9            ; String-print Function
            INT  21h
  •
  •
```

Fig. 2-18. Displaying a string of characters.

To use Function 0A, store in DS:DX the pointer to the first auxiliary byte (the byte that defines the maximum buffer size), which is located two bytes in front of the text. Store 0A in register AH and issue Interrupt 21. Figure 2-19 shows how to use this function.

Function 0B: Keyboard Status. There may be times when you do not want to wait for character input. You can avoid waiting by using Int 21 Function 0B to check the keyboard status. Store a 0B in the AH register and execute INT 21. On return, register AL contains a value if a character is waiting; it holds a zero if no key has been pressed.

Function 0B does not read the character. You must use Function 1, 7, or 8 for that.

Interrupt 21 Error Return Codes. Many system calls return values in a register that specify whether or not the operation succeeded. Your program can handle error conditions by checking the register that contains the error code (AX) and taking appropriate action. Figure 2-20 lists the error codes.

Since the newer versions of MS-DOS allow extended error handling, we included a procedure (EXTERROR—see Chapter 5 for a description and listing). This procedure allows you to access additional information on errors, a great help during program debugging.

Interrupt 23: Intercept Ctrl-Break

Users generally stop program execution by holding the Ctrl key and pressing Break (Ctrl-C often does the same thing). These keystrokes cause a branch to Interrupt 23 and then to an MS-DOS routine to stop the program.

You can keep users from interrupting a program (or enhance what happens when they do) by changing the Interrupt 23 so that it branches into your program. Then, when your user hits what she thinks is a Break key, you take control. When you've finished, you may wish the new value to remain in effect until the system

```
Program
  :
INPUT—STR  DB    23 DUP (?)
  :
           MOV   INPUT—STR,20    ; Maximum allowed on input
           LEA   DX,INPUT—STR    ; Point to string for input
           MOV   AH,0Ah          ; Buffered keyboard input function
           INT   21h
```

Fig. 2-19. Buffered keyboard input example.

Fig. 2-20. Error return codes.

Code	Meaning
1	Invalid Function Number
2	File Not Found
3	Path Not Found
4	Too Many Open Files
5	Access Denied
6	Invalid File Handle
7	Memory Control Blocks Destroyed
8	Insufficient Memory
9	Invalid Memory Block Address
10	Invalid Environment
11	Invalid Format
12	Invalid Access Code
13	Invalid Data
14	(Not Used)
15	Invalid Drive Specified
16	Attempted to Remove Current Directory
17	Not Same Device
18	No More Files

is shut off, or you may wish to restore the original value before the program finishes. With Interrupt 23, MS-DOS always restores the original value when the current program finishes.

Using the Numeric Coprocessor

Numeric coprocessors, also called math coprocessors, reduce the amount of time you spend waiting for math functions to be performed. An 80287 works with machines that have an 80286 CPU (such as IBM's PC AT and compatibles and the Personal System/2 Models 50 and 60). The 80386 chip recognizes the 80287 and will use it or the 80387, whichever is available. Note that the 8087 works only with the 8086 and 8088 (in systems such as the IBM PC and PC XT).

Installing the coprocessor is easy. Generally, there's an empty slot on the motherboard (often labeled) in which to insert the coprocessor. Be sure that the metal legs are in the proper slots in the socket. Most systems automatically recognize the chip, although some may require you to run a setup program in CMOS

RAM to complete installation (just as you do if you install a new video card or another disk drive).

Be sure to match or exceed the speed of your CPU when you buy a numeric coprocessor.

Common DOS File Name Extensions

The Microsoft system programs and language products commonly use the following file name extensions. They're included here so you'll know what they are if/when they appear in any of your libraries.

Extension	***Description***
.@@@	Backup ID file
.ASC	ASCII text file
.ASM	MASM uses this for assembly language source code
.BAK	Backup file
.BAT	Batch file which contains MS-DOS commands
.BIN	Binary file
.COD	Object listing file
.COM	Executable program file
.CRF	MASM cross-reference file
.DAT	Data file
.DOC	Documentation or document file
.DRV	Driver file
.ERR	Error file
.EXE	Executable program file
.FNT	Font file
.HEX	Intel hexadecimal format file
.HLP	Help file
.INC	Include file
.LIB	Library file
.MAP	Address map file
.MOD	Module file
.OBJ	Relocatable object module
.OVL	Overlay file
.QLB	Library file, Microsoft *Quick* products
.REF	Cross-reference listing file
.SCR	Script file
.SYM	Symbol file
.SYS	System file or device driver
.TMP	Temporary file
.TXT	Text file or *Windows* Notepad file

An Undocumented Link Editor Error

If you create a source file without the USE16 directive and assemble it, it will assemble correctly. If you then link it with modules which have USE16, you'll receive an error message that reads:

```
FATAL ERROR L1123: <this is blank>
POS: nnnn RECORD TYPE: yy
```

where (we're not sure) the *nnnn* position is a number of bytes into the file. The record type *yy* refers to Intel's relocatable object module format. See the Intel documentation for further details.

This error does not appear in any Microsoft documentation we've been able to find. Add the USE16 to the proper line in your program and reassemble and link. This error goes away.

3

80386 Programming Notes and Tips

In general, software developed for one generation of the Intel microprocessor family works without alteration on the next higher (more modern) level. This chapter lists various facts you need to remember when you program or design around the 80386 chip.

First, we address the current software/hardware environment with a list of guidelines for software developers. Then the chapter reviews certain aspects of programming for the 80386 where you will want to keep an eye out for problems. Although the operating systems being offered by the major companies force the use of USE16 in programs (which limits the effectiveness of the 80386), there are some very nice items programmers can use.

The greatest thing the 80386 does is provide large segments, which virtually eliminate the 64K segment-limit headaches.

The fact that there isn't an operating system (among the very popular operating systems) which supports the large model is an irritant. A large model provides easy array indexing and makes very good use of the 80386 instructions. As shown by many of the programs in this book, you can make use of the extended addressing features as long as you're careful about overflows of 64K words. You can use SIB *byte* for indexing, which is a real pleasure to use because it provides you with a "high-level language" for indexing. You don't have to load values, multiply them by the appropriate other values and load into registers. The instruction does it for you.

The addition of another byte in the jump instructions (this allows the use of a 16-bit displacement instead of the 8-bit) gives a much wider range of displacement addresses. It eases a lot of programming problems of jumping only certain bytes ahead or behind. Other useful instructions are the bit test instructions that are useful in doing bitmap operations, such as handling the Task State Segment (TSS). See Appendix A for a discussion of this segment.

Even with the limitations of current operating systems, the 80386 is a very powerful and capable processor.

With MS-DOS in real mode and OS/2 in protected mode providing only a 16-bit address capability, effectively the 80386 runs as a fast 80286. That limits you in terms of 32-bit addressing, which is (in our opinion) the most significant capability the 80386 has. The additional instructions are useful, but they do things that you could do some other way. You *can* get around the addressing (which we show in the array routines in Chapter 9) but, running in protected mode, programs are more expensive in machine cycles to run. In addition to the overhead and keeping track of where you are, there are additional descriptors, which impose the overhead of having to load them—where what you'd like to do is load the descriptor to your array, mush around in the array, and never have to load the descriptor again.

(There are DOS's available that do provide 32-bit addressing. UNIX for the 80386 runs normally in the USE32 mode; we've heard very good things about it.)

Terminology

First, let's look at some 80386 definitions. You can find fuller descriptions of the terms in Appendix A, "80386 Architectural Overview."

Descriptor—Descriptors are data structures used to define the characteristics of a program element. For example, descriptors describe a data record, a segment, or a task.

Flag—A flag is an indicator whose state is used to inform a later section of a program that a condition has occurred. The condition is identified with the flag and designated by the state of the flag; that is, the flag is either set (ON = 1) or not set (OFF = 0).

Gates—A gate is a logic design that allows only certain processes to pass through it. The 80386 provides protection for control transfers among executable segments at differing privilege levels by use of gate descriptors. There are four: Call gates, Trap gates, Interrupt gates, and Task gates.

Segment—Beginning with the 8086, Intel introduced the concept of segments, which were defined as units of contiguous (adjacent) address space. In the 8086, this space had a maximum of 64K or 65536 bytes. In the 80386, that limitation no longer applies. You can now view segments as one-dimensional subspaces, each with some specified length up to 4 gigabytes.

Linear Address Space—An address indicates the location of a register, a particular place in storage, or some other data source or destination. In the 80386, the memory's linear address space runs from byte 0 to 4 gigabytes. A linear address points to a particular byte within this space.

Logical Address—First, there is no conceptual parallel from linear address space to the space used by logical addressing. A logical address consists of a selector and offset. The selector points to some segment descriptor (part of which is that segment's linear base address). The offset tells how far into the segment the required byte is. In the programs in this book, you see notations like DS:DX that often point to a memory buffer. What this notation means is that the contents of the DX register [DX] point to bytes at an offset from the data segment [DS] beginning.

Physical Address—The address which actually selects the memory where a required byte is located. In the 80386, linear and physical addresses differ only when paging is in effect.

Task—A task is a basic, unique function of a program or system. It can be one instance of the execution of a program.

Task State Segment (TSS)—A TSS is a data structure delineated and pointed to by a descriptor, wherein the interrupted state of a task is stored each time the task is interrupted. Systems software creates the TSS's and places the initial information in them, such as correct stack pointers for interrupt handlers. TSS's are described in detail in Appendix A.

Paging—Paging refers to a procedure which transmits the consecutive bytes called a page between locations, such as between disk storage and memory. A paging function simplifies the operating system swapping algorithms because it provides a uniform mechanism for managing the physical structure of memory.

Software Guidelines

Applications designed for the 8086/8088 execute transparently in the 80386's virtual-8086 mode. Virtual environments bridge existing applications to new microprocessor systems and provide upward compatibility while offering the new environment with enhanced functions and performance. Remember that performance of applications executed in virtual-8086 mode tends to be lower than in real mode in the same processor. This occurs because an operating system intervenes to handle interrupts and emulate certain instructions. To this intervention time is added the execution time of the code that saves and restores machine state and emulates the instruction. The primary impact is in interrupt-intensive programs, because straight code tends to execute unimpeded in virtual-8086 mode.

Until an operating system is designed specifically for the 80386, certain guidelines should be kept in mind when developing a software product that is intended to run on 80386 systems; those guidelines are summarized in Fig. 3-1.

- ☐ The 80386 tends to execute specific code sequences significantly faster than earlier processors. Any code that interacts with real-time events or that depends on its execution time to perform its function should use a timing source independent of the 80386 clock speed.
- ☐ Routines written to run specifically on an 80386 system should be insensitive to the state of the PE (Protection Enable) bit in the Machine Status Word (MSW) of CR0. Setting PE causes the processor to begin executing in protected mode. The visibility of the PE bit via the Store Machine Status Word (SMSW) instruction may cause problems for code that attempts to act differently based on whether protected mode.
- ☐ Avoid any implicit or explicit use of register bits, flags, or data structures that are declared undefined or reserved for future Intel development.
- ☐ If the software is intended to run on various levels of processors (8086/8088, 80286 or 80386), write to the lowest common denominator: the 8086/8088.

Guidelines Overview
* The 80386 is faster so don't depend on real-time events as with earlier chips. Use a timing source independent of the 80386. * Avoid defining any bits that are Intel-reserved. * If writing for entire chip family (8086 thru 80386), write for 8086. 80386 instruction set is a superset of all previous generations. * Values in various registers are different on the earlier micorprocessors. Load values explicitly. * Only use instruction Opcodes that are explicitly defined.

Fig. 3-1. Software guidelines overview.

- ☐ The value of various registers and flags after reset is different on the different processors. Do not depend on the power-on state of a particular processor. A program should explicitly load the required values.
- ☐ Do not use instruction opcodes that are not explicitly documented in Intel literature. An opcode that is not part of the supported instruction set may be defined differently in a later generation, even if it seemed to have a function in the earlier processor.

Programming for the 80386

The 80386 provides compatibility with applications developed for earlier Intel processors, while providing a full 32-bit, large linear address programming environment. There are several issues to keep in mind when programming specifically for the 80386 environment that may not be clear from the documentation. Those issues are noted below.

The 80386 and OS/2

The current OS/2 operating system does not support 80386 32-bit protected mode. In the assembler directives, you tell it to assemble 80386 instructions. You also have to tell it the operating system is dispatching you in 16-bit mode. Otherwise, it generates 32-bit addresses. USE16 in all procedures requires that all 32-bit instructions be preceded by a 32-bit ESC.

Program Instructions

The 80286 implements the bus lock function differently than the 80386. Programs that use forms of memory locking specific to the 80286 may not execute correctly when transported to a specific program on the 80386.

LOCK may only be used with certain 80386 instructions (as shown in Fig. 3-2) when they modify memory. An undefined opcode exception results from using LOCK before any other instruction.

1. One-operand arithmetic and logical: INC, DEC, NOT, and NEG.
2. Two-operand arithmetic and logical: ADD, ADC, SBB, SUB, AND, OR, and XOR.
3. Exchange: XCHG.
4. Bit test and change: BTS, BTR, BTC.

The LOCK prefix and its corresponding output signal should only be used to prevent other bus masters from interrupting a data movement operation.

LOCK works *only* with:

BT, BTC, BTR, BTS	Memory, Reg/Imm
ADD, OR, ADC, SBB, AND, SUB, XOR .	Memory, Reg/Imm
DEC, INC, NEG, NOT	Memory
XCHG	Reg/Memory or Memory/Reg

Fig. 3-2. LOCK limits.

A locked instruction is guaranteed to lock only the areas of memory specifically defined by the destination operand. Typical 8086 and 80286 configurations lock the entire physical memory space. With the 80386, the defined area of memory is guaranteed to be locked against access by a processor executing a locked instruction on *exactly* the same memory area; that is, only with an operand with *identical* starting address and identical length.

The 80386 allows a CALL or JMP directly to another segment only if one of the following rules is satisfied: (1) the conforming bit of the target code-segment descriptor is set *and* the DPL of the target is less than or equal to the CPL; or (2) the DPL of the target is equal to the CPL. Most code segments are *not* conforming. For these segments, control can be transferred without a gate only to executable segments at the same privilege level. To transfer control to numerically smaller privilege levels, the CALL instruction is used with call gate descriptors. The JMP instruction may never transfer control to a nonconforming segment whose DPL does not equal CPL.

Only CALL instructions can use gates to transfer to lower numeric privilege levels. A gate may be used by a JMP instruction only to transfer to an executable segment with the same privilege level or to a conforming segment.

The BSF (Bit Scan Forward) instruction scans a word or doubleword for a one bit and stores the index of the first set bit into a register. The bit string being scanned may be either in a register or in memory. ZF is set if the entire word is zero; that is, no set bits are found. ZF is cleared if a one-bit is found. Note: If no set bit is found, the value of the destination register is undefined.

With the DIV (Unsigned Integer Divide) instruction, non-integer quotients are truncated to integers toward zero. The remainder is always less than the divisor. For unsigned byte division, the largest quotient is 255; for unsigned word division, it is 65535. For unsigned doubleword division, it is $2^{32} - 1$. For shift instructions such as SAL, CF (Carry Flag) always contains the value of the last bit shifted out of the destination operand. In a single-bit shift, OF (Overflow Flag) is set if the value of the high-order (the sign) bit was changed by the operation. If the sign bit was not changed, OF is cleared. After a multi-bit shift, the contents of OF is *always* undefined.

The difference between TEST (Logical Compare) and AND is that TEST does *not* alter the destination operand. TEST differs from BT (Bit Test) in that TEST tests the value of multiple bits in one operation, while BT tests a single bit.

Memory

Physical address formation in real-address mode: Unlike the 8086, when calculating the effective address the 80386's resulting linear address may have up to 21 significant bits. There is a possibility of a carry when the base address is added to the effective address. On the 8086, the carry bit is truncated. On the 80386,

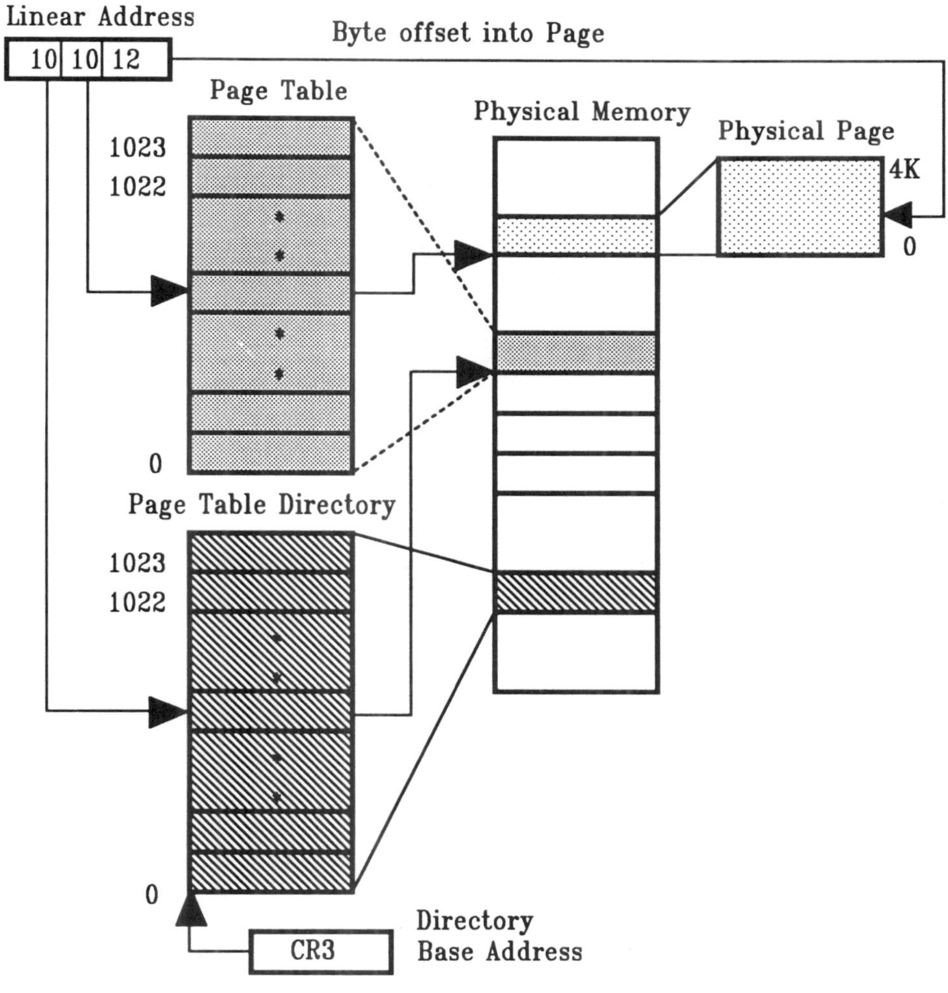

Fig. 3-3. Linear to physical address mapping.

the carry bit is stored in bit position 20 of the linear address. See Fig. 3-3 for an overview look at how the 80386 maps a linear address to a physical address.

Unlike the 8086 and the 80286, 32-bit effective addresses can be generated via the address-size prefix. However, the value of a 32-bit address in real mode may not exceed 65536 or it will cause an exception.

With the 80286, any base and offset combination that addresses beyond 16 megabytes wraps around to the first megabyte of the 80286 address space. Since the 80386 has greater physical address space, any such address falls into the 17th megabyte. In the event that any software depends on this anomaly, the same effect can be simulated on the 80386 by using paging to map the first 64K bytes of the 17th megabyte of logical address to physical addresses in the first megabyte.

To allow maximum flexibility in data structures' efficient memory utilization, words do *not* need to be aligned at even-numbered addresses. Also, doublewords do *not* need to be aligned at addresses evenly divisible by four. When using a system with a 32-bit bus, however, actual transfers of data between processor and memory take place in units of doublewords that begin at addresses evenly divisible by four. The misaligned words cause an increase in the number of memory cycles to fetch data, thus decreasing performance.

It may be expedient to turn off the 80386 segmentation when the 80386 is used to execute software designed for special architectures that do not have segments. The processor does not have a specific mode to disable segmentation. However, the same effect is achieved by initially loading the segment registers with selectors for descriptors that encompass the entire 32-bit linear address space. Once the descriptors are loaded, the segment registers are not changed. The 80386 instructions' 32-bit offsets address the entire linear-address space.

In a write cycle (with 8-bit I/O devices), if BE3# and/or BE2# but not BE1# or BE0#, the write data on the top half of the data bus is duplicated on the bottom half. If the addresses of two devices differ only in the values of BE3#–BE0# (that is, the addresses lie within the same doubleword boundaries), BE3#–BE0# must be decoded to provide a chip select signal that prevents a write to one device from erroneously performing a write to the other. This chip select can be generated using an address decoder PAL device or TTL logic.

Descriptors

Because the 80386 uses the contents of the reserved word (the last word) of every descriptor, 80286 programs that place values in this word may not execute correctly on the 80386. See Fig. 3-4 for the format of segment descriptors.

Code that manages space in descriptor tables often uses an invalid value in the access-rights field of descriptor-table entries to identify unused entries. Access rights values of 80h and 00h remain invalid on the 80386. Other values that may have been invalid for the 80286 may now be valid for the 80386 because of new descriptor types.

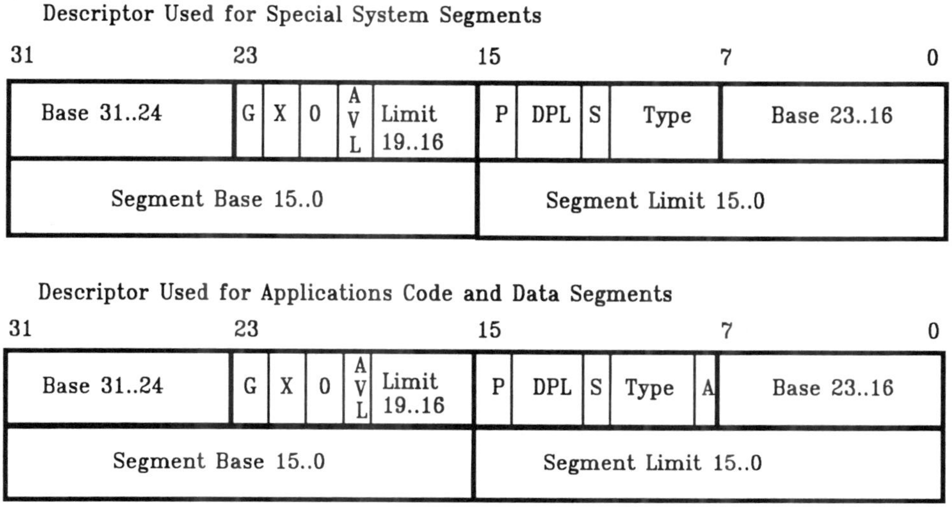

Fig. 3-4. General Segment Descriptor format.

To tell the difference between an 80286-type descriptor and an 80386-type descriptor, the processor checks the upper word. If the word is zero, then the descriptor is an 80286-type.

An executable segment whose descriptor has the conforming bit (bit 10) set is called a *conforming segment.* The conforming segment allows sharing of procedures that may be called from differing privilege levels but should execute at the privilege level of the calling procedure. When control is transferred to a conforming segment, the CPL does not change. This is the only case when CPL may be unequal to the DPL of the currently executable segment.

Registers

Certain bits in various registers are shown as either "reserved" or "undefined." When using registers with these bits, treat the bits as truly undefined. Do not depend on the states of any undefined bits when testing the values of defined register bits. Mask the undefined ones out. Do not depend on the states of any undefined bits when storing them to memory or to another register or on the ability of these bits to retain information. When loading registers, always load the undefined or reserved bits as zeros or unchanged from their values as stored.

The VM bit of the EFLAGS register can be set only two ways: in protected mode, by the IRET instruction, and only if the current privilege level is zero; and by task switches at any privilege level.

The low-order 16 bits of the CR0 register is the 80286 Machine Status Word and can be addressed separately as the MSW. See Fig. 3-5 for the format of Control Register Zero (CR0).

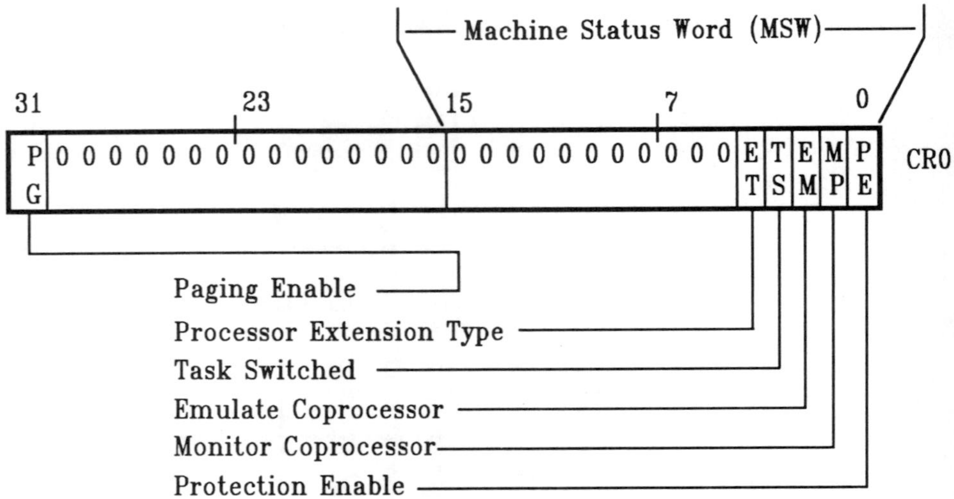

Fig. 3-5. Control Register Zero (CR0) with MSW. (Zero entries indicate Intel reserved bits; do not define.)

Tasks

The only way to leave real-address mode is to deliberately switch to protected mode. The 80386 enters protected mode when a MOV to CR0 instruction sets the protection enable (PE) bit in CR0.

A Task State Segment (TSS) may reside anywhere in the linear address space. The single caution is when the TSS spans a page boundary. In this case, the 80386 raises an exception if it encounters the not-present page while reading the TSS during a task switch.

To avoid this, either allocate the TSS so that it does not cross a page boundary, or ensure that both pages are either both present or both not-present at the time of a task switch. In this latter case, if both pages are not-present, the page-fault handler makes both pages present before restarting the instruction that caused the page default.

Tasks are *not* re-entrant. The B-bit on the TSS descriptor allows the processor to detect an attempt to switch to a task that is already busy.

In the TSS descriptor, the LIMIT defines the size of the segment. This LIMIT must contain a value of 103 or higher. An attempt to switch to a task whose LIMIT is less than 103 causes an exception.

Every task switch sets the TS bit in the MSW (in CR0). The TS bit signals that the context of a numeric coprocessor *may not correspond* to the current 80386 task.

Privilege and Protection

The privilege level at which execution restarts in the incoming task is not restricted in any way by the privilege level of the outgoing task.

When paging is enabled, the processor first checks segment protection, then evaluates page protection. If the 80386 detects a protection violation at either level, it cancels the requested operation and generates a protection exception.

The processor examines type information (in segment descriptors) on two sets of occasions. The first is when a selector of a descriptor is loaded into a segment register. Certain segment registers can contain only fixed descriptor types, such as:

- ☐ Only selectors of writable data segments can be loaded into SS.
- ☐ The CS register can be loaded only with a selector of an executable segment.
- ☐ Selectors of executable segments (that are not readable) cannot be loaded into data-segment registers.

The second class of occasion is when an instruction implicitly or explicitly refers to a segment register. Some segments can be used by instructions only in certain ways, such as:

- ☐ Unless the readable bit is set, no instruction may read an executable segment.
- ☐ Unless the writable bit is set, no instruction may write into a data segment.
- ☐ No instruction may write into an executable segment.

To combine page and segment protection, it is possible to define a large enough data segment which has some subunits that are read-only and other subunits that are read-write. If you do, the page directory or page table entries for the read-only subunits would have the U/S (User or Supervisor) and the R/W (Read/Write) bits set to *x*0. This indicates that there are no write rights for all the pages described by that directory entry or for the individual pages.

This technique could be useful in a UNIX-like system to define a large data segment, part of which is read-only (for shared data or ROMmed constants). This would enable the system to define a "flat" data space as one large segment, use "flat" pointers to address within this space, and yet be able to protect shared data, supervisor areas, and shared files mapped into virtual space.

Code segments can hold constants, but cannot be written to. There are three methods of reading data in code segments:

1. Use a CS override prefix to read a readable, executable segment whose selector is already loaded in the CS register.

2. Load a data-segment register with a selector or a non-conforming, readable, executable segment.
3. Load a data-segment register with a selector of a conforming, readable, executable segment.

Case 1 is always valid because the DPL of the code segment in CS is, by definition, equal to CPL. Case 2 uses the same rules as for access to data segments. Case 3 is always valid because the privilege level of a segment whose conforming bit is set is effectively the same as CPL, regardless of its DPL.

Testing and Debugging

Since the first entry of the Global Descriptor Table (GDT) is not used by the processor, a selector that has an index of zero and a table indicator of zero can be used as a null selector. This process does *not* cause an exception when a segment register (other than CS or SS) is loaded with a null selector. It *will* cause an exception when the segment register is used to access memory. This feature is useful for initializing unused segment registers so as to trap accidental references.

The Translation Lookaside Buffer (TLB) is a cache used for translating linear addresses to physical addresses. Figure 3-6 shows the general structure of the TLB. Note that the TLB testing mechanism is unique to the 80386 and may not be continued in the same way in future processors. Software that uses this mechanism as it currently is implemented may be incompatible with future processors.

The complement of the Dirty, User, and Writable bits in Test Register 6 (TR6) are provided to force a hit or miss for TLB lookups. A lookup operation with a bit and its complement both low is forced to be a miss. If both bits are high, a hit is forced. A write operation is *always* performed when a bit and its complement have opposite values.

It is important *not* to write the same linear address to more than one Translation Lookaside Buffer (TLB) entry. Otherwise, hit information returned during a TLB lookup operation is undefined. To look up or read a TLB entry:

1. Move a doubleword to TR6 that contains the appropriate linear address and attributes. Be sure C = 1 for lookup.
2. Store TR7. If the HT bit in TR7 is 1, then other values reveal the TLB contents. If HT = 0, then the other values are undefined. See Fig. 3-7 for Test Registers TR6 and TR7 formats.
3. For the purposes of testing, the V bit acts as another bit of address. The V bit for a lookup request should be set, so that uninitialized tags do not match. Lookups with V = 0 are unpredictable if any tags are uninitialized.

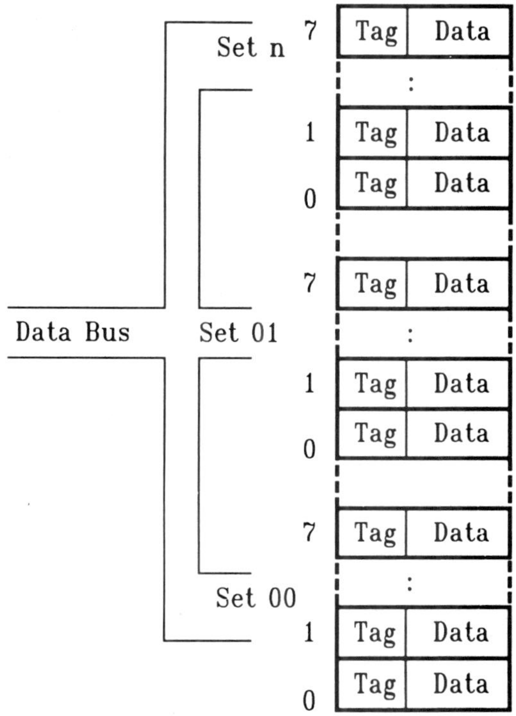

Fig. 3-6. Translation Lookaside Buffer (TLB) structure.

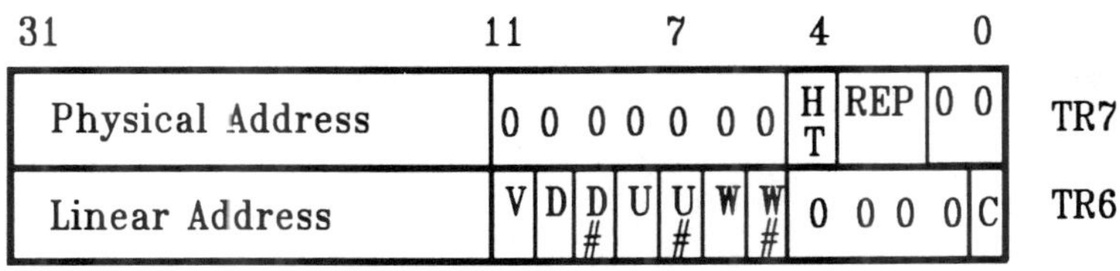

Fig. 3-7. Test Registers TR6 and TR7. (Zero entries indicate Intel reserved bits; do not define.)

TR7	HT	= Lookup was a HIT=1, MISS=0
	REP	= Block where tag was found, if HT=1, Undefined if HT=0.
TR6	V	= Valid bit
	D/D#	= Dirty bit
	U/U#	= User bit
	W/W#	= Read/Write bit
	C	= Command bit

To write a TLB entry:

1. Move a doubleword to TR7 that contains the desired physical address, HT, and REP values. HT must contain a 1. REP must point to the associative block in which to place the entry.
2. Move a doubleword to TR6 that contains the appropriate linear address, and values for V, D, U, and W. Be sure C = 0 for write command.
3. Be careful not to write duplicate tags. The results are undefined.

4

Arithmetic

Computers were designed as fast arithmetic engines that solve a variety of problems. In most computers, a single number occupies a single memory unit, usually labeled a *word*. Such word-length numbers are called *single precision*, in contrast to double-precision numbers. Double-precision numbers occupy two words (doublewords or dwords) and are used when you require additional accuracy.

Programmers work with numbers in the powers of two (2). Figure 4-1 shows the abbreviations, the powers of two, and decimal values.

A given number may be stored as fixed-point, floating-point, or binary-coded decimal (BCD). In fixed-point, the binary point (the *decimal* or *radix point*) is assumed to be at a "fixed" place, such as at the left end of the number. The mechanics of fixed-point arithmetic are essentially those of ordinary binary arithmetic, given the restriction that negative numbers are usually stored and manipulated in some complement form.

The major snare in fixed-point addition and subtraction is the phenomenon known as *overflow*. Since not only the two operands but also the result in addition and subtraction must be less than 1 in magnitude, a result greater than this will not be handled correctly. Overflow occurs when the high-order numeric bit has a carry-out into the sign bit. Normally, this is indicated by setting an internal switch which the programmer can test.

Hardware that stored and manipulated numbers in fixed-point form was the only kind available in early computers, but handling them and doing arithmetic with them created major problems. For instance, how could numbers with magnitudes of 1 or greater be handled? More significantly, how could numbers be han-

Fig. 4-1. Numeric abbreviations.

Programmer Notation	Power of Two	Decimal Value
1K	2^{10}	1024
4K	2^{12}	4096
16K	2^{14}	16,384
32K	2^{15}	32,768
64K	2^{16}	65,536
2G	2^{31}	2,147,483,648
4G	2^{32}	4,294,967,296

dled whose implicit decimal points were in different positions? How could they be added, subtracted, divided, or multiplied?

To do this arithmetic, programs shift the contents of the words, bit by bit, relative to the others. The process of such shifting and the associated problem of choosing the location of the implicit binary point for numbers before they are stored is called *scaling.* The difficulty of scaling for all but the simplest computations led to the introduction of *floating-point* hardware capabilities.

As with other processors, the 80386 supports the basic unsigned number data in byte (8-bit), word (16-bit), and dword (32-bit) lengths. Figure 4-2 shows those types. The most significant bit (MSB) of unsigned numbers is bit 7 for bytes, 15 for words, and 31 for dwords. By extension, the least significant bit (LSB) is at 0 for all types.

A sign is a binary indicator of the position of the size (magnitude) of a number, relative to zero. Sign magnitude in computer numbers has a bit that represents the sign, 0 if positive and 1 if negative. The remainder of the bits gives the absolute value of the number.

Exponents use *biased numbers* for expressing values of floating-point exponents. Biases are 127, 1023, and 16383 for short, long, and temporary real formats. Biased numbers ease numeric comparisons (e.g., greater than or less than) and are computed by taking the initial positive or negative number and adding a bias value to it. This bias makes sure that the most positive number allowable becomes the largest value of the representation and the most negative number becomes zero.

Two's complement represents signed integers. The 80386 supports both two's complement and unsigned data. In two's complement, the simple binary adder used for unsigned numbers also adds two numbers in two's complement format with no additional transformations. Two's complement is formed by computing the one's

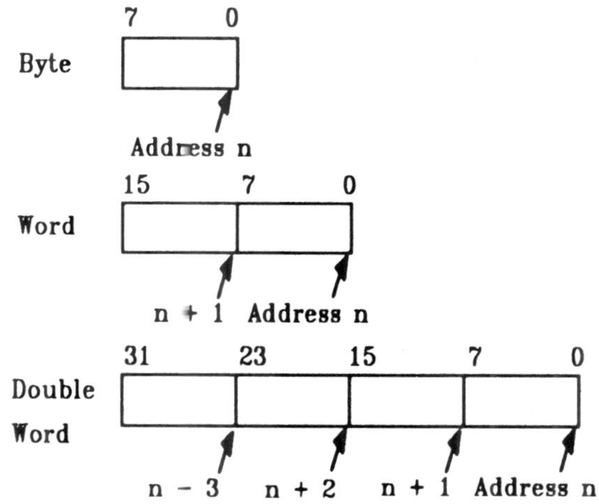

Fig. 4-2. 80386 basic data types, shown as it appears in registers (not as it appears in memory).

complement of the number and adding 1 to the result. (A one's complement number is computed by inverting every bit, including the most significant bit, or MSB.) The MSB of the byte, word, or dword is the sign bit. MSB = 1 shows a negative number and MSB = 0 indicates a positive number.

In binary arithmetic, the product of two bits is 1 if and only if both bits are 1. In adding two bits, the sum is 1 if and only if one but not both summands have the value of 1; the carry bit is 1 if and only if both summands have the value 1. Thus we compute the sum bit by using the logical inequivalence (the exclusive OR) operation and the carry bit by using the logical conjunction (the AND) operation. Since the negative of an integer is normally represented by a complementary bit pattern (two's complement), arithmetic negation is accomplished by logical negation (or boolean complementation) and adding one to form the two's complement.

Binary Addition and Subtraction

The rules of binary addition are the same as for decimal values. In decimal, adding a 9 and 1 results in a 10. We call this value "ten," but it really is this: "We've exceeded the count for the units position and this is the base number in the units position and a carry to the tens position." The same occurs in binary addition. Adding 1 and 1 results in a zero in that position with a 1 carry to the left. The rules of binary addition are shown in Fig. 4-3.

Computers don't subtract, so you have to do some fancy footwork to make them appear to (if you choose not to use the "SUB" instruction). Of the two numbers you want to work with, the first (that appears on top) is called the *minuend*. The second (that appears underneath) is called the *subtrahend*. To get a correct answer,

Rule 1: ZERO plus ZERO equals ZERO
Rule 2: ZERO plus ONE equals ONE
Rule 3: ONE plus ONE equals ZERO, with a carry to the left

Rule 1:	Rule 2:	Rule 3:
0	0	1
+ 0	+ 1	+ 1
0	1	10

Examples:

BINARY	DECIMAL	BINARY	DECIMAL
0011	3	1001	9
+ 0111	+ 7	+0101	+ 5
1010	10	1110	14

Fig. 4-3. Rules of binary addition.

Rule: Take the two's complement of the subtrahend and add to the minuend

Regular	BINARY	DECIMAL	
	S		S=Sign
Minuend	0 1010	10	
Subtrahend	0 0111	7	

The Two's complement is taken by inverting all bits and adding 1 to the low bit

	S		
Minuend	0	1010	10
Subtrahend	1	1001	−7
	C	0011	3

Fig. 4-4. Binary subtraction.

take the two's complement of the subtrahend and add it to the minuend. Figure 4-4 shows how this is done.

Binary addition and subtraction are cumbersome for humans once you get into numbers of any size. Thus, designers came up with *binary coded decimal*, which is easy for humans and more difficult for computers.

Binary Coded Decimal (BCD)

Binary-coded decimal (BCD) is a system of number representation where each decimal digit is represented by a combination of four binary digits (bits), as shown in Fig. 4-5. The largest single digit in BCD is 9 decimal, or 1001 binary.

BCD arithmetic is accurate because there is no limit to the size of the operands and the decimal point can be repositioned easily. The BCD system is based on the fact that each of the decimal digits 0 through 9 can be held conveniently in a single 4-bit nibble (half-byte). One format, called *packed BCD*, uses the two nibbles of a byte to represent two decimal digits. *Unpacked BCD* ignores the upper half of a byte and uses the lower nibble to hold a decimal digit.

BCD arithmetic involves conversion overhead before and after each operation. Packed BCD requires that two digits be packed into a series of bytes before the operation and then unpacked into ASCII representation in order to display them. Unpacked BCD is simpler because the ASCII digits 0 through 9 start out in the correct format; for example, the low nibble of the ASCII character "6" is a binary 6 (See Appendix E for additional numeric translations).

Binary	Decimal
0000	0
0001	1
0010	2
0011	3
0100	4
0101	5
0110	6
0111	7
1000	8
1001	9

Convert 3571 to BCD

Digit	3	5	7	1
Binary	0011	0101	0111	0001

Fig. 4-5. *Binary Coded Decimal (BCD) representation.*

A 64-Bit Addition/Subtraction Program

BIN64ADD, (Program 4-1 at the end of this chapter) provides a 64-bit binary add and subtract. The numbers are considered to be 63 bits long, with the high-order bit being a sign (negative numbers are kept in two's complement form). BIN64ADD uses the 32-bit integer form of the 80386.

DS:SI points to one number and DS:DI points to the other. For subtraction, the minuend is the number at DS:SI and the subtrahend is at DS:DI. The arithmetic result is stored at DS:BX. The condition codes are returned exactly as if a simple add or subtract had been done. Zero, Carry, Sign, and Overflow flags are all returned, depending on the result of the add or subtract.

Packed Decimal Routines

A BCD Driver Program

BCDDRIVE (Program 4-2 at the end of the chapter) drives the BCD routines. It allows you to enter numbers and converts them to BCD. The "standard" BCD convention used in the routines is 8 bytes long, which is 14 BCD digits with one byte taken for the sign. The routines are easily extensible to use some bits of the sign byte for a floating decimal. The BCD routines make use of the 80386 extended register set.

The BCD routines avoid creating the anomaly of a "negative zero" by testing the number to determine if it is zero and forcing the sign byte to reflect the result of the test.

BCD Pack and Unpack Programs

BCDUNPK (Program 4-3) accepts a signed BCD number with the form

SSdddddddddddddd

where *SS* is the sign byte and the 7 pairs of *dd*'s are the BCD digits. BCDUNPK creates, as output, an ASCIIZ string in the form

[–] *NNNNNNNNNNNNNN*\0

The ASCIIZ string may have a leading minus sign if the BCD number was negative. At least a single zero will be produced and the number will be terminated with a null (hex 00).

DS:BX points to the BCD number coming in and ES:DI points to the ASCII string. The number pointed to by BX will first have its sign transferred to the output string if it is negative. Leading zero digits are bypassed until the final digit, which is converted and output as are all digits after the first non-zero. The resulting ASCII string is then terminated with a null, which makes it an ASCIIZ string.

BCDPACK (Program 4-4) does the reverse. It produces a signed BCD number in the form

SSdddddddddddddd

(where *SS* is the sign byte and the 7 pairs of dd's are the BCD digits) from an ASCII string in the form of

[+/−] *NNNNNNNNNNNNNN*

The ASCII string may have a leading plus or minus sign. Up to 14 ASCII digits will be packed. Within the 14-digit limit, packing stops at the first non-digit.

DS:BX points to the BCD number and DS:SI points to the ASCII string. The number pointed to by BX is first cleared to zero. If the ASCII string has a leading minus, the sign will be tentatively set minus. The string will be examined from left to right to determine its numeric length. It will then be packed, right to left, into the target BCD number. An invalid numeric terminates the scan of the source number. The Zero Flag (ZF) is set if the result of the pack was zero. At the end of the procedure, SI points to the character beyond the converted number. The area pointed to by BX contains the packed number.

Signed Test of a BCD Number

Program 4-5, BCDTST, provides a signed test of a BCD number in the form

SSdddddddddddddd

where *SS* is the sign byte (bit 7 is on for minus, off for plus) and the 7 pairs of *dd*'s make up a 14-digit packed BCD number. BCDTST uses the 80386 expanded register set, so the routine ends up being half the size it would be if it were written for an 80286-based system (or earlier generation of chip).

DS:BX points to the BCD number. The number is tested for zero. If it is, the sign is forced to zero and a zero condition code is returned. Otherwise, the sign is set according to the value of the number's sign. Register AL contains a −1, 0, or +1, depending on the result of the comparison. The Zero Flag (ZF) and the Sign Flag (SF) are also set, depending on the results of the comparison.

Signed Comparison of BCD Numbers

BCDCMP (Program 4-6) performs a signed comparison of BCD numbers in the form

SSdddddddddddddd

where *SS* is the sign byte (bit 7 on for minus, off for plus) and the 7 pairs of *dd*'s make up a 14-digit packed BCD number. If the signs of the two numbers being compared are the same, the numbers are compared. If the signs are different, the numbers cannot be the same, so the one with the negative sign is taken to be the lower number. If both numbers are negative, the "smaller" absolute-value is determined to be closer to zero, so is therefore greater.

BCD Shift Left and Shift Right

BCDSHL (Program 4-7) provides a BCD left shift of an accumulator (double-precision) or a standard BCD value. The reason for the shifting of an accumulator is to allow the scaling before a division. If working with an implied decimal point, you can scale it left to provide decimals in the quotient.

The number of digits shifted can be from zero to the size of the input number. AL contains the size code of the value to be shifted, with zero indicating a standard number. Non-zero indicates a double-precision accumulator. AH contains the number of digits to shift and BX contains the address of the field to shift.

The size code is replaced with the size of the number in bytes (less one) for use in computing the rightmost byte address. It is also used to select a comparand for the check of the shift amount; an oversized shift (more than 13 digits for this example) results in zero and a zero condition code is set. If an odd number of digits is requested, the number is shifted left one digit. The shift amount is divided by two and the number is moved left. If a non-zero digit was shifted out of the number, the Carry Flag (CF) is set to indicate the loss of significance.

Program 4-8, BCDSHR, provides a BCD right shift of an accumulator (double-precision) or a standard BCD value. The reason for the shifting of an accumulator is to allow for scaling after a multiplication. If working with an implied decimal point, you can scale it back to get rid of the unwanted decimals.

The number of digits shifted can be from zero to the size of the input number. AL contains the size code of the value to be shifted. Zero indicates a standard number. Non-zero indicates a double-precision accumulator. AH contains the number of digits to shift. BX contains the address of the field to shift.

The size code is replaced with the size of the number in bytes (less one) for use in computing the rightmost byte address. It is also used to select a comparand for the check of the shift amount; an oversized shift (more than 13 digits for this example) results in zero and a zero condition code is set. If an odd number of digits is requested, the number is shifted right one digit. The shift amount is divided by two and the number is moved right, with zeros filling the vacated positions.

BCD Arithmetic Programs

BCD Addition and Subtraction

BCD add and subtract are combined into one procedure, BCDADD (Program 4-9). This is done because the two arithmetic functions differ only in that the sign of the subtrahend is inverted for subtraction.

Stack space is reserved as a work area for computing the result. If the signs of the two numbers are the same, the result is computed directly by addition and receives the same sign. If the signs differ, the number with the smaller absolute value is subtracted from the larger and the result receives the sign of the larger. If the result is zero, the sign is forced to positive. If an overflow occurs, the Carry Flag will be set.

BCD Multiplication

BCDMPY (Program 4-10) provides signed multiplication for BCD numbers in the form

SSdddddddddddddd

where *SS* is the sign byte (bit 7 is on for minus, off for plus) and the 7 pairs of *dd*'s make up a 14-digit packed BCD number, packed two digits per byte. The product is placed in the 16-byte accumulator specified by DS:BX. If the accumulator overlaps either the multiplier or the multiplicand, the results are undefined.

DS:SI points to one BCD number and DS:DI points to the other. DS:BX points to the accumulator where the product is formed. The sign of the product is computed and set, and the accumulator is cleared to zero. The algorithm used to form the product is an adaptation of a simple manual multiplication.

The product is formed by selecting each digit of the multiplier from right to left and performing a right-to-left, digit-by-digit multiplication, adding the result to the accumulator. Because there are two decimal digits in each byte, we have four variants of the multiply. That is, if we are multiplying 76 by 34, we have to multiply 6 by 4, getting a product of 24. We then multiply 70 by 4 and add that partial product (280) to the 24 to get 304. We then multiply 6 by 30 to get 180 as a partial product which, when added, gives 484. Finally, we multiply 70 by 30 to get the partial product 2100 which we add to our previous sum, to get the final result of 2584.

BCD Division

BCDDIV (Program 4-11) provides a signed division of an accumulator, a 16-byte product:

SSxxdddddddddddddddddddddddddddd

(where in this case *xx* is filler to force the sign to the leftmost byte of the high-order word) by a BCD number:

SSdddddddddddddd

BCDDIV uses the technique of repeated subtraction to form the quotient. It subtracts the divisor from the left digits of the dividend until the result goes negative, counting the number of times it was subtracted and adding back to get a positive value, then shift right one nibble. This creates a signed quotient in the upper half of the double-wide accumulator and a signed remainder in the lower portion.

DS:DI points to the BCD number which is the divisor and DS:BX points to the dividend (accumulator). Division by zero is checked. In the case of an overflow, the Carry Flag is set and no quotient or remainder is formed.

Program 4-1: BIN64ADD

```
Microsoft (R) Macro Assembler Version 5.00


                                        PAGE      55,132
                                        .386
0000                             code   SEGMENT   para 'CODE' PUBLIC USE16
                                        ASSUME    CS:code, DS:code, SS:code

                                 ; Name:    BIN64ADD
                                 ;
                                 ; Purpose: The following procedure provides a 64 bit binary add
                                 ;          and subtract. The numbers are considered to be 63 bits
                                 ;          long with the high order bit being a sign.  Negative
                                 ;          numbers are kept in 2's compliment form.
                                 ;          It uses the 32 bit integer form of the 80386.
                                 ;
                                 ;
                                 ;
                                 ; Inputs:   DS:SI points to one number, DS:DI points to the other.
                                 ;           For subtraction the minuend is the number at DS:SI, the
                                 ;           subtrahend is at DS:DI.  (i.e. DS:BX=DS:SI-DS:DI)
                                 ;           DS:BX points to the location for the sum (or difference).
                                 ;
                                 ; Process:  The add entry point preserves EAX and EDX and loads them
                                 ;           with the number at DS:DI.  The subtract entry does the
                                 ;           same and in addition takes the 2's compliment of the
                                 ;           number.  The number at DS:SI is then added and the result
                                 ;           is stored at DS:BX.
                                 ;
                                 ; Output:  The arithmetic result is stored at DS:BX.  The condition
                                 ;          code is returned exactly as if a simple add or subtract had
                                 ;          been done.   Zero, carry, sign, and overflow are all
                                 ;          returned.
                                 ;
                                          PUBLIC  Bin64add
                                 ;
0000                             Bin64add PROC
0000  66| 52                              push    EDX                   ; Save entry registers
0002  66| 50                              push    EAX
0004  66| 8B 05                           mov     EAX,DWORD PTR[DI+0]   ; Load low 32
0007  66| 8B 55 04                        mov     EDX,DWORD PTR[DI+4]   ; and high 32.
000B  EB 18 90                            jmp     goaddem               ; Go do addition.

                                 ;
                                 ; Entry point for subtract.
                                 ;
                                          PUBLIC  Bin64sub
000E                             Bin64sub:
000E  66| 52                              push    EDX                   ; Save entry registers
0010  66| 50                              push    EAX
0012  66| 8B 05                           mov     EAX,DWORD PTR[DI+0]   ; Load low 32
0015  66| 8B 55 04                        mov     EDX,DWORD PTR[DI+4]   ; and high 32.
0019  66| F7 D0                           not     EAX                   ; Get the one's compliment.
001C  66| F7 D2                           not     EDX
001F  66| 40                              inc     EAX                   ; Add one for two's compliment
0021  66| 83 D2 00                        adc     EDX,0                 ; propagate the carry if any.
                                 ;
                                 ; The routines are the same from here out.
                                 ;
0025                             goaddem:
```

```
0025  66| 03 04                     add     EAX,DWORD PTR[SI+0] ; Add the low 32 bits
0028  66| 89 07                     mov     DWORD PTR[BX+0],EAX ; and store the result.
002B  9F                            lahf                        ; Preserve the condition code.
002C  8A C4                         mov     AL,AH               ; In AL.
002E  66| 13 54 04                  adc     EDX,DWORD PTR[SI+4] ; Include carry in the high 32.
0032  66| 89 57 04                  mov     DWORD PTR[BX+4],EDX ; Store the result.
0036  9F                            lahf                        ; Get the condition code.
0037  B6 00                         mov     DH,0                ; assume no overflow
0039  0F 81 003F R                  jno     didnt               ; and skip if it didn't
003D  B6 80                         mov     DH,080h             ; set to cause one otherwise.
003F                        didnt:
                            ;
                            ; We need to combine the condition codes from the two adds as follows:
                            ; Sign and carry from the high order add, aux-carry and parity from
                            ; the low order add, and zero is set only if on in both.
                            ;
003F  B2 40                         mov     DL,01000000b        ; mask to preserve zero flag.
0041  22 D4                         and     DL,AH
0043  22 D0                         and     DL,AL               ; Zero is set if on in both.
                            ;                  AH high AL low    cc from add of
                            ;                  szxaxpxcszxaxpxc  bits
0045  25 AB3E                       and     AX,1010101100111110b ;
0048  0A E0                         or      AH,AL               ; Combine low half flags and high
004A  0A E2                         or      AH,DL               ; With zero if necessary.
004C  02 F6                         add     DH,DH               ; Reset overflow if needed then
004E  9E                            sahf                        ; set the combined other flags.
004F  66| 58                        pop     EAX                 ; Restore the entry registers
0051  66| 5A                        pop     EDX
0053  C3                            ret                         ; and return.
0054                        Bin64add ENDP
0054                        code    ENDS
                                    END
```

Program 4-2: DRIVEBCD

```
Microsoft (R) Macro Assembler Version 5.00


                                        PAGE    55,132
                                        .386

                              ;
                              ; Name:    DRIVEBCD
                              ;
                              ; Purpose: This program demonstrates the BCD package.
                              ;
                              ; Inputs:  We prompt for three numbers to be entered: A first number,
                              ;          a second number, and a number to divide.
                              ;
                              ; Process: The program loops requesting the first number (we end if an
                              ;          empty line is entered), and a second number.  We then add
                              ;          the numbers and display the result, subtract the numbers
                              ;          and display the result, multiply the numbers and display
                              ;          the result.  We then prompt for a third number and divide
                              ;          it by the second.  We display the resulting quotient and
                              ;          remainder.  We then shift the quotient left 5 and right 3
                              ;          displaying the results.  We shift the product left 4 and
                              ;          right 2 displaying the results.  We test number 1 and
                              ;          display the result.  We compare number 2 to number 1 and
                              ;          display the result.  We then loop.
                              ;
                              ; Outputs: All output is displayed as the result of the above tests.
                              ;
                              ;
                              ; Declare the routines we are going to use
                              ;
                                        EXTRN   BCDPACK:NEAR
                                        EXTRN   BCDUNPK:NEAR
                                        EXTRN   BCDSUB:NEAR
                                        EXTRN   BCDADD:NEAR
                                        EXTRN   BCDMPY:NEAR
                                        EXTRN   BCDDIV:NEAR
                                        EXTRN   BCDCMP:NEAR
                                        EXTRN   BCDTST:NEAR
                                        EXTRN   BCDSHL:NEAR
                                        EXTRN   BCDSHR:NEAR

0000                          stack     SEGMENT para 'STACK' STACK
0000  0100[                             dq      256 DUP(?)
          ???????????????
          ?
                  ]

0800                          stack     ENDS
0000                          data      SEGMENT para
0000  0100[                   string    db      256 DUP(?)          ; String scratch area
           ??
                  ]
0100  0008[                   bcdno1    db      8 DUP(?)            ; First BCD number
           ??
                  ]

0108  0008[                   bcdno2    db      8 DUP(?)            ; Second BCD number
           ??
```

```
                               ]

0110  0010[                     bcdacum    db      16 DUP(?)          ; Accumulator
           ??
                               ]

0120  0010[                     bcdacum1   db      16 DUP(?)          ; Accumulator 2
           ??
                               ]

0130  80 00 00 00 00 00 00      minus1     db      128,0,0,0,0,0,0,1  ; minus one
      01
0138  00 00 00 00 00 00 00      zero       db      0,0,0,0,0,0,0,0    ; and zero
      00
0140  00 00 00 00 00 00 00      plus1      db      0,0,0,0,0,0,0,1    ; plus one
      01
0148  0A 0A 0A 0D 45 6E 74      query1     db      10,10,10,13,"Enter first number: $"
      65 72 20 66 69 72 73
      74 20 6E 75 6D 62 65
      72 3A 20 24
0161  0A 0D 45 6E 74 65 72      query2     db      10,13,"Enter second number: $"
      20 73 65 63 6F 6E 64
      20 6E 75 6D 62 65 72
      3A 20 24
0179  0A 0D 45 6E 74 65 72      query3     db      10,13,"Enter a number to divide: $"
      20 61 20 6E 75 6D 62
      65 72 20 74 6F 20 64
      69 76 69 64 65 3A 20
      24
0196  53 75 6D 20 20 20 3D      output1    db     "Sum   = $"
      20 24
019F  44 69 66 66 20 20 3D      output2    db     "Diff  = $"
      20 24
01A8  50 72 6F 64 20 20 3D                 db     "Prod  = $"
      20 24
01B1  51 75 6F 74 20 20 3D                 db     "Quot  = $"
      20 24
01BA  52 65 6D 20 20 20 3D                 db     "Rem   = $"
      20 24
01C3  53 68 6C 20 35 20 3D                 db     "Shl 5 = $"
      20 24
01CC  53 68 72 20 33 20 3D                 db     "Shr 3 = $"
      20 24
01D5  53 68 6C 20 34 20 3D                 db     "Shl 4 = $"
      20 24
01DE  53 68 72 20 32 20 3D                 db     "Shr 2 = $"
      20 24
01E7  54 73 74 20 31 20 3D                 db     "Tst 1 = $"
      20 24
01F0  43 6D 70 31 3A 32 3D                 db     "Cmp1:2= $"
      20 24
01F9  0000                      nxtdisp    dw     0                   ; output pointer
01FB                            data       ENDS
0000                            code       SEGMENT   para 'CODE' USE16 PUBLIC
                                           ASSUME    CS:code, DS:data
                                ;
                                ; Set up the environment
                                ;
0000                            Begin:
0000  B8 ---- R                            mov    AX,data             ; Get data segment pointer
0003  8E D8                                mov    DS,AX               ; into DS,
0005  8E C0                                mov    ES,AX               ; and ES.
```

```
0007  2B F6                   sub     SI,SI               ; Clear indices
0009  2B FF                   sub     DI,DI
000B                  nextnum:
000B  8D 16 0196 R            lea     DX,output1          ; Set output pointer
000F  89 16 01F9 R            mov     nxtdisp,DX          ; initially for add.
0013  8D 16 0148 R            lea     DX,query1           ; ask for it
0017  E8 0110 R               call    getinp              ; get first number
001A  0B C9                   or      CX,CX               ; Is it null
001C  0F 84 00FD R            jz      Exit                ; If null - quit
0020  8B F3                   mov     SI,BX               ; Point to string,
0022  8D 1E 0100 R            lea     BX,bcdno1           ; number, and
0026  E8 0000 E               call    bcdpack             ; convert it.
0029                  getsecnd:
0029  8D 16 0161 R            lea     DX,query2           ; ask for it
002D  E8 0110 R               call    getinp              ; get first number
0030  E3 F7                   jcxz    getsecnd            ; If null - try again
0032  8B F3                   mov     SI,BX               ; Point to string,
0034  8D 1E 0108 R            lea     BX,bcdno2           ; number, and
0038  E8 0000 E               call    bcdpack             ; convert it.
                      ;
                      ; Add them and display the result
                      ;
003B  8D 1E 0110 R            lea     BX,bcdacum          ; Point to result
003F  8D 36 0100 R            lea     SI,bcdno1           ; first number,
0043  8D 3E 0108 R            lea     DI,bcdno2           ; second number,
0047  E8 0000 E               call    bcdadd              ; and add them.
004A  E8 0137 R               call    display             ; Put out a line.
                      ;
                      ; Subtract them and display the result
                      ;
004D  E8 0000 E               call    bcdsub              ; subtract them
0050  E8 0137 R               call    display             ; Put out a line
                      ;
                      ; Multiply them and display the result
                      ;
0053  8D 1E 0120 R            lea     BX,bcdacum1         ; Use alt accum
0057  E8 0000 E               call    bcdmpy              ; multiply them
005A  A0 0120 R               mov     AL,bcdacum1         ; Get sign
005D  8D 1E 0128 R            lea     BX,bcdacum1+8       ; point to it.
0061  88 07                   mov     BYTE PTR [BX],AL    ; Position the sign.
0063  E8 0137 R               call    display             ; display it
                      ;
                      ; Get a number for the dividend
                      ;
0066                  getdiv:
0066  8D 16 0179 R            lea     DX,query3           ; ask for it
006A  E8 0110 R               call    getinp              ; get first dividend
006D  E3 F7                   jcxz    getdiv              ; If null - try again
006F  8B F3                   mov     SI,BX               ; Point to string,
0071  8D 1E 0118 R            lea     BX,bcdacum+8        ; number, and
0075  E8 0000 E               call    bcdpack             ; convert it.
0078  66| 2B C0               sub     EAX,EAX             ; Get leading zeros
007B  66| A3 0114 R           mov     DWORD PTR bcdacum+4,EAX ; force leading zeros
007F  86 06 0118 R            xchg    AL,bcdacum+8        ; Get sign and clear old
0083  66| A3 0110 R           mov     DWORD PTR bcdacum,EAX ; force leading zeros
                      ;
                      ; Divide by the second number and display both quotient and remainder.
                      ;
0087  8D 1E 0110 R            lea     BX,bcdacum          ; Point to accum
008B  8D 36 0108 R            lea     SI,bcdno2           ; second number,
008F  E8 0000 E               call    bcddiv              ; and divide
0092  E8 0137 R               call    display             ; display the quotient
0095  8D 1E 0118 R            lea     BX,bcdacum+8
```

```
0099  E8 0137 R                 call    display             ; and remainder.
                        ;
                        ; Shift the quotient as a number and display it.
                        ;
009C  8D 1E 0110 R              lea     BX,bcdacum          ; Quotient
00A0  B0 00                     mov     AL,0                ; as a number
00A2  B4 05                     mov     AH,5                ; shift count
00A4  E8 0000 E                 call    bcdshl              ; and shift it left 5
00A7  E8 0137 R                 call    display             ; and display the number
                        ;
                        ; Shift it back three and display it.
                        ;
00AA  8D 1E 0110 R              lea     BX,bcdacum          ; Quotient
00AE  B0 00                     mov     AL,0                ; as a number
00B0  B4 03                     mov     AH,3                ; shift count
00B2  E8 0000 E                 call    bcdshr              ; and shift it right 3
00B5  E8 0137 R                 call    display             ; and display the number
                        ;
                        ; Shift the product and display it as an accumulator.
                        ;
00B8  8D 1E 0120 R              lea     BX,bcdacum1         ; Product
00BC  B0 01                     mov     AL,1                ; as an accum
00BE  B4 04                     mov     AH,4                ; shift count
00C0  E8 0000 E                 call    bcdshl              ; and shift it left 4
00C3  8D 1E 0128 R              lea     BX,bcdacum1+8       ; shift for number display
00C7  E8 0137 R                 call    display             ; and display the number
00CA  8D 1E 0120 R              lea     BX,bcdacum1         ; Product
00CE  B0 01                     mov     AL,1                ; as an accum
00D0  B4 02                     mov     AH,2                ; shift count
00D2  E8 0000 E                 call    bcdshr              ; and shift it right 2
00D5  8D 1E 0128 R              lea     BX,bcdacum1+8       ; shift for number display
00D9  E8 0137 R                 call    display             ; and display the number
                        ;
                        ; Test the first number and display the result
                        ;
00DC  8D 1E 0100 R              lea     BX,bcdno1           ; point to number
00E0  E8 0000 E                 call    bcdtst              ; check it
00E3  E8 0103 R                 call    pzmpoint            ; Get value pointer
00E6  E8 0137 R                 call    display             ; Display the result
                        ;
                        ; Compare number2 to number1 and display the result.
                        ;
00E9  8D 3E 0108 R              lea     DI,bcdno2           ; point to comparand 2
00ED  8D 36 0100 R              lea     SI,bcdno1           ; point to comparand 1
00F1  E8 0000 E                 call    bcdcmp              ; compare them
00F4  E8 0103 R                 call    pzmpoint            ; Get value pointer
00F7  E8 0137 R                 call    display             ; Display the result
                        ;
                        ; Get another set of test values and repeat.
                        ;
00FA  E9 000B R                 jmp     nextnum
00FD                    Exit:
00FD  B0 00                     mov     AL,0                ; Set return code
00FF  B4 4C                     mov     AH,04ch             ; Set good-by
0101  CD 21                     int     21h                 ; Return to the system

                        ;
                        ; Point to a -1, 0, or +1 based on AL  (preserve flags too)
                        ;
0103                    pzmpoint        PROC
0103  9C                        pushf                       ; save flags
0104  98                        cbw                         ; get a word index
```

```
0105  C1 E0 03                      shl     AX,3                ; times 8
0108  8D 1E 0138 R                  lea     BX,zero             ; Point to the number
010C  03 D8                         add     BX,AX               ; matching the return code
010E  9D                            popf
010F  C3                            ret
0110                      pzmpoint  ENDP
                          ;
                          ; Read a string in response to a prompt
                          ; The prompt must be in DX.  The string will be returned in string.
                          ; The length of string is returned in CX.
                          ; BX points to the start of the string.
                          ;
0110                      getinp    PROC
0110  50                            push    AX                  ; Save registers
0111  56                            push    SI
0112  B4 09                         mov     AH,9                ; and dos request
0114  CD 21                         int     21h                 ; put out the string
0116  8D 16 0000 R                  lea     DX,string           ; point to input area
011A  C6 06 0000 R FE               mov     string,254          ; Set max length in
011F  B4 0A                         mov     AH,10               ; Ask for read of string
0121  CD 21                         int     21h                 ; from DOS.
0123  8D 1E 0002 R                  lea     BX,string+2         ; Point to just read data
0127  8A 0E 0001 R                  mov     CL,string+1         ; Get length read
012B  B5 00                         mov     CH,0                ; as a word.
012D  8B F1                         mov     SI,CX               ; Set length
012F  C6 84 0002 R 00               mov     string+2[SI],0      ; and make an asciiz string.
0134  5E                            pop     SI
0135  58                            pop     AX                  ; Restore registers
0136  C3                            ret                         ; and return.
0137                      getinp    ENDP

                          ;
                          ; Display the number pointed to by BX.
                          ;
0137                      display   PROC
0137  60                            pusha                       ; Save registers
0138  B8 0D0A                       mov     AX,0d0ah            ; Set c/r lf
013B  A3 0000 R                     mov     WORD PTR string,AX  ; into output
013E  66| B8 534F435A               mov     EAX,'SOCZ'          ; All on
0144  66| A3 0002 R                 mov     DWORD PTR string+2,EAX ; into output
0148  B8 2420                       mov     AX,'$ '             ; Stopper
014B  A3 0006 R                     mov     WORD PTR string+6,AX ; into output
014E  0F 84 0155 R                  jz      nonzer
0152  A2 0002 R                     mov     BYTE PTR string+2,AL ; If flag not set - blank it
0155                      nonzer:
0155  0F 82 015C R                  jc      noncry
0159  A2 0003 R                     mov     BYTE PTR string+3,AL ; If flag not set - blank it
015C                      noncry:
015C  0F 80 0163 R                  jo      nonovf
0160  A2 0004 R                     mov     BYTE PTR string+4,AL ; If flag not set - blank it
0163                      nonovf:
0163  0F 88 016A R                  js      nonsgn
0167  A2 0005 R                     mov     BYTE PTR string+5,AL ; If flag not set - blank it
016A                      nonsgn:
016A  8D 16 0000 R                  lea     DX,string           ; Point to output
016E  B4 09                         mov     AH,9                ; set dos code.
0170  CD 21                         int     21h                 ; Write it
0172  8B 16 01F9 R                  mov     DX,nxtdisp          ; Get output type
0176  CD 21                         int     21h                 ; Put it out
0178  83 C2 09                      add     DX,output2-output1  ; step it
017B  89 16 01F9 R                  mov     nxtdisp,DX          ; and save it
017F  8D 3E 0000 R                  lea     DI,string           ; output pointer
```

```
0183  E8 0000 E                        call    bcdunpk           ;
0186  C6 85 0000 R 24                  mov     string[DI],'$'    ; set ender
018B  8D 16 0000 R                     lea     DX,string         ; Point to it
018F  B4 09                            mov     AH,9              ; set print
0191  CD 21                            int     21h               ; and do it.

0193  61                               popa                      ; Restore registers
0194  C3                               ret                       ; and return
0195                         display   ENDP

0195                         code      ENDS
                                       END     Begin
```

Program 4-3: BCDUNPK

```
Microsoft (R) Macro Assembler Version 5.00


                                        PAGE    55,132
                                        .386
 0000                           code    SEGMENT para 'CODE' PUBLIC USE16
                                        ASSUME  CS:code, DS:code, SS:code

                                ; Name:    BCDUNPK
                                ;
                                ; Purpose: The following procedure accepts a signed BCD number in
                                ;          the 'standard' form of SSdddddddddddddd and creates an
                                ;          ASCIIZ string of the form [-]NNNNNNNNNNNNNN\0.
                                ;          Where SS is the sign byte (bit 7 is on for minus, off for
                                ;          plus) and the 7 pairs of dd's make up a 14 digit packed BCD
                                ;          number.  The ascii string may have a leading minus sign if
                                ;          the bcd number was negative.  At least a single zero will
                                ;          be produced.  The number will be terminated with a null.
                                ;
                                ;
                                ; Inputs:  DS:BX points to the BCD number ES:DI points to the ascii
                                ;          string.
                                ;
                                ; Process: The number pointed to by BX will first have its sign
                                ;          transferred to the output string if it is negative.  Leading
                                ;          zero digits are bypassed until the final digit which is
                                ;          converted and output as are all digits after the first
                                ;          non-zero.  The resulting ascii string is then terminated
                                ;          with a null.
                                ;
                                ; Output:  The ascii representation of the number will be placed into
                                ;          ES:DI and DI will point to the null following the number.
                                ;
                                ;
                                ;
                                ;
                                         PUBLIC  Bcdunpk
                                         PUBLIC  Bcdunpka
                                ;
 0000                           Bcdunpk  PROC
 0000  50                                push    AX                  ; Save work registers
 0001  51                                push    CX
 0002  B9 0007                           mov     CX,7                ; Set count of pairs.
 0005  EB 06 90                          jmp     setsi
 0008                           Bcdunpka:
 0008  50                                push    AX                  ; Save work registers
 0009  51                                push    CX
 000A  B9 000F                           mov     CX,15               ; Set count of pairs.
 000D                           setsi:
 000D  56                                push    SI
 000E  BE 0001                           mov     SI,1                ; Set source index

 0011  FC                                cld                         ; Set direction to up.
 0012  F6 07 80                          test    BYTE PTR[BX+0],080h ; is the number negative?
 0015  0F 84 001C R                      jz      leadzero            ; no - skip
 0019  B0 2D                             mov     AL,'-'              ; Get minus sign
 001B  AA                                stosb                       ; into number.

 001C                           leadzero:
 001C  8A 00                             mov     AL,BYTE PTR[BX+SI]  ; Get pair of digits
 001E  46                                inc     SI                  ; Point to next
```

```
001F  0A C0                    or      AL,AL                ; check it
0021  0F 85 0028 R             jnz     leadzero1            ; A digit! Go check high/low.
0025  E2 F5                    loop    leadzero             ; Check all pairs.
                        ;
                        ; The number was zero - just plug a zero and a null and exit.
                        ;
0027  41                       inc     CX                   ; We want to stop below too.
0028                    leadzero1:
0028  A8 F0                    test    AL,0f0h              ; Is high nibble zero?
002A  0F 84 0040 R             jz      highzero             ; Yes just store low.
002E  EB 04 90                 jmp     highdig              ; No go do both
0031                    moredigs:
0031  8A 00                    mov     AL,BYTE PTR[BX+SI]   ; Get pair of digits
0033  46                       inc     SI                   ; Point to next
0034                    highdig:
0034  8A E0                    mov     AH,AL                ; Copy to save low nibble
0036  C0 E8 04                 shr     AL,4                 ; Get a digit from the high
0039  0C 30                    or      AL,'0'               ; Put proper zone in.
003B  AA                       stosb                        ; Then store digit.
003C  8A C4                    mov     AL,AH                ; Get low digit in AL.
003E  24 0F                    and     AL,00fh              ; Clear high nibble
0040                    highzero:
0040  0C 30                    or      AL,'0'               ; Set the zone
0042  AA                       stosb                        ; and place the digit
0043  E2 EC                    loop    moredigs             ; Go do all the rest.
                        ;
                        ; All digit pairs have been translated
                        ;
0045  B0 00                    mov     AL,0                 ; Get a null
0047  AA                       stosb                        ; use it to follow the number
0048  5E                       pop     SI                   ; Restore registers
0049  59                       pop     CX
004A  58                       pop     AX
004B  C3                       ret                          ; and return.
004C                    Bcdunpk         ENDP
004C                    code            ENDS
                                END
```

Program 4-4: BCDPACK

```
Microsoft (R) Macro Assembler Version 5.00


                                        PAGE      55,132
                                        .386
0000                            code    SEGMENT   para 'CODE' PUBLIC USE16
                                        ASSUME    CS:code, DS:code, SS:code

                                ; Name:     BCDPACK
                                ;
                                ; Purpose: The following procedure produces a signed BCD number in
                                ;           the 'standard' form of SSdddddddddddddd from an ascii
                                ;           string of the form [+/-]NNNNNNNNNNNNNN.
                                ;           Where SS is the sign byte (bit 7 is on for minus, off for
                                ;           plus) and the 7 pairs of dd's make up a 14 digit packed BCD
                                ;           number.  The ascii string may have a leading plus or minus
                                ;           sign.  Up to 14 ascii digits will be packed. Within the 14
                                ;           digit limit, packing stops at the first non digit.
                                ;
                                ;
                                ; Inputs:  DS:BX points to the BCD number DS:SI points to the ascii
                                ;           string.
                                ;
                                ; Process: The number pointed to by BX is cleared to zero. If the
                                ;           ASCII string has a leading -, the sign will be tentatively
                                ;           set minus.  The string will be examined left to right to
                                ;           determine its numeric length.  It will then be packed,
                                ;           right to left into the target BCD number.  An invalid
                                ;           numeric terminates the scan of the source number.
                                ;
                                ; Output:  The zero flag will be set if the result of the pack was
                                ;           zero.
                                ;           SI will point to the character beyond the converted number.
                                ;           The area pointed to by BX will contain the packed number.
                                ;
                                ;
                                          PUBLIC   Bcdpack
                                ;
0000                            Bcdpack   PROC
0000  66| 50                              push     EAX                   ; Save work registers
0002  51                                  push     CX
0003  57                                  push     DI

0004  66| 2B C0                           sub      EAX,EAX               ; Get a double word of zero.
0007  66| 89 07                           mov      DWORD PTR[BX+0],EAX ; Load the first half
000A  66| 89 47 04                        mov      DWORD PTR[BX+4],EAX ; and the second half.
000E  80 3C 2B                            cmp      BYTE PTR[SI],'+'      ; Leading plus?
0011  0F 84 001F R                        jz       leadplus              ; If so - just skip it
0015  80 3C 2D                            cmp      BYTE PTR[SI],'-'      ; Negative number?
0018  0F 85 0020 R                        jnz      notminus              ; no - skip
001C  C6 07 80                            mov      BYTE PTR[BX+0],080h ; set number negative
001F                            leadplus:
001F  46                                  inc      SI                    ; and skip the sign.
0020                            notminus:
0020  B9 000E                             mov      CX,14                 ; Set maximum number of digits
0023  FC                                  cld                            ; and set direction up.
0024                            chknbr:
0024  AC                                  lodsb                          ; Get a byte from the string.
0025  34 30                               xor      AL,'0'                ; Check if it is a number
```

```
0027  3C 09                    cmp     AL,9                   ;
0029  0F 87 0030 R             ja      endnbr                 ; if >9 we are done.
002D  E2 F5                    loop    chknbr                 ; try next one
002F  46                       inc     SI                     ; Pretend we went too far.
0030                    endnbr:
0030  4E                       dec     SI                     ; Point to stopper byte.
0031  56                       push    SI                     ; Save location of next char.
0032  4E                       dec     SI                     ; Point to last digit
0033  B8 000E                  mov     AX,14                  ; Prepare to get number of
0036  2B C1                    sub     AX,CX                  ; digits in the string.
0038  8B C8                    mov     CX,AX                  ; Set in count position.
003A  E3 1E                    jcxz    donenbr                ; If none - get out
003C  BF 0007                  mov     DI,7                   ; Get right-hand index to dest.
003F  FD                       std                            ; Work right to left
0040                    nextpair:
0040  AC                       lodsb                          ; Get a digit
0041  E2 07                    loop    havetop                ; If it has a top half - get it
0043  24 0F                    and     AL,0fh                 ; set top half zero.
0045  88 01                    mov     BYTE PTR[BX+DI],AL     ; Put into number
0047  EB 11 90                 jmp     donenbr                ; and exit.
004A                    havetop:
004A  8A E0                    mov     AH,AL                  ; Save AL for
004C  AC                       lodsb                          ; load of high order digit.
004D  25 0F0F                  and     AX,0f0fh               ; Isolate digits
0050  C0 E0 04                 shl     AL,4                   ; Position high as high,
0053  0A C4                    or      AL,AH                  ; and combine into AL.
0055  88 01                    mov     BYTE PTR[BX+DI],AL     ; Put into number
0057  4F                       dec     DI                     ; point to next digit
0058  E2 E6                    loop    nextpair               ; Go do another pair
005A                    donenbr:
005A  5E                       pop     SI                     ; Restore pointer to next char.
005B  66| 8B 07                mov     EAX,[BX+0]             ; Get top word
005E  B0 00                    mov     AL,0                   ; less sign
0060  66| 0B 47 04             or      EAX,[BX+4]             ; Combine with the low word
0064  0F 85 006A R             jnz     donenbr0               ; Go
0068  88 07                    mov     BYTE PTR[BX+0],AL      ; Plug sign with zero.
006A                    donenbr0:
006A  5F                       pop     DI                     ; Restore registers
006B  59                       pop     CX
006C  66| 58                   pop     EAX
006E  C3                       ret                            ; and return.
006F                    Bcdpack ENDP
006F                    code    ENDS
                               END
```

Program 4-5: BCDTST

```
Microsoft (R) Macro Assembler Version 5.00


                                        PAGE      55,132
                                        .386
 0000                           code    SEGMENT   para 'CODE' PUBLIC USE16
                                        ASSUME    CS:code, DS:code, SS:code

                                ; Name:    BCDTST
                                ;
                                ; Purpose: The following procedure provides a signed test of a
                                ;          BCD number in the 'standard' form of SSdddddddddddddd.
                                ;          Where SS is the sign byte (bit 7 is on for minus, off for
                                ;          plus) and the 7 pairs of dd's make up a 14 digit packed
                                ;          BCD number.
                                ;
                                ;
                                ; Inputs:  DS:BX points to the BCD number.
                                ;
                                ; Process: The number pointed to by BX is tested for zero. If it is,
                                ;          the sign is forced to zero and a zero cc is returned.
                                ;          Otherwise, the sign is set according to the value of the
                                ;          number's sign.
                                ;
                                ;
                                ;
                                ; Output:  Register AL will contain -1, 0, +1 depending on the result
                                ;          of the comparison.
                                ;          The zero and sign flags will also be set.
                                ;
                                ;
                                        PUBLIC  Bcdtst
                                ;
 0000                           Bcdtst  PROC
 0000  66| 50                           push    EAX                    ; Save work register
 0002  80 27 80                         and     BYTE PTR[BX+0],080h    ; Force good sign byte
 0005  66| 8B 07                        mov     EAX,DWORD PTR[BX+0]    ; Load the first half
 0008  B0 00                            mov     AL,0                   ; Clear the sign byte
 000A  66| 0B 47 04                     or      EAX,DWORD PTR[BX+4]    ; Combine with second half
 000E  66| 58                           pop     EAX                    ; restore entry register
 0010  B0 00                            mov     AL,0                   ; set for zero
 0012  0F 85 0017 R                     jnz     notyet                 ; Return zero
 0016  C3                               ret
 0017                           notyet:
 0017  F6 07 80                         test    BYTE PTR[BX+0],080h    ; check the sign
 001A  0F 85 0021 R                     jnz     minus                  ; it is negative
 001E  FE C0                            inc     AL                     ; set AL and cc
 0020  C3                               ret
 0021                           minus:
 0021  FE C8                            dec     AL                     ; Set AL and cc
 0023  C3                               ret                            ; and return.
 0024                           Bcdtst  ENDP
 0024                           code    ENDS
                                        END
```

Program 4-6: BCDCMP

```
                                        .386
0000                            code    SEGMENT   para 'CODE' PUBLIC USE16
                                        ASSUME    CS:code, DS:code, SS:code
                                ;
                                ; Name:     BCDCMP
                                ;
                                ; Purpose: The following procedure provides signed comparison
                                ;          of BCD numbers in the 'standard' form of
                                ;          SSdddddddddddddd.  Where SS is the sign byte (bit 7 is on
                                ;          for minus, off for plus) and the 7 pairs of dd's make up a
                                ;          14 digit packed BCD number.
                                ;
                                ; Inputs:  DS:SI points to one BCD number, DS:DI points to the other.
                                ;
                                ; Process: The number pointed to by SI is compared to the number
                                ;          pointed to by DI.  (Conceptually the number (DI) is
                                ;          subtracted from the number (SI).)  The comparison is
                                ;          performed to determine relative magnitude and the
                                ;          result is adjusted depending on the signs of the numbers.
                                ;
                                ; Output:  Register AL will contain -1, 0, +1 depending on the result
                                ;          of the comparison (SI)<(DI), (SI)=(DI), (SI)>(DI).  The
                                ;          zero and sign flags will also be set.
                                ;
                                         PUBLIC  Bcdcmp
                                ;
0000                            Bcdcmp   PROC
0000  51                                 push    CX                  ; Save entry registers
0001  56                                 push    SI
0002  57                                 push    DI
0003  06                                 push    ES
0004  8C D9                              mov     CX,DS
0006  8E C1                              mov     ES,CX

0008  FC                                 cld                         ; Set direction for compare.
0009  8A 24                              mov     AH,BYTE PTR [SI]    ; Get the sign of SI's number
000B  8A 05                              mov     AL,BYTE PTR [DI]    ; and the sign of DI's number
000D  25 8080                            and     AX,08080h           ; Isolate the signs.
0010  0F 84 001C R                       jz      bothpos             ; Both numbers are positive.
0014  3A C4                              cmp     AL,AH               ; Are the signs the same?
0016  0F 85 0029 R                       jne     signset             ; Are both are negative?
001A  87 F7                              xchg    SI,DI               ; Reverse the compare if so.
001C                            bothpos:
001C  B9 0007                            mov     CX,7                ; Set count to compare.
001F  46                                 inc     SI
0020  47                                 inc     DI
0021  F3/ A6                             repz cmpsb                  ; and compare magnitudes.
0023  B0 00                              mov     AL,0                ; Set for equal
0025  0F 84 0031 R                       je      done                ; and get out if they were.

0029                            signset:
0029  B0 01                              mov     AL,1                ; Set (SI)>(DI)
002B  0F 87 0031 R                       ja      done                ; Get out if true.
002F  B0 FF                              mov     AL,0ffh             ; Set (SI)<(DI)
0031                            done:

0031  07                                 pop     ES                  ; Restore the entry registers
0032  5F                                 pop     DI
0033  5E                                 pop     SI
0034  59                                 pop     CX
```

```
0035  C3                              ret                       ; and return.
0036                    Bcdcmp        ENDP
0036                    code          ENDS
                                      END
```

Program 4-7: BCDSHL

```
Microsoft (R) Macro Assembler Version 5.00


                                      PAGE      55,132
                                      .386
 0000                   code          SEGMENT   para 'CODE' PUBLIC USE16
                                      ASSUME    CS:code, DS:code, SS:code

                        ;
                        ; Name:     BCDSHL
                        ;
                        ; Purpose: The following procedure provides a BCD left shift of
                        ;          an accumulator (double precision) or a standard BCD
                        ;          value.  The number of digits shifted can be from zero
                        ;          to the size of the input number.
                        ;
                        ;
                        ; Inputs:  AL contains the size code of the value to be shifted.
                        ;          Zero indicates a standard number.  Non zero indicates
                        ;          a double precision accumulator.
                        ;          AH contains the number of digits to shift.
                        ;          BX contains the address of the field to shift.
                        ;
                        ; Process: The size code is replaced with the size of the number in
                        ;          bytes less one (for use in computing the rightmost byte
                        ;          address).  It is also used to select a comparand for the
                        ;          check of the shift amount (an oversized shift results in
                        ;          zero).
                        ;
                        ;          The shift amount is divided by two and the number is
                        ;          moved left the required number of bytes.  The overlaid
                        ;          bytes are checked for zero and if not, the fact is
                        ;          remembered so that carry can be set.  Remaining bytes to
                        ;          the right are zeroed.
                        ;
                        ;          If an odd number of digits was requested, the number is
                        ;          shifted left one digit.  The leftmost bcd digit is also
                        ;          checked for zero to allow setting of carry.
                        ;
                        ;
                        ; Output:  The number is shifted left the desired number of digits.
                        ;          If the result is zero, a zero condition code is set.
                        ;          If a non-zero digit was shifted out of the number,
                        ;          carry is set to indicate the loss of significance.
                        ;
                        ;
                                       PUBLIC  Bcdshl


 0000                   Bcdshl         PROC
 0000  66| 52                          push    EDX              ; Save entry registers
 0002  51                              push    CX
 0003  53                              push    BX
 0004  66| 50                          push    EAX
```

```
0006  56                      push    SI
0007  57                      push    DI
0008  06                      push    ES
0009  8C DA                   mov     DX,DS               ; Set ES to DS
000B  8E C2                   mov     ES,DX
000D  B9 000D                 mov     CX,13               ; set max digits for non-zero
0010  0A C0                   or      AL,AL               ; Accumulator size
0012  B0 07                   mov     AL,7                ; Assume not
0014  0F 84 0020 R            jz      notaccum            ; Good guess
0018  B0 0E                   mov     AL,14               ; Need 14 digit pairs
001A  B1 1B                   mov     CL,27               ; and more digits for non zero.
001C  C6 47 01 00             mov     BYTE PTR [BX+1],0   ; Force extra digit to zero.
0020                  notaccum:
0020  B6 00                   mov     DH,0                ; Set flag for no carry
0022  80 27 80                and     BYTE PTR [BX],080h  ; Clear all but the sign bit
0025  3A E1                   cmp     AH,CL               ; Shift to zero?
0027  0F 8F 00BD R            jg      zeroit              ; if so - clear the field
002B  8A D4                   mov     DL,AH               ; copy the amount to shift
                      ;
                      ; Shift the even digit pairs if any.
                      ;
002D  D0 EC                   shr     AH,1                ; Get the number of pairs
002F  0F 84 0054 R            jz      oddshiftq           ; If no pairs - check if odd.
0033  50                      push    AX                  ; Save size value
0034  8B FB                   mov     DI,BX               ;
0036  8A CC                   mov     CL,AH               ; Get bytes to check
0038  47                      inc     DI                  ; Point to leftmost destination
0039  3C 07                   cmp     AL,7                ; If number - ok
003B  0F 84 0040 R            jz      notaccum1           ;
003F  47                      inc     DI                  ; Need to skip top accum byte
0040                  notaccum1:
0040  8B F7                   mov     SI,DI               ; Get leftmost byte for check
                      ;
                      ; Check overlaid digit pairs for zero (remember the result in DH).
                      ;
0042                  checkzer:
0042  0A 34                   or      DH,BYTE PTR [SI]    ; Combine to check significance
                                                          ; loss
0044  46                      inc     SI                  ; Shift to next source
0045  E2 FB                   loop    checkzer            ; and check all overlaid bytes
                      ;
                      ; Now we can overlay the leftmost digit pairs with the remainder of
                      ; the original number.
                      ;
0047  8A C8                   mov     CL,AL               ; Get count of bytes to process
0049  2A CC                   sub     CL,AH               ; less number checked.
004B  F3/ A4                  rep movsb                   ; Close over those checked.
                      ;
                      ; Fill the remainder with zeros.
                      ;
004D  8A CC                   mov     CL,AH               ; Get count to set zero.
004F  B0 00                   mov     AL,0                ; Get the zero value
0051  F3/ AA                  rep stosb                   ; and fill zeros to the right.
0053  58                      pop     AX                  ; Restore size value
                      ;
                      ; Now take care of any odd shift necessary.
                      ;
0054                  oddshiftq:
0054  F6 C2 01                test    DL,1                ; Was the amount to shift odd?
0057  0F 84 0089 R            jz      shiftx              ; No - skip odd shift
005B  50                      push    AX                  ; Save digit count
                      ;
```

```
                            ; Shift the odd digit
                            ;
005C  8A C8                           mov     CL,AL               ; Set count to shift
005E  2A CC                           sub     CL,AH               ; (bytes less zeros filled)
0060  8B F3                           mov     SI,BX               ; Point SI to leftmost pair
0062  46                              inc     SI
0063  3C 07                           cmp     AL,7                ; Is it a number?
0065  0F 84 006A R                    jz      number              ; Yes - we are set
0069  46                              inc     SI                  ; Accumulators have an extra
006A                        number:
006A  8B FE                           mov     DI,SI               ; Set destination too
006C  FC                              cld                         ; Set direction to up.
006D  8A 04                           mov     AL, BYTE PTR [SI]   ; Get value of top pair
006F  24 F0                           and     AL,0f0h             ; Get the digit lost
0071  0A F0                           or      DH,AL               ; and save for significance
                                                                  ; loss check
0073                        shift1:
0073  8A 24                           mov     AH, BYTE PTR [SI]   ; Get a byte into AH
0075  E2 08                           loop    shift2              ; Skip special handling of last
                            ;
                            ; Last pair of digits cannot fetch the next pair (it doesn't exist);
                            ; We need to fill a zero to the right.
                            ;
0077  C0 E4 04                        shl     AH,4                ; Fill zeros on right
007A  88 25                           mov     BYTE PTR [DI],AH    ; and put down in place.
007C  EB 0A 90                        jmp     shift3              ; we are done.
007F                        shift2:
007F  46                              inc     SI                  ; point source to next pair
0080  8A 04                           mov     AL, BYTE PTR [SI]   ; and get for top nibble
0082  C1 E8 04                        shr     AX,4                ; Shift right one nibble
0085  AA                              stosb                       ; Put shifted byte back
0086  EB EB                           jmp     shift1              ; and do next one
0088                        shift3:
0088  58                              pop     AX                  ; Restore digit count

                            ;
                            ; The shift is completed - check if result is zero and set cc and sign
                            ;
0089                        shiftx:
0089  52                              push    DX                  ; Save significance loss
008A  8A C8                           mov     CL,AL               ; Set size in CX
008C  C0 E9 02                        shr     CL,2                ; Divide by word size (4)
008F  8B F3                           mov     SI,BX               ; Set start
0091  66| AD                          lodsd                       ; Get first word
0093  B0 00                           mov     AL,0                ; less the sign byte
0095  66| 8B D0                       mov     EDX,EAX             ; set into accumulator.
0098                        shiftx0:
0098  66| AD                          lodsd                       ; Get the next double word
009A  66| 0B D0                       or      EDX,EAX             ; combine and set z/nz
009D  E2 F9                           loop    shiftx0             ; do for 1 or 3 more dwords
009F  0F 85 00A6 R                    jnz     shiftx1             ; Done if non zero
00A3  C6 07 00                        mov     BYTE PTR [BX],0     ; force sign to positive
00A6                        shiftx1:
00A6  0F 94 C0                        setz    AL                  ; Put a 1 in AL if zero result
00A9  5A                              pop     DX                  ; Restore significance loss
00AA  0A F6                           or      DH,DH               ; check if we lost significance
00AC  0F 84 00B1 R                    jz      shiftx2             ; If not carry is off from or.
00B0  F9                              stc                         ; Force it on.
00B1                        shiftx2:
00B1  FE C8                           dec     AL                  ; Reset zero flag from setz.
00B3  07                              pop     ES                  ; Restore the entry registers
00B4  5F                              pop     DI
```

```
00B5  5E                       pop     SI
00B6  66| 58                   pop     EAX
00B8  5B                       pop     BX
00B9  59                       pop     CX
00BA  66| 5A                   pop     EDX
00BC  C3                       ret                     ; and return.
                       ;
                       ; The shift would result in zeros - clear the result.  First we must
                       ; check if we would loose significance.
                       ;
00BD                   zeroit:
00BD  50                       push    AX              ; Save sizes
00BE  8A C8                    mov     CL,AL           ; Set size in CX
00C0  C0 E9 02                 shr     CL,2            ; Divide by word size (4)
00C3  8B F3                    mov     SI,BX           ; Set start
00C5  66| AD                   lodsd                   ; Get first word
00C7  B0 00                    mov     AL,0            ; less the sign byte
00C9  66| 8B D0                mov     EDX,EAX         ; set into accumulator.
00CC                   zerock0:
00CC  66| AD                   lodsd                   ; Get the next double word
00CE  66| 0B D0                or      EDX,EAX         ; combine and set z/nz
00D1  E2 F9                    loop    zerock0         ; do for 1 or 3 more dwords
00D3  0F 95 C6                 setnz   DH              ; Done with significance check
00D6  58                       pop     AX
                       ;
                       ; DH is set if we lost significance so we can clear the field.
                       ;
00D7  50                       push    AX              ; Re-save sizes
00D8  8B FB                    mov     DI,BX           ; Set destination,
00DA  8A C8                    mov     CL,AL           ; and count,
00DC  C1 E9 02                 shr     CX,2            ; divide by word size
00DF  41                       inc     CX              ; include sign word.
00E0  66| 2B C0                sub     EAX,EAX         ; Get a double zero
00E3  FC                       cld                     ; Set direction up
00E4  F3/ 66| AB               rep stosd               ; Fill with zeros
00E7  58                       pop     AX              ; Restore sizes
00E8  EB 9F                    jmp     shiftx          ; exit (cc is set)
00EA                   Bcdshl  ENDP
00EA                   code    ENDS
                               END
```

Program 4-8: BCDSHR

```
Microsoft (R) Macro Assembler Version 5.00


                                                PAGE     55,132
                                                .386
 0000                                   code    SEGMENT  para 'CODE' PUBLIC USE16
                                                ASSUME   CS:code, DS:code, SS:code

                                        ;
                                        ; Name:     BCDSHR
                                        ;
                                        ; Purpose: The following procedure provides a BCD right shift of
                                        ;           an accumulator (double precision) or a standard BCD
                                        ;           value.  The number of digits shifted can be from zero
                                        ;           to the size of the input number.
                                        ;
                                        ;
                                        ; Inputs:   AL contains the size code of the value to be shifted.
                                        ;           Zero indicates a standard number.  Non zero indicates
                                        ;           a double precision accumulator.
                                        ;           AH contains the number of digits to shift.
                                        ;           BX contains the address of the field to shift.
                                        ;
                                        ; Process: The size code is replaced with the size of the number in
                                        ;           bytes less one (for use in computing the rightmost byte
                                        ;           address).  It is also used to select a comparand for the
                                        ;           check of the shift amount (an oversized shift results in
                                        ;           zero).
                                        ;
                                        ;           If an odd number of digits is requested, the number is
                                        ;           shifted right one digit.
                                        ;
                                        ;           The shift amount is divided by two and the number is
                                        ;           moved right
                                        ;
                                        ; Output:   The number is shifted right the desired number of digits.
                                        ;           If the result is zero, a zero condition code is set.
                                        ;
                                        ;
                                        ;
                                        ;

                                                  PUBLIC  Bcdshr

 0000                                   Bcdshr    PROC
 0000  66| 52                                     push    EDX              ; Save entry registers
 0002  51                                         push    CX
 0003  53                                         push    BX
 0004  66| 50                                     push    EAX
 0006  56                                         push    SI
 0007  57                                         push    DI
 0008  06                                         push    ES
 0009  8C DA                                      mov     DX,DS            ; Set ES to DS
 000B  8E C2                                      mov     ES,DX
 000D  B9 000D                                    mov     CX,13            ; set max digits for non-zero
                                                                           ; (note that this clears CH)
 0010  0A C0                                      or      AL,AL            ; Accumulator size
 0012  B0 07                                      mov     AL,7             ; Assume not
 0014  0F 84 0020 R                               jz      notaccum         ; Good guess
 0018  B0 0F                                      mov     AL,15            ; Need 14 digit pairs of 15
```

```
001A  B1 1B                    mov     CL,27                ; and more digits for non zero.
001C  C6 47 01 00              mov     BYTE PTR [BX+1],0    ; Force extra digit to zero.
0020                     notaccum:
0020  80 27 80                 and     BYTE PTR [BX],080h   ; Clear all but the sign bit
0023  3A E1                    cmp     AH,CL                ; Shift to zero?
0025  0F 87 008B R             ja      zeroit               ; if so - clear the field
0029  8A D4                    mov     DL,AH                ; copy the amount to shift
                         ;
                         ; Shift the even digit pairs if any.
                         ;
002B  FD                       std                          ; Set decrement
002C  D0 EC                    shr     AH,1                 ; Any pairs to shift?
002E  0F 84 0048 R             jz      oddshift             ; No - go check for odd shift
0032  50                       push    AX                   ; Save digit count
0033  8B FB                    mov     DI,BX                ;
0035  8A C8                    mov     CL,AL                ; Get bytes to rightmost
0037  03 F9                    add     DI,CX                ; Get destination rightmost
0039  8B F3                    mov     SI,BX                ;
003B  2A CC                    sub     CL,AH                ; Get bytes to rightmost source
003D  03 F1                    add     SI,CX                ; and rightmost source.
003F  F3/ A4                   rep movsb                    ; Now shift pairs
0041  8A CC                    mov     CL,AH                ; Get count to set zero
0043  B0 00                    mov     AL,0                 ; and a zero to set
0045  F3/ AA                   rep stosb                    ; Clear each pair.
0047  58                       pop     AX                   ; Restore size value
                         ;
                         ; Shift the odd digit
                         ;
0048                     oddshift:
0048  F6 C2 01                 test    DL,1                 ; Is there an odd digit?
004B  0F 84 0064 R             jz      shiftx               ; No, we are done.
004F  50                       push    AX                   ; save lengths
0050  8A C8                    mov     CL,AL                ; Set count to rightmost.
0052  8B F3                    mov     SI,BX                ; Point SI to Rightmost pair
0054  03 F1                    add     SI,CX                ;
0056  8B FE                    mov     DI,SI                ; Set destination too
                                                            ; Direction is down.
0058  2A CC                    sub     CL,AH                ; Take out the pairs we zeroed.
005A                     shift1:
005A  AC                       lodsb                        ; Get a byte into AL
005B  8A 24                    mov     AH, BYTE PTR [SI]    ; Get the next byte to the left
005D  C1 E8 04                 shr     AX,4                 ; Shift right one nibble
0060  AA                       stosb                        ; Put shifted byte back
0061  E2 F7                    loop    shift1               ; and do next one
0063  58                       pop     AX                   ; Restore digit count
                         ;
                         ; The shift is completed - check if result is zero and set cc and sign
                         ;
0064                     shiftx:
0064  FC                       cld                          ; Set direction up
0065  8A C8                    mov     CL,AL                ; Set size in CX
0067  C0 E9 02                 shr     CL,2                 ; Divide by word size (4)
006A  8B F3                    mov     SI,BX                ; Set start
006C  66| AD                   lodsd                        ; Get first word
006E  B0 00                    mov     AL,0                 ; less the sign byte
0070  66| 8B D0                mov     EDX,EAX              ; set into accumulator.
0073                     shiftx0:
0073  66| AD                   lodsd                        ; Get the next double word
0075  66| 0B D0                or      EDX,EAX              ; combine and set z/nz
0078  E2 F9                    loop    shiftx0              ; do for 1 or 3 more dwords
007A  0F 85 0081 R             jnz     shiftx1              ; Done if non zero
007E  C6 07 00                 mov     BYTE PTR [BX],0      ; force sign to positive
0081                     shiftx1:
```

```
0081  07                         pop     ES              ; Restore the entry registers
0082  5F                         pop     DI
0083  5E                         pop     SI
0084  66| 58                     pop     EAX
0086  5B                         pop     BX
0087  59                         pop     CX
0088  66| 5A                     pop     EDX
008A  C3                         ret                     ; and return.
                        ;
                        ; The shift would result in zeros - clear the result, and set cc z.
                        ;
008B                    zeroit:
008B  8B FB                      mov     DI,BX           ; Set destination,
008D  8A C8                      mov     CL,AL           ; and count,
008F  C0 E9 02                   shr     CL,2            ; divided by 4.
0092  FE C1                      inc     CL              ; plus 1.
0094  B5 00                      mov     CH,0            ; Set CX by zeroing upper half.
0096  66| 2B C0                  sub     EAX,EAX         ; Get a double zero
0099  FC                         cld                     ; Set direction up
009A  F3/ 66| AB                 rep stosd
009D  EB E2                      jmp     shiftx1         ; exit (cc is set)
009F                    Bcdshr   ENDP
009F                    code     ENDS
                                 END
```

Program 4-9: BCDADD

```
Microsoft (R) Macro Assembler Version 5.00


                                        PAGE      55,132
                                        .386
 0000                           code    SEGMENT   para 'CODE' PUBLIC USE16
                                        ASSUME    CS:code, DS:code, SS:code

                                ; Name:     BCDADD
                                ;
                                ; Purpose:  The following procedures provides signed addition and
                                ;           subtraction of BCD numbers in the 'standard' form of
                                ;           SSdddddddddddddd.  Where SS is the sign byte (bit 7 is on
                                ;           for minus, off for plus) and the 7 pairs of dd's make up
                                ;           a 14 digit packed BCD number.
                                ;
                                ;
                                ; Inputs:   DS:SI points to one BCD number, DS:DI points to the other.
                                ;           DS:BX points to the area for the sum (BX may be the same
                                ;           as SI or DI).
                                ;
                                ; Process:  The entry points, bcdadd and bcdsub differ as entry points
                                ;           in bcdsub's inversion of the sign of the second number.
                                ;           Both then use the common routine addsub to compute the
                                ;           sum or difference.
                                ;
                                ;           Stack space is reserved as a work area for computing the
                                ;           result.  If the signs of the two numbers are the same, the
                                ;           result is computed directly by addition and receives the
                                ;           same sign.  If the signs differ, the number with the
                                ;           smaller absolute value is subtracted from the larger and
                                ;           the result receives the sign of the larger.  (If the result
                                ;           is zero, the sign is forced to positive (0)).
                                ;
                                ;           The result is copied from the work area to the desired
                                ;           location.  If an overflow occurred carry will be set on
                                ;           exit, otherwise reset.
                                ;
                                ;
                                ; Output:   The sum or difference of the two numbers will be returned
                                ;           in the area indicated.  Carry will be on if the result
                                ;           overflowed.
                                ;
                                ;
                                          PUBLIC  Bcdadd
                                          PUBLIC  Bcdsub
                                ;
 0000                           Bcdadd    PROC
 0000  66| 50                             push    EAX                 ; Save AX for sign use.
 0002  8A 05                              mov     AL, BYTE PTR [DI]   ; Get sign of 'b'.
 0004  0F 8A 000E R                       jp      saverest
 0008                           Bcdsub:
 0008  66| 50                             push    EAX                 ; Save AX for sign use.
 000A  8A 05                              mov     AL, BYTE PTR [DI]   ; Get sign of 'b'
 000C  34 80                              xor     AL,080h             ; and flip it for subtract.

 000E                           saverest:
 000E  52                                 push    DX                  ; Save entry registers
 000F  51                                 push    CX
```

```
0010  53                         push   BX
0011  56                         push   SI
0012  57                         push   DI
0013  06                         push   ES
0014  8C D9                      mov    CX,DS
0016  8E C1                      mov    ES,CX
0018  C8 0008 00                 enter  8,0                   ; Reserve 8 byte work area
                            ;
                            ; First check for signs the same.
                            ;
001C  8A 24                      mov    AH, BYTE PTR [SI]     ; Get sign byte of 'a',


001E  32 C4                      xor    AL,AH                 ; Check if they are the same.
0020  24 80                      and    AL,080h               ; (remove all but the sign.)
0022  0F 84 0058 R               jz     samesign              ; They were the same!
                            ;
                            ; We will find the one with the largest magnitude and then subtract
                            ; the other one from it.  The sign will be taken from the larger
                            ; number.
                            ;
0026  53                         push   BX                    ; Save result pointer
0027  B9 0007                    mov    CX,7                  ; Get loop count
002A  8B D6                      mov    DX,SI                 ; Save number pointers
002C  8B DF                      mov    BX,DI
002E  46                         inc    SI
002F  47                         inc    DI                    ; and step over sign byte
0030  FC                         cld                          ; Set to increment
0031  F3/ A6                     repz cmpsb                   ; locate larger (or equal)
0033  0F 83 0039 R               jnb    dilower               ; SI has larger.
0037  87 D3                      xchg   DX,BX                 ; Flip the pointers.
0039                        dilower:
0039  8B F2                      mov    SI,DX                 ; Restore pointer to larger
003B  8B FB                      mov    DI,BX                 ; and smaller.
003D  B9 0007                    mov    CX,7                  ; Prepare to point to
                                                              ; rightmost.
0040  03 F1                      add    SI,CX                 ; do so for 'a'
0042  03 F9                      add    DI,CX                 ; and 'b'.
0044  FD                         std                          ; Set direction for auto dec.
0045  F8                         clc                          ; and clear carry
0046                        subtloop:
0046  AC                         lodsb                        ; get a byte (2 digits) of 'a'.
0047  1A 05                      sbb    AL, BYTE PTR [DI]     ; subtract 'b' & carry from it.
0049  2F                         das                          ; Decimal adjust the result.
004A  4F                         dec    DI                    ; Position to next byte and
004B  88 46 00                   mov    BYTE PTR [BP+0],AL    ; store result temporarily.
004E  4D                         dec    BP                    ; Step target pointer.
004F  E2 F5                      loop   subtloop              ; Subtract all seven pairs
0051  AC                         lodsb                        ; get the sign of the larger
0052  24 80                      and    AL,080h               ; with any garbage removed.
0054  5B                         pop    BX                    ; Restore target pointer
0055  EB 1B 90                   jmp    setreslt              ; and go set the result.


0058                        samesign:
0058  B9 0007                    mov    CX,7                  ; Prepare to point to
                                                              ; rightmost
005B  03 F1                      add    SI,CX                 ; do so for 'a'
005D  03 F9                      add    DI,CX                 ; and 'b'.
005F  FD                         std                          ; Set direction for auto dec.
0060  80 E4 80                   and    AH,080h               ; Get sign isolated. (clears
                                                              ; carry)
0063                        samesloop:
```

```
0063  AC                        lodsb                           ; get a byte (2 digits) of 'a'.
0064  12 05                     adc     AL, BYTE PTR [DI]       ; add 'b' and carry to it.
0066  27                        daa                             ; Decimal adjust the result.
0067  4F                        dec     DI                      ; Position to next byte and
0068  88 46 00                  mov     BYTE PTR [BP+0],AL      ; store result temporarily.
006B  4D                        dec     BP                      ; Step target pointer.
006C  E2 F5                     loop    samesloop               ; Add all seven pairs
006E  8A C4                     mov     AL,AH                   ; position the sign.
0070  14 00                     adc     AL,0                    ; Add carry from high digit.

0072              setreslt:
0072  53                        push    BX                      ; Save output pointer
0073  88 07                     mov     BYTE PTR [BX],AL        ; store sign
0075  43                        inc     BX                      ; and step pointer.
0076  B9 0007                   mov     CX,7                    ; Get loop count.
0079  45                        inc     BP                      ; point to digit pair
007A              nextreslt:
007A  8A 46 00                  mov     AL, BYTE PTR [BP+0]     ; Get digits
007D  88 07                     mov     BYTE PTR [BX],AL        ; into target
007F  45                        inc     BP
0080  43                        inc     BX                      ; Adjust pointers
0081  E2 F7                     loop    nextreslt               ; and move next result.
0083  4D                        dec     BP                      ; Correct for one too far.
0084  5B                        pop     BX                      ; Get output pointer
0085  66| 8B 07                 mov     EAX,DWORD PTR[BX]       ; Check the result for
0088  B0 00                     mov     AL,0                    ; zero except for the sign.
008A  66| 0B 47 04              or      EAX,DWORD PTR[BX+4]     ; Check for a zero result.
008E  0F 85 0094 R              jnz     exit                    ; Leave sign alone if not.
0092  88 07                     mov     BYTE PTR[BX],AL         ; Avoid -0.
0094              exit:

0094  C9                        leave                           ; Restore the entry registers
0095  07                        pop     ES
0096  5F                        pop     DI
0097  5E                        pop     SI
0098  5B                        pop     BX
0099  59                        pop     CX
009A  5A                        pop     DX
009B  66| 58                    pop     EAX
009D  F6 07 0F                  test    BYTE PTR [BX],0fh       ; check if an overflow occurred,
00A0  0F 84 00A5 R              jz      nooflow                 ; if not - skip (carry is off)
00A4  F9                        stc                             ; set of carry on
00A5              nooflow:
00A5  C3                        ret                             ; and return.
00A6              Bcdadd        ENDP
00A6              code          ENDS
                                END
```

Program 4-10: BCDMPY

```
Microsoft (R) Macro Assembler Version 5.00


                                         PAGE      55,132
                                         .386
 0000                          code      SEGMENT   para 'CODE' PUBLIC USE16
                                         ASSUME    CS:code, DS:code, SS:code
                               ;
                               ; Name:    BCDMPY
                               ;
                               ; Purpose: The following procedure provides signed multiplication for
                               ;          BCD numbers in the 'standard' form of SSdddddddddddddd.
                               ;          Where SS is the sign byte (bit 7 is on for minus, off for
                               ;          plus) and the 7 pairs of dd's make up a 14 digit packed BCD
                               ;          number.  (Packed two digits per byte.)
                               ;
                               ;          The product is placed in the 16 byte accumulator specified
                               ;          by DS:BX.  If the accumulator overlaps either the multiplier
                               ;          or the multiplicand the results are undefined.
                               ;
                               ; Inputs:  DS:SI points to one BCD number, DS:DI points to the other.
                               ;          DS:BX points to the accumulator where the product is formed.
                               ;
                               ; Process: The sign of the product is computed and set and the
                               ;          accumulator is cleared to zero.  The algorithm used to form
                               ;          the product is an adaptation of simple manual
                               ;          multiplication.  The product is formed by selecting each
                               ;          digit of the multiplier from right to left and performing a
                               ;          right to left digit by digit multiplication, adding the
                               ;          result to the accumulator.
                               ;
                               ;          Because there are two decimal digits in each byte, we have
                               ;          four variants of the multiply.  (assume 76 * 34, we
                               ;          multiply 6 by 4, getting a product of 24.  We then multiply
                               ;          70 by 4 and add that partial product (280) to 24 to get 304.
                               ;          We then multiply 6 by 30 to get 180 as a partial product
                               ;          which gives us 484.  Finally, we multiply 70 by 30 to get
                               ;          the partial product 2100 which we add to our product to get
                               ;          the final result of 2584.)  The aam instruction assumes the
                               ;          product was formed from two bcd digits so we adjust our
                               ;          point of addition into the product.
                               ;
                               ; Output:  The product will be returned in the accumulator as a signed
                               ;          double precision value.
                               ;
                                         PUBLIC Bcdmpy
                               ;
 0000                          Bcdmpy    PROC
 0000  06                                push     ES
 0001  52                                push     DX                 ; Save entry registers
 0002  51                                push     CX
 0003  53                                push     BX
 0004  50                                push     AX
 0005  56                                push     SI
 0006  57                                push     DI
                               ;
                               ; clear the accumulator and set its sign
                               ;
 0007  8A 04                             mov      AL,[SI]            ; Get multiplier sign byte
```

```
0009  32 05                         xor     AL,[DI]               ; Combine with multiplicand's
000B  25 0080                       and     AX,00080h             ; Isolate the sign
000E  8C D9                         mov     CX,DS                 ; Get DS
0010  8E C1                         mov     ES,CX                 ; into ES,
0012  FC                            cld                           ; set direction to incr,
0013  87 FB                         xchg    DI,BX                 ; and prepare to clear accum.
0015  AB                            stosw                         ; Set sign value and 00
0016  8A C4                         mov     AL,AH                 ; Get word of zeros,
0018  B9 0007                       mov     CX,7                  ; the count to clear and
001B  F3/ AB                        rep stosw                     ; clear words 1 - 7
001D  87 FB                         xchg    DI,BX                 ; Get DI back again.
001F  4B                            dec     BX                    ; Point to rightmost accum loc.
                         ;
                         ; point to the rightmost byte of each of the other fields.
                         ;
0020  B9 0007                       mov     CX,7                  ; Get count of bytes.
0023  03 F1                         add     SI,CX                 ; Multiplier and
0025  03 F9                         add     DI,CX                 ; Multiplicand


                         ;
                         ; Begin the bytewise selection of multiplier digits
                         ;
0027                     nextmpyr:
0027  51                            push    CX                    ; Save byte count remaining.
0028  8A 14                         mov     DL, BYTE PTR [SI]     ; Load a pair of digits.
002A  8A F2                         mov     DH,DL                 ; Save the top digit
002C  80 E2 0F                      and     DL,0fh                ; Isolate the low digit
002F  0F 84 0096 R                  jz      dohigh                ; If zero - go do high digit.
0033  53                            push    BX                    ; Save BX for high digit
0034  57                            push    DI                    ; Save right hand m'p'cand ptr.
0035  B9 0007                       mov     CX,7                  ; Get count of digit pairs
                         ;
                         ; This section multiplies the right nibble of the multiplicand by the
                         ; right nibble of the multiplier and adds the result to the right
                         ; nibble of the accumulator.   i.e.   z := z + x * y
                         ;                                  ss dd dd dd dd dd dd dx   Multiplicand
                         ;                                  ss dd dd dd dd dd dd dy   Multiplier
                         ;    ss dd dd dd dd dd dd dd dd dd dd dd dd dd dd dz   Product
                         ;
0038                     nextmpcnd:
0038  8A 05                         mov     AL, BYTE PTR [DI]     ; Get digit pair
003A  24 0F                         and     AL,0fh                ; Isolate right one.
003C  0F 84 005E R                  jz      donert                ; If zero - do leftmost.
0040  F6 E2                         mul     DL                    ; Multiply
0042  D4 0A                         aam                           ; adjust product and get
0044  C0 E4 04                      shl     AH,4                  ; high digit positioned
0047  0A C4                         or      AL,AH                 ; for bcd combination with low.
0049  02 07                         add     AL, BYTE PTR [BX]     ; add to product.
004B  27                            daa                           ; Adjust back to bcd
004C  88 07                         mov     BYTE PTR [BX],AL      ; and put it back
004E  0F 83 005E R                  jnc     donert                ; Done if no carry to propagate
0052  53                            push    BX                    ; Save product pointer
0053                     undonert:
0053  4B                            dec     BX                    ; step to next pair
0054  B0 00                         mov     AL,0                  ; We just need to propagate cy.
0056  12 07                         adc     AL, BYTE PTR [BX]     ; add to product.
0058  27                            daa                           ; Adjust back to bcd
0059  88 07                         mov     BYTE PTR [BX],AL      ; and put it back
005B  72 F6                         jc      undonert              ; If no more carry - done.
005D  5B                            pop     BX                    ; Restore product pointer
005E                     donert:
                         ;
```

```
                        ; This section multiplies the left nibble of the multiplicand by the
                        ; right nibble of the multiplier and adds the result to the left
                        ; nibble of the accumulator.     i.e.    z := z + x * y
                        ;                                ss dd dd dd dd dd dd xd   Multiplicand
                        ;                                ss dd dd dd dd dd dd dy   Multiplier
                        ;     ss dd dd dd dd dd dd dd dd dd dd dd dd dd dd zd   Product
                        ;
005E  8A 05                     mov     AL, BYTE PTR [DI]    ; Get digit pair
0060  24 F0                     and     AL,0f0h              ; isolate leftmost digit
0062  0F 84 0090 R              jz      donelft              ; If zero - pair is done.
0066  C0 E8 04                  shr     AL,4                 ; Get it into low nibble
0069  F6 E2                     mul     DL                   ; Multiply
006B  D4 0A                     aam                          ; adjust partial product
006D  C0 E0 04                  shl     AL,4                 ; and get it positioned for
0070  02 07                     add     AL, BYTE PTR [BX]    ; add to product.
0072  27                        daa                          ; Adjust back to bcd
0073  88 07                     mov     BYTE PTR [BX],AL     ; and put it back
0075  4B                        dec     BX                   ; Point to next pair
0076  8A 07                     mov     AL, BYTE PTR [BX]    ; load it
0078  12 C4                     adc     AL,AH                ; add the upper nibble + carry
007A  27                        daa                          ; adjust to bcd pair
007B  88 07                     mov     BYTE PTR [BX],AL     ; and put it back
007D  0F 83 0091 R              jnc     donelft0             ; Done if no carry to propagate
0081  53                        push    BX                   ; Save product pointer
0082                    undonelft:
0082  4B                        dec     BX                   ; step to next pair
0083  B0 00                     mov     AL,0                 ; We need to propagate carry.
0085  12 07                     adc     AL, BYTE PTR [BX]    ; add to product.
0087  27                        daa                          ; Adjust back to bcd
0088  88 07                     mov     BYTE PTR [BX],AL     ; and put it back
008A  72 F6                     jc      undonelft            ; If carry to propagate, do it
008C  5B                        pop     BX                   ; Restore product pointer
008D  EB 02 90                  jmp     donelft0             ; (Already at next higher.)
0090                    donelft:
0090  4B                        dec     BX                   ; Next higher product digits
0091                    donelft0:
0091  4F                        dec     DI                   ; and multiplicand digits
0092  E2 A4                     loop    nextmpcnd            ; To do all 7 pairs.
0094  5F                        pop     DI                   ; Get multiplicand right hand.
0095  5B                        pop     BX                   ; Get product byte pointer.
                        ;
                        ; Process the next (left) multiplier digit.  This process is similar
                        ; to the above but the point of addition into the product is shifted
                        ; left one nibble.  Thus the above routine is reversed.  Note that
                        ; the point at which we begin adding to the product has shifted by a
                        ; nibble.
                        ;
                        ;
                        ;
                        ; This section multiplies the right nibble of the multiplicand by the
                        ; left nibble of the multiplier and adds the result to the left
                        ; nibble of the accumulator.     i.e.    z := z + x * y
                        ;                                ss dd dd dd dd dd dd dx   Multiplicand
                        ;                                ss dd dd dd dd dd dd yd   Multiplier
                        ;     ss dd dd dd dd dd dd dd dd dd dd dd dd dd dd zd   Product
                        ;
0096                    dohigh:
0096  80 E6 F0                  and     DH,0f0h              ; isolate the high digit
0099  0F 84 0103 R              jz      donehigh             ; Exit if zero - no mpy needed.
009D  C0 EE 04                  shr     DH,4                 ; Position the high digit
00A0  57                        push    DI                   ; Save right hand multiplicand
00A1  53                        push    BX                   ; Save BX for next pair
```

```
                                                                ; pointer.
00A2  B9 0007                       mov     CX,7                ; Get count of digit pairs

00A5                        nextmpcnd2:
00A5  8A 05                         mov     AL, BYTE PTR [DI]   ; Get digit pair
00A7  24 0F                         and     AL,0fh              ; Isolate right one.
00A9  0F 84 00D4 R                  jz      dolef2              ; If zero - do leftmost.
00AD  F6 E6                         mul     DH                  ; Multiply
00AF  D4 0A                         aam                         ; adjust partial product
00B1  C0 E0 04                      shl     AL,4                ; and get positioned for
00B4  02 07                         add     AL, BYTE PTR [BX]   ; add to product.
00B6  27                            daa                         ; Adjust back to bcd
00B7  88 07                         mov     BYTE PTR [BX],AL    ; and put it back
00B9  4B                            dec     BX                  ; Point to next pair
00BA  8A 07                         mov     AL, BYTE PTR [BX]   ; load it
00BC  12 C4                         adc     AL,AH               ; add the upper nibble + carry
00BE  27                            daa                         ; adjust to bcd pair
00BF  88 07                         mov     BYTE PTR [BX],AL    ; and put it back
00C1  0F 83 00D5 R                  jnc     donert20            ; Done if no carry to propagate
00C5  53                            push    BX                  ; Save product pointer
00C6                        undonert2:
00C6  4B                            dec     BX                  ; step to next pair
00C7  B0 00                         mov     AL,0                ; Just need to propagate carry.
00C9  12 07                         adc     AL, BYTE PTR [BX]   ; add to product.
00CB  27                            daa                         ; Adjust back to bcd
00CC  88 07                         mov     BYTE PTR [BX],AL    ; and put it back
00CE  72 F6                         jc      undonert2           ; Done if no carry.
00D0  5B                            pop     BX                  ; Restore product pointer
00D1  EB 02 90                      jmp     donert20            ; Skip product ptr adjust

00D4                        dolef2:
                            ;
                            ; This section multiplies the left nibble of the multiplicand by the
                            ; left nibble of the multiplier and adds the result to the right
                            ; nibble of the accumulator.    i.e.    z := z + x * y
                            ;                                 ss dd dd dd dd dd dd xd   Multiplicand
                            ;                                 ss dd dd dd dd dd dd yd   Multiplier
                            ;     ss dd dd dd dd dd dd dd dd dd dd dd dd dd dz dd   Product
                            ;
00D4  4B                            dec     BX                  ; Next higher product digits
00D5                        donert20:
00D5  8A 05                         mov     AL, BYTE PTR [DI]   ; Get digit pair
00D7  24 F0                         and     AL,0f0h             ; isolate leftmost digit
00D9  0F 84 00FE R                  jz      donelf2             ; If zero - done with pair.
00DD  C0 E8 04                      shr     AL,4                ; Get it into low nibble
00E0  F6 E6                         mul     DH                  ; Multiply,
00E2  D4 0A                         aam                         ; adjust partial product,
00E4  C0 E4 04                      shl     AH,4                ; and get digit positioned
00E7  0A C4                         or      AL,AH               ; for bcd combination with low.
00E9  02 07                         add     AL, BYTE PTR [BX]   ; add into product.
00EB  27                            daa                         ; Adjust back to bcd
00EC  88 07                         mov     BYTE PTR [BX],AL    ; and put it back
00EE  0F 83 00FE R                  jnc     donelf2             ; If no carry - done
00F2  53                            push    BX                  ; Save product pointer
00F3                        undonelf2:
00F3  4B                            dec     BX                  ; step to next pair
00F4  B0 00                         mov     AL,0                ; Just need to propagate carry.
00F6  12 07                         adc     AL, BYTE PTR [BX]   ; add to product.
00F8  27                            daa                         ; Adjust back to bcd
00F9  88 07                         mov     BYTE PTR [BX],AL    ; and put it back
00FB  72 F6                         jc      undonelf2           ; If carry to propagate do it.
00FD  5B                            pop     BX                  ; Restore product pointer
```

```
00FE                        donelf2:
                                                                ; We have the next product ptr.
00FE  4F                              dec     DI                ; and multiplicand digits
00FF  E2 A4                           loop    nextmpcnd2        ; to do all 7 pairs.
0101  5B                              pop     BX                ; Restore product pointer and
0102  5F                              pop     DI                ; right-hand multiplicand digit.
                            ;
                            ; The point at which we want to begin adding to our product is now
                            ; two digits to the left (one byte).  BX needs to be adjusted to
                            ; reflect this.
                            ;
0103                        donehigh:
0103  59                              pop     CX                ; Restore outer loop count
0104  49                              dec     CX                ; subtract one from pair count
0105  0F 84 010E R                    jz      mpydone           ; If zero - skip the adjustment
0109  4B                              dec     BX                ; to product formation
010A  4E                              dec     SI                ; next multiplier and go
010B  E9 0027 R                       jmp     nextmpyr          ; to do seven pairs.

010E                        mpydone:
010E  5F                              pop     DI                ; Restore the entry registers
010F  5E                              pop     SI
0110  58                              pop     AX
0111  5B                              pop     BX
0112  59                              pop     CX
0113  5A                              pop     DX
0114  07                              pop     ES
0115  C3                              ret                       ; and return.
0116                        Bcdmpy    ENDP
0116                        code      ENDS
                                      END
```

Program 4-11: BCDDIV

Microsoft (R) Macro Assembler Version 5.00

```
                                        PAGE     55,132
                                        .386
0000                            code    SEGMENT  para 'CODE' PUBLIC USE16
                                        ASSUME   CS:code, DS:code, SS:code

                                ; Name:     BCDDIV
                                ;
                                ; Purpose:  The following procedure provides signed division of an
                                ;           accumulator (16 byte product
                                ;           SSxxdddddddddddddddddddddddddddd)
                                ;           by a BCD number in the 'standard' form of SSdddddddddddddd.
                                ;           Where SS is the sign byte (bit 7 is on for minus, off for
                                ;           plus) and the 7 pairs of dd's make up a 14 digit packed BCD
                                ;           number.
                                ;
                                ;
                                ; Inputs:   DS:SI points to the BCD number which is the divisor, DS:BX
                                ;           points to the dividend (accumulator).
                                ;
                                ; Process:  The number pointed to by BX is divided by the number
                                ;           pointed to by SI.  The algorithm uses repeated subtraction
                                ;           to generate each quotient digit (Subtract, if the result is
                                ;           not negative add one to the quotient digit and repeat.
                                ;           Otherwise, add back, preserve the quotient digit and shift
                                ;           the point of subtraction one digit right.)  This is applied
                                ;           twice per byte (once for each packed digit), then a pair of
                                ;           quotient digits are stored.  When the quotient has been
                                ;           formed, the sign of the dividend is placed in the
                                ;           remainder's sign position.  The sign of the quotient is
                                ;           computed from the signs of the divisor and dividend.
                                ;
                                ; Output:   The quotient is returned in the leftmost 8 bytes of the
                                ;           accumulator.  The remainder is returned in the right 8
                                ;           bytes.  (i.e. SSqqqqqqqqqqqqqqSSrrrrrrrrrrrrrr replaces
                                ;           the dividend.)
                                ;
                                ;           In the case of an overflow, carry will be set - this
                                ;           includes division by zero.  In this case, no quotient or
                                ;           remainder is formed.
                                ;
                                ;
                                            PUBLIC  Bcddiv
                                ;
0000                            Bcddiv      PROC
0000  66| 50                                push    EAX             ; Save entry registers
0002  53                                    push    BX
0003  51                                    push    CX
0004  52                                    push    DX
0005  56                                    push    SI
0006  57                                    push    DI
0007  06                                    push    ES
0008  8C D9                                 mov     CX,DS
000A  8E C1                                 mov     ES,CX
000C  C8 0020 00                            enter   32,0            ; Get some work space.
                                ;
                                ; We will copy the divisor into our work space twice.  Shifted left
```

```
                              ; one nibble and standard without sign.
                              ;
0010  8A 24                           mov     AH,BYTE PTR[SI]       ; Get the sign
0012  80 E4 80                        and     AH,080h               ; isolated to the bit
0015  88 66 F1                        mov     BYTE PTR[BP-15],AH    ; in our work area.
                              ;
                              ; The first copy checks for division by zero
                              ;
0018  BF FFF9                         mov     DI,-7                 ; index for shifted number
001B  56                              push    SI                    ; Save number's index

                              ;
                              ; Shift left one nibble
                              ;
001C  B6 00                           mov     DH,0                  ; Clear for div by zero check
001E  B9 0007                         mov     CX,7                  ; Set count to shift
0021  FC                              cld                           ; Set direction to up.
0022  B4 00                           mov     AH,0                  ; Get leading zero
0024                          shift2:
0024  46                              inc     SI                    ; point source to next pair
0025  8A 04                           mov     AL, BYTE PTR [SI]     ; and get for top nibble
0027  C1 E8 04                        shr     AX,4                  ; Shift right one nibble
002A  88 03                           mov     BYTE PTR [BP+DI],AL   ; Put shifted byte back
002C  47                              inc     DI
002D  8A 24                           mov     AH, BYTE PTR [SI]     ; Get a byte into AH
002F  0A F4                           or      DH,AH                 ; For zero check
0031  E2 F1                           loop    shift2                ; Skip special handling of
                                                                    ; last pair
                              ;
                              ; Last pair of digits cannot fetch the next pair (it doesn't exist);
                              ; We need to fill a zero to the right.
                              ;
0033  C0 E4 04                        shl     AH,4                  ; Fill zeros on right
0036  88 23                           mov     BYTE PTR [BP+DI],AH   ; and put down in place.
0038  5E                              pop     SI                    ; Restore index to number
0039  0A F6                           or      DH,DH                 ; Divide by zero?
003B  0F 84 0102 R                    jz      zerodiv               ; Yes - error.
                              ;
                              ; Now copy the unshifted number over.
                              ;
003F  46                              inc     SI                    ; Step over sign.
0040  BF FFF2                         mov     DI,-14                ; Set start of unshifted no.
0043  B1 07                           mov     CL,7                  ; Get count of digits
0045                          copyno:
0045  8A 04                           mov     AL, BYTE PTR[SI]      ;
0047  88 03                           mov     BYTE PTR [BP+DI],AL   ; Copy a digit pair.
0049  46                              inc     SI
004A  47                              inc     DI                    ; Step the pointers
004B  E2 F8                           loop    copyno                ; and do all digit pairs.
                              ;
                              ; Begin the division process.  We use repeated subtraction in each
                              ; digit position.  This involves two subtract loops, the first to
                              ; create the high nibble subtracts the shifted divisor, the second
                              ; which creates the low nibble subtracts the original divisor.
                              ;
                              ;
004D  BF 0009                         mov     DI,9                  ; Set beginning displacement
0050                          highsub:
0050  66| 2B C0                       sub     EAX,EAX               ; Initialize quotient pair
0053                          highsub0:
0053  57                              push    DI                    ; Save displacement into
                                                                    ; divisor.
```

```
0054  BE 0000                    mov    SI,0                    ; Set right digit pair.
0057  B9 0008                    mov    CX,8                    ; Set count of digits.

005A  F8                         clc                            ; and clear carry for first
                                                                ; subtract.
005B                    highsub1:
005B  8A 01                      mov    AL, BYTE PTR[BX+DI]     ; Get digit pair
005D  1A 02                      sbb    AL, BYTE PTR[BP+SI]     ; Subtract with any borrow
                                                                ; needed.
005F  2F                         das                            ; adjust to bcd.
0060  88 01                      mov    BYTE PTR[BX+DI],AL      ; and put it back
0062  4F                         dec    DI                      ; Point to next dividend pair
0063  4E                         dec    SI                      ; and divisor pair
0064  E2 F5                      loop   highsub1                ; Do all pairs.
0066  5F                         pop    DI                      ; Restore dividend displacement
0067  0F 82 0073 R               jc     highadd                 ; We went minus - pass is done.
006B  66| 05 00001000            add    EAX,01000h              ; Add to high nibble and note
                                                                ; overflow from byte.
0071  EB E0                      jmp    highsub0                ; Go subtract again.
                        ;
                        ; We need to add back having gone too far.
                        ;
0073                    highadd:
0073  57                         push   DI                      ; Save displacement
0074  BE 0000                    mov    SI,0                    ; Point to right digit pair
0077  B9 0008                    mov    CX,8                    ; Set count to add back
007A  F8                         clc                            ; Clear carry for first add.
007B                    highadd0:
007B  8A 01                      mov    AL, BYTE PTR[BX+DI]     ; Get pair,
007D  12 02                      adc    AL, BYTE PTR[BP+SI]     ; add back,
007F  27                         daa                            ; adjust to bcd,
0080  88 01                      mov    BYTE PTR[BX+DI],AL      ; and set result back.
0082  4F                         dec    DI
0083  4E                         dec    SI                      ; Adjust pointers and
0084  E2 F5                      loop   highadd0                ; do all 8 digits.
0086  5F                         pop    DI                      ; Restore displacement
                        ;
                        ; Check for overflow (quotient digit > 9)
                        ;
0087  66| 3D 000090FF            cmp    EAX,090ffh              ; Did we overflow (first
                                                                ; time only)?
008D  0F 87 0102 R               ja     zerodiv                 ; If so - same as zero divide.
                        ;
                        ; Subtract the unshifted number from the same displacement.
                        ;
0091                    lowsub:
0091  57                         push   DI                      ; Save displacement
0092  BE FFF8                    mov    SI,-8                   ; Set right digit pair,
0095  B9 0007                    mov    CX,7                    ; count of digits, and
0098  F8                         clc                            ; clear carry for first sbb.
0099                    lowsub0:
0099  8A 01                      mov    AL, BYTE PTR[BX+DI]     ; Get digit pair
009B  1A 02                      sbb    AL, BYTE PTR[BP+SI]     ; Subtract with borrow needed.
009D  2F                         das                            ; adjust to bcd.
009E  88 01                      mov    BYTE PTR[BX+DI],AL      ; and put it back
00A0  4F                         dec    DI                      ; Point to next dividend pair
00A1  4E                         dec    SI                      ; and divisor pair
00A2  E2 F5                      loop   lowsub0                 ; Do all pairs.
00A4  5F                         pop    DI                      ; Restore dividend displacement
00A5  0F 82 00AD R               jc     lowadd                  ; We went minus - pass is done.
00A9  FE C4                      inc    AH                      ; Add to low nibble.
00AB  EB E4                      jmp    lowsub                  ; Go subtract again.
```

```
                          ;
                          ; We need to add back having gone too far.
                          ;
00AD                      lowadd:
00AD  57                          push    DI                      ; Save displacement
00AE  BE FFF8                     mov     SI,-8                   ; Point to right digit pair
00B1  B9 0007                     mov     CX,7                    ; Set count to add back
00B4  F8                          clc                             ; Clear carry for first add.
00B5                      lowadd0:
00B5  8A 01                       mov     AL, BYTE PTR[BX+DI]     ; Get pair,
00B7  12 02                       adc     AL, BYTE PTR[BP+SI]     ; add back,
00B9  27                          daa                             ; adjust to bcd,
00BA  88 01                       mov     BYTE PTR[BX+DI],AL      ; and set result back.
00BC  4F                          dec     DI
00BD  4E                          dec     SI                      ; Adjust pointers and
00BE  E2 F5                       loop    lowadd0                 ; do all 8 digits.
00C0  5F                          pop     DI                      ; Restore displacement
                          ;
                          ; Store the pair of quotient digits which we have produced.
                          ;
00C1  8B F7                       mov     SI,DI                   ; Copy displacement into accum
00C3  83 EE 08                    sub     SI,8                    ; Back up by number size
00C6  88 20                       mov     BYTE PTR[BX+SI],AH      ; and store digit pair.
00C8  47                          inc     DI                      ; Need to do the next pair
00C9  83 FF 10                    cmp     DI,16                   ; Check if we are done
00CC  7C 82                       jl      highsub                 ; loop to do all pairs.
                          ;
                          ; We have generated the quotient, the remainder is in the low 8
                          ; bytes of the accumulator.
                          ; We need to set the signs for each number.  The remainder keeps
                          ; the sign of the original dividend (if it isn't zero) and the
                          ; quotient is positive if the dividend and divisor signs were the
                          ; same (or if it is zero) and negative otherwise.
                          ;
00CE  8A 07                       mov     AL,BYTE PTR[BX+0]       ; Get dividend sign
00D0  88 47 08                    mov     BYTE PTR[BX+8],AL       ; Into remainder.
00D3  32 46 F1                    xor     AL,BYTE PTR[BP-15]      ; Combine with divisor sign
00D6  88 07                       mov     BYTE PTR[BX+0],AL       ; to make the quotient's sign.
                          ;
                          ; Check for the zero cases.
                          ;
00D8  66| 8B 07                   mov     EAX,DWORD PTR[BX+0]     ; Get first 4 bytes
00DB  B0 00                       mov     AL,0                    ; (without sign)
00DD  66| 0B 47 04                or      EAX,DWORD PTR[BX+4]     ; and combine with low 4.
00E1  0F 85 00E7 R                jnz     quotnz                  ; If not zero - skip
00E5  88 07                       mov     BYTE PTR[BX+0],AL       ; plug of zero sign
00E7                      quotnz:
00E7  66| 8B 47 08                mov     EAX,DWORD PTR[BX+8]     ; Get first 4 bytes
00EB  B0 00                       mov     AL,0                    ; (without sign)
00ED  66| 0B 47 0C                or      EAX,DWORD PTR[BX+12]    ; and combine with low 4.
00F1  0F 85 00F8 R                jnz     remdrnz                 ; If not zero - skip
00F5  88 47 08                    mov     BYTE PTR[BX+8],AL       ; plug of zero sign
00F8                      remdrnz:


00F8                      divexit:
00F8  C9                          leave                           ; Return work space
00F9  07                          pop     ES                      ; Restore the entry registers
00FA  5F                          pop     DI
00FB  5E                          pop     SI
00FC  5A                          pop     DX
00FD  59                          pop     CX
```

```
00FE  5B                              pop     BX
00FF  66| 58                          pop     EAX
0101  C3                              ret                          ; and return.
                          ;
                          ; Zero divide or overflow.
                          ;
0102                      zerodiv:
0102  F9                              stc                          ; set carry
0103  EB F3                           jmp     divexit              ; and get out
0105                      Bcddiv      ENDP
0105                      code        ENDS
                                      END
```

5

Interrupts and Exceptions

Performing an interrupt means to stop a current sequence and pay attention to another request. Program interrupts enable processors to respond to these requests in a controlled manner. For example, unpredictable incidents can be:

- Signals generated by an error condition (such as an array subscript that goes beyond the bounds of the array).
- Signals sent by an external device (such as a storage device responding that the requested data has been found and is ready for use).
- A user signaling the end of a typed message (with a carriage return) that requires analysis and response.

Interrupts have no relation to the instruction executing when the interrupt is received. The interrupt calls a responding program or subroutine (an *interrupt handler*) and control is turned over to that program or subroutine. Figure 5-1 gives a general overview of how a program interrupts and transfers control. First, the processor stores the current condition of the executing program and then changes the flow of program control to link to (and execute) that subroutine. The interrupt handler processes its code and, if appropriate, the original program is restarted at the point where the interrupt came in. To do this, the interrupt handler executes an IRET instruction.

The 80386 has both hardware- and software-generated interrupts that alter the programmed execution. A hardware-generated interrupt occurs in response to an

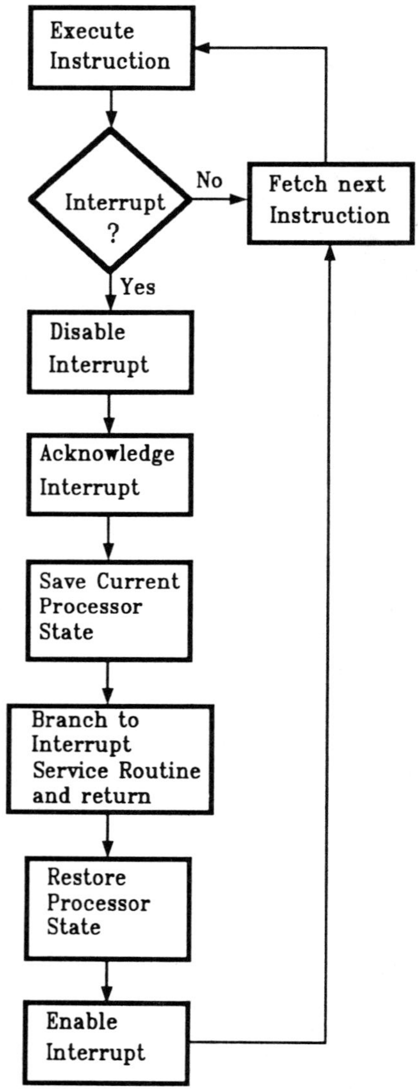

Fig. 5-1. Diagram for a program interrupt transfer.

active input on one of the two 80386 interrupt inputs: NMI, which is non-maskable, or INTR, which is maskable. A software-generated interrupt occurs in response to an INT instruction or an exception (a software condition that requires servicing). Figure 5-2 gives valid 80386 interrupt and exception ID assignments.

Exceptions are unusual or invalid conditions that are detected during instruction execution. The key difference between an interrupt and an exception is that exceptions are directly associated with the interrupted instruction, while interrupts

Identifier	Description
0	Divide Error
1	Debug Exception
2	Nonmaskable Interrupt
3	Breakpoint
4	Overflow
5	Bounds Check
6	Invalid Opcode
7	Coprocessor Not Available
8	Double Fault
9	Coprocessor Segment Overrun
10	Invalid TSS
11	Segment Not Present
12	Stack Exception
13	General Protection
14	Page Fault
15	(RESERVED)
16	Coprocessor Error
17–31	(RESERVED)
32–255	Available for External Interrupts via the INTR Pin

Fig. 5-2. Interrupt and exception ID assignments.

are not. For example, the "software interrupt" instruction INT *n* is classified as an exception rather than interrupt since its execution causes an exception.

BIOS and MS-DOS Interrupts

BIOS and MS-DOS interrupts were introduced in Chapter 2, and are detailed in Appendix G. In this chapter, we want to look at working with them. BIOS vectors are located at the beginning of memory and are followed by the MS-DOS interrupt vectors. Each vector uses 4 bytes, so a quick calculation of the location of interrupt *n* is *n**4. Therefore, the INT 10 vector is located at location 0000:0040.

One of the programs in this chapter, INTHNDLR, allows you to intercept an MS-DOS or BIOS interrupt and replace it with one of your own. You replace the BIOS or MS-DOS interrupt vector with a vector that points to your routine by using Function 25 of INT 21. Remember to change the vector back before ending your program.

Masked and Unmasked Exceptions

A *mask* is a machine word that specifies which part(s) of another machine word are to be operated on. *Masking* is the technique for sensing specific binary conditions and ignoring others. It is typically accomplished by placing zeros in bit positions of no interest and ones in bit positions to be sensed.

Certain conditions and flags cause the 80386 to ignore interrupts and debug exceptions. In those cases, the 80386 holds the interrupts pending and discards the debug exceptions. Those cases are:

- ☐ If the RF (Resume Flag) bit in the EFLAGS register is 1, debug faults (but not traps) are masked.
- ☐ If the IF bit (Interrupt Enable Flag) in EFLAGS is zero, INTR interrupts are masked.
- ☐ If the STI (Set Interrupt Flag) instruction executes with IF = 0, INTR interrupts are masked until after the next instruction.
- ☐ A POP or MOV instruction (with the SS register as the destination) masks interrupts and debug exceptions until after the next instruction.
- ☐ After reporting an NMI, further NMIs are masked until an IRET instruction executes.

80386 Interrupts

The 80386 handles both interrupts and exceptions between instructions. Instructions such as repeated string instructions are built so that they update pointer and count registers. Thus they handle interrupts after each repeat step, which provides good interrupt response while ensuring that the string instruction finishes.

Figure 5-2 shows that each interrupt and exception has an identification or vector number. The vector number selects the handler for a particular interrupt or exception from the interrupt descriptor table. Exceptions have preassigned vector numbers that range from 0 to 31. While you can assign your own numbers (from 0 to 255) to your interrupts and exceptions, it's best if you stick to the range of 32 to 255.

The 80386 recognizes 16 defined error codes, which are described briefly below.

Interrupt 0: Divide Error. The divide error occurs during a DIV (unsigned Divide) or IDIV (Signed Divide) instruction when the divisor is zero.

Interrupt 1: Debug Exceptions. The 80386 generates this interrupt for five general conditions.

1. Task-switch breakpoint trap.
2. General detect fault.
3. Data address breakpoint trap.
4. Instruction address breakpoint fault.
5. Single-step trap.

Interrupt 2: Nonmaskable Interrupt

Interrupt 3: Breakpoint. INT 3 (Call to Interrupt Procedure) causes this trap. INT 3 is one byte long, which makes it easy to replace an opcode in an executable segment with the breakpoint opcode. The saved CS:EIP (Code Segment, Instruction Pointer) points to the byte following the breakpoint.

Interrupt 4: Overflow. When the 80386 executes an INTO (Call to Interrupt Procedure for Overflow) and the OF (Overflow) flag is set, this interrupt is triggered. Both signed and unsigned arithmetic use the same arithmetic instructions. Since the 80386 cannot judge which is meant, it does not cause overflow exceptions automatically.

Interrupt 5: Bounds Check. While executing a BOUND (Check Array Index Against Bounds) instruction, if the 80386 finds that the operand is greater than the limit, the processor signals this fault. Software can also use BOUND to check a signed array index against signed limits that are defined in a block of memory.

Interrupt 6: Invalid Opcode. This fault occurs if an invalid opcode is found by the execution unit. That exception is not detected until the processor attempts to execute the invalid opcode. That is, prefetching the invalid opcode does not trigger this interrupt. Also, no error code is pushed on the stack. Another problem can cause this exception. If the type of operand is invalid for a given opcode, the fault is triggered. For example, an interrupt will occur if an LES (Load Full Pointer into ES Register) uses a register source operand.

Interrupt 7: Coprocessor Not Available. This exception occurs in one of two conditions, either (1) the processor encounters either the WAIT instruction or an ESC (Escape, the signal that this is a coprocessor instruction) and both the MP (Monitor Coprocessor) and the TS (Task Switched) bits of Control Register Zero (CR0) are set; or (2) the 80386 finds an ESC instruction and the EM (Emulate) bit of CR0 is set.

Interrupt 8: Double Fault. The 80386 generally handles exceptions serially. If it cannot, it signals a double-fault condition. To be able to determine if the error is a double-fault condition, the 80386 divides exceptions into three classes: benign exceptions, contributory exceptions, and page faults. These are shown in Fig. 5-3.

The 80386 always pushes an error code onto the stack of the double-fault handler. That error code is *always* zero. The faulting instruction may not be restarted. If another exception occurs while the processor is attempting to handle a double fault, the processor shuts down.

Class	Identification	Description
Benign Exceptions	1 2 3 4 5 6 7 16	Debug Exceptions NMI Breakpoint Overflow Bounds Check Invalid Opcode Coprocessor Not Available Coprocessor Error
Contributory Exceptions	0 9 10 11 12 13	Divide Error Coprocessor Segment Overrun Invalid TSS Segment Not Present Stack Exception General Protection
Page Fault	14	Page Fault

Fig. 5-3. Three classes of double faults.

Interrupt 9: Coprocessor Segment Overrun. In the protected mode, if the 80386 detects a page or segment violation while transferring the middle portion of a coprocessor operand to the NPX, this exception is raised.

Interrupt 10: Invalid Task State Segment (TSS). An attempt to switch to an invalid TSS causes this exception. Eleven conditions can cause a TSS to be considered invalid and Fig. 5-4 lists the conditions. An error code is pushed onto the stack to help identify which cause it is. The EXT (External) bit indicates if the exception was caused by a condition outside the control of the program, such as an external interrupt via a task gate which triggered the switch to an invalid TSS. To ensure a correct TSS to process this condition, the exception handler must be a task call via a task gate.

Interrupt 11: Segment Not Present. This exception occurs when the 80386 finds that the P (Present) bit of a descriptor is zero. This fault is restartable. The exception handler makes the segment present and returns. The interrupted program then resumes execution. Generally, an operating system uses this exception to implement virtual memory at the segment level.

Interrupt 12: Stack Exception. Interrupt 12 occurs in either of two conditions. The first is if the 80386 attempts to load the SS register with a descriptor that is marked as not-present but is otherwise valid. This can occur in an interlevel CALL, an interlevel return, in a task switch, an LSS instruction, or a MOV or POP instruction to SS.

Error Code	Conditions
TSS id + EXT	The limit in the TSS Descriptor is less than 103
LTD id + EXT	Invalid LDT selector, or LDT not present
SS id + EXT	Stack segment selector is outside table limit
SS id + EXT	Stack segment is not a writeable segment
SS id + EXT	Stack segment selector RPL; not equal to CPL
CS id + EXT	Code segment selector is outside table limit
CS id + EXT	Code segment selector does not refer to code segment
CS id + EXT	DPL of non-conforming code segment is not equal to the new CPL
CS id + EXT	DPL of conforming code segment is greater than new CPL
DS/ES/FS/GS id + EXT	DS, ES, FS, or GS segment selector is outside table limits
DS/ES/FS/GS id + EXT	DS, ES, FS, or GS is not a readable segment

Fig. 5-4. Conditions invalidating a TSS.

The second Interrupt 12 exception condition is any operation that refers to the SS register and has a limit violation. This includes stack-oriented instructions such as ENTER, LEAVE, POP, and PUSH. It also includes other memory references that imply use of the SS register. An instruction that causes this interrupt is restartable in all cases. The return pointer pushed onto the exception handler's stack points to the instruction to be restarted.

Interrupt 13: General Protection Exception. This exception is the "catch-all." All protection violations that do not cause another exception cause a

Number	Description	Return to Faulting Instruction	Caused By
0	Divide Error	Yes	DIV, IDIV
1	Debug Exceptions	Yes	Any
3	Breakpoint	No	One-Byte INT3
4	Overflow	No	INTO
5	Bounds Check	Yes	BOUND
6	Invalid Opcode	Yes	Any illegal
7	Coprocessor Not Available	Yes	ESC, WAIT
8	Double Fault	Yes	Any exception
9	Coprocessor Segment Overrun	No	Any Op of ESC that wraps a segment
10	Invalid TSS	Yes	JMP, CALL, IRET interrupt
11	Segment Not Present	Yes	Any segment-register modification
12	Stack Exception	Yes	Any memory reference through SS
13	General Protection	Yes	Any memory reference or code fetch
14	Page Fault	Yes	Any memory reference or code fetch
16	Coprocessor Error	No	ESC, WAIT
0–255	Two-Byte SW Interrupt	No	Int n

Fig. 5-5. Exception summary.

general exception. The following are sample causes:

1. Writing into a read-only data segment or into a code segment.
2. Switching to a busy task.
3. Violating privilege rules.
4. Exceeding segment limit when using CS, DS, ES, FS, or GS.
5. Transferring control to a segment that is not executable.

Interrupt 14: Page Fault. Interrupt 14 occurs when paging is enabled (PG = 1) and the processor finds one of the two following conditions when translating a linear address to a physical address. The first is when the current procedure does not have enough privilege to access the indicated page; the second is when the page-table entry or page-directory that is needed for the address translation has a zero in its P (Present) bit.

Interrupt 15: Reserved for future Intel use.

Interrupt 16: Coprocessor Error. The 80386 issues an Interrupt 16 if it detects a signal on its own ERROR# pin, from the numeric coprocessor (the 80287 or 80387). The 80386 only tests this ERROR# pin twice: at the beginning of certain ESC (Escape) instructions and when the 80386 finds a WAIT instruction while the EM (Emulate) bit of the MSW (Machine Status Word) is zero (that is, no emulation).

Coprocessor Error Exceptions

The 80387 numeric coprocessor has a Control Word register that can be set by program control. Figure 5-6 shows the format of this register. Part of the register controls how the coprocessor handles error conditions. There are three fields in the Control Word register.

- **Bits 0–5** contain the exception mask for exception status and mask bits. A list is shown in Fig. 5-7. If the 80387 detects an exception, the mask bit for that exception is tested to see if the exception should be passed to a software error handler (mask = 0) or handled by an 80387 default error handler (mask = 1).
- **Bits 8–9** comprise the Precision Control Field. Results of floating-point arithmetic are rounded to one of the three precisions before being stored in the destination. The various precision decisions are shown in Fig. 5-8.

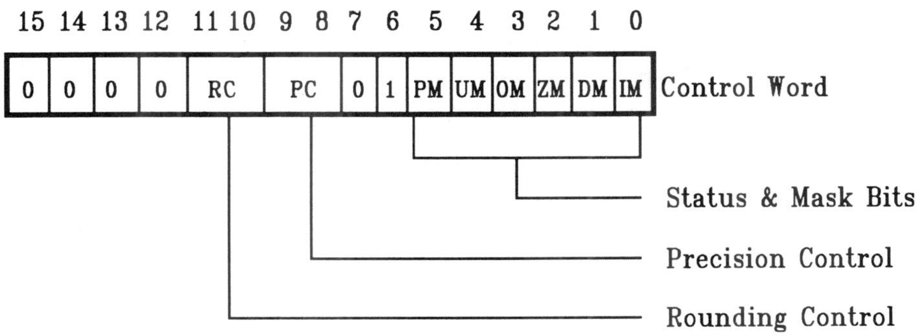

Fig. 5-6. 80387 Control Word register.

Fig. 5-7. 80387 Exception Status and Mask bits.

Bit	Status	Mask	Condition
0	IE	IM	invalid Operation
1	DE	DM	Denormal
2	ZE	ZM	Zero Divide
3	OE	OM	Overflow
4	UE	UM	Underflow
5	PE	PM	Precision

Fig. 5-8. 80387 Precision Control bits.

PC Bits 8 & 9	Precision Control of Significand
00	24 bits - Short Real
01	(Reserved for Future Use)
10	53 bits - Long Real
11	64 bits - Temporary Real

- ☐ **Bits 10–11** comprise the Rounding Control field. The four rounding modes are shown in Fig. 5-9. They are available to round results of floating-point arithmetic.

Coprocessor error exceptions group into six categories, listed in Fig. 5-10. If an exception is detected, the mask bit in the Control Word register determines what action is taken. If the mask bit is 1, the exception is masked and processing continues without reporting the condition. If the mask bit is 0, the exception is unmasked, and is reported and then processed.

Interrupt and Error Code Handling

BIOS and MS-DOS interrupt vectors are located in low memory. You can use MS-DOS interrupts to locate the vectors if you want to see how MS-DOS handles the interrupts (by unassembling the code with a debug package). You also can change how the interrupts are handled by intercepting the calls and replacing the interrupt handlers with ones you have written.

RC Bits 10 & 11	Rounding Control Rounding Mode
00	Round toward nearest or even
01	Round toward – infinity
10	Round toward + infinity
11	Chop or Truncate toward zero

Fig. 5-9. 80387 Rounding Control bits.

Intercepting BIOS/DOS Interrupts

In INTHNDLR (Program 5-1 at the end of this chapter) we replace PrtSc (INT 5) with a handler for the BOUND interrupt. Although the example is simple, it illustrates the best method for replacing interrupt vectors. The early operating system designers for the PC used reserved but unused BIOS interrupt vectors, which is why there is overlap and confusion today.

Another way you may want to invalidate an interrupt is to use INT 21 Function 35 and get the interrupt vector into DX. Subtract one byte and you run into the IRET of the previous interrupt. If you substitute the new address as the vector of the interrupt you intercept, nothing happens. The interrupt simply returns.

Let's use a debug package (SYMDEB, an overview of which appears in Appendix I) and find the vector of an interrupt, say INT 5 (see Fig. 5-11).

A Read/Write Error Message Program

Program 5-2, ERRORMSG, is a "simple-minded" example of showing how to index into an error table. It links with another procedure CODEHXTB (described

Mask	Code	Status	Condition	Precedence
IM	I, IS	IE	Invalid Operation (stack, numeric)	Highest
DM	D	DE	Denormal	↓
ZM	Z	ZE	Zero Divide	
OM	O	OE	Overflow	
UM	U	UE	Underflow	
PM	P	PE	Precision – IEEE inexact	Lowest

Fig. 5-10. Coprocessor error exceptions.

```
Microsoft (R) Symbolic Debug Utility  Version 4.00
Copyright (C) Microsoft Corp 1984, 1985.  All rights reserved.

Processor is [80286]
-D 0000:0000
0000:0000  00 4E 2E 01 F0 01 70 00-1B 2C B4 0C F0 01 70 00  .N..p.p..,4.p.p.
0000:0010  F0 01 70 00 54 FF 00 F0-6F EF 00 F0 6F EF 00 F0  p.p.T..poo.poo.p
0000:0020  A5 FE 00 F0 AD 2B B4 0C-6F EF 00 F0 6F EF 00 F0  %~.p-+4.oo.poo.p
0000:0030  6F EF 00 F0 BE 01 00 C8-57 EF 00 F0 F0 01 70 00  oo.p>..HWo.pp.p.
0000:0040  65 F0 00 F0 4D F8 00 F0-41 F8 00 F0 AB 09 70 00  ep.pMx.pAx.p+.p.
0000:0050  39 E7 00 F0 59 F8 00 F0-2E E8 00 F0 D2 EF 00 F0  9g.pYx.p.h.pRo.p
0000:0060  AD E3 00 F0 DD 0A 70 00-6E FE 00 F0 F2 00 E6 07  -c.p].p.n~.pr.f.
0000:0070  53 FF 00 F0 A4 F0 00 F0-22 05 00 00 00 00 00 00  S..p$p.p".......
-DW 0000:0014 0017
0000:0014  FF54 F000
-U F000:FF53
F000:FF53 CF             IRET
F000:FF54 50             PUSH   AX
F000:FF55 53             PUSH   BX
F000:FF56 51             PUSH   CX
F000:FF57 52             PUSH   DX
F000:FF58 1E             PUSH   DS
F000:FF59 B84000         MOV    AX,0040
F000:FF5C 8ED8           MOV    DS,AX
```

Fig. 5-11. SYMDEB run, finding INT 5 vector and unassembling code.

```
C:\ASM>DIR A:

 Volume in drive A is TESTIT
 Directory of  A:\

THISFILE           28   2-17-88   3:57p
        1 File(s)    361472 bytes free

C:\ASM>IOWRITE

Write to which file? A:THISFILE
Enter the bytes? Overwrite other bytes.

 ERROR FOUND
 Error code:        File already exists
 Error class:       Already exists
 Suggested action: Prompt user to enter corrected information
 Location:          Block device

C:\ASM>
```

Fig. 5-12. IOWRITE example, with EXTERROR messages.

and listed in Chapter 7), which converts hexadecimal input to binary. For the purpose of this example, ERRORMSG reads in a number from the keyboard and then looks up that message in the error table. In practice, you will want to pass ERRORMSG a number in an array and have ERRORMSG look up that passed parameter.

To link, you enter:

```
LINK ERR__MSG + CODEHXTB,,,;
```

or, using the library on the available diskette:

```
LINK ERR__MSG,,,LIBRARY;
```

Since we entered only four sample messages into the error table in the program, only type a number between 1 and 4. The program checks and blocks you if you type another number. If ERRORMSG were to be part of a final program, you would test for the limits of input so that your user could not receive unexpected output.

Extended Error Messages

The extended error codes returned by INT 21 Function 59 correspond to error values that are returned in AX by various MS-DOS functions (level 3.0 and later) that set the Carry Flag = 1. If a function call results in an error, INT 21 Function 59 returns meaningful information—but only if it is the next call to MS-DOS, after the one which received the error. Any other intervening call to another MS-DOS function, whether explicit or indirect, causes the error value for the unsuccessful function to be lost. We hard-coded the error messages into the procedure EXTERROR (Program 5-3) and used the return values in the various registers to index into the messages.

To use INT 21 Function 59, store 59 in AH, a hex 0 (00) in BX and issue INT 21. Unlike many MS-DOS functions, this function modifies registers, so we do a PUSHA in the beginning to save the registers and a POPA at the end to restore them. Function 59 returns the extended error code in AX, the error class in BH, a suggested action in BL, and the location of the error in CH. Shown in Fig. 5-12 is a sample run in which an attempt was made to write to a file (using IOWRITE, listed and explained in Chapter 8) that already existed.

Program 5-1: INTHNDLR

```
Microsoft (R) Macro Assembler Version 5.00


                                        PAGE    55,132
                                        .386
                                ;
                                ; Name: INTHNDLR
                                ;
                                ; Purpose: This program shown an example of intercepting an
                                ;          interrupt and replacing it with one specially written.
                                ;          The intercepted interrupt could just as well be an MS-DOS
                                ;          interrupt.  We replace interrupt 5 (print screen) with
                                ;          a handler for the bound interrupt.
                                ;
                                ; Inputs:  The program itself embodies a simple game of guessing the
                                ;          bounds.  All input is prompted for.
                                ;
                                ; Process: The program preserves the original value of the interrupt
                                ;          vector for the INT 5h handler.  It then sets its interrupt
                                ;          handler vector in DS:DX and requests MS-DOS to replace the
                                ;          vector.  The program then prompts for guesses and using the
                                ;          bound instruction checks whether the guesses are in bounds.
                                ;          Messages are produced for high, low and in bounds.
                                ;          The game is over when both upper and lower bounds are
                                ;          found.
                                ;
                                ; Outputs: All outputs are displayed.
                                ;
                                ; Note:    The program demonstrates techniques for swapping interrupt
                                ;          vectors.
                                ;


                                ;
                                ;
                                ; Declare the routines we are going to use
                                ;
                                        EXTRN   CODEASB:PROC
                                        EXTRN   CODEBAS:PROC
                                ;
                                ; Define a range of values for our bound test
                                ;
=-000D                          lowval  EQU     -13
= 0002                          valid   EQU     2
= 0017                          hival   EQU     23

0000                            stack   SEGMENT para 'STACK' STACK
0000  0100[                             dq      256 DUP(?)
          ???????????????
          ?
                         ]

0800                            stack   ENDS

0000                            data    SEGMENT para
0000  0000 0000                 int5save dw     0,0             ; Will save it here

0004  FFF3 0017                 okbound dw      lowval,hival    ; target for our bound check
0008  00                        fndlow  db      0
0009  00                        fndhi   db      0
```

```
000A  0100[                 string     db      256 DUP(?)           ; String scratch area
          ??
                   ]

010A  0A 0D 59 6F 75 20 67  rules      db      10,13,"You get to find the lowest and highest"
      65 74 20 74 6F 20 66
      69 6E 64 20 74 68 65
      20 6C 6F 77 65 73 74
      20 61 6E 64 20 68 69
      67 68 65 73 74
0132  20 76 61 6C 69 64 20             db      " valid array bounds."
      61 72 72 61 79 20 62
      6F 75 6E 64 73 2E
0146  0A 0D 20 49 66 20 79             db      10,13," If you get tired, a null entry will exit.$"
      6F 75 20 67 65 74 20
      74 69 72 65 64 2C 20
      61 20 6E 75 6C 6C 20
      65 6E 74 72 79 20 77
      69 6C 6C 20 65 78 69
      74 2E 24

0173  0A 0D 49 74 20 69 73  itisin     db      10,13,"It is in.$"
      20 69 6E 2E 24
017F  0A 0A 0D 45 6E 74 65  query      db      10,10,13,"Enter a number to test: $"
      72 20 61 20 6E 75 6D
      62 65 72 20 74 6F 20
      74 65 73 74 3A 20 24
019B  0A 0D 59 6F 75 20 67  gotlow     db      10,13,"You got the low value!$"
      6F 74 20 74 68 65 20
      6C 6F 77 20 76 61 6C
      75 65 21 24
01B4  0A 0D 59 6F 75 20 67  gothigh    db      10,13,"You got the high value!$"
      6F 74 20 74 68 65 20
      68 69 67 68 20 76 61
      6C 75 65 21 24
01CE                        data       ENDS
0000                        code       SEGMENT para 'CODE' USE16 PUBLIC
                                       ASSUME  CS:code, DS:data
                            ;
                            ; Set up the environment
                            ;
0000                        Begin:
0000  B8 ---- R                        mov     AX,data              ; Get data segment pointer
0003  8E D8                            mov     DS,AX                ; into DS,
                            ;
                            ; Get int 5's current handler and save it.
                            ;
0005  B8 3505                          mov     AX,3505h             ; Set both AH and AL
0008  CD 21                            int     21h
000A  8C 06 0000 R                     mov     int5save,ES          ; save segment
000E  89 1E 0002 R                     mov     int5save+2,BX        ; and offset
0012  8D 16 0095 R                     lea     DX,ibound            ; Point DX to the routine
0016  8C C9                            mov     CX,CS                ; Get the CS value
0018  8C DB                            mov     BX,DS                ; Save our DS
001A  8E D9                            mov     DS,CX                ; set segment for move
001C  B8 2505                          mov     AX,2505h             ; Set int code
001F  CD 21                            int     21h                  ; and put our handler in
0021  8E DB                            mov     DS,BX                ; restore DS
0023  8D 16 010A R                     lea     DX,rules             ; point to our simple rules
0027  B4 09                            mov     AH,9
0029  CD 21                            int     21h
002B                        getnbr:
```

```
002B  8D 16 017F R                  lea     DX,query            ; get a number
002F  E8 009B R                     call    getinp
0032  E3 52                         jcxz    Exit                ; got tired
0034  8B F3                         mov     SI,BX               ; Set input pointer
0036  E8 0000 E                     call    Codeasb             ; Do the convert
0039  72 F0                         jc      getnbr              ; Go get a good one
003B  BB 0001                       mov     BX,1                ; Set the good signal
003E  62 06 0004 R                  bound   AX,DWORD PTR okbound ; Do the bound instruction
0042  0B DB                         or      BX,BX               ; was it valid?
0044  74 E5                         jz      getnbr              ; no - try again
0046  50                            push    AX                  ; Save the number
0047  8D 16 0173 R                  lea     DX,itisin           ; Point to the ok msg
004B  B4 09                         mov     AH,9
004D  CD 21                         int     21h                 ; and put it out
004F  58                            pop     AX
0050  3D FFF3                       cmp     AX,lowval           ; is it the low
0053  0F 84 0073 R                  jz      foundlow            ; yes
0057  3D 0017                       cmp     AX,hival            ; is it the high?
005A  75 CF                         jnz     getnbr              ; no
005C  FE 06 0009 R                  inc     fndhi               ; set non zero
0060  8D 16 01B4 R                  lea     DX,gothigh
0064  B4 09                         mov     AH,9
0066  CD 21                         int     21h                 ; write message
0068  A0 0008 R                     mov     AL,fndlow           ; both found?
006B  0A C0                         or      AL,AL               ;
006D  0F 85 0086 R                  jnz     Exit
0071  EB B8                         jmp     getnbr              ; nope
0073                        foundlow:
0073  FE 06 0008 R                  inc     fndlow              ; set non zero
0077  8D 16 019B R                  lea     DX,gotlow
007B  B4 09                         mov     AH,9
007D  CD 21                         int     21h                 ; write message
007F  A0 0009 R                     mov     AL,fndhi            ; both found?
0082  0A C0                         or      AL,AL               ;
0084  74 A5                         jz      getnbr


0086                        Exit:
0086  C5 16 0000 R                  lds     DX,DWORD PTR int5save ; point to original
008A  B8 2505                       mov     AX,2505h            ; Set the code and int no.
008D  CD 21                         int     21h
008F  B0 00                         mov     AL,0                ; Set return code
0091  B4 4C                         mov     AH,04ch             ; Set good-by
0093  CD 21                         int     21h                 ; Return to the system
                            ;
                            ; Interrupt 5 handler.
                            ;       This is a simplified handler for the bound interrupt.
                            ;       It corrects the value in AX to an in-bound value and
                            ;       clears BX to indicate the error.  It then returns.
                            ;
0095                        ibound:
0095  2B DB                         sub     BX,BX               ; clear the flag register
0097  B8 0002                       mov     AX,valid            ; Set a valid value
009A  CF                            iret                        ; and return
                            ;
                            ; Read a string in response to a prompt
                            ; The prompt must be in DX.  The string will be returned in string.
                            ;
009B                        getinp      PROC
```

```
009B  50                      push   AX                ; Save registers
009C  56                      push   SI
009D  B4 09                   mov    AH,9              ; and dos request
009F  CD 21                   int    21h               ; put out the string
00A1  8D 16 000A R            lea    DX,string         ; point to input area
00A5  C6 06 000A R FE         mov    string,254        ; Set max length in
00AA  B4 0A                   mov    AH,10             ; Ask for read of string
00AC  CD 21                   int    21h               ; from DOS.
00AE  8D 1E 000C R            lea    BX,string+2       ; Point to just read data
00B2  8A 0E 000B R            mov    CL,string+1       ; Get length read
00B6  B5 00                   mov    CH,0              ; as a word.
00B8  8B F1                   mov    SI,CX             ; Set length
00BA  C6 84 000C R 00         mov    string+2[SI],0    ; and make an asciiz string.
00BF  5E                      pop    SI
00C0  58                      pop    AX                ; Restore registers
00C1  C3                      ret                      ; and return.
00C2                  getinp  ENDP

00C2                  code    ENDS
                              END    Begin
```

Program 5-2: ERRORMSG

```
Microsoft (R) Macro Assembler Version 5.00


                                                 PAGE    55,132
                                                 .386
                                          ;
                                          ; Declare the external procedure used to change hex to binary
                                          ;
                                                 EXTRN  CODEHXTB:PROC
                                          ;
 0000                                     STACK  SEGMENT 'STACK' STACK
 0000  0064[                                     DW      100 DUP(?)
           ????
                              ]

 00C8                                     STACK  ENDS
 0000                                     CODE   SEGMENT para 'CODE' PUBLIC USE16
                                                 ASSUME  CS:CODE, DS:CODE, SS:STACK
                                          ;
                                          ; Name: ERRORMSG
                                          ;
                                          ; Purpose:       This program has a table of error messages.  It uses
                                          ;                messages of the same length, to ease the indexing into
                                          ;                the table.  Note that each messages ends with a "$"
                                          ;                which is not printed.  Function 9 of INT 21 uses the
                                          ;                "$" as an end of text symbol.  Also "0Dh" is a
                                          ;                carriage return and "0Ah" is a line feed.
                                          ;
                                          ; Inputs:        The hex error number is read into AH,AL (AX).  This
                                          ;                program then calls CODEHXTB, which converts hex to
                                          ;                binary of whatever value is in AX.  If only a single
                                          ;                digit is passed to CODEHXTB, then AH must be set to
                                          ;                "30".  CODEHXTB is described in Chapter 7, Code
                                          ;                Conversion of the "80386 Assembly Language Toolkit"
                                          ;                from TAB Books Inc.
                                          ;
                                          ; Process:       DX points to the address of the beginning of the
                                          ;                error table.  The error number is the index into the
                                          ;                table.  Once the message is found, it prints on the
                                          ;                screen.
                                          ;
                                          ; Outputs:       A printed message on the screen.
                                          ;
                                          ; NOTE:          For the purposes of this example, a number is read in
                                          ;                from the keyboard.
                                          ;
 0000                                     ERRORMSG:
 0000  8C C8                                             MOV     AX,CS           ; Prepare to set DS
 0002  8E D8                                             MOV     DS,AX           ;   and set it.
 0004  E9 009E R                                         JMP     BEGINHERE
                                          ;
 0007  0028[                              INPUTSTR       DB      40 DUP(?)
             ??
                              ]
 002F  54 79 70 65 20 61 20               QUERY          DB      'Type a number 0-3 $'
       6E 75 6D 62 65 72 20
       30 2D 33 20 24
 0042  55 6E 61 62 6C 65 20               MESSAGES       DB      'Unable to open file.',0Dh,0Ah,'$'
       74 6F 20 6F 70 65 6E
```

```
      20 66 69 6C 65 2E 0D
      0A 24
0059  46 69 6C 65 20 64 6F                DB     'File does not exist.',0Dh,0Ah,'$'
      65 73 20 6E 6F 74 20
      65 78 69 73 74 2E 0D
      0A 24
0070  49 6E 76 61 6C 69 64                DB     'Invalid file name.  ',0Dh,0Ah,'$'
      20 66 69 6C 65 20 6E
      61 6D 65 2E 20 20 0D
      0A 24
0087  44 61 74 61 20 6E 6F                DB     'Data not found.     ',0Dh,0Ah,'$'
      74 20 66 6F 75 6E 64
      2E 20 20 20 20 20 0D
      0A 24
009E                       BEGINHERE:
009E  8D 16 002F R                        LEA    DX,QUERY        ; Print the prompt
00A2  B4 09                               MOV    AH,9h
00A4  CD 21                               INT    21h
00A6  8D 16 0007 R                        LEA    DX,INPUTSTR     ; Point to input buffer
00AA  C6 06 0007 R 25                     MOV    INPUTSTR,37     ; This max to read in
00AF  B4 0A                               MOV    AH,0Ah          ; Get ready to read in a value
00B1  CD 21                               INT    21h
00B3  A0 0009 R                           MOV    AL,INPUTSTR+2   ; Get the digit into AL
00B6  B4 30                               MOV    AH,30h          ; Since only 1 input digit
                           ;
                           ; Turn the hex into binary
                           ;
00B8  E8 0000 E                           CALL   CODEHXTB
                           ;
                           ; Now point to table entry
                           ;
00BB  3D 0003                             CMP    AX,3            ; Check value
00BE  77 DE                               JA     BEGINHERE       ; If bad try again
00C0  8D 16 0042 R                        LEA    DX,MESSAGES     ; Load in Table entry point
00C4  B1 17                               MOV    CL,23           ; Each message is 23 bytes
00C6  F6 E1                               MUL    CL              ; CL X AL = Result in AL
00C8  03 D0                               ADD    DX,AX           ; Add this result to entry
00CA  B4 09                               MOV    AH,9h           ; Get ready to print
00CC  CD 21                               INT    21h
                           ;
                           ; End of Program - Wrap-Up
                           ;
00CE                       ENDHERE:
00CE  B4 4C                               MOV    AH,4Ch          ; Standard Ending
00D0  CD 21                               INT    21h
00D2                       CODE           ENDS
                                          END    ERRORMSG
```

Program 5-3: EXTERROR

```
Microsoft (R) Macro Assembler Version 5.00


                                                PAGE    55,132
                                                .386
0000                                    STACK   SEGMENT 'STACK' STACK
0000  00C8[                                     DW      200 DUP(?)
          ????
                             ]

0190                                    STACK   ENDS
0000                                    CODE    SEGMENT para 'CODE' PUBLIC USE16
                                                ASSUME  CS:CODE, DS:CODE, SS:STACK
                                        ;
                                        ; Name:         EXTERROR
                                        ;
                                        ; Purpose:      This program reads the error code and gives an
                                        ;               extended code, with additional information in other
                                        ;               registers.  These extended error codes are especially
                                        ;               helpful when attempting to create new files or to
                                        ;               modify existing ones.
                                        ;
                                        ;               The extended error codes returned by INT 21 Function 59
                                        ;               correspond to the error values returned in AX by
                                        ;               functions in MS-DOS, versions 2.0 and later, that set
                                        ;               the Carry Flag=1.
                                        ;
                                        ; Inputs:       Store 59 in AH, 00 in BX and issue INT 21h.
                                        ;
                                        ; Process:      INT 21 Function 59 modifies registers CL, DX, SI,
                                        ;               DI, ES and DS.  These registers must be preserved
                                        ;               prior to invoking Function 59, if their contents are
                                        ;               needed for later processing.
                                        ;
                                        ; Outputs:      AX = extended error code.
                                        ;               BX = Error class and action
                                        ;                    BH = Error class
                                        ;                    BL = Suggested Action
                                        ;               CH = Location of Error
                                        ;
                                                        PUBLIC  EXTERROR
0000                                    EXTERROR        PROC
0000  E9 1379 R                                         JMP     BEGINHERE
                                        ;
0003  0A 0D 20 45 52 52 4F              HEADER          DB      0Ah,0Dh,' ERROR FOUND$'
      52 20 46 4F 55 4E 44
      24
0012  0A 0D 20 45 72 72 6F              CODES           DB      0Ah,0Dh,' Error code:       $'
      72 20 63 6F 64 65 3A
      20 20 20 20 20 20 20
      24
0028  0A 0D 20 45 72 72 6F              CLASS           DB      0Ah,0Dh,' Error class:      $'
      72 20 63 6C 61 73 73
      3A 20 20 20 20 20 20
      24
003E  0A 0D 20 53 75 67 67              ACTION          DB      0Ah,0Dh,' Suggested action: $'
      65 73 74 65 64 20 61
      63 74 69 6F 6E 3A 20
      24
```

```
0054  0A 0D 20 4C 6F 63 61     LOCATION        DB      0Ah,0Dh,' Location:         $'
      74 69 6F 6E 3A 20 20
      20 20 20 20 20 20 20
      24
006A  0A 0D 24                 CR_LF           DB      0Ah,0Dh,'$'
                               ;
                               ; AX Error Codes
006D  4E 6F 20 65 72 72 6F     AX00     DB     'No error encountered                   $'
      72 20 65 6E 63 6F 75
      6E 74 65 72 65 64 20
      20 20 20 20 20 20 20
      20 20 20 20 20 20 20
      20 20 20 20 20 20 24
0097  49 6E 76 61 6C 69 64     AX01     DB     'Invalid function number                $'
      20 66 75 6E 63 74 69
      6F 6E 20 6E 75 6D 62
      65 72 20 20 20 20 20
      20 20 20 20 20 20 20
      20 20 20 20 20 20 24
00C1  46 69 6C 65 20 6E 6F     AX02     DB     'File not found                         $'
      74 20 66 6F 75 6E 64
      20 20 20 20 20 20 20
      20 20 20 20 20 20 20
      20 20 20 20 20 20 20
      20 20 20 20 20 20 24
00EB  50 61 74 68 20 6E 6F     AX03     DB     'Path not found                         $'
      74 20 66 6F 75 6E 64
      20 20 20 20 20 20 20
      20 20 20 20 20 20 20
      20 20 20 20 20 20 20
      20 20 20 20 20 20 24
0115  54 6F 6F 20 6D 61 6E     AX04     DB     'Too many files open, no handles available$'
      79 20 66 69 6C 65 73
      20 6F 70 65 6E 2C 20
      6E 6F 20 68 61 6E 64
      6C 65 73 20 61 76 61
      69 6C 61 62 6C 65 24
013F  41 63 63 65 73 73 20     AX05     DB     'Access denied                          $'
      64 65 6E 69 65 64 20
      20 20 20 20 20 20 20
      20 20 20 20 20 20 20
      20 20 20 20 20 20 20
      20 20 20 20 20 20 24
0169  49 6E 76 61 6C 69 64     AX06     DB     'Invalid handle                         $'
      20 68 61 6E 64 6C 65
      20 20 20 20 20 20 20
      20 20 20 20 20 20 20
      20 20 20 20 20 20 20
      20 20 20 20 20 20 24
0193  4D 65 6D 6F 72 79 20     AX07     DB     'Memory control blocks destroyed        $'
      63 6F 6E 74 72 6F 6C
      20 62 6C 6F 63 6B 73
      20 64 65 73 74 72 6F
      79 65 64 20 20 20 20
      20 20 20 20 20 20 24
01BD  49 6E 73 75 66 66 69     AX08     DB     'Insufficient memory                    $'
      63 69 65 6E 74 20 6D
      65 6D 6F 72 79 20 20
      20 20 20 20 20 20 20
      20 20 20 20 20 20 20
      20 20 20 20 20 20 24
01E7  49 6E 76 61 6C 69 64     AX09     DB     'Invalid memory-block address           $'
```

```
      20 6D 65 6D 6F 72 79
      2D 62 6C 6F 63 6B 20
      61 64 64 72 65 73 73
      20 20 20 20 20 20 20
      20 20 20 20 20 20 24
0211  49 6E 76 61 6C 69 64    AX0A   DB    'Invalid environment                $'
      20 65 6E 76 69 72 6F
      6E 6D 65 6E 74 20 20
      20 20 20 20 20 20 20
      20 20 20 20 20 20 20
      20 20 20 20 20 20 24
023B  49 6E 76 61 6C 69 64    AX0B   DB    'Invalid format                     $'
      20 66 6F 72 6D 61 74
      20 20 20 20 20 20 20
      20 20 20 20 20 20 20
      20 20 20 20 20 20 20
      20 20 20 20 20 20 24
0265  49 6E 76 61 6C 69 64    AX0C   DB    'Invalid access code                $'
      20 61 63 63 65 73 73
      20 63 6F 64 65 20 20
      20 20 20 20 20 20 20
      20 20 20 20 20 20 20
      20 20 20 20 20 20 24
028F  49 6E 76 61 6C 69 64    AX0D   DB    'Invalid data                       $'
      20 64 61 74 61 20 20
      20 20 20 20 20 20 20
      20 20 20 20 20 20 20
      20 20 20 20 20 20 20
      20 20 20 20 20 20 24
02B9  52 65 73 65 72 76 65    AX0E   DB    'Reserved                           $'
      64 20 20 20 20 20 20
      20 20 20 20 20 20 20
      20 20 20 20 20 20 20
      20 20 20 20 20 20 20
      20 20 20 20 20 20 24
02E3  49 6E 76 61 6C 69 64    AX0F   DB    'Invalid disk drive                 $'
      20 64 69 73 6B 20 64
      72 69 76 65 20 20 20
      20 20 20 20 20 20 20
      20 20 20 20 20 20 20
      20 20 20 20 20 20 24
030D  41 74 74 65 6D 70 74    AX10   DB    'Attempt to remove current directory $'
      20 74 6F 20 72 65 6D
      6F 76 65 20 63 75 72
      72 65 6E 74 20 64 69
      72 65 63 74 6F 72 79
      20 20 20 20 20 20 24
0337  44 65 76 69 63 65 20    AX11   DB    'Device not the same                $'
      6E 6F 74 20 74 68 65
      20 73 61 6D 65 20 20
      20 20 20 20 20 20 20
      20 20 20 20 20 20 20
      20 20 20 20 20 20 24
0361  4E 6F 20 6D 6F 72 65    AX12   DB    'No more files                      $'
      20 66 69 6C 65 73 20
      20 20 20 20 20 20 20
      20 20 20 20 20 20 20
      20 20 20 20 20 20 20
      20 20 20 20 20 20 24
038B  57 72 6F 74 65 2D 70    AX13   DB    'Wrote-protected disk               $'
      72 6F 74 65 63 74 65
      64 20 64 69 73 6B 20
```

```
      20 20 20 20 20 20 20
      20 20 20 20 20 20 20
      20 20 20 20 20 20 24
03B5  55 6E 6B 6E 6F 77 6E     AX14    DB     'Unknown unit                  $'
      20 75 6E 69 74 20 20
      20 20 20 20 20 20 20
      20 20 20 20 20 20 20
      20 20 20 20 20 20 20
      20 20 20 20 20 20 24
03DF  44 72 69 76 65 20 6E     AX15    DB     'Drive not ready               $'
      6F 74 20 72 65 61 64
      79 20 20 20 20 20 20
      20 20 20 20 20 20 20
      20 20 20 20 20 20 20
      20 20 20 20 20 20 24
0409  49 6E 76 61 6C 69 64     AX16    DB     'Invalid command               $'
      20 63 6F 6D 6D 61 6E
      64 20 20 20 20 20 20
      20 20 20 20 20 20 20
      20 20 20 20 20 20 20
      20 20 20 20 20 20 24
0433  44 61 74 61 20 65 72     AX17    DB     'Data error based on CRC       $'
      72 6F 72 20 62 61 73
      65 64 20 6F 6E 20 43
      52 43 20 20 20 20 20
      20 20 20 20 20 20 20
      20 20 20 20 20 20 24
045D  4C 65 6E 67 74 68 20     AX18    DB     'Length of request structure invalid      $'
      6F 66 20 72 65 71 75
      65 73 74 20 73 74 72
      75 63 74 75 72 65 20
      69 6E 76 61 6C 69 64
      20 20 20 20 20 20 24
0487  53 65 65 6B 20 65 72     AX19    DB     'Seek error                    $'
      72 6F 72 20 20 20 20
      20 20 20 20 20 20 20
      20 20 20 20 20 20 20
      20 20 20 20 20 20 20
      20 20 20 20 20 20 24
04B1  4E 6F 6E 2D 4D 53 2D     AX1A    DB     'Non-MS-DOS disk               $'
      44 4F 53 20 64 69 73
      6B 20 20 20 20 20 20
      20 20 20 20 20 20 20
      20 20 20 20 20 20 20
      20 20 20 20 20 20 24
04DB  53 65 63 74 6F 72 20     AX1B    DB     'Sector not found              $'
      6E 6F 74 20 66 6F 75
      6E 64 20 20 20 20 20
      20 20 20 20 20 20 20
      20 20 20 20 20 20 20
      20 20 20 20 20 20 24
0505  50 72 69 6E 74 65 72     AX1C    DB     'Printer out of paper          $'
      20 6F 75 74 20 6F 66
      20 70 61 70 65 72 20
      20 20 20 20 20 20 20
      20 20 20 20 20 20 20
      20 20 20 20 20 20 24
052F  57 72 69 74 65 20 66     AX1D    DB     'Write fault                   $'
      61 75 6C 74 20 20 20
      20 20 20 20 20 20 20
      20 20 20 20 20 20 20
      20 20 20 20 20 20 20
```

```
     20 20 20 20 20 20 24
0559 52 65 61 64 20 66 61    AX1E    DB    'Read fault                        $'
     75 6C 74 20 20 20 20
     20 20 20 20 20 20 20
     20 20 20 20 20 20 20
     20 20 20 20 20 20 20
     20 20 20 20 20 20 24
0583 47 65 6E 65 72 61 6C    AX1F    DB    'General failure                   $'
     20 66 61 69 6C 75 72
     65 20 20 20 20 20 20
     20 20 20 20 20 20 20
     20 20 20 20 20 20 20
     20 20 20 20 20 20 24
05AD 53 68 61 72 69 6E 67    AX20    DB    'Sharing violation                 $'
     20 76 69 6F 6C 61 74
     69 6F 6E 20 20 20 20
     20 20 20 20 20 20 20
     20 20 20 20 20 20 20
     20 20 20 20 20 20 24
05D7 4C 6F 63 6B 20 76 69    AX21    DB    'Lock violation                    $'
     6F 6C 61 74 69 6F 6E
     20 20 20 20 20 20 20
     20 20 20 20 20 20 20
     20 20 20 20 20 20 20
     20 20 20 20 20 20 24
0601 49 6E 76 61 6C 69 64    AX22    DB    'Invalid disk change               $'
     20 64 69 73 6B 20 63
     68 61 6E 67 65 20 20
     20 20 20 20 20 20 20
     20 20 20 20 20 20 20
     20 20 20 20 20 20 24
062B 46 69 6C 65 20 43 6F    AX23    DB    'File Control Block unavailable    $'
     6E 74 72 6F 6C 20 42
     6C 6F 63 6B 20 75 6E
     61 76 61 69 6C 61 62
     6C 65 20 20 20 20 20
     20 20 20 20 20 20 24
0655 53 68 61 72 69 6E 67    AX24    DB    'Sharing buffer exceeded           $'
     20 62 75 66 66 65 72
     20 65 78 63 65 65 64
     65 64 20 20 20 20 20
     20 20 20 20 20 20 20
     20 20 20 20 20 20 24
067F 52 65 73 65 72 76 65    AX25    DB    'Reserved                          $'
     64 20 20 20 20 20 20
     20 20 20 20 20 20 20
     20 20 20 20 20 20 20
     20 20 20 20 20 20 20
     20 20 20 20 20 20 24
06A9 52 65 73 65 72 76 65    AX26    DB    'Reserved                          $'
     64 20 20 20 20 20 20
     20 20 20 20 20 20 20
     20 20 20 20 20 20 20
     20 20 20 20 20 20 20
     20 20 20 20 20 20 24
06D3 52 65 73 65 72 76 65    AX27    DB    'Reserved                          $'
     64 20 20 20 20 20 20
     20 20 20 20 20 20 20
     20 20 20 20 20 20 20
     20 20 20 20 20 20 20
     20 20 20 20 20 20 24
06FD 52 65 73 65 72 76 65    AX28    DB    'Reserved                          $'
```

```
      64 20 20 20 20 20 20
      20 20 20 20 20 20 20
      20 20 20 20 20 20 20
      20 20 20 20 20 20 20
      20 20 20 20 20 20 24
0727  52 65 73 65 72 76 65    AX29   DB    'Reserved                        $'
      64 20 20 20 20 20 20
      20 20 20 20 20 20 20
      20 20 20 20 20 20 20
      20 20 20 20 20 20 20
      20 20 20 20 20 20 24
0751  52 65 73 65 72 76 65    AX2A   DB    'Reserved                        $'
      64 20 20 20 20 20 20
      20 20 20 20 20 20 20
      20 20 20 20 20 20 20
      20 20 20 20 20 20 20
      20 20 20 20 20 20 24
077B  52 65 73 65 72 76 65    AX2B   DB    'Reserved                        $'
      64 20 20 20 20 20 20
      20 20 20 20 20 20 20
      20 20 20 20 20 20 20
      20 20 20 20 20 20 20
      20 20 20 20 20 20 24
07A5  52 65 73 65 72 76 65    AX2C   DB    'Reserved                        $'
      64 20 20 20 20 20 20
      20 20 20 20 20 20 20
      20 20 20 20 20 20 20
      20 20 20 20 20 20 20
      20 20 20 20 20 20 24
07CF  52 65 73 65 72 76 65    AX2D   DB    'Reserved                        $'
      64 20 20 20 20 20 20
      20 20 20 20 20 20 20
      20 20 20 20 20 20 20
      20 20 20 20 20 20 20
      20 20 20 20 20 20 24
07F9  52 65 73 65 72 76 65    AX2E   DB    'Reserved                        $'
      64 20 20 20 20 20 20
      20 20 20 20 20 20 20
      20 20 20 20 20 20 20
      20 20 20 20 20 20 20
      20 20 20 20 20 20 24
0823  52 65 73 65 72 76 65    AX2F   DB    'Reserved                        $'
      64 20 20 20 20 20 20
      20 20 20 20 20 20 20
      20 20 20 20 20 20 20
      20 20 20 20 20 20 20
      20 20 20 20 20 20 24
084D  52 65 73 65 72 76 65    AX30   DB    'Reserved                        $'
      64 20 20 20 20 20 20
      20 20 20 20 20 20 20
      20 20 20 20 20 20 20
      20 20 20 20 20 20 20
      20 20 20 20 20 20 24
0877  52 65 73 65 72 76 65    AX31   DB    'Reserved                        $'
      64 20 20 20 20 20 20
      20 20 20 20 20 20 20
      20 20 20 20 20 20 20
      20 20 20 20 20 20 20
      20 20 20 20 20 20 24
08A1  55 6E 73 75 70 70 6F    AX32   DB    'Unsupported network request     $'
      72 74 65 64 20 6E 65
      74 77 6F 72 6B 20 72
```

```
      65 71 75 65 73 74 20
      20 20 20 20 20 20 20
      20 20 20 20 20 20 24
08CB  52 65 6D 6F 74 65 20     AX33   DB    'Remote machine not listening        $'
      6D 61 63 68 69 6E 65
      20 6E 6F 74 20 6C 69
      73 74 65 6E 69 6E 67
      20 20 20 20 20 20 20
      20 20 20 20 20 20 24
08F5  44 75 70 6C 69 63 61     AX34   DB    'Duplicate name on network           $'
      74 65 20 6E 61 6D 65
      20 6F 6E 20 6E 65 74
      77 6F 72 6B 20 20 20
      20 20 20 20 20 20 20
      20 20 20 20 20 20 24
091F  4E 65 74 77 6F 72 6B     AX35   DB    'Network name not found              $'
      20 6E 61 6D 65 20 6E
      6F 74 20 66 6F 75 6E
      64 20 20 20 20 20 20
      20 20 20 20 20 20 20
      20 20 20 20 20 20 24
0949  4E 65 74 77 6F 72 6B     AX36   DB    'Network busy                        $'
      20 62 75 73 79 20 20
      20 20 20 20 20 20 20
      20 20 20 20 20 20 20
      20 20 20 20 20 20 20
      20 20 20 20 20 20 24
0973  44 65 76 69 63 65 20     AX37   DB    'Device no longer exists on network  $'
      6E 6F 20 6C 6F 6E 67
      65 72 20 65 78 69 73
      74 73 20 6F 6E 20 6E
      65 74 77 6F 72 6B 20
      20 20 20 20 20 20 24
099D  4E 65 74 20 42 49 4F     AX38   DB    'Net BIOS command limit exceeded     $'
      53 20 63 6F 6D 6D 61
      6E 64 20 6C 69 6D 69
      74 20 65 78 63 65 65
      64 65 64 20 20 20 20
      20 20 20 20 20 20 24
09C7  45 72 72 6F 72 20 69     AX39   DB    'Error in network adapter hardware   $'
      6E 20 6E 65 74 77 6F
      72 6B 20 61 64 61 70
      74 65 72 20 68 61 72
      64 77 61 72 65 20 20
      20 20 20 20 20 20 24
09F1  49 6E 63 6F 72 72 65     AX3A   DB    'Incorrect response from network     $'
      63 74 20 72 65 73 70
      6F 6E 73 65 20 66 72
      6F 6D 20 6E 65 74 77
      6F 72 6B 20 20 20 20
      20 20 20 20 20 20 24
0A1B  55 6E 65 78 70 65 63     AX3B   DB    'Unexpected network error            $'
      74 65 64 20 6E 65 74
      77 6F 72 6B 20 65 72
      72 6F 72 20 20 20 20
      20 20 20 20 20 20 20
      20 20 20 20 20 20 24
0A45  52 65 6D 6F 74 65 20     AX3C   DB    'Remote adapt incompatible           $'
      61 64 61 70 74 20 69
      6E 63 6F 6D 70 61 74
      69 62 6C 65 20 20 20
      20 20 20 20 20 20 20
```

```
      20 20 20 20 20 20 24
0A6F  50 72 69 6E 74 20 71     AX3D    DB     'Print queue full                $'
      75 65 75 65 20 66 75
      6C 6C 20 20 20 20 20
      20 20 20 20 20 20 20
      20 20 20 20 20 20 20
      20 20 20 20 20 20 24
0A99  51 75 65 75 65 20 6E     AX3E    DB     'Queue not full                  $'
      6F 74 20 66 75 6C 6C
      20 20 20 20 20 20 20
      20 20 20 20 20 20 20
      20 20 20 20 20 20 20
      20 20 20 20 20 20 24
0AC3  4E 6F 74 20 65 6E 6F     AX3F    DB     'Not enough room for print file  $'
      75 67 68 20 72 6F 6F
      6D 20 66 6F 72 20 70
      72 69 6E 74 20 66 69
      6C 65 20 20 20 20 20
      20 20 20 20 20 20 24
0AED  4E 65 74 77 6F 72 6B     AX40    DB     'Network name deleted            $'
      20 6E 61 6D 65 20 64
      65 6C 65 74 65 64 20
      20 20 20 20 20 20 20
      20 20 20 20 20 20 20
      20 20 20 20 20 20 24
0B17  41 63 63 65 73 73 20     AX41    DB     'Access denied                   $'
      64 65 6E 69 65 64 20
      20 20 20 20 20 20 20
      20 20 20 20 20 20 20
      20 20 20 20 20 20 20
      20 20 20 20 20 20 24
0B41  49 6E 63 6F 72 72 65     AX42    DB     'Incorrect network device type   $'
      63 74 20 6E 65 74 77
      6F 72 6B 20 64 65 76
      69 63 65 20 74 79 70
      65 20 20 20 20 20 20
      20 20 20 20 20 20 24
0B6B  4E 65 74 77 6F 72 6B     AX43    DB     'Network name not found          $'
      20 6E 61 6D 65 20 6E
      6F 74 20 66 6F 75 6E
      64 20 20 20 20 20 20
      20 20 20 20 20 20 20
      20 20 20 20 20 20 24
0B95  4E 65 74 77 6F 72 6B     AX44    DB     'Network name limit exceeded     $'
      20 6E 61 6D 65 20 6C
      69 6D 69 74 20 65 78
      63 65 65 64 65 64 20
      20 20 20 20 20 20 20
      20 20 20 20 20 20 24
0BBF  4E 65 74 20 42 49 4F     AX45    DB     'Net BIOS session limit exceeded $'
      53 20 73 65 73 73 69
      6F 6E 20 6C 69 6D 69
      74 20 65 78 63 65 65
      64 65 64 20 20 20 20
      20 20 20 20 20 20 24
0BE9  54 65 6D 70 6F 72 61     AX46    DB     'Temporary pause                 $'
      72 79 20 70 61 75 73
      65 20 20 20 20 20 20
      20 20 20 20 20 20 20
      20 20 20 20 20 20 20
      20 20 20 20 20 20 24
0C13  4E 65 74 77 6F 72 6B     AX47    DB     'Network request not accepted    $'
```

```
      20 72 65 71 75 65 73
      74 20 6E 6F 74 20 61
      63 63 65 70 74 65 64
      20 20 20 20 20 20 20
      20 20 20 20 20 20 24
0C3D  50 72 69 6E 74 20 6F    AX48    DB    'Print or disk redirection paused      $'
      72 20 64 69 73 6B 20
      72 65 64 69 72 65 63
      74 69 6F 6E 20 70 61
      75 73 65 64 20 20 20
      20 20 20 20 20 20 24
0C67  52 65 73 65 72 76 65    AX49    DB    'Reserved                              $'
      64 20 20 20 20 20 20
      20 20 20 20 20 20 20
      20 20 20 20 20 20 20
      20 20 20 20 20 20 20
      20 20 20 20 20 20 24
0C91  52 65 73 65 72 76 65    AX4A    DB    'Reserved                              $'
      64 20 20 20 20 20 20
      20 20 20 20 20 20 20
      20 20 20 20 20 20 20
      20 20 20 20 20 20 20
      20 20 20 20 20 20 24
0CBB  52 65 73 65 72 76 65    AX4B    DB    'Reserved                              $'
      64 20 20 20 20 20 20
      20 20 20 20 20 20 20
      20 20 20 20 20 20 20
      20 20 20 20 20 20 20
      20 20 20 20 20 20 24
0CE5  52 65 73 65 72 76 65    AX4C    DB    'Reserved                              $'
      64 20 20 20 20 20 20
      20 20 20 20 20 20 20
      20 20 20 20 20 20 20
      20 20 20 20 20 20 20
      20 20 20 20 20 20 24
0D0F  52 65 73 65 72 76 65    AX4D    DB    'Reserved                              $'
      64 20 20 20 20 20 20
      20 20 20 20 20 20 20
      20 20 20 20 20 20 20
      20 20 20 20 20 20 20
      20 20 20 20 20 20 24
0D39  52 65 73 65 72 76 65    AX4E    DB    'Reserved                              $'
      64 20 20 20 20 20 20
      20 20 20 20 20 20 20
      20 20 20 20 20 20 20
      20 20 20 20 20 20 20
      20 20 20 20 20 20 24
0D63  52 65 73 65 72 76 65    AX4F    DB    'Reserved                              $'
      64 20 20 20 20 20 20
      20 20 20 20 20 20 20
      20 20 20 20 20 20 20
      20 20 20 20 20 20 20
      20 20 20 20 20 20 24
0D8D  46 69 6C 65 20 61 6C    AX50    DB    'File already exists                   $'
      72 65 61 64 79 20 65
      78 69 73 74 73 20 20
      20 20 20 20 20 20 20
      20 20 20 20 20 20 20
      20 20 20 20 20 20 24
0DB7  52 65 73 65 72 76 65    AX51    DB    'Reserved                              $'
      64 20 20 20 20 20 20
      20 20 20 20 20 20 20
```

```
       20 20 20 20 20 20 20
       20 20 20 20 20 20 20
       20 20 20 20 20 20 24
0DE1   43 61 6E 6E 6F 74 20    AX52   DB    'Cannot make directory                $'
       6D 61 6B 65 20 64 69
       72 65 63 74 6F 72 79
       20 20 20 20 20 20 20
       20 20 20 20 20 20 20
       20 20 20 20 20 20 24
0E0B   46 61 69 6C 75 72 65    AX53   DB    'Failure on Interrupt 24h (Critical Error)$'
       20 6F 6E 20 49 6E 74
       65 72 72 75 70 74 20
       32 34 68 20 28 43 72
       69 74 69 63 61 6C 20
       45 72 72 6F 72 29 24
0E35   4F 75 74 20 6F 66 20    AX54   DB    'Out of structures                    $'
       73 74 72 75 63 74 75
       72 65 73 20 20 20 20
       20 20 20 20 20 20 20
       20 20 20 20 20 20 20
       20 20 20 20 20 20 24
0E5F   41 6C 72 65 61 64 79    AX55   DB    'Already assigned                     $'
       20 61 73 73 69 67 6E
       65 64 20 20 20 20 20
       20 20 20 20 20 20 20
       20 20 20 20 20 20 20
       20 20 20 20 20 20 24
0E89   49 6E 76 61 6C 69 64    AX56   DB    'Invalid password                     $'
       20 70 61 73 73 77 6F
       72 64 20 20 20 20 20
       20 20 20 20 20 20 20
       20 20 20 20 20 20 20
       20 20 20 20 20 20 24
0EB3   49 6E 76 61 6C 69 64    AX57   DB    'Invalid parameter                    $'
       20 70 61 72 61 6D 65
       74 65 72 20 20 20 20
       20 20 20 20 20 20 20
       20 20 20 20 20 20 20
       20 20 20 20 20 20 24
0EDD   4E 65 74 20 77 72 69    AX58   DB     Net write fault                      $'
       74 65 20 66 61 75 6C
       74 20 20 20 20 20 20
       20 20 20 20 20 20 20
       20 20 20 20 20 20 20
       20 20 20 20 20 20 24

                               ;
                               ; BH = Error Class
                               ;
0F07   4F 75 74 20 6F 66 20    BH01   DB    'Out of resource (such as storage)              $'
       72 65 73 6F 75 72 63
       65 20 28 73 75 63 68
       20 61 73 20 73 74 6F
       72 61 67 65 29 20 20
       20 20 20 20 20 20 20
       20 20 20 20 20 20 20
       24
0F39   54 65 6D 70 6F 72 61    BH02   DB    'Temporary situation, will end, not an error    $'
       72 79 20 73 69 74 75
       61 74 69 6F 6E 2C 20
       77 69 6C 6C 20 65 6E
       64 2C 20 6E 6F 74 20
       61 6E 20 65 72 72 6F
```

```
      72 20 20 20 20 20 20
      24
0F6B  41 75 74 68 6F 72 69   BH03   DB   'Authorization problem                         $'
      7A 61 74 69 6F 6E 20
      70 72 6F 62 6C 65 6D
      20 20 20 20 20 20 20
      20 20 20 20 20 20 20
      20 20 20 20 20 20 20
      20 20 20 20 20 20 20
      24
0F9D  49 6E 74 65 72 6E 61   BH04   DB   'Internal error in system hardware             $'
      6C 20 65 72 72 6F 72
      20 69 6E 20 73 79 73
      74 65 6D 20 68 61 72
      64 77 61 72 65 20 20
      20 20 20 20 20 20 20
      20 20 20 20 20 20 20
      24
0FCF  48 61 72 64 77 61 72   BH05   DB   'Hardware failure                              $'
      65 20 66 61 69 6C 75
      72 65 20 20 20 20 20
      20 20 20 20 20 20 20
      20 20 20 20 20 20 20
      20 20 20 20 20 20 20
      20 20 20 20 20 20 20
      24
1001  53 79 73 74 65 6D 20   BH06   DB   'System software failure, not active process fault$'
      73 6F 66 74 77 61 72
      65 20 66 61 69 6C 75
      72 65 2C 20 6E 6F 74
      20 61 63 74 69 76 65
      20 70 72 6F 63 65 73
      73 20 66 61 75 6C 74
      24
1033  41 70 70 6C 69 63 61   BH07   DB   'Application program error                     $'
      74 69 6F 6E 20 70 72
      6F 67 72 61 6D 20 65
      72 72 6F 72 20 20 20
      20 20 20 20 20 20 20
      20 20 20 20 20 20 20
      20 20 20 20 20 20 20
      24
1065  46 69 6C 65 20 6F 72   BH08   DB   'File or item not found                        $'
      20 69 74 65 6D 20 6E
      6F 74 20 66 6F 75 6E
      64 20 20 20 20 20 20
      20 20 20 20 20 20 20
      20 20 20 20 20 20 20
      20 20 20 20 20 20 20
      24
1097  46 69 6C 65 2F 69 74   BH09   DB   'File/item an invalid format/type or unsuitable   $'
      65 6D 20 61 6E 20 69
      6E 76 61 6C 69 64 20
      66 6F 72 6D 61 74 2F
      74 79 70 65 20 6F 72
      20 75 6E 73 75 69 74
      61 62 6C 65 20 20 20
      24
10C9  46 69 6C 65 20 6F 72   BH0A   DB   'File or item interlocked                      $'
      20 69 74 65 6D 20 69
      6E 74 65 72 6C 6F 63
      6B 65 64 20 20 20 20
```

```
      20 20 20 20 20 20 20
      20 20 20 20 20 20 20
      20 20 20 20 20 20 20
      24
10FB  44 72 69 76 65 20 68   BH0B    DB 'Drive has wrong disk or storage medium problem   $'
      61 73 20 77 72 6F 6E
      67 20 64 69 73 6B 20
      6F 72 20 73 74 6F 72
      61 67 65 20 6D 65 64
      69 75 6D 20 70 72 6F
      62 6C 65 6D 20 20 20
      24
112D  41 6C 72 65 61 64 79   BH0C    DB 'Already exists                                   $'
      20 65 78 69 73 74 73
      20 20 20 20 20 20 20
      20 20 20 20 20 20 20
      20 20 20 20 20 20 20
      20 20 20 20 20 20 20
      20 20 20 20 20 20 20
      24
115F  55 6E 6B 6E 6F 77 6E   BH0D    DB 'Unknown                                          $'
      20 20 20 20 20 20 20
      20 20 20 20 20 20 20
      20 20 20 20 20 20 20
      20 20 20 20 20 20 20
      20 20 20 20 20 20 20
      20 20 20 20 20 20 20
      24
                             ;
                             ; BL = Suggested action
                             ;
1191  52 65 74 72 79 20 62   BL01    DB 'Retry before prompting user to Abort or Ignore
      65 66 6F 72 65 20 70
      72 6F 6D 70 74 69 6E
      67 20 75 73 65 72 20
      74 6F 20 41 62 6F 72
      74 20 6F 72 20 49 67
      6E 6F 72 65 20 20 20
      20 20 20 20 20 20 20
      20 20 24
11CC  52 65 74 72 79 20 77   BL02    DB 'Retry with pause before prompt to user to Abort or Ignore $'
      69 74 68 20 70 61 75
      73 65 20 62 65 66 6F
      72 65 20 70 72 6F 6D
      70 74 20 74 6F 20 75
      73 65 72 20 74 6F 20
      41 62 6F 72 74 20 6F
      72 20 49 67 6E 6F 72
      65 20 24
1207  50 72 6F 6D 70 74 20   BL03    DB 'Prompt user to enter corrected information             $'
      75 73 65 72 20 74 6F
      20 65 6E 74 65 72 20
      63 6F 72 72 65 63 74
      65 64 20 69 6E 66 6F
      72 6D 61 74 69 6F 6E
      20 20 20 20 20 20 20
      20 20 20 20 20 20 20
      20 20 24
1242  43 6C 65 61 6E 20 75   BL04    DB 'Clean up and exit the application                      $'
      70 20 61 6E 64 20 65
      78 69 74 20 74 68 65
      20 61 70 70 6C 69 63
```

```
      61 74 69 6F 6E 20 20
      20 20 20 20 20 20 20
      20 20 20 20 20 20 20
      20 20 20 20 20 20 20
      20 20 24
127D  45 78 69 74 20 69 6D  BL05    DB  'Exit immediately without cleanup                       $'
      6D 65 64 69 61 74 65
      6C 79 20 77 69 74 68
      6F 75 74 20 63 6C 65
      61 6E 75 70 20 20 20
      20 20 20 20 20 20 20
      20 20 20 20 20 20 20
      20 20 20 20 20 20 20
      20 20 24
12B8  49 67 6E 6F 72 65 20  BL06    DB  'Ignore - informational error                           $'
      2D 20 69 6E 66 6F 72
      6D 61 74 69 6F 6E 61
      6C 20 65 72 72 6F 72
      20 20 20 20 20 20 20
      20 20 20 20 20 20 20
      20 20 20 20 20 20 20
      20 20 20 20 20 20 20
      20 20 24
12F3  50 72 6F 6D 70 74 20  BL07    DB  'Prompt user to correct error (like change disk) then retry$'
      75 73 65 72 20 74 6F
      20 63 6F 72 72 65 63
      74 20 65 72 72 6F 72
      20 28 6C 69 6B 65 20
      63 68 61 6E 67 65 20
      64 69 73 6B 29 20 74
      68 65 6E 20 72 65 74
      72 79 24
                            ;
                            ; CH = Location of error
                            ;
132E  55 6E 6B 6E 6F 77 6E  CH01    DB  'Unknown       $'
      20 20 20 20 20 20 20
      24
133D  42 6C 6F 63 6B 20 64  CH02    DB  'Block device  $'
      65 76 69 63 65 20 20
      24
134C  4E 65 74 77 6F 72 6B  CH03    DB  'Network       $'
      20 20 20 20 20 20 20
      24
135B  53 65 72 69 61 6C 20  CH04    DB  'Serial device $'
      64 65 76 69 63 65 20
      24
136A  4D 65 6D 6F 72 79 20  CH05    DB  'Memory related$'
      72 65 6C 61 74 65 64
      24

                            ;
                            ;
1379                        BEGINHERE:
1379  60                                PUSHA                   ; Save all registers
137A  8D 16 006A R                      LEA     DX,CR_LF        ; Space error away
137E  B4 09                             MOV     AH,9
1380  CD 21                             INT     21h
                            ;
1382  8D 16 0003 R                      LEA     DX,HEADER
1386  B4 09                             MOV     AH,9
1388  CD 21                             INT     21h
                            ;
```

```
138A  8D 16 0012 R          LEA     DX,CODES
138E  B4 09                 MOV     AH,9
1390  CD 21                 INT     21h
                    ;
1392  BB 0000               MOV     BX,00           ; Zero out BX
1395  B4 59                 MOV     AH,59h
1397  CD 21                 INT     21h
                    ;
                    ; Print the AX message
                    ;  AX = Extended error code
                    ;
1399  87 CD                 XCHG    CX,BP           ; Save CX (the error location)
139B  2B C9                 SUB     CX,CX           ; Use CX for multiplication
139D  B1 2A                 MOV     CL,42           ; Each AX message is 42 bytes
139F  F7 E1                 MUL     CX              ; Mul AX x CX, result in AX
13A1  8D 16 006D R          LEA     DX,AX00         ; Point to beginning of AX messages
13A5  03 D0                 ADD     DX,AX           ; Point at correct message
13A7  B4 09                 MOV     AH,9            ; Now print AX message
13A9  CD 21                 INT     21h
                    ;
                    ; Print the BH Error Class message
                    ;  BH = Error class
                    ;
13AB  8D 16 0028 R          LEA     DX,CLASS        ; Print the "prefix"
13AF  B4 09                 MOV     AH,9
13B1  CD 21                 INT     21h
                    ;
13B3  2B C0                 SUB     AX,AX
13B5  8A C7                 MOV     AL,BH           ; Error class
13B7  2B C9                 SUB     CX,CX           ; Use CX for multiplication
13B9  B1 32                 MOV     CL,50           ; Each BH message is 50 bytes
13BB  F7 E1                 MUL     CX              ; Mul AX x CX, result in AX
13BD  8D 16 0F07 R          LEA     DX,BH01         ; Point to beginning of BH messages
13C1  03 D0                 ADD     DX,AX           ; Point at correct message
13C3  83 EA 32              SUB     DX,50           ; Correct position
13C6  B4 09                 MOV     AH,9            ; Now print AX message
13C8  CD 21                 INT     21h
                    ;
                    ; Print the BL Suggested Action message
                    ;  BL = Suggested action
                    ;
13CA  8D 16 003E R          LEA     DX,ACTION       ; Print the "prefix"
13CE  B4 09                 MOV     AH,9
13D0  CD 21                 INT     21h
                    ;
13D2  2B C0                 SUB     AX,AX
13D4  8A C3                 MOV     AL,BL           ; Suggested Action
13D6  2B C9                 SUB     CX,CX           ; Use CX for multiplication
13D8  B1 3B                 MOV     CL,59           ; Each BL message is 59 bytes
13DA  F7 E1                 MUL     CX              ; Mul AX x CX, result in AX
13DC  8D 16 1191 R          LEA     DX,BL01         ; Point to beginning of BL messages
13E0  03 D0                 ADD     DX,AX           ; Point at correct message
13E2  83 EA 3B              SUB     DX,59
13E5  B4 09                 MOV     AH,9            ; Now print AX message
13E7  CD 21                 INT     21h
                    ;
                    ; Print the CX Location message
                    ;  CH = Location of error
                    ;
13E9  8D 16 0054 R          LEA     DX,LOCATION     ; Print the "prefix"
13ED  B4 09                 MOV     AH,9
13EF  CD 21                 INT     21h
```

```
                                ;
13F1  87 CD                          XCHG    CX,BP        ; Retrieve the location
13F3  2B C0                          SUB     AX,AX
13F5  8A C5                          MOV     AL,CH        ; Location
13F7  2B C9                          SUB     CX,CX        ; Use CX for multiplication
13F9  B1 0F                          MOV     CL,15        ; Each CH message is 15 bytes
13FB  F7 E1                          MUL     CX           ; Mul AX x CL, result in AX
13FD  8D 16 132E R                   LEA     DX,CH01      ; Point to beginning of CH messages
1401  03 D0                          ADD     DX,AX        ; Point at correct message
1403  83 EA 0F                       SUB     DX,15        ; Correct position
1406  B4 09                          MOV     AH,9         ; Now print AX message
1408  CD 21                          INT     21h
                                ;
                                ;
140A  8D 16 006A R                   LEA     DX,CR_LF     ; Space errors
140E  B4 09                          MOV     AH,9
1410  CD 21                          INT     21h
                                ;
1412  61                             POPA                 ; Retrieve all registers
1413  C3                             RET
1414                            EXTERROR  ENDP
1414                            CODE      ENDS
                                          END
```

6

Bit and String Manipulation

New to the 80386 is bit manipulation support, with instructions that can change anything from single bits to bit strings up to 2^{32} bits long. Bit manipulation becomes important for system control, such as modifying bitmaps and semaphores. For example, each bit in a bitmap can represent a *pixel*—each dot on the display—and you may wish to turn the bits on and off. You may also need to know the status of a bit that keeps track of whether an overflow has occurred. That bit is called a signal flag or semaphore. When you use a semaphore, the bit is either set (ON = 1) when busy or reset (OFF = 0) when free.

Register bytes, words, and doublewords are actually templates for other objects, each with its own meaning. Each bit in the register can have a separate meaning, such as each bit in the EFLAGS register (see Appendix B for a detailed format of EFLAGS). The 80386 accesses each individual bit: reads it, writes it, or tests it.

80386 Bit Manipulation Instructions

Simply, the 80386 bit manipulation instructions manipulate bit patterns within registers and memory locations. The instructions divide into three groups: logical, shift, and rotate.

Logical Bit Manipulation

Logical instructions follow rules of logic. That is, they check that if Fact One is true and Fact Two is true, then it concludes that the answer is true. To use this logic, assembly language uses the AND, OR, XOR, NOT, and TEST instructions. See Fig. 6-1 for an overview of the results of these instructions.

Any bit ANDed with 0 is set to 0, while any bit ANDed with 1 retains its original value. OR, on the other hand, is used to force specific bits to 1. The OR instruction checks bits in each position of the operands. If either or both bits are 1, OR forces the destination to be a 1. The XOR (exclusive-OR) also checks each bit position of the operands. XOR sets a 1 in the destination operand for every bit position in which the operands *differ*. Where one operand has a 0 and the other has a 1, XOR sets a 1 in the destination; it sets 0 if they are the same.

	AND	OR	XOR	NOT	TEST
Operand 1	1010	1010	1010	1010	1010
Operand 2	0111	1100	1110		0111
Result	0010	1110	0100	0101	1010
Flags Modified	SF ZF PF	SF ZF PF	SF ZF PF	SF ZF PF	SF ZF PF
Flags Reset	OF CF	OF CF	OF CF	OF CF	OF CF

CF Carry Flag – Set on high-order bit carry or borrow

PF Parity Flag – Set if low-order 8 bits of result contain an even number of 1 bits; cleared otherwise

AF Adjust Flag – Set on carry from or borrow to the low order 4 bits of AL; cleared otherwise

ZF Zero Flag – Set if result is 0; cleared otherwise

SF Sign Flag – Set if high–order bit of result is 0=positive, 1=negative

OF Overflow Flag – Set if result is too large a positive number or too small a negative number (excluding the sign-bit) to fit in the destination operand; cleared otherwise

Fig. 6-1. Overview of AND, OR, XOR, NOT, and TEST.

NOT reverses the setting of each bit in a register or memory location. It effectively does a one's complement. However, NOT has no effect on the flags. TEST does an AND of its operands but only changes the flags, not the contents of the operands.

Bit Scanning

Instructions such as BSF (Bit Scan Forward) and BSR (Bit Scan Reverse) work only on 16-bit or 32-bit registers. They cannot be used on memory operands or 8-bit registers. The source register (the first operand in the instruction) contains the value to be scanned. The destination register is set to the number of the position of the first or last set bit. See Fig. 6-2 for scanning examples.

BSF scans the bits of the source register starting with the 0 bit (the rightmost bit) and works toward the most significant bit (MSB), the leftmost bit. BSR works just the opposite; it scans the bits in the source register starting with the MSB and going toward the 0 bit.

Shift and Rotate

The shift and rotate instructions have been with the Intel family of chips since the 8086. Bits can be moved left (toward the most significant bit, MSB) or right (toward 0). Values that shift off the end go into the CF (Carry Flag). See Fig. 6-3 for examples of how shifts and rotates move in and out of CF.

The shift instructions move the bits whatever number of positions you tell them to. The last bit in the direction of the shift "falls off" (actually it goes into CF). The first bit is then filled with 0 or with the value of the preceding first bit. Rotate

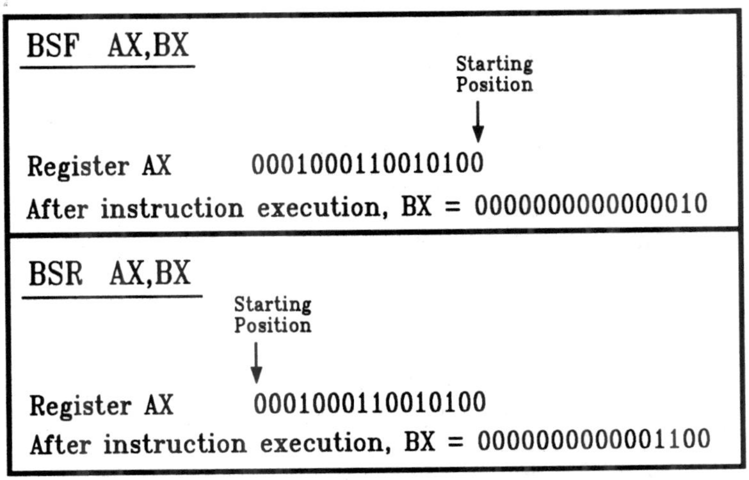

Fig. 6-2. Bit scanning examples.

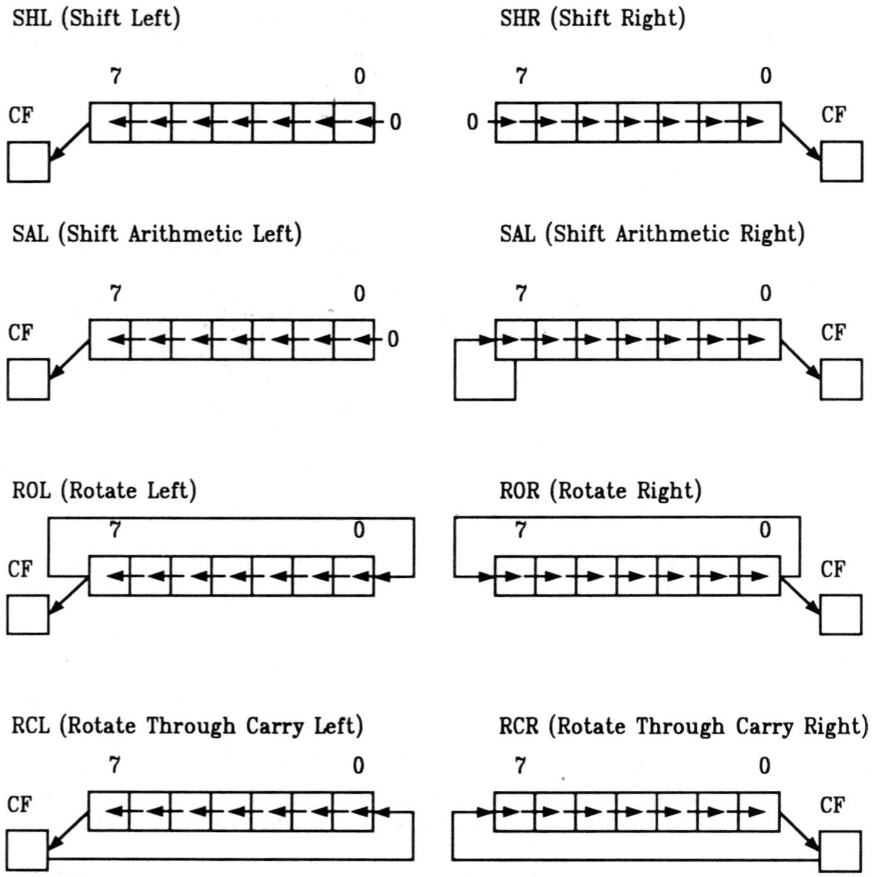

Fig. 6-3. Examples of shifts and rotates, using the Carry Flag (CF).

moves bits in a circle. The specified number of places move to the right or left as you code. For each bit rotated, the last bit in the direction of the rotate moves into the first bit position at the other end of the operand. See Appendix C for a complete description of each instruction used in the 80386 and Appendix D for the 80387 instructions.

Bit Manipulation Programs

Bitmaps are often used to store information about a set of items which can be mapped to integers, e.g., the sectors on a disk. If done, the in-use state of each sector would be recorded in a bitmap (1 = available, 0 = in-use). As another example, 4K pages of real memory can also have their in-use state mapped by a bitmap. A second bitmap could record the "dirty" or changed bit for the page.

The first program, CAP_IT, is not a bit manipulation program per se, because it is a simple subtraction of 20h to change a lowercase character into an uppercase character. The program does logically fit here, however, because no matter how simplistic the case, the bits are changed before displaying on the screen.

Alphabetic Character Case Conversion

CAP-IT (Program 6-1 at the end of the chapter) asks for a character to be input via the keyboard. Then it does a simple edit to be sure that an uppercase character was entered. It subtracts 20 from the character and prints the result.

A Bitmap Driver Program

BITMAPDV (Program 6-2) drives the BITMAPS procedure. All inputs are provided within the program. Basic tests of the bitmap routines are made and the results are reported on the screen.

The BITMAPS Procedure

The BITMAPS procedure (Program 6-3) provides a means of setting a bit in a bitmap which corresponds to the number provided. AX has the number of the bit to be set, changed from 0 to 1. BX points at the bitmap. The process is to convert the number into a doubleword (dword) displacement into the map by dividing by 32, multiplying the quotient by 4, and using the remainder as a bit number. The bit in the word is then set to 1. The Carry Flag reflects the previous setting of the bit; that is, if the bit was zero, CF will be set.

BITMAPS contains several procedures which provide a complete set of bitmap operations.

- ☐ **BITMAPR** provides a means of clearing a bit in a bitmap which corresponds to the number provided. AX has the number of the bit to be reset (changed from 1 to 0). BX points to the bitmap. The process is to convert the number into a doubleword displacement into the map by dividing by 32, multiplying the quotient by 4, and using the remainder as a bit number. The bit in the word is then set to 0. Carry reflects the previous setting of the bit.
- ☐ **BITMAPT** provides a means of testing a bit in a bitmap which corresponds to the number provided. AX has the number of the bit to be tested and BX points to the bitmap. The process is to convert the number into a doubleword displacement into the map by dividing by 32, multiplying the quotient by 4, and using the remainder as a bit number. The bit in the word is then tested. The Carry Flag (CF) reflects the setting of the bit.

☐ **BITMAPL** provides a means of locating the first 1 bit in a bitmap. BX points to the bitmap and CX has the number of doublewords in the map. The process is to scan the bitmap for a doubleword which is non-zero. The word is then scanned for the first 1 bit. A bit number is returned as doubleword number * 32, plus the bit number. Note: Doublewords are numbered from zero. If the bit is located, its number will be in AX and Carry will be reset (CF = 0). If the map is empty, AX is undefined and Carry is set (CF = 1).

Manipulating EFLAGS Bits

EFLAGSCH (Program 6-4) demonstrates the bit test and complement instruction that is unique to the 80386. EFLAGSCH captures the bit flags in the EFLAGS register and allows a change. EFLAGSCH prints a menu of items to be changed and prints EFLAGS prior to the change. The flag to change is entered via the keyboard. It is estimated that this program in its current form will *not* work under OS/2 in protected mode. You could cause it to get the lower 16 bits, called FLAGS, which would work in protected mode.

String Manipulation

The word *string* generally refers to a sequence of characters. The usage is analogous to physical objects strung together, one after another, such as a string of beads. As we look at them, strings are typically written from left to right. Thus, XYZ is a string of three characters, the first being X and the last being Z. In principle, strings may be arbitrarily any length, but there are always restrictions in practice.

Two strings joined together form another string that is the result of the joining. Appending (one way to join strings) one string to another is called *concatenation*. A *null string* contains no characters and is important because it is the identity with respect to concatenation. Note that concatenating the null string onto a second string does not change either string. A sequence of consecutive characters within a string is a *substring*. Thus, MAC is a substring of MACRO, but MC is not.

Almost all computer input and output consists of strings, including programs and data. One important aspect of strings is the characters they may contain. This is determined by the character set of the computer on which the string is represented. Character sets differ in specific characters, the number of characters they contain, and the order in which they are arranged. (Most common are ASCII and EBCDIC.)

Characters arranged in order of their internal numerical representation are said to be in *collating sequence* or *lexical order*. For letters, this order corresponds to ordinary alphabetical order. Note that in ASCII the digits come before the letters, while in EBCDIC the converse is true. The lexical order extends to strings, which allows strings to be compared lexically (for their relative alphabetical order). This comparison is the basis for string sorting.

To sort strings, the leftmost character in the string is the most significant one for the purposes of determining lexical order; the next character is the second most important, and so on. Characters, digits, and special characters all can be sorted.

A graphic is the printed representation of a character, and one character set can differ widely from another character set in their individual printed representations, especially of special characters. The character sets sometimes vary for other characters, depending on the printer or printing device and the representation chosen (generally several character sets are built into laser printers as internal fonts). Not all characters have graphics, the blank for example. In addition, there are characters which perform control functions (such as "line feed" and "tab") which affect the behavior of the output device.

String Operations

There were no generally agreed-upon string operations when string processing was first developed. However by now, four operations have achieved general

Operation	Logical Instruction	Result
Concatenation (Appending)	Concatenate 1,2	AAAA000AXXXX
Substring	Place 2 inside 1 beginning with position 3	AAXXXXAA000A
Pattern Matching	Find String 3 inside String 1	AAAA000A ↑ Position 5
Transformation	Find String 3 inside String 1 and replace with 3 bytes of String 2	AAAA000A ↑ Find it at Position 5 Then make it into: AAAAXXXA
Where: String 1 = AAAA000A String 2 = XXXX String 3 = 000		

Fig. 6-4. Generic string manipulation examples.

acceptance: concatenation, identification of substrings, pattern matching, and transformation of strings to replace identified substrings by other strings.

Concatenation is the process of appending one string to another to produce a longer string. The result of concatenating the string XYZ to ABC is the string ABC-XYZ. This operation is the natural extension of the idea of a string as a sequence of characters. *Substring* is a string within another string, where DEF is a substring of CDEFGH. *Pattern matching* is the most important and far-reaching string operation. It is the process of examining a string to locate substrings or to determine if a string has certain properties. *Transformation* typically is accomplished in conjunction with pattern matching and uses the results of matching to effect a replacement of substrings. Figure 6-4 shows examples of these four generic types of string operations.

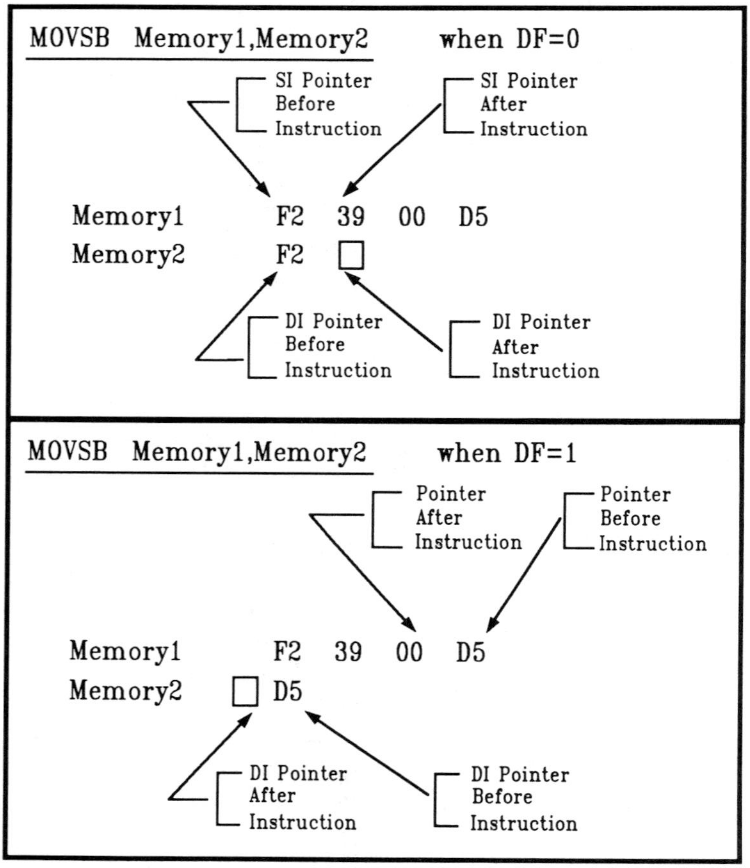

Fig. 6-5. Examples of a string move with the Direction Flag (DF) set.

80386 String Instructions

80386 string instructions operate on blocks of consecutive bytes or words in memory. These strings can consist of either text characters or numeric values and can be up to 4 gigabytes (using ECX). There are seven types of 80386 string instructions: input, output, compare, scan, load, move, and store.

After the string instruction operates, the pointer moves either higher or lower in memory. Its direction is set by use of the Direction Flag (DF) in EFLAGS, which is set by using the STD (Set Direction Flag) or CLD (Clear Direction Flag) instructions. If DF = 0, the pointer increases (moves upward to the next element). IF DF = 1, it decreases (moves downward to the previous element). See Fig. 6-5 and Fig. 6-6 for examples of direction and repetition.

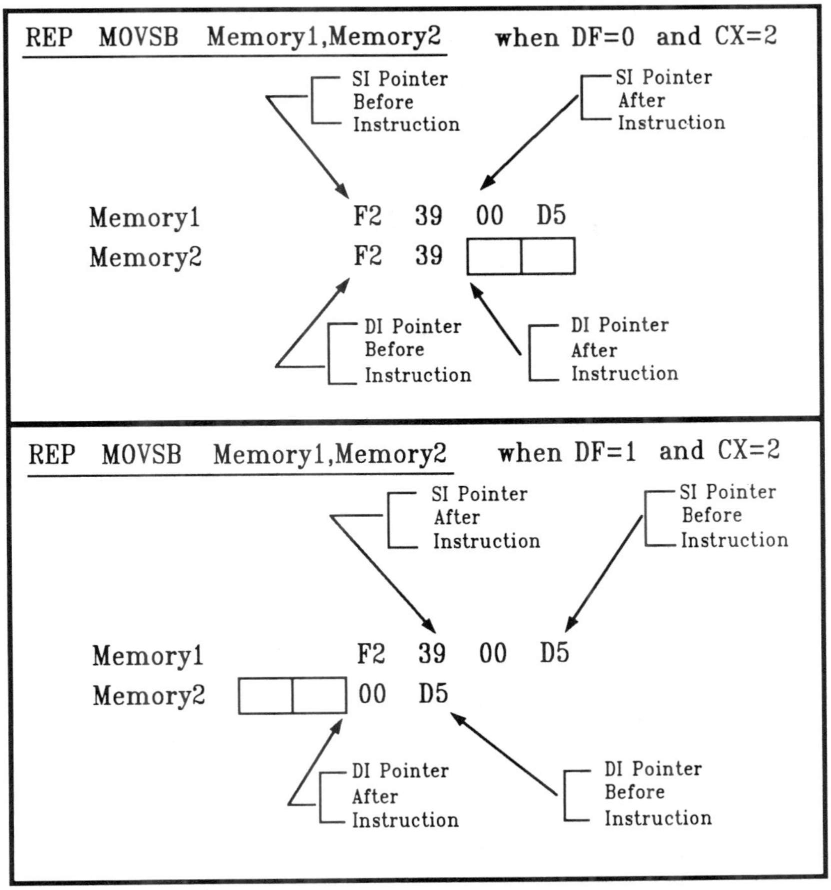

Fig. 6-6. Example of a string move with direction set and the REP prefix used.

String Search Routines

String instructions can operate on a series of elements. To do this, use the repeat prefix (REP). The 80386 then repeats the instruction based on a count you move into the CX register. On each iteration of the string instruction, the 80386 decrements the count by one. There are two additional aids in the REP prefix. They involve the Zero Flag (ZF) but can only be used with Scan String (SCAS) and Compare String (CMPS). Repeat While Not Equal (REPNE) repeats the instruction as long as ZF is 0 and CX is not 0. Repeat While Equal (REPE) repeats as long as ZF is 1 and CX is not 0.

Searching for Substrings

STRSRCH (Program 6-5) searches for the first occurrence of a specified substring within another given string. If the substring is found, the starting location (byte) returns in register DX.

A target string of some length is offered and its length in bytes determined. A second string is specified, with its length. The strings are checked for simple validity: Was anything entered in each and was the search string longer than the target string? If the strings pass, go to search. If not, an error message is written, DX set to 0, and the program ended. To print the byte, the external procedure CODEBAS is called. (See Chapter 7 for a description of CODEBAS.) CODEBAS turns binary characters into printable ASCII.

Inserting Substrings

STRINSRT (Program 6-6) asks for a target string to be input from the keyboard. Next it asks for a second string to insert into the target and the position in the target string in which to insert the second string. Notice the compactness of the code which does the actual insert—no more than 14 instructions.

Working with Strings

STRWORKS (Program 6-7) demonstrates the shell-sort algorithm, as demonstrated in the procedure SHELLSRT (described in Chapter 9). It requests a series of variable-length alphabetic words (not to be confused with computer memory words) until the user inputs a null string (carriage return). STRWORKS forces them to an ASCIIZ strings and put them into preallocated memory area, one right after another, and builds an array of displacements. After the null entry is entered, the array of displacements are passed to SHELLSRT. The strings are sorted and, once finished, printed out in sequence.

Comparing Two Strings

STRZCOMP (Program 6-8) compares two ASCIIZ strings and returns the resulting condition code flags. ASCIIZ (with its hex 00 terminating byte) is a common string form used by C programs and has become a standard because of that. Because STRZCOMP doesn't know the length of the two strings, it does a compare on each byte and, if equal, it checks that it hasn't reached the terminator. Otherwise, it terminates if the two strings are equivalent down to some point and one string is longer, the longer string will be considered the "greater" in the comparison.

DS:SI contains the address of String1. ES:DI contains the address of String2. The comparison is String1 minus String2. STRZCOMP compares byte for byte with each equal compare checked for a null (end-of-string indicator). An unequal or a null terminates the compare. Appropriate flags are set with the result of the subtraction of String2 from String1. Only the flags are set, with no other change.

Determining String Length

STRZLNG (Program 6-9) finds the length of an ASCIIZ string. ES:DI points to the string to examine and CX has the maximum length to examine. The registers are set for a repeated SCASB. The length of the string is scanned, excluding the null (hex 00) that ends the string. On return, AX has the count of bytes in the string, excluding the null. Carry is reset if the null was found. Otherwise, Carry is set to 1 and AX is returned equal to the input CX value.

String Parsing Routines

Parsing is the process by which the phrases in a string of characters are associated with the component names of the grammar that generated the string. Parsing is the heart of the process of compilation of source programs in a high-level language into machine language. The compiler must take the string of characters written by the programmer and associate appropriate substrings of characters with the syntactic components of the high-level language in order to determine the structure of the given program so that it can be translated into machine code.

Parsing also is important when editing input from a keyboard and to "fill in the blanks"; that is, to separate pieces of input and assign them to variables or fields which the program needs to process data.

In the program shown in this section, the procedure parses input text into a token which it returns to the driver. We decided to run parsing from a driver, to allow you to enter a string of characters, special characters, blanks, and so on from a keyboard and watch the output. The parsing routine uses punctuation and blanks to recognize the division between tokens. Note that if you enter a "$" character, the parser quits scanning. This is because INT 21 Function 9 is used to read in the keyboard input; this Function recognizes "$" as the end of a string.

A Parsing Driver

PARSEDRV (Program 6-10) provides a test for the parser, PARSING, and an example of its use. The program prompts for a line to be parsed and reads the input from the keyboard. The input is passed to PARSING until an end-of-data token is returned. Each token is displayed as it is returned. At end-of-data, another line of input is requested. If a null line (Enter only is pressed) comes in, the program terminates.

A String Parsing Program

PARSING (Program 6-11) is an example of how you may wish to write a parser. PARSING parses input text into tokens and returns them to the driving process. It demonstrates many of the standard operations in a parsing routine: skip leading spaces, checks for end of text string, identification of the types of input (numeric, alphabetic), and so on.

If a number is encountered, PARSING verifies that the following non-space, non-punctuation is also a number. It repeats until a proper end is detected and returns the number token. If an unknown character is encountered, it scans until a space or punctuation is detected to identify the unknown token's size and return as an unknown. If the non-blank is a capital letter, PARSING potentially identifies the token as a capitalized word. If lowercase, it potentially identifies the token as a lowercase word. In either alphabetic case, check the following characters for either lowercase letters or a proper ending (spaces or punctuation). If a non-space is a punctuation mark, PARSING returns the proper token type.

PARSING reads the string of characters in the input string which the DRIVER passes to it. It divides the input string into tokens and prints them back with a code that identifies it as:

Cwd Capitalized word
Lwd Lowercase word
Nbr Number
Per Period
Com Comma
Exc Exclamation point
Qmk Question mark
Unk Unknown

Program 6-1: CAP_IT

```
Microsoft (R) Macro Assembler Version 5.00


                                                PAGE     55,132
                                                .386
 0000                                   STACK   SEGMENT 'STACK' STACK
 0000   0064[                                   DW       100 DUP(?)
            ????
                          ]

 00C8                                   STACK   ENDS
 0000                                   CODE    SEGMENT para 'CODE' PUBLIC
                                                ASSUME   CS:CODE, DS:CODE, SS:STACK
                                        ;
                                        ; Name:          CAP_IT
                                        ;
                                        ; Purpose:       This program reads in a character from the keyboard
                                        ;                and, if it is a lower case character, converts it to
                                        ;                upper case.
                                        ;
                                        ; Inputs:        A character from the keyboard.
                                        ;
                                        ; Process:       Since the ASCII representation of a lower-case character
                                        ;                is 20h greater than a capital letter, the character is
                                        ;                read in, checked to see that it is an alphabetic character
                                        ;                between "a" and "z", then 20h is subtracted from it and
                                        ;                it is printed.
                                        ;
                                        ; Outputs:       Error message if a non-lowercase alpha character is typed.
                                        ;                If the input character is lower case alphabetic character,
                                        ;                it's capitalized and printed back to the screen.
                                        ;
 0000                                   CAP_IT:
 0000   66| 8C C8                                        MOV      AX,CS          ; Prepare to set DS
 0003   66| 8E D8                                        MOV      DS,AX          ;   and set it.
 0006   E9 0000008B R                                    JMP      BEGINHERE
                                        ;
 000B   20 2D 20 4E 6F 74 20            NOT_ALPHA        DB       ' - Not a lower-case alpha character.',0Ah,0Dh,'$'
        61 20 6C 6F 77 65 72
        2D 63 61 73 65 20 61
        6C 70 68 61 20 63 68
        61 72 61 63 74 65 72
        2E 0A 0D 24
 0032   20 20 20 20 20 20 20            NOT_2ND          DB                                  Re-enter.',0Ah,0Dh,'$'
        20 20 20 20 20 20 20
        20 20 20 20 20 20 20
        20 20 20 52 65 2D 65
        6E 74 65 72 2E 0A 0D
        24
 0056   45 6E 74 65 72 20 61            PROMPT           DB       'Enter a character > $'
        20 63 68 61 72 61 63
        74 65 72 20 3E 20 24
 006B   54 68 65 20 63 61 70            CAPS             DB       'The capitalized character = $'
        69 74 61 6C 69 7A 65
        64 20 63 68 61 72 61
        63 74 65 72 20 3D 20
        24
 0088   0A 0D 24                        CR_LF            DB       0Ah,0Dh,'$'
                                        ;
```

```
008B                          BEGINHERE:
008B  8D 15 00000056 R                    LEA     DX,PROMPT      ; Print prompt
0091  B4 09                               MOV     AH,9
0093  CD 21                               INT     21h
0095  B4 01                               MOV     AH,1           ; Read in the character
0097  CD 21                               INT     21h
                              ;
0099  3C 60                               CMP     AL,60h         ; See what input char was
009B  0F 8E 000000CC R                    JLE     OOPS           ; Less than an "a"?
00A1  3C 7B                               CMP     AL,7Bh         ; Past a "z"?
00A3  0F 8D 000000CC R                    JGE     OOPS
                              ;
00A9  2C 20                               SUB     AL,20h         ; Lower case, so subtract to upper
00AB  8A C8                               MOV     CL,AL          ; Save character
                              ;
                              ;       Go to new line on screen
                              ;
00AD  8D 15 00000088 R                    LEA     DX,CR_LF       ; Carriage Ret/Line Feed
00B3  B4 09                               MOV     AH,9
00B5  CD 21                               INT     21h
00B7  8D 15 0000006B R                    LEA     DX,CAPS        ; Print message
00BD  B4 09                               MOV     AH,9
00BF  CD 21                               INT     21h
                              ;
00C1  8A D1                               MOV     DL,CL          ; Move char to DL & Print
00C3  B4 02                               MOV     AH,2
00C5  CD 21                               INT     21h
00C7  EB 17 90 90 90                      JMP     ENDHERE
                              ;
00CC                          OOPS:
00CC  8D 15 0000000B R                    LEA     DX,NOT_ALPHA   ; Print error and go get char
00D2  B4 09                               MOV     AH,9
00D4  CD 21                               INT     21h
00D6  8D 15 00000032 R                    LEA     DX,NOT_2ND
00DC  CD 21                               INT     21h
00DE  EB AB                               JMP     BEGINHERE
                              ;
00E0                          ENDHERE:
00E0  B4 4C                               MOV     AH,4Ch         ; Standard Ending
00E2  CD 21                               INT     21h
00E4                          CODE        ENDS
                                          END     CAP_IT
```

Program 6-2: BITMAPDV

```
Microsoft (R) Macro Assembler Version 5.00


                                                PAGE    55,132
                                                .386
                                        ;
                                        ; Name:     BITMAPDV
                                        ;
                                        ; Purpose: This program exercises the bitmap routines.
                                        ;
                                        ; Inputs:   All inputs are provided within the program.
                                        ;
                                        ; Process: Basic tests of the bitmap routines are made and the results
                                        ;          are reported on the screen.
                                        ;
                                        ; Outputs: The only outputs are to the screen.
                                        ;
                                        ;
                                        ; Declare the routines we are going to use
                                        ;
                                                EXTRN   BITMAPS:PROC        ; Set bit
                                                EXTRN   BITMAPR:PROC        ; Reset bit
                                                EXTRN   BITMAPT:PROC        ; Test bit
                                                EXTRN   BITMAPL:PROC        ; Locate bit
0000                                    stack   SEGMENT para 'STACK' STACK
0000    0100[                                   dq      256 DUP(?)
            ???????????????
            ?
                        ]

0800                                    stack   ENDS
0000                                    data    SEGMENT para
0000    000A[                           empty   dd      10 DUP(0)
            00000000
                        ]

0028    000A[                           full    dd      10 DUP(-1)
            FFFFFFFF
                        ]


0050    0100[                           string  db      256 DUP(?)          ; String scratch area
             ??
                        ]

0150    0A 0D 45 6D 70 74 79            emptyms db      10,13,"Empty detected.$"
        20 64 65 74 65 63 74
        65 64 2E 24
0162    0A 0D 46 75 6C 6C 20            fullms  db      10,13,"Full returned bit 0.$"
        72 65 74 75 72 6E 65
        64 20 62 69 74 20 30
        2E 24
0179    0A 0D 4C 61 73 74 20            lastm1  db      10,13,"Last bit was on.$"
        62 69 74 20 77 61 73
        20 6F 6E 2E 24
018C    0A 0D 4C 61 73 74 20            lastm2  db      10,13,"Last bit was off.$"
        62 69 74 20 77 61 73
        20 6F 66 66 2E 24
```

```
01A0  0A 0A 0A 0D 45 20 52      errom      db      10,10,10,13,"E R R O R $"
      20 52 20 4F 20 52 20
      24
01AF  0A 0A 0D 41 20 4C 20      lastm3     db      10,10,13,"A L L   O K ! ! $"
      4C 20 20 20 4F 20 4B
      20 21 20 21 20 24
01C3                            data       ENDS
0000                            code       SEGMENT para 'CODE' USE16 PUBLIC
                                           ASSUME  CS:code, DS:data
                                ;
                                ; Set up the environment
                                ;
0000                            Begin:
0000  B8 ---- R                            mov     AX,data             ; Get data segment pointer
0003  8E D8                                mov     DS,AX               ; into DS,
0005  8E C0                                mov     ES,AX               ; and ES.
0007  2B F6                                sub     SI,SI               ; Clear indices
0009  2B FF                                sub     DI,DI
                                ;
                                ; Locate bit in empty map
                                ;
000B  B9 000A                              mov     CX,10               ; Set count
000E  8D 1E 0000 R                         lea     BX,empty            ; map pointer
0012  E8 0000 E                            call    Bitmapl             ; Try a locate
0015  0F 83 00A8 R                         jnc     fullerr             ; Should be empty
0019  8D 16 0150 R                         lea     DX,emptyms          ; point to message
001D  B4 09                                mov     AH,9
001F  CD 21                                int     21h                 ; and write it
                                ;
                                ; locate bit in full map
                                ;
0021  8D 1E 0028 R                         lea     BX,full             ; use full map
0025  E8 0000 E                            call    Bitmapl             ; Try a locate
0028  0F 82 00A8 R                         jc      fullerr             ; error if not found
002C  0B C0                                or      AX,AX               ; was proper bit found
002E  0F 85 00A8 R                         jnz     fullerr
0032  8D 16 0162 R                         lea     DX,fullms           ; Point to message
0036  B4 09                                mov     AH,9
0038  CD 21                                int     21h                 ; and write it
                                ;
                                ; reset last bit
                                ;
003A  B8 013F                              mov     AX,320-1            ; number of last bit
003D  E8 0000 E                            call    Bitmapr             ; Go reset it
0040  0F 83 00A8 R                         jnc     fullerr             ; If it was off - bad
0044  8D 16 0179 R                         lea     DX,lastm1           ; Point to message
0048  B4 09                                mov     AH,9
004A  CD 21                                int     21h                 ; and write it
                                ;
                                ; now set it again
                                ;
004C  B8 013F                              mov     AX,320-1            ; Number of last bit
004F  E8 0000 E                            call    Bitmaps             ; Go set it
0052  0F 82 00A8 R                         jc      fullerr             ; If bad - out
0056  8D 16 018C R                         lea     DX,lastm2           ; Point to message
005A  B4 09                                mov     AH,9
005C  CD 21                                int     21h                 ; and write it
                                ;
                                ; Test last bit in full
                                ;
005E  B8 013F                              mov     AX,320-1            ; number of last bit
0061  E8 0000 E                            call    Bitmapt             ; Go test it
```

```
0064  0F 83 00A8 R              jnc     fullerr             ; If it was off - bad
0068  8D 16 0179 R              lea     DX,lastm1           ; Point to message
006C  B4 09                     mov     AH,9
006E  CD 21                     int     21h                 ; and write it
                        ;
                        ; now test it in the empty
                        ;
0070  8D 1E 0000 R              lea     BX,empty            ; Point to the empty
0074  B8 013F                   mov     AX,320-1            ; Number of last bit
0077  E8 0000 E                 call    Bitmapt             ; Go set it
007A  0F 82 00A8 R              jc      fullerr             ; If bad - out
007E  8D 16 018C R              lea     DX,lastm2           ; Point to message
0082  B4 09                     mov     AH,9
0084  CD 21                     int     21h                 ; and write it
0086  8D 1E 0028 R              lea     BX,full             ; point back to full
                        ;
                        ; copy full to empty
                        ;
008A                    fullcopy:
008A  B9 000A                   mov     CX,10               ; Count of words
008D  8D 1E 0028 R              lea     BX,full             ; Bitmap
0091  E8 0000 E                 call    Bitmapl             ; Find a bit
0094  0F 82 00B3 R              jc      fulldone            ; When empty we are done
0098  E8 0000 E                 call    Bitmapr             ; Clear the bit
009B  0F 83 00A8 R              jnc     fullerr             ; error if not on for clear
009F  8D 1E 0000 R              lea     BX,empty            ; Point to empty
00A3  E8 0000 E                 call    Bitmaps             ; copy bit into it
00A6  73 E2                     jnc     fullcopy            ; As long as it was off - ok
00A8                    fullerr:
00A8  8D 16 01A0 R              lea     DX,errom            ; Set error message
00AC  B4 09                     mov     AH,9
00AE  CD 21                     int     21h
00B0  EB 24 90                  jmp     Exit
00B3                    fulldone:
00B3  66| 2B C0                 sub     EAX,EAX             ; Set comparand
00B6  8D 3E 0028 R              lea     DI,full             ; check all off in full
00BA  B9 000A                   mov     CX,10
00BD  F3/ AE                    repe scasb                  ; Check
00BF  75 E7                     jne     fullerr             ; Error if not empty
00C1  66| 48                    dec     EAX                 ; Get all ones
00C3  8D 3E 0000 R              lea     DI,empty            ; Should be full now
00C7  B9 000A                   mov     CX,10
00CA  F3/ AE                    repe scasb                  ; Check
00CC  75 DA                     jne     fullerr             ; Error if not full

00CE  8D 16 01AF R              lea     DX,lastm3           ; Point to message
00D2  B4 09                     mov     AH,9
00D4  CD 21                     int     21h                 ; and write it
00D6                    Exit:
00D6  B0 00                     mov     AL,0                ; Set return code
00D8  B4 4C                     mov     AH,04ch             ; Set good-by
00DA  CD 21                     int     21h                 ; Return to the system
                        ;
                        ; Read a string in response to a prompt
                        ; The prompt must be in DX.  The string will be returned in string.
                        ;
00DC                    getinp  PROC
00DC  50                        push    AX                  ; Save registers
00DD  56                        push    SI
00DE  B4 09                     mov     AH,9                ; and dos request
00E0  CD 21                     int     21h                 ; put out the string
00E2  8D 16 0050 R              lea     DX,string           ; point to input area
```

```
00E6  C6 06 0050 R FE                 mov     string,254          ; Set max length in
00EB  B4 0A                           mov     AH,10               ; Ask for read of string
00ED  CD 21                           int     21h                 ; from DOS.
00EF  8D 1E 0052 R                    lea     BX,string+2         ; Point to just read data
00F3  8A 0E 0051 R                    mov     CL,string+1         ; Get length read
00F7  B5 00                           mov     CH,0                ; as a word.
00F9  8B F1                           mov     SI,CX               ; Set length
00FB  C6 84 0052 R 00                 mov     string+2[SI],0      ; and make an asciiz string.
0100  5E                              pop     SI
0101  58                              pop     AX                  ; Restore registers
0102  C3                              ret                         ; and return.
0103                          getinp  ENDP

0103                          code    ENDS
                                      END     Begin
```

Program 6-3: BITMAPS

```
Microsoft (R) Macro Assembler Version 5.00


                                           PAGE      55,132
                                           .386
0000                              code     SEGMENT   para 'CODE' USE16 PUBLIC
                                           ASSUME    CS:code, DS:code, SS:code
                                  ;
                                  ; Name:     BITMAPS
                                  ;
                                  ; Purpose: The following procedure provides a means of setting a bit
                                  ;           in a bitmap which corresponds to the number provided.
                                  ;
                                  ; Inputs:   AX has the number of the bit to be set (changed from 0 to
                                  ;           1).
                                  ;           BX points to the bitmap.
                                  ;
                                  ; Process: The process is to convert the number into a double word
                                  ;           displacement into the map by dividing by 32, multiplying
                                  ;           the quotient by 4 and using the remainder as a bit number.
                                  ;           The bit in the word is then set to 1.
                                  ;
                                  ; Output:   The carry flag reflects the previous setting of the bit.
                                  ;           i.e. if the bit was zero, the carry flag will be set.
                                  ;
                                  ;
                                  ;
                                  ;
                                           PUBLIC   Bitmaps             ; Make the name usable
0000                              Bitmaps  PROC
0000  66| 51                               push     ECX                 ; Save entry registers
0002  53                                   push     BX
0003  50                                   push     AX
0004  66| 2B C9                            sub      ECX,ECX             ; clear bit register
0007  8A C8                                mov      CL,AL               ; copy bit number
0009  80 E1 1F                             and      CL,31               ; clear garbage
000C  24 E0                                and      AL,0e0h             ; and bit number from AX
000E  C1 E8 03                             shr      AX,3                ; Get proper word index
0011  03 D8                                add      BX,AX               ; point to the word
0013  66| 0F AB 0F                         bts      [BX],ECX            ; Reset the bit
0017  58                                   pop      AX                  ; Restore the entry registers
0018  5B                                   pop      BX
0019  66| 59                               pop      ECX
001B  C3                                   ret                          ; and return.
001C                              Bitmaps  ENDP


                                  ;
                                  ; Name:     BITMAPR
                                  ;
                                  ; Purpose: The following procedure provides a means of clearing a bit
                                  ;           in a bitmap which corresponds to the number provided.
                                  ;
                                  ; Inputs:   AX has the number of the bit to be reset (changed from 1 to
                                  ;           0).
                                  ;           BX points to the bitmap.
                                  ;
                                  ; Process: The process is to convert the number into a double word
                                  ;           displacement into the map by dividing by 32, multiplying
```

```
                                ;           the quotient by 4 and using the remainder as a bit number.
                                ;           The bit in the word is then set to 0.
                                ;
                                ; Output:   The carry flag reflects the previous setting of the bit.
                                ;           i.e. if the bit was carry, the zero flag will be set.
                                ;
                                ;
                                ;
                                ;
                                            PUBLIC  Bitmapr             ; Make the name usable
001C                            Bitmapr     PROC
001C  66| 51                                push    ECX                 ; Save entry registers
001E  53                                    push    BX
001F  50                                    push    AX
0020  66| 2B C9                             sub     ECX,ECX             ; clear bit register
0023  8A C8                                 mov     CL,AL               ; copy bit number
0025  80 E1 1F                              and     CL,31               ; clear garbage
0028  24 E0                                 and     AL,0e0h             ; and bit number from AX
002A  C1 E8 03                              shr     AX,3                ; Get proper word index
002D  03 D8                                 add     BX,AX               ; point to the word
002F  66| 0F B3 0F                          btr     [BX],ECX            ; Reset the bit
0033  58                                    pop     AX                  ; Restore the entry registers
0034  5B                                    pop     BX
0035  66| 59                                pop     ECX
0037  C3                                    ret                         ; and return.
0038                            Bitmapr     ENDP


                                ;
                                ; Name:     BITMAPT
                                ;
                                ; Purpose:  The following procedure provides a means of testing a bit
                                ;           in a bitmap which corresponds to the number provided.
                                ;
                                ; Inputs:   AX has the number of the bit to be tested.
                                ;           BX points to the bitmap.
                                ;
                                ; Process:  The process is to convert the number into a double word
                                ;           displacement into the map by dividing by 32, multiplying
                                ;           the quotient by 4 and using the remainder as a bit number.
                                ;           The bit in the word is then tested.
                                ;
                                ; Output:   The carry flag reflects the setting of the bit.
                                ;           i.e. if the bit was carry, the zero flag will be set.
                                ;
                                ;
                                ;
                                            PUBLIC  Bitmapt             ; Make the name usable
0038                            Bitmapt     PROC
0038  66| 51                                push    ECX                 ; Save entry registers
003A  53                                    push    BX
003B  50                                    push    AX
003C  66| 2B C9                             sub     ECX,ECX             ; clear bit register
003F  8A C8                                 mov     CL,AL               ; copy bit number
0041  80 E1 1F                              and     CL,31               ; clear garbage
0044  24 E0                                 and     AL,0e0h             ; and bit number from AX
0046  C1 E8 03                              shr     AX,3                ; Get proper word index
0049  03 D8                                 add     BX,AX               ; point to the word
004B  66| 0F A3 0F                          bt      [BX],ECX            ; Test the bit
004F  58                                    pop     AX                  ; Restore the entry registers
0050  5B                                    pop     BX
0051  66| 59                                pop     ECX
0053  C3                                    ret                         ; and return.
```

```
0054                        Bitmapt   ENDP



                            ;
                            ; Name:     BITMAPL
                            ;
                            ; Purpose: The following procedure provides a means of locating the
                            ;          first one bit in a bitmap.
                            ;
                            ; Inputs:  BX points to the bitmap.
                            ;          CX has the number of double words in the map.
                            ;
                            ; Process: The process is to scan the bitmap for a double word which
                            ;          is non zero.  The word is then scanned for the first one
                            ;          bit.  A bit number is returned as double word number * 32
                            ;          plus the bit number.  (double words are numbered from
                            ;          zero.)
                            ;
                            ; Output:  If a bit is located, its number will be in AX and carry
                            ;          will be reset.  If the map is empty, AX is undefined and
                            ;          carry is set.
                            ;
                            ;
                            ;
                                      PUBLIC  Bitmapl             ; Make the name usable
0054                        Bitmapl   PROC
0054  06                              push    ES                  ; Save entry registers
0055  57                              push    DI
0056  51                              push    CX
0057  53                              push    BX
0058  51                              push    CX                  ; save count again
0059  66| 2B C0                       sub     EAX,EAX             ; Get comparand
005C  8C DF                           mov     DI,DS               ; Get DS into
005E  8E C7                           mov     ES,DI               ; ES
0060  8B FB                           mov     DI,BX               ; and map into DI
0062  F3/ 66| AF                      repe scasd                  ; look for non zero dword
0065  5B                              pop     BX                  ; get original count in BX
0066  0F 84 007F R                    jz      errorl              ; Map is empty
006A  83 EF 04                        sub     DI,4                ; point to the word
006D  2B D9                           sub     BX,CX               ; Get its word number +1
006F  4B                              dec     BX
0070  66| 0F BC 05                    bsf     EAX,DWORD PTR [DI]  ; Get the bit number
0074  C1 E3 05                        shl     BX,5                ; Word number times 32
0077  03 C3                           add     AX,BX               ; Plus bit number
0079  F8                              clc                         ; clear carry
007A                        exitl:
007A  5B                              pop     BX                  ; Restore the entry registers
007B  59                              pop     CX
007C  5F                              pop     DI
007D  07                              pop     ES
007E  C3                              ret                         ; and return.
007F                        errorl:
007F  F9                              stc                         ; Return with carry set
0080  EB F8                           jmp     exitl
0082                        Bitmapl   ENDP
0082                        code      ENDS
                                      END
```

Program 6-4: EFLAGSCH

```
Microsoft (R) Macro Assembler Version 5.00


                                        PAGE    55,132
                                        .386
 0000                           STACK   SEGMENT 'STACK' STACK
 0000  0064[                            DW      100 DUP(?)
           ????
                       ]

 00C8                           STACK   ENDS
 0000                           CODE    SEGMENT para 'CODE' PUBLIC USE16
                                        ASSUME  CS:CODE, DS:CODE, SS:STACK
                                ;
                                ; Name:     EFLAGSCH
                                ;
                                ; Purpose:  This routine captures the bit flags in EFLAGS and
                                ;           allows a change.  The flag to change is entered via
                                ;           the keyboard.
                                ;
                                ; Inputs:   Enter the flag to be changed, the choice coming from a
                                ;           menu printed at the beginning.  EFLAGS is printed as it
                                ;           is prior to the change.
                                ;
                                ; Process:  The EFLAGS register is captured and then we loop getting
                                ;           the number of a bit to change and changing the bit until
                                ;           a null line is entered.  At this time, we place the new
                                ;           value into EFLAGS.
                                ;
                                ; Outputs:  EFLAGS is printed after the change.
                                ;
                                        EXTRN   CODEASB:PROC
 0000                           EFLAGSCH:
 0000  8C C8                            MOV     AX,CS           ; Prepare to set DS
 0002  8E D8                            MOV     DS,AX           ;   and set it.
 0004  E9 02ED R                        JMP     BEGINHERE
                                ;
 0007  0100[                    string  db      256 DUP(?)          ;
           ??
                       ]

                                ;
 0107  0A 0D 45 46 4C 41 47     BEFORE  DB      0Ah,0Dh,'EFLAGS before change: $'
       53 20 62 65 66 6F 72
       65 20 63 68 61 6E 67
       65 3A 20 24
 0120  0A 0D 45 46 4C 41 47     AFTER   DB      0Ah,0Dh,'EFLAGS after change:  $'
       53 20 61 66 74 65 72
       20 63 68 61 6E 67 65
       3A 20 20 24
 0139  0A 0D 45 46 4C 41 47     MENU    DB      0Ah,0Dh,'EFLAGS bits: '
       53 20 62 69 74 73 3A
       20
 0148  0A 0D 31 37 2E 20 20             DB      0Ah,0Dh,'17.  VM = Virtual 8086 Mode '
       56 4D 20 3D 20 56 69
       72 74 75 61 6C 20 38
       30 38 36 20 4D 6F 64
       65 20
 0166  0A 0D 31 36 2E 20 20             DB      0Ah,0Dh,'16.  RF = Resume Flag '
```

```
     52 46 20 3D 20 52 65
     73 75 6D 65 20 46 6C
     61 67 20
017E 0A 0D 31 34 2E 20 20              DB     0Ah,0Dh,'14.  NT = Nested Task Flag'
     4E 54 20 3D 20 4E 65
     73 74 65 64 20 54 61
     73 6B 20 46 6C 61 67
019A 0A 0D 31 33 2E 20 20              DB     0Ah,0Dh,'13.  IOPL = I/O Privilege Level'
     49 4F 50 4C 20 3D 20
     49 2F 4F 20 50 72 69
     76 69 6C 65 67 65 20
     4C 65 76 65 6C
01BB 0A 0D 31 31 2E 20 20              DB     0Ah,0Dh,'11.  OF = Overflow'
     4F 46 20 3D 20 4F 76
     65 72 66 6C 6F 77
01CF 0A 0D 31 30 2E 20 20              DB     0Ah,0Dh,'10.  DF = Direction Flag'
     44 46 20 3D 20 44 69
     72 65 63 74 69 6F 6E
     20 46 6C 61 67
01E9 0A 0D 20 39 2E 20 20              DB     0Ah,0Dh,' 9.  IF = Interrupt Enable Flag'
     49 46 20 3D 20 49 6E
     74 65 72 72 75 70 74
     20 45 6E 61 62 6C 65
     20 46 6C 61 67
020A 0A 0D 20 38 2E 20 20              DB     0Ah,0Dh,' 8.  TF = Trap Flag'
     54 46 20 3D 20 54 72
     61 70 20 46 6C 61 67
021F 0A 0D 20 37 2E 20 20              DB     0Ah,0Dh,' 7.  SF = Sign Flag'
     53 46 20 3D 20 53 69
     67 6E 20 46 6C 61 67
0234 0A 0D 20 36 2E 20 20              DB     0Ah,0Dh,' 6.  ZF = Zero Flag'
     5A 46 20 3D 20 5A 65
     72 6F 20 46 6C 61 67
0249 0A 0D 20 34 2E 20 20              DB     0Ah,0Dh,' 4.  AF = Auxiliary Carry Flag'
     41 46 20 3D 20 41 75
     78 69 6C 69 61 72 79
     20 43 61 72 72 79 20
     46 6C 61 67
0269 0A 0D 20 32 2E 20 20              DB     0Ah,0Dh,' 2.  PF = Parity Flag'
     50 46 20 3D 20 50 61
     72 69 74 79 20 46 6C
     61 67
0280 0A 0D 20 30 2E 20 20              DB     0Ah,0Dh,' 0.  CF = Carry Flag'
     43 46 20 3D 20 43 61
     72 72 79 20 46 6C 61
     67
                              ;
0296 0A 0D 20 4E 6F 74 65     NOTE     DB     0Ah,0Dh,' Note: unlisted bits are reserved.$'
     3A 20 75 6E 6C 69 73
     74 65 64 20 62 69 74
     73 20 61 72 65 20 72
     65 73 65 72 76 65 64
     2E 24
02BB 0A 0D 24                 CR_LF    DB     0Ah,0Dh,'$'
02BE 0A 0D 45 6E 74 65 72     PROMPT   DB     0Ah,0Dh,'Enter the bit number of the flag to'
     20 74 68 65 20 62 69
     74 20 6E 75 6D 62 65
     72 20 6F 66 20 74 68
     65 20 66 6C 61 67 20
     74 6F
02E3 20 63 68 61 6E 67 65              DB     ' change: $'
     3A 20 24
```

```
                                ;
02ED                            BEGINHERE:
02ED  66| 9C                            pushfd                          ; Get EFLAGS
02EF  66| 5B                            pop     EBX                     ; locally
02F1                            showflags:
02F1  8D 16 0107 R                      lea     DX,before               ; Set message
02F5  B4 09                             mov     AH,9
02F7  CD 21                             int     21h                     ; and display it
02F9  E8 0331 R                         call    outbits                 ; followed by the bits
02FC  8D 16 0139 R                      lea     DX,menu                 ; Point to menu
0300  B4 09                             mov     AH,9
0302  CD 21                             int     21h                     ; and write it
0304                            getnbr:
0304  8D 16 02BE R                      lea     DX,prompt               ;
0308  E8 034A R                         call    getinp                  ; Get bit to change
030B  E3 0F                             jcxz    donechg                 ; If null entered -
030D  E8 0000 E                         call    Codeasb                 ; Convert the bit number
0310  66| 83 F8 1F                      cmp     EAX,31                  ; check bit number
0314  77 EE                             ja      getnbr                  ; If bad - try again.
                                ;
                                ; Note how easy the bit gets flipped!
                                ;
0316  66| 0F BB C3                      btc     EBX,EAX                 ; change the bit
031A  EB D5                             jmp     showflags               ; loop
031C                            donechg:
031C  8D 16 0120 R                      lea     DX,after                ; message
0320  B4 09                             mov     AH,9
0322  CD 21                             int     21h                     ; out followed by
0324  E8 0331 R                         call    outbits                 ; bits
0327  66| 53                            push    EBX                     ; Stack the flags
0329  66| 9D                            popfd                           ; and set them

032B                            ENDHERE:
032B  2A C0                             sub     AL,AL                   ; Set return code 0
032D  B4 4C                             MOV     AH,4Ch                  ; Standard Ending
032F  CD 21                             INT     21h
                                ;
                                ; Display the bits of EBX as they are set.
                                ;
0331                            outbits PROC
0331  66| 53                            push    EBX                     ; Don't destroy the bits
0333  B4 02                             mov     AH,2                    ; We do a character at a time
0335  B9 0020                           mov     CX,32                   ; Full register worth
0338                            onebit:
0338  B2 31                             mov     DL,'1'                  ; Assume bit is 1
033A  66| D1 E3                         shl     EBX,1                   ; check it
033D  0F 82 0343 R                      jc      isaone                  ; We were right
0341  FE CA                             dec     DL                      ; Set it zero
0343                            isaone:
0343  CD 21                             int     21h                     ; put the bit out.
0345  E2 F1                             loop    onebit                  ; Do all 32
0347  66| 5B                            pop     EBX                     ; Restore our bits
0349  C3                                ret                             ; and return
034A                            outbits ENDP


                                ;
                                ; Read a string in response to a prompt
                                ; The prompt must be in DX.  The string will be returned in string.
                                ;
034A                            getinp  PROC
034A  50                                push    AX                      ; Save registers
```

```
034B  B4 09                         mov     AH,9              ; and dos request
034D  CD 21                         int     21h               ; put out the string
034F  8D 16 0007 R                  lea     DX,string         ; point to input area
0353  C6 06 0007 R FE               mov     string,254        ; Set max length in
0358  B4 0A                         mov     AH,10             ; Ask for read of string
035A  CD 21                         int     21h               ; from DOS.
035C  8D 36 0009 R                  lea     SI,string+2       ; Point to just read data
0360  8A 0E 0008 R                  mov     CL,string+1       ; Get length read
0364  B5 00                         mov     CH,0              ; as a word.
0366  03 F1                         add     SI,CX             ; Set length
0368  C6 04 00                      mov     BYTE PTR [SI],0   ; and make an asciiz string.
036B  2B F1                         sub     SI,CX
036D  58                            pop     AX                ; Restore registers
036E  C3                            ret                       ; and return.
036F                        getinp  ENDP

036F                        CODE    ENDS
                                    END     EFLAGSCH
```

Program 6-5: STRSRCH

```
Microsoft (R) Macro Assembler Version 5.00


                                        PAGE    55,132
                                        .386
                                        EXTRN   CODEBAS:PROC
 0000                         STACK     SEGMENT 'STACK' STACK
 0000   0064[                           DW      100 DUP(?)
            ????
                        ]

 00C8                         STACK     ENDS
 0000                         CODE      SEGMENT para 'CODE' PUBLIC
                                        ASSUME  CS:CODE, DS:CODE, SS:STACK
                              ;
                              ; Name:   STRSRCH
                              ;
                              ; Purpose:        This program searches for the first occurrence of a
                              ;          specified substring within another given string.  If
                              ;          the substring is found, the starting location (byte)
                              ;          returns in register DX.
                              ;
                              ; Inputs:  A string is specified.  The search string is also
                              ;          specified.
                              ;
                              ; Process: A target string of some length is offered.  Its length
                              ;          in bytes is determined.  Then a second string is
                              ;          specified, with its length.  The strings are checked
                              ;          for simple validity: was anything entered in each and
                              ;          was the SEARCH string longer than the TARGET string. If
                              ;          the strings pass, go to search.      If not, an error message
                              ;          is written, DX set to 0, and the program ended.
                              ;
                              ;          To print the byte, the external procedure CODEBAS
                              ;          is called.  CODEBAS turns binary characters into
                              ;          printable ASCII for 80286-based computers.  The program
                              ;          is described in Chapter 7 of the "80386 Assembly
                              ;          Language Toolkit" from TAB Books.
                              ;
                              ; Outputs: If the substring is found, its offset in bytes is
                              ;          in DX.  If it is not found, DX=0.
                              ;
 0000                         STRSRCH:
 0000   66| 8C C8                       MOV     AX,CS                   ; Prepare to set DS
 0003   66| 8E D8                       MOV     DS,AX                   ;    and set it.
 0006   66| 8E C0                       MOV     ES,AX                   ; Also set ES
 0009   E9 000001CF R                   JMP     BEGINHERE
                              ;
 000E   0064[                 TARGET_STR DB     100 DUP(?)
             ??
                        ]

 0072   0064[                 SEARCH_STR DB     100 DUP(?)
             ??
                        ]

 00D6   49 6E 70 75 74 20 74     PROMPT     DB      'Input the Target string>$'
        68 65 20 54 61 72 67
        65 74 20 73 74 72 69
```

```
      6E 67 3E 24
00EF  0A 0D 49 6E 70 75 74   PROMPT1    DB    0Ah,0Dh,'Input the Search string>$'
      20 74 68 65 20 53 65
      61 72 63 68 20 73 74
      72 69 6E 67 3E 24
010A  0A 0D 54 68 65 20 53   TOO_LONG   DB    0Ah,0Dh,'The Search string is longer than the Target
      65 61 72 63 68 20 73                      string.$'
      74 72 69 6E 67 20 69
      73 20 6C 6F 6E 67 65
      72 20 74 68 61 6E 20
      74 68 65 20 54 61 72
      67 65 74 20 73 74 72
      69 6E 67 2E 24
0140  0A 0D 54 68 65 20 54   EMPTY      DB    0Ah,0Dh,'The Target string is empty.$'
      61 72 67 65 74 20 73
      74 72 69 6E 67 20 69
      73 20 65 6D 70 74 79
      2E 24
015E  0A 0D 54 68 65 20 53   EMPTY1     DB    0Ah,0Dh,'The Search string is empty.$'
      65 61 72 63 68 20 73
      74 72 69 6E 67 20 69
      73 20 65 6D 70 74 79
      2E 24
017C  0A 0D 54 68 65 20 53   NOT_HERE   DB    0Ah,0Dh,'The Search string is not in the Target
      65 61 72 63 68 20 73                      string.',0Ah,0Dh,'$'
      74 72 69 6E 67 20 69
      73 20 6E 6F 74 20 69
      6E 20 74 68 65 20 54
      61 72 67 65 74 20 73
      74 72 69 6E 67 2E 0A
      0D 24
01AF  0A 0D 4D 61 74 63 68   IS_HERE    DB    0Ah,0Dh,'Match found.  Starts in byte $'
      20 66 6F 75 6E 64 2E
      20 20 53 74 61 72 74
      73 20 69 6E 20 62 79
      74 65 20 24
                             ;
01CF                         BEGINHERE:
                             ;
                             ; Get the strings from the keyboard.  They go into a keyboard buffer
                             ;        which has two bytes at the beginning of the buffer.  The first
                             ;        byte is your statement of the maximum number allowed in the
                             ;        buffer.  The second byte is MS-DOS's count of how many bytes
                             ;        were ACTUALLY entered.  The character string begins at byte
                             ;        2 (counting from 0), or the third byte of the buffer.
                             ;
01CF  66| 2B DB                          SUB   BX,BX            ; Be sure count variables are
01D2  66| 2B C9                          SUB   CX,CX            ;   zero
01D5  C6 05 0000000E R 62                MOV   TARGET_STR,98    ; Maximum entry
01DC  8D 15 000000D6 R                   LEA   DX,PROMPT
01E2  B4 09                              MOV   AH,9
01E4  CD 21                              INT   21h
01E6  8D 15 0000000E R                   LEA   DX,TARGET_STR    ; Point to input buffer
01EC  B4 0A                              MOV   AH,0Ah           ; Get ready to read in
01EE  CD 21                              INT   21h
01F0  8A 0D 0000000F R                   MOV   CL,TARGET_STR+1 ; The number actually read in
01F6  8A F9                              MOV   BH,CL            ; Save it in BH
                             ;
01F8  C6 05 00000072 R 62                MOV   SEARCH_STR,98    ; Maximum entry
01FF  8D 15 000000EF R                   LEA   DX,PROMPT1
0205  B4 09                              MOV   AH,9
0207  CD 21                              INT   21h
```

```
0209  8D 15 00000072 R              LEA     DX,SEARCH_STR
020F  B4 0A                         MOV     AH,0Ah
0211  CD 21                         INT     21h
0213  8A 1D 00000073 R              MOV     BL,SEARCH_STR+1      ; The number of bytes read in
                        ;
                        ; Check validity of strings
                        ;
0219  0A FF                         OR      BH,BH                ; Is target string empty?
021B  0F 84 000002C5 R              JZ      MSG1                 ; Give msg if so
0221  0A DB                         OR      BL,BL                ; Is substring empty?
0223  0F 84 000002D0 R              JZ      MSG2                 ; Message if so
0229  3A DF                         CMP     BL,BH                ; Is substring too large?
022B  0F 87 000002DB R              JA      MSG3                 ; If so - message
0231  FE CB                         DEC     BL                   ; Since we look for the first
                                                                 ; byte, then scan for the rest
                                                                 ; we only need length -1.
                        ;
0233  FC                            CLD                          ; Increment after scan

0234  8D 3D 00000010 R              LEA     DI,TARGET_STR+2      ; Point to one to find it in
                        ;
                        ;    Scan for match
                        ;         The target of SCASB is in AL.  REPNE uses the count
                        ;         in CX and decrements CX at each pass.
                        ;
023A                    SEARCH1:
023A  8D 35 00000074 R              LEA     SI,SEARCH_STR+2      ; Point to string to find
0240  67| 8A 04                     MOV     AL,[SI]              ; Scan target
0243  F2/ AE                        REPNE SCASB
0245  0F 85 000002B2 R              JNE     NOT_FOUND            ; If no match at all
                        ;
                        ;    Got a match on first character
                        ;

024B  3A CB                         CMP     CL,BL                ; Enough left in target?
024D  0F 82 000002B2 R              JB      NOT_FOUND            ; If not - don't look.
0253  66| 8B EF                     MOV     BP,DI                ; Save offset of next
0256  66| 8B D1                     MOV     DX,CX                ; and count remaining.
                        ;
                        ;    DI points at target (current location)
                        ;    SI at search (current location)
                        ;
0259  8A CB                         MOV     CL,BL                ; Is next n chars = ?
025B  66| 46                        INC     SI                   ; Go to next value in Search
025D  66| E3 18                     JCXZ    FOUND                ; If only one byte - found
0260  F3/ A6                        REPZ CMPSB                   ; Compare two strings
0262  0F 84 00000278 R              JE      FOUND                ; If = for count - got it.
                        ;
                        ; Otherwise, found a non-match, so resume our scansb at the location
                        ; and with the count we saved.
                        ;
0268  66| 8B FD                     MOV     DI,BP                ; Offset where to start looking
026B  66| 8B CA                     MOV     CX,DX                ; and count remaining.
026E  3A CB                         CMP     CL,BL                ; Count remaining > search-1
0270  0F 86 000002B2 R              JNA     NOT_FOUND            ; No - not there.
0276  EB C2                         JMP     SEARCH1
                        ;
                        ;
0278                    FOUND:
0278  2A FA                         SUB     BH,DL                ; Loc = count - count remaining
027A  8D 15 000001AF R              LEA     DX,IS_HERE
0280  B4 09                         MOV     AH,9
```

```
0282  CD 21                              INT      21h
0284  8A C7                              MOV      AL,BH             ; Get offset
0286  B4 00                              MOV      AH,0              ; As a word
0288  98                                 CWDE                       ; (double)
0289  E8 00000000 E                      CALL     CODEBAS           ; DI=pointer to converted data
028E  67| 8A 15                          MOV      DL,BYTE PTR [DI]  ; VALUE that DI points to
0291  B4 02                              MOV      AH,2              ; Print that value
0293  CD 21                              INT      21h
0295  67| 8A 55 01                       MOV      DL,BYTE PTR [DI+1] ; Another digit?
0299  80 FA 30                           CMP      DL,30h            ; Less than zero?
029C  0F 8C 000002EA R                   JL       ENDHERE
02A2  80 FA 39                           CMP      DL,39h            ; Greater than 9 ?
02A5  0F 87 000002EA R                   JA       ENDHERE
02AB  CD 21                              INT      21h               ; Otherwise print it
02AD  EB 3B 90 90 90                     JMP      ENDHERE
02B2                         NOT_FOUND:
02B2  8D 15 0000017C R                   LEA      DX,NOT_HERE
02B8  66| BE 0000                        MOV      SI,0
02BC  B4 09                              MOV      AH,9
02BE  CD 21                              INT      21h
02C0  EB 28 90 90 90                     JMP      ENDHERE
                             ;
                             ;
                             ; Error messages
                             ;
02C5                         MSG1:
02C5  8D 15 00000140 R                   LEA      DX,EMPTY          ; Target is empty
02CB  EB 14 90 90 90                     JMP      MSG99
02D0                         MSG2:
02D0  8D 15 0000015E R                   LEA      DX,EMPTY1         ; Substring is empty
02D6  EB 09 90 90 90                     JMP      MSG99
02DB                         MSG3:
02DB  8D 15 0000010A R                   LEA      DX,TOO_LONG       ; Print error and exit
02E1                         MSG99:
02E1  B4 09                              MOV      AH,9
02E3  CD 21                              INT      21h
02E5  EB 03 90 90 90                     JMP      ENDHERE
                             ;
                             ;
02EA                         ENDHERE:
02EA  B4 4C                              MOV      AH,4Ch            ; Standard Ending
02EC  CD 21                              INT      21h
02EE                         CODE        ENDS
                                         END      STRSRCH
```

Program 6-6: STRINSRT

```
Microsoft (R) Macro Assembler Version 5.00


                                                PAGE    55,132
                                                .386
 0000                                   STACK   SEGMENT 'STACK' STACK
 0000  0064[                                    DW      100 DUP(?)
           ????
                        ]

 00C8                                   STACK   ENDS
 0000                                   CODE    SEGMENT para 'CODE' PUBLIC USE16
                                                ASSUME  CS:CODE, DS:CODE, SS:STACK
                                        ;
                                        ; Name:     STRINSRT
                                        ;
                                        ; Purpose:  This program inserts a source string into a
                                        ;           specified place in a target string.  Both
                                        ;           strings are input via the keyboard.
                                        ;
                                        ; Inputs:   The Target string and the Insert strings both are
                                        ;           keyed into the program.  The place to insert is also.
                                        ;
                                        ; Process:  We prompt for and read the target string, the string to
                                        ;           insert and the location (0 to the end of the target) to
                                        ;           insert the string.  We then form the new string by
                                        ;           copying the leading bytes of the target (if any), the
                                        ;           insert string, and any remaining bytes of the target.
                                        ;
                                        ; Outputs:  After the run, the resulting string is displayed.
                                        ;           The beginning byte where the insertion was done is
                                        ;           given.  Also, the new length of the resulting string
                                        ;           is given.
                                        ;
                                                EXTRN   CODEBAS:PROC
                                                EXTRN   CODEASB:PROC
 0000                                   STRINSRT:
 0000  8C C8                                    MOV     AX,CS                   ; Prepare to set DS
 0002  8E D8                                    MOV     DS,AX                   ;   and set it.
 0004  8E C0                                    MOV     ES,AX                   ;   (ES too)
 0006  E9 0257 R                                JMP     BEGINHERE
                                        ;
 0009  0A 0A 0D 41 6E 20 65             PROMPT  DB      10,10,13,'An empty target string ends the program.'
       6D 70 74 79 20 74 61
       72 67 65 74 20 73 74
       72 69 6E 67 20 65 6E
       64 73 20 74 68 65 20
       70 72 6F 67 72 61 6D
       2E
 0034  0A 0D 45 6E 74 65 72                     DB      10,13,'Enter the Target String: $'
       20 74 68 65 20 54 61
       72 67 65 74 20 53 74
       72 69 6E 67 3A 20 24
 0050  0A 0D 45 6E 74 65 72             PROMPT1 DB      10,13,'Enter the Insert String: $'
       20 74 68 65 20 49 6E
       73 65 72 74 20 53 74
       72 69 6E 67 3A 20 24
 006C  0A 0D 45 6E 74 65 72             PROMPT2 DB      10,13,'Enter the position to insert after: $'
       20 74 68 65 20 70 6F
```

```
     73 69 74 69 6F 6E 20
     74 6F 20 69 6E 73 65
     72 74 20 61 66 74 65
     72 3A 20 24
0093 0A 0D 54 68 65 20 74    NEW_LENGTH DB    0Ah,0Dh,'The total length is: $'
     6F 74 61 6C 20 6C 65
     6E 67 74 68 20 69 73
     3A 20 24
00AB 0064[                   TARGET     DB    100 DUP(?)
          ??
                    ]

010F 0064[                   INSERT     DB    100 DUP(?)
          ??
                    ]

0173 0A 0D 54 68 65 20 72    RESULTM    DB    0Ah,0Dh,'The resulting string is:',10,13
     65 73 75 6C 74 69 6E
     67 20 73 74 72 69 6E
     67 20 69 73 3A 0A 0D
018F 00C8[                   RESULT     DB    200 DUP(?)
          ??
                    ]

                             ;
0257                         BEGINHERE:
0257 8D 1E 00AB R                       LEA     BX,TARGET       ; Point to input buffer
025B 8D 16 0009 R                       LEA     DX,PROMPT       ; and prompt
025F E8 02EF R                          CALL    GETIN           ; Do prompt and get input
0262 0B C9                              OR      CX,CX           ; was a target entered?
0264 0F 85 026B R                       JNZ     ASKAGAIN        ; yes.
0268 E9 02EB R                          JMP     ENDHERE         ; Quit on a null
026B                         ASKAGAIN:
026B 8D 1E 010F R                       LEA     BX,INSERT       ; Point to input buffer
026F 8D 16 0050 R                       LEA     DX,PROMPT1      ; prompt, and
0273 E8 02EF R                          CALL    GETIN           ; get input.
0276 E3 F3                              JCXZ    ASKAGAIN        ; null insert not allowed.
0278                         GETNUMB:
0278 8D 16 006C R                       LEA     DX,PROMPT2      ; Point to prompt,
027C 8D 1E 018F R                       LEA     BX,RESULT       ; input buffer, and
0280 E8 02EF R                          CALL    GETIN           ; get number.
0283 E3 F3                              JCXZ    GETNUMB         ; (required)
0285 8D 36 0191 R                       LEA     SI,RESULT+2     ; Set the number pointer.
0289 E8 0000 E                          CALL    CODEASB         ; Convert the number.
028C 72 EA                              JC      GETNUMB         ; Overflow?
028E 0B C0                              OR      AX,AX           ; how about negative
0290 78 E6                              JS      GETNUMB         ; Try again on minus.
0292 8A 0E 00AC R                       MOV     CL,TARGET+1     ; Get target size.
0296 3B C1                              CMP     AX,CX           ; In or at end is ok.
0298 7F DE                              JG      GETNUMB         ; beyond is not!
029A 8D 3E 018F R                       LEA     DI,RESULT       ; Point at result.
029E 8D 36 00AD R                       LEA     SI,TARGET+2     ; Target string to move.
02A2 2B C8                              SUB     CX,AX           ; Get size left.
02A4 91                                 XCHG    AX,CX           ; Count to move in CX.
02A5 E3 02                              JCXZ    DOINSERT        ; If insert in front - ok
02A7 F3/ A4                             REP MOVSB               ; Move first part of string
02A9                         DOINSERT:
02A9 56                                 PUSH    SI              ; Save loc in target
02AA 8D 36 0111 R                       LEA     SI,INSERT+2     ; Set string to insert.
02AE 8A 0E 0110 R                       MOV     CL,INSERT+1     ; and its length.
02B2 F3/ A4                             REP MOVSB               ; Move insert
02B4 5E                                 POP     SI              ; Get target back.
```

```
02B5  8B C8                        MOV     CX,AX                  ; and remaining length
02B7  E3 02                        JCXZ    MOVDONE                ; if none _ done.
02B9  F3/ A4                       REP MOVSB                      ; Put rest of target out
02BB                   MOVDONE:
02BB  C6 05 24                     MOV     BYTE PTR [DI],'$'      ; Follow with stopper.
02BE  A0 00AC R                    MOV     AL,TARGET+1            ; Get length of target,
02C1  8A 0E 0110 R                 MOV     CL,INSERT+1            ; and length of insert.
02C5  03 C1                        ADD     AX,CX                  ; add to get total length.
02C7  8D 3E 00AB R                 LEA     DI,TARGET              ; Convert area
02CB  E8 0000 E                    CALL    CODEBAS                ; get length as ASCII
02CE  8D 16 0173 R                 LEA     DX,RESULTM             ; point to results
02D2  B4 09                        MOV     AH,9                   ;
02D4  CD 21                        INT     21h                    ; and print them.
02D6  8D 16 0093 R                 LEA     DX,NEW_LENGTH          ;
02DA  CD 21                        INT     21h
02DC  B4 02                        MOV     AH,2                   ; Number follows
02DE                   PRTNUMB:
02DE  8A 15                        MOV     DL,BYTE PTR[DI]        ; Get a digit
02E0  0A D2                        OR      DL,DL                  ; if zero _ done
02E2  0F 84 0257 R                 JZ      BEGINHERE              ; Let it be done again!
02E6  CD 21                        INT     21h
02E8  47                           INC     DI
02E9  EB F3                        JMP     PRTNUMB                ; Do all digits

02EB                   ENDHERE:
02EB  B4 4C                        MOV     AH,4Ch            ; Standard Ending
02ED  CD 21                        INT     21h
02EF                   GETIN       PROC
02EF  B4 09                        MOV     AH,9                   ; Set write
02F1  CD 21                        INT     21h                    ; of prompt
02F3  8B D3                        MOV     DX,BX                  ; point to input buffer
02F5  C6 07 62                     MOV     BYTE PTR[BX],98        ; set max length.
02F8  B4 0A                        MOV     AH,10                  ; Set read to buffer
02FA  CD 21                        INT     21h                    ; and read it.
02FC  8A 4F 01                     MOV     CL,BYTE PTR [BX+1]     ; get length
02FF  2A ED                        SUB     CH,CH                  ; as a word in CX
0301  C3                           RET                            ; Return
0302                   GETIN       ENDP
0302                   CODE        ENDS
                                   END     STRINSRT
```

Program 6-7: STRWORKS

```
Microsoft (R) Macro Assembler Version 5.00


                                        PAGE    55,132
                                        .386

                                ;
                                ; Name:         STRWORKS
                                ;
                                ; Purpose: This program does several things:
                                ;              1.  Sets up an ordered list of ASCIIZ strings
                                ;              2.  Requests an input string
                                ;              3.  Finds the position within the ordered list
                                ;              4.  Inserts the new string
                                ;
                                ; Inputs:  A series of variable length alphabetic words are typed
                                ;          in, until a word of null length (a carriage return).
                                ;          Then a Source word is entered.
                                ;
                                ; Process: We loop, requesting strings be entered until an empty
                                ;          line is entered.  Each string is copied into a string
                                ;          area and its displacement is saved in the array 'ordered'
                                ;          (We check for and also stop if we run out of either array
                                ;          space or string space.)
                                ;          We call the shell sort routine to sort the strings and
                                ;          print the ordered result.
                                ;
                                ; Outputs: The ordered list is displayed, with the Source word
                                ;          in its correct position.

                                        EXTRN   SHELLSRT:PROC

0000                            stack   SEGMENT para 'STACK' STACK
0000  0100[                             dq      256 DUP(?)
        ???????????????
        ?
                    ]

0800                            stack   ENDS
0000                            data    SEGMENT para
0000  0100[                     string  db      256 DUP(?)          ; String scratch area
        ??
                    ]

0100  0A 0A 0D 45 6E 74 65      query   db      10,10,13,"Enter the next string: $"
      72 20 74 68 65 20 6E
      65 78 74 20 73 74 72
      69 6E 67 3A 20 24
011B  0A 0A 0D 41 72 72 61      toomany db      10,10,13,"Array space is full!$"
      79 20 73 70 61 63 65
      20 69 73 20 66 75 6C
      6C 21 24
0133  0A 0A 0D 53 74 72 69      toobig  db      10,10,13,"String storage space is full!$"
      6E 67 20 73 74 6F 72
      61 67 65 20 73 70 61
      63 65 20 69 73 20 66
      75 6C 6C 21 24
0154  0A 0A 0D 54 68 65 20      heading db      10,10,13,"The ordered list is:",10,"$"
      6F 72 64 65 72 65 64
```

```
      20 6C 69 73 74 20 69
      73 3A 0A 24
                                        ;
                                        ; The following contains the array of displacements into the string
                                        ;     area.  If the number of strings grows beyond the size of the
                                        ;     array, it may be necessary to increase not only the size but
                                        ;     the method of storage
                                        ;
 = 0200                                 maxnbr      EQU     512
 016D  90                                           ALIGN   2
 016E  0200[                            ordered     dw      maxnbr DUP(?)        ; ordered string displacements
          ????
                        ]

                                        ;
                                        ; String storage area - Once placed here, the strings are not moved
                                        ; again.  Only their displacements are manipulated.
                                        ;
 056E  1400[                            strarea     db      maxnbr*10 DUP(?)
          ??
                        ]

 = 196E                                 strend      EQU     $
 196E  0000                             count       dw      0                    ; count of strings
 1970  056E                             nextstrp    dw      strarea-data         ; displacement into string area
 1972                                   data        ENDS
 0000                                   code        SEGMENT para 'CODE' USE16 PUBLIC
                                                    ASSUME  CS:code, DS:data
                                        ;
                                        ;
 0000                                   STRWORKS:
 0000  B8 ---- R                                    mov     AX,data              ; Prepare to set DS
 0003  8E D8                                        mov     DS,AX                ;   and set it.
 0005  8E C0                                        mov     ES,AX                ;   (ES too)
 0007  8B 36 1970 R                                 mov     SI,nextstrp          ; Set first SI
 000B  8D 1E 016E R                                 lea     BX,ordered           ; Set pointer to array
                                        ;
                                        ; Loop getting words (or strings) until a null string is entered or
                                        ; we run out of string storage space.
                                        ;
 000F                                   nextstr:
 000F  8D 16 0100 R                                 lea     DX,query             ; Point to message
 0013  E8 008C R                                    call    getinp               ; Get a word,string or a null
 0016  E3 3D                                        jcxz    endinp               ; Null ends our loop
 0018  41                                           inc     CX                   ; Include the zero in the move
 0019  8B C1                                        mov     AX,CX                ; Copy string length
 001B  03 C6                                        add     AX,SI                ; Add the starting loc
 001D  8D 3E 196E R                                 lea     DI,strend            ; Get the last +1 loc
 0021  3B C7                                        cmp     AX,DI                ; is there room?
 0023  0F 83 004D R                                 jnb     outroom              ; No - do message
 0027  8D 3E 0002 R                                 lea     DI,string+2          ; Point to string location
 002B  89 37                                        mov     WORD PTR[BX],SI      ; Save the destination displ.
 002D  83 C3 02                                     add     BX,2                 ; Point to the next area.
 0030  87 F7                                        xchg    SI,DI                ; Flip source and destination
 0032  F3/ A4                                       rep movsb                    ; put string in position.
 0034  8B F7                                        mov     SI,DI                ; Get pointer back
 0036  FF 06 196E R                                 inc     count                ; Add to the count
 003A  81 3E 196E R 0200                            cmp     count,maxnbr         ; At the max?
 0040  75 CD                                        jne     nextstr              ; No - get another.
 0042  8D 16 011B R                                 lea     DX,toomany           ; Point to the message
 0046  B4 09                                        mov     AH,9
 0048  CD 21                                        int     21h                  ; and put it out
```

```
004A  EB 09 90                 jmp     endinp              ; go sort
004D                   outroom:
004D  8D 16 0133 R             lea     DX,toobig           ; set message
0051  B4 09                    mov     AH,9
0053  CD 21                    int     21h                 ; and put it out
0055                   endinp:
0055  8B 0E 196E R             mov     CX,count            ; Get count in CX
0059  8D 1E 016E R             lea     BX,ordered          ; Point to the array of displ.
005D  E8 0000 E                call    Shellsrt            ; Order them
0060  8D 16 0154 R             lea     DX,heading          ; Put out the heading
0064  B4 09                    mov     AH,9
0066  CD 21                    int     21h
0068  B4 02                    mov     AH,2                ; Set code for rest
006A                   display:
006A  B2 0A                    mov     DL,10               ; l/f
006C  CD 21                    int     21h
006E  B2 0D                    mov     DL,13               ; cr
0070  CD 21                    int     21h
0072  8B 37                    mov     SI,WORD PTR[BX]     ; get string pointer
0074                   outstr:
0074  AC                       lodsb                       ; Get byte in AL
0075  0A C0                    or      AL,AL               ; check it
0077  0F 84 0081 R             jz      donestr             ; zero is done
007B  8A D0                    mov     DL,AL               ; position it
007D  CD 21                    int     21h                 ; put it out
007F  EB F3                    jmp     outstr              ; and get next
0081                   donestr:
0081  83 C3 02                 add     BX,2                ; Step string pointer.
0084  E2 E4                    loop    display             ; and do till done


0086                   endhere:
0086  2A C0                    sub     AL,AL               ; Return ok
0088  B4 4C                    mov     AH,4Ch              ; Standard Ending
008A  CD 21                    int     21h

                       ;
                       ; Read a string in response to a prompt
                       ; The prompt must be in DX.  The string will be returned in string.
                       ;
008C                   getinp  PROC
008C  50                       push    AX                  ; Save registers
008D  56                       push    SI
008E  B4 09                    mov     AH,9                ; and dos request
0090  CD 21                    int     21h                 ; put out the string
0092  8D 16 0000 R             lea     DX,string           ; point to input area
0096  C6 06 0000 R FE          mov     string,254          ; Set max length in
009B  B4 0A                    mov     AH,10               ; Ask for read of string
009D  CD 21                    int     21h                 ; from DOS.
009F  8A 0E 0001 R             mov     CL,string+1         ; Get length read
00A3  B5 00                    mov     CH,0                ; as a word.
00A5  8B F1                    mov     SI,CX               ; Set length
00A7  C6 84 0002 R 00          mov     string+2[SI],0      ; and make an asciiz string.
00AC  5E                       pop     SI
00AD  58                       pop     AX                  ; Restore registers
00AE  C3                       ret                         ; and return.
00AF                   getinp  ENDP

00AF                   CODE    ENDS
                               END     STRWORKS
```

Program 6-8: STRZCOMP

```
Microsoft (R) Macro Assembler Version 5.00

                                      PAGE      55,132
                                      .386
 0000                         code    SEGMENT   para 'CODE' PUBLIC USE16
                                      ASSUME    CS:code, DS:code, SS:code

                              ; Name:    STRZCOMP
                              ;
                              ; Purpose: The following procedure compares two ASCIIZ strings
                              ;          and returns the resulting condition code flags.
                              ;
                              ;
                              ; Inputs:  DS:SI contains the address of string 1.
                              ;          ES:DI contains the address of string 2.
                              ;          (The comparison is string 1 - string 2.)
                              ;
                              ; Process: A byte by byte comparison is performed with each equal
                              ;          compare checked for a null (end of string indicator).
                              ;          An unequal or a null terminates the compare.
                              ;
                              ; Output:  The flags are set with the result of the subtraction
                              ;          of string 2 from string 1 (only the flags are set no
                              ;          other changes are returned).
                              ;
                              ; Note:    No procedure for fixed length strings is provided - see
                              ;          the text (repe cmpsb is used - no proc is needed).
                              ;
                                       PUBLIC  Strzcomp
                              ;
0000                          Strzcomp PROC
0000  56                               push    SI              ; Save entry registers
0001  57                               push    DI
0002  50                               push    AX
0003                          cmpnext:
0003  AC                               lodsb                   ; Get string 1 byte in AL
0004  AE                               scasb                   ; Compare to string 2 byte
0005  0F 85 000D R                     jne     cmpdone         ; Not equal - done
0009  3C 00                            cmp     AL,0            ; Equal at end of string?
000B  75 F6                            jne     cmpnext         ; Not yet!
000D                          cmpdone:
000D  58                               pop     AX              ; Restore the entry registers
000E  5F                               pop     DI
000F  5E                               pop     SI
0010  C3                               ret                     ; and return.
0011                          Strzcomp ENDP
0011                          code     ENDS
                                       END
```

Program 6-9: STRZLNG

```
Microsoft (R) Macro Assembler Version 5.00


                                PAGE      55,132
                                .386
 0000                   code    SEGMENT   para 'CODE' PUBLIC USE16
                                ASSUME    CS:code, DS:code, SS:code
                        ;
                        ; Name:     STRZLNG
                        ;
                        ; Purpose: The following procedure scans an ASCIIZ string and
                        ;          returns its length.
                        ;
                        ;
                        ; Inputs:  ES:DI has the address of the string to examine.
                        ;          CX has the maximum length to examine.
                        ;
                        ; Process: We set the registers for a repeated scasb and do it.
                        ;          Compute the length excluding the null and return it.
                        ;
                        ; Output:  AX has the count of bytes in the string (excluding the
                        ;          terminating null).  Carry is reset if the null was found,
                        ;          otherwise carry is set and AX is returned equal to the
                        ;          input CX value.
                        ;
                                 PUBLIC  Strzlng
                        ;
 0000                   Strzlng  PROC
 0000  57                        push    DI              ; Save entry registers
 0001  51                        push    CX              ; Save CX twice for length
 0002  51                        push    CX              ; computation.
 0003  2B C0                     sub     AX,AX           ; Clear AX (AL for scan)
 0005  0B C9                     or      CX,CX           ; is CX zero
 0007  0F 84 001A R              jz      outbad          ; Exit if none to scan
 000B  FC                        cld                     ; Scan low to high
 000C  F2/ AE                    repne scasb             ; Condition for terminating
                                                         ; scan is a null.
 000E  0F 85 001A R              jne     outbad          ; If count ran out - die
 0012  41                        inc     CX              ; Don't include the terminator
 0013  58                        pop     AX              ; Get saved length
 0014  2B C1                     sub     AX,CX           ; and the count processed.
 0016  F8                        clc                     ; Ensure carry is reset
 0017  59                        pop     CX
 0018  5F                        pop     DI              ; Restore registers
 0019  C3                        ret                     ; and return with length.
 001A                   outbad:
 001A  F9                        stc                     ; Indicate an error
 001B  58                        pop     AX
 001C  59                        pop     CX
 001D  5F                        pop     DI              ; Restore registers
 001E  C3                        ret                     ; and return AX=CX.
 001F                   Strzlng  ENDP
 001F                   code     ENDS
                                 END
```

Program 6-10: PARSEDRV

```
Microsoft (R) Macro Assembler Version 5.00


                                        PAGE    55,132
                                        .386

                              ;
                              ; Name:    PARSEDRV
                              ;
                              ; Purpose: The following program provides a simple test for the
                              ;          sample parser PARSING.
                              ;
                              ;
                              ;
                              ; Inputs:  The program prompts for a line to be parsed and reads
                              ;          the input.
                              ;
                              ; Process: The input is passed to the parsing routine until the
                              ;          end of data token is returned.  Each token is displayed
                              ;          as it is returned.  At end of data, another line of input
                              ;          is requested.  If a null line (enter only) is input, the
                              ;          program terminates.
                              ;
                              ; Output:  The output is the displayed tokens.
                              ;

                              ;
                              ; Declare the routine we are going to use
                              ;
                                        EXTRN    PARSING:PROC

0000                          stack     SEGMENT  para 'STACK' STACK
0000  0100[                             dq       256 DUP(?)
       ???????????????
       ?
                    ]

0800                          stack     ENDS
0000                          data      SEGMENT  para
0000  0100[                   string    db       256 DUP(?)          ; String scratch area
         ??
                    ]

0100  0100[                   outwork   db       256 DUP(?)          ; Output work area
         ??
                    ]

0200  0D 0A 45 6E 74 65 72    query     db       13,10,"Enter a string to parse: $"
      20 61 20 73 74 72 69
      6E 67 20 74 6F 20 70
      61 72 73 65 3A 20 24
021C  0D 0A 54 6F 6B 65 6E    sayret    db       13,10,"Token="
      3D
0224  0004[                   rettokt   db       4 DUP(?)            ; Type of token
         ??
                    ]

0228  73 74 72 69 6E 67 3D              db       "string=",34        ; ending quote by 34
      22
0230  0080[                   rettokv   db       128 DUP(?)          ; Lots of room for the token
```

```
         ??
                      ]

02B0  24                            db        "$"              ; Ender just in case
02B1  55 6E 6B 20         tokent    db        "Unk "           ; Type zero
02B5  43 77 64 20                   db        "Cwd "           ; 1
02B9  4C 77 64 20                   db        "Lwd "           ; 2
02BD  4E 62 72 20                   db        "Nbr "           ; 3
02C1  50 20 2E 20                   db        "P . "           ; 4
02C5  50 20 2C 20                   db        "P , "           ; 5
02C9  50 20 21 20                   db        "P ! "           ; 6
02CD  50 20 3F 20                   db        "P ? "           ; 7
02D1                      data      ENDS
                          ;
                          ;
                          ; Standard equates for token types
                          ;
= 0001                    tokencwd   EQU     1                 ; Capitalized word
= 0002                    tokenlwd   EQU     2                 ; Lower-Case word
= 0003                    tokennbr   EQU     3                 ; Number
= 0004                    tokenper   EQU     4                 ; Period
= 0005                    tokencom   EQU     5                 ; Comma
= 0006                    tokenexc   EQU     6                 ; Exclamation point
= 0007                    tokenqmk   EQU     7                 ; Question mark
= 0000                    tokenunk   EQU     0                 ; Unknown type
= 00FF                    tokeneod   EQU     255               ; End of data
                          ;

0000                      code      SEGMENT   para 'CODE' USE16 PUBLIC
                                    ASSUME    CS:code, DS:data
                          ;
                          ; Set up the environment
                          ;
0000                      Begin:
0000  B8 ---- R                       mov     AX,data          ; Get data segment pointer
0003  8E D8                           mov     DS,AX            ; into DS,
0005  8E C0                           mov     ES,AX            ; and ES.
0007  2B F6                           sub     SI,SI            ; Clear indices
0009  2B FF                           sub     DI,DI
                          ;
                          ; Parse a line entered from the keyboard and repeat until a null
                          ; line is entered.
                          ;
000B                      getparse:
000B  E8 0049 R                       call    getinp           ; Get a line in
000E  E3 33                           jcxz    endit            ; if empty - exit.
                          ;
                          ; Loop thru the parse routine until an end of data is returned.
                          ;
0010                      nexttoken:
0010  E8 0000 E                       call    parsing          ; Go isolate token
0013  3C FF                           cmp     AL,tokeneod      ; End of data?
0015  74 F4                           jz      getparse         ; Need more data if so
                          ;
                          ; Put out the data which was returned.
                          ;
0017  53                              push    BX
0018  51                              push    CX               ; Save next pointers
0019  98                              cbw                      ; Get token number
001A  66| 98                          cwde                     ; as double word index.
001C  67| 66| 8B 0485 0000            mov     EAX,DWORD PTR tokent[EAX*4] ; Get into register
```

```
     02B1 R
0025 66| A3 0224 R              mov     DWORD PTR rettokt,EAX ; and into message.
0029 8B CA                      mov     CX,DX                 ; Set the length
002B 8D 3E 0230 R               lea     DI,rettokv            ; and destination.
002F F3/ A4                     rep movsb                     ; then move token,
0031 B0 22                      mov     AL,34                 ; ending quote,
0033 AA                         stosb                         ;
0034 B0 24                      mov     AL,'$'                ; and stopper.
0036 AA                         stosb
0037 B4 09                      mov     AH,9                  ; Set code,
0039 8D 16 021C R               lea     DX,sayret             ; text pointer,
003D CD 21                      int     21h                   ; and do the message.
003F 59                         pop     CX
0040 5B                         pop     BX                    ; Restore our registers and
0041 EB CD                      jmp     nexttoken             ; try for next token



0043                    endit:
0043 B0 00                      mov     AL,0                  ; Set return code
0045 B4 4C                      mov     AH,04ch               ; Set good-by
0047 CD 21                      int     21h                   ; Return to the system
                        ;
                        ; Read a string in response to a prompt
                        ;
0049                    getinp  PROC
0049 52                         push    DX                    ; Save registers
004A 50                         push    AX
004B 56                         push    SI
004C 8D 16 0200 R               lea     DX,query              ; Set output prompt
0050 B4 09                      mov     AH,9                  ; and dos request
0052 CD 21                      int     21h                   ; put out the string
0054 8D 16 0000 R               lea     DX,string             ; point to input area
0058 C6 06 0000 R FE            mov     string,254            ; Set max length in
005D B4 0A                      mov     AH,10                 ; Ask for read of string
005F CD 21                      int     21h                   ; from DOS.
0061 8D 1E 0002 R               lea     BX,string+2           ; Point to just read data
0065 8A 0E 0001 R               mov     CL,string+1           ; Get length read
0069 B5 00                      mov     CH,0                  ; as a word.
006B 8B F1                      mov     SI,CX                 ; Set length
006D C6 84 0002 R 00            mov     string+2[SI],0        ; and make an asciiz string.
0072 5E                         pop     SI
0073 58                         pop     AX
0074 5A                         pop     DX                    ; Restore registers
0075 C3                         ret                           ; and return.
0076                    getinp  ENDP

0076                    code    ENDS
                                END     Begin
```

Program 6-11: PARSING

```
Microsoft (R) Macro Assembler Version 5.00


                                       PAGE      55,132
                                       .386
 0000                          code    SEGMENT   para 'CODE' USE16 PUBLIC
                                       ASSUME    CS:code, DS:code, SS:code
                               ;
                               ; Name:    PARSING
                               ;
                               ; Purpose: The following procedure parses input text into a token
                               ;          which it returns to the driving process.
                               ;
                               ;
                               ; Inputs:  DS:BX points to the next text to parse.  CX has the
                               ;          length of text remaining.  If CX is zero, end of data
                               ;          is returned.
                               ;
                               ; Process: Leading spaces are skipped. If we ran out of data, return
                               ;          end of data.  Examine the non-blank we located.
                               ;
                               ;          If it's a number, verify that the following non-space, non-
                               ;          punctuation is also a number.  Repeat until a proper end
                               ;          is detected and return the number token.  If an unknown
                               ;          is detected, scan until a space or punctuation is detected
                               ;          to identify the unknown token's size and return an unknown.
                               ;
                               ;          If it's a capital letter, potentially identify the token as
                               ;          a capitalized word.
                               ;          If it's a lower-case letter, potentially identify the token
                               ;          as a lower-case word.
                               ;          In either case, check the following for either lower-case
                               ;          letters or a proper ending (space or punctuation).  Treat
                               ;          an unknown token the same as above.
                               ;
                               ;          Otherwise check if the non-space is a punctuation mark
                               ;          and if so return the proper token type.  Otherwise, treat
                               ;          the unknown token as above.
                               ;
                               ; Output:  AL will contain the type of token detected.  SI will point
                               ;          to the start of the token and DX will contain its length.
                               ;          BX will point to the character which stopped the scan and
                               ;          CX will contain the count of characters remaining.
                               ;
                               ;
                               ;
                               ; Standard equates for token types
                               ;
 = 0001                        tokencwd   EQU    1                ; Capitalized word
 = 0002                        tokenlwd   EQU    2                ; Lower-Case word
 = 0003                        tokennbr   EQU    3                ; Number
 = 0004                        tokenper   EQU    4                ; Period
 = 0005                        tokencom   EQU    5                ; Comma
 = 0006                        tokenexc   EQU    6                ; Exclamation point
 = 0007                        tokenqmk   EQU    7                ; Question mark
 = 0000                        tokenunk   EQU    0                ; Unknown type
 = 00FF                        tokeneod   EQU    255              ; End of data
                               ;
                                          PUBLIC Parsing
```

```
                                   ;
0000                               Parsing    PROC
0000  06                                      push    ES                 ; Save entry registers
0001  E3 32                                   jcxz    enddata            ; If no more data - say so
                                   ;
                                   ; Skip all leading spaces
                                   ;
0003  8C D8                                   mov     AX,DS              ; Set up for scan
0005  8E C0                                   mov     ES,AX              ; ES
0007  8B FB                                   mov     DI,BX              ; and DI
0009  FC                                      cld                        ; Go up scanning
000A  B0 20                                   mov     AL,' '             ; for non space.
000C  F3/ AE                                  repe scasb                 ; skip all leading spaces.
000E  0F 84 0035 R                            jz      enddata            ; End of data if all spaces.
0012  41                                      inc     CX                 ; Add overage back
                                   ;
                                   ; Identify the kind of token found.  Our repe took us one too far.
                                   ; We need to back the pointer up one and ultimately count this byte
                                   ; out of CX.  We need to delay counting the byte until after we
                                   ; determine the type in order to handle single byte tokens at the
                                   ; end of the input.
                                   ;
                                   ; We change ES here to allow its use in checkend where it could be
                                   ; set multiple times.  (Protected mode checking makes segment
                                   ; register setting more expensive. 18 clocks.)
                                   ;
0013  8C CE                                   mov     SI,CS              ; Prepare for check ending
0015  8E C6                                   mov     ES,SI              ; Set ES
0017  8B F7                                   mov     SI,DI              ; Need to check each byte
0019  4E                                      dec     SI                 ; Point to token start.
001A  56                                      push    SI                 ; Save the start.
001B  AC                                      lodsb                      ; Get a byte (step SI).
001C  34 30                                   xor     AL,'0'             ;
001E  3C 09                                   cmp     AL,9               ; Is it a number
0020  0F 87 0048 R                            ja      checkalph          ; No - go check for alpha
0024  EB 0A 90                                jmp     numbere            ; Yes, go count char found
                                   ;
                                   ; We have either a number or an unknown
                                   ;
0027                               number:
0027  AC                                      lodsb                      ; Get the next byte
0028  34 30                                   xor     AL,'0'             ; Check if a number
002A  3C 09                                   cmp     AL,9               ; Is it
002C  0F 87 0039 R                            ja      numbend            ; No - check proper endings.
0030                               numbere:
0030  E2 F5                                   loop    number             ; go check the next
                                   ;
                                   ; We ended on a valid number.
                                   ;
0032  EB 0F 90                                jmp     goodnum            ; We are OK.
                                   ;
                                   ; End of data - return token type saying so
                                   ;
0035                               enddata:
0035  B0 FF                                   mov     AL,tokeneod        ; Set token type
0037  07                                      pop     ES                 ; restore register
0038  C3                                      ret                        ; and exit.
                                   ;
                                   ; We had a number up to this byte - if it is punctuation or a space
                                   ; the number is valid.  Otherwise we have an unknown.
                                   ;
0039                               numbend:
0039  4E                                      dec     SI                 ; We went one too far!
```

```
003A  34 30                 xor     AL,'0'            ; Put it back as it was.
003C  E8 00AE R             call    checkend          ; Is it an ending
003F  0F 85 0095 R          jne     unklook           ; Bad so scan to a good one.
                   ;
                   ; Our token is a number
                   ;
0043               goodnum:
0043  B0 03                 mov     AL,tokennbr       ; Set the type
0045  EB 5E 90              jmp     outtoken          ; Build token for return.
                   ;
                   ; We may have a lower-case or capitalized word.
                   ;
0048               checkalph:
0048  34 30                 xor     AL,'0'            ; Fix char again.
004A  B4 01                 mov     AH,tokencwd       ; Assume it is.
004C  3C 41                 cmp     AL,'A'            ; Check if it is a cap
004E  0F 82 0066 R          jb      checkpunct        ; No - go check punctuation.
0052  3C 5A                 cmp     AL,'Z'            ; Is it a cap
0054  0F 86 0082 R          jna     checkworde        ; Yes - it may be a word!
0058  B4 02                 mov     AH,tokenlwd       ; Assume a lower-case word.
005A  3C 61                 cmp     AL,'a'            ; Check if it is a lower
                   ;                                    Note: in case we add punct-
005C  0F 82 0066 R          jb      checkpunct        ; uation we go check here.
0060  3C 7A                 cmp     AL,'z'            ; Is it a-z?
0062  0F 86 0082 R          jna     checkworde        ; yes -
                   ;
                   ; It may be punctuation
                   ;
0066               checkpunct:
0066  E8 00AE R             call    checkend          ; Check for punctuation ending.
0069  0F 85 009D R          jne     unknown           ; If not - go find some.
                   ;
                   ; We need to adjust the count for the single byte processed.
                   ;
006D  49                    dec     CX                ; So count this out.
006E  B0 03                 mov     AL,tokenper-1     ; Set the amount to add
0070  02 C4                 add     AL,AH             ; and add to get token type.
0072  EB 31 90              jmp     outtoken          ; Go build token pointers.
                   ;
                   ; Check for more lower-case alpha with a proper ending.
                   ;
0075               checkword:
0075  AC                    lodsb                     ; Get the next byte
0076  3C 61                 cmp     AL,'a'            ; Is it a
0078  0F 82 0089 R          jb      wordendq          ; If low - can't be
007C  3C 7A                 cmp     AL,'z'            ; thru z?
007E  0F 87 0089 R          ja      wordendq          ; if high - is isn't
0082               checkworde:
0082  E2 F1                 loop    checkword         ; If another - check it
0084  8A C4                 mov     AL,AH             ; Set the token type and
0086  EB 1D 90              jmp     outtoken          ; go build pointers.
                   ;
                   ; A word has ended - check for proper ending.
                   ;
0089               wordendq:
0089  4E                    dec     SI                ; We went too far by 1.
008A  50                    push    AX                ; Save our possible token type
008B  E8 00AE R             call    checkend          ; check for proper ending.
008E  58                    pop     AX                ; Restore token type
008F  8A C4                 mov     AL,AH             ; into proper register
0091  0F 84 00A5 R          je      outtoken          ; If proper ending - done.
                   ;
```

```
                          ; Scan forward to a proper ending
                          ;
0095                      unklook:
0095  AC                            lodsb                       ; Get the next byte
0096  E8 00AE R                     call    checkend            ; Is it a good ending?
0099  0F 84 00A2 R                  je      unknowne            ; It is - get out
009D                      unknown:
009D  E2 F6                         loop    unklook             ; Count it and if more - check
009F  EB 02 90                      jmp     outunknown
00A2                      unknowne:
00A2  4E                            dec     SI                  ; Back up to punctuation
00A3                      outunknown:
00A3  B0 00                         mov     AL,tokenunk         ; Set type as unknown
                          ;
                          ; Build the token pointer and length for return.
                          ;
00A5                      outtoken:
00A5  8B DE                         mov     BX,SI               ; Set next char pointer.
00A7  5E                            pop     SI                  ; Get start
00A8  8B D3                         mov     DX,BX               ; Set next into length.
00AA  2B D6                         sub     DX,SI               ; Get the length=next-start
00AC  07                            pop     ES                  ; Restore ES
00AD  C3                            ret                         ; and return.
00AE                      checkend  PROC
                          ;
                          ; Check if the byte in AL is one of our delimiters.  If it is, we exit
                          ; with AH set to the remaining count from CX and the zero flag set.
                          ; Otherwise, the zero flag is not set on exit.
                          ;
                          ;
                          ;
00AE  51                            push    CX                  ; Save current count left
00AF  8D 3E 00BD R                  lea     DI,CS:punct         ; Point to the proper endings
00B3  B9 0005 90                    mov     CX,punctct          ; Set the proper count.
                          ;
                          ; The following is a good way to test for set inclusion.  AL (AX or
                          ; EAX) is tested against all CX items until a match is found.  The
                          ; number of clocks (5+8n) is small enough to make even moderate
                          ; size lists efficient.  Of course, large lists are more efficiently
                          ; searched with a non-linear technique such as a binary search or
                          ; hashing.
                          ;
00B7  F2/ AE                        repne scasb                 ; Check if any of the endings.
00B9  8A E1                         mov     AH,CL               ; Save residual
00BB  59                            pop     CX                  ; Restore count left
00BC  C3                            ret

00BD                      checkend  ENDP

00BD  3F 21 2C 2E 20      punct     db      '?!,. '             ; Proper endings
= 0005                    punctct   EQU     $-punct

00C2                      Parsing   ENDP
00C2                      code      ENDS
                                    END
```

7

Code Conversion

Conversion is the process of changing information from one form to another. Often you have little control over the form of input and must convert numbers from one base to another, or character sets from one to another, in order to better handle a process within a program. A second need for conversion comes when the hardware and/or software of the host system cannot easily handle a particular input set.

80386 Data Handling

Memory is viewed from the processor as if it were a sequential array of bytes. Think of it as beginning from your left hand, moving to your right and continuing to the right for as many bytes as are built into your system. However, the bits within the bytes are counted (or positioned) from right to left, as shown in Fig. 7-1. The byte address starts at the left with zero and moves to the right. In the example, the byte for "40" is stored in memory storage location zero (0). Yet, the least significant bit (LSB) is on the right and the most significant bit (MSB) is on the left.

The 80386 moves data from memory a byte at a time into the specified registers. The registers begin their counting from the right. So, the 80386 stores it from the the first byte in the right-hand slot (the AL byte register in the example). The second byte goes in the second slot (the AH register in the example). Therefore, if you look at a dump of a location in memory, it probably will *not* look like a dump of a register that holds the same data.

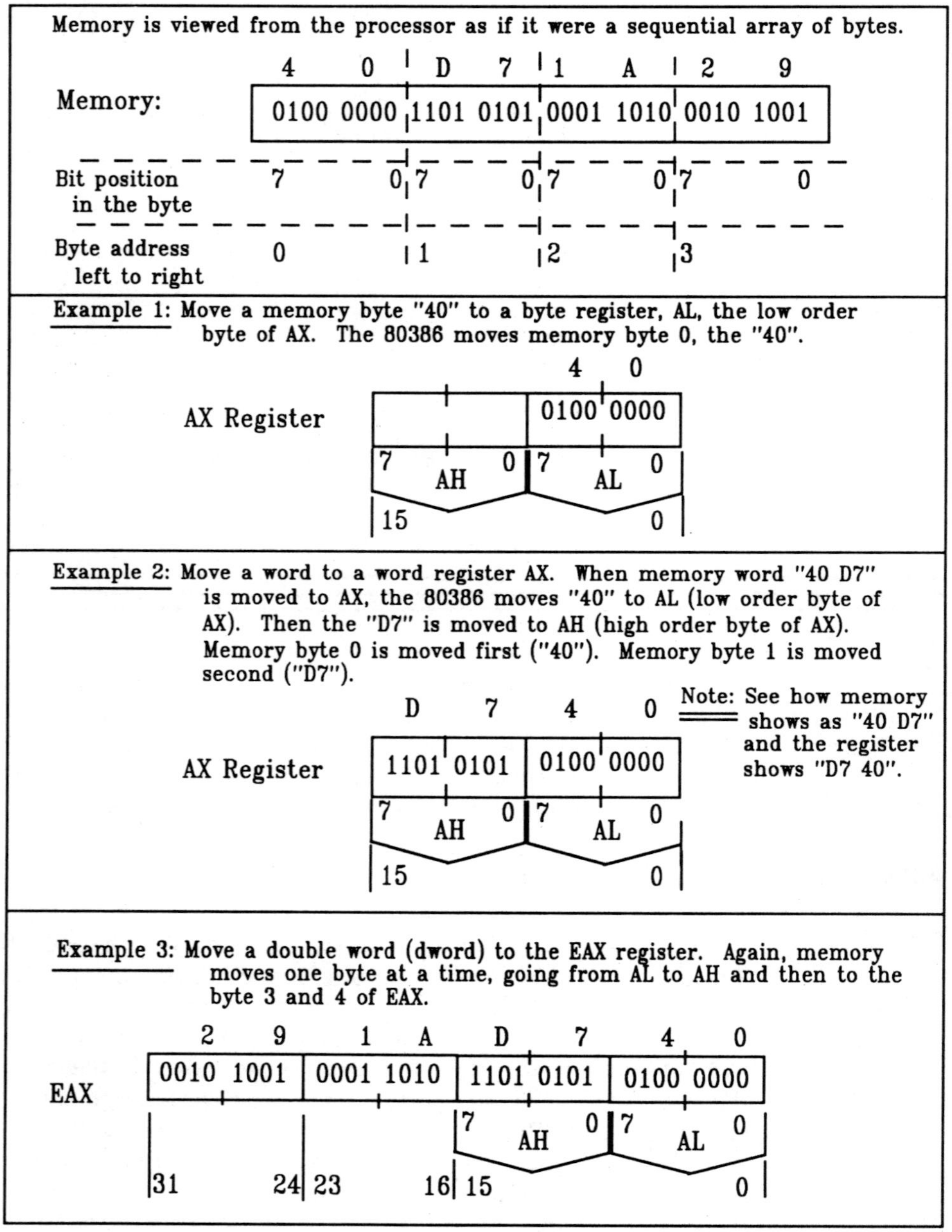

Fig. 7-1. Storage examples of memory and registers.

80386 and 80387 Data Types

The 80386 operates on signed and unsigned integers, BCD (binary coded decimal)—both packed and unpacked, floating-point, bits, and strings. The 80386 uses 8-bit bytes, 16-bit words, and 32-bit doublewords (dwords). The dword is new to the 80386; none of the previous Intel chips supported the 32-bit length.

The 80386 processor and 80387 numeric coprocessor support seven data types: word integer, short integer, long integer, BCD, short real, long real, and temporary real. The 80387 was built to handle both real and integer data types so that, if an arithmetic computation is sent to the 80387, there is no *required* transfer between the 80386 and the 80387 other than the original transfer of the arithmetic elements and the returned answer. The coprocessor handles the entire computation.

New to the 80386 is support of bit manipulation, from a single bit to bit strings up to 2^{32} bits in length. Bit manipulation is important for use in bitmaps and as semaphores. For example, a bitmap can represent each pixel, i.e., each dot on the display. When used as a semaphore, the bit is either set (ON = 1) when busy or reset (OFF = 0) when free. Bit and string manipulation are discussed in detail in Chapter 6.

Floating-Point Numbers

Floating-point numbers allow computations where the range of the magnitude of the numbers is very large, larger than can be handled with fixed-point numbers (except with great difficulty). Floating-point representation of numbers corresponds to what is usually called scientific notation. That is, each number is represented as the product of a normal number with a decimal point and an integral power of the radix. For example, the number 57.2233 is expressed in scientific notation as 0.57223×10^2, with the 0.57223 being called the *fractional* part and the 2 the *exponent* part. This notation is called floating-point in computer arithmetic because the radix point of the entire number is not fixed but can float, depending on the value of the exponent.

The most difficult operations in floating-point arithmetic are addition and subtraction. Overflow can occur in all floating-point operations when the magnitude of the result exceeds the capacity of the floating-point number system. The result of floating-point overflow is handled either by making the result the largest number possible and setting an indicator that the programmer can test, or by stopping the computation with an appropriate error message.

Underflow, which results from the attempt to produce a nonzero result too small in magnitude to be accommodated, can also result from any floating-point operation. The usual response is to generate a zero result. Often, an indicator is set which you can check with your program code.

Floating-point multiplication and division require only performing the appropriate action on the fractional parts, rounding the results, adding (for multiplication) or subtracting (for division) the exponents, and then normalizing if necessary.

Real numbers are floating-point numbers. Their formats are composed of significand, exponent, and sign. Figure 7-2 shows the bits which are used for the real formats and the general format of real numbers.

The *sign* is a sign bit, at the MSB location. If the sign = 0, the number is positive; if sign = 1, it is negative. The *significand* hold the significant bits of the number, often called the *mantissa*. To show maximum precision, the results of arithmetic computations are *normalized*, i.e., numbers have their exponent adjusted so that the most significant bit of the binary significand is 1. The binary point is then to the right of this 1. The correct normalized result of the number 1 is $1.0*10^0$. Note that an exponent of zero means the value of one.

The *exponent* field holds the power of two needed to scale the significand to get the final result. The exponent is stored in biased form to ease numerical comparisons.

The 80387 numeric coprocessor converts all data types into temporary real, no matter what it was originally passed. This is done to maximize the precision and the range of computations. The temporary real has no hidden bit, so bit 63 is always 1 in a normalized number.

Conversion Routines

The conversion routines (Programs 7-1 through 7-15 at the end of the chapter) are meant to ease your programming to convert number representation. We included

Data Type	Total Bits	Significand	Exponent	Sign
Short	32	23	8	1
Long	64	52	11	1
Temporary	80	64	15	1

Sign	Exponent	Significand

General Format

Fig. 7-2. Real-number data format.

a driver so you can test the routines and see how they are called and implemented, before you use or modify them.

A Code Conversion Driver Program

CODEDRV (Program 7-1) drives the various code conversion routines in this book. This provides both a test for the conversion routines themselves and a working example of the calling sequences. Input is typed at the keyboard in response to prompts. The input is passed through the conversion routines, first converting from the ASCII to either binary or EBCDIC. The reverse conversion is then done and the output displayed. Output should equal input. The reverse conversion results are displayed.

Hex to Binary and Back

Hexadecimal representation is condensed visual representation, where each hex digit (0–9, A–F) represents a 4-bit value. Since a byte is 8 bits, it can be represented visually by two hex digits. This is the most compact representation which also allows easy mental conversion to bit form. A pair of hex digits is converted into a binary byte. The left hex digit becomes the most significant nibble (4 bits). The right hex digit becomes the least significant nibble.

CODEHXTB (Program 7-2) converts a displayable hexadecimal number into its binary equivalent. It accepts two ASCII hex digits and returns a byte. Each input nibble is converted and, at the same time, edited to ensure that the presented value is 0–9 or A–F (or a–f). An error causes a set Carry Flag and an immediate return.

After subtracting the character 0 (hex 30), it ANDS bit 5 off (which would be on for a lowercase character). This allows it to treat all alphabetic character inputs (the A–F of hex notation) without special handling of case. This AND replaces a comparison, a branch, and special handling with a single instruction.

Binary numbers generally are too clumsy for easy use. The base-16 hexadecimal (hex) numbering system evolved as the most convenient one for assembly language programming largely for two reasons. First, conversions are easily done between hex and binary, and second, programmers are more accustomed to the digits 0–9 and A–F.

CODEBTHX (Program 7-3) provides a single-byte conversion from binary to displayable hexadecimal. The calling program passes the byte to be converted in AL. CODEBTHX converts the left nibble of AL and returns it in AH, then converts the right nibble and returns it in AL. The program BUFFER (described and listed in Chapter 9) calls CODEBTHX to display a memory register.

ASCII to EBCDIC and Back

Bytes are units of information and consist of 8 bits. Besides carrying numeric entities, bytes also represent alphabetic and special characters. The American

Standard Code for Information Interchange (ASCII) is an assignment of a numeric value to each digit, letter, and special character. ASCII also has control codes that carry special information, such as "carriage return." (See Appendix 5 for the full ASCII character set.)

On the other hand, BCDIC (Binary-Coded Decimal Interchange Code) developed because alphabetic data could not be represented in any combination of 4 bits, the basic BCD representation (see Chapter 4 for more information). To get around this, BCD was expanded by the addition of two extra bits, called B and A bits, which were used extensively in second-generation computers. The A and B bits were used to record the zone portion of alphabetic data as coded in the standard (Hollerith) punched card. Figure 7-3 shows where they were placed.

When third-generation computers came along, the 6-bit BCDIC was discarded for an 8-bit coding scheme—EBCDIC (Extended Binary-Coded Decimal Interchange Code)—that allowed both upper- and lowercase alphabetic characters, as well as a lot of special characters. Two versions of the 8-bit code were devised: EBCDIC and ASCII. In each, two sets of 4-bit codes were used, with each 4-bit set being coded with the "8-4-2-1" scheme. ASCII became the industry standard for data exchange between computers. In the 1960s, IBM adopted 8-bit EBCDIC for their

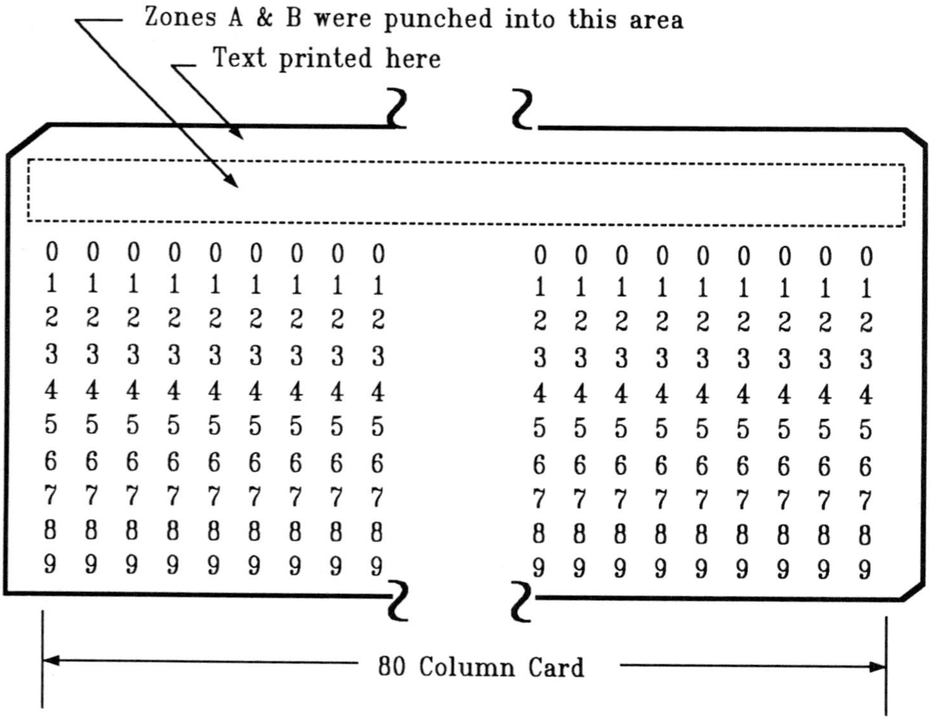

Fig. 7-3. Standard punched card format.

System/360 mainframes, while much of the remainder of the industry adopted ASCII. Today, ASCII is used on most microcomputers.

CODEASB converts an ASCII numeric string to its doubleword binary equivalent. Because the end number is a doubleword, CODEASB uses the 80386 extended register set. This routine is useful in pulling multiple numbers out of a long string, where the numbers are separated by commas or by spaces. You could intersperse this routine with scanning of text, for instance.

The procedure scans the string to get the count of digits. The technique of the routine is new: CODEASB fetches decimal digit pairs from left to right. The prior result is multiplied by 100 and the new pair converted to binary and added to the prior result. Each pair in the source is processed. If an odd number of digits is presented, the first digit is processed alone before going on to the pairs.

It turns out that the 8086 through 80386 ASCII Adjust for Division (AAD) will take a pair of digits and do the combination and multiplication to get them into a range from 0 to 99 in a single binary byte. This is less expensive in terms of machine cycles than a multiply for each character.

CODEEBAS (Program 7-4) provides a conversion from EBCDIC (the code used by IBM/370 mainframes) to ASCII. Notice the EBCDIC to ASCII translation table that is included with the program. This routine and its partner CODEASEB, (Program 7-5) are effectively the same. The instructions used in them are the same, except the conversion is done in an opposite direction.

The technique of combining error bits and leaving them in the translate table if the value did not translate validly to EBCDIC is interesting. It costs very little to initially clear a register and OR each character into the register, but at the end you have an easy method to detect "bad" characters. The character translates to a character with the high bit on and can be identified.

Binary to ASCII and Back

CODEBAS (Program 7-6) converts a binary doubleword to an ASCII decimal string. CODEBAS uses the fact that the 80386 ASCII Adjust for Multiply (AAM) instruction will effectively do a divide by 10 and separate the two digits in the proper registers. This ends up having the program check to eliminate leading zeros.

EAX contains the double word to be converted and ES:DI contains the pointer to a 12-byte area for the converted data. The sign is captured and, if negative, the absolute value of the number is used. Next, we divide the number by 100. The two-decimal digit remainder is converted and stored in the target string from right to left. The procedure is repeated until the quotient is zero. We chose this technique of repeated division because it is easily expandable to larger binary numbers, as well as for its simplicity. CODEASB (Program 7-7) converts in the other direction.

A Floating-Point Routine Driver Program

FPDRIVE (Program 7-8) exercises the floating-point conversion routines. You are prompted for a floating-point number, which must be in the form:

(–)*d**.*d***e*(–)*d**

where (–) is an optional minus sign, *d** is one or more numeric digits, the decimal "." is a required decimal, and *e* is a required start-of-exponent signal; *e* may be either upper- or lowercase. Inputting a null (pressing Enter) ends the program.

The floating-point number is converted to an IEEE long floating-point number; an error causes a re-prompt. The floating-point number is then converted to ASCII and displayed. It is displayed in hexadecimal, converted to IBM format, displayed in hex, converted to IEEE format and displayed in hex again. The number is then converted to short floating-point form, displayed in hex, converted to long form, displayed in hex and converted to ASCII and displayed again. The program then loops back to the original user prompt for input.

Single to Double Precision and Back

FPLONGTS (Program 7-9) converts an IEEE format long floating-point number to an IEEE short format floating-point number. Intel provides both a short floating-point and a long floating-point; you may need to convert from one to the other. IEEE long format has an 11-digit binary exponent biased by 1023. It appears in memory reversed from its form in registers. IEEE short format has 8 bits of exponent biased by 127 and a 23-bit fraction. Conversion from long to short can either overflow or underflow the short exponent. An overflow returns a short infinity, while an underflow returns a short zero. In either case, the Carry Flag is set upon return.

DS:SI points to an IEEE format long floating-point number in memory, which is assumed to be a normalized number. The exponent is unbiased and checked for over- or underflow and, if found, the Carry Flag is set. Otherwise, the exponent is biased as a short number and the fraction truncated to 23 bits and combined with the new exponent and sign. The converted number is returned in EAX.

FPSTLONG (Program 7-10) does the opposite. This conversion is simpler. It's a matter of rebiasing the exponent and adding some zeros at the end of the number. Conversion from short to long can neither over- nor underflow the long exponent. Zero and short infinity must be checked for and preserved. Infinity is recognized and the Carry Flag set on return. The converted number is returned in EAX:EDX.

IEEE to IBM Double Precision and Back

FPIBMEEE (Program 7-11) provides a conversion of an IBM-format long floating-point number to an IEEE long-format floating-point number. The IBM/370 format is hexadecimal-based and appears in memory in the same form as it does in registers. The IEEE format is binary-based and, on the 80386, appears reversed in memory from its form in registers.

IEEE format appears to have 4 bits less precision than IBM format, but the average precision of IBM format is 54.5 bits because it is hexadecimal. The hidden bit in front of the fraction of the IEEE format extends its precision to 53 bits. The conversion routines ignore this discrepancy. The IBM format's exponent base (16) provides a maximum value of $2^{(64 \times 4)}$ or 2^{256}. The IEEE format provides a maximum of 2^{1023}. Therefore, there is no problem converting from IBM to IEEE.

DS:SI points to an IBM-format long floating-point number in memory. This is assumed to be a normalized number. It is in IBM order as it would be if read from a network, IBM file, or magnetic tape. The number is reversed into 80386 format. The exponent is then converted from IBM to IEEE base in signed form. The fraction is then renormalized from IBM to IEEE form and shifted right to make room for the biased exponent and sign. The exponent is then biased by 1023, the sign appended, and the resulting 12 bits are combined with the fraction. The result is stored over the original number.

FPIEEEBM (Program 7-12) does the reverse. Both routines use 80386 instructions (double shift left and right, for example) which eases the conversion, in addition to using the larger 80386 registers.

Note: When going IBM to IEEE, you can't overflow. However, when going from IEEE to IBM, you can both over- and underflow because there are more positions in the exponent of IEEE numbers. As an implementation decision, if you underflow, the routine returns zero; if you overflow, it provides the maximum IBM floating-point number. If either occurs, the Carry Flag is set.

IEEE Long Float to ASCII and Back

In floating-point numbers, the binary point is allowed to float. A portion of the data shows the location of the binary point and the rest specifies the significant data bits. This allows you to extend the representable range of numbers, at the same time providing you with precision over the entire range. The 80386 processor with the 80387 numeric coprocessor supports the IEEE floating-point standard.

FPLFPASC (Program 7-13) converts from an Intel IEEE-format long floating-point number to an ASCII representation of a floating-point number. The technique used is a binary search of exponents, to reduce the number of floating-point multiplication to be done (divides are avoided wherever possible). We scaled exponents to an appropriate power and multiplied by ten. Then, we multiplied by 100 and ASCII Adjusted after Multiplication (AAM) to convert to character. This cut the number of machine cycles in half, over a multiply by 10.

IEEE long format has an 11-digit binary exponent biased by 1023. It appears in memory reversed from its form in registers. An ASCII representation is a string in the form:

[–]*digit.digits*E[–]

where [–] indicates an optional minus sign; *digit* is an ASCII digit preceding the decimal point (.); *digits* is one or more ASCII digits following the decimal point; and E begins the exponent.

Conversion to ASCII of a valid long floating-point number is always possible. Infinity is checked for and is returned as 9.9E999 or – 9.9E999, depending on the number's sign. Zero is returned as 0.0E0. Zero and infinity are returned for exponents of 00000000000 and 11111111111, respectively. The fraction is not checked in either case (ignoring NaNs).

EAX:EDX contains the long floating-point number. BX is assumed to point to a string area of (at least) 25 bytes. The sign is transferred to the output and the number is replaced by its absolute value if it is negative. The decimal exponent is then created by scaling the number to a value between 1.0 and 10.0. The digit is extracted, converted to ASCII, and placed in the output followed by a decimal point.

FPASCLFP (Program 7-14) does the opposite conversion. Both routines make extensive use of the 80386 extended register set. They also assume the presence of a numeric coprocessor (in our case, an 80287). The functioning of an 80387 is essentially the same.

Conversion can over- or underflow, which results in a zero or infinity, depending on whether you under- or overflowed. FPASCLFP converts the digits into a quadword, binary number, and then counts digits beyond to convert to the proper exponent value. Then FPASCLFP converts the exponent and combines the two to form the number. The final exponent is formed by using a binary search.

IBM System/370 to Intel and Back

FLIPS (Program 7-15) provides data conversions for a word, a doubleword, and a quadword from mainframe style (such as used on IBM mainframes) to the Intel style. Intel stores the registers low-order byte to low-order address and high-order byte to high-order address. In memory, then, it makes the bytes look "reversed" on a byte basis. Mainframes generally store bytes exactly as they appear in registers.

If you're getting data from a mainframe, either through a communications line or on magnetic tape, that data will be in the mainframe order. Before you can actually work with it on a system based on an Intel microprocessor, you have to flip it around to make it usable.

Program 7-1: CODEDRV

```
Microsoft (R) Macro Assembler Version 5.00

                                        PAGE    55,132
                                        .386
                                ;
                                ; Name:     CODEDRV
                                ;
                                ; Purpose:  This program drives the various code conversion routines.
                                ;           This provides both a test for the routines themselves and
                                ;           a working example of the calling sequences.
                                ;
                                ; Inputs:   Input is typed at the keyboard in response to prompts.
                                ;
                                ; Process:  The input is passed through the conversion routines, first
                                ;           converting from the ASCII to either binary or EBCDIC.  The
                                ;           reverse conversion is then done and the output displayed.
                                ;
                                ; Outputs:  The reverse conversion results are displayed for
                                ;           inspection.
                                ;
                                ; Declare the routines we are going to use
                                ;
                                        EXTRN   CODEEBAS:PROC
                                        EXTRN   CODEASEB:PROC
                                        EXTRN   CODEASB:PROC
                                        EXTRN   CODEBAS:PROC
                                        EXTRN   CODEHXTB:PROC
                                        EXTRN   CODEBTHX:PROC

 0000                           stack   SEGMENT para 'STACK' STACK
 0000  0100[                            dq      256 DUP(?)
        ???????????????
        ?
                        ]

 0800                           stack   ENDS
 0000                           data    SEGMENT para
 0000  00000000                 number  dd      0
 0004  0100[                    string1 db      256 DUP(?)          ; String scratch area
         ??
                        ]

 0104  0100[                    string2 db      256 DUP(?)          ; Second scratch area
         ??
                        ]

 0204  0A 0D                    string3p db     10,13
 0206  0100[                    string3 db      256 DUP(?)          ; Third scratch area
         ??
                        ]

 0306  0A 0D 49 6E 76 61 6C     badhexm db      10,13,"Invalid hex entered.$"
       69 64 20 68 65 78 20
       65 6E 74 65 72 65 64
       2E 24
 031D  0A 0D 4E 75 6D 62 65     oflowmsg db     10,13,"Number overflows extended register.$"
       72 20 6F 76 65 72 66
       6C 6F 77 73 20 65 78
```

```
      74 65 6E 64 65 64 20
      72 65 67 69 73 74 65
      72 2E 24
0343  0A 0D 43 6F 6E 76 65     numbert    db       10,13,"Converted to: $"
      72 74 65 64 20 74 6F
      3A 20 24
0354  0A 0A 0D 45 6E 74 65     query1     db       10,10,13,"Enter a string to convert: $"
      72 20 61 20 73 74 72
      69 6E 67 20 74 6F 20
      63 6F 6E 76 65 72 74
      3A 20 24
0373  0A 0A 0D 45 6E 74 65     query2     db       10,10,13,"Enter a number to convert: $"
      72 20 61 20 6E 75 6D
      62 65 72 20 74 6F 20
      63 6F 6E 76 65 72 74
      3A 20 24
0392  0A 0A 0D 45 6E 74 65     query3     db       10,10,13,"Enter a string of hex digits "
      72 20 61 20 73 74 72
      69 6E 67 20 6F 66 20
      68 65 78 20 64 69 67
      69 74 73 20
03B2  74 6F 20 63 6F 6E 76                db       "to convert: $"
      65 72 74 3A 20 24
03BF                           data       ENDS
0000                           code       SEGMENT para 'CODE' USE16 PUBLIC
                                          ASSUME   CS:code, DS:data
                               ;
                               ; Set up the environment
                               ;
0000                           Begin:
0000  B8 ---- R                           mov      AX,data            ; Get data segment pointer
0003  8E D8                               mov      DS,AX              ; into DS,
0005  8E C0                               mov      ES,AX              ; and ES.
0007  2B F6                               sub      SI,SI              ; Clear indices
0009  2B FF                               sub      DI,DI
                               ;
                               ; First convert ascii to ebcdic and back
                               ;
000B                           nexttry:
000B  8D 16 0354 R                        lea      DX,query1          ; Get a string to convert
000F  E8 00D2 R                           call     getinp             ;
0012  0B C9                               or       CX,CX              ; Was any entered?
0014  0F 84 00CC R                        jz       Exit               ; No - simple exit
0018  8D 36 0006 R                        lea      SI,string1+2       ; Source string
001C  8D 3E 0104 R                        lea      DI,string2         ; destination string
0020  51                                  push     CX                 ; Save CX
0021  E8 0000 E                           call     Codeaseb           ; Make ebcdic
0024  8D 36 0104 R                        lea      SI,string2         ; Set ebcdic source
0028  8D 3E 0206 R                        lea      DI,string3         ; and ascii destination
002C  59                                  pop      CX                 ; length
002D  51                                  push     CX                 ; save it
002E  E8 0000 E                           call     Codeebas           ; back to ascii
0031  5B                                  pop      BX                 ; Get length back
0032  C6 87 0206 R 24                     mov      string3[BX],'$'    ; Set stopper
0037  8D 16 0204 R                        lea      DX,string3p        ; Point to lf/cr
003B  B4 09                               mov      AH,9               ; Set code for DOS
003D  CD 21                               int      21h                ; and put it out.
                               ;
                               ; Do ascii to binary and back
                               ;
003F  8D 16 0373 R                        lea      DX,query2          ; Point to number query.
0043  E8 00D2 R                           call     getinp             ; read a number to convert
```

```
0046  8D 36 0006 R                  lea     SI,string1+2        ; Point to string entered.
004A  E8 0000 E                     call    Codeasb             ; Convert it to binary.
004D  0F 82 00C2 R                  jc      oflomsg             ; If too large - do message
0051  66| A3 0000 R                 mov     number,EAX          ; Save the number
0055  8D 3E 0104 R                  lea     DI,string2          ; Point to output string.
0059  E8 0000 E                     call    Codebas             ; Convert it back.
005C  8D 16 0343 R                  lea     DX,numbert          ; Point to text
0060  B4 09                         mov     AH,9
0062  CD 21                         int     21h                 ; and write it
0064  B4 02                         mov     AH,2                ; Set code for single byte
0066                        numbout:
0066  8A 15                         mov     DL,BYTE PTR [DI]    ; Get a byte
0068  0A D2                         or      DL,DL               ; test for stopper
006A  0F 84 0073 R                  jz      numbout0            ; done
006E  CD 21                         int     21h
0070  47                            inc     DI                  ; Point to next
0071  EB F3                         jmp     numbout             ; Do the next.
0073                        numbout0:
                            ;
                            ; Do hex to binary and back
                            ;
0073  8D 16 0392 R                  lea     DX,query3           ; Request the data
0077  E8 00D2 R                     call    getinp              ; in the string1 area.
007A  D1 E9                         shr     CX,1                ; Get number of pairs.
007C  E3 F5                         jcxz    numbout0            ; require one.
007E  8D 36 0006 R                  lea     SI,string1+2        ; Point to the input data
0082  8D 3E 0104 R                  lea     DI,string2          ; and to the output.
0086  51                            push    CX                  ; Save the count
0087  FC                            cld                         ; Set direction up.
0088                        nexthex:
0088  8A 24                         mov     AH,BYTE PTR[SI]     ; Get the high byte
008A  46                            inc     SI
008B  AC                            lodsb                       ; and the low
008C  E8 0000 E                     call    Codehxtb            ; Convert them
008F  0F 82 00B6 R                  jc      badhex              ; If an error - quit
0093  AA                            stosb                       ; Store the converted byte.
0094  E2 F2                         loop    nexthex             ; Back for the next pair.
0096  59                            pop     CX                  ; Restore the pair count
0097  8D 36 0104 R                  lea     SI,string2          ; Set the binary pointer
009B  8D 3E 0206 R                  lea     DI,string3          ; and the display pointer
009F                        nextbin:
009F  AC                            lodsb                       ; Get a byte
00A0  E8 0000 E                     call    codebthx            ; convert it to display form
00A3  86 C4                         xchg    AL,AH               ; Flip the bytes
00A5  AB                            stosw                       ; and put them down
00A6  E2 F7                         loop    nextbin             ; do all pairs
00A8  C6 05 24                      mov     BYTE PTR[DI],'$'    ; Terminate the string
00AB  8D 16 0204 R                  lea     DX,string3p         ; put it out
00AF  B4 09                         mov     AH,9                ;
00B1  CD 21                         int     21h
00B3  E9 000B R                     jmp     nexttry             ; Go try again
00B6                        badhex:
00B6  59                            pop     CX                  ; clear the stack
00B7  8D 16 0306 R                  lea     DX,badhexm          ; Point to the message
00BB  B4 09                         mov     AH,9                ; Set code
00BD  CD 21                         int     21h                 ; display it
00BF  E9 000B R                     jmp     nexttry             ; and loop
00C2                        oflomsg:
00C2  8D 16 031D R                  lea     DX,oflowmsg         ; Set message
00C6  B4 09                         mov     AH,9
00C8  CD 21                         int     21h                 ; put it out
00CA  EB A7                         jmp     numbout0            ; continue
```

```
00CC                            Exit:
00CC  B0 00                             mov     AL,0                ; Set return code
00CE  B4 4C                             mov     AH,04ch             ; Set good-by
00D0  CD 21                             int     21h                 ; Return to the system
                                ;
                                ; Read a string in response to a prompt
                                ; The prompt must be in DX.  The string will be returned in string.
                                ;
00D2                            getinp  PROC
00D2  50                                push    AX                  ; Save registers
00D3  56                                push    SI
00D4  B4 09                             mov     AH,9                ; and dos request
00D6  CD 21                             int     21h                 ; put out the string
00D8  8D 16 0004 R                      lea     DX,string1          ; point to input area
00DC  C6 06 0004 R FE                   mov     string1,254         ; Set max length in
00E1  B4 0A                             mov     AH,10               ; Ask for read of string
00E3  CD 21                             int     21h                 ; from DOS.
00E5  8D 1E 0006 R                      lea     BX,string1+2        ; Point to just read data
00E9  8A 0E 0005 R                      mov     CL,string1+1        ; Get length read
00ED  B5 00                             mov     CH,0                ; as a word.
00EF  8B F1                             mov     SI,CX               ; Set length
00F1  C6 84 0006 R 00                   mov     string1+2[SI],0     ; and make an asciiz string.
00F6  5E                                pop     SI
00F7  58                                pop     AX                  ; Restore registers
00F8  C3                                ret                         ; and return.
00F9                            getinp  ENDP

00F9                            code    ENDS
                                        END     Begin
```

Program 7-2: CODEHXTB

```
Microsoft (R) Macro Assembler Version 5.00


                                        PAGE      55,132
                                        .386
0000                            code    SEGMENT   para 'CODE' PUBLIC USE16
                                        ASSUME    CS:code, DS:code, SS:code
                                ;
                                ; Name:     Codehxtb
                                ;
                                ; Purpose: The following procedure provides conversion from
                                ;          hexadecimal representation into binary.
                                ;
                                ;
                                ; Inputs:  AH has the hex value for the left nibble.
                                ;          AL has the hex value for the right nibble.
                                ;
                                ; Process: Each nibble is converted and at the same time edited to
                                ;          ensure that the presented value is 0-9 or A-F (a-f).
                                ;          An error causes carry to be set and an immediate return.
                                ;
                                ;          The high nibble value is shifted left 4 bits and combined
                                ;          with the low nibble in AL, carry is reset and we return.
                                ;
                                ; Output:  AL has the binary value if the hex values were valid.
                                ;          Carry is reset.
                                ;
                                ;          If the hex values are in error, AL is undefined and
                                ;          Carry is set.
                                ;
                                ;
                                          PUBLIC  Codehxtb          ; Make name known.
                                ;
0000                            Codehxtb  PROC
0000  80 EC 30                            sub     AH,'0'            ; Convert the high nibble
0003  0F 88 0040 R                        js      badhex            ; Negative is bad
0007  80 FC 09                            cmp     AH,9              ; Was it 0-9?
000A  0F 86 001F R                        jna     gothi             ; Yes, High is converted.
000E  80 E4 DF                            and     AH,0dfh           ; Make lower into upper case.
0011  80 EC 07                            sub     AH,'@'-'9'        ; Must have been A-F
0014  0F 88 0040 R                        js      badhex            ; No - was between 9 and A
0018  80 FC 0F                            cmp     AH,15             ; Check if valid.
001B  0F 87 0040 R                        ja      badhex            ; Above is bad!
001F                            gothi:
001F  2C 30                               sub     AL,'0'            ; Convert the low nibble
0021  0F 88 0040 R                        js      badhex            ; Negative is bad
0025  3C 09                               cmp     AL,9              ; Was it 0-9?
0027  0F 86 0039 R                        jna     gotlo             ; Yes, low is converted.
002B  24 DF                               and     AL,0dfh           ; Make lower into upper case.
002D  2C 07                               sub     AL,'@'-'9'        ; Must have been A-F
002F  0F 88 0040 R                        js      badhex            ; No - was between 9 and A
0033  3C 0F                               cmp     AL,15             ; Check if valid.
0035  0F 87 0040 R                        ja      badhex            ; Above is bad!
0039                            gotlo:
0039  C0 E4 04                            shl     AH,4              ; Position high nibble
003C  02 C4                               add     AL,AH             ; Combine with low
003E  F8                                  clc                       ; Clear the carry flag
003F  C3                                  ret                       ; and return.
0040                            badhex:
```

```
0040  F9                              stc                               ; Set the carry flag
0041  C3                              ret                               ; and return.
0042                     Codehxtb     ENDP
0042                     code         ENDS
                                      END
```

Program 7-3: CODEBTHX

```
Microsoft (R) Macro Assembler Version 5.00

                                     PAGE      55,132
                                     .386
0000                     code        SEGMENT   para 'CODE' PUBLIC USE16
                                     ASSUME    CS:code, DS:code, SS:code
                         ;
                         ; Name:     CODEBTHX
                         ;
                         ; Purpose: The following procedure provides a single byte conversion
                         ;          from binary to displayable hexadecimal (base 16).
                         ;
                         ;
                         ; Inputs:  The byte to be converted is passed in AL.
                         ;
                         ; Process: The left nibble is converted into AH.
                         ;          The right nibble is converted into AL.
                         ;
                         ; Output:  The converted data is returned in AH and AL.
                         ;
                                      PUBLIC   Codebthx
                         ;
0000                     Codebthx     PROC
0000  8A E0                           mov      AH,AL              ; Copy the byte and
0002  C0 EC 04                        shr      AH,4               ; isolate the left nibble.
0005  24 0F                           and      AL,15              ; Isolate the right nibble.
0007  80 C4 30                        add      AH,'0'             ; Add the zone for 0-9
000A  80 FC 39                        cmp      AH,'9'             ; Is it above 9?
000D  0F 86 0014 R                    jna      highok             ; If not - we are ok.
0011  80 C4 07                        add      AH,'@'-'9'         ; Shift to A-F.
0014                     highok:
0014  04 30                           add      AL,'0'             ; We do the same for the low 4.
0016  3C 39                           cmp      AL,'9'             ; Is it ok?
0018  0F 86 001E R                    jna      lowisok            ; Yes, skip
001C  04 07                           add      AL,'@'-'9'         ; shift to A-F
001E                     lowisok:
001E  C3                              ret                         ; and return.
001F                     Codebthx     ENDP
001F                     code         ENDS
                                      END
```

Program 7-4: CODEEBAS

```
Microsoft (R) Macro Assembler Version 5.00


                                        PAGE      55,132
                                        .386
 0000                           code    SEGMENT   para 'CODE' PUBLIC USE16
                                        ASSUME    CS:code, DS:code, SS:code

                                ; Name:     CODEEBAS
                                ;
                                ; Purpose:  The following procedure provides a conversion from
                                ;           EBCDIC (the code used by the IBM 370 mainframes) to
                                ;           ASCII.
                                ;
                                ;
                                ; Inputs:   CX has the count of bytes to translate.
                                ;           DS:SI points to the EBCDIC source to translate.
                                ;           ES:DI points to the destination ASCII data.
                                ;
                                ;
                                ; Process:  The routine simply loops loading, translating, flagging any
                                ;           untranslatable data, and storing the result for CX bytes.
                                ;
                                ; Output:   The area pointed to by ES:DI will have CX bytes of
                                ;           ASCII data as translated from DS:SI.
                                ;           If any of the data presented has no ASCII representation
                                ;           carry will be set on exit, otherwise carry is reset.
                                ;
                                ; Notes:    There are other considerations if general data is to be
                                ;           transferred from 370 class machines.  The 370 orders bytes
                                ;           in memory the same as it does in registers.  This requires
                                ;           that binary data be re-arranged in order to make it usable.
                                ;           i.e. A two byte integer (370 halfword) appears in memory as
                                ;                AH,AL.  An 8086 word appears as AL,AH.
                                ;           The 370 does not use IEEE format floating point so floating
                                ;           point numbers must be converted.
                                ;
                                            PUBLIC Codeebas
                                ;
 0000                           Codeebas    PROC
 0000  E3 1C                                jcxz    getout          ; If count is zero - exit
 0002  57                                   push    DI              ; Save entry registers
 0003  56                                   push    SI
 0004  51                                   push    CX
 0005  53                                   push    BX
 0006  50                                   push    AX
 0007  2A E4                                sub     AH,AH           ; Indicate no error.
 0009  8D 1E 0020 R                         lea     BX,CS:toasc     ; Get translate table offset
 000D  FC                                   cld                     ; Ensure direction is 'up'.
 000E                           ebasnxt:
 000E  AC                                   lodsb                   ; Get a byte to translate
 000F  2E: D7                               xlat    CS:[BX]         ; Translate the byte.
 0011  0A E0                                or      AH,AL           ; Combine for check later.
 0013  AA                                   stosb                   ; Place the result
 0014  E2 F8                                loop    ebasnxt         ; Do CX bytes
 0016  D0 E4                                shl     AH,1            ; Was there an error?
 0018  58                                   pop     AX              ; Restore the entry registers
 0019  5B                                   pop     BX
 001A  59                                   pop     CX
```

```
001B  5E                                pop     SI
001C  5F                                pop     DI
001D  C3                                ret                             ; return.
001E                            getout:
001E  F8                                clc                             ; indicate no error
001F  C3                                ret                             ; and return.

                                ;
                                ; EBCDIC to ASCII translation table
                                ;       Note that extended ASCII is not included in the table.
                                ;       EBCDIC values with no corresponding ASCII translate to
                                ;       values with bit 7 set.  This allows easy detection.
                                ;       If your application defines translations beyond the ASCII
                                ;       character set, this table may be filled in and the error
                                ;       check in the translate routine removed or changed.
                                ;
                                ;       Also note that the full ASCII graphic set is not defined
                                ;       in the EBCDIC graphics.  Where possible, the IBM U.S.
                                ;       standard bit pattern assignments were used.  [ and ] are
                                ;       taken from the 120 graphic print chain.  ^ is taken from
                                ;       the not character.
                                ;
                                ;
                                ;
0020  00 01 02 03 84 09 86      toasc   db      000h,001h,002h,003h,084h,009h,086h,07Fh
      7F
                                ;          0x    NUL  SOH  STX  ETX  SEL   HT  RNL  DEL
0028  88 89 8A 0B 0C 0D 0E              db      088h,089h,08Ah,00Bh,00Ch,00Dh,00Eh,00Fh
      0F
                                ;                 GE  SPS  RPT   VT   FF   CR   SO   SI
0030  10 11 12 13 84 85 08              db      010h,011h,012h,013h,084h,085h,008h,087h
      87
                                ;          1x    DLE  DC1  DC2  DC3  RES   NL   BS  POC
0038  18 19 8A 8B 8C 1D 1E              db      018h,019h,08Ah,08Bh,08Ch,01Dh,01Eh,01Fh
      1F
                                ;                CAN   EM  UBS  CU1  IFS  IGS  IRS  IUS
0040  80 81 1C 83 84 0A 17              db      080h,081h,01Ch,083h,084h,00Ah,017h,01Bh
      1B
                                ;          2x     DS  SOS   FS  WUS  BYP   LF  ETB  ESC
0048  88 89 8A 8B 8C 05 06              db      088h,089h,08Ah,08Bh,08Ch,005h,006h,007h
      07
                                ;                 SA  SFE   SM  CSP  MFA  ENQ  ACK  BEL
0050  80 81 16 83 84 85 86              db      080h,081h,016h,083h,084h,085h,086h,004h
      04
                                ;          3x    -?-  -?-  SYN   IR   PP  TRN  NBS  EOT
0058  88 89 8A 8B 14 15 8E              db      088h,089h,08Ah,08Bh,014h,015h,08Eh,01Ah
      1A
                                ;                SBS   IT  RFF  CU3  DC4  NAK  -?-  SUB
0060  20 81 82 83 84 85 86              db      020h,081h,082h,083h,084h,085h,086h,087h
      87
                                ;          4x         -?-  -?-  -?-  -?-  -?-  -?-  -?-
0068  88 89 8A 2E 3C 28 2B              db      088h,089h,08Ah,02Eh,03Ch,028h,02Bh,08Fh
      8F
                                ;                -?-  -?-  -?-    .    <    (    +  -?-
0070  26 81 82 83 84 85 86              db      026h,081h,082h,083h,084h,085h,086h,087h
      87
                                ;          5x      &  -?-  -?-  -?-  -?-  -?-  -?-  -?-
0078  88 89 21 24 2A 29 3B              db      088h,089h,021h,024h,02Ah,029h,03Bh,05Eh
      5E
                                ;                -?-  -?-    !    $    *    )    ;    ^
0080  2D 2F 82 83 84 85 86              db      02Dh,02Fh,082h,083h,084h,085h,086h,087h
      87
```

```
                              ;      6x    -   / -?-  -?-  -?-  -?-  -?-  -?-
0088  88 89 7C 2C 25 5F 3E          db      088h,089h,07Ch,02Ch,025h,05Fh,03Eh,03Fh
      3F
                              ;            -?-  -?-   |    ,    %    _    >    ?
0090  80 81 82 83 84 85 86          db      080h,081h,082h,083h,084h,085h,086h,087h
      87
                              ;      7x    -?-  -?-  -?-  -?-  -?-  -?-  -?-  -?-
0098  88 60 3A 23 40 27 3D          db      088h,060h,03Ah,023h,040h,027h,03Dh,022h
      22
                              ;            -?-   `    :    #    @    '    =    "
00A0  80 61 62 63 64 65 66          db      080h,061h,062h,063h,064h,065h,066h,067h
      67
                              ;      8x    -?-   a    b    c    d    e    f    g
00A8  68 69 8A 8B 8C 8D 8E          db      068h,069h,08Ah,08Bh,08Ch,08Dh,08Eh,08Fh
      8F
                              ;             h    i  -?-  -?-  -?-  -?-  -?-  -?-
00B0  80 6A 6B 6C 6D 6E 6F          db      080h,06Ah,06Bh,06Ch,06Dh,06Eh,06Fh,070h
      70
                              ;      9x    -?-   j    k    l    m    n    o    p
00B8  71 72 8A 8B 8C 8D 8E          db      071h,072h,08Ah,08Bh,08Ch,08Dh,08Eh,08Fh
      8F
                              ;             q    r  -?-  -?-  -?-  -?-  -?-  -?-
00C0  80 7E 73 74 75 76 77          db      080h,07Eh,073h,074h,075h,076h,077h,078h
      78
                              ;      Ax    -?-   ~    s    t    u    v    w    x
00C8  79 7A 8A 8B 8C 5B 8E          db      079h,07Ah,08Ah,08Bh,08Ch,05Bh,08Eh,08Fh
      8F
                              ;             y    z  -?-  -?-  -?-   [  -?-  -?-
00D0  80 81 82 83 84 85 86          db      080h,081h,082h,083h,084h,085h,086h,087h
      87
                              ;      Bx    -?-  -?-  -?-  -?-  -?-  -?-  -?-  -?-
00D8  88 89 8A 8B 8C 5D 8E          db      088h,089h,08Ah,08Bh,08Ch,05Dh,08Eh,08Fh
      8F
                              ;            -?-   ]  -?-  -?-  -?-  -?-  -?-  -?-
00E0  7B 41 42 43 44 45 46          db      07Bh,041h,042h,043h,044h,045h,046h,047h
      47
                              ;      Cx     {    A    B    C    D    E    F    G
00E8  48 49 8A 8B 8C 8D 8E          db      048h,049h,08Ah,08Bh,08Ch,08Dh,08Eh,08Fh
      8F
                              ;             H    I  -?-  -?-  -?-  -?-  -?-  -?-
00F0  7D 4A 4B 4C 4D 4E 4F          db      07Dh,04Ah,04Bh,04Ch,04Dh,04Eh,04Fh,050h
      50
                              ;      Dx     }    J    K    L    M    N    O    P
00F8  51 52 8A 8B 8C 8D 8E          db      051h,052h,08Ah,08Bh,08Ch,08Dh,08Eh,08Fh
      8F
                              ;             Q    R  -?-  -?-  -?-  -?-  -?-  -?-
0100  5C 81 53 54 55 56 57          db      05Ch,081h,053h,054h,055h,056h,057h,058h
      58
                              ;      Ex     \  -?-    S    T    U    V    W    X
0108  59 5A 8A 8B 8C 8D 8E          db      059h,05Ah,08Ah,08Bh,08Ch,08Dh,08Eh,08Fh
      8F
                              ;             Y    Z  -?-  -?-  -?-  -?-  -?-  -?-
0110  30 31 32 33 34 35 36          db      030h,031h,032h,033h,034h,035h,036h,037h
      37
                              ;      Fx     0    1    2    3    4    5    6    7
0118  38 39 8A 8B 8C 8D 8E          db      038h,039h,08Ah,08Bh,08Ch,08Dh,08Eh,08Fh
      8F
                              ;             8    9  -?-  -?-  -?-  -?-  -?-  -?-
0120                          Codeebas      ENDP
0120                          code          ENDS
                                            END
```

Program 7-5: CODEASEB

```
Microsoft (R) Macro Assembler Version 5.00


                                        PAGE     55,132
                                        .386
 0000                           code    SEGMENT  para 'CODE' PUBLIC USE16
                                        ASSUME   CS:code, DS:code, SS:code

                                ; Name:     CODEASEB
                                ;
                                ; Purpose: The following procedure provides a conversion from ASCII
                                ;          to EBCDIC (the code used by the IBM 370 mainframes).
                                ;
                                ;
                                ; Inputs:  CX has the count of bytes to translate.
                                ;          DS:SI points to the source to translate.
                                ;          ES:DI points to the destination EBCDIC data.
                                ;
                                ;
                                ; Process: The routine simply loops loading, masking, translating and
                                ;          storing the result for CX bytes.
                                ;
                                ; Output:  The area pointed to by ES:DI will have CX bytes of
                                ;          EBCDIC data as translated from DS:SI.
                                ;
                                ; Notes:   There are other considerations if general data is to be
                                ;          transferred to 370 class machines.  The 370 orders bytes
                                ;          in memory the same as it does in registers.  This requires
                                ;          that binary data be re-arranged in order to make it usable.
                                ;          i.e. A two byte integer (word) appears in memory as AL,AH
                                ;               a 370 halfword would appear as AH,AL.
                                ;          The 370 does not use IEEE format floating point so floating
                                ;          point numbers must be converted.
                                ;
                                        PUBLIC   Codeaseb
                                ;
 0000                           Codeaseb PROC
 0000  E3 19                            jcxz     getout              ; If count is zero - exit
 0002  57                               push     DI                  ; Save entry registers
 0003  56                               push     SI
 0004  51                               push     CX
 0005  53                               push     BX
 0006  50                               push     AX
 0007  B4 7F                            mov      AH,7Fh              ; Set the mask for ASCII
 0009  8D 1E 001C R                     lea      BX,CS:ascto         ; Get translate table offset
 000D  FC                               cld                          ; Ensure direction is 'up'.
 000E                           asebnxt:
 000E  AC                               lodsb                        ; Get a byte to translate
 000F  22 C4                            and      AL,AH               ; Don't allow extended bit.
 0011  2E: D7                           xlat     CS:[BX]             ; Translate the byte.
 0013  AA                               stosb                        ; Place the result
 0014  E2 F8                            loop     asebnxt             ; Do CX bytes
 0016  58                               pop      AX                  ; Restore the entry registers
 0017  5B                               pop      BX
 0018  59                               pop      CX
 0019  5E                               pop      SI
 001A  5F                               pop      DI
 001B                           getout:
 001B  C3                               ret                          ; and return.
```

```
                                ;
                                ; ASCII to EBCDIC translation table
                                ;       Note that extended ASCII is not included in the table.
                                ;       If your application defines translations beyond the ASCII
                                ;       character set, this table may be extended and the masking
                                ;       in the translate routine removed.
                                ;
                                ;       Also note that the ASCII graphics are not all defined in
                                ;       the EBCDIC graphic set.  The IBM standard U.S. bit patterns
                                ;       conflict with the bit patterns used for their 120 graphic
                                ;       character print trains.  The translate table uses the IBM
                                ;       standard except for [ and ] which only appear in the 120
                                ;       graphic set.  ^ is translated as the not sign.
                                ;
                                ;
001C  00 01 02 03 37 2D 2E      ascto   db      000h,001h,002h,003h,037h,02Dh,02Eh,02Fh
      2F
                                ;                NUL  SOH  STX  ETX  EOT  ENQ  ACK  BEL
0024  16 05 25 0B 0C 0D 0E              db      016h,005h,025h,00Bh,00Ch,00Dh,00Eh,00Fh
      0F
                                ;                 BS  TAB   LF   VT   FF   CR   SO   SI
002C  10 11 12 13 3C 3D 32              db      010h,011h,012h,013h,03Ch,03Dh,032h,026h
      26
                                ;                DLE  DC1  DC2  DC3  DC4  NAK  SYN  ETB
0034  18 19 3F 27 22 1D 1E              db      018h,019h,03Fh,027h,022h,01Dh,01Eh,01Fh
      1F
                                ;                CAN   EM  SUB  ESC   FS   GS   RS   US
003C  40 5A 7F 7B 5B 6C 50              db      040h,05Ah,07Fh,07Bh,05Bh,06Ch,050h,07Dh
      7D
                                ;                       !    "    #    $    %    &    '
0044  4D 5D 5C 4E 6B 60 4B              db      04Dh,05Dh,05Ch,04Eh,06Bh,060h,04Bh,061h
      61
                                ;                  (    )    *    +    ,    -    .    /
004C  F0 F1 F2 F3 F4 F5 F6              db      0F0h,0F1h,0F2h,0F3h,0F4h,0F5h,0F6h,0F7h
      F7
                                ;                  0    1    2    3    4    5    6    7
0054  F8 F9 7A 5E 4C 7E 6E              db      0F8h,0F9h,07Ah,05Eh,04Ch,07Eh,06Eh,06Fh
      6F
                                ;                  8    9    :    ;    <    =    >    ?
005C  7C C1 C2 C3 C4 C5 C6              db      07Ch,0C1h,0C2h,0C3h,0C4h,0C5h,0C6h,0C7h
      C7
                                ;                  @    A    B    C    D    E    F    G
0064  C8 C9 D1 D2 D3 D4 D5              db      0C8h,0C9h,0D1h,0D2h,0D3h,0D4h,0D5h,0D6h
      D6
                                ;                  H    I    J    K    L    M    N    O
006C  D7 D8 D9 E2 E3 E4 E5              db      0D7h,0D8h,0D9h,0E2h,0E3h,0E4h,0E5h,0E6h
      E6
                                ;                  P    Q    R    S    T    U    V    W
0074  E7 E8 E9 AD E0 BD 5F              db      0E7h,0E8h,0E9h,0ADh,0E0h,0BDh,05Fh,06Dh
      6D
                                ;                  X    Y    Z    [    \    ]    ^    _
007C  79 81 82 83 84 85 86              db      079h,081h,082h,083h,084h,085h,086h,087h
      87
                                ;                  `    a    b    c    d    e    f    g
0084  88 89 91 92 93 94 95              db      088h,089h,091h,092h,093h,094h,095h,096h
      96
                                ;                  h    i    j    k    l    m    n    o
008C  97 98 99 A2 A3 A4 A5              db      097h,098h,099h,0A2h,0A3h,0A4h,0A5h,0A6h
      A6
                                ;                  p    q    r    s    t    u    v    w
0094  A7 A8 A9 C0 6A D0 A1              db      0A7h,0A8h,0A9h,0C0h,06Ah,0D0h,0A1h,007h
      07
```

```
                                    ;                 x    y    z    {    |    }    ~    DEL
009C                                Codeaseb  ENDP
009C                                code      ENDS
                                              END
```

Program 7-6: CODEBAS

```
                                              PAGE      55,132
                                              .386
 0000                                code     SEGMENT   para 'CODE' PUBLIC USE16
                                              ASSUME    CS:code, DS:code, SS:code
                                    ;
                                    ; Name:    CODEBAS
                                    ;
                                    ; Purpose: The following converts a binary double word to an ASCII
                                    ;          decimal string.
                                    ;
                                    ;
                                    ;
                                    ; Inputs:  EAX contain the double word to be converted.
                                    ;          ES:DI contains the pointer to a 12 byte area for the
                                    ;                converted data.
                                    ;
                                    ; Process: The sign is 'captured' and if negative, the absolute
                                    ;          value is used.  The conversion divides the number by 100.
                                    ;          The 2 decimal digit remainder is converted and stored in
                                    ;          the target string from right to left.
                                    ;          The preceding is repeated until the quotient is zero.
                                    ;          If there is a leading zero, it is removed from the string.
                                    ;          (A zero value converts to a single ASCII zero.)
                                    ;
                                    ; Output:  ES:DI point to the first byte of the ASCIIZ string
                                    ;          containing the converted value.
                                    ;
                                    ;
                                    ; Notes:   The technique of repeated division is essentially a brute
                                    ;          force method.  It was chosen because it is easily
                                    ;          expandable to larger binary numbers as well as for its
                                    ;          simplicity.
                                    ;
                                    ;
                                              PUBLIC  Codebas
                                    ;
0000                                Codebas   PROC
0000  66| 52                                  push    EDX                    ; Save entry registers
0002  66| 51                                  push    ECX
0004  66| 50                                  push    EAX
0006  66| 0B C0                               or      EAX,EAX                ; check the sign.
0009  0F 89 0012 R                            jns     positive               ; If positive, no problem.
000D  66| F7 D0                               not     EAX                    ; Get the inverted number
0010  66| 40                                  inc     EAX                    ; plus one.
0012                                positive:
0012  FD                                      std                            ; We create digits from right
0013  83 C7 0B                                add     DI,11                  ; to left.
0016  26: C6 45 01 00                         mov     BYTE PTR ES:1[DI],0    ; Set ASCIIZ terminator.
001B  66| B9 00000064                         mov     ECX,100                ; and the divisor.
0021  66| 2B D2                               sub     EDX,EDX                ; prepare to do division
0024                                divdh:
```

```
0024  66| F7 F1                     div    ECX                 ; Divide by 100
0027  66| 92                        xchg   EDX,EAX             ; Flip quotient and remainder.
                         ;
                         ;  The remainder is the next 2 digits of the number.
                         ;
0029  D4 0A                         aam                        ; We expand the two digits,
002B  0D 3030                       or     AX,'00'             ; put zones on them,
002E  AA                            stosb
002F  8A C4                         mov    AL,AH
0031  AA                            stosb                      ; and store the pair.
0032  66| 2B C0                     sub    EAX,EAX             ; Clear our working register
0035  66| 92                        xchg   EAX,EDX             ; Get quotient for division.
0037  66| 0B C0                     or     EAX,EAX             ; Is there more left?
003A  75 E8                         jnz    divdh               ; Yes - go do it
003C  26: 80 7D 01 30               cmp    BYTE PTR ES:1[DI],'0' ; Leading zero?
0041  0F 85 0046 R                  jne    nolead0             ; No, don't
0045  47                            inc    DI                  ; back up over it.
0046                     nolead0:
0046  66| 58                        pop    EAX                 ; Get number back,
0048  66| 0B C0                     or     EAX,EAX             ; check its sign, and
004B  0F 89 0054 R                  jns    positive2           ; skip if positive.
004F  26: C6 05 2D                  mov    BYTE PTR ES:[DI],'-' ; Set sign
0053  4F                            dec    DI                  ; and make room for it.
0054                     positive2:
0054  47                            inc    DI                  ; Point to first digit.
0055  66| 59                        pop    ECX
0057  66| 5A                        pop    EDX
0059  C3                            ret                        ; and return.
005A                     Codebas    ENDP
005A                     code       ENDS
                                    END
```

Program 7-7: CODEASB

```
                                    PAGE      55,132
                                    .386
0000                        code    SEGMENT   para 'CODE' USE16 PUBLIC
                                    ASSUME    CS:code, DS:code, SS:code

                            ; Name:     CODEASB
                            ;
                            ; Purpose: The following procedure converts an ASCII numeric string
                            ;          to a double word binary equivalent.
                            ;
                            ;
                            ;
                            ; Inputs:  SI points to the string which is to be converted.  It is
                            ;             edited to ensure it is valid data.
                            ;          CX has the count of ASCII characters which may exceed the
                            ;             count of digits.
                            ;
                            ; Process: The procedure scans the string to get the count of digits.
                            ;          The procedure fetches decimal digit pairs from left to
                            ;          right.  The prior result is multiplied by 100, the new pair
                            ;          is converted to binary and added to to the prior result.
                            ;          Each pair in the source is processed.  (If an odd number of
                            ;          digits are presented, the first digit is processed alone.)
                            ;
                            ;
                            ; Output:  If the conversion is without overflow, carry is reset and
                            ;             EAX contains the result.
                            ;          If the conversion overflows, carry is set and EAX is
                            ;             undefined.
                            ;          If no digits are valid, the result is zero in EAX.
                            ;          SI points to the digit following the last character
                            ;             converted and
                            ;          CX contains the remaining count.
                            ;
                            ;
                                    PUBLIC  Codeasb
                            ;
0000                        Codeasb PROC
0000  66| 53                        push    EBX                 ; Save work registers
0002  66| 52                        push    EDX
0004  57                            push    DI
0005  56                            push    SI                  ; Save first character pointer
0006  66| 2B DB                     sub     EBX,EBX             ; Clear the result
0009  66| 2B C0                     sub     EAX,EAX             ; and rest of EAX.
000C  FC                            cld                         ; Force direction to up.
000D  80 3C 2D                      cmp     BYTE PTR[SI],'-'    ; Negative?
0010  0F 84 001B R                  je      signed              ; Yes
0014  80 3C 2B                      cmp     BYTE PTR[SI],'+'    ; Positive
0017  0F 85 001D R                  jne     unsigned            ; No - skip
001B                        signed:
001B  46                            inc     SI                  ; step over of sign.
001C  49                            dec     CX                  ; and counting it
001D                        unsigned:
001D  56                            push    SI                  ; Save for conversion pass
001E  8B F9                         mov     DI,CX               ; Save char count.
0020  BA 0930                       mov     DX,0930h            ; set '0' in DL and 9 in DH.
0023  E3 0B                         jcxz    numdone             ;
0025                        numscan:
0025  AC                            lodsb                       ; Get a possible digit
0026  32 C2                         xor     AL,DL               ;
```

```
0028  3A C6                      cmp    AL,DH               ; Check if it is a digit.
002A  0F 87 0030 R               ja     numdone             ; get out if not
002E  E2 F5                      loop   numscan             ; try another digit.
0030                   numdone:
0030  5E                         pop    SI                  ; Restore for conversion pass
0031  87 CF                      xchg   CX,DI               ; Set original count
0033  2B CF                      sub    CX,DI               ; and get digit count
0035  F6 C1 01                   test   CL,1                ; Is the count odd?
0038  0F 84 0041 R               jz     cxeven              ; No, skip
003C  AC                         lodsb                      ; the load of the first byte
003D  24 0F                      and    AL,15               ; as a binary value.
003F  8A D8                      mov    BL,AL               ; We have a starting value.
0041                   cxeven:
0041  D1 E9                      shr    CX,1                ; divide the count by 2
0043  0F 84 0077 R               jz     outgood             ; If the result is zero - out.
0047  66| 55                     push   EBP                 ;
0049  66| BD 00000064            mov    EBP,100             ; Get multiplier in a register
004F                   dopair:
004F  AD                         lodsw                      ; Get pair of bytes (reversed)
0050  86 C4                      xchg   AL,AH               ; back in proper order
0052  25 0F0F                    and    AX,0F0fh            ; clear zones
0055  D5 0A                      aad                        ; convert pair to binary.
0057  66| 93                     xchg   EAX,EBX             ; Position accum for mpy
0059  66| F7 E5                  mul    EBP                 ; and make room for digits.
005C  66| 0B D2                  or     EDX,EDX             ; Check if overflow
005F  0F 85 008E R               jnz    outoflo             ; Out if it did
0063  66| 0B C0                  or     EAX,EAX             ; Check overflow into sign.
0066  0F 88 008E R               js     outoflo             ; Out if it did
006A  66| 03 C3                  add    EAX,EBX             ; Add new pair in.
006D  0F 80 008E R               jo     outoflo             ; exit if overflow occurred
0071  66| 93                     xchg   EAX,EBX             ; Put registers back
0073  E2 DA                      loop   dopair              ; Do each pair
0075  66| 5D                     pop    EBP                 ; Restore EBP
0077                   outgood:                             ; Go back
0077  66| 8B C3                  mov    EAX,EBX             ; with number in EAX.
007A  8B CF                      mov    CX,DI               ; Remaining count in CX
007C  5B                         pop    BX                  ; Restore the sign pointer.
007D  80 3F 2D                   cmp    BYTE PTR [BX],'-'   ; Was a minus entered?
0080  0F 85 0087 R               jne    positive            ; nope
0084  66| F7 D8                  neg    EAX                 ; Force it minus
0087                   positive:
0087  F8                         clc                        ; Clear carry (neg could set)
0088  5F                         pop    DI                  ; Restore the entry registers
0089  66| 5A                     pop    EDX
008B  66| 5B                     pop    EBX
008D  C3                         ret                        ; and return.
008E                   outoflo:
008E  66| 5D                     pop    EBP                 ; Restore work register.
0090  F9                         stc                        ; Set error then
0091  5F                         pop    DI                  ; Clear sign pointer
0092  5F                         pop    DI                  ; Restore the entry registers
0093  66| 5A                     pop    EDX
0095  66| 5B                     pop    EBX
0097  C3                         ret                        ; and return.
0098                   Codeasb   ENDP
0098                   code      ENDS
                                 END
```

Program 7-8: FPDRIVE

```
Microsoft (R) Macro Assembler Version 5.00


                                                PAGE    55,132
                                                .386
                                        ;
                                        ; Name:     FPDRIVE
                                        ;
                                        ; Purpose:  This program exercises the floating point conversion
                                        ;           routines.
                                        ;
                                        ; Inputs:   The user is prompted for a floating point number.
                                        ;           The number must be of the form (-)d*.d*e(-)d* where
                                        ;           (-) is an optional minus sign, d* is one or more numeric
                                        ;           digits, . is a required decimal and e is a required start
                                        ;           of exponent signal.  e may be either upper or lower case.
                                        ;
                                        ; Process:  The user is prompted for a floating-point number.  A null
                                        ;           terminates the program.  The floating-point number will be
                                        ;           converted to an IEEE long floating-point number, an error
                                        ;           causes a reprompt.  The floating-point number is then
                                        ;           converted to ASCII and displayed.  It is displayed in
                                        ;           hexadecimal, converted to IBM format, displayed in
                                        ;           hexadecimal, converted to IEEE format and displayed in
                                        ;           hexadecimal again.  The number is then converted to short
                                        ;           form, displayed in hexadecimal, converted to long form,
                                        ;           displayed in hexadecimal and converted to ASCII and
                                        ;           displayed again.  The program then loops.
                                        ;
                                        ; Outputs:  The output is the displayed results of each conversion.
                                        ;
                                        ;
                                        ; Declare the routines we are going to use
                                        ;


                                        ;
                                        ; Declare those routines we are going to use
                                        ;
                                                EXTRN   Fpasclfp:PROC
                                                EXTRN   Fplfpasc:PROC
                                                EXTRN   Fpieeebm:PROC
                                                EXTRN   Fpibmeee:PROC
                                                EXTRN   Fplongts:PROC
                                                EXTRN   Fpstlong:PROC
                                                EXTRN   Codebthx:PROC
0000                                    stack   SEGMENT para 'STACK' STACK
0000  0100[                                     dq      256 DUP(?)
        ???????????????
        ?
                    ]

0800                                    stack   ENDS
0000                                    data    SEGMENT para
0000  0100[                             string  db      256 DUP(?)          ; String scratch area
        ??
                    ]

0100  0100[                             string2 db      256 DUP(?)
```

```
          ??
                    ]

0200  0A 0D 24               lfcr      db      10,13,'$'           ; linefeed and carriage return
0203  0A 0D 45 6E 74 65 72   query     db      10,13,"Enter a floating point number: $"
      20 61 20 66 6C 6F 61
      74 69 6E 67 20 70 6F
      69 6E 74 20 6E 75 6D
      62 65 72 3A 20 24
0225  9A99993E                         dd      3.0e-1
0229  333333333333D33F                 dq      3.0e-1
0231                         data       ENDS
0000                         code      SEGMENT para 'CODE' USE16 PUBLIC
                                       ASSUME  CS:code, DS:data

                             ;
                             ; Set up the environment
                             ;
0000                         Begin:
0000  B8 ---- R                        mov     AX,data             ; Get data segment pointer
0003  8E D8                            mov     DS,AX               ; into DS,
0005  8E C0                            mov     ES,AX               ; and ES.
0007  2B F6                            sub     SI,SI               ; Clear indices
0009  2B FF                            sub     DI,DI
000B                         cvtloop:
000B  8D 16 0203 R                     lea     DX,query            ; point to query
000F  E8 00CB R                        call    getinp              ; Get a number
0012  8D 16 0200 R                     lea     DX,lfcr             ; space down
0016  B4 09                            mov     AH,9                ;
0018  CD 21                            int     21h
001A  E3 5E                            jcxz    Exit                ; A null ends the program
001C  8B F3                            mov     SI,BX               ; Point to the number
001E  E8 0000 E                        call    fpasclfp            ; convert it
0021  72 E8                            jc      cvtloop             ; If error get another
0023  66| A3 0100 R                    mov     DWORD PTR string2,EAX ; set low half
0027  66| 89 16 0104 R                 mov     DWORD PTR string2+4,EDX ; set high half
002C  E8 00A6 R                        call    cvtprt              ; convert it and print
002F  E8 0080 R                        call    hexprt2             ; dump it in hex
0032  8D 36 0100 R                     lea     SI,string2          ; Point to it
0036  E8 0000 E                        call    Fpieeebm            ; convert to IBM format
0039  E8 0080 R                        call    hexprt2             ; dump it
003C  E8 0000 E                        call    Fpibmeee            ; re-convert it
003F  E8 0080 R                        call    hexprt2             ; dump it
0042  66| A1 0100 R                    mov     EAX,DWORD PTR string2 ; Prepare to print
0046  66| 8B 16 0104 R                 mov     EDX,DWORD PTR string2+4
004B  E8 00A6 R                        call    cvtprt              ; convert it again
004E  E8 0000 E                        call    Fplongts            ; Get as short
0051  66| 8B D0                        mov     EDX,EAX             ; Set number as 'high'
0054  66| 2B C0                        sub     EAX,EAX             ; Clear low half
0057  66| A3 0100 R                    mov     DWORD PTR string2,EAX ; set low half
005B  66| 89 16 0104 R                 mov     DWORD PTR string2+4,EDX ; set high half
0060  E8 0080 R                        call    hexprt2             ; dump it
0063  66| 8B C2                        mov     EAX,EDX             ; Set short to cvt
0066  E8 0000 E                        call    Fpstlong            ; convert to long
0069  66| A3 0100 R                    mov     DWORD PTR string2,EAX ; set low half
006D  66| 89 16 0104 R                 mov     DWORD PTR string2+4,EDX ; set high half
0072  E8 0080 R                        call    hexprt2             ; dump it
0075  E8 00A6 R                        call    cvtprt              ; convert it again
0078  EB 91                            jmp     cvtloop             ; Go get another number

007A                         Exit:
007A  B0 00                            mov     AL,0                ; Set return code
007C  B4 4C                            mov     AH,04ch             ; Set good-by
007E  CD 21                            int     21h                 ; Return to the system
```

```
                                ;
                                ; display the 8 byte string2 area in hex
                                ;
0080                            hexprt2   PROC
0080  66| 60                              pushad
0082  8D 36 0100 R                        lea    SI,string2         ; point to string
0086  B9 0008                             mov    CX,8               ; Want 8 bytes
0089                            hexstrl:
0089  AC                                  lodsb                     ; get a byte
008A  E8 0000 E                           call   Codebthx           ; Convert them
008D  8B D0                               mov    DX,AX              ; save them
008F  86 F2                               xchg   DH,DL              ; print left first
0091  B4 02                               mov    AH,2               ; set dos code
0093  CD 21                               int    21h                ; print it
0095  8A D6                               mov    DL,DH              ; Do right byte
0097  CD 21                               int    21h
0099  E2 EE                               loop   hexstrl            ; loop to do all 8
009B  B4 09                               mov    AH,9               ;
009D  8D 16 0200 R                        lea    DX,lfcr            ; point to lf/cr
00A1  CD 21                               int    21h                ; put it out
00A3  66| 61                              popad
00A5  C3                                  ret
00A6                            hexprt2   ENDP

                                ;
                                ; convert the long float in EAX:EDX to a string and display it.
                                ;
00A6                            cvtprt    PROC
00A6  66| 60                              pushad                    ; save the registers
00A8  8D 1E 0000 R                        lea    BX,string          ; Point to string work
00AC  E8 0000 E                           call   Fplfpasc           ; Convert to string
00AF  8B D9                               mov    BX,CX
00B1  C6 87 0000 R 0D                     mov    string[BX],13
00B6  C6 87 0001 R 0A                     mov    string[BX+1],10    ; c/r lf
00BB  C6 87 0002 R 24                     mov    string[BX+2],'$'   ; and dos stopper
00C0  8D 16 0000 R                        lea    DX,string          ; point to string
00C4  B4 09                               mov    AH,9               ; Request print
00C6  CD 21                               int    21h                ;
00C8  66| 61                              popad
00CA  C3                                  ret
00CB                            cvtprt    ENDP
                                ;
                                ; Read a string in response to a prompt
                                ; The prompt must be in DX.  The string will be returned in string.
                                ;
00CB                            getinp    PROC
00CB  50                                  push   AX                 ; Save registers
00CC  56                                  push   SI
00CD  B4 09                               mov    AH,9               ; and dos request
00CF  CD 21                               int    21h                ; put out the string
00D1  8D 16 0000 R                        lea    DX,string          ; point to input area
00D5  C6 06 0000 R FE                     mov    string,254         ; Set max length in
00DA  B4 0A                               mov    AH,10              ; Ask for read of string
00DC  CD 21                               int    21h                ; from DOS.
00DE  8D 1E 0002 R                        lea    BX,string+2        ; Point to just read data
00E2  8A 0E 0001 R                        mov    CL,string+1        ; Get length read
00E6  B5 00                               mov    CH,0               ; as a word.
00E8  8B F1                               mov    SI,CX              ; Set length
00EA  C6 84 0002 R 00                     mov    string+2[SI],0     ; and make an asciiz string.
00EF  5E                                  pop    SI
00F0  58                                  pop    AX                 ; Restore registers
00F1  C3                                  ret                       ; and return.
```

```
00F2                    getinp  ENDP

00F2                    code    ENDS
                                END     Begin
```

Program 7-9: FPLONGTS

```
                                PAGE    55,132
                                .386
0000                    code    SEGMENT para 'CODE' PUBLIC USE16
                                ASSUME  CS:code, DS:code, SS:code
                        ;
                        ; Name:     FPLONGTS
                        ;
                        ; Purpose:  The following procedure provides a conversion of an IEEE
                        ;           format long floating point number to an IEEE short format
                        ;           floating point number.
                        ;           IEEE long format has an 11 digit binary exponent biased by
                        ;           1023.  It appears in memory reversed from its form in
                        ;           registers. i.e.
                        ;   bbbbcccc9999aaaa77778888555566663333444411112222eeee0000seeeeeee
                        ;   0       1       2       3       4       5       6       7
                        ;
                        ;           IEEE short format has 8 bits of exponent biased by 127,
                        ;           a 23 bit fraction and appears in memory as:
                        ;           3444455512222333e0000111seeeeeee
                        ;           0       1       2       3
                        ;
                        ;           Conversion from long to short can either overflow or
                        ;           underflow the short exponent.  An overflow will return a
                        ;           short infinity while an underflow will return a short zero.
                        ;           In either case the carry flag will be set at return.
                        ;
                        ;
                        ; Inputs:   DS:SI points to an IEEE format long floating point number
                        ;           in memory.  (This is assumed to be a normalized number.)
                        ;
                        ; Process:  The exponent is unbiased and checked for over or underflow.
                        ;           If either occurs, infinity or zero is returned with carry
                        ;           set.  Otherwise, the exponent is biased as a short number,
                        ;           the fraction is truncated to 23 bits, and combined with the
                        ;           new exponent and sign.
                        ;
                        ; Output:   The converted number is returned in EAX.  Carry is set if
                        ;           over or underflow occurred and reset otherwise.
                        ;
                        ;
                                PUBLIC  Fplongts
                        ;
0000                    Fplongts PROC
0000  66| 52                    push    EDX                 ; Save entry registers
0002  66| 53                    push    EBX
0004  66| 2B C0                 sub     EAX,EAX             ; Clear short number

                        ;
                        ; Get the biased exponent.
                        ;
0007  8B 5C 06                  mov     BX,WORD PTR [SI+6]  ; Get seeeeeeeeeee1111
```

```
000A  8B D3                        mov   DX,BX              ; preserve sign.
000C  C1 EB 04                     shr   BX,4               ; then 0000seeeeeeeeee
000F  81 E3 07FF                   and   BX,07ffh           ; and  00000eeeeeeeeee
0013  0F 84 0058 R                 jz    alldone            ; Get out if zero.
0017  81 EB 03FF                   sub   BX,1023            ; Unbias the exponent.
001B  83 C3 7F                     add   BX,127             ; Re-bias as short.
001E  83 FB 01                     cmp   BX,1               ; check for short underflow.
0021  0F 8C 005D R                 jl    setcyz             ; If so - exit with a zero+cy
0025  8A E6                        mov   AH,DH              ; Copy sign to return reg.
0027  0D 7F80                      or    AX,07f80h          ; Set signed short infinity.
002A  66| C1 E0 10                 shl   EAX,16             ; Position exponent and sign.
002E  81 FB 00FE                   cmp   BX,254             ; check to max exponent.
0032  0F 8F 0058 R                 jg    alldone            ; and get out if >= to max.
                          ;
                          ; Position as short exponent and get the sign back
                          ;
0036  C1 E3 07                     shl   BX,7               ; position exponent.
0039  81 E2 8000                   and   DX,08000h          ; Isolate the sign
003D  0B DA                        or    BX,DX              ; and combine with exponent.
003F  66| C1 E3 10                 shl   EBX,16             ; Position for short fraction.
                          ;
                          ; Prepare to get the fraction into position.
                          ;
0043  66| 8B 44 04                 mov   EAX,DWORD PTR [SI+4] ; Load high 32 bits
0047  66| 8B 14                    mov   EDX,DWORD PTR [SI]   ; and low 32 bits.
004A  66| 0F A4 D0 03              shld  EAX,EDX,3          ; Keep 23 fraction bits.
004F  66| 25 007FFFFF              and   EAX,007fffffh      ; Clear top 9 to
0055  66| 0B C3                    or    EAX,EBX            ; combine with sign + exponent.
                          ;                                   (also clears carry flag)
                          ;
                          ; and exit
                          ;
0058                      alldone:
0058  66| 5B                       pop   EBX                ; Restore the entry registers
005A  66| 5A                       pop   EDX
005C  C3                           ret                      ; and return.
005D                      setcyz:
005D  0A C0                        or    AL,AL              ; Force a zero
005F  F9                           stc                      ; and a carry
0060  EB F6                        jmp   alldone            ; and exit
0062                      Fplongts ENDP
0062                      code     ENDS
                                   END
```

Program 7-10: FPSTLONG

```
Microsoft (R) Macro Assembler Version 5.00


                                      PAGE      55,132
                                      .386
0000                          code    SEGMENT   para 'CODE' PUBLIC USE16
                                      ASSUME    CS:code, DS:code, SS:code

                              ; Name:     FPSTLONG
                              ;
                              ; Purpose: The following procedure provides a conversion of an IEEE
                              ;          format short floating point number to an IEEE long format
                              ;          floating point number.
                              ;          IEEE long format has an 11 digit binary exponent biased by
                              ;          1023.  It appears in memory reversed from its form in
                              ;          registers. i.e.
                              ;   bbbbcccc9999aaaa7777888855556666333344441111222eeee0000seeeeeee
                              ;   0       1       2       3       4       5       6       7
                              ;
                              ;          IEEE short format has 8 bits of exponent biased by 127, a
                              ;          23 bit fraction and appears in memory as:
                              ;          34444555512222333e0000111seeeeeee
                              ;          0       1       2       3
                              ;
                              ;          Conversion from short to long can neither overflow nor
                              ;          underflow the long exponent.  Zero and short infinity must
                              ;          be checked for and preserved.  Infinity will be recognized
                              ;          and carry set on its return.
                              ;
                              ;
                              ; Inputs:  EAX contains an IEEE format short floating point number.
                              ;          (This is assumed to be a normalized number.)
                              ;
                              ; Process: The exponent is unbiased and checked for zero or infinity.
                              ;          If zero, return is made with a long zero.
                              ;          Infinity is converted to long infinity and returned with
                              ;          carry set.  Otherwise, the exponent is biased as a long
                              ;          number, the fraction's 23 bits are extended with zeros and
                              ;          combined with the new exponent and sign.
                              ;
                              ; Output:  The converted number is returned in EAX:EDX.  Carry is set
                              ;          if infinity is returned and reset otherwise.
                              ;
                              ;
                                      PUBLIC  Fpstlong
                              ;
0000                          Fpstlong  PROC
0000  66| 53                          push    EBX               ; Save work register.
0002  66| 2B D2                       sub     EDX,EDX           ; Clear rest of long number.
0005  66| 92                          xchg    EAX,EDX           ; Position high to EDX.
                              ;
                              ; Get the biased exponent.
                              ;
0007  66| 8B DA                       mov     EBX,EDX           ; Copy number
000A  66| C1 EB 17                    shr     EBX,23            ; Get 0000000seeeeeeee
000E  81 E3 00FF                      and     BX,0ffh           ; isolate exponent
0012  0F 84 0039 R                    jz      alldone           ; If zero - we are done.
0016  81 FB 00FF                      cmp     BX,0ffh           ; Check if infinity
```

```
001A  0F 84 003C R                  jz      infinity          ; If so - return such.
001E  81 C3 0380                    add     BX,1023-127       ; get new bias.
0022  66| 0F AC D0 03               shrd    EAX,EDX,3         ; Shift the fraction into EAX
0027  66| C1 FA 03                  sar     EDX,3             ; make room for long exponent
002B  66| C1 E3 14                  shl     EBX,20            ; Get 0eeeeeeeeeee0000 in high
002F  66| 81 E2 800FFFFF            and     EDX,0800fffffh    ; save sign and clear for
0036  66| 0B D3                     or      EDX,EBX           ; insert of exponent.
                          ;                                     (also clears carry flag)
                          ;
                          ; and exit
                          ;
0039                      alldone:
0039  66| 5B                        pop     EBX               ; Restore the entry registers
003B  C3                            ret                       ; and return.
                          ;
                          ; Form long infinity over short
                          ;
003C                      infinity:
003C  66| 81 E2 80000000            and     EDX,080000000h    ; Preserve sign of infinity
0043  66| 81 CA 7FF00000            or      EDX,07ff00000h    ; make long infinity
004A  F9                            stc                       ; Set carry flag
004B  EB EC                         jmp     alldone           ; and exit.
004D                      Fpstlong  ENDP
004D                      code      ENDS
                                    END
```

Program 7-11: FPIBMEEE

Microsoft (R) Macro Assembler Version 5.00

```
                                        PAGE     55,132
                                        .386
 0000                           code    SEGMENT  para 'CODE' PUBLIC USE16
                                        ASSUME   CS:code, DS:code, SS:code

                                ; Name:     FPIBMEEE
                                ;
                                ; Purpose: The following procedure provides a conversion of an IBM
                                ;           format long floating point number to an IEEE long format
                                ;           floating point number.  The IBM 370 format is hexadecimal
                                ;           based and appears in memory in the same form as it does in
                                ;           registers.  i.e.
                                ;    seeeeeee0000111122223333444455556666777788889999aaaabbbbccccdddd
                                ;    0       1       2       3       4       5       6       7
                                ;           IEEE format is binary based and on the 80386 appears
                                ;           reversed in memory from its form in registers. i.e.
                                ;    bbbbcccc9999aaaa777788885555666633334444111122222eeee0000seeeeeee
                                ;    0       1       2       3       4       5       6       7
                                ;
                                ;           IEEE format appears to have 4 bits less precision than IBM
                                ;           format but the average precision of IBM format is 54.5 bits
                                ;           because it is hexadecimal.  The hidden bit in front of the
                                ;           fraction of the IEEE format extends its precision to 53
                                ;           bits.
                                ;
                                ;           The conversion routines ignore this discrepancy.
                                ;
                                ;           The IBM format's exponent base (16) provides a maximum
                                ;           value of 2**(64*4) or 2**(256).  The IEEE format provides a
                                ;           maximum of 2**(1023).  Therefore, there is no problem
                                ;           converting from IBM to IEEE.
                                ;
                                ;
                                ;
                                ;
                                ;
                                ; Inputs:   DS:SI points to an IBM format long floating point number in
                                ;           memory.  (This is assumed to be a normalized number.)  It
                                ;           is in IBM order as it would be if read from a network or
                                ;           file.
                                ;
                                ; Process:  The number is reversed into 80386 format.  The exponent is
                                ;           then converted from IBM to IEEE base in signed form.  The
                                ;           fraction is then re-normalized from IBM to IEEE form.  It
                                ;           is then shifted right to make room for the biased exponent
                                ;           and sign.  The exponent is then biased by 1023, the sign is
                                ;           appended, and the resulting 12 bits are combined with the
                                ;           fraction.  The result is stored over the original number.
                                ;
                                ; Output:   The converted number replaces the input number.
                                ;
                                ;
                                ; Note:     This requires the procedure flip8 from the file FLIPS.
                                ;
                                            EXTRN   Flip8:NEAR
                                            PUBLIC  Fpibmeee
                                ;
```

```
0000                          Fpibmeee    PROC
0000  66| 52                              push    EDX                ; Save entry registers
0002  66| 53                              push    EBX
0004  66| 50                              push    EAX

                              ;
                              ; Get number re-ordered to 80386 order.
                              ;
0006  66| 8B 04                           mov     EAX,DWORD PTR [SI]   ; Get
                              ;                             44445555222233330000l111seeeeeee
0009  8A D8                               mov     BL,AL              ; Save exponent and sign.
000B  66| 8B 54 04                        mov     EDX,DWORD PTR [SI+4] ; and
                              ;                             ccccddddaaaabbbb8888999966667777
000F  E8 0000 E                           call    Flip8              ; convert to
                              ;                        EDX  seeeeeee000011112222333344445555
                              ;                        EAX  66667777888899999aaaabbbbccccdddd
0012  66| 81 E2 00FFFFFF                  and     EDX,00ffffffh      ; Clear out seeeeeee
0019  0F 85 0024 R                        jnz     havenbr            ; Fraction is non zero
001D  66| 0B C0                           or      EAX,EAX            ; Have we got one?
0020  0F 84 006D R                        jz      alldone            ; If zero, we're done.
0024                          havenbr:
                              ;
                              ; Left adjust the fraction's leftmost hex digit
                              ;
0024  66| 0F A4 C2 08                     shld    EDX,EAX,8          ; Get bits shifted to high
0029  66| C1 E0 08                        shl     EAX,8              ; complete shift in low.

                              ;
                              ; Re-scale the exponent.
                              ;
002D  83 E3 7F                            and     BX,07fh            ; and clear out the sign.
0030  83 EB 40                            sub     BX,040h            ; Get as signed, unbiased number.
0033  C1 E3 02                            shl     BX,2               ; Multiply by 4 to get binary exp.
                              ;                                        (2**4)**x=2**(4*x)
                              ;
                              ; Adjust normalization from hexadecimal to IEEE binary.
                              ;       (IBM uses 0.x, IEEE uses 1.b and hides the 1)
                              ;
0036                          normq:
0036  4B                                  dec     BX                 ; Count out the shift.
0037  66| 0F A4 C2 01                     shld    EDX,EAX,1          ; Shift one bit left
003C  0F 82 0045 R                        jc      normal             ; Done if normalized
0040  66| D1 E0                           shl     EAX,1              ; Adjust the lower bits.
0043  EB F1                               jmp     normq              ; Go check if normalized
0045                          normal:
0045  66| D1 E0                           shl     EAX,1              ; Complete the shift of the fraction.

                              ;
                              ; Re-bias the exponent to IEEE (add 1023) and insert the sign.
                              ;
0048  81 C3 03FF                          add     BX,1023            ; Add bias amount
004C  F6 04 80                            test    BYTE PTR [SI],080H ; Check the original sign.
004F  0F 84 0056 R                        jz      positive           ; If ok as is skip the
0053  80 CF 08                            or      BH,08h             ; set of the sign minus.
0056                          positive:
                              ;
                              ; Make room for the exponent and sign.
                              ;
0056  66| 0F AC D0 0C                     shrd    EAX,EDX,12         ; From low of EDX to EAX
005B  66| C1 EA 0C                        shr     EDX,12             ; then make room in EDX.
005F  66| C1 E3 14                        shl     EBX,20             ; Position the exponent and sign
0063  66| 0B D3                           or      EDX,EBX            ; and combine with the fraction.
                              ;
```

```
                                ;  The conversion is done.
                                ;
0066  66| 89 54 04                        mov    DWORD PTR [SI+4],EDX  ; Put number's high 32 down
006A  66| 89 04                            mov    DWORD PTR [SI],EAX   ; and the low 32

006D                            alldone:
006D  66| 58                               pop    EAX                  ; Restore the entry registers
006F  66| 5B                               pop    EBX
0071  66| 5A                               pop    EDX
0073  C3                                   ret                         ; and return.
0074                            Fpibmeee   ENDP
0074                            code       ENDS
                                           END
```

Program 7-12: FPIEEEBM

```
                                        PAGE      55,132
                                        .386
0000                            code    SEGMENT   para 'CODE' PUBLIC USE16
                                        ASSUME    CS:code, DS:code, SS:code

                                ;
                                ; Name:     FPIEEEBM
                                ;
                                ; Purpose: The following procedure provides a conversion of an IEEE
                                ;          format long floating point number to an IBM long format
                                ;          floating point number.  The IBM 370 format is hexadecimal
                                ;          based and appears in memory in the same form as it does in
                                ;          registers.  i.e.
                                ;    seeeeeee00001111222233334444555566667777888899999aaaabbbbccccdddd
                                ;    0        1        2        3        4        5        6        7
                                ;          IEEE format is binary based and on the 80386 appears
                                ;          reversed in memory from its form in registers. i.e.
                                ;    bbbbcccc9999aaaa8888777766665555444433332222111eeee0000seeeeeee
                                ;    0        1        2        3        4        5        6        7
                                ;
                                ;          IEEE format has 10 bits of exponent while IBM format has
                                ;          only 8 (reduced to 6 because IBM uses hexadecimal).
                                ;          Therefore, while the IBM format can hold the IEEE fraction
                                ;          (including the hidden 1. bit) an exponent overflow or
                                ;          underflow could occur.
                                ;
                                ;          The conversion routine represents an underflow as zero and
                                ;          an overflow as the maximum possible number.  If either
                                ;          occurs, the routine returns with carry set (otherwise carry
                                ;          is reset).
                                ;
                                ;
                                ; Inputs:  DS:SI points to an IEEE format long floating point number
                                ;          in memory.  (This is assumed to be a normalized number.)
                                ;
                                ; Process: The exponent is unbiased and the fraction is converted to
                                ;          0.1 format.  The exponent is checked for zero and an IBM
                                ;          format zero is returned if it is.  The exponent is checked
                                ;          for underflow and if so, zero and carry are returned.  The
                                ;          exponent is then checked for overflow and if so, a maximum
                                ;          value IBM number is returned with carry set.  A convertible
```

```
                                ;          number has its exponent converted to a base 16 exponent by
                                ;          shifting right two bits.  The fraction is adjusted to
                                ;          hexadecimal by shifting right for the count given by the
                                ;          two bits shifted out of the exponent.  The exponent is
                                ;          then biased by 64, the sign is appended and the resulting
                                ;          number is stored in reverse form as expected by an IBM 370.
                                ;          Carry is cleared and the routine returns.
                                ;
                                ; Output:  The converted number replaces the input number.  Carry is
                                ;          set if over or underflow occurred and reset otherwise.

                                ;
                                           PUBLIC  Fpieeebm
                                           EXTRN   Flip8:PROC
                                ;
0000                            Fpieeebm   PROC
0000  66| 52                               push    EDX                  ; Save entry registers
0002  66| 51                               push    ECX
0004  66| 53                               push    EBX
0006  66| 50                               push    EAX

                                ;
                                ; Get number in 80386 order.
                                ;
0008  66| 8B 04                            mov     EAX,DWORD PTR [SI]   ; Get low order 32
000B  66| 8B 54 04                         mov     EDX,DWORD PTR [SI+4] ; and the high.
000F  8B 5C 06                             mov     BX,WORD PTR [SI+6]   ; Get seeeeeeeeeee0000
0012  66| 0F A4 C2 0B                      shld    EDX,EAX,11           ; Position fraction to bits 62
0017  66| C1 E0 0B                         shl     EAX,11               ; through 11
001B  66| 0F BA EA 1F                      bts     EDX,31               ; Set hidden one bit.
                                ;
                                ; The fraction is now left adjusted in EAX:EDX
                                ;
0020  2B C9                                sub     CX,CX                ; Assume ok conversion.
0022  C1 EB 04                             shr     BX,4                 ; Position biased exponent
0025  81 E3 07FF                           and     BX,07ffh             ; isolate it
0029  0F 84 0043 R                         jz      iszero               ; and exit if zero.
002D  81 EB 03FF                           sub     BX,03ffh             ; remove the bias
0031  43                                   inc     BX                   ; add one for the right shift.
                                ;
                                ; Check for exponent overflow.
                                ;
0032  81 FB 00FF                           cmp     BX,255               ; check to maximum positive
0036  0F 8F 004C R                         jg      overflow             ; out if overflow.
003A  81 FB FEFD                           cmp     BX,-259              ; check for minimum negative
003E  0F 8D 005C R                         jnl     neither              ; continue if it converts.
0042  49                                   dec     CX                   ; Flag as underflow
0043                            iszero:
0043  66| 2B C0                            sub     EAX,EAX              ; Zero the completed
0046  66| 2B D2                            sub     EDX,EDX              ; 8 byte float number
0049  EB 43 90                             jmp     setit                ; and go put it down.
004C                            overflow:
004C  49                                   dec     CX                   ; Flag as overflow
004D  66| BA 7FFFFFFF                      mov     EDX,7fffffffh        ; Set maximum exponent,
0053  66| B8 FFFFFFFF                      mov     EAX,-1               ; and a fraction of
0059  EB 33 90                             jmp     setit                ; all one bits.
005C                            neither:
005C  8A CB                                mov     CL,BL                ; Get low two
005E  80 E1 03                             and     CL,3                 ; exponent bits as shift count.
0061  80 E9 04                             sub     CL,4
0064  F6 D9                                neg     CL
0066  66| 0F AD D0                         shrd    EAX,EDX,CL           ; Shift fraction to
006A  66| D3 EA                            shr     EDX,CL               ; hexadecimal normalization.
```

```
006D  C1 FB 02                    sar     BX,2                ; Divide exponent by 4
0070  83 C3 41                    add     BX,64+1             ; and add IBM bias amount.
                                                              ; +1 for point position.
0073  80 E3 7F                    and     BL,07fh             ; Clear sign bit and
0076  8A 4C 07                    mov     CL,BYTE PTR [SI+7]  ; Get the sign of the fraction
0079  80 E1 80                    and     CL,080h             ; isolate it and
007C  0A D9                       or      BL,CL               ; Set if negative.
007E  66| C1 E3 18                shl     EBX,24              ; Position new exponent & sign
0082  66| 0F AC D0 08             shrd    EAX,EDX,8           ; make room for it
0087  66| C1 EA 08                shr     EDX,8               ; in EDX
008B  66| 0B D3                   or      EDX,EBX             ; and combine them
                          ;
                          ; Re-order the bytes as we store them into IBM order.
                          ;
008E                      setit:
008E  E8 0000 E                   call    Flip8               ; Reorder the bytes
0091  66| 89 04                   mov     DWORD PTR [SI],EAX  ; Put them down
0094  66| 89 54 04                mov     DWORD PTR [SI+4],EDX  ;
                          ;
                          ; Set carry if needed
                          ;
0098  D0 E5                       shl     CH,1                ; Shift sign into carry.
                          ;
                          ; and exit
                          ;
009A  66| 58                      pop     EAX                 ; Restore the entry registers
009C  66| 5B                      pop     EBX
009E  66| 59                      pop     ECX
00A0  66| 5A                      pop     EDX
00A2  C3                          ret                         ; and return.
00A3                      Fpieeebm  ENDP
00A3                      code      ENDS
                                  END
```

Program 7-13: FPLFPASC

```
Microsoft (R) Macro Assembler Version 5.00


                                        PAGE    55,132
                                        .386
                                        .287
 0000                           code    SEGMENT para 'CODE' USE16 PUBLIC
                                        ASSUME  CS:code, DS:code, SS:code
                                ;
                                ; Name:    FPLFPASC
                                ;
                                ; Purpose: The following procedure provides a conversion from an IEEE
                                ;          format long floating point number to an ASCII
                                ;          representation of a floating point number. IEEE long format
                                ;          has an 11 digit binary exponent biased by 1023.  It appears
                                ;          in memory reversed from its form in registers. i.e.
                                ;   bbbbcccc9999aaaa77778888555566663333444411112222eeee0000seeeeeee
                                ;   0       1       2       3       4       5       6       7
                                ;
                                ;          An ASCII representation is a string of the form:
                                ;          [-]digit.digitsE[-]digits  Where:
                                ;          [-] indicates an optional minus sign,
                                ;          digit is an ASCII digit preceding the decimal point (.),
                                ;          digits is one or more ASCII digits following the decimal
                                ;          point, the E which begins the exponent or the minus sign if
                                ;          the exponent is negative.
                                ;
                                ;          Some possible values are: 0.0E0 for zero, -1.0E0 for -1,
                                ;          -2.345E-3 for -.002345.
                                ;
                                ;          Conversion to ASCII of a valid long floating point number
                                ;          is always possible.  Infinity is checked for and is
                                ;          returned as 9.9E999 or -9.9E999 depending on the number's
                                ;          sign.  Zero is returned as 0.0E0.
                                ;          Zero and infinity are returned for exponents of 00000000000
                                ;          and 11111111111 respectively.  The fraction is not checked
                                ;          in either case.
                                ;
                                ;
                                ; Inputs:  EAX:EDX contains the long floating point number.  BX is
                                ;          assumed to point to a string area of at least 25 bytes.
                                ;
                                ; Process: The number is checked for infinity or zero and if either,
                                ;          is detected, the appropriate values are returned.
                                ;          The sign is transferred to the output and the number is
                                ;          replaced by its absolute value if it was negative.
                                ;          The decimal exponent is then created by scaling the number
                                ;          to a value between 1.0 and 10.0.  The digit is extracted,
                                ;          converted to ASCII and placed in the output followed by a
                                ;          decimal point.
                                ;
                                ;          We then enter the following loop:
                                ;          The integer portion is subtracted from our scaled number.
                                ;          The result is checked for zero and if it is we exit this
                                ;          loop.  Otherwise the result is multiplied by 100.  The
                                ;          result is a new integer portion in the range 100>i>=0
                                ;          which is extracted, converted to ASCII and placed in the
                                ;          output. If our fraction is 15 digits long we exit the loop.
                                ;
```

```
                              ;          If the fraction is 15 digits long, we round it to 14 digits
                              ;          by adding 1 to the 14th digit if digit 15 is 5 or more. If
                              ;          the result is over 9 we 'eat' the digit and propagate the
                              ;          carry to the next digit to the left for as many digits as
                              ;          necessary.
                              ;
                              ;
                              ; Output:  The converted number is returned memory as an ASCIIZ string
                              ;          in the area pointed to by DS:BX.  The length of the string
                              ;          is returned in CX.  All other registers are preserved.
                              ;
                              ;
                              ;
                              ;
 =                            fpnohi     EQU     SS:DWORD PTR[BP-4]   ; High part of float
 =                            fpnolo     EQU     SS:DWORD PTR[BP-8]   ; Low part of float
 =                            fpnumb     EQU     SS:QWORD PTR[BP-8]   ; Complete number
 =                            fpcntl     EQU     SS:WORD PTR[BP-12]   ; Save area for control flags

                              ;
                                         PUBLIC  Fplfpasc
                              ;
0000                          Fplfpasc   PROC
0000  C8 0010 00                         enter   16,0                 ; Get work space
0004  66| 89 56 FC                       mov     fpnohi,EDX           ; Store the number.
0008  66| 89 46 F8                       mov     fpnolo,EAX
000C  57                                 push    DI                   ; Save work registers.
000D  56                                 push    SI
000E  66| 52                             push    EDX
0010  66| 50                             push    EAX
0012  2B FF                              sub     DI,DI                ; Clear index registers
0014  2B F6                              sub     SI,SI
0016  66| 81 E2 7FF00000                 and     EDX,07ff00000h       ; isolate binary exponent
001D  0F 84 0045 R                       jz      outzero              ; Exit if zero.
                              ;
                              ; Infinity may be positive or negative as may the number.
                              ;
0021  66| 0F BA 76 FC 1F                 btr     fpnohi,31            ; Check sign of number
0027  0F 83 002F R                       jnc     positive             ; Positive
002B  C6 07 2D                           mov     BYTE PTR [BX+0],'-'  ; Negative
002E  46                                 inc     SI                   ; count the sign.
002F                          positive:
002F  66| 81 FA 7FF00000                 cmp     EDX,07ff00000h       ; Check if infinity
0036  0F 85 0059 R                       jnz     number               ; No - need to convert.
003A  B9 0007 90                         mov     CX,infsize           ; Set count of bytes.
003E  8D 3E 0262 R                       lea     DI,infinity          ; and address.
0042  EB 09 90                           jmp     moveit               ; go copy infinity.
0045                          outzero:
0045  B9 0005 90                         mov     CX,zersize           ; set count of bytes
0049  8D 3E 0269 R                       lea     DI,zero              ; and address
004D                          moveit:
004D  2E: 8A 05                          mov     AL,BYTE PTR CS:[DI]  ; Get a byte
0050  88 00                              mov     BYTE PTR [BX+SI],AL  ; and put it down
0052  46                                 inc     SI                   ; step indices
0053  47                                 inc     DI
0054  E2 F7                              loop    moveit               ; and copy constant.
0056  E9 01A3 R                          jmp     exit                 ; Then get out
                              ;
                              ; A number needs to be converted.
                              ;
                              ; First we scale the number to the range 1.0<=n<10.0
                              ;
```

```
0059                              number:
0059  9B DB E3                            finit                        ; Reset the box.
005C  D9 7E F4                            fnstcw  fpcntl               ; Preserve control flag state.
005F  8B 46 F4                            mov     AX,fpcntl            ; changing only the round
0062  0D 0C00                             or      AX,0000110000000000b ; Set rounding to truncate
0065  89 46 F4                            mov     fpcntl,AX            ; Put back in memory and
0068  9B D9 6E F4                         fldcw   fpcntl               ; cause truncation not rounding
006C  56                                  push    SI                   ; Save possible sign.
006D  BF 0040                             mov     DI,8*8               ; Set index of powers
0070  BE 0010                             mov     SI,8*2
0073  66| 2B D2                           sub     EDX,EDX              ; Clear accum of powers stepped
0076  DD 46 F8                            fld     fpnumb               ; Set number into unit.
0079  2E: DC 16 0200 R                    fcom    CS:conof1            ; Check to 1.0
007E  9B DF E0                            fstsw   AX                   ; Get results into AX
0081  9E                                  sahf                         ; and then into flags.
0082  0F 82 00AA R                        jb      mustgoup             ; If ST low - need to scale up
                                  ;
                                  ; We need to scale down
                                  ;
0086                              nextdown:
0086  2E: DC 95 01B0 R                    fcom    CS:pospower[DI]      ; Check to positive power
008B  9B DF E0                            fstsw   AX                   ; of ten.
008E  9E                                  sahf
008F  0F 82 009F R                        jb      below                ; If we are under, leave alone.
0093  2E: DD 85 0208 R                    fld     CS:negpower[DI]      ; Bring it down a step
0098  DE C9                               fmul
009A  2E: 03 94 0250 R                    add     DX,CS:valpower[SI]   ; Add the power we stepped.
009F                              below:
009F  83 EE 02                            sub     SI,2
00A2  83 EF 08                            sub     DI,8                 ; Try next lower
00A5  79 DF                               jns     nextdown             ; Go try it
00A7  EB 35 90                            jmp     convert              ; Done - go convert the number.
                                  ;
                                  ; We need to scale up
                                  ;
00AA                              mustgoup:
00AA  2E: DC 95 0208 R                    fcom    CS:negpower[DI]      ; Check to next negative power
00AF  9B DF E0                            fstsw   AX                   ; of ten.
00B2  9E                                  sahf
00B3  0F 87 00C3 R                        ja      above                ; If not lower - leave alone.
00B7  2E: DD 85 01B0 R                    fld     CS:pospower[DI]      ; Bring it up a step
00BC  DE C9                               fmul
00BE  2E: 2B 94 0250 R                    sub     DX,CS:valpower[SI]   ; Down the power we stepped.
00C3                              above:
00C3  83 EF 08                            sub     DI,8                 ; Try next higher
00C6  83 EE 02                            sub     SI,2
00C9  79 DF                               jns     mustgoup             ; Go try it
                                  ;
                                  ; The above can leave us with a value less than 1 - check if it did.
                                  ;
00CB  2E: DC 16 0200 R                    fcom    CS:conof1            ; Check to 1.0
00D0  9B DF E0                            fstsw   AX                   ; Get results into AX
00D3  9E                                  sahf                         ; and then into flags.
00D4  0F 83 00DE R                        jnb     convert              ; If ST isn't low - skip
00D8  2E: DC 0E 01B0 R                    fmul    CS:conof10           ; Get leading digit non zero
00DD  4A                                  dec     DX                   ; and account for it.
                                  ;
                                  ; Now convert the first digit, place it in the output followed by a
                                  ; decimal point.  If the fraction is zero a zero is placed after the
                                  ; decimal and we are done.
                                  ;
00DE                              convert:
00DE  5E                                  pop     SI                   ; Get output pointer back.
```

```
00DF  DD D1                  fst    ST(1)                  ; Copy the number from ST.
00E1  DF 18                  fistp  WORD PTR[BX+SI]        ; Put word in user's area
00E3  DF 00                  fild   WORD PTR[BX+SI]        ; and get the integer back.
00E5  80 08 30               or     BYTE PTR[BX+SI],'0'    ; Put the zone on it
00E8  46                     inc    SI                     ; point to the point position
00E9  C6 00 2E               mov    BYTE PTR[BX+SI],'.'    ; and put it there
00EC  46                     inc    SI                     ; Point to next position.

00ED                 hundreds:
00ED  DE E9                  fsub                          ; Subtract integer ST=ST(1)-ST
00EF  2E: DC 0E 01B8 R       fmul   CS:con100              ; Fraction times 100
00F4  DD D1                  fst    ST(1)                  ; Save a copy.
00F6  DF 5F 18               fistp  WORD PTR[BX+24]        ; Copy integer to memory
00F9  DF 47 18               fild   WORD PTR[BX+24]        ; and back on stack.
00FC  8B 47 18               mov    AX,WORD PTR[BX+24]     ; Get into AX in order to
00FF  D4 0A                  aam                           ; spread to two digits,
0101  0D 3030                or     AX,'00'                ; and place zones on them.
0104  86 E0                  xchg   AH,AL                  ; Reverse them
0106  89 00                  mov    WORD PTR[BX+SI],AX     ; and store them
0108  83 C6 02               add    SI,2                   ; Step the destination
010B  83 FE 10               cmp    SI,16                  ; Did we fill last part
010E  0F 83 0126 R           jnb    donefull               ; Yes, check for rounding.
0112  D8 D1                  fcom                          ; Was this the last pair?
                                                           ; i.e. would ST(1)-ST be <= 0?
0114  9B DF E0               fstsw  AX                     ; Get the resulting condition
0117  9E                     sahf                          ; code into the flags.
                                                           ; Exit if it would. (C0=0)
0118  72 D3                  jc     hundreds               ; Go do more digits.

                     ;
                     ; All digits of the number have been converted.
                     ;
011A  80 78 FF 30            cmp    BYTE PTR[BX+SI-1],'0'  ; Was a zero the last digit?
011E  0F 85 016E R           jnz    doexponent             ; No, leave it alone, but
0122  4E                     dec    SI                     ; overlay it otherwise.
0123  EB 3B 90               jmp    trail0s                ; Go get rid of others.

                     ;
                     ; The fraction filled all digits of the output -
                     ; round it up if ST+.5-ST(1)<=0
                     ;
0126                 donefull:
0126  2E: DC 06 01F8 R       fadd   CS:point5              ; Add the rounding value.
012B  D8 D1                  fcom                          ; Check if we need to round.
012D  9B DF E0               fstsw  AX                     ; Get condition code
0130  9E                     sahf                          ; into the flags
0131  0F 87 0160 R           ja     trail0s                ; If no rounding needed - out.
0135                 donefull0:
0135  4E                     dec    SI                     ; Need to round up
0136  80 38 2E               cmp    BYTE PTR[BX+SI],'.'    ; At decimal point?
0139  0F 84 0148 R           je     moveptq                ; We may have to move it
013D  FE 00                  inc    BYTE PTR[BX+SI]        ; So do it.
013F  80 38 39               cmp    BYTE PTR[BX+SI],'9'    ; Do we have a carry?
0142  77 F1                  ja     donefull0              ; Yes. propagate it.
0144  46                     inc    SI                     ; No. leave it.
0145  EB 19 90               jmp    trail0s                ; Go do trailing zeros

                     ;
                     ; The rounding went into the decimal point.
                     ;
0148                 moveptq:
0148  4E                     dec    SI                     ; Get leading digit
0149  80 38 39               cmp    BYTE PTR[BX+SI],'9'    ; Need to adjust exponent?
014C  0F 85 0154 R           jne    moveptq1               ; We may have to move it
```

```
0150  C6 00 30                         mov     BYTE PTR[BX+SI],'0' ; We do - and make 1.0
0153  42                               inc     DX                  ; Add one to exponent.
0154                          moveptq1:
0154  FE 00                            inc     BYTE PTR[BX+SI]     ; Step the digit
0156  83 C6 02                         add     SI,2                ; point to trailing zero
0159  C6 00 30                         mov     BYTE PTR[BX+SI],'0' ; fill it in
015C  46                               inc     SI                  ; Get next position
015D  EB 0F 90                         jmp     doexponent          ; Go do exponent
                              ;
                              ; Eliminate any trailing zeros
                              ;
0160                          trail0s:
0160  83 FE 03                         cmp     SI,3                ; Check where we are
0163  0F 86 016E R                     jna     doexponent          ; if just x.x - leave it
0167  4E                               dec     SI
0168  80 38 30                         cmp     BYTE PTR[BX+SI],'0' ; Trailing zero
016B  74 F3                            je      trail0s             ; Yes - get rid of most
016D  46                               inc     SI
                              ;
                              ; We only need to convert the power of ten
                              ;
016E                          doexponent:
016E  9B DB E3                         finit                       ; Leave the box neutral.
0171  C6 00 45                         mov     BYTE PTR[BX+SI],'E' ; Set exponent indicator
0174  46                               inc     SI
0175  2B C0                            sub     AX,AX               ; Clear leading digit
0177  0B D2                            or      DX,DX               ; Check sign
0179  0F 89 0183 R                     jns     posexpon            ; and if it is positive - skip
017D  C6 00 2D                         mov     BYTE PTR[BX+SI],'-' ; setting exponent sign.
0180  46                               inc     SI                  ; leave room
0181  F7 DA                            neg     DX                  ; force positive
0183                          posexpon:
0183  83 EA 64                         sub     DX,100              ; Back out the hundreds
0186  0F 88 018D R                     js      backin              ; too far - back it in
018A  40                               inc     AX                  ; Add the digit.
018B  EB F6                            jmp     posexpon            ; Go do another
018D                          backin:
018D  83 C2 64                         add     DX,100              ; Put it back
0190  0C 30                            or      AL,'0'              ; set zone
0192  88 00                            mov     BYTE PTR[BX+SI],AL  ; and put digit out
0194  8B C2                            mov     AX,DX               ; position low two
0196  D4 0A                            aam                         ; and convert them
0198  0D 3030                          or      AX,'00'             ; to ASCII digits
019B  86 E0                            xchg    AH,AL               ; reverse them
019D  89 40 01                         mov     WORD PTR[BX+SI+1],AX ; and store them.
01A0  83 C6 03                         add     SI,3                ; count them

01A3                          exit:
01A3  C6 00 00                         mov     BYTE PTR [BX+SI],0  ; Follow with a null
01A6  8B CE                            mov     CX,SI               ; set the count of bytes.
01A8  66| 58                           pop     EAX                 ; Restore work registers
01AA  66| 5A                           pop     EDX
01AC  5E                               pop     SI
01AD  5F                               pop     DI
01AE  C9                               leave
01AF  C3                               ret                         ; and return.
                              ;
                              ; Power of ten conversion - positive and negative to |511|
                              ;
                                       ALIGN   4

01B0  0000000000002440        pospower dq      1.0E+001            ; Positive powers of ten
```

```
=                               conof10     equ     pospower
01B8  0000000000005940          con100      dq      1.0E+002
01C0  00000000088C340                       dq      1.0E+004
01C8  0000000084D79741                      dq      1.0E+008
01D0  0080E03779C34143                      dq      1.0E+016
01D8  176E05B5B5B89346                      dq      1.0E+032
01E0  F5F93FE9034F384D                      dq      1.0E+064
01E8  321D30F94877825A                      dq      1.0E+128
01F0  3CBF737FDD4F1575                      dq      1.0E+256
01F8  000000000000E03F          point5      dq      5.0E-001          ; .5
0200  000000000000F03F          conof1      dq      1.0
0208  9A999999999B93F           negpower    dq      1.0E-001          ; Negative powers of ten
0210  7B14AE47E17A843F                      dq      1.0E-002
0218  2D431CEBE2361A3F                      dq      1.0E-004
0220  3A8C30E28E79453E                      dq      1.0E-008
0228  BC89D897B2D29C3C                      dq      1.0E-016
0230  33A7A8D523F64939                      dq      1.0E-032
0238  3DA7F444FD0FA532                      dq      ^ 0E-064
0240  9D978CCF08BA5B25                      dq      ı.0E-128
0248  436FAC642806C80A                      dq      1.0E-256
0250  0001                      valpower    dw      1                 ; Table of powers stepped
0252  0002                                  dw      2
0254  0004                                  dw      4
0256  0008                                  dw      8
0258  0010                                  dw      16
025A  0020                                  dw      32
025C  0040                                  dw      64
025E  0080                                  dw      128
0260  0100                                  dw      256
                                ;
                                ; Easy conversions
                                ;
0262  39 2E 39 45 39 39 39      infinity    db      '9.9E999'
= 0007                          infsize     equ     $-infinity
0269  30 2E 30 45 30            zero        db      '0.0E0'
= 0005                          zersize     equ     $-zero

026E                            Fplfpasc    ENDP
026E                            code        ENDS
                                            END
```

Program 7-14: FPASCLFP

Microsoft (R) Macro Assembler Version 5.00

```
                                        PAGE     55,132
                                        .386
                                        .287
 0000                           code    SEGMENT  para 'CODE' USE16 PUBLIC
                                        ASSUME   CS:code, DS:code, SS:code

                                ; Name:     FPASCLFP
                                ;
                                ; Purpose: The following procedure provides a conversion to an IEEE
                                ;          format long floating point number from an ASCII
                                ;          representation of a floating point number.
                                ;          IEEE long format has an 11 digit binary exponent biased by
                                ;          1023. It appears in memory reversed from its form in
                                ;          registers. i.e.
                                ;   bbbbcccc9999aaaa77778888555566663333444411112222eeee0000seeeeeee
                                ;   0       1       2       3       4       5       6       7
                                ;
                                ;          An ASCII representation is a string of the form:
                                ;          [+/-] [digits].[digits][E[+/-]digits] where [+/-] indicates
                                ;          an optional sign of either + or -, [digits] indicates
                                ;          possible digits (0 - 9), a required decimal point (.)
                                ;          potentially followed by digits and an optional exponent
                                ;          which if present must be E followed by an optional sign and
                                ;          1 to 3 digits.  Possible numbers are:
                                ;          5.,  -., (or .  both giving the same as 0.0), -5.3E-2 etc.
                                ;          The numbers are ASCII strings in memory.
                                ;
                                ;          Conversion from ASCII to long can either underflow or
                                ;          overflow the long exponent.  Zero and infinity are returned
                                ;          respectively and flagged with a carry.
                                ;
                                ;
                                ; Inputs:  DS:SI point to the ASCII string, CX has its maximum length.
                                ;
                                ; Process: The string is parsed from left to right with possible
                                ;          leading spaces ignored.  The sign is assumed + if omitted.
                                ;          Digits are converted into a quadword integer.  Digits to
                                ;          the right of the decimal also are counted in the exponent.
                                ;          The exponent is converted and added to the count of digits
                                ;          to the right of the decimal point.
                                ;
                                ;          The quadword integer is converted to a long floating point
                                ;          number.  (If zero we are done.)  The exponent is created
                                ;          as 64-the number of leading zero bits in the quadword.
                                ;          The resulting floating point number is further scaled by
                                ;          the power of ten given in the decimal exponent.
                                ;
                                ;          A malformed number is returned as zero with carry set.
                                ;          i.e. -5E (no decimal) 55a (invalid digit) would both
                                ;          be returned as zero.
                                ;
                                ; Output:  The converted number is returned in EAX:EDX.  Carry is set
                                ;          if infinity is returned and reset otherwise.  SI points
                                ;          beyond the last digit converted and CX has the remaining
                                ;          length.
                                ;
```

```
                                   ;
                                   ;
                                   ;
 =                                 fpnohi     EQU     SS:DWORD PTR[BP-4]  ; High part of float
 =                                 fpnolo     EQU     SS:DWORD PTR[BP-8]  ; Low part of float
 =                                 fpnumb     EQU     SS:QWORD PTR[BP-8]  ; Complete number
                                   ;
                                              PUBLIC  Fpasclfp
                                   ;
0000                               Fpasclfp   PROC
0000  C8 0010 00                              enter   16,0                ; Get work space
0004  66| 53                                  push    EBX                 ; Save work registers.
0006  57                                      push    DI
0007  E3 59                                   jcxz    badnum              ; If no digits - exit
0009  06                                      push    ES
000A  8C DB                                   mov     BX,DS
000C  8E C3                                   mov     ES,BX
000E  8B FE                                   mov     DI,SI
0010  66| 2B DB                               sub     EBX,EBX             ; Clear first part of long
0013  66| 2B D2                               sub     EDX,EDX             ; Clear rest of long number.
0016  66| 0F B7 C9                            movzx   ECX,CX              ; Clear sign indicator
001A  FC                                      cld                         ; Force direction to up.

                                   ;
                                   ; Strip leading blanks
                                   ;

001B  B0 20                                   mov     AL,' '              ; Set space as skip
001D  F3/ AE                                  repe scasb                  ;
001F  4F                                      dec     DI                  ; Point back to non-space.
0020  41                                      inc     CX                  ; back count up too
0021  8B F7                                   mov     SI,DI               ; Use SI for lodsb
0023  07                                      pop     ES                  ; Restore ES
0024  E3 3C                                   jcxz    badnum              ; If all spaces - exit
0026  2B FF                                   sub     DI,DI               ; Clear exponent digit count
0028  AC                                      lodsb                       ; Get the non blank and step SI
0029  34 30                                   xor     AL,'0'              ; Check if sign omitted
002B  3C 09                                   cmp     AL,9                ; Is it a digit?
002D  0F 86 0059 R                            jna     isdigit             ; Yes - start number
0031  3C 1E                                   cmp     AL,'.' XOR '0'      ; Is it a period?
0033  0F 84 0072 R                            jz      decpoint            ; Yes - Number may be valid
0037  3C 1D                                   cmp     AL,'-' XOR '0'      ; Is it a minus
0039  0F 85 0045 R                            jnz     checkpl             ; No - maybe a plus?
003D  66| 0F BA E9 1F                         bts     ECX,31              ; Remember in high bit of ECX.
0042  EB 07 90                                jmp     sign                ; Yes - skip the sign.
0045                               checkpl:
0045  3C 1B                                   cmp     AL,'+' XOR '0'      ; Is it a plus sign
0047  0F 85 0062 R                            jnz     badnum              ; If not - error
004B                               sign:
004B  49                                      dec     CX                  ; Count the character
004C  0F 84 0062 R                            jz      badnum              ; Can't end with sign!
                                   ;
                                   ; Collect leading digits
                                   ;
0050                               digitq:
0050  AC                                      lodsb                       ; Get the next byte and step SI
0051  34 30                                   xor     AL,'0'              ; Check if it is a digit
0053  3C 09                                   cmp     AL,9                ; Is it a digit?
0055  0F 87 006E R                            ja      decptq              ; No - leading digits are gone
0059                               isdigit:
0059  E8 0240 R                               call    accumd              ; accumulate leading digits.
005C  0F 82 0088 R                            jc      skiprest            ; for 64 bits max.
0060  E2 EE                                   loop    digitq              ; Count it and try next
```

```
                                ;                                          No decimal point!
                                ;
                                ; An error in the number's format was encountered.  Exit with an
                                ; error.
                                ;
0062                            badnum:
0062  5F                                pop     DI                      ; Restore work registers
0063  66| 5B                            pop     EBX
0065  66| 2B C0                         sub     EAX,EAX                 ; Clear the number
0068  66| 2B D2                         sub     EDX,EDX
006B  F9                                stc                             ; Set carry on and
006C  C9                                leave
006D  C3                                ret                             ; return.
                                ;
                                ; We must encounter a decimal point now.
                                ;
006E                            decptq:
006E  3C 1E                             cmp     AL,'.' XOR '0'          ; Is it a decimal point?
0070  75 F0                             jnz     badnum                  ; If not - too bad.
0072                            decpoint:
0072  AC                                lodsb                           ; Get the next byte and step SI
0073  34 30                             xor     AL,'0'                  ; Check for digit
0075  3C 09                             cmp     AL,9                    ; Is it?
0077  0F 87 00A3 R                      ja      checke                  ; If not - it must be exponent
007B  E8 0240 R                         call    accumd                  ; accumulate another digit
007E  0F 82 0097 R                      jc      skiprestp               ; No more will fit!
0082  4F                                dec     DI                      ; Reduce exponent by a power
                                                                        ; of 10.
0083  E2 ED                             loop    decpoint                ; Get more digits
0085  E9 0110 R                         jmp     scandone                ; If no more - done
                                ;
                                ; Precision has been exceeded but we have significant digits of
                                ; the number.  We skip digits to the decimal point, counting
                                ; places into the exponent.
                                ;
0088                            skiprest:
0088  49                                dec     CX                      ; Count the digit out
0089  74 D7                             jz      badnum                  ; All digits and no decimal!
008B  47                                inc     DI                      ; Add to exponent count
008C  AC                                lodsb                           ; get next byte
008D  34 30                             xor     AL,'0'                  ; Check for another digit
008F  3C 09                             cmp     AL,9                    ; Is it?
0091  76 F5                             jna     skiprest                ; Yes - go count for exponent
                                ;
                                ; We must have a decimal point here or we will bomb out.
                                ;
0093  3C 1E                             cmp     AL,'.' XOR '0'          ; Is it?
0095  75 CB                             jnz     badnum                  ; No - too bad
                                ;
                                ; Now we skip unusable fraction digits.  An exponent may be present
                                ; so we must look for it but we don't require one.
                                ;
0097                            skiprestp:
0097  49                                dec     CX                      ; Count the digit out
0098  0F 84 0110 R                      jz      scandone                ; If no more - scan is done.
009C  AC                                lodsb                           ; Get next digit
009D  34 30                             xor     AL,'0'                  ; Check if it is
009F  3C 09                             cmp     AL,9                    ;
00A1  76 F4                             jna     skiprestp               ; loop if so
                                ;
                                ; We now expect an exponent - E (or e) followed by an optionally
                                ; signed number.
```

```
                                ;
00A3                            checke:
00A3  3C 55                                 cmp     AL,'e' XOR '0'       ; Is it lower case
00A5  0F 84 00AD R                          jz      havee                ; Yes - go get exponent.
00A9  3C 75                                 cmp     AL,'E' XOR '0'       ; Is it upper case?
00AB  75 B5                                 jnz     badnum               ; No - It is bad.
00AD                            havee:
00AD  49                                    dec     CX                   ; Count out the E
00AE  74 B2                                 jz      badnum               ; error if no number after.
00B0  AC                                    lodsb                        ; Get next character.
00B1  3C 2D                                 cmp     AL,'-'               ; Is it minus?
00B3  0F 85 00BF R                          jnz     posexpon             ; no - check further
00B7  66| 0F BA E9 1E                       bts     ECX,30               ; remember it was minus
00BC  EB 07 90                              jmp     getexpd              ;
00BF                            posexpon:
00BF  3C 2B                                 cmp     AL,'+'               ; Is it plus?
00C1  0F 85 00C9 R                          jnz     expond               ; No - must be digit.
00C5                            getexpd:
00C5  49                                    dec     CX                   ; Count the exponent's sign
00C6  74 9A                                 jz      badnum               ; Just a sign is an error.
00C8  AC                                    lodsb                        ; Get next byte
                                ;
                                ; We now collect the exponent digits.
                                ;
00C9                            expond:
00C9  3C 30                                 cmp     AL,'0'               ; Check if under zero
00CB  72 95                                 jb      badnum               ; if so - bad
00CD  3C 39                                 cmp     AL,'9'               ; is it over 9
00CF  77 91                                 ja      badnum               ; if so - bad
00D1  66| 52                                push    EDX                  ; Save accumed number
00D3  66| 53                                push    EBX
00D5  66| 2B DB                             sub     EBX,EBX              ; Clear for accum of exponent
00D8  66| 2B D2                             sub     EDX,EDX
00DB  EB 09 90                              jmp     expond1              ; Digit is loaded
00DE                            expond2:
00DE  66| 5B                                pop     EBX                  ; Clean up the stack
00E0  66| 5A                                pop     EDX
00E2  E9 0062 R                             jmp     badnum               ; and report the error
00E5                            expond0:
00E5  AC                                    lodsb                        ; Get the next digit (if any)
00E6                            expond1:
00E6  34 30                                 xor     AL,'0'               ; check if digit
00E8  3C 09                                 cmp     AL,9                 ;
00EA  0F 87 00F5 R                          ja      expond3              ; We have trailing other data
00EE  E8 0240 R                             call    accumd               ; accumulate digit
00F1  72 EB                                 jc      expond2              ; Too many exponent digits.
00F3  E2 F0                                 loop    expond0              ; Go try another.
00F5                            expond3:
                                ;
                                ; EBX has the power of ten - Need to feed in the sign and combine
                                ; with the value in DI.
                                ;
00F5  66| 81 FB 000001FF                    cmp     EBX,511              ; check if exponent too big.
00FC  77 E0                                 ja      expond2              ; If so - number is malformed.
00FE  66| 0F BA E1 1E                       bt      ECX,30               ; check if exponent negative.
0103  0F 83 010A R                          jnc     expplus              ; If not - EBX is ok as is.
0107  66| F7 DB                             neg     EBX                  ; Get 2's compliment
010A                            expplus:
010A  03 FB                                 add     DI,BX                ; Get the exponent into DI
010C  66| 5B                                pop     EBX                  ; Restore the 64 bit number
010E  66| 5A                                pop     EDX
                                ;
                                ; The exponent (as a power of ten) is now in DI, and the 64 bit
```

```
                        ; number is in EDX:EBX.  CX has the remaining count of characters.
                        ; SI points to the character after the last number digit.
                        ;
0110                    scandone:
0110  51                          push   CX                  ; Save character count and
0111  56                          push   SI                  ; pointer for work registers.
                        ;
                        ; First we normalize the 64 bit number.  Doing this we create a binary
                        ; exponent in the range of 0 to 63.  Then we form a long floating
                        ; point by combining the exponent and the fraction.  Finally we need
                        ; to apply the proper power of ten to the result.
0112  66| 0B D2                   or     EDX,EDX             ; Is the top dword occupied?
0115  0F 84 012F R                jz     topzero             ; No, exponent range is 0 - 31.
0119  66| 0F BD C2                bsr    EAX,EDX             ; Get bit number of highest on.
011D  B9 0020                     mov    CX,32               ; 32-(bit#) is the shift amount
0120  2B C8                       sub    CX,AX               ; in CX.
0122  05 0020                     add    AX,32               ; 32+(bit#) is exponent in AX.
0125  66| 0F A5 DA                shld   EDX,EBX,CL          ; Adjust to get top bit out
0129  66| D3 E3                   shl    EBX,CL              ; and fill zeros to right.
012C  EB 17 90                    jmp    makefp              ; and go make the number
012F                    topzero:
012F  66| 0B D3                   or     EDX,EBX             ; Shift 32 bits
0132  0F 84 01A5 R                jz     outzero             ; If zero - done - totally!
0136  66| 2B DB                   sub    EBX,EBX             ; Fill 32 zero bits to right.
0139  66| 0F BD C2                bsr    EAX,EDX             ; Get bit number of highest on.
                        ;                                      It is the exponent!
013D  B9 0020                     mov    CX,32               ; 32-bit number is shift amount
0140  2B C8                       sub    CX,AX               ; in CX.
0142  66| D3 E2                   shl    EDX,CL              ; Do the shift.
                        ;
                        ; We have the sign, exponent, and the fraction; now put them together.
                        ;
0145                    makefp:
0145  66| 0F AC D3 0C             shrd   EBX,EDX,12          ; push bits into right part
014A  66| C1 EA 0C                shr    EDX,12              ; and zeros into left part
014E  05 03FF                     add    AX,1023             ; Bias the exponent,
0151  66| C1 E0 14                shl    EAX,20              ; position it,
0155  66| 0B D0                   or     EDX,EAX             ; and combine with number.
0158  66| 0F BA E1 1F             bt     ECX,31              ; Do we want minus?
015D  0F 83 0166 R                jnc    makefp1             ; No - We are done.
0161  66| 0F BA EA 1F             bts    EDX,31              ; Yes - set the sign minus.
0166                    makefp1:
0166  66| 89 56 FC                mov    fpnohi,EDX          ; Put number into work memory
016A  66| 89 5E F8                mov    fpnolo,EBX          ; (both halves)
                        ;
                        ; The power of ten is the only thing left to handle.
                        ;
016E  0B FF                       or     DI,DI               ; Check the exponent
0170  0F 84 01A8 R                jz     alldone             ; If zero - we are done.
0174  8D 1E 01B0 R                lea    BX,CS:pospower      ; Assume positive.
0178  0F 89 0187 R                jns    itispos             ; It is.
017C  81 C3 0048                  add    BX,negpower-pospower ; shift to negative exponents
0180  8B C7                       mov    AX,DI               ; Get exponent's
0182  BF 0000                     mov    DI,0                ;
0185  2B F8                       sub    DI,AX               ; absolute value.
0187                    itispos:
0187  DD 46 F8                    fld    fpnumb              ; Get the number
018A                    nextpowr:
018A  D1 EF                       shr    DI,1                ; shift a bit out of exponent
018C  0F 83 0193 R                jnc    skipmpy             ; If not a one - don't mpy
0190  2E: DC 0F                   fmul   QWORD PTR CS:[BX+0] ; multiply by power of ten
0193                    skipmpy:
```

```
0193  83 C3 08                      add    BX,8            ; Step power pointer
0196  0B FF                         or     DI,DI           ; Check if done
0198  75 F0                         jnz    nextpowr        ; if not - do again
019A  DD 56 F8                      fst    fpnumb          ; Get the number from the unit.
019D  66| 8B 56 FC                  mov    EDX,fpnohi      ; Get number from work memory
01A1  66| 8B 5E F8                  mov    EBX,fpnolo      ; (both halves)
01A5                       outzero:
01A5  66| 8B C3                     mov    EAX,EBX         ; Position number as EAX:EDX

01A8                       alldone:
01A8  5E                            pop    SI              ; Restore work registers
01A9  59                            pop    CX
01AA  5F                            pop    DI
01AB  66| 5B                        pop    EBX             ; Restore the entry registers
01AD  C9                            leave
01AE  C3                            ret                    ; and return.
                           ;
                           ; Power of ten conversion - positive and negative to |511|
                           ;
01AF  90                            ALIGN  4
01B0  0000000000002440     pospower dq     1.0E+001
01B8  0000000000005940              dq     1.0E+002
01C0  00000000088C340               dq     1.0E+004
01C8  0000000084D79741              dq     1.0E+008
01D0  0080E03779C34143              dq     1.0E+016
01D8  176E05B5B5B89346              dq     1.0E+032
01E0  F5F93FE9034F384D              dq     1.0E+064
01E8  321D30F94877825A              dq     1.0E+128
01F0  3CBF737FDD4F1575              dq     1.0E+256
01F8  9A9999999999B93F     negpower dq     1.0E-001
0200  7B14AE47E17A843F              dq     1.0E-002
0208  2D431CEBE2361A3F              dq     1.0E-004
0210  3A8C30E28E79453E              dq     1.0E-008
0218  BC89D897B2D29C3C              dq     1.0E-016
0220  33A7A8D523F64939              dq     1.0E-032
0228  3DA7F444FD0FA532              dq     1.0E-064
0230  9D978CCF08BA5B25              dq     1.0E-128
0238  436FAC642806C80A              dq     1.0E-256
                           ;
                           ; Accumulate another digit into our 64 bit number
                           ;
                           ; The 64 bit number is accumulated in EBX:EDX, the new digit is passed
                           ; in AL (the rest of EAX is assumed to be zero).  If the digit can be
                           ; accommodated, it is, and return is made with carry reset.  Otherwise,
                           ; carry is set and EBX:EDX is returned unchanged.
                           ;
0240                       accumd   PROC   NEAR
0240  66| 51                        push   ECX             ; Save work register
0242  66| 53                        push   EBX             ; Save the low 32 bits.
0244  66| 52                        push   EDX             ; Save high 32 bits

0246  66| 50                        push   EAX             ; Save the digit
0248  66| 52                        push   EDX             ; Save high 32 bits
024A  66| 8B C3                     mov    EAX,EBX         ; Get low 32 bits in EAX
024D  66| B9 0000000A               mov    ECX,10          ; Get the multiplier
0253  66| F7 E1                     mul    ECX             ; multiply low 32 bits
0256  66| 8B D8                     mov    EBX,EAX         ; save low 32 bits of product
0259  66| 58                        pop    EAX             ; Get high 32 bits of number
025B  66| 52                        push   EDX             ; Save overflow from low mpy
025D  66| F7 E1                     mul    ECX             ; multiply high 32 bits by 10
0260  66| 0B D2                     or     EDX,EDX         ; if we overflow beyond 64 bits
0263  66| 5A                        pop    EDX             ; Possible overflow of low
0265  0F 85 0288 R                  jnz    toobig          ; We must quit.
```

```
0269  66| 03 D0                    add     EDX,EAX        ; add result of the high mpy
026C  0F 82 0288 R                 jc      toobig         ; If it carried - we must quit.
0270  66| 58                       pop     EAX            ; Restore the new digit
0272  66| 83 E0 0F                 and     EAX,0fh        ; Clear all but digit
0276  66| 03 D8                    add     EBX,EAX        ; and add it to low 32 bits.
0279  66| 83 D2 00                 adc     EDX,0          ; Propagate the possible carry
027D  0F 82 028B R                 jc      toobig1        ; If carry out of top 32, quit.
0281  66| 59                       pop     ECX            ; The new number is OK
0283  66| 59                       pop     ECX            ; so we don't need the old one.
0285  66| 59                       pop     ECX            ; Finally, restore the work reg
0287  C3                           ret                    ; and return (carry is off).
0288                    toobig:
0288  F9                           stc                    ; Set the carry flag
0289  66| 58                       pop     EAX            ; Clear stack of digit
028B                    toobig1:
028B  66| 5A                       pop     EDX            ; Get old high 32
028D  66| 5B                       pop     EBX            ; and low 32.
028F  66| 59                       pop     ECX            ; Restore work register
0291  C3                           ret                    ; and return (carry is set)
0292                    accumd     ENDP

0292                    Fpasclfp   ENDP
0292                    code       ENDS
                                   END
```

Program 7-15: FLIPS

```
Microsoft (R) Macro Assembler Version 5.00


                                        PAGE      55,132
                                        .386
 0000                           code    SEGMENT   para 'CODE' USE16 PUBLIC
                                        ASSUME    CS:code, DS:code, SS:code
                                ; Name:    FLIPS  (Flip2, Flip4, and Flip8)
                                ;
                                ; Purpose: The following procedures provide data conversions for
                                ;          a word (for completeness), a double word and a quadword
                                ;          from Intel ordering to its reverse (or visa-versa).
                                ;
                                ; Inputs:  AX has the word to be flipped.
                                ;
                                ; Process: AL and AH are exchanged.
                                ;
                                ; Output:  AX has the reversed word.
                                ;
                                ;
                                ;
                                         PUBLIC  Flip2               ; Make the name usable
 0000                           Flip2    PROC
 0000  86 C4                             xchg    AL,AH               ; Reverse the byte order
 0002  C3                                ret                         ; and return.
 0003                           Flip2    ENDP
                                ;
                                ;
                                ; Inputs:  EAX has the 32 bit double word to reorder.
                                ;
                                ; Process: see below
                                ;
                                ; Output:  EAX has the reversed word.
                                ;
                                ;
                                ;
                                         PUBLIC  Flip4               ; Make the name usable
 0003                           Flip4    PROC
                                ;                          Assume:     0123
 0003  66| C1 C8 08                      ror     EAX,8               ; get 3012
 0007  86 C4                             xchg    AL,AH               ;     3021
 0009  66| C1 C0 10                      rol     EAX,16              ;     2130
 000D  86 C4                             xchg    AL,AH               ;     2103
 000F  66| C1 C8 08                      ror     EAX,8               ; and 3210
 0013  C3                                ret                         ; then return.
 0014                           Flip4    ENDP
                                ;
                                ;
                                ; Inputs:  EAX:EDX has the 64 bit quadword to reorder
                                ;          Loaded as:   mov  EAX,qword
                                ;                       mov  EDX,qword+4
                                ;
                                ; Process: see below
                                ;
                                ; Output:  EAX:EDX has the reversed quadword.
                                ;          To store as:  mov   qword,EAX
                                ;                        mov   qword+4,EDX
                                ;
                                ;
                                ;
```

```
                                    ;
                                              PUBLIC  Flip8              ; Make the name usable
0014                                Flip8     PROC
                                    ;                                         EAX: EDX
                                    ;                                          HL   HL
                                    ;                                 Assume:  4567 0123
0014  66| C1 C2 10                            rol     EDX,16                 ; 4567 2301
0018  86 D4                                   xchg    DL,AH                  ; 4517 2306
001A  86 F0                                   xchg    DH,AL                  ; 4510 2376
001C  66| C1 C2 10                            rol     EDX,16                 ; 4510 7623
0020  66| C1 C0 10                            rol     EAX,16                 ; 1045 7623
0024  86 D4                                   xchg    DL,AH                  ; 1035 7624
0026  86 F0                                   xchg    DH,AL                  ; 1032 7654
0028  66| C1 C0 10                            rol     EAX,16                 ; 3210 7654
002C  C3                                      ret                            ; and return.
002D                                Flip8     ENDP
002D                                code      ENDS
                                              END
```

8

Input/Output and File Manipulation

The primary reason for the initial development (and later growth) of operating systems concerns the handling of input and output (I/O) operations. Simply, computers take data in, crunch it, and send it back out. Input is the translation of incoming information into useful formats suitable for storage and future handling. That handling could be within a program, for display on a screen, or storage within a data file. Output is the reverse process. Output generally goes to a disk, screen, or printer.

Responsibility for processor-level I/O moved from the programmer to the operating system for several reasons. First, the construction of code for handling I/O deserves the reputation for being one of the more demanding and contrary aspects of programming. By not forcing everyone to savor the intricate I/O, programming became accessible to a greater number of people. Second, a common set of I/O routines executed by all system facilities and user programs saves duplicated effort, storage, and development dollars. In addition, carefully debugged routines provide a measure of protection against destruction of important data files caused by incomplete knowledge of what the system *really* needed that particular flag for.

Standard Input/Output

By *standard input* and *standard output*, we understand the transfer of data to (from) a computer from (to) an external agent, generally a human operator. Input may originate at a keyboard and output may go to a display screen. In any case, its characteristics are that it is readable and typically consists of a sequence of characters. This readability condition is responsible for another complication incurred in most I/O operations. Apart from the actual data transfer, I/O also involves a transformation of representation. For example, numbers represented (internally in the computer) in binary form need to be transformed into readable, decimal notation.

The most common handling of input data is to edit it to a previously known standard. For example, when requesting a date input, you put limits on the year, such as no earlier than 1900 or later than 2000. You restrict months to numbers between (and including) 1 and 12; days are no fewer than 1 nor more than 31. And so on.

Text editing implies a "reasonability check," e.g., allowing only characters between A and Z (in addition to the lowercase equivalents), digits 0 through 9, and special characters (decimal point, dollar sign, parentheses, and percent).

I/O goes between your fingertips and some storage medium. The most common storage is diskettes, which have their own formats for you to remember.

Disk Organization

Disks are divided into *tracks* with an equal number of bytes available on each track for storage; there are 40 tracks on normal, double-density floppy diskettes. Hard disks also have tracks. However, the hard disk is composed of a number of parallel hard disks with a read/write head per surface. These heads move in and out together on a single actuator, so they use the concept of cylinders. As Fig. 8-1 shows, a *cylinder* is simply a convenient idea that all tracks a certain number (radius) from the center are thought of as a logical unit. Hard disks use cylinders to minimize read/write head movement, which gives you faster I/O seek times. When data is stored on a hard disk, the storage algorithm uses all the tracks (up and down) on a cylinder before moving over to a new cylinder.

Sectors

Tracks divide into 512-byte *sectors* under most MS-DOS formats. Sectors are grouped into *clusters* and MS-DOS keeps track of clusters individually, each as one entry in the *File Allocation Table* (FAT), which keeps a record of which clusters are used and which are free. The number of sectors in a cluster varies from disk format to disk format. Double-sided diskettes have two sectors to a cluster, while high-density diskettes have only one sector to a cluster. File clusters may be scattered all over the disk, matching the available space. The FAT chains them so that your program can read from the beginning of your data to the end. Since files can be broken up into pieces for efficient disk storage, some size limitation had to be made for minimal space, and that limit is 1024 bytes.

The first sector of a double-sided diskette contains the boot record, stored on logical sector 0. The next two pairs of sectors (1–2 and 3–4) each contain a copy

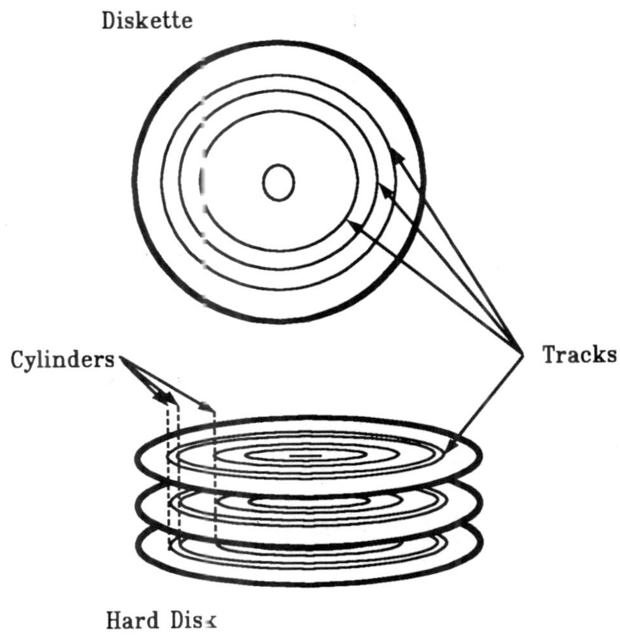

Fig. 8-1. Hard disk cylinders versus diskette tracks.

of the FAT. DOS maintains two copies to compare each for correctness; if the FAT goes bad, your data becomes garbage. Next come the directories, which occupy seven sectors and fills logical sectors 5–11 on every double-sided, nine-sectored disk.

If you've loaded COMMAND.COM onto your formatted diskette, the file IBMBIO.COM (the disk interface to BIOS) starts right after the directory. Next comes IBMDOS.COM; then begins the actual data area (your files).

Directories

Directory entries are 32 bytes long and, on a double-sided diskette, there are seven sectors of directory. This means that there are 112 directory entries possible; this is calculated by multiplying the number of sectors (7) by 512 bytes per sector, and then dividing by 32 bytes per entry.

The first 8 directory bytes (0–7) contain the file's name, and the next three bytes (8–10) hold the file's extension. Byte 11 has the file's attribute (normal, read-only, hidden, system, subdirectory, and the archive bit). Bytes 12–21 are reserved for future use. Bytes 22–25 contain the file creation time of day, calculated with this formula:

$$\text{TIME} = (\textit{seconds}/2) + 2^5 * (\textit{minutes}) + 2^{11} * (\textit{hours})$$

Bytes 24–25 contain the date, calculated by:

$$\text{DATE} = (\textit{days}) + 2^5 * (\textit{months}) + 2^9 * (\textit{year} - 1980)$$

If you dumped the directory entry for AUTOEXEC.BAT, you'd see the directory entry like in Fig. 8-2.

Bytes 26–27 contain the file's starting cluster number, and the next four (28–31) contain the file size, which is the only place MS-DOS keeps accurate track of the file's size. Bytes 26–27 tell you where the first 1024 bytes of your file are located. Bytes 26–31 are useful in case you accidentally delete a file. You can use a debugger to modify the entries to "recreate" your file, but only if you haven't used any of the chained clusters in another file. Remember, when you released those clusters back to the FAT, MS-DOS thought that it could use them for storage.

80386 Input/Output

The 80386 processor supports 8-, 16-, and 32-bit input/output (I/O) devices; I/O can be mapped either onto the 4-gigabyte physical memory address space using general-purpose operand manipulation instructions, or onto the 64-kilobyte I/O address space using specific I/O instructions. I/O mapping and memory mapping differ in three major ways.

- ☐ Memory mapping offers more flexibility in protection than I/O mapping does, because memory-mapped devices are protected by memory management and protection features.

Byte	0	1	2	3	4	5	6	7
0	A	U	T	O	E	X	E	C
8	B	A	T	File Attrib	Reserved			
16	Reserved						Time file created or updated	
24	Date file created or updated		Starting Cluster		File size in bytes: Low Order		File size in bytes: High Order	

Fig. 8-2. AUTOEXEC.BAT directory entry.

- ☐ The address decoding necessary to generate chip select for I/O-mapped devices is generally simpler than for memory-mapped devices. I/O mapped devices reside in the 64-kilobyte I/O space of the 80386, while memory-mapped devices reside in much larger memory space that makes use of more address lines, the 4 gigabytes.
- ☐ Memory-mapped devices can be accessed using any 80386 instruction. This allows efficient coding of I/O-to-memory, memory-to-I/O, and I/O-to-I/O transfers. I/O mapped devices can be accessed through four instructions: IN, INS, OUT, OUTS. All I/O transfers are done via the AL (8-bit), AX (16-bit), or EAX (32-bit) registers. See Fig. 8-3, which shows the general layout of EAX. The first 256 bytes of I/O space are directly addressable and the entire 64-kilobyte I/O space is indirectly addressable through the DX register.

The 80386 has a separate I/O address space distinct from physical memory and which can be used to address the I/O ports that are used for external 16-bit devices. This I/O address space is made up of 2^{16} (64K) individually addressable 8-bit ports. Any even-numbered consecutive 8-bit port can be treated as a 16-bit port and any doubleword-addressed consecutive 8-bit port can be treated as a 32-bit port. This means that the total I/O address space accommodates up to:

Ports	*Quantity*	*Numbered*
8-bit	64K	0, 1, 2, . . . , 65535
16-bit	32K	0, 2, 4, . . . , 65534
32-bit	16K	0, 4, 8, . . . , 65532

Figure 8-4 diagrams these divisions of the I/O address space.

I/O Instructions

The 80386 I/O instructions give access to the processor's I/O ports for data transfer to and from peripheral devices. Instructions that directly use addresses

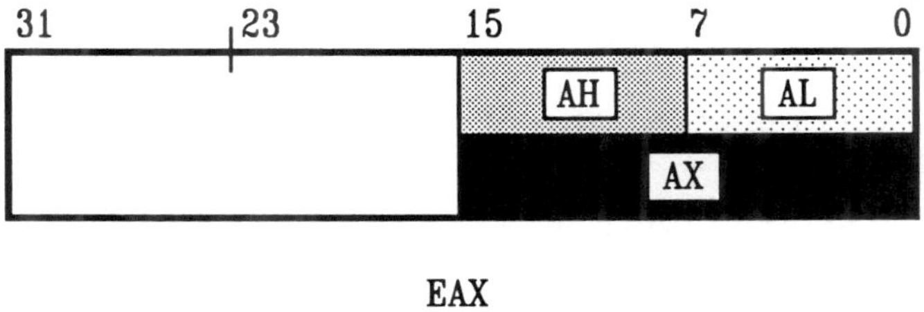

Fig. 8-3. General layout of the EAX register.

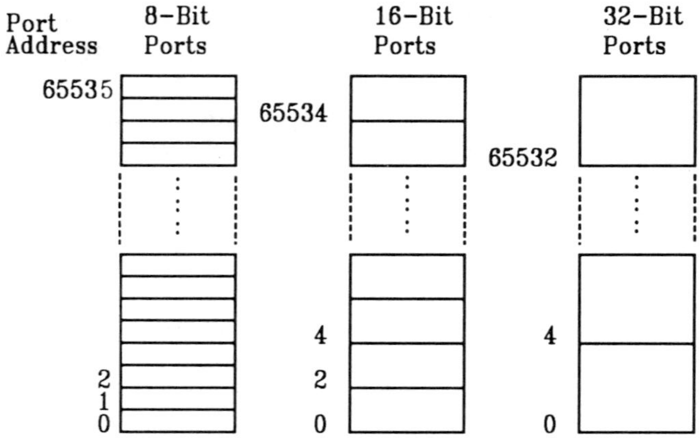

Fig. 8-4. I/O address spaces.

in the 80386's I/O space are IN, INS, OUT, and OUTS. These instructions have, as one operand, the address of a port in the I/O space. There are two classes of I/O instructions: those that transfer strings of items located in memory (known as "string I/O instructions" or "block I/O instructions") and those that transfer a single byte, word, or doubleword located in a register.

The block I/O instructions, INS and OUTS, move blocks of data between I/O ports and memory space. These instructions use the DX register to specify the address of a port in the I/O address space. INS uses ES:DI to specify the memory space in which to input; OUTS uses DS:SI.

The IN and OUT instructions move data between I/O ports and the AL register for 8-bit I/O, AX for 16-bit I/O, and EAX for 32-bit I/O. IN and OUT addresses I/O ports either directly (with the addresses of one of up to 256 port addresses coded in the instruction) or indirectly (using the DX register to one of up to 64K port addresses). See Appendix C for a complete alphabetic list of 80386 instructions and Appendix D for the 80387 instructions.

I/O Privilege

At privilege level 0, all I/O instructions are allowed. Instructions that deal with I/O not only need to be restricted, they need to be executed by procedures which execute at privilege levels other than zero. To allow this, the 80386 uses two bits of the EFLAGS register to store the IOPL (I/O Privilege Level). The IOPL defines the privilege level needed to execute I/O related instructions.

In protected mode, IOPL offers protection by allowing a task to access I/O devices which are flagged accessible in the task's I/O Bitmap or by preventing a task from accessing any I/O device. In virtual-8086 mode (V86), the I/O Permission Bitmap is not checked. The I/O Permission Bitmap is the controlling factor in whether or not I/O is allowed. See Fig. 8-5 and Fig. 8-6 to see where the bitmap is stored in the TSS.

The TSS consists of 3 parts: the Intel-defined minimum, an operating system defined extension, and the I/O bitmap itself.

I/O protection is provided in two ways: the I/O Permission Bitmap in the TSS defines the right to use ports in the I/O address space, and the IOPL (I/O Privilege Level) flag in the EFLAGS register defines the right to use I/O-related instruc-

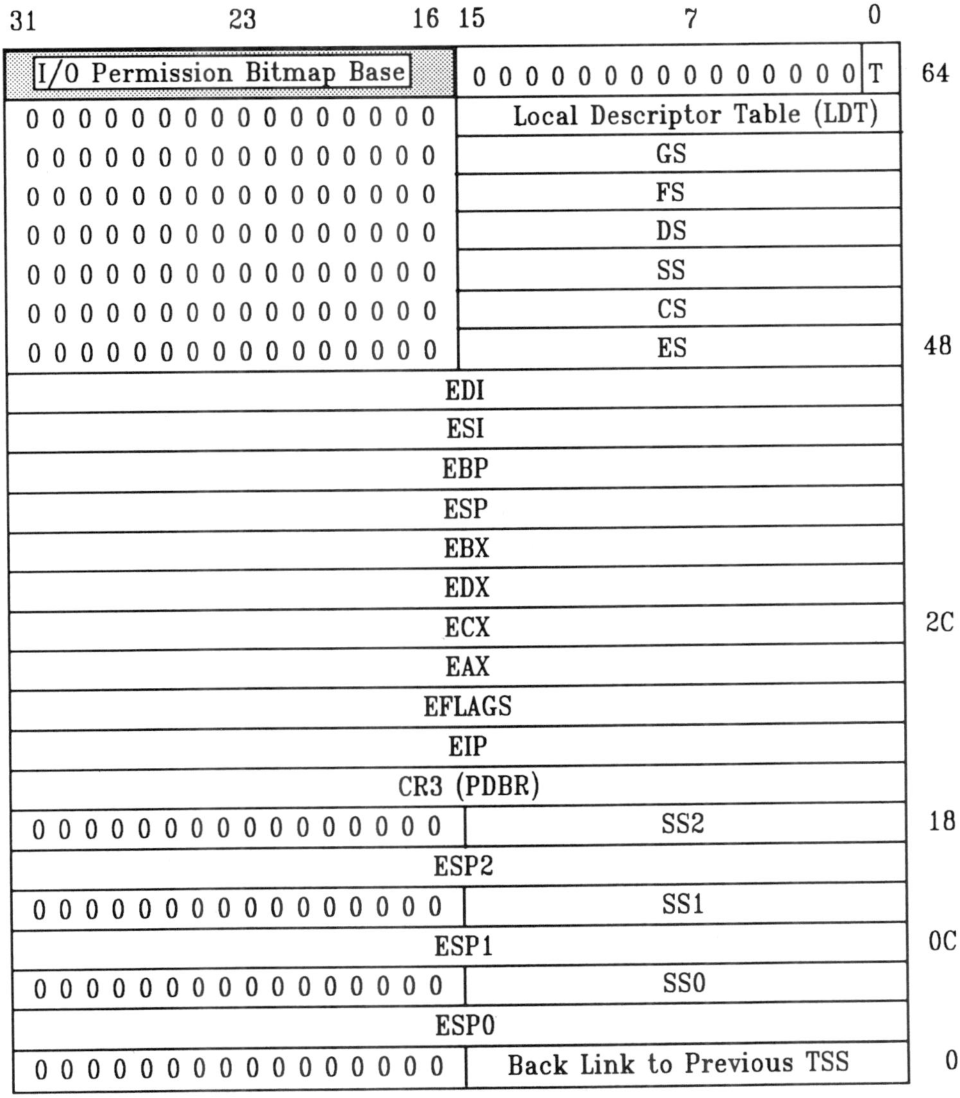

Fig. 8-5. TSS with I/O Permission Bitmap. (Zero entries indicate Intel reserved bits; do not define.)

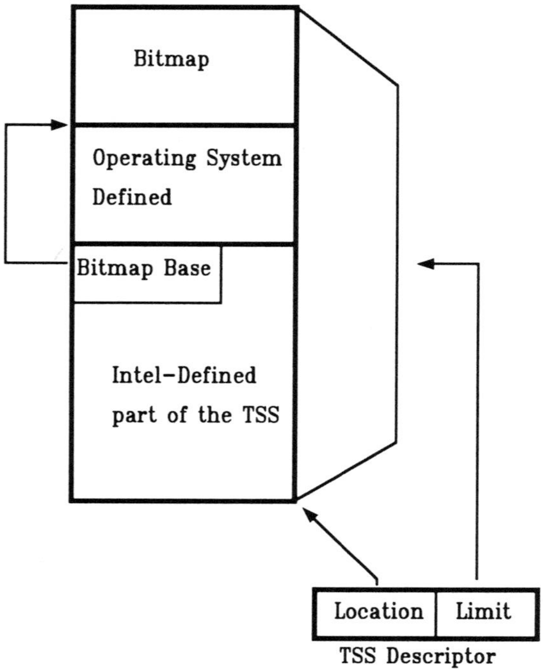

Fig. 8-6. Schematic of the TSS with Bitmap.

tions. See Appendix B for a detailed description of the EFLAGS format. These mechanisms work only in protected mode, which includes the virtual-8086 mode. They do not work in real mode. In real mode, any procedure executes I/O instructions and any I/O port can be addressed by any of those instructions.

The 80386 selectively traps references to specific I/O addresses. The mechanism that allows this trapping is the I/O Permission Bitmap in the TSS. The Bitmap is a bit vector and its size and location in the TSS are variable. The 80386 locates the Bitmap by means of the 16-bit *I/O Map Base* field in the fixed portion of the TSS which contains the offset to the beginning of the Bitmap. The upper limit of the Bitmap is the same as the limit of the TSS segment. Because the Bitmap is in the TSS, different tasks can have different Bitmaps. Thus, the operating system can allocate ports to a task by changing the I/O Permission Bitmap in the task's TSS.

Each bit in the Bitmap corresponds to an I/O port byte address. For instance, the bit for port 41 is found at I/O Bitmap Base+5, bit offset 1. The 80386 tests all bits that correspond to the I/O addresses spanned by an I/O operation. That is, a doubleword operation will test four bits that correspond to four adjacent byte addressees. If any tested bit is set, the 80386 signals a general protection exception. If all tested bits are zero, the I/O operation proceeds.

Each task in the system has its own unique copy of the EFLAGS register. Therefore, each task can have a different IOPL. A task can change the IOPL *only* with a POPF instruction. Such changes are privileged. No procedure may alter IOPL in EFLAGS unless the procedure is executing at privilege level zero.

An Input Editing Program

As time goes on, no doubt you'll be writing your own I/O routines. If you haven't done this in the past, you may wish to practice using the routines below. Try them out as they appear, running a dump program which will step through them one at a time so you can see the various register, flag, and memory changes. Then customize them into the shape you need for your programming.

There are two very common input/output routines that most programs contain. Those are editing input and handling carriage returns and line feeds. Editing input tends to lie in the area of verification of numbers and alphabetic characters. Whether the numbers are single or multiple digits, the individual numbers are limited to the 0–9 range. Alphabetic characters are almost as straightforward. They must be in the range of uppercase A–Z, or lowercase a–z. Alphabetic characters can be part of character strings that are divided by blanks or special characters, such as a slash (/) or punctuation like a semicolon (;).

IOEDIT (Program 8-1) is meant to show how to handle input buffers and to edit single digits. More complex editing is an extension of the simple methods shown.

In MS-DOS, an input buffer is composed of the input data and two auxiliary bytes. You supply the first byte, a count of the maximum number of characters allowed before MS-DOS beeps and disallows more entry. MS-DOS uses the second byte to indicate the actual number of characters entered. An input buffer may look like the example shown in Fig. 8-7. Notice that the counts and digits are displayed in hex (although they are actually stored as binary), and that the amount actually entered is less than the maximum allowable.

IOEDIT uses an input buffer called INPUT_STR. In the data initialization area, INPUT_STR is established to be 4 bytes long and initialized. Later, a hex 4 is moved into the first byte. Then the index into the buffer is moved two bytes (from byte 0 to byte 2) because actual input goes into byte 2.

The carriage return (0D) is captured on input, but MS-DOS does not count that character as part of the count in byte 1. If you're working with an ASCIIZ string (which must end in hex 00 by definition), you would take the count from byte 1, add 2 to it, and replace that byte with hex 00. That byte is the 0D. Note that the 0D is shown in Fig. 8-6. If you're not working with ASCIIZ strings, you may not care that the 0D remains in the string, as we didn't in IOEDIT.

Figure 8-8 shows three lines of code from IOEDIT which we think merit your attention. (We've never seen them coded anywhere.) They make the decision as to whether or not a character is numeric into a very few lines of code. You move

Program Code

```
    *
    *
INPUT_STR   DB   6 DUP (?)
    *
    *
        MOV   INPUT_STR,4      ; Maximum count into string
        LEA   DX,INPUT_STR     ; Move pointer to buffer into DX
        ADD   DX,2             ; Skip auxiliary bytes
        MOV   AH,0Ah           ; Buffered keyboard input function
        INT   21h
    *
    *
```

Assume the entered data is two digits: 1 and 4
After entry, the buffer would appear like:

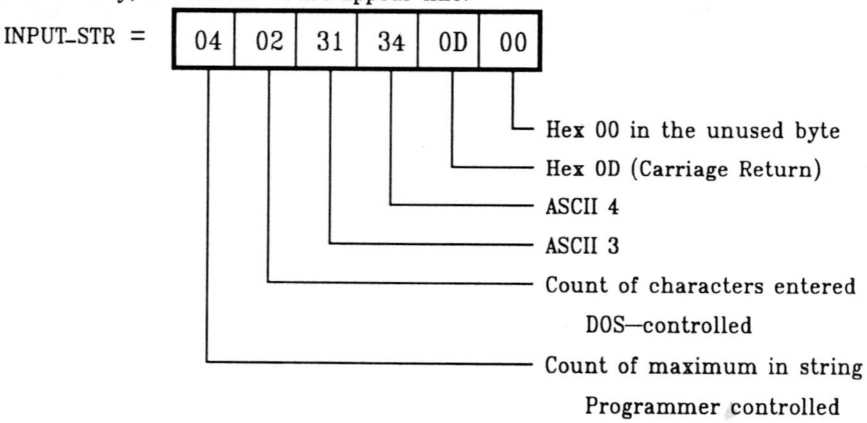

Fig. 8-7. Input Buffer with auxiliary bytes.

```
; Assume INPUT_STR is an input buffer that has a character
; entered into byte 2.  Byte 0 and 1 are auxiliary bytes for an
; input buffer.

        MOV   CL,BYTE PTR INPUT_STR[2]
        XOR   CL,30h
        CMP   CL,9h
```

Fig. 8-8. Easy method to determine if a character is numeric.

a byte from the input buffer into a byte register, exclusive-or (XOR) it against 30 hex (which is an ASCII zero) and then compare (CMP) the result against a 9 hex. A value greater than 9 is non-numeric.

File Manipulation

A file is a collection of data that has been stored on some external storage device (such as a magnetic disk) for use at a future time. Files have structures that determine how the records in the file are organized.

Structure subdivides into logical structure and physical structure. The *logical* structure of a file is the user's view of the file. A file declaration that appears in a program is basically a logical structure specification and generally involves defining the attribute(s) of the record type(s) and possibly specifying a relationship (e.g., an ordering relationship) on the record occurrences.

Physical structure, on the other hand, is associated with how a file actually is organized on the storage medium on which it resides. This normally involves pointers, indexes, and how the records are laid out on the external storage device. Note the differences between logical and physical structure shown in Fig. 8-9.

You access files in various ways. The most common access method is sequential, because computer files were first stored on inherently sequential storage media

Logical File Format:

Title:	Dr.
First Name:	Elizabeth
Last Name:	Doe
Street Address:	111 Main Street
City:	Anytown
State:	California
Zip:	95117
Telephone:	(408) 555-1212

Physical File Format:

Text Representation:

D	r	.	E	l	••	9	5	1	1	7

ASCII Representation:

44	72	2E	45	6C	••	39	35	31	31	37

Fig. 8-9. Differences between logical and physical file structures.

such as magnetic tape. To access a record in a sequential file, the "earlier" records must be passed over (read and ignored). A second and more widely used access method is random (direct) access of records. With direct access, any record in a file can be retrieved without looking first at the records that precede it. Techniques for implementing direct access generally involve some method for translating a key that identifies the record sought into the (absolute or relative) address of the corresponding record on the device on which it is stored. This translation is normally done via an index (or indexes) or a key-to-address transformation function (called a *hashing function*) that computes the address of the record from the key (or keys). See Chapter 9 for information on hashing.

Checking, Renaming, and Deleting a File

IOWORKS (Program 8-2) performs several functions. It deletes an existing file, renames an existing file, and checks for the existence of a file. It uses Interrupt 21 Function 41 to delete a file, Interrupt 21 Function 56 to rename a file, and Interrupt 21 Function 4E to find a file. A Disk Transfer Area (DTA) is established when a file is found. Inside the DTA is the file size (see Fig. 8-10).

If an error is found, this program uses EXTERROR (described and listed in Chapter 5) to determine the extended error and to print error messages. EXTERROR uses Interrupt 21 Function 59, which returns an extended error code, an error class and action, plus the location of the error.

You'll probably notice that most of the programs in this book have "positive responses" to users. This is a human engineering feature often left out (because not thought of) by programmers. Users request an action and the computer goes off and does something. They know it does because the disk read light comes on. Then the next thing a user sees is a system prompt. What happened? It's often a matter of faith (or of checking some other way) that the proposed action was accomplished. Rather than leave a user guessing, display a message that states the conclusion of a "user-invisible" action.

Fig. 8-10. DTA layout. Note that there is no drive or library name (e.g., no path name).

Bytes	Contents
0–20	Reserved
21	Found Attribute
22–23	File's Time
24–25	File's Date
26–27	File's Size, Low word
28–29	File's Size, High word
30–42	Name and Extension

Opening and Reading an Existing File

To read from a file, you must open it (use INT 21 Function 3D). First, store the attribute into AX. The attribute is how you want to access the file (0 = read, 1 = write, 2 = read/write). Store the pointer to the ASCIIZ file name (an ASCII string that ends in hex 00) into DS:DX and issue the open. The file handle returns in AX. Since the other file-handle functions use BX for the file name, move the handle into BX immediately.

When the file is opened, the Read/Write pointer points at the first byte. After each read, the pointer moves to the first byte past the end of the read. To read bytes in, set up a memory buffer, with two auxiliary bytes at the front of the buffer. You set the first one (byte 0) with the maximum number of bytes in the buffer (counting the carriage return). DOS sets the second byte (byte 1) as how many were actually entered. However, DOS does *not* count the carriage return in the bytes read, although the 0Dh is in the buffer. The actual bytes you want to read (or write with INT 21 Function 3F) go into bytes 2 through *n*, where *n* is the end of the memory buffer.

Figure 8-11 shows a SYMDEB dump of an actual memory buffer used in IOREAD (Program 8-3). The memory buffer holds the ASCIIZ string of the file name that IOREAD requested. The dump first sets a breakpoint (BP) in the IOREAD program; the location was determined from the assembly listing of the

```
C:\ASM>SYMDEB IOREAD.EXE
Microsoft (R) Symbolic Debug Utility  Version 4.00
Copyright (C) Microsoft Corp 1984, 1985.  All rights reserved.

Processor is [80286]
-BP 03D3
-G
AX=0A0D  BX=0000  CX=0013  DX=0041  SP=00C8  BP=0000  SI=0013  DI=0000
DS=15D7  ES=15BA  SS=15CA  CS=15D7  IP=03D3   NV UP EI PL NZ NA PO NC
15D7:03D3 8D161900       LEA    DX,[0019]                    ;BR0 DS:0019=0D0A
-DB 0041 0055
15D7:0040     1E 11 43 3A 5C 41 53-4D 5C 49 4F 52 45 41 44   ..C:\ASM\IOREAD
15D7:0050  2E 41 53 4D 00 00                                .ASM..
-DA 0041 0055
15D7:0041  ..C:\ASM\IOREAD.ASM..
-Q

C:\ASM>
```

Fig. 8-11. SYMDEB dump of memory buffer, showing auxiliary bytes.

program. The file name is asked for and the program goes on. It stops at the breakpoint and displays the current register contents.

Then a display of bytes (SYMDEB DB command) at the memory buffer location (taken from the assembled listing of the program) shows how the buffer appears in memory. Byte zero is 1E, which shows that a total of 30 bytes could be read in. Byte one shows an 11, which says that 17 bytes actually were read in. A count of "C:\ASM\IOREAD.ASM" shows 17 bytes. The carriage return does not appear because the program has already overwritten the 0D with 00 (see the IOREAD program listing), since we needed an ASCIIZ string. Finally, an ASCII dump was taken to show how you can read the file using ASCII dumps. Then SYMDEB was exited using the "Q" (quit) command.

```
 IOREAD.ASM sectors 23,931-23,934            Cursor at offset 0, hex 0
09504147 45093535 2C313332 0D0A092E 3238360D 0A094558  PAGE    55,132
        .286
        EX
54524E09 434F4445 41534232 3A50524F 430D0A53 5441434B TRN      CODEASB2:PROC
STACK
09534547 4D454E54 20275354 41434B27 20535441 434B0D0A  SEGMENT 'STACK' STACK

09445709 31303020 44555028 3F290D0A 53544143 4B09454E  DW      100 DUP(?)
STACK   EN
44530D0A 434F4445 09534547 4D454E54 09706172 61202743 DS
CODE    SEGMENT para 'C
4F444527 20505542 4C49430D 0A094153 53554D45 0943533A ODE' PUBLIC
        ASSUME  CS:
434F4445 2C204453 3A434F44 452C2053 533A5354 41434B0D CODE, DS:CODE, SS:STACK
0A3B0D0A 3B204E61 6D653A09 09494F52 4541440D 0A3B0D0A
                                                      ;
; Name:          IOREAD
;

3B205075 72706F73 653A2009 54686973 2070726F 63656475 ; Purpose:  This procedu
72652072 65616473 20627974 65732066 726F6D20 61206669 re reads bytes from a fi
6C652E0D 0A3B0D0A 3B20496E 70757473 3A202009 41534349 le.
;
; Inputs:        ASCI
49204669 6C652069 73207370 65636966 69656420 28647269 I File is specified (dri
76655C70 6174685C 66696C65 6E616D65 292C2061 6C6F6E67 ve\path\filename), along
200D0A3B 09097769 74682074 6865206E 756D6265 72206F66
;                with the number of
20627974 65732074 6F207265 61642066 726F6D20 74686520  bytes to read from the
66696C65 2E202054 6865200D 0A3B0909 66696C65 20636861 file.  The
;                file cha
72616374 65727320 61726520 6C696D69 74656420 746F2061 racters are limited to a
206D6178 696D756D 206F6620 33302E20 20497420 63616E20  maximum of 30.  It can
0D0A3B09 09626520 616E7920 6E756D62 65722079 6F752077
;                be any number you w
616E7420 746F2073 70656369 66792C20 7768656E 20796F75 ant to specify, when you
20636861 6E676520 69740D0A 3B090974 6F20796F 75722063  change it
;                to your c
6F64652E 0D0A3B0D             Press Enter for help      ode.
;
```

Fig. 8-12. Hex dump of IOREAD.ASM.

If there is an error in the file read, the Carry Flag is set to 1. Then you examine AX, where the error code was returned. If CF = 0, the read was successful.

IOREAD was run, to read from an assembly language source file, IOREAD.ASM, in the C:\ASM\ path. A hex dump (using the *Norton Utilities*) of IOREAD.ASM, in Fig. 8-12, shows the first bytes of the program. Compare that with Fig. 8-13, the IOREAD run. As you can see, some of the ASCII characters in the file do not print. You can attack this difference several ways. For example, you could (1) change IOREAD to print binary equivalents of the non-printable ASCII characters, (2) use a utility program to see the actual non-printable characters and decide if you actually need to know them, or (3) change IOREAD to print periods "." for non-printable characters.

Creating, Writing, and Closing a File

Creating a file used to be a difficult problem. Today it is much easier, using file handles. Program 8-4, IOWRITE, illustrates the process. You create an ASCIIZ string (an ASCII string which ends with a hex 00) with the file name and point to it with DS:DX. Then you decide which file attribute you want (0 = normal, 01 = read-only, 02 = hidden file, 04 = system file, 08 = volume label, 10 = subdirectory, and 20 = archive) and store that value in CX. Then you use INT 21 Function 5B. If the create is successful, the Carry Flag = 0 and the file handle returns in AX. If unsuccessful, CF = 1 and AX holds the extended error code.

To get additional information about the error, use Interrupt 21 Function 59, which returns a great deal of information in various registers. (For a list of extended error codes, see EXTERROR in Chapter 6, a procedure that contains the codes and an explanation of their use.)

```
C:\ASM>IOREAD
Read which file? C:\ASM\IOREAD.ASM
How many bytes? 15
Read from file:    PAGE  55,132

C:\ASM>
```

Fig. 8-13. *IOREAD run, reading the IOREAD.ASM file.*

To open the file after creation, use Interrupt 21 Function 3D. This function requires the same ASCIIZ file name. Store the access code (0 = read, 1 = write, and 2 = read/write) in AL. After the interrupt, AL holds the file handle or an error code if the Carry Flag is set. To write to the file, use the file handle and Interrupt 21 Function 40. If the write is successful, CF = 0 and AX has the number of bytes written. If unsuccessful, CF = 1 and AX holds the error code.

When you finish writing to a file, you must close the file (use INT 21 Function 3E). If you fail to, the disk directory is incorrect and the file almost useless. Furthermore, INT 21 Function 3E releases the assigned handle so that it can be reused for the next file-handle operation. It isn't a requirement to close files that were opened only for reading, since they did not change length, but closing them releases the file handle. See Fig. 8-14 for a sample run of IOWRITE.

Prior to the sample run, a diskette was formatted and a directory taken to show an empty disk. Then IOWRITE ran, requesting a path/file name be entered. Next it prompted for the bytes to write to the file. Once the bytes were written and the file closed, a message displayed on the screen. The next step in the sample run was to use the DOS command TYPE to show the contents of A:THISFILE. The contents were identical to what had been entered from the keyboard. Next, a DIR was requested which showed that THISFILE now exists and contains data. As

```
C:\ASM>DIR A:

 Volume in drive A is TESTIT
 Directory of  A:\

File not found

C:\ASM>IOWRITE

Write to which file? A:THISFILE
Enter the bytes? These are the entered bytes.
Closing the file.

C:\ASM>TYPE A:THISFILE
These are the entered bytes.
C:\ASM>DIR A:

 Volume in drive A is TESTIT
 Directory of  A:\

THISFILE          28   2-17-88   3:57p
        1 File(s)    361472 bytes free

C:\ASM>
```

Fig. 8-14. IOWRITE sample run.

you can see, the date and time of the file update was automatically stored in the directory.

Setting up the memory buffer for the file name is discussed in the section on IOREAD. The same process is used with IOWRITE. Then IOWRITE asks for input from the keyboard that it is to write to the file. Once the data has been written to the file, the file is closed using INT 21 Function 3E.

Program 8-1: IOEDIT

```
Microsoft (R) Macro Assembler Version 5.00


                                          PAGE     55,132
                                          .386
 0000                             STACK   SEGMENT 'STACK' STACK
 0000   0064[                             DW       100 DUP(?)
             ????
                             ]

 00C8                             STACK   ENDS
 0000                             CODE    SEGMENT para 'CODE' PUBLIC USE16
                                          ASSUME   CS:CODE, DS:CODE, SS:STACK
                                  ;
                                  ; Name:          IOEDIT
                                  ;
                                  ; Purpose:       This program uses an input buffer to edit numeric and
                                  ;                alpha characters.  It also shows how to set up and
                                  ;                print Carriage Return/Line Feed.  To print CR/LF, the
                                  ;                hex characters (0A=Line Feed, 0D=Carriage Return) are
                                  ;                placed in a character string which ends with a "$",
                                  ;                so that Interrupt 21 Function 9A can print it.
                                  ;
                                  ;                On input, the 0D (carriage return) is kept in the input
                                  ;                string by DOS.  If the program worked with the entire
                                  ;                string, the 0D would have to be figured into the program
                                  ;                logic.
                                  ;
                                  ; Inputs:        A single digit number or alpha character is requested.
                                  ;                It is entered via keyboard into a buffered input area.
                                  ;                Only a single character is entered.  Additional numbers
                                  ;                could be requested and CODEASB (convert ASCII to Binary)
                                  ;                called to convert the larger number for verification.
                                  ;                The alpha characters could be checked one at a time by
                                  ;                stepping through the input string.
                                  ;
                                  ; Process:       First the entered character is checked to see if it is
                                  ;                a number. If so, it is checked to see that it is between
                                  ;                0 and 9.  For purposes of this example, negative numbers
                                  ;                are ignored.  If it's alpha, its checked to see if it is
                                  ;                between A-Z or a-z.
                                  ;
                                  ; Outputs:       Messages with the results of each action.  Note that
                                  ;                carriage return and line feed are the first two characters
                                  ;                of each output line.
                                  ;
 0000                             IOEDIT:
 0000   8C C8                                      MOV     AX,CS          ; Prepare to set DS
 0002   8E D8                                      MOV     DS,AX          ;   and set it.
 0004   E9 00E7 R                                  JMP     BEGINHERE
                                  ;
 0007   0A 0D 20 45 6E 74 65      PROMPT           DB      0Ah,0Dh,' Enter a number or character > $'
        72 20 61 20 6E 75 6D
        62 65 72 20 6F 72 20
        63 68 61 72 61 63 74
        65 72 20 3E 20 24
 0029   0A 0D 24                  CR_LF            DB      0Ah,0Dh,'$'
 002C   0004[                     INPUT_STR        DB      4 DUP(?)
             ??
```

```
                                 ]

0030  0A 0D 20 54 68 69 73  ERR_NUM          DB      0Ah,0Dh,' This number is not a positive 0-9.$'
      20 6E 75 6D 62 65 72
      20 69 73 20 6E 6F 74
      20 61 20 70 6F 73 69
      74 69 76 65 20 30 2D
      39 2E 24
0056  0A 0D 20 54 68 69 73  ERR_CHAR         DB      0Ah,0Dh,' This is not an alphabetic character.$'
      20 69 73 20 6E 6F 74
      20 61 6E 20 61 6C 70
      68 61 62 65 74 69 63
      20 63 68 61 72 61 63
      74 65 72 2E 24
007E  0A 0D 20 54 68 69 73  NUM_FOUND        DB      0Ah,0Dh,' This is a positive number 0-9.$'
      20 69 73 20 61 20 70
      6F 73 69 74 69 76 65
      20 6E 75 6D 62 65 72
      20 30 2D 39 2E 24
00A0  0A 0D 20 54 68 69 73  CHAR_FOUND       DB      0Ah,0Dh,' This is a lower-case character.$'
      20 69 73 20 61 20 6C
      6F 77 65 72 2D 63 61
      73 65 20 63 68 61 72
      61 63 74 65 72 2E 24
00C3  0A 0D 20 54 68 69 73  CHAR1_FOUND      DB      0Ah,0Dh,' This is an upper-case character.$'
      20 69 73 20 61 6E 20
      75 70 70 65 72 2D 63
      61 73 65 20 63 68 61
      72 61 63 74 65 72 2E
      24
                            ;
00E7                        BEGINHERE:
00E7  8D 16 0007 R                           LEA     DX,PROMPT         ; Print the request for input
00EB  B4 09                                  MOV     AH,9
00ED  CD 21                                  INT     21h
                            ;
00EF  C6 06 002C R 04                        MOV     INPUT_STR,4       ; Max number of chars in string
00F4  8D 16 002C R                           LEA     DX,INPUT_STR      ; Input Buffer
00F8  B4 0A                                  MOV     AH,0Ah
00FA  CD 21                                  INT     21h               ; Buffered keyboard input
                            ;
                            ; Now edit the input.
                            ;
00FC  2B C9                                  SUB     CX,CX             ; Be sure CX is empty
00FE  8D 36 002C R                           LEA     SI,INPUT_STR      ; Point to input buffer
0102  83 C6 02                               ADD     SI,2              ; Skip the auxiliary bytes
                            ;
                            ;  See if it is a number - no matter how many are entered, only one
                            ;       is checked, for this example.  See Prolog for other ways to
                            ;       check multiple digits.
                            ;
0105  8A 0E 002E R                           MOV     CL,BYTE PTR INPUT_STR[2]
0109  80 F1 30                               XOR     CL,30h
010C  80 F9 09                               CMP     CL,9              ; Is this a number?
010F  0F 86 0116 R                           JBE     EDIT0
0113  EB 2F 90                               JMP     CHAR0             ; Go see if it is a character
0116                        EDIT0:
0116  0B C0                                  OR      AX,AX             ; Is the number negative?
0118  0F 89 011F R                           JNS     EDIT2             ; If it is, it's called an error
011C  EB 0C 90                               JMP     ERR0              ;   and a new request is made
011F                        EDIT2:
011F  8D 16 007E R                           LEA     DX,NUM_FOUND      ; Print message
0123  B4 09                                  MOV     AH,9
```

```
0125  CD 21                             INT     21h
0127  EB 55 90                          JMP     ENDHERE
                    ;
                    ; Input error - neither positive number or character
                    ;
012A                ERR0:
012A  8D 16 0030 R                      LEA     DX,ERR_NUM      ; Error message
012E  EB 05 90                          JMP     ERR2
0131                ERR1:
0131  8D 16 0056 R                      LEA     DX,ERR_CHAR
0135                ERR2:
0135  B4 09                             MOV     AH,9
0137  CD 21                             INT     21h
0139  8D 16 0029 R                      LEA     DX,CR_LF        ; Space up a line
013D  B4 09                             MOV     AH,9
013F  CD 21                             INT     21h
0141  EB 3B 90                          JMP     ENDHERE         ; Go get next entry
                    ;
                    ; Was it an alphabetic character - A single character is checked.  See
                    ;       the Prolog for ways to check more than one character.
                    ;
0144                CHAR0:
0144  2B C9                             SUB     CX,CX           ; Zero out CX
0146  8A 0E 002E R                      MOV     CL,BYTE PTR INPUT_STR[2]
014A  80 F9 41                          CMP     CL,41h          ; Capital Letter?
014D  0F 8D 0153 R                      JGE     CHAR1
0151  EB DE                             JMP     ERR1            ; No, less than "A"
0153                CHAR1:
0153  80 F9 5A                          CMP     CL,5Ah          ; Is this <= a "Z" ?
0156  0F 8D 0161 R                      JGE     CHAR3           ; Go see if it's a small letter
015A  8D 16 00C3 R                      LEA     DX,CHAR1_FOUND
015E  EB 17 90                          JMP     CHAR5           ; It's upper case, go print message
0161                CHAR3:
0161  80 F9 61                          CMP     CL,61h          ; Lower case letter?
0164  0F 8D 016A R                      JGE     CHAR4
0168  EB C7                             JMP     ERR1
016A                CHAR4:
016A  80 F9 7A                          CMP     CL,7Ah          ; Is this <= "z" ?
016D  8D 16 00A0 R                      LEA     DX,CHAR_FOUND   ; Print message
0171  0F 8E 0177 R                      JLE     CHAR5           ; Yes, go print message
0175  EB BA                             JMP     ERR1            ; Not alpha character
0177                CHAR5:
0177  B4 09                             MOV     AH,9
0179  CD 21                             INT     21h
017B  EB 01 90                          JMP     ENDHERE
                    ;
                    ;
017E                ENDHERE:
017E  8D 16 0029 R                      LEA     DX,CR_LF        ; Space up one line
0182  B4 09                             MOV     AH,9
0184  CD 21                             INT     21h
                    ;
0186  B4 4C                             MOV     AH,4Ch          ; Standard Ending
0188  CD 21                             INT     21h
018A                CODE                ENDS
                                        END     IOEDIT
```

Program 8-2: IOWORKS

```
Microsoft (R) Macro Assembler Version 5.00


                                        PAGE     55,132
                                        .386
                                        EXTRN    CODEBAS:PROC
                                        EXTRN    EXTERROR:PROC
                                        EXTRN    CODEASB:PROC
0000                           STACK    SEGMENT 'STACK' STACK
0000  00C8[                             DW       200 DUP(?)
          ????
                            ]

0190                           STACK    ENDS
0000                           CODE     SEGMENT para 'CODE' PUBLIC USE16
                                        ASSUME   CS:CODE, DS:CODE, SS:STACK
                               ;
                               ; Name:           IOWORKS
                               ;
                               ; Purpose:        This program performs several functions:
                               ;                 1. Delete a file
                               ;                 2. Rename a file
                               ;                 3. Checking for Existing/non-existing files
                               ;
                               ;                 To see how to create a file, see IOWRITE
                               ;                               open a file, see IOREAD
                               ;                               Read from a file, see IOREAD
                               ;                               Write to a file, see IOWRITE
                               ;                               Close a file, see IOWRITE
                               ;                 All these programs are documented in Chapter 8
                               ;                 of "80386 Assembly Language Toolkit."  They are also
                               ;                 available on disk from TAB Books.
                               ;
                               ; Inputs:         File names are requested.  They are entered via
                               ;                 keyboard.
                               ;
                               ; Process:        1. Delete a file:   INT 21 Function 41
                               ;                 2. Rename a file:   INT 21 Function 56
                               ;                 3. Find first file: INT 21 Function 4E
                               ;                        Once the file is found, file size is printed.
                               ;                        A Disk Transfer Area (DTA) is set up.
                               ;
                               ;                 If any of the processes find an error, they go to
                               ;                 an error location that calls EXTERROR, a procedure
                               ;                 that finds the extended error code and associated
                               ;                 messages to aid debug.  See Chapter 5 of "80386
                               ;                 Assembly Language Toolkit" for a description of all
                               ;                 the processes of EXTERROR.
                               ;
                               ;                 To find the file, a DTA needs to be established.  Once
                               ;                 it is, and the file is found, then you can find the file
                               ;                 size.  Use CODEBAS to convert the binary size to printable
                               ;                 ASCII.
                               ;
                               ; Outputs:        Messages with the results of each action.
                               ;
0000                           IOWORKS:
0000  8C C8                                      MOV      AX,CS             ; Prepare to set DS
```

```
0002  8E D8                                   MOV    DS,AX            ;   and set it.
0004  8E C0                                   MOV    ES,AX
0006  E9 01F7 R                               JMP    BEGINHERE
                                  ;
0009  0A 0D 20 43 68 6F 6F        MENU        DB     0Ah,0Dh,' Choose a number: $'
      73 65 20 61 20 6E 75
      6D 62 65 72 3A 20 24
001E  0A 0D 20 31 2E 20 44                    DB     0Ah,0Dh,' 1. Delete a file $'
      65 6C 65 74 65 20 61
      20 66 69 6C 65 20 24
0033  0A 0D 20 32 2E 20 52                    DB     0Ah,0Dh,' 2. Rename a file $'
      65 6E 61 6D 65 20 61
      20 66 69 6C 65 20 24
0048  0A 0D 20 33 2E 20 46                    DB     0Ah,0Dh,' 3. Find a file   $'
      69 6E 64 20 61 20 66
      69 6C 65 20 20 20 24
005D  0A 0D 20 30 2E 20 54                    DB     0Ah,0Dh,' 0. To end        $'
      6F 20 65 6E 64 20 20
      20 20 20 20 20 20 24
                                  ;
0072  0A 0D 20 45 6E 74 65        PROMPT      DB     0Ah,0Dh,' Enter a number > $'
      72 20 61 20 6E 75 6D
      62 65 72 20 3E 20 24
0087  0A 0D 20 45 6E 74 65        PROMPT1     DB     0Ah,0Dh,' Enter new name > $'
      72 20 6E 65 77 20 6E
      61 6D 65 20 3E 20 24
009C  0A 0D 20 45 6E 74 65        PROMPT2     DB     0Ah,0Dh,' Enter file name> $'
      72 20 66 69 6C 65 20
      6E 61 6D 65 3E 20 24
00B1  0A 0D 20 49 6E 63 6F        ERR1        DB     0Ah,0Dh,' Incorrect. Re-enter.$'
      72 72 65 63 74 2E 20
      52 65 2D 65 6E 74 65
      72 2E 24
00C9  0A 0D 24                    CR_LF       DB     0Ah,0Dh,'$'
00CC  000A[                       INPUT_STR   DB     10 DUP(?)
          ??
                         ]

00D6  0024[                       FILE_NAME   DB     36 DUP(?)
          ??
                         ]

00FA  0024[                       NEWFILE     DB     36 DUP(?)
          ??
                         ]

011E  0A 0D 20 54 68 65 20        SUCCESS     DB     0Ah,0Dh,' The process was successful.$'
      70 72 6F 63 65 73 73
      20 77 61 73 20 73 75
      63 63 65 73 73 66 75
      6C 2E 24
013D  0A 0D 20 46 6F 75 6E        FILESIZE    DB     0Ah,0Dh,' Found it.  Its size in bytes is : $'
      64 20 69 74 2E 20 20
      49 74 73 20 73 69 7A
      65 20 69 6E 20 62 79
      74 65 73 20 69 73 20
      3A 20 24
0163  0014[                       SIZE1       DB     20 DUP(?)
          ??
                         ]

0177  0080[                       DTA_AREA    DB     128 DUP(?)
```

```
          ??
                      ]

                             ;
01F7                         BEGINHERE:
01F7  B9 0005                              MOV    CX,5            ; Number of menu items to print
01FA  8D 16 0009 R                         LEA    DX,MENU
01FE  B4 09                                MOV    AH,9
0200                         MENUPRT:
0200  CD 21                                INT    21h
0202  83 C2 15                             ADD    DX,21           ; Each prompt is 21 bytes long
0205  E2 F9                                LOOP   MENUPRT
0207                         MENUPRT1:
0207  8D 16 00C9 R                         LEA    DX,CR_LF        ; Space down a line
020B  B4 09                                MOV    AH,9
020D  CD 21                                INT    21h
020F  8D 16 0072 R                         LEA    DX,PROMPT
0213  B4 09                                MOV    AH,9
0215  CD 21                                INT    21h
                             ;
0217  C6 06 00CC R 0A                      MCV    INPUT_STR,10    ; Max number of chars in string
021C  8D 16 00CC R                         LEA    DX,INPUT_STR    ; Input Buffer
0220  B4 0A                                MOV    AH,0Ah
0222  CD 21                                INT    21h             ; Buffered keyboard input
                             ;
                             ; Now edit the input.  First CALL CODEASB to turn the entered ASCII
                             ;        number into a binary number.
                             ;        SI - points to the string to be converted
                             ;        CX - the count of characters
                             ;        If successful, Carry Flag = 0 and AX holds the returned number
                             ;        If not, Carry Flag = 1
                             ;
0224  2B C9                                SUB    CX,CX           ; Be sure CX is empty
0226  8A 0E 00CD R                         MOV    CL,INPUT_STR[1] ; The count of characters entered
022A  8D 36 00CC R                         LEA    SI,INPUT_STR
022E  83 C6 02                             ADD    SI,2            ; Now points to char string
                             ;
                             ;  See if it is a number before calling CODEASB
                             ;
0231  8A 0E 00CE R                         MOV    CL,BYTE PTR INPUT_STR[2]
0235  80 F1 30                             XOR    CL,30h
0238  80 F9 09                             CMP    CL,9            ; Is this a number?
023B  0F 86 0242 R                         JBE    EDIT0
023F  EB 29 90                             JMP    ERR0
0242                         EDIT0:
0242  E8 0000 E                            CALL   CODEASB
0245  0F 83 024C R                         JNC    EDIT1           ; Carry Flag set?
0249  EB 1F 90                             JMP    ERR0
024C                         EDIT1:
024C  0B C0                                OR     AX,AX           ; Is the number negative?
024E  0F 89 0255 R                         JNS    EDIT2
0252  EB 16 90                             JMP    ERR0
0255                         EDIT2:
0255  2B C9                                SUB    CX,CX           ; Zero out CX
0257  8A C8                                MOV    CL,AL           ; AL holds the number in binary
0259  80 F9 00                             CMP    CL,0            ; End?
025C  0F 8F 0263 R                         JG     EDIT3
0260  E9 035E R                            JMP    ENDHERE
0263                         EDIT3:
0263  80 F9 04                             CMP    CL,4            ; Too high?
0266  0F 8C 027D R                         JL     GETFILE
                             ;
                             ; Input error
```

```
                                  ;
026A                              ERRO:
026A  8D 16 00B1 R                               LEA     DX,ERR1          ; Error message
026E  B4 09                                      MOV     AH,9
0270  CD 21                                      INT     21h
0272  8D 16 00C9 R                               LEA     DX,CR_LF         ; Space up a line
0276  B4 09                                      MOV     AH,9
0278  CD 21                                      INT     21h
027A  E9 01F7 R                                  JMP     BEGINHERE        ; Go get next entry
                                  ;
027D                              GETFILE:
027D  8D 16 009C R                               LEA     DX,PROMPT2       ; Ask for file name
0281  B4 09                                      MOV     AH,9
0283  CD 21                                      INT     21h
0285  C6 06 00D6 R 24                            MOV     FILE_NAME,36     ; Max chars to enter
028A  8D 16 00D6 R                               LEA     DX,FILE_NAME
028E  B4 0A                                      MOV     AH,0Ah           ; Buffered keyboard entry
0290  CD 21                                      INT     21h
0292  83 C2 02                                   ADD     DX,2             ; Point at path/file
0295  2B C0                                      SUB     AX,AX            ; Zero out AX
0297  A0 00D7 R                                  MOV     AL,[FILE_NAME+1] ; Count of actually entered bytes
029A  04 02                                      ADD     AL,2             ; Find position after last char
029C  8B F0                                      MOV     SI,AX            ; Move count to an index register
029E  C6 84 00D6 R 00                            MOV     FILE_NAME[SI],00 ; Make into ASCIIZ string
                                  ;
                                  ; Delete a file
                                  ;       INT 21 Function 41
                                  ;       DS:DX = segment:offset of ASCIIZ file name
                                  ;       If successful, Carry Flag = 0
                                  ;        unsuccessful, Carry Flag = 1 and AX has error
                                  ;
02A3  80 F9 01                                   CMP     CL,1             ; Delete a file choice ?
02A6  0F 8F 02BF R                               JG      RENAME
02AA  2B C0                                      SUB     AX,AX
02AC  B4 41                                      MOV     AH,41h           ; Delete file from directory
02AE  CD 21                                      INT     21h
02B0  0F 82 0358 R                               JC      ERROR_MSG
02B4  8D 16 011E R                               LEA     DX,SUCCESS       ; Give positive results
02B8  B4 09                                      MOV     AH,9
02BA  CD 21                                      INT     21h
02BC  E9 035E R                                  JMP     ENDHERE
                                  ;
                                  ; Rename a file
                                  ;       INT 21 Function 56
                                  ;       DS:DX = segment:offset of ASCIIZ file name
                                  ;       ES:DI = segment:offset of new ASCIIZ pathname for file
                                  ;
02BF                              RENAME:
02BF  80 F9 02                                   CMP     CL,2             ; Rename a file choice ?
02C2  0F 8F 0304 R                               JG      CHECK
02C6  87 D5                                      XCHG    DX,BP            ; Save pointer to old name
02C8  8D 16 0087 R                               LEA     DX,PROMPT1       ; Ask for new name
02CC  B4 09                                      MOV     AH,9
02CE  CD 21                                      INT     21h
02D0  C6 06 00FA R 24                            MOV     NEWFILE,36       ; Max chars to be entered
02D5  8D 16 00FA R                               LEA     DX,NEWFILE       ; Point to new file name
02D9  B4 0A                                      MOV     AH,0Ah           ; Buffered keyboard input
02DB  CD 21                                      INT     21h
02DD  2B C0                                      SUB     AX,AX            ; Zero out AX
02DF  A0 00FB R                                  MOV     AL,[NEWFILE+1]   ; How many chars entered
02E2  04 02                                      ADD     AL,2             ; Find position after last char
02E4  8B F0                                      MOV     SI,AX            ; Move count to index register
```

```
02E6  C6 84 00FA R 00              MOV     NEWFILE[SI],00   ; Make new name into ASCIIZ str
02EB  8D 3E 00FC R                 LEA     DI,NEWFILE+2     ; Point to new name
02EF  87 D5                        XCHG    DX,BP            ; Retrieve pointer to old name
02F1  B4 56                        MOV     AH,56h           ; Rename function
02F3  CD 21                        INT     21h
02F5  0F 82 0358 R                 JC      ERROR_MSG        ; Was there an error?
02F9  8D 16 011E R                 LEA     DX,SUCCESS       ; Give positive results
02FD  B4 09                        MOV     AH,9
02FF  CD 21                        INT     21h
0301  EB 5B 90                     JMP     ENDHERE
                        ;
                        ;
                        ; Check for existing file name
                        ;       INT 21 Function 4E
                        ;       DS:DX = segment:offset of ASCIIZ filename
                        ;       CX = attribute word (0=normal file, 1=read only, 2=hidden,
                        ;               4=system, 8=volume label, 10=subdirectory, and
                        ;               20=archive)  For a multipurpose procedure/program,
                        ;               request this from the user.  0 Used for this example.
                        ;
                        ;       If successful, Carry Flag=0, and DTA holds:
                        ;               Offset  length  Value
                        ;               00      21      MS-DOS reserved
                        ;               15       1      file attribute
                        ;               16       2      Time of last write
                        ;               18       2      Date of last write
                        ;               1A       2      Low word of file size
                        ;               1C       2      High word of file size
                        ;               1E      13      Filename & extension in ASCIIZ
                        ;
                        ;       If unsuccessful, Carry Flag = 1, AX has error code
                        ;
0304                    CHECK:
0304  80 F9 03                     CMP     CL,3             ; File size choice?
0307  0F 8F 0358 R                 JG      ERROR_MSG
                        ; Set up DTA area
030B  8D 16 0177 R                 LEA     DX,DTA_AREA
030F  B4 1A                        MOV     AH,1Ah           ; Set the DTA address
0311  CD 21                        INT     21h
                        ;
                        ; Get the file attributes.  Attribute returns in CX
                        ;       DS:DX points to file name
                        ;
0313  8D 16 00D6 R                 LEA     DX,FILE_NAME
0317  83 C2 02                     ADD     DX,2
031A  B4 43                        MOV     AH,43h           ; Get attributes function
031C  B0 00                        MOV     AL,00
031E  CD 21                        INT     21h              ; Return attrib in CX
                        ;
0320  B4 4E                        MOV     AH,4Eh           ; Check for file
0322  CD 21                        INT     21h
0324  0F 82 0358 R                 JC      ERROR_MSG        ; Was there an error?
                        ;
                        ; Print file size.  CALL CODEBAS : AX word to be converted
                        ;                                  DI char string returned
                        ;
0328  8D 16 013D R                 LEA     DX,FILESIZE      ; Print file size header
032C  B4 09                        MOV     AH,9
032E  CD 21                        INT     21h
                        ;
0330  A1 0191 R                    MOV     AX,WORD PTR [DTA_AREA+1Ah] ; Get word
0333  66| 98                       CWDE                     ; As a double
```

```
0335  8D 3E 0163 R                  LEA     DI,SIZE1        ; The pointer to string
0339  E8 0000 E                     CALL    CODEBAS         ; Convert to ASCII
033C  2B D2                         SUB     DX,DX           ; Be sure DX is empty to start
033E                      SIZEPRT:
033E  8A 15                         MOV     DL,BYTE PTR [DI]
0340  0A D2                         OR      DL,DL           ; Is this byte a hex 00 ?
0342  0F 84 034D R                  JE      MSG
0346  B4 02                         MOV     AH,2
0348  CD 21                         INT     21h
034A  47                            INC     DI
034B  EB F1                         JMP     SIZEPRT
034D                      MSG:
034D  8D 16 011E R                  LEA     DX,SUCCESS      ; Give positive results
0351  B4 09                         MOV     AH,9
0353  CD 21                         INT     21h
0355  EB 07 90                      JMP     ENDHERE
                          ;
                          ;
                          ; If any of the processes find an error, they come to this section
                          ; which calls EXTERROR, to determine the extended error and the
                          ; messages to help pinpoint the problem.
                          ;
0358                      ERROR_MSG:
0358  E8 0000 E                     CALL    EXTERROR
035B  EB 01 90                      JMP     ENDHERE
                          ;
035E                      ENDHERE:
035E  8D 16 00C9 R                  LEA     DX,CR_LF        ; Space up one line
0362  B4 09                         MOV     AH,9
0364  CD 21                         INT     21h
                          ;
0366  B4 4C                         MOV     AH,4Ch          ; Standard Ending
0368  CD 21                         INT     21h
036A                      CODE      ENDS
                                    END     IOWORKS
```

Program 8-3: IOREAD

```
Microsoft (R) Macro Assembler Version 5.00


                                        PAGE     55,132
                                        .386
                                        EXTRN    CODEASB:PROC
 0000                          STACK    SEGMENT 'STACK' STACK
 0000   0064[                           DW       100 DUP(?)
            ????
                        ]

 00C8                          STACK    ENDS
 0000                          CODE     SEGMENT para 'CODE' PUBLIC USE16
                                        ASSUME   CS:CODE, DS:CODE, SS:STACK
                               ;
                               ; Name:           IOREAD
                               ;
                               ; Purpose:        This procedure reads bytes from a file.
                               ;
                               ; Inputs:         ASCII File is specified (drive\path\filename), along
                               ;                 with the number of bytes to read from the file.  The
                               ;                 file characters are limited to a maximum of 30.  It can
                               ;                 be any number you want to specify, when you change it
                               ;                 to your code.
                               ;
                               ;                 For purposes of this example, the bytes to be read
                               ;                 are limited to a 40 characters.  This eliminates having
                               ;                 format the screen printout.
                               ;
                               ; Process:        INT 21 Function 3D is used to open the file.  This
                               ;                 function requires the ASCIIZ filename to be in DS:DX.
                               ;                 AL is the Access code (0=reading, 1=writing, 3=both
                               ;                 reading and writing).  If open is successful, AX
                               ;                 contains the file handle.  If not, AL has an error
                               ;                 code.  For error codes, see Appendix 6 of "80386
                               ;                 Assembly Language Toolkit."
                               ;
                               ;                 Once the bytes are read, the file is closed using INT
                               ;                 21 Function 3E.  BX holds the valid file handle.  If
                               ;                 an unsuccessful close, AL=6 which says invalid handle.
                               ;
                               ; Outputs:        The bytes read are displayed.
                               ;
 0000                          IOREAD:
 0000   8C C8                                    MOV      AX,CS             ; Prepare to set DS
 0002   8E D8                                    MOV      DS,AX             ;   and set it.
 0004   E9 03AE R                                JMP      BEGINHERE
                               ;
 0007   52 65 61 64 20 77 68   PROMPT            DB       'Read which file? $'
        69 63 68 20 66 69 6C
        65 3F 20 24
 0019   0A 0D 48 6F 77 20 6D   PROMPT1           DB       0Ah,0Dh,'How many bytes? $'
        61 6E 79 20 62 79 74
        65 73 3F 20 24
 002C   0A 0D 52 65 61 64 20   HEADER            DB       0Ah,0Dh,'Read from file:   $'
        66 72 6F 6D 20 66 69
        6C 65 3A 20 20 20 24
 0041   0020[                  FILE_NAME         DB       32 DUP(?)
             ??
```

```
                          ]

0061  0020[                       BYTE_NO        DB      32 DUP(?)
           ??
                          ]

0081  0028[                       INPUT_STR      DB      40 DUP(?)
           ??
                          ]

00A9  0A 0D 24                    CR_LF          DB      0Ah,0Dh,'$'
00AC  0A 0D 20 45 52 52 4F        ERROR_MSG      DB      0Ah,0Dh,' ERROR - $'
      52 20 2D 20 24
00B8  0A 0D 20 49 6E 76 61        INVALID_NO     DB      0Ah,0Dh,' Invalid Number entered.$'
      6C 69 64 20 4E 75 6D
      62 65 72 20 65 6E 74
      65 72 65 64 2E 24
                                  ;
                                  ; Error Return Codes
                                  ;
00D3  20 46 75 6E 63 74 69        ERROR1         DB      ' Function number not valid.            $'
      6F 6E 20 6E 75 6D 62
      65 72 20 6E 6F 74 20
      76 61 6C 69 64 2E 20
      20 20 20 20 20 20 20
      20 20 20 20 20 20 20
      24
00FE  20 46 69 6C 65 20 6E        ERROR2         DB      ' File not found.                       $'
      6F 74 20 66 6F 75 6E
      64 2E 20 20 20 20 20
      20 20 20 20 20 20 20
      20 20 20 20 20 20 20
      20 20 20 20 20 20 20
      24
0129  20 49 6E 76 61 6C 69        ERROR3         DB      ' Invalid path.                         $'
      64 20 70 61 74 68 2E
      20 20 20 20 20 20 20
      20 20 20 20 20 20 20
      20 20 20 20 20 20 20
      20 20 20 20 20 20 20
      24
0154  20 54 6F 6F 20 6D 61        ERROR4         DB      ' Too many files open at the same time. $'
      6E 79 20 66 69 6C 65
      73 20 6F 70 65 6E 20
      61 74 20 74 68 65 20
      73 61 6D 65 20 74 69
      6D 65 2E 20 20 20 20
      24
017F  20 41 63 63 65 73 73        ERROR5         DB      ' Access is denied.                     $'
      20 69 73 20 64 65 6E
      69 65 64 2E 20 20 20
      20 20 20 20 20 20 20
      20 20 20 20 20 20 20
      20 20 20 20 20 20 20
      24
01AA  20 46 69 6C 65 20 68        ERROR6         DB      ' File handle is invalid.               $'
      61 6E 64 6C 65 20 69
      73 20 69 6E 76 61 6C
      69 64 2E 20 20 20 20
      20 20 20 20 20 20 20
      20 20 20 20 20 20 20
      24
```

```
01D5  20 4D 65 6D 6F 72 79     ERROR7      DB     ' Memory control blocks destroyed.          $'
      20 63 6F 6E 74 72 6F
      6C 20 62 6C 6F 63 6B
      73 20 64 65 73 74 72
      6F 79 65 64 2E 20 20
      20 20 20 20 20 20 20
      24
0200  20 4E 6F 74 20 65 6E     ERROR8      DB     ' Not enough memory.                        $'
      6F 75 67 68 20 6D 65
      6D 6F 72 79 2E 20 20
      20 20 20 20 20 20 20
      20 20 20 20 20 20 20
      20 20 20 20 20 20 20
      24
022B  20 4D 65 6D 6F 72 79     ERROR9      DB     ' Memory block address is invalid.          $'
      20 62 6C 6F 63 6B 20
      61 64 64 72 65 73 73
      20 69 73 20 69 6E 76
      61 6C 69 64 2E 20 20
      20 20 20 20 20 20 20
      24
0256  20 45 6E 76 69 72 6F     ERROR10     DB     ' Environment String is invalid.            $'
      6E 6D 65 6E 74 20 53
      74 72 69 6E 67 20 69
      73 20 69 6E 76 61 6C
      69 64 2E 20 20 20 20
      20 20 20 20 20 20 20
      24
0281  20 46 6F 72 6D 61 74     ERROR11     DB     ' Format invalid.                           $'
      20 69 6E 76 61 6C 69
      64 2E 20 20 20 20 20
      20 20 20 20 20 20 20
      20 20 20 20 20 20 20
      20 20 20 20 20 20 20
      24
02AC  20 41 63 63 65 73 73     ERROR12     DB     ' Access code invalid.                      $'
      20 63 6F 64 65 20 69
      6E 76 61 6C 69 64 2E
      20 20 20 20 20 20 20
      20 20 20 20 20 20 20
      20 20 20 20 20 20 20
      24
02D7  20 44 61 74 61 20 69     ERROR13     DB     ' Data invalid.                             $'
      6E 76 61 6C 69 64 2E
      20 20 20 20 20 20 20
      20 20 20 20 20 20 20
      20 20 20 20 20 20 20
      20 20 20 20 20 20 20
      24
0302  20 49 6E 76 61 6C 69     ERROR15     DB     ' Invalid drive specified.                  $'
      64 20 64 72 69 76 65
      20 73 70 65 63 69 66
      69 65 64 2E 20 20 20
      20 20 20 20 20 20 20
      20 20 20 20 20 20 20
      24
032D  20 41 74 74 65 6D 70     ERROR16     DB     ' Attempt made to remove current directory.$'
      74 20 6D 61 64 65 20
      74 6F 20 72 65 6D 6F
      76 65 20 63 75 72 72
      65 6E 74 20 64 69 72
      65 63 74 6F 72 79 2E
```

```
      24
0358  20 4E 6F 74 20 73 61     ERROR17        DB      ' Not same device.                 $'
      6D 65 20 64 65 76 69
      63 65 2E 20 20 20 20
      20 20 20 20 20 20 20
      20 20 20 20 20 20 20
      20 20 20 20 20 20 20
      24
0383  20 4E 6F 20 6D 6F 72     ERROR18        DB      ' No more files found.             $'
      65 20 66 69 6C 65 73
      20 66 6F 75 6E 64 2E
      20 20 20 20 20 20 20
      20 20 20 20 20 20 20
      20 20 20 20 20 20 20
      24

                               ;
03AE                           BEGINHERE:
03AE  8D 16 0007 R                            LEA     DX,PROMPT          ; Print the file prompt
03B2  B4 09                                   MOV     AH,9
03B4  CD 21                                   INT     21h
03B6  C6 06 0041 R 1E                         MOV     FILE_NAME,30       ; Max characters in input
03BB  8D 16 0041 R                            LEA     DX,FILE_NAME       ; Get file name/path (if any)
03BF  B4 0A                                   MOV     AH,0Ah
03C1  CD 21                                   INT     21h
03C3  8A 0E 0042 R                            MOV     CL,[FILE_NAME+1] ; How many bytes read in
03C7  80 C1 02                                ADD     CL,2               ; Find position after last char
03CA  B5 00                                   MOV     CH,00
03CC  8B F1                                   MOV     SI,CX              ; Move to index register
03CE  C6 84 0041 R 00                         MOV     FILE_NAME[SI],00 ; Make into ASCIIZ string
                               ;
03D3  8D 16 0019 R                            LEA     DX,PROMPT1         ; Now read how many bytes
03D7  B4 09                                   MOV     AH,9
03D9  CD 21                                   INT     21h
03DB  C6 06 0061 R 26                         MOV     BYTE_NO,38
03E0  8D 16 0061 R                            LEA     DX,BYTE_NO
03E4  B4 0A                                   MOV     AH,0Ah             ; Read in digit(s)
03E6  CD 21                                   INT     21h
                               ;
                               ;      Convert to a binary number
                               ;      SI points to the string which is to be converted
                               ;      CX has the count of ASCII characters
                               ;      If CALL is Successful, Carry Flag = 0
                               ;                                AX has result
                               ;      If not successful,      Carry Flag = 1
                               ;                                AX = 0
                               ;
03E8  2B C9                                   SUB     CX,CX
03EA  8A 0E 0062 R                            MOV     CL,BYTE_NO[1]     ; Number of bytes read in
03EE  8D 36 0063 R                            LEA     SI,BYTE_NO[2]     ; The character string
03F2  E8 0000 E                               CALL    CODEASB
                               ;
03F5  2B C9                                   SUB     CX,CX              ; Zero CX
03F7  A2 0061 R                               MOV     BYTE_NO,AL         ; Save the Number
03FA  0F 82 0407 R                            JC      INVALID            ; Was Carry Flag Set?
03FE  80 3E 0061 R 00                         CMP     BYTE_NO,0          ; Was a zero entered?
0403  0F 85 0412 R                            JNE     OPEN0
0407                           INVALID:
0407  8D 16 00B8 R                            LEA     DX,INVALID_NO      ; Error on entry
040B  B4 09                                   MOV     AH,9
040D  CD 21                                   INT     21h
040F  EB 6A 90                                JMP     ENDHERE
                               ;
```

```
                        ; Open file
                        ;       DX = ASCIIZ string with file name
                        ;       AL = File attribute (0=read only, 1=write only,
                        ;            2=read/write)
                        ;         Successful read, AX = File handle
                        ;       Unsuccessful read, AX = Error Code and CF=1
                        ;
0412                    OPEN0:
0412  8D 16 0043 R              LEA     DX,FILE_NAME+2  ; The file/path
0416  B0 00                     MOV     AL,0            ; Read file only
0418  B4 3D                     MOV     AH,3Dh
041A  CD 21                     INT     21h
041C  8B F8                     MOV     DI,AX           ; Save file handle
                        ;
                        ;       Check for errors
                        ;       If there's an error, Carry Flag is set and error number in AL
                        ;
041E                    ERROR_HERE:
041E  0F 83 0448 R              JNC     READ0
0422  95                        XCHG    AX,BP           ; Save error number
0423  8D 16 00A9 R              LEA     DX,CR_LF        ; Carriage Return/Line Feed
0427  B4 09                     MOV     AH,9
0429  CD 21                     INT     21h
042B  8D 16 00AC R              LEA     DX,ERROR_MSG    ; Print that there is an error
042F  B4 09                     MOV     AH,9
0431  CD 21                     INT     21h
0433  95                        XCHG    AX,BP           ; Get error number back
0434  8D 16 00D3 R              LEA     DX,ERROR1       ; Print which error was found
0438  B1 2B                     MOV     CL,43           ; Each error is 43 bytes
043A  F6 E1                     MUL     CL              ; CL x AX = Result in AL
043C  2D 002B                   SUB     AX,43           ; Back up to correct position
043F  03 D0                     ADD     DX,AX           ; Index into error messages
0441  B4 09                     MOV     AH,9
0443  CD 21                     INT     21h
0445  EB 34 90                  JMP     ENDHERE
                        ;
                        ; Read from file
                        ;       DI = File Handle, Moved into BX
                        ;       BYTE_NO = Number of bytes to read from file
                        ;               Successful read, AX has Number actually read
                        ;             Unsuccessful read, AX has error number
                        ;
0448                    READ0:
0448  8B DF                     MOV     BX,DI           ; File handle
044A  8D 16 0081 R              LEA     DX,INPUT_STR
044E  8A 0E 0061 R              MOV     CL,BYTE_NO      ; Number of bytes to read
0452  B4 3F                     MOV     AH,3Fh          ; Read function number
0454  CD 21                     INT     21h
0456  8B C8                     MOV     CX,AX           ; Number actually read
                        ;
                        ; If an error on read Carry Flag is set
                        ;
0458  0F 83 0466 R              JNC     DISPLAY0
045C  3D 0005                   CMP     AX,5
045F  74 BD                     JE      ERROR_HERE
0461  3D 0006                   CMP     AX,6
0464  74 B8                     JE      ERROR_HERE
                        ;
                        ; Display the bytes read
                        ;       CX has the number of bytes, so use CX as loop index
                        ;       INPUT_STR is the buffer with the characters read from
                        ;               the ASCII file
                        ;
```

```
                                     ;
0466                                 DISPLAY0:
0466  8D 16 002C R                                  LEA     DX,HEADER         ; Output header
046A  B4 09                                         MOV     AH,9
046C  CD 21                                         INT     21h
046E  2B F6                                         SUB     SI,SI             ; Initialize index
0470                                 SHOW0:
0470  46                                            INC     SI                ; Index into INPUT_STR
0471  8A 94 0081 R                                  MOV     DL,INPUT_STR[SI]  ; Load character into DX
0475  B4 02                                         MOV     AH,2              ; Print the character
0477  CD 21                                         INT     21h
0479  E0 F5                                         LOOPNZ  SHOW0
                                     ;
                                     ;
047B                                 ENDHERE:
047B  B4 4C                                         MOV     AH,4Ch            ; Standard Ending
047D  CD 21                                         INT     21h
047F                                 CODE           ENDS
                                                    END     IOREAD
```

Program 8-4: IOWRITE

```
Microsoft (R) Macro Assembler Version 5.00


                                           PAGE    55,132
                                           .386
                                           EXTRN   EXTERROR:PROC
 0000                             STACK    SEGMENT 'STACK' STACK
 0000   00C8[                              DW      200 DUP(?)
            ????
                        ]

 0190                             STACK    ENDS
 0000                             CODE     SEGMENT para 'CODE' PUBLIC USE16
                                           ASSUME  CS:CODE, DS:CODE, SS:STACK
                                  ;
                                  ; Name:          IOWRITE
                                  ;
                                  ; Purpose:       This procedure creates a file, then writes bytes
                                  ;                to that file, and then closes the file.
                                  ;
                                  ; Inputs:        An ASCII File is specified (drive\path\filename).
                                  ;                For purposes of this example, the path/file characters
                                  ;                are limited to a maximum of 30.  It can be any number
                                  ;                you want to specify, when you change it to your code.
                                  ;
                                  ;                Also, for purposes of this example, the bytes to be
                                  ;                written are limited to 40 characters.  Again this was
                                  ;                arbitrary for the purposes of an example.
                                  ;
                                  ;                This program calls EXTERROR to process errors. EXTERROR
                                  ;                contains the extended error codes and uses INT 21
                                  ;                Function 59 to get them.  After INT 21 Function 59
                                  ;                is issued, AX holds the extended error code, BH holds
                                  ;                the error class, BL holds the suggested action, and
                                  ;                CH holds the location of the error.  See EXTERROR in
                                  ;                Chapter 5 of the "80386 Assembly Language Toolkit"
                                  ;                for further information.
                                  ;
                                  ; Process:       INT 21 Function 5B creates a file handle, with DS:DX
                                  ;                pointing to the ASCIIZ string with path/file name, and
                                  ;                CX pointing to the file attribute (0=normal file, 1=read
                                  ;                only, 2=hidden file, 4=system file, 8=volume label,
                                  ;                10=subdirectory, and 20=archive).  Note that if the
                                  ;                file already exists, INT 21 Function 5B will return with
                                  ;                an error message.  Use INT 21 Function 59 to get what
                                  ;                the extended error message is.  EXTERROR gets the error
                                  ;                and prints explanatory messages.
                                  ;
                                  ;                INT 21 Function 3D is used to open the file.  This
                                  ;                function requires the ASCIIZ filename to be in DS:DX.
                                  ;                AL is the Access code(0=read only, 1=write only, and
                                  ;                2=read/write).  If open is successful, AX
                                  ;                contains the file handle.  If not, AL has an error
                                  ;                code.  For error codes, see Appendix 6 of "80386
                                  ;                Assembly Language Toolkit."  Also, codes are in
                                  ;                EXTERROR.
                                  ;
                                  ;                INT 21 40 is used to write the bytes to the file.  Once
                                  ;                they are written the read/write pointer is automatically
```

```
                                        ;               updated so that the next write goes to the byte that
                                        ;               follows the end of the previous write.
                                        ;
                                        ;               Once the bytes are written, the file is closed using INT
                                        ;               21 Function 3E.  BX holds the valid file handle.  If
                                        ;               an unsuccessful close, AL=6 which says invalid handle.
                                        ;
                                        ; Outputs:      A File Closed message is displayed on the screen.
                                        ;
                                        ; Note:         INT 21 Function 5B will abort with a "File already
                                        ;               exists if the file has been ERASED from the disk (when a
                                        ;               file is erased the first character is overwritten but
                                        ;               INT 21 Function 5B still "finds" the file.
                                        ;
0000                                    IOWRITE:
0000  8C C8                                             MOV     AX,CS           ; Prepare to set DS
0002  8E D8                                             MOV     DS,AX           ;   and set it.
0004  E9 00B4 R                                         JMP     BEGINHERE
                                        ;
0007  0A 0D 57 72 69 74 65              PROMPT          DB      0Ah,0Dh,'Write to which file? $'
      20 74 6F 20 77 68 69
      63 68 20 66 69 6C 65
      3F 20 24
001F  0A 0D 45 6E 74 65 72              PROMPT1         DB      0Ah,0Dh,'Enter the bytes? $'
      20 74 68 65 20 62 79
      74 65 73 3F 20 24
0033  0A 0D 43 6C 6F 73 69              CLOSEFILE       DB      0Ah,0Dh,'Closing the file.$'
      6E 67 20 74 68 65 20
      66 69 6C 65 2E 24
0047  0020[                             FILE_NAME       DB      32 DUP(?)
          ??
                        ]

0067  0020[                             BYTE_NO         DB      32 DUP(?)
          ??
                        ]

0087  002A[                             INPUT_STR       DB      42 DUP(?)
          ??
                        ]

00B1  0A 0D 24                          CR_LF           DB      0Ah,0Dh,'$'
                                        ;
00B4                                    BEGINHERE:
00B4  8D 16 0007 R                                      LEA     DX,PROMPT       ; Print the file prompt
00B8  B4 09                                             MOV     AH,9
00BA  CD 21                                             INT     21h
00BC  C6 06 0047 R 1E                                   MOV     FILE_NAME,30    ; Max characters in input
00C1  8D 16 0047 R                                      LEA     DX,FILE_NAME    ; Get file name/path (if any)
00C5  B4 0A                                             MOV     AH,0Ah
00C7  CD 21                                             INT     21h
00C9  8A 0E 0048 R                                      MOV     CL,[FILE_NAME+1] ; How many bytes read in
00CD  80 C1 02                                          ADD     CL,2            ; Find position after last char
00D0  B5 00                                             MOV     CH,00
00D2  8B F1                                             MOV     SI,CX           ; Move count to index register
00D4  C6 84 0047 R 00                                   MOV     FILE_NAME[SI],00 ; Make into ASCIIZ string
                                        ;
00D9  8D 16 001F R                                      LEA     DX,PROMPT1      ; Request input
00DD  B4 09                                             MOV     AH,9
00DF  CD 21                                             INT     21h
00E1  C6 06 0087 R 26                                   MOV     INPUT_STR,38    ; Max 38 characters
00E6  8D 16 0087 R                                      LEA     DX,INPUT_STR
```

```
00EA  B4 0A                        MOV     AH,0Ah          ; Read in data
00EC  CD 21                        INT     21h
                          ;
                          ; Create a File Handle, Create a new file
                          ;       Note: If file already exists, its length is set to 0
                          ;             at the end of this routine
                          ;       DS:DX holds the pointer to path/file name
                          ;       CX = file attribute (see prolog information)
                          ;       On return, if Carry Flag = 0, successful and AX holds handle
                          ;                  if Carry Flag = 1, unsuccessful, AX=error code
                          ;
00EE  8D 16 0047 R                 LEA     DX,FILE_NAME    ; Load pointer to file name
00F2  83 C2 02                     ADD     DX,2            ; Skip auxiliary bytes
00F5  B9 0000                      MOV     CX,0            ; Normal file
00F8  B4 5B                        MOV     AH,5Bh          ; Create handle
00FA  CD 21                        INT     21h
00FC  0F 83 0106 R                 JNC     OPEN0           ; Was Carry Flag set?
                          ;
                          ; Error while trying to create a file
                          ;
0100  E8 0000 E                    CALL    EXTERROR        ; Get error code & print messages
0103  EB 4F 90                     JMP     ENDHERE

                          ; Open file
                          ;       DX = ASCIIZ string with file name
                          ;       AL = File attribute (0=read only, 1=write only,
                          ;            2=read/write)
                          ;          Successful read, AX = File handle
                          ;        Unsuccessful read, AX = Error Code and CF=1
                          ;
0106                      OPEN0:
0106  8D 16 0049 R                 LEA     DX,FILE_NAME+2  ; The file/path
010A  B0 02                        MOV     AL,2            ; Read/write file
010C  B4 3D                        MOV     AH,3Dh
010E  CD 21                        INT     21h
0110  8B F8                        MOV     DI,AX           ; Save file handle
                          ;
                          ;       Check for errors
                          ;       If there's an error, Carry Flag is set and error number
                          ;               returned in AL
                          ;
0112  0F 83 011C R                 JNC     WRITE0
0116  E8 0000 E                    CALL    EXTERROR        ; Get error & print messages
0119  EB 39 90                     JMP     ENDHERE
                          ;
                          ; Write to file
                          ;       DI = File Handle, Moved into BX
                          ;       CX = Number of bytes to write (from 2nd byte of INPUT_STR)
                          ;       INPUT_STR = The bytes to write to file
                          ;               Successful write, Carry Flag = 0
                          ;                       AX has Number actually written
                          ;             Unsuccessful write, Carry Flag = 1
                          ;                       AX has error number
                          ;
011C                      WRITE0:
011C  8B DF                        MOV     BX,DI           ; File handle
011E  8D 16 0089 R                 LEA     DX,INPUT_STR[2]
0122  8A 0E 0088 R                 MOV     CL,INPUT_STR[1] ; Number of bytes to read
0126  B4 40                        MOV     AH,40h          ; Write function number
0128  CD 21                        INT     21h
012A  8B C8                        MOV     CX,AX           ; Number actually written
                          ;
```

```
                                ; If an error on read Carry Flag is set
                                ;
012C  0F 83 0136 R                          JNC     DISPLAY0
0130  E8 0000 E                             CALL    EXTERROR        ; Get error & print message
0133  EB 1F 90                              JMP     ENDHERE
                                ;
                                ; Now close the file so that end-of-file (EOF) is correct
                                ;       BX still contains the file handle
                                ;       If successful, Carry Flag = 0
                                ;        unsuccessful, Carry Flag = 1, AX holds error code
                                ;
0136                            DISPLAY0:
0136  8D 16 0033 R                          LEA     DX,CLOSEFILE    ; Output close file message
013A  B4 09                                 MOV     AH,9
013C  CD 21                                 INT     21h
                                ;
013E  B4 3E                                 MOV     AH,3Eh          ; Close file function
0140  CD 21                                 INT     21h
                                ;
0142  0F 83 014C R                          JNC     DISPLAY1
0146  E8 0000 E                             CALL    EXTERROR        ; Get error & print messages
0149  EB 09 90                              JMP     ENDHERE
                                ;
014C                            DISPLAY1:
014C  8D 16 00B1 R                          LEA     DX,CR_LF        ; Put out one last CR/LF
0150  B4 09                                 MOV     AH,9            ; for prettier screen format
0152  CD 21                                 INT     21h
                                ;
                                ;
0154                            ENDHERE:
0154  B4 4C                                 MOV     AH,4Ch          ; Standard Ending
0156  CD 21                                 INT     21h
0158                            CODE        ENDS
                                            END     IOWRITE
```

9

Algorithms

An algorithm is a prescribed set of well-defined rules or processes for the solution of a problem in a finite number of steps. For instance, a transfer algorithm is a specific algorithm design used in a demand-fetching system to determine the order in which segments demanded by concurrent processes transfer from storage to internal memory.

An object is said to be *recursive* if it partially consists or is defined in terms of itself. Recursion is encountered not only in mathematics, but in daily life; for instance, product advertising often shows a picture that includes a picture of itself. Recursion is particularly powerful in mathematical definitions.

The power of recursion lies in the possibility of defining an infinite set of objects by a finite statement. Recursive algorithms are appropriate when the problem to be solved (or the function to be computed or the data structure to be processed) already is defined in recursive terms. This does not mean that such recursive definitions guarantee that a recursive algorithm is the best way to solve the problem. Often, it is plain that recursion can be replaced by simple iteration within the main program.

The necessary and sufficient tool for expressing recursive programs is the *procedure* or *subroutine*. They allow a statement to be given a name by which this code may be invoked. If a procedure (X) contains an explicit reference to itself, it is said to be *directly recursive*. If X contains reference to another procedure (Y) which contains a reference to X, then X is said to be *indirectly recursive*.

Searching

The task of searching is one of the most frequent operations in computer programming. There are several basic variations of the theme of searching, and each has many algorithms developed for it (and proponents who swear that their way is best). The basic assumption in searching a group of data is that the group is finite; that is, it is a fixed group. The task is to locate the element of the group which is equal to a given search argument, or to determine that the match does not exist within the given group.

Linear Search

When no further information is given about a group of data, the obvious approach is to proceed sequentially through the group (array)—to increase step by step the size of the selection where the desired element is known not to exist. This approach is called *linear search*. There are two conditions which terminate the linear search: the element is found, or the entire array has been scanned and no match was found.

Termination of linear searches is eventually guaranteed, because in each step the index increases by one and therefore will reach the limit after a finite number of steps. Each step requires the incrementing of the index and the evaluation of whether or not the search element matches the array element. A linear search may be the only way to locate an element in an unsorted array; that is, in a group which isn't ordered in any manner. We haven't demonstrated a linear search for a couple of reasons. First, it's easy to do (so you can do it on your own). Second, we feel that it is worth the time and resources to order an array prior to searching.

A Binary Search Program

A search for a particular element in an array or a table can be speeded up considerably if the elements are already ordered (sorted). In this case, the principle of repeated halving of the interval where the desired element must be is common. This is called *binary search*. In each repetition, the inspected interval between the indices is bisected to give a point where it is assumed the match will be made. If a match is not made, the half of the interval which potentially contains the desired element becomes the interval to check. The number of required comparisons is therefore at most $[\log_2(N)]$, where N is the total number of elements in the array. Figure 9-1 illustrates this binary search technique.

The goal of binary searching is to eliminate in each step as many elements as possible from further searches, no matter what the outcome of the comparison is. The optimal solution is to choose the middle element because this eliminates half the array (the search value either matches the middle, is larger or smaller than the middle).

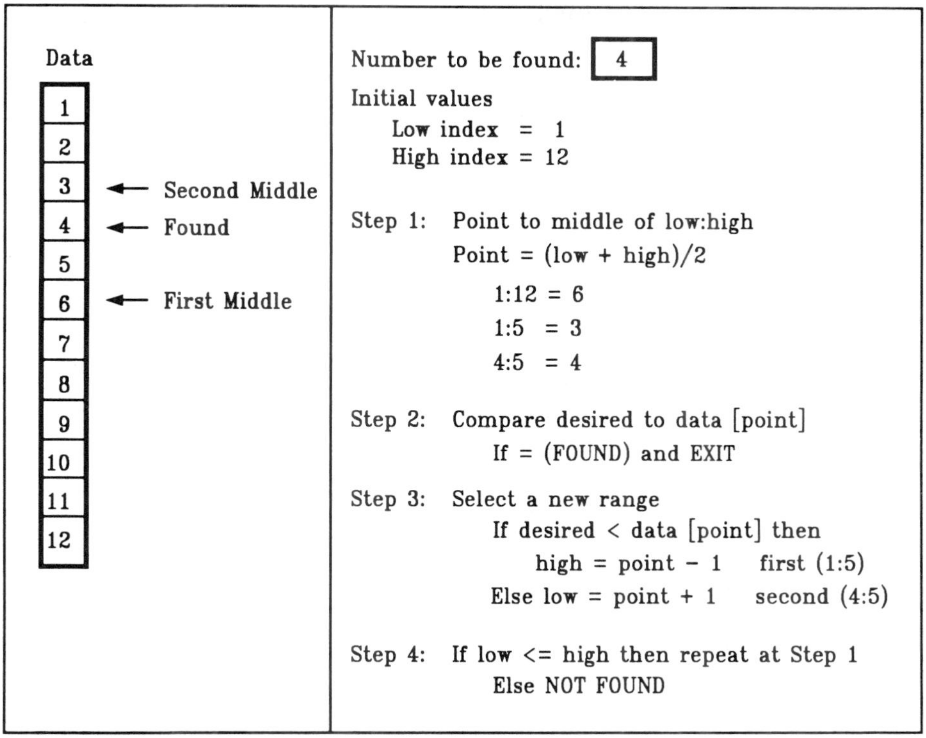

Fig. 9-1. Binary search technique.

BNSEARCH (Program 9-1) implements the standard binary search algorithm. While the shell sort routine was built for variable-length string, BNSEARCH and QSORT are for fixed-length data. In BNSEARCH, BX points to an array description. SI points to an array of index elements which provide a set of ordered pointers to the keys to be searched. DI points to the key to locate.

The binary search algorithm searches an ordered array. The initial partition has 1 as its left index and the maximum as its right index. The algorithm computes the index of the center of the partition (left plus right divided by 2). The center is compared to the target. If the target is equal to the center, we found the match. If the target is greater, a new left limit is set as center + 1; otherwise, a new right limit is set as center-1. If the indices cross, there is no match in the array; otherwise, we repeat. At the end, ES:DI points to the record located.

KEYCOMP. This is a routine within BNSEARCH that compares the source key to the desired key. This assumes that the desired key is pointed to by DS:BP, and is a fixed length. (This is common in the data processing industry. For example, employee records may be indexed by Social Security Number or company employee number.) The index of the comparison element is in AX, so the comparison is always A(SI(AX)):*desired*. This comparison routine is particularized for purposes of testing and demonstrating the algorithm. The location of the key in a record is not necessarily at the beginning. The length is not always 11. Keys are not always character strings, either; numbers (both floating-point and binary) are popular, too. AX indexes the desired element on input. ES:DI points to the desired element on exit and the flags reflect the result of the key comparison.

ARRANDXP. This procedure provides a method for computing a usable array element address. This is required for accessing elements of large arrays (over 64K bytes in size) in a USE16 task. It is a modification of the full routine shown below. AX has the index of the array element (1 . . . LAST) desired. BX has the segment array pointer. The DS array is assumed to be of the form built by the ARRABLDP.ASM routine (see below). AX is decremented to get a zero base and DX is zeroed. DX – AX is divided by the number of elements per segment. The quotient is multiplied by 2 and used to select the ES value. The remainder multiplied by the element size becomes the DI value. At output, if the element is found, DI has the displacement to the record. AX has the segment register value.

Buffers

When data are transferred to or from a secondary storage device, the individual bits are transferred as a stream. Because each secondary device imposes timing constraints on the transmission, gaps of time are left between the data transmitted and the data which follows later. To achieve a high density of data (which leads to faster throughput), the number of time gaps ought to be kept small. To keep them as small as possible, data to be transferred are buffered. That is, they are collected in an intermediate storage area (called a *buffer*) and transferred when a sufficient amount of data is accumulated.

Think of a buffer as a logical device inserted between other devices or program elements to match impedances or peripheral speeds, to prevent mixed interactions, to supply additional drive or relay capability, or to simply modify the rate of information flow. While data are being buffered, the processor goes on to do other things.

A simple buffer, therefore, is a technique for obtaining simultaneous performance of input/output operations and computing. This involves associating a buffer with only one input or output file (or data set) for the entire duration of the activity on that file (or data set). For example, a data communications buffer enables devices to operate at different speeds independent of communications line speeds.

A buffer acts as a first-in-first-out (FIFO) queue. If it is declared as an array, two index variables (for example, *in* and *out*) mark the positions of the next location to be written into and to be read from.

Memory buffers, as used in the programs in this book and with MS-DOS interrupts, are storage devices that allow input and output of strings of characters. For most MS-DOS interrupts, input buffers have two auxiliary bytes at the front of the buffer. You store the first byte, byte 0, which is the total number of bytes possible in the buffer. MS-DOS stores the second byte, byte 1, which is the actual number of characters entered. For instance, Interrupt 21 Function 0A requires this type of memory buffer. Several of the procedures for code conversion (See Chapter 7) use memory buffers, but generally without the two auxiliary bytes because they aren't input buffers.

A note about the counts in memory buffers is in order here. If, for instance, you wish to input 10 characters, your buffer must be defined with 13 bytes. The first two bytes are the auxiliary bytes; the next ten are the entered characters. The final byte is for the 0D carriage return.

A Buffer Handling Program

There are many instances throughout the various programs and procedures in this book showing how to handle memory buffers for input and output. BUFFER (Program 9-2) gives a standalone example of an input buffer, filled by using Interrupt 21 Function 0A. It proves also to be of secondary interest. We wanted to convert the binary bytes to printable hex in order to be able to display how the memory buffer changes depending on your input, so we coded BUFFER to call CODEBTHX (described and listed in Chapter 7). What turned out was that BUFFER now gives you a quick hex translation of your keyboard characters, along with a demonstration of memory buffers. A sample run of BUFFER is shown in Fig. 9-2.

```
C:\ASM>BUFFER

 Type up to ten characters > 1234567890

 Here is the memory buffer >0B 0A 31 32 33 34 35 36 37 38 39 30 0D

C:\ASM>BUFFER

 Type up to ten characters > ABC

 Here is the memory buffer >0B 03 41 42 43 0D 00 00 00 00 00 00 00

C:\ASM>BUFFER

 Type up to ten characters > $%&

 Here is the memory buffer >0B 03 24 25 26 0D 00 00 00 00 00 00 00

C:\ASM>
```

Fig. 9-2. Sample run of BUFFER program.

Circular Buffers

Buffers such as keyboard buffers allow you to read and write to them independently. Circular buffering allows you to put in and take out keys easily. At any point, one of the 16 words (in the keyboard buffer) is at a place called the "head," which is the position that the next character can be read from. The "tail" is the position that the next character can be written to. When keys are typed in, the tail advances. When you read one, the head advances. When either comes to the end of their 16-word queue, they wrap around to the beginning again. Two bytes in the BIOS data area hold the current addresses of the head and tail.

When everything has been read, the head catches up with the tail and the two are at the same address. This means that the buffer is empty. On the other hand, if the tail comes around and catches the head, the buffer is full.

The keyboard buffer, by the way, holds only 15 bytes before it is filled. The reason is that the tail word is where the next character goes. If the tail is looped around right behind the head with 15 characters input, the next character coming in would overwrite the head. Since an overlap signals an empty buffer, BIOS doesn't allow 16 characters in or it wouldn't know if the buffer were full or empty.

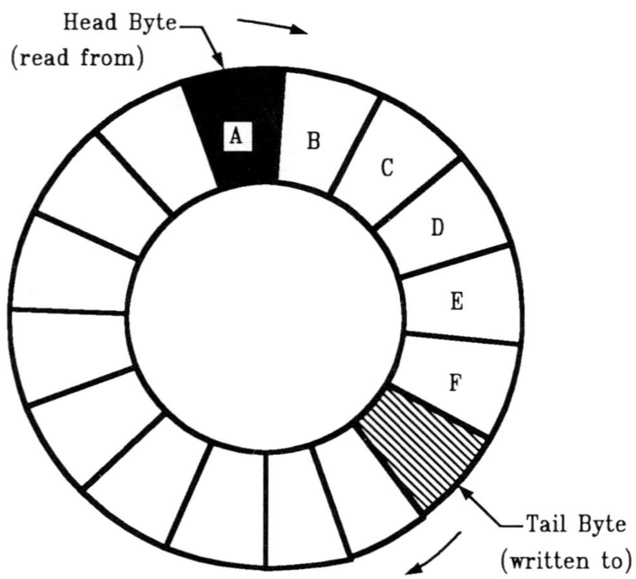

Fig. 9-3. Circular buffer with head and tail.

Clearing Buffers

Application programs meant for end users should clear the keyboard buffer before prompting for input, eliminating any inadvertent keystrokes that may be waiting in the buffer. The keyboard buffer holds up to 15 keystrokes, whether they are one-byte ASCII codes or two-byte extended codes. There are instances where you want to flush the buffer, such as when there is an unexpected or critical prompt the user may not have expected.

Interrupt 21 Function 0C clears the keyboard buffer and then performs one of the other keyboard input functions (01, 06, 07, 08, or 0A). If AL contains 0A, DS:DX must point to the buffer in which MS-DOS is to place the string read from the keyboard. Move 0C into AH and the other function into AL. With early versions of MS-DOS, Function 0C emptied the type-ahead buffer before executing the input function specified in AL. With versions 2.0 and later, if input has been redirected to a file, Function 0C does nothing before carrying out the input function specified in AL. If input is not redirected, the type-ahead buffer is flushed.

With a function number other than 01, 06, 07, 08, or 0A in AL, Function 0C simply flushes the standard-input buffer and returns control to the calling program. Because the buffer is flushed before the input function is carried out, any Ctrl-C (Break) character pending in the buffer is discarded. If subsequent input is a Ctrl-C, Interrupt 23 (Ctrl-C handler address) is called.

Encryption

The need for security measures to protect computer data was recognized from the beginnings of computer usage. This was accomplished in early batch-operated computers, which were made to perform one job completely before going to the next. Security was merely adapted from techniques used in the protection of manual handling of assets. Problems arose when technical advances allowed the sharing of resources by more than one job at a time and when storage media (such as diskettes) became extremely easy to transport.

At the same time, computers are being used for more purposes where the possibilities for unauthorized or malicious acts could result in serious losses. Money in electronic form and data records representing valuable property are being moved from vaults to computers at a rapid rate, resulting in computers becoming the new vaults.

Computer security has several dimensions. It consists of physical, personnel, operational, data, program, and hardware protection. Security functions are avoidance, deterrence, prevention, detection, recovery, and correction. These areas are too broad for a book like this one. This section directs attention to data protection.

While an ideal protection of data is available with the use of data encryption techniques, the administration of encryption keys remains a problem. That is, a programmer can come up with an encryption technique but someone in the company must know it and decide to implement it. If that key is not kept secure, then the encryption is simply an exercise. Again, this issue is outside the province of this book. Here, we're showing one method of encrypting data.

The program ENCRYPT (Program 9-3) uses a simple Caesar cipher, which simply adds one to the character. Thus, A becomes B, B becomes C, and so on. Decryption is the same operation in reverse—subtracting 1 from the character.

Another simple approach is straight exchange. There, you set up an exchange table. You establish the first half of the table with all the characters and the second half for their replacement values. For instance, you might say that every A is exchanged with an X. Every B is exchanged with a slash (\). And so on.

While these appear simplistic, they often serve the purpose of protecting data from the casual hacker or a deliberately malicious employee. There are other methods which are more complex and can be studied by programmers who must code more tightly secure programs.

ENCRYPT uses Interrupt 21 Function 0A to capture an input string into a memory buffer and displays it prior to encryption. It uses the Caesar cipher to encrypt the input characters and then displays the encrypted characters. The characters are decrypted and displayed.

Hashing Schemes

Hashing is a word coined to describe a general class of operations done to transform one or more fields (usually a key) into a different and more compact arrangement. The justification for hashing derives from being able to convert naturally occurring, ill-structured, scattered key fields into compact, easily manipulated fields—usually some numeric, computer-oriented field such as a word or double word, or a computer memory address to facilitate subsequent references.

The transformation from the "natural" field to the hash address is a one-way process, however; the natural field cannot be decoded or reconstructed from the hash. The hashed field also may not necessarily represent only one unique natural field, since many natural fields could hash to the same value. Ideally, the hashing scheme would convert the original keys to transformed keys with no duplicates. While schemes can be constructed to minimize *collisions* (called "hash clash"), their possibility cannot be eliminated completely and the original key should be stored along with the newly computed hash value.

One simple hashing scheme is the division-remainder method. Here, you choose a number close to the number of table positions needed. Use that number as a divisor to extract a quotient and a remainder from the dividend (which is the original key). The remainder so obtained is the transformed key.

Other schemes are *folding* and *digit rearrangement*. Folding consists of splitting the original key into two or more parts, then adding the parts together or (sometimes) using the exclusive OR operator. This sum, or some part of it, is then used as the transformed key. For example, using the key of 11 5234 9999, split and add

"11 + 5234 + 9999" to get 15244. Discard the high-order digit of "1" to obtain the four-digit transformed key of 5244.

Digit rearrangement consists simply of selecting and shifting digits of the original key. For example, an original key of 123456 could be transformed to a four-digit key of 5432 by selecting digit positions 2 through 5 and reversing their order.

A Hashing Driver

HASHDRV (Program 9-4) demonstrates the hashing routine that is coded in the HASHING program. Strings to hash are entered in response to a query. The strings are passed to HASHING and then the returned hashed answer is printed.

A Hashing Program

HASHING (Program 9-5) is a procedure called by HASHDRV, and which gives an example of a simple hashing routine. The method used is typical of many hashing algorithms. Perform some operation on the key to form it into a number within the range of a set of indices. As explained above, hash totals can be duplicated. There is no attempt in this example to avoid the duplication, which you would want to take care of in your main-line program.

ES:DI points to an ASCIIZ string to be hashed and CX has the maximum length of the strings to be hashed. The string is obtained from HASHDRV. The first two bytes and the last byte of the string are combined to form a word which is then multiplied by the length. The result is divided by 8 and ANDed against 511 to form the hash value. AX returns a hashed value in the range 0–511, which represents the string.

Sorting

Sorting is generally understood to be the process of rearranging a given set of objects in a specific order (usually ascending or descending). The purpose of sorting is to expedite the later search for members of the sorted set. (See the binary search description and program in this chapter.) As such, sorting is an almost universally performed, fundamental activity. It's estimated that sorting occupies about 25 percent of all computer time. Objects are sorted in telephone books, tables of contents, dictionaries, warehouse inventories—and so on, wherever objects must be searched and retrieved.

There aren't many techniques that do not occur somewhere in connection with sorting algorithms. In particular, sorting is an ideal subject to demonstrate a great diversity of algorithms, all having the same purpose and many being optimal in some sense, and most having advantages over others. The predominant requirement that has to be made for sorting methods is an economical use of the available storage.

There are several factors that influence the effectiveness of a sorting algorithm. This is why there is no best sorting algorithm for all situations. Some of the factors are:

- ☐ The number of records to be sorted.
- ☐ Whether or not all records fit into available internal memory.
- ☐ The degree to which the records are already sorted.
- ☐ The type of storage media on which the records are sorted.
- ☐ The complexity and storage requirements of the sorting algorithm.

Sorting methods generally are classified into two categories: sorting of arrays and sorting of files. The two classes are often called internal and external sorting, because arrays are stored in the fast, high-speed, random-access "internal" store of computers, while files are located on the slower, but more spacious "external" stores based on mechanically moving devices such as disks.

The importance of this internal/external distinction is obvious from an example of sorting a deck of cards. Structuring the cards as an array corresponds to laying them out in front of the sorter so that each card is visible and individually accessible. Structuring them as a file implies that from each pile only the card on the top is visible. Such a restriction has serious consequences on the sorting method to be used, but is unavoidable if the number of cards to be laid out is larger than the available table.

As previously stated, the major requirement for sorting arrays is an economical use of the available store. This implies that the permutation of items which brings the array contents into order is performed *in situ*, and that methods which transport items from an input array to a result array are intrinsically of minor interest.

A good measure of efficiency is obtained by counting the numbers of needed comparisons and moves (transportation) of items. These numbers are a function of the total number of items to be sorted. Sorting methods *in situ* can be classified into three principal categories: sorting by insertion, sorting by selection, and sorting by exchange.

Sorting by straight insertion is widely used by card players. The items (cards) are conceptually divided into a destination sequence and a source sequence. In each step, the *X*th element of the source is picked and transferred into the destination sequence by inserting it at the appropriate place. Sorting by selection is based on the following principles. First, select the item with the least key value. Then, second, exchange it with the first item. Finally, repeat these operations until only one item, the largest is left. Straight selection considers all items in the source array to find the one with the least key and to be deposited as the one next item of the destination sequence.

Sorting by straight exchange is based on the principle of comparing and exchanging pairs of adjacent items until all items are sorted. As with the previous methods of sorting, we make repeated passes over the array, each time sifting the least item of the remaining set to the left end of the array. If we view the array in a vertical instead of horizontal position, the items can be bubbles in water with weights according to their keys. Each pass over the array results in the ascension of a bubble to its appropriate level of weight. This method is widely known as the *bubble sort*. It is also the slowest and will not be shown in this book as there are very many examples already extant. We do show two of the fastest: the shell sort (for variable-length records), and the quicksort (for fixed-length records).

The Sorting Driver Program

SORTDRV (Program 9-6) demonstrates the binary search and the QSORT (Quicksort) routines. The driver has a pre-built test case in it. It builds an array of items which are created in such a fashion that they go across a pseudo-segment boundary; the routine which locates records in multiple segments gets exercised without having to build a truly multiple-segment database.

SORTDRV points to the array descriptor, builds the segment-pointer portion of a standard array descriptor, points to the array descriptor and calls QSORT. When QSORT returns, the standard array and the sorted array are both printed. The reason SORTDRV can do this is that SORTDRV uses the indirect pointers returned from QSORT.

After that, SORTDRV loops asking for entry of keys. It then uses a binary search routine to locate the desired target within the sorted list. Try SORTDRV and experiment with it.

Shell Sort

SHELLSRT (Program 9-7) sorts variable-length strings. SHELLSRT is a more compact implementation than QSORT, but is not as fast a sort. It does not show evidence of degenerate cases, which Quicksort algorithms can have. SHELLSRT uses the STRZCOMP (Chapter 6) routine because of the ASCIIZ strings. SHELLSRT is a straight "vanilla" algorithm.

DS:BX points to an array of displacements into a string area. All strings are assumed to be standard ASCIIZ strings. CX holds the count of strings to sort. A distance of CX/2 is used for the first pass of compares. Elements of the array are compared and exchanged if the value of the lower indexed element is greater than the higher. When all pairs of the given distance have been compared, the distance is halved and the process is repeated until the distance is zero.

On output, SHELLSRT returns an array (of displacements into the string area) which is in alphabetic sequence.

Quicksort

Quicksort (invented by C.A.R. Hoare) is based on the fact that exchanges should preferably be performed over large distance in order to be most effective. Assume N items are given in reverse order of their keys. It is possible to sort them by performing only N/2 exchanges, first taking the leftmost and the rightmost and gradually progressing inward from both sides. Naturally, this is possible only if we know that their order is exactly inverse.

The Quicksort algorithm is as follows: Pick any item at random and call it X. Scan the array from the left until an item of greater value than X is found. Then scan from the right until an item of less value than X is found. Now exchange the two items and continue this scan and swap process until the two scans meet somewhere in the middle of the array. The result is that the array is now partitioned into a left part with keys less than (or equal to) X and a right part with keys greater than (or equal to) X.

After partitioning the array, apply the same process to both partitions, then to the partitions of the partitions and so on, until every partition consists of a single item only.

To do a Quicksort, we first select a bound X, which sweeps the entire array. Therefore, exactly N comparisons are performed. With a fixed bound X, the expected number of exchange operations is equal to the number of elements in the left part of the partition, namely N – 1, multiplied by the probability that such an element reached its place by an exchange.

The crucial step is the selection of the comparand X. Hoare suggests that the choice of X be made at random, or by selecting it as the median of a small sample of, say, three keys. (This is the method we used in our implementation of Quicksort.) The median of N items is defined as that item which is less than (or equal to) half of the N items and which is larger than (or equal to) the other half of the N items. For example, the median of the string of numbers [16 12 99 95 18 87 10] is 18. The problem of finding the median is customarily connected with that of sorting because the obvious method of determining the median is to sort the N items and then to pick the item in the middle. But partitioning yields a potentially much faster way of finding the median.

Sorting is not useful if the data does not fit into a computer's main storage, but it is if some of the data can come from an external file. In this case, we describe the data as a sequential file whose characteristic is that at each moment one and only one component is directly accessible. This is a severe restriction compared to the possibilities offered by the array structure, and therefore different sorting techniques have to be used. The most important one is sorting by merging.

Merging (or collating) means combining two (or more) ordered sequences into a single, ordered sequence by repeated selection among the currently accessible components. Merging is a much simpler operation than sorting, and it is used as an auxiliary operation in the more complex process of sequential sorting. One way of sorting on the basis of merging is called *straight merging*. Straight merging works by first splitting the sequence A into two halves called B and C. Then B and C are merged by combining single items into ordered pairs. Steps one and two are repeated, this time merging ordered pairs into ordered quadruples. The previous steps are repeated yet again, merging quadruples into octets. The process continues doing this, each time doubling the lengths of the merged sequences, until the entire sequence is ordered.

Each operation that treats the entire set of data once is called a *phase,* and the smallest subprocess that by repetition constitutes the sort process is called a *pass* or *stage*. Figure 9-4 shows an example of this sorting by straight merging.

QSORT (Program 9-8) provides an implementation of the Quicksort algorithm, which is one of the fastest of the minimum-core sorts. It can degenerate to a slow sort, however, depending on how the partitions are decided upon. This implementation attempts to avoid that by taking any partition that is at size 4 or greater and taking the median of the left, center, and right key as a comparison value as a pivot point. If the partition is 3 or less, the median-taking operation simply sorts the partition so you don't have to worry about it. Care is taken to stack the largest of the partitions and sort the shortest of the partitions.

QSORT uses the comparison of a fixed-length key; it assumes a fixed-length record in its index calculations but not in the elementary algorithm of the sort. QSORT could be modified fairly easily to work off the same type of array that the shell sort (SHELLSRT) algorithm does.

QSORT provides an example of the 80386 Scale Index Byte type of addressing (see Appendix C) in the way QSORT uses the indirect array. Notice the way it exchanges the index values.

DS:BX points to a standard array descriptor. DS:SI points to an index array. The index array is initialized with sequential index values. This indirection is done because exchanging index values is faster than exchanging records which might be very large. The Quicksort algorithm is then applied using the indirection of the index array. On output, the index array contains pointers to records with ascending key values. Neither the array descriptor nor the record array is changed.

The way QSORT is implemented uses the 80386's stack instead of an array. This is a non-recursive implementation, but it uses the natural stacking of the 80386—as opposed to separate arrays for indices in the stack partition.

In QSORT, there are two comparison routines and a procedure to compute a usable array element address. The first, COMPARE, compares two keys together (needed for getting the median key value of the keys) and a compare of the pivot element, PIVOTC. The pivot element never changes during the partitioning operation.

The sort operates by splitting a large partition into two partitions, one having nothing but key values less than or equal to the pivot key and the other having keys larger. The pivot compare doesn't have to compute the index of the pivot, so it gets away "cheaper" that way. COMPARE, PIVOTC, and ARRANDXP are explained more fully in the next three paragraphs.

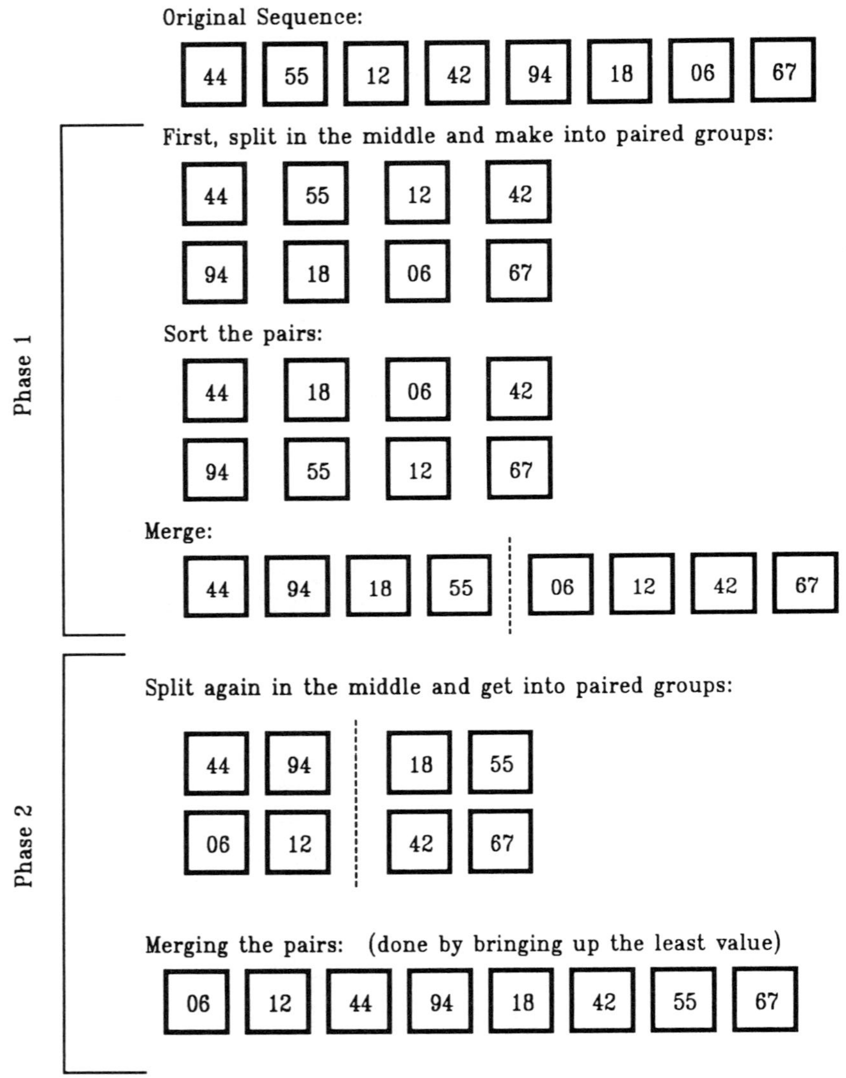

Fig. 9-4. *Sorting by straight merging.*

COMPARE. This routine compares the key in the record at SI(AX) to the key in the record at this location:

[SI(CX) *key* (SI(AX)) – *key*(SI(CX))]

It returns with the flags set. The usage is such that a call to COMPARE is followed by a conditional jump using the flag settings. The *key* as used in the demo

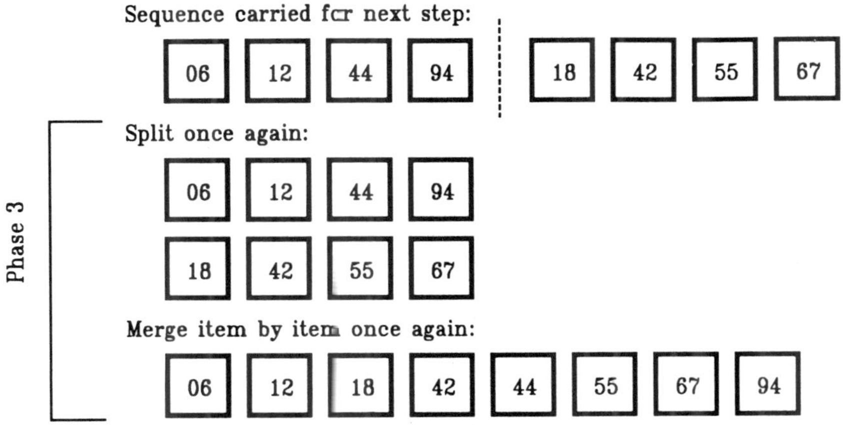

(Fig. 9-4 ends.)

program is a Social Security number with dashes, 000-00-0000 for instance. This is the first field in the record.

PIVOTC. This compares to the pivot element. It's similar to the COMPARE, but assumes that the segment and offset for the pivot are set in ES:DI. Thus, the comparison is always A(SI(AX)):pivot.

ARRANDXP. This routine computes a usable array element address. This is required for accessing elements of large arrays (over 64K bytes) in a USE16 task. It is a modification of the full routine described later in this chapter. AX has the index of the array element (1 . . LAST) desired and BX has the segment array pointer. The DS array is assumed to be of the form built by the ARRABLDP.ASM routine. AX is decremented to get a zero base and DX is zeroed. DX – AX is divided by the number of elements per segment. The quotient is multiplied by 2 and used to select the ES value. The remainder is multiplied by the element size and becomes the SI value. On return, SI has the displacement to the record and AX has the segment register value.

One additional thing that QSORT makes use of is one of the new 80386 segment registers, GS. It turns out that a third segment base (GS) made it much easier.

Array Manipulation and Indexing

The array is probably the most widely known data structure. An array consists of a series of items arranged in a meaningful pattern. The array is also a random-access structure; all components can be selected at random and are equally accessible. In order to point to an individual component, the name of the entire structure is augmented by an index selecting the component, as shown in Fig. 9-5.

The handy thing about an index is that it can be computed—a general index expression can be substituted in place of an index constant. This expression is evalu-

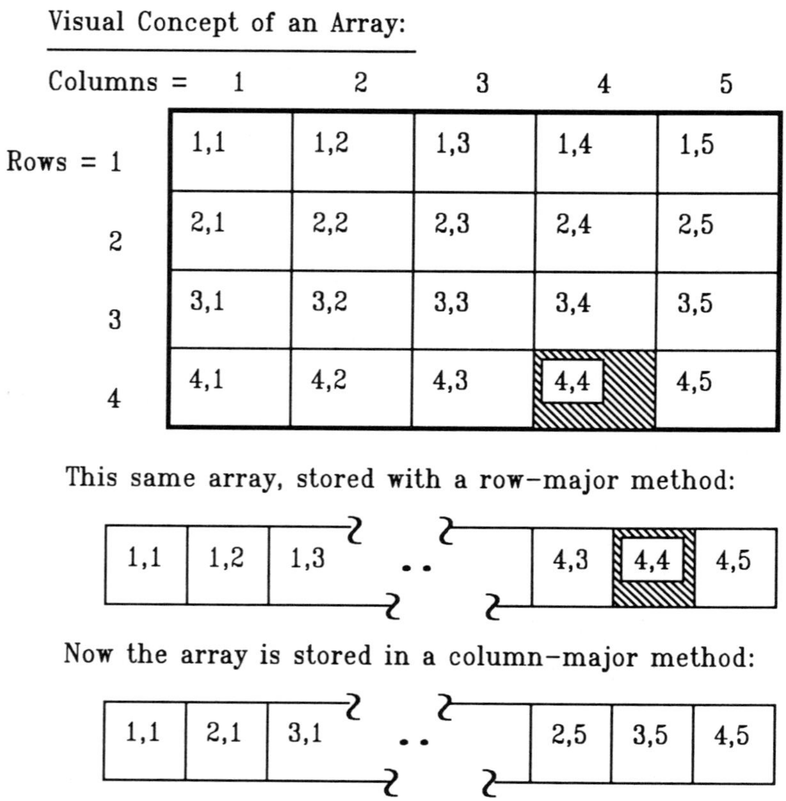

Fig. 9-5. Conceptual image versus actual storage of an array.

ated and the result identifies (points to) the selected component. This generality not only provides a powerful programming facility, but at the same time it also gives rise to one of the most frequently encountered mistakes: the resulting computation is outside the interval specified as the range of indices of the array, in which case you get a BOUNDS exception. Furthermore, when you calculate indices you have to know a basic fact: Is the array stored by rows or columns? For instance, the array position 4,4 (stored in a row-major method) will be at a different location in memory than the same 4,4 that's stored in a column-major method.

The common way of operating with arrays, particularly large ones, is to update selectively single components of the array, rather than to construct entirely new structured values. Although selective updating causes only a single component value to change, from a conceptual point of view we regard the entire composite value as having changed, too.

We have provided some routines in this section to take care of a problem which OS/2 does not solve. That is, OS/2 still requires that you run in a USE16 partition, which keeps you from using the extended addressing capabilities and the large segment size of the 80386. The build routine gets from MS-DOS or OS/2 blocks of memory which are nearly a full segment in size and builds a table of segment descriptors for building the arrays.

An Array Driver Program

Program 9-9, ARRADRV, drives the array building and indexing procedures. You are prompted for an element size and a number of elements. The program then calls ARRABLDP to get the memory and fill in the ARRADESC structure. The structure is displayed in hex. The program then prompts for element numbers to locate; it displays the resulting segment and displacement into that segment in hex.

Note: Under MS-DOS using Microsoft's linker, you must link with the option /CP:*nnnn*, where *nnnn* is the maximum number of paragraphs to be allocated to your program. If it is less than the size of the program, the program size will be used. This option overrides the default memory allocation, which allocates all free memory to your program.

Building an Array Larger than 64K

ARRABLDP (Program 9-10) provides a means to build an array which exceeds the size of a single segment (64K). BX points to the structure ARRADESC with the fields *ndxmax* and *elesize* set. First, the maximum number of elements per segment is computed. The size to get is computed (the MS-DOS Allocate Memory call is used in the example, so the size is rounded up to the nearest paragraph). The number of segments to get is computed, and we loop getting them until we either have them all or an error is returned.

The field *elepseg* is set and the DS array is filled in with segment descriptors for each section of the array. If an error occurs, the Carry Flag (CF) is set.

The ARRANDXP companion routine (Program 9-11) provides a way to compute an array element address. This is useful for accessing elements of large arrays and is an 80286 protected-mode routine. It is also usable in real mode on all 8086-family processors, and is usable on the 80386 in protected mode for USE16 tasks. (USE32 tasks, with 32-bit displacements available, normally get a segment of the array size and index it directly.) ARRANDXP uses the previously established array of segment descriptor values (as created by ARRABLDP) in computing the actual segment and offset of an individual record.

Both routines assume a fixed-length record. They provide a way around the annoying protected mode problem of overrunning segment boundaries.

Computing a Usable 80386 Array Element Address

ARRANDXR (Program 9-12) assumes you've obtained a large block of memory over a segment in size and that you have a segment beginning address. Given an index value, ARRANDXR returns to you a new segment pointer and a displacement into that segment, which allows you to access the entire record without quietly wrapping around the original segment. The 80386 won't allow this wrap-around in protected mode (neither will the 80286), but in real mode the segments wrap—which can be very surprising if you aren't expecting it.

AX has the index of the array element (1 . . LAST), BX has the DS value for element 1. CX has the element size in bytes and DX has the offset of element 1. The element index is converted into a byte offset into the array [(*index*-1)***size*]. The array offset is added to the result and the carry (if any) is propagated to DX. This gives you the byte offset from the array's segment descriptor. The lower bits of the result form the element's offset in SI. The total offset is divided by 16 and added to the segment's descriptor to form the descriptor for ES. We used shifts instead of a divide for speed (taking about a third of the time). On return, ES has the segment descriptor and SI the offset (0–15) of addressing the desired element.

Miscellaneous Routines

The following routines do a number of things, a grab bag of items. Let's take a few examples as to why these routines may be useful. For instance, if you're designing large programs and/or large databases, you may need to know your configuration (or the configuration of your end user, which may be vastly different from the system on which you designed your code). Second, if you move data from one storage medium to another, you'll need to know if your destination drive has sufficient free space to contain the new data. Finally, you may be designing a graphics package where you want the screen display to pause to allow your user to see and understand what's happening.

Determining Host System Configuration

For many systems the amount of memory on the system board and the number of peripherals are encoded in two bytes stored at address 410 hex in the BIOS data area. You can find out what it says by either reading the two bytes directly, or by using BIOS Interrupt 11. In most systems, INT 11 returns the information in the AX register. Figure 9-6 identifies the bits. When you purchase your system, you should receive material that tells you what your BIOS interrupts do and how they interact.

FIND_CFG (Program 9-13) does several things. First it uses INT 21 Function 2A to get the date, which it prints after using CODEBAS (see Chapter 7) to convert the binary characters to printable ASCII. Then it uses INT 11 (equipment determination), which returns bits in the AX register. Those bits are broken down as shown in Fig. 9-7. FIND_CFG uses Interrupt 21 Function 19 to find the default drive, which it prints. One of the things you can examine is how FIND_CFG sets up arrays of fixed-length messages and uses bits to index into the correct messages.

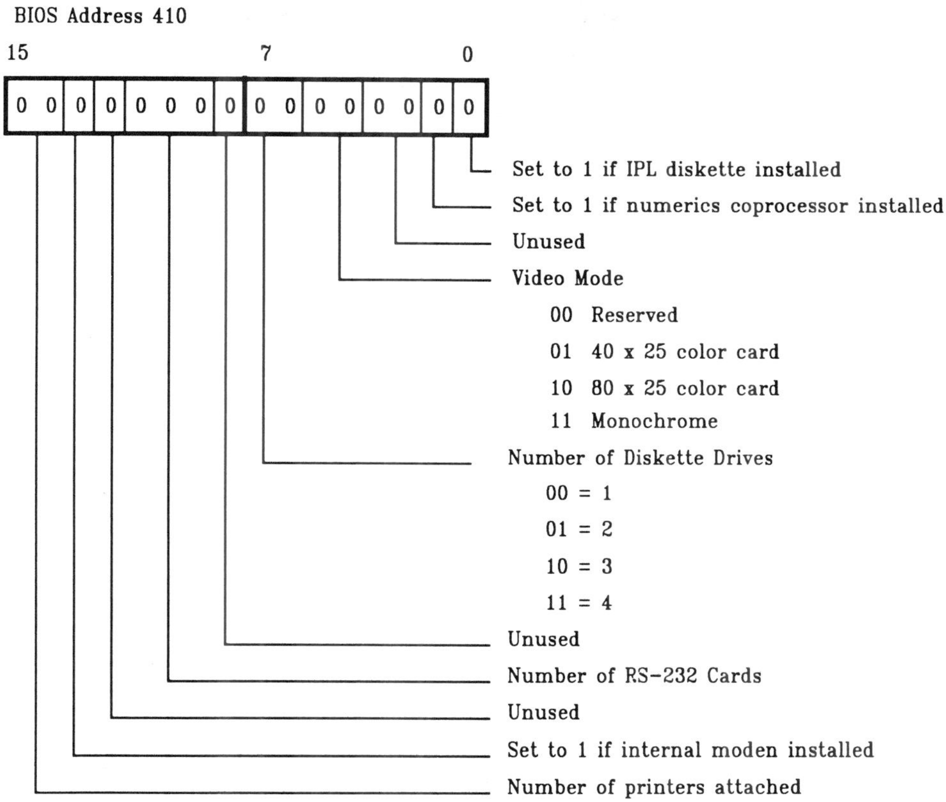

Fig. 9-6. BIOS equipment list bits.

If your system does not return the correct bits, as one of our clones did not, use Microsoft's SYMDEB debugger to find out what AX should be. Appendix H has a good overview of SYMDEB, along with the major SYMDEB commands. See Fig. 9-8 to follow this example.

First, execute SYMDEB. Use the display (D) option on address 0:44 (-D 0:44 47), to display the four bytes we're interested in. Since each interrupt uses 4 bytes, 4*11 is the offset of low memory.

Then use the unassemble (U) option on the first four bytes, to see where INT 10 returns the byte of configuration information. As you can see, the memory address of 0040 is moved into AX and then to DX. Then the offset of 10 is moved into AX. In the example, those bytes are 4D F8 00 F0. Since memory is reversed, you'll want to Unassemble with the command -U F000:F84D.

In this third step, we display a word (DW) at location 40:10 11 (start at byte 10 and go to byte 11). We see that the two bytes are 84 33. SYMDEB has swapped the memory to show the bytes as they would appear in a register, as shown in Fig. 9-9.

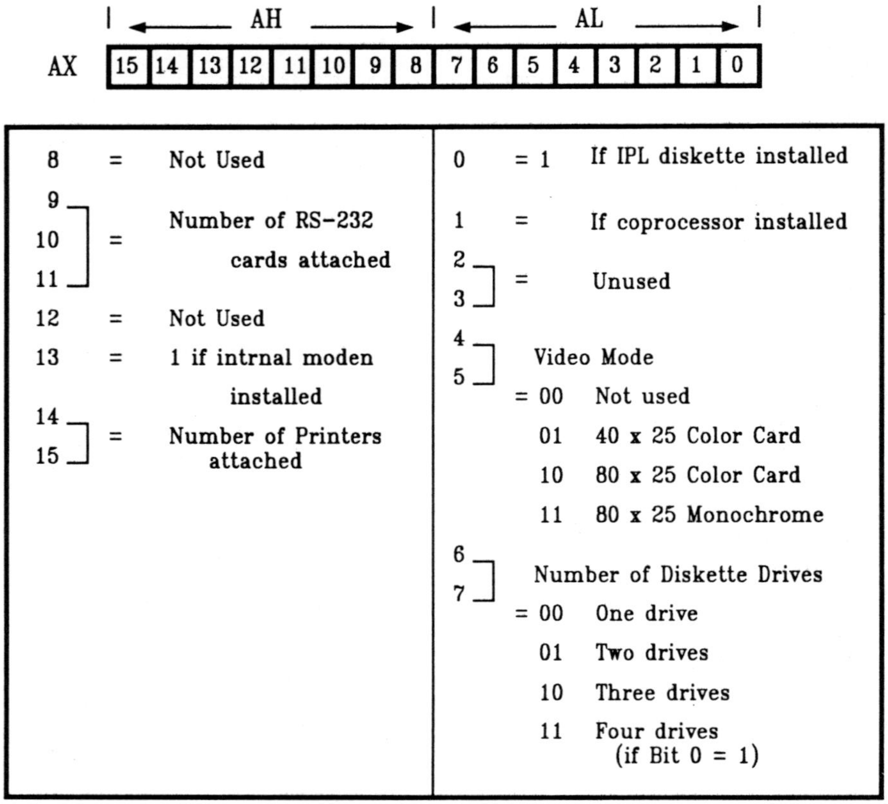

Fig. 9-7. AX register bits after INT 11.

Here's a word of warning: If you simply do a display (D) of 40:10 and let the full eight lines of hex and ASCII print, the bytes show—as they actually do in memory—as 33 84. Then you have to reverse those two and register AX will show 84 33. That means that this particular system has:

Date = 2/28/88
One drive
80 × 25 monochrome
Two RS-232 cards
No internal modem
Two printers
There is a coprocessor installed
The default drive is C
An IPL diskette is installed

Note that FIND__CFG also uses INT 21 Function 2A to get the date and calls

```
C:\ASM>SYMDEB
Microsoft (R) Symbolic Debug Utility  Version 4.00
Copyright (C) Microsoft Corp 1984, 1985.  All rights reserved.

Processor is [80286]
-D 0:44 47
0000:0040             4D F8 00 F0                         Mx.p
-U F000:F84D
F000:F84D 1E            PUSH   DS
F000:F84E B84000        MOV    AX,0040
F000:F851 8ED8          MOV    DS,AX
F000:F853 A11000        MOV    AX,[0010]
F000:F856 1F            POP    DS
F000:F857 CF            IRET
F000:F858 61            POPA
F000:F859 E91EC0        JMP    B87A
-DW 40:10 11
0040:0010  8471
-Q

C:\ASM>
```

Fig. 9-8. Locating configuration information in memory.

CODEBAS to turn the binary digits into printable ASCII. FIND_CFG also uses INT 21 Function 19 to find out the default drive.

Free Bytes on a Disk Drive

GET_FREE (Program 9-14) asks which drive (and gives you a choice of three) that it is to check for available space. Once you input the drive number, it calls CODEASB to convert the typed ASCII into binary. It then uses INT 21 Function 36, which returns number of sectors per cluster, the number of bytes per sector, and the number of available clusters. Multiply those values together and you have (in binary) the number of free bytes. GET_FREE then uses CODEBAS to convert the binary to printable ASCII and prints the results to the screen. After assembly, GET_FREE was linked with CODEASB and CODEBAS.

Checking for a Coprocessor

The program FIND_COP (Program 9-15) was run on an 80386 system built for programs in this book (and, of course, to stay current with the new thrust of the micro world). The engineers installed an 80287 numeric coprocessor. There are a couple of ways you can find out if a numerics coprocessor is installed on your

```
C:\ASM>SYMDEB
Microsoft (R) Symbolic Debug Utility  Version 4.00
Copyright (C) Microsoft Corp 1984, 1985.  All rights reserved.

Processor is [80286]
-D 0:44
0000:0040              4D F8 00 F0-41 F8 00 F0 AB 09 70 00       Mx.pAx.p+.p.
0000:0050  39 E7 00 F0 59 F8 00 F0-2E E8 00 F0 D2 EF 00 F0   9g.pYx.p.h.pRo.p
0000:0060  AD E3 00 F0 DD 0A 70 00-6E FE 00 F0 F2 00 E6 07   -c.p].p.n~.pr.f.
0000:0070  53 FF 00 F0 A4 F0 00 F0-22 05 00 00 00 00 00 00   S..p$p.p".......
0000:0080  C3 12 2E 01 E4 12 2E 01-8E 09 1E 0E 2B 0A 1E 0E   C...d.......+...
0000:0090  56 09 1E 0E 5B 14 2E 01-9E 14 2E 01 4D 5B 2E 01   V...[.......M[..
0000:00A0  C9 12 2E 01 EF 02 E6 07-C9 12 2E 01 C9 12 2E 01   I...o.f.I...I...
0000:00B0  C9 12 2E 01 C9 12 2E 01-57 02 CD 0B AB 15 2E 01   I...I...W.M.+...
0000:00C0  EA CA 12 2E                                       jJ..
-D 0:44 47
0000:0040              4D F8 00 F0                               Mx.p
-DW 0:44 47
0000:0044  F84D F000
-Q
```

Note how the display changes when you dump memory addresses D 0:44, to the four bytes when you use D 0:44 45 for a range, or dump words with DW 0:44 45.

Fig. 9-9. SYMDEB dump differences.

system. FIND_CFG (see above) does it one way. FIND_COP uses INT 21 Function 14.

Determining the DOS Version

FIND_VER (Program 9-16) finds which version of MS-DOS is installed on a computer. Interrupt 21 Function 30 returns the MS-DOS number. The major version of the number (e.g., the "3" of 3.10) returns in AL. The minor version (e.g., the "10" of 3.10) returns in AH. Note that this function of Interrupt 21 destroys registers BX and CX.

Making a Program Wait

The procedure PAUSE (Program 9-17) provides a means of pausing for a time span from 0.02 seconds to 59.99 seconds. The system clock does not increment smoothly but in "clumps," so the granularity within PAUSE is not to the hundredths. A calling program passes parameters of seconds and hundredths to PAUSE, which edits them for conformance to the value range.

When you call this procedure, store the number of seconds to delay in DH and the number of hundredths to DL. The seconds and hundredths are edited for conformance with their value range (0–59 in DH, and 0–99 in DL, with DX less than 1). If invalid, the Carry Flag is set and the procedure returns. If valid, the procedure delays for the desired length of time and returns with Carry Flag = 0.

A Driver for the PAUSE Program

CHKPAUSE (Program 9-18) provides a simple visual check of the PAUSE routine. It displays a tick, calls PAUSE for a 0.5 second delay, then flips to tock. It repeats this 200 times.

Finding Computer's "Name"

Most PCs currently on the market identify themselves in a one-byte identification in location F000:FFFE, the penultimate location in regular memory. PCNAME (Program 9-19) reads that location and indexes into an array that converts the answer into the name. The array is set up to contain:

FF = Original PC
FE = PC XT
FD = PC Jr
FC = PC AT

When the program assembles, the data segment is set into DS, the data segment pointer register. The location 0F000 is moved into BX and from there to DS, which changes the data segment pointer to F000. Then the offset is loaded into BX and the contents of that address moved into AL.

A Random Number Generator

RANDNUM (Program 9-20) generates a random number between 0 and 1. The program gets the time of day and uses the hundredths of a second as a key. It then rotates the answer three times (an arbitrary design decision). Then it calls CODEBAS (see Chapter 7) to turn the resultant binary into a printable ASCII.

Calculating Square Roots

This procedure calculates the square root by following Newton's Method, which says that if A is an approximation for the square root of a number N, then A1 = (N/A + A)/2 is a better approximation. To get the first approximation, the routine uses (N/200) + 2, where N is the contents of DX:AX and the value 200 is arbitrary. To get the next approximation, the program divides N by the first and averages the two. For the third, it divides N by the second approximation and averages again. This repeats until it finds two approximations that are identical (or differ only by 1, whether positive or negative).

After input of the number (any number up to 9,999,999), it is multiplied by 100 to get some decimal precision. On return, DS:BX holds the square root. The routine "hard codes" a single decimal figure and prints the figure with the decimal point.

Program 9-1: BNSEARCH

```
Microsoft (R) Macro Assembler Version 5.00


                                      PAGE    55,132
                                      .386
0000                          code    SEGMENT para 'CODE' USE16 PUBLIC
                                      ASSUME  CS:code, DS:code, SS:code
                              ;
                              ; Name;     BNSEARCH
                              ;
                              ; Purpose: The following procedure implements the binary search
                              ;           algorithm.
                              ;
                              ;
                              ; Inputs:   BX points to an array description.  SI points to an array
                              ;           of index elements which provide a set of ordered pointers
                              ;           to the keys to be searched.  DI points to the key to locate.
                              ;
                              ; Process: The binary search algorithm searches an ordered array.
                              ;           The initial partition has 1 as its left index and the
                              ;           maximum as its right index.  The algorithm computes the
                              ;           index of the center of the partition as (left+right)/2.
                              ;           The center is compared to the target.  If the target is
                              ;           equal to the center, we have found our match.  If the
                              ;           target is greater, a new left limit is set as center+1
                              ;           otherwise a new right limit is set as center-1.  If the
                              ;           indices cross there is no match in the array, otherwise
                              ;           we repeat.
                              ;
                              ; Output:   ES:DI will point to the record located and the zero flag
                              ;           will be set if the record was located.
                              ;
                              ;
                              ;

                              ;
                              arradesc  STRUC
0000  0000                    ndxmax    dw      0                 ; Maximum element index
0002  0000                    elesize   dw      0                 ; Size of an element
0004  0000                    elepseg   dw      0                 ; Elements per segment
0006  0000                    elesegs   dw      0                 ; First element of the DS
                              ;                                     array.  Further elements
                              ;                                     follow sequentially.
0008                          arradesc  ENDS
                              ;
                              ;
                              ;
                                        PUBLIC  Bnsearch          ; Make the name usable
0000                          Bnsearch  PROC
0000  66| 52                            push    EDX               ; Save entry registers
0002  66| 51                            push    ECX
0004  66| 50                            push    EAX
0006  66| 56                            push    ESI
0008  66| 55                            push    EBP
000A  66| B8 0000FFFF                   mov     EAX,0000ffffh     ; Get mask
0010  66| 23 F0                         and     ESI,EAX           ; and ensure high bytes clear
0013  66| 23 F8                         and     EDI,EAX
0016  66| 8B EF                         mov     EBP,EDI           ; Save search target's loc.
0019  66| 23 D8                         and     EBX,EAX
001C  66| 23 C8                         and     ECX,EAX
```

```
001F  66| 23 D0                      and     EDX,EAX
0022  8B 0F                          mov     CX,[BX].ndxmax      ; Get rightmost index
0024  BA 0001                        mov     DX,1                ; and leftmost.
0027                         center:
0027  8B C2                          mov     AX,DX               ; Prepare to get center
0029  03 C1                          add     AX,CX               ; Left + right
002B  D1 E8                          shr     AX,1                ; div 2 gives the center
002D  E8 0050 R                      call    Keycomp             ; Compare to the desired key
0030  0F 84 0045 R                   je      Alldone             ; We have it
0034  0F 82 003E R                   jb      toolow              ; Our
0038  8B D0                          mov     DX,AX               ; Set left to center
003A  42                             inc     DX                  ; and add one.
003B  EB 04 90                       jmp     checkend            ; See if we are done.
003E                         toolow:
003E  8B C8                          mov     CX,AX               ; set right to center
0040  49                             dec     CX                  ; less one.
0041                         checkend:
0041  3B D1                          cmp     DX,CX               ; Check if we have a miss
0043  76 E2                          jna     center              ; if not - look again.
                             ;
                             ; We fall through with zero not set.  If we branch - it is set.
                             ;
0045                         Alldone:
0045  66| 5D                         pop     EBP
0047  66| 5E                         pop     ESI
0049  66| 58                         pop     EAX
004B  66| 59                         pop     ECX
004D  66| 5A                         pop     EDX
004F  C3                             ret                         ; and return.

                             ;
                             ; Compare to the desired key.  This assumes that the desired key is
                             ; pointed to by DS:BP.  The index of the comparison element is in AX
                             ; so the comparison is always A(SI(AX)):desired.
                             ;
                             ; This comparison routine is particularized for purposes of testing
                             ; and demonstrating the algorithm.  The location of the key in a
                             ; record is not necessarily at the beginning.  The length is not
                             ; always 11.  Keys are not always character strings either, numbers
                             ; both floating point and binary, are popular too.
                             ;
                             ; AX indexes the desired element on input.
                             ; ES:DI points to the desired element on exit, the flags reflect the
                             ; result of the key comparison.
                             ;
0050                         Keycomp    PROC
0050  56                             push    SI                  ; Save registers used
0051  50                             push    AX
0052  51                             push    CX
0053  48                             dec     AX                  ; Get indices on zero base.
0054  67| 8B 0446                    mov     AX,WORD PTR [ESI+EAX*2] ; Get indirect index AX
0058  E8 006A R                      call    arrandxp            ; Get the record location AX
005B  57                             push    DI                  ; First save the record's disp.
                                                                 ; Add key's displacement to DI
005C  8E C0                          mov     ES,AX               ; Set the base
005E  8B F5                          mov     SI,BP               ; Get key displacement in SI
0060  B9 000B                        mov     CX,11               ; Set count to compare
                                                                 ; This would also change.
0063  F3/ A6                         repz cmpsb                  ; Compare,
                                                                 ; (for character strings)
0065  5F                             pop     DI                  ; Restore record's displacement
0066  59                             pop     CX                  ; restore registers,
0067  58                             pop     AX
```

```
0068  5E                          pop     SI
0069  C3                          ret                         ; and return.
006A                    Keycomp   ENDP
                        ;
                        ;
                        ; Purpose: The following procedure provides a method for computing
                        ;          a usable array element address.  This is required for
                        ;          accessing elements of large arrays (over 64k bytes in
                        ;          size) in a USE16 task.  It is a modification of the full
                        ;          routine.
                        ;
                        ;
                        ; Inputs:  AX has the index of the array element (1 .. LAST) desired.
                        ;          BX has the segment array pointer.
                        ;
                        ;          The DS array is assumed to be of the form built by the
                        ;          ARRABLDP.ASM routine.
                        ;
                        ; Process: AX is decremented to get a zero base and DX is zeroed.
                        ;          DX-AX is divided by the number of elements per segment.
                        ;          The quotient is multiplied by 2 and used to select the
                        ;          ES value.  The remainder multiplied by the element size
                        ;          becomes the DI value.
                        ;
                        ; Output:  DI has the displacement to the record.  AX has the segment
                        ;          register value.
                        ;
006A                    Arrandxp  PROC
006A  52                          push    DX                  ; Save entry registers
006B  51                          push    CX
006C  53                          push    BX
006D  48                          dec     AX                  ; Get index based on zero
006E  2B D2                       sub     DX,DX               ; Clear upper word of dividend
0070  F7 77 04                    div     [BX].elepseg        ; Divide by elements / segment
0073  8B C8                       mov     CX,AX               ; Save the quotient
0075  8B C2                       mov     AX,DX               ; Position the remainder
0077  F7 67 02                    mul     [BX].elesize        ; Get the element's offset
007A  8B F8                       mov     DI,AX               ; Into DI
007C  03 D9                       add     BX,CX               ; Add the quotient to BX
007E  03 D9                       add     BX,CX               ; twice to get the displacement
0080  8B 47 06                    mov     AX,[BX].elesegs     ; of the descriptor.
0083  5B                          pop     BX                  ; Restore the entry registers
0084  59                          pop     CX
0085  5A                          pop     DX
0086  C3                          ret                         ; and return.
0087                    Arrandxp  ENDP

0087                    Bnsearch  ENDP
0087                    code      ENDS
                                  END
```

Program 9-2: BUFFER

```
                                        PAGE    55,132
                                        .386
                                        EXTRN   CODEBTHX:PROC
0000                            STACK   SEGMENT 'STACK' STACK
0000   0064[                            DW      100 DUP(?)
           ????
                      ]

00C8                            STACK   ENDS

0000                            CODE    SEGMENT para 'CODE' PUBLIC USE16
                                        ASSUME  CS:CODE, DS:CODE, SS:STACK
                                ;
                                ; Name:          BUFFER
                                ;
                                ; Purpose:       This program gives a graphic demonstration of what a
                                ;                memory buffer looks like once it has been loaded with
                                ;                data.
                                ;
                                ; Inputs:        A string of characters is entered via the keyboard.
                                ;
                                ; Process:       A memory buffer is established.  Interrupt 21 Function
                                ;                0A (buffered keyboard entry) is used to capture the
                                ;                input into a memory buffer called INPUT_STR.  Then
                                ;                CODEBTHX is called to transform the binary memory into
                                ;                printable hex.
                                ;
                                ;                A note on the counts.  If you store 10 (meaning you want
                                ;                10 characters), you can only type 9 before the beep, since
                                ;                your count includes the 0D carriage return.  The count
                                ;                that DOS puts in does NOT count the 0D.  Therefore, if you
                                ;                want 10 characters in, your buffer must be 13 to hold the
                                ;                two auxiliary bytes and the carriage return along with your
                                ;                10 characters.
                                ;
                                ; Outputs:       A message and the contents of the buffer.


                                ;
0000                            BUFFER:
0000   8C C8                                    MOV     AX,CS           ; Prepare to set DS
0002   8E D8                                    MOV     DS,AX           ;   and set it.
0004   EB 52 90                                 JMP     BEGINHERE
                                ;
0007   000D[                    INPUT_STR       DB      13 DUP (?)
           ??
                      ]

0014   0A 0D 20 54 79 70 65     PROMPT          DB      0Ah,0Dh,' Type up to ten characters > $'
       20 75 70 20 74 6F 20
       74 65 6E 20 63 68 61
       72 61 63 74 65 72 73
       20 3E 20 24
0034   0A 0D 20 48 65 72 65     HEADER          DB      0Ah,0Dh,' Here is the memory buffer >$'
       20 69 73 20 74 68 65
       20 6D 65 6D 6F 72 79
       20 62 75 66 66 65 72
       20 3E 24
0053   0A 0D 24                 CR_LF           DB      0Ah,0Dh,'$'
0056   20 24                    BLANK           DB      ' $'
```

```
                              ;
0058                          BEGINHERE:
                              ;
0058  8D 16 0014 R                      LEA    DX,PROMPT        ; Print the prompt
005C  B4 09                             MOV    AH,9h
005E  CD 21                             INT    21h
0060  C6 06 0007 R 0B                   MOV    INPUT_STR,11     ; Max 10 chars input (see Prolog)
0065  8D 16 0007 R                      LEA    DX,INPUT_STR     ; Point at buffer
0069  B4 0A                             MOV    AH,0Ah           ; Buffered keyboard input
006B  CD 21                             INT    21h
                              ;
006D  8D 16 0053 R                      LEA    DX,CR_LF         ; Space up a line
0071  B4 09                             MOV    AH,9
0073  CD 21                             INT    21h
                              ;
                              ;       Convert the binary bytes to printable hex by calling CODEHXTB.
                              ;       CODEHXTB requires:
                              ;       AL = the byte to be converted
                              ;       If successful, Carry Flag = 0
                              ;               AH = Left nibble
                              ;               AL = Right nibble
                              ;       If not, Carry Flag = 1
                              ;
0075  8D 16 0034 R                      LEA    DX,HEADER        ; Print the header
0079  B4 09                             MOV    AH,9
007B  CD 21                             INT    21h
                              ;
007D  2B C0                             SUB    AX,AX            ; Clear out AX
007F  2B C9                             SUB    CX,CX            ; Also CX
0081  BF 0000                           MOV    DI,0             ; Index through INPUT_STR
0084                          CONVERT:
0084  8A 85 0007 R                      MOV    AL,BYTE PTR INPUT_STR[DI]
0088  E8 0000 E                         CALL   CODEBTHX         ; Convert to printable hex
                              ;
008B  2B D2                             SUB    DX,DX            ; Clear out DX
008D  8B D8                             MOV    BX,AX            ; Save the byte, AX used to print
008F  8A D7                             MOV    DL,BH            ; Left nibble
0091  B4 02                             MOV    AH,2             ; Print it
0093  CD 21                             INT    21h
0095  8A D3                             MOV    DL,BL            ; Right nibble
0097  CD 21                             INT    21h              ; Print it
0099  8D 16 0056 R                      LEA    DX,BLANK         ; Print a space between bytes
009D  B4 09                             MOV    AH,9
009F  CD 21                             INT    21h
00A1  47                                INC    DI               ; Go to next byte
00A2  83 FF 0D                          CMP    DI,13            ; Done?
00A5  0F 84 00AB R                      JE     ENDHERE          ; Yes, go end program
00A9  EB D9                             JMP    CONVERT
                              ;
00AB                          ENDHERE:
00AB  8D 16 0053 R                      LEA    DX,CR_LF         ; Space up one line
00AF  B4 09                             MOV    AH,9
00B1  CD 21                             INT    21h
                              ;
00B3  B4 4C                             MOV    AH,4Ch           ; Standard Ending
00B5  CD 21                             INT    21h
00B7                          CODE      ENDS
                                        END    BUFFER
```

Program 9-3: ENCRYPT

```
Microsoft (R) Macro Assembler Version 5.00


                                        PAGE     55,132
                                        .386
                                        EXTRN    CODEBTHX:PROC
 0000                           STACK   SEGMENT 'STACK' STACK

 0000  0064[                            DW       100 DUP(?)
          ????
                        ]

 00C8                           STACK   ENDS
 0000                           CODE    SEGMENT para 'CODE' PUBLIC USE16
                                        ASSUME   CS:CODE, DS:CODE, SS:STACK
                                ;
                                ; Name:          ENCRYPT
                                ;
                                ; Purpose:       This program takes an input string and uses a Caesar
                                ;                Cipher (add 1) to encrypt the input characters.  Then it
                                ;                gives a graphic demonstration of what the characters
                                ;                looks like once they have been changed.
                                ;
                                ;                Then the characters are decrypted (subtract 1) and
                                ;                displayed.
                                ;
                                ; Inputs:        A string of characters is entered via the keyboard.
                                ;
                                ; Process:       A memory buffer is established.  Interrupt 21 Function
                                ;                0A (buffered keyboard entry) is used to capture the
                                ;                input into a memory buffer called INPUT_STR.  The
                                ;                characters are encrypted.  Then CODEBTHX is called to
                                ;                transform the binary memory into printable hex.
                                ;
                                ;                A note on the counts.  If you store 10 (meaning you want
                                ;                10 characters), you can only type 9 before the beep, since
                                ;                your count includes the 0D carriage return.  The count
                                ;                that DOS puts in does NOT count the 0D.  Therefore, if you
                                ;                want 10 characters in, your buffer must be 13 to hold the
                                ;                two auxiliary bytes and the carriage return along with your
                                ;                10 characters.
                                ;
                                ; Outputs:       A message and the contents of the buffer.
                                ;
0000                            ENCRYPT:
0000  8C C8                                      MOV      AX,CS            ; Prepare to set DS
0002  8E D8                                      MOV      DS,AX            ;   and set it.
0004  E9 0099 R                                  JMP      BEGINHERE
                                ;
0007  000D[                     INPUT_STR        DB       13 DUP (?)
         ??
                        ]

0014  0A 0D 20 54 79 70 65      PROMPT           DB       0Ah,0Dh,' Type up to ten characters > $'
      20 75 70 20 74 6F 20
      74 65 6E 20 63 68 61
      72 61 63 74 65 72 73
      20 3E 20 24
```

```
0034  0A 0D 20 50 72 69 6F   HEADER0       DB      0Ah,0Dh,' Prior to encryption      > $'
      72 20 74 6F 20 65 6E
      63 72 79 70 74 69 6F
      6E 20 20 20 20 20 20
      20 3E 20 24
0054  0A 0D 20 54 68 65 20   HEADER1       DB      0Ah,0Dh,' The encrypted characters  > $'
      65 6E 63 72 79 70 74
      65 64 20 63 68 61 72
      61 63 74 65 72 73 20
      20 3E 20 24
0074  0A 0D 20 54 68 65 20   HEADER2       DB      0Ah,0Dh,' The decrypted characters  > $'
      64 65 63 72 79 70 74
      65 64 20 63 68 61 72
      61 63 74 65 72 73 20
      20 3E 20 24
0094  0A 0D 24               CR_LF         DB      0Ah,0Dh,'$'
0097  20 24                  BLANK         DB      ' $'
                             ;
0099                         BEGINHERE:
                             ;
0099  8D 16 0014 R                         LEA     DX,PROMPT        ; Print the prompt
009D  B4 09                                MOV     AH,9h
009F  CD 21                                INT     21h
00A1  C6 06 0007 R 0B                      MOV     INPUT_STR,11     ; Max 10 chars input (see Prolog)
00A6  8D 16 0007 R                         LEA     DX,INPUT_STR     ; Point at buffer
00AA  B4 0A                                MOV     AH,0Ah           ; Buffered keyboard input
00AC  CD 21                                INT     21h
                             ;
00AE  8D 16 0094 R                         LEA     DX,CR_LF         ; Space up a line
00B2  B4 09                                MOV     AH,9
00B4  CD 21                                INT     21h
                             ;
00B6  8D 16 0034 R                         LEA     DX,HEADER0       ; Print the header
00BA  B4 09                                MOV     AH,9
00BC  CD 21                                INT     21h
00BE  E8 0106 R                            CALL    PRINT            ; Internal procedure
                             ;
                             ; Encrypt the characters by adding a binary 1 to them
                             ;
00C1  2B C9                                SUB     CX,CX
00C3  8A 0E 0008 R                         MOV     CL,BYTE PTR INPUT_STR[1] ; Number of chars entered
00C7  8D 3E 0007 R                         LEA     DI,INPUT_STR     ; Point at the first character
00CB  83 C7 02                             ADD     DI,2             ; Skip the two aux bytes
00CE                         ENCRY:
00CE  8A 05                                MOV     AL,BYTE PTR [DI]
00D0  04 01                                ADD     AL,1
00D2  88 05                                MOV     BYTE PTR [DI],AL
00D4  47                                   INC     DI
00D5  E2 F7                                LOOP    ENCRY
                             ;
00D7  8D 16 0054 R                         LEA     DX,HEADER1       ; Print the header
00DB  B4 09                                MOV     AH,9
00DD  CD 21                                INT     21h
                             ;
00DF  E8 0106 R                            CALL    PRINT
                             ;
                             ; Decrypt the characters by subtracting a binary 1 to them
                             ;
00E2  2B C9                                SUB     CX,CX
00E4  8A 0E 0008 R                         MOV     CL,BYTE PTR INPUT_STR[1] ; Number of chars entered
00E8  8D 3E 0007 R                         LEA     DI,INPUT_STR     ; Point at the first character
00EC  83 C7 02                             ADD     DI,2             ; Skip the two aux bytes
```

```
00EF                    DECRY:
00EF  8A 05                         MOV     AL,BYTE PTR [DI]
00F1  2C 01                         SUB     AL,1
00F3  88 05                         MOV     BYTE PTR [DI],AL
00F5  47                            INC     DI
00F6  E2 F7                         LOOP    DECRY
                        ;
00F8  8D 16 0074 R                  LEA     DX,HEADER2       ; Print the header
00FC  B4 09                         MOV     AH,9
00FE  CD 21                         INT     21h
                        ;
0100  E8 0106 R                     CALL    PRINT
0103  EB 2D 90                      JMP     ENDHERE
                        ;
                        ;       Convert the binary bytes to printable hex by calling CODEHXTB.
                        ;       CODEHXTB requires:
                        ;       AL = the byte to be converted
                        ;       If successful, Carry Flag = 0
                        ;               AH = Left nibble
                        ;               AL = Right nibble
                        ;       If not, Carry Flag = 1
                        ;
0106                    PRINT       PROC
0106  2B C0                         SUB     AX,AX            ; Clear out AX
0108  2B C9                         SUB     CX,CX
010A  8A 0E 0008 R                  MOV     CL,BYTE PTR INPUT_STR[1]
010E  BF 0002                       MOV     DI,2             ; Index through INPUT_STR
0111                    PRINT0:
0111  8A 85 0007 R                  MOV     AL,BYTE PTR INPUT_STR[DI]
0115  E8 0000 E                     CALL    CODEBTHX         ; Convert to printable hex
                        ;
0118  2B D2                         SUB     DX,DX            ; Clear out DX
011A  8B D8                         MOV     BX,AX            ; Save the byte, AX used to print
011C  8A D7                         MOV     DL,BH            ; Left nibble
011E  B4 02                         MOV     AH,2             ; Print it
0120  CD 21                         INT     21h
0122  8A D3                         MOV     DL,BL            ; Right nibble
0124  CD 21                         INT     21h              ; Print it
0126  8D 16 0097 R                  LEA     DX,BLANK         ; Print a space between bytes
012A  B4 09                         MOV     AH,9
012C  CD 21                         INT     21h
012E  47                            INC     DI               ; Go to next byte
012F  E2 E0                         LOOP    PRINT0
                        ;
0131  C3                            RET
0132                    PRINT       ENDP
                        ;
0132                    ENDHERE:
0132  8D 16 0094 R                  LEA     DX,CR_LF         ; Space up one line
0136  B4 09                         MOV     AH,9
0138  CD 21                         INT     21h
                        ;
013A  B4 4C                         MOV     AH,4Ch           ; Standard Ending
013C  CD 21                         INT     21h
013E                    CODE        ENDS
                                    END     ENCRYPT
```

Program 9-4: HASHDRV

```
Microsoft (R) Macro Assembler Version 5.00


                                        PAGE    55,132
                                        .386
                                ;
                                ; Name:    HASHDRV
                                ;
                                ; Purpose: This program demonstrates the hashing routine.
                                ;
                                ; Inputs:  Strings to hash are entered in response to the query.
                                ;
                                ; Process: The program requests a string to hash, passes it to
                                ;          the hashing routine and displays the resulting number.
                                ;
                                ; Outputs: The hash index is displayed.
                                ;
                                ;
                                ; Declare the routines we are going to use
                                ;
                                        EXTRN   HASHING:PROC
                                        EXTRN   CODEBAS:PROC

0000                            stack   SEGMENT para 'STACK' STACK
0000  0100[                             dq      256 DUP(?)
          ???????????????
          ?
                       ]

0800                            stack   ENDS
0000                            data    SEGMENT para
0000  0100[                     string  db      256 DUP(?)          ; String scratch area
           ??
                       ]

0100  0A 0A 0D 45 6E 74 65      query   db      10,10,13,"Enter a string to hash: $"
      72 20 61 20 73 74 72
      69 6E 67 20 74 6F 20
      68 61 73 68 3A 20 24
011C  0A 0D 49 74 20 68 61      result  db      10,13,"It hashes to index $"
      73 68 65 73 20 74 6F
      20 69 6E 64 65 78 20
      24
0132                            data    ENDS
0000                            code    SEGMENT para 'CODE' USE16 PUBLIC
                                        ASSUME  CS:code, DS:data
                                ;
                                ; Set up the environment
                                ;
0000                            Begin:
0000  B8 ---- R                         mov     AX,data             ; Get data segment pointer
0003  8E D8                             mov     DS,AX               ; into DS,
0005  8E C0                             mov     ES,AX               ; and ES.
0007  2B F6                             sub     SI,SI               ; Clear indices
0009  2B FF                             sub     DI,DI
000B                            gethash:
000B  8D 16 0100 R                      lea     DX,query            ; Get the string to hash
000F  E8 0040 R                         call    getinp              ; From the keyboard
0012  E3 26                             jcxz    Exit                ; Empty string exits
```

```
0014  8B FB                        mov     DI,BX               ; Set the pointer
0016  B9 0064                      mov     CX,100              ; and an arbitrary length
0019  E8 0000 E                    call    Hashing             ; Get a hash value
001C  66| 98                       cwde                        ; as a double word
001E  8D 3E 0000 R                 lea     DI,string           ;
0022  E8 0000 E                    call    Codebas             ; and convert it
0025  8D 16 011C R                 lea     DX,result           ; point to header
0029  B4 09                        mov     AH,9
002B  CD 21                        int     21h                 ; and put it out
002D  B4 02                        mov     AH,2
002F                       outnbr:
002F  8A 15                        mov     DL, BYTE PTR [DI]   ; get number
0031  47                           inc     DI
0032  0A D2                        or      DL,DL               ; are we at end?
0034  74 D5                        jz      gethash             ; Yes - try again
0036  CD 21                        int     21h
0038  EB F5                        jmp     outnbr              ; do another digit
003A                       Exit:
003A  B0 00                        mov     AL,0                ; Set return code
003C  B4 4C                        mov     AH,04ch             ; Set good-by
003E  CD 21                        int     21h                 ; Return to the system

                           ;
                           ; Read a string in response to a prompt
                           ; The prompt must be in DX.  The string will be returned in string.
                           ;
0040                       getinp  PROC
0040  50                           push    AX                  ; Save registers
0041  56                           push    SI
0042  B4 09                        mov     AH,9                ; and dos request
0044  CD 21                        int     21h                 ; put out the string
0046  8D 16 0000 R                 lea     DX,string           ; point to input area
004A  C6 06 0000 R FE              mov     string,254          ; Set max length in
004F  B4 0A                        mov     AH,10               ; Ask for read of string
0051  CD 21                        int     21h                 ; from DOS.
0053  8D 1E 0002 R                 lea     BX,string+2         ; Point to just read data
0057  8A 0E 0001 R                 mov     CL,string+1         ; Get length read
005B  B5 00                        mov     CH,0                ; as a word.
005D  8B F1                        mov     SI,CX               ; Set length
005F  C6 84 0002 R 00              mov     string+2[SI],0      ; and make an asciiz string.
0064  5E                           pop     SI
0065  58                           pop     AX                  ; Restore registers
0066  C3                           ret                         ; and return.
0067                       getinp  ENDP

0067                       code    ENDS
                                   END     Begin
```

Program 9-5: HASHING

```
                                        .386
0000                            code    SEGMENT   para 'CODE' USE16 PUBLIC
                                        ASSUME    CS:code, DS:code, SS:code
                                ;
                                ; Name;   HASHING
                                ;
                                ; Purpose: The following procedure provides an instance of a hashing
                                ;          algorithm.
                                ;
                                ; Inputs:  ES:DI points to an asciiz string to be hashed.
                                ;          CX has the maximum length of strings to be hashed.
                                ;
                                ; Process: The string length is obtained.  The first two bytes
                                ;          and the last byte of the string are combined to form
                                ;          a word which is then multiplied by the length.  The result,
                                ;          divided by 8, is ANDed against 511 to form the hash value.
                                ;
                                ; Output:  AX returns a hashed value in the range 0-511 which
                                ;          represents the string.
                                ;
                                ; Note:    The method used here is typical of many hashing algorithms.
                                ;          Perform some operation on the key to form it into a number
                                ;          within the range of a set of indices.  Not shown here is
                                ;          the method used to handle items which hash to the same
                                ;          number.  Linked lists which are then searched sequentially
                                ;          can be headed by an index word at the hash index are one
                                ;          method.
                                ;
                                        PUBLIC  Hashing               ; Make the name usable
                                        EXTRN   STRZLNG:PROC
0000                            Hashing PROC
0000  52                                push    DX                    ; Save entry registers
0001  51                                push    CX
0002  53                                push    BX
0003  E8 0000 E                         call    Strzlng               ; Get the string's length.
0006  0F 83 000C R                      jnc     hashln                ; If not oversize, use length
000A  8B C1                             mov     AX,CX                 ; Else use maximum.
000C                            hashln:
000C  0B C0                             or      AX,AX                 ; Zero length strings
000E  0F 84 0026 R                      jz      hashexit              ; return a zero hash value.
0012  8B D8                             mov     BX,AX                 ; Save the length
0014  26: 8B 05                         mov     AX,ES:[DI]            ; Get the first two chars
0017  4B                                dec     BX                    ;
0018  26: 32 21                         xor     AH,BYTE PTR ES:[BX+DI] ; Fold in the last
001B  43                                inc     BX                    ; Get length back
001C  F7 E3                             mul     BX                    ;
001E  03 C2                             add     AX,DX
0020  C1 E8 03                          shr     AX,3                  ; and divide by 8
0023  25 01FF                           and     AX,01ffh              ; Truncate to 0-511
0026                            hashexit:
0026  5B                                pop     BX
0027  59                                pop     CX
0028  5A                                pop     DX
0029  C3                                ret                           ; and return.
002A                            Hashing ENDP
002A                            code    ENDS
                                        END
```

Program 9-6: SORTDRV

```
Microsoft (R) Macro Assembler Version 5.00


                                        PAGE    55,132
                                        .386

                              ;
                              ; Name:   SORTDRV
                              ;
                              ; Purpose: This program demonstrates the Quicksort and Binary search
                              ;         routines.
                              ;
                              ; Inputs:  The program has the array to be sorted within itself.
                              ;         Search arguments are prompted for.
                              ;
                              ; Process: We first set up a 'standard' array description used for
                              ;         arrays of fixed length records which contain too many
                              ;         elements to fit within a single 64K segment.  We break
                              ;         our array artificially to test the ability of the sort
                              ;         and search to cross segment bounds. We then call the
                              ;         qsort routine and print both the original and ordered
                              ;         arrays.  We then loop getting search targets, searching
                              ;         for them and reporting the results until a null target
                              ;         is entered.
                              ;
                              ; Outputs: All outputs are displayed.
                              ;


                              ;
                              ; Declare the routines we are going to use
                              ;
                                        EXTRN   BNSEARCH:PROC
                                        EXTRN   QSORT:PROC

0000                          stack     SEGMENT para 'STACK' STACK
0000  0100[                             dq      256 DUP(?)
          ???????????????
          ?
                        ]

0800                          stack     ENDS
0000                          data      SEGMENT para
0000  0100[                   string    db      256 DUP(?)          ; String scratch area
           ??
                        ]

0100  0A 0D 45 6E 74 65 72    query     db      10,13,"Enter an SSN to find: $"
      20 61 6E 20 53 53 4E
      20 74 6F 20 66 69 6E
      64 3A 20 24
0119  0A 0D 46 20 4F 20 55    found     db      10,13,"F O U N D  I T!! $"
      20 4E 20 44 20 20 49
      20 54 21 21 20 24
012D  0A 0D 4E 6F 74 20 74    notfound  db      10,13,"Not there. $"
      68 65 72 65 2E 20 24
013B  0A 0D 24                newline   db      10,13,"$"
013E  20 20 20 20 20 20 24    spaces    db      "      $"
0145  90                                ALIGN   WORD
0146  0014                    arradesc  dw      20                  ; Small test case
```

```
0148  000C                          elesize    dw      12                 ; Size
014A  0010                          elepseg    dw      16                 ; Count
014C  0000                          elesegs    dw      0                  ; filled in
014E  0000                                     dw      0
0150  0014[                         indirect   dw      20 DUP(?)          ; indirect array for sort
          ????
                         ]

0178  90 90 90 90 90 90 90                     ALIGN   16
      90
0180  30 39 39 2D 31 32 2D          sortit     db      "099-12-3452$"     ; 1
      33 34 35 32 24
018C  33 30 30 2D 32 32 2D                     db      "300-22-3452$"     ; 2
      33 34 35 32 24
0198  33 30 30 2D 31 32 2D                     db      "300-12-3452$"     ; 3
      33 34 35 32 24
01A4  32 30 30 2D 31 32 2D                     db      "200-12-3452$"     ; 4
      33 34 35 32 24
01B0  33 31 30 2D 31 32 2D                     db      "310-12-3452$"     ; 5
      33 34 35 32 24
01BC  33 30 31 2D 31 32 2D                     db      "301-12-3452$"     ; 6
      33 34 35 32 24
01C8  30 31 30 2D 31 32 2D                     db      "010-12-3452$"     ; 7
      33 34 35 32 24
01D4  33 31 31 2D 31 32 2D                     db      "311-12-3452$"     ; 8
      33 34 35 32 24
01E0  30 32 30 2D 31 32 2D                     db      "020-12-3452$"     ; 9
      33 34 35 32 24
01EC  32 30 30 2D 31 32 2D                     db      "200-12-3451$"     ; 10
      33 34 35 31 24
01F8  32 31 30 2D 31 32 2D                     db      "210-12-3452$"     ; 11
      33 34 35 32 24
0204  30 30 30 2D 31 32 2D                     db      "000-12-3452$"     ; 12
      33 34 35 32 24
0210  34 30 30 2D 31 32 2D                     db      "400-12-3452$"     ; 13
      33 34 35 32 24
021C  33 35 30 2D 31 32 2D                     db      "350-12-3452$"     ; 14
      33 34 35 32 24
0228  32 32 30 2D 31 32 2D                     db      "220-12-3452$"     ; 15
      33 34 35 32 24
0234  39 39 30 2D 31 32 2D                     db      "990-12-3452$"     ; 16
      33 34 35 32 24
0240  39 30 30 2D 31 32 2D          sortit0    db      "900-12-3452$"     ; 17
      33 34 35 32 24
024C  30 35 30 2D 31 32 2D                     db      "050-12-3452$"     ; 18
      33 34 35 32 24
0258  30 37 30 2D 31 32 2D                     db      "070-12-3452$"     ; 19
      33 34 35 32 24
0264  31 30 30 2D 31 32 2D                     db      "100-12-3452$"     ; 20
      33 34 35 32 24
0270  37 30 30 2D 31 32 2D                     db      "700-12-3452$"     ; 21
      33 34 35 32 24
027C                                data       ENDS
0000                                code       SEGMENT para 'CODE' USE16 PUBLIC
                                               ASSUME  CS:code, DS:data
                                    ;
                                    ; Set up the environment
                                    ;
0000                                Begin:
0000  B8 ---- R                                mov     AX,data            ; Get data segment pointer
0003  8E D8                                    mov     DS,AX              ; into DS,
0005  8E C0                                    mov     ES,AX              ; and ES.
```

```
0007  2B F6                    sub     SI,SI              ; Clear indices
0009  2B FF                    sub     DI,DI
000B  8D 1E 0146 R             lea     BX,arradesc        ; point to array descriptor
000F  8D 36 0150 R             lea     SI,indirect        ; and to indirect array
0013  8D 0E 0180 R             lea     CX,sortit          ; point to data to sort
0017  C1 E9 04                 shr     CX,4               ; make into a descriptor
001A  03 C8                    add     CX,AX              ;
001C  89 0E 014C R             mov     elesegs,CX         ; For the table
0020  8D 0E 0240 R             lea     CX,sortit0         ; Get second segment
0024  C1 E9 04                 shr     CX,4               ; as a descriptor
0027  03 C8                    add     CX,AX              ; in
0029  89 0E 014E R             mov     elesegs+2,CX       ; table
002D  E8 0000 E                call    qsort              ; call the sort
0030  8B 0E 0146 R             mov     CX,arradesc        ; get the count to print
0034  8D 1E 0180 R             lea     BX,sortit          ; point to the data
0038  B4 09                    mov     AH,9               ; set DOS code
                        ;
                        ; Print the original and sorted arrays
                        ;
003A                    printit:
003A  8D 16 013B R             lea     DX,newline         ; Point to new line
003E  CD 21                    int     21h
0040  8B D3                    mov     DX,BX              ; point to key
0042  CD 21                    int     21h                ; write it
0044  8D 16 013E R             lea     DX,spaces          ; and some white space
0048  CD 21                    int     21h
004A  03 1E 0148 R             add     BX,elesize         ; Step to next
004E  8B 04                    mov     AX,WORD PTR[SI]    ; Get index value
0050  48                       dec     AX                 ; based on zero
0051  F7 26 0148 R             mul     elesize            ; times size.
0055  83 C6 02                 add     SI,2               ; Next entry
0058  8D 16 0180 R             lea     DX,sortit          ;
005C  03 D0                    add     DX,AX              ; Get displacement of entry
005E  B4 09                    mov     AH,9               ; Set code
0060  CD 21                    int     21h                ; and print it
0062  E2 D6                    loop    printit            ;
                        ;
                        ; Use the binary search routine to locate various keys.
                        ;
0064                    nextsch:
0064  8D 16 0100 R             lea     DX,query           ; point to query
0068  E8 0097 R                call    getinp             ; and get a search target
006B  E3 24                    jcxz    Exit               ; A null response quits.
006D  83 F9 0B                 cmp     CX,11              ; Check size
0070  75 F2                    jne     nextsch            ; If not right - loop
0072  8B FB                    mov     DI,BX              ; Set pointer of target,
0074  8D 1E 0146 R             lea     BX,arradesc        ; point to array descriptor,
0078  8D 36 0150 R             lea     SI,indirect        ; and to indirect array.
007C  E8 0000 E                call    Bnsearch           ; Try to locate it
007F  8D 16 0119 R             lea     DX,found           ; assume we did
0083  0F 84 008B R             je      putout             ; We did.
0087  8D 16 012D R             lea     DX,notfound        ; not
008B                    putout:
008B  B4 09                    mov     AH,9               ; Set DOS code
008D  CD 21                    int     21h                ; and put message out.
008F  EB D3                    jmp     nextsch            ; and try again.

0091                    Exit:
0091  B0 00                    mov     AL,0               ; Set return code
0093  B4 4C                    mov     AH,04ch            ; Set good-by
0095  CD 21                    int     21h                ; Return to the system
                        ;
```

```
                               ; Read a string in response to a prompt
                               ; The prompt must be in DX.  The string will be returned in string.
                               ;
0097                           getinp    PROC
0097  50                                 push    AX                 ; Save registers
0098  56                                 push    SI
0099  B4 09                              mov     AH,9               ; and dos request
009B  CD 21                              int     21h                ; put out the string
009D  8D 16 0000 R                       lea     DX,string          ; point to input area
00A1  C6 06 0000 R FE                    mov     string,254         ; Set max length in
00A6  B4 0A                              mov     AH,10              ; Ask for read of string
00A8  CD 21                              int     21h                ; from DOS.
00AA  8D 1E 0002 R                       lea     BX,string+2        ; Point to just read data
00AE  8A 0E 0001 R                       mov     CL,string+1        ; Get length read
00B2  B5 00                              mov     CH,0               ; as a word.
00B4  8B F1                              mov     SI,CX              ; Set length
00B6  C6 84 0002 R 00                    mov     string+2[SI],0     ; and make an asciiz string.
00BB  5E                                 pop     SI
00BC  58                                 pop     AX                 ; Restore registers
00BD  C3                                 ret                        ; and return.
00BE                           getinp    ENDP

00BE                           code      ENDS
                                         END     Begin
```

Program 9-7: SHELLSRT

```
Microsoft (R) Macro Assembler Version 5.00


                                        PAGE      55,132
                                        .386
0000                            code    SEGMENT   para 'CODE' USE16 PUBLIC
                                        ASSUME    CS:code, DS:code, SS:code
                                ;
                                ; Name;    SHELLSRT
                                ;
                                ; Purpose: The following procedure implements the shellsort algorithm.
                                ;
                                ;
                                ;
                                ; Inputs:  DS:BX points to an array of displacements into a string
                                ;          area.  All strings are assumed to be standard asciiz
                                ;          strings.  CX holds the count of strings to sort.
                                ;
                                ; Process: A distance of CX/2 is used for the first pass of compares.
                                ;          Elements of the array are compared and exchanged if the
                                ;          value of the lower indexed element is greater than the
                                ;          higher.  When all pairs of the given distance have been
                                ;          compared, the distance is halved and the process is
                                ;          repeated until the distance is zero.
                                ;
                                ;
                                ; Output: The output is an array of displacements into the string
                                ;         area which is in alphabetic sequence.
                                ;
                                ;
                                ;
                                        EXTRN     STRZCOMP:PROC
                                        PUBLIC    Shellsrt             ; Make the name usable
0000                            Shellsrt PROC
0000  52                                push      DX                   ; Save entry registers
0001  51                                push      CX
0002  53                                push      BX
0003  50                                push      AX
0004  56                                push      SI
0005  57                                push      DI
0006  55                                push      BP
0007  8B E9                             mov       BP,CX                ; Save limit value
                                ;
                                ; This loop computer closer and closer distances to compare at.
                                ;      i.e. for 15 items we compare 7, 3, and 1 apart.
                                ;
0009                            nextdist:
0009  D1 E9                             shr       CX,1                 ; Get the next distance
000B  0F 84 0052 R                      jz        sortdone             ; If at zero - we are done.
000F  8B D5                             mov       DX,BP                ; get original top
0011  2B D1                             sub       DX,CX                ; less our new distance.
0013  B8 0001                           mov       AX,1                 ; j=1 to limit
                                ;
                                ; This loop steps us up the array from 1 to our limit comparing items
                                ; which are 'distance' apart.  i.e. for our distance of 7 we compare
                                ;      1:8, 2:9, 3:10, 4:11 ... 8:15.  for the 3 distance we compare
                                ;      1:4, 2:5, 3:6, 4:7 ... 12:15, for the 1 distance we compare
                                ;      1:2, 2:3, 3:4, 4:5 ... 14:15 which completes the sort.
                                ;
```

```
0016                       nextj:
0016  50                            push    AX                  ; save J and init I
                           ;
                           ; This loop compares and if an out of sequence condition is found,
                           ; steps back down the array to force the out of sequence item as far
                           ; to the left as possible.  i.e if we find an out of sequence in our
                           ; 3 distance at 4:7, we ensure that the 1:4 is in sequence after
                           ; we exchange 4 and 7.
                           ;
0017                       nexti:
0017  8B F0                         mov     SI,AX
0019  8B F8                         mov     DI,AX
001B  03 F1                         add     SI,CX               ; Get I+distance
001D  4E                            dec     SI
001E  4F                            dec     DI                  ; zero base for indexed loads
001F  03 FF                         add     DI,DI
0021  03 F6                         add     SI,SI
0023  8B 30                         mov     SI,WORD PTR DS:[BX+SI] ; Load string displacements
0025  8B 39                         mov     DI,WORD PTR DS:[BX+DI]
0027  E8 0000 E                     call    Strzcomp            ; compare the strings
002A  0F 83 004A R                  jnb     inseq               ; If in sequence - skip
002E  48                            dec     AX                  ; Get zero base
002F  96                            xchg    AX,SI
0030  03 F6                         add     SI,SI               ; Get as index
0032  89 00                         mov     WORD PTR DS:[BX+SI],AX ; exchange the string
0034  D1 EE                         shr     SI,1
0036  8B C6                         mov     AX,SI
0038  40                            inc     AX
0039  8B F0                         mov     SI,AX
003B  03 F1                         add     SI,CX
003D  4E                            dec     SI
003E  03 F6                         add     SI,SI
0040  89 38                         mov     WORD PTR DS:[BX+SI],DI ; displacements
0042  2B C1                         sub     AX,CX               ; next to compare
0044  0F 88 004A R                  js      inseq               ; If negative - out
0048  75 CD                         jnz     nexti               ; If positive - check again
004A                       inseq:
004A  58                            pop     AX                  ; Get j back
004B  40                            inc     AX                  ; add 1
004C  3B D0                         cmp     DX,AX               ; Are we at our limit
004E  73 C6                         jnb     nextj               ; No - loop again
0050  EB B7                         jmp     nextdist            ; loop until distance = 0
0052                       sortdone:
0052  5D                            pop     BP                  ; Restore the entry registers
0053  5F                            pop     DI
0054  5E                            pop     SI
0055  58                            pop     AX
0056  5B                            pop     BX
0057  59                            pop     CX
0058  5A                            pop     DX
0059  C3                            ret                         ; and return.
005A                       Shellsrt ENDP
005A                       code     ENDS
                                    END
```

Program 9-8: QSORT

```
                                  .386
0000                      code    SEGMENT  para 'CODE' USE16 PUBLIC
                                  ASSUME   CS:code, DS:code, SS:code
                          ;
                          ; Name;     QSORT
                          ;
                          ; Purpose: The following procedure provides an implementation of the
                          ;          quicksort algorithm.
                          ;
                          ; Inputs:  DS:BX points to a standard array descriptor.
                          ;          DS:SI points to an index array
                          ;
                          ; Process: The index array is initialized with sequential index
                          ;          values.  This indirection is done for two reasons:
                          ;          1. Exchanging index values is faster than exchanging
                          ;             records (which may be very large).
                          ;          2. Often we don't want to change the original order
                          ;             we only want a differently ordered set of pointers.
                          ;          The quicksort algorithm is then applied using the
                          ;          indirection of the index array.
                          ;
                          ; Output:  The index array will contain pointers to records with
                          ;          ascending key values.  Neither the array descriptor nor
                          ;          the record array is changed.
                          ;
                          arradesc  STRUC
0000  0000                ndxmax    dw      0                   ; Maximum element index
0002  0000                elesize   dw      0                   ; Size of an element
0004  0000                elepseg   dw      0                   ; Elements per segment
0006  0000                elesegs   dw      0                   ; First element of the DS
                          ;                                       array.  Further elements
                          ;                                       follow sequentially.
0008                      arradesc  ENDS
                          ;
                          ;
=                         left      EQU     WORD PTR SS:[BP-1]  ; Save area for working left
=                         right     EQU     WORD PTR SS:[BP-3]  ; and right of partition.
                          ;
                                    PUBLIC  Qsort
0000                      Qsort     PROC
0000  66| 52                        push    EDX                 ; Save entry registers
0002  66| 51                        push    ECX
0004  66| 53                        push    EBX
0006  66| 50                        push    EAX
0008  66| 56                        push    ESI
000A  66| 57                        push    EDI
000C  06                            push    ES
000D  0F A0                         push    FS
000F  0F A8                         push    GS
0011  C8 0008 00                    enter   8,0                 ; Get some work area
0015  8C D8                         mov     AX,DS               ; Move DS to GS for use.
0017  8E E8                         mov     GS,AX               ; We will need ES and DS
0019  8E C0                         mov     ES,AX               ; for comparisons later.
001B  66| B8 0000FFFF               mov     EAX,0000ffffh       ; Get mask
0021  66| 23 F0                     and     ESI,EAX             ; and ensure high bytes clear
0024  66| 23 F8                     and     EDI,EAX
0027  66| 23 D8                     and     EBX,EAX
002A  66| 23 C8                     and     ECX,EAX
002D  66| 23 D0                     and     EDX,EAX
                          ;
```

```
                              ; Form the index array as pointed to by DS:SI.
                              ;
0030  8B FE                             mov     DI,SI                   ; Set pointer
0032  B8 0001                           mov     AX,1                    ; Set initial index value
0035  FC                                cld                             ; and set direction to up.
0036                          formit:
0036  AB                                stosw                           ; store index value
0037  40                                inc     AX                      ; step the index
0038  3B 07                             cmp     AX,ndxmax.[BX]          ; are we done?
003A  76 FA                             jna     formit                  ; No - go back for next.
003C  2B C0                             sub     AX,AX                   ; Set stopper on stack
003E  50                                push    AX                      ; left index
003F  50                                push    AX                      ; and right for a partition.
0040  40                                inc     AX                      ; get a 1
0041  8B 0F                             mov     CX,ndxmax.[BX]          ; and the top
0043  EB 03 90                          jmp     qbegin                  ; Go
                              ;
                              ; Unstack a new partition, the previous is in order.
                              ;
0046                          unstack:
0046  59                                pop     CX                      ; Get right index
0047  58                                pop     AX                      ; and left.


                              ;
                              ; Start a new partitioning process.
                              ;
                              ; We have a left and right index in AX and CX respectively.  We first
                              ; check for the completion condition - 0,0.
                              ;
0048                          qbegin:
0048  50                                push    AX                      ; save our left in case
0049  0B C1                             or      AX,CX                   ; we are not done.
004B  58                                pop     AX
004C  0F 84 0127 R                      jz      alldone                 ; We have unstacked our stop.
                              ;
                              ; If our partition is of size 3 or less, we just sort it without
                              ; partitioning.
                              ;
0050  8B D1                             mov     DX,CX                   ; Copy for our test
0052  2B D0                             sub     DX,AX                   ; Check distance
0054  74 F0                             jz      unstack                 ; Single element is in order.
                              ;
                              ; We can have a partition of size 2, or more.
                              ;
0056  E8 013E R                         call    compare                 ; check a(l) to a(r)
0059  0F 86 0070 R                      jna     order1                  ; In order - could be done.
005D  48                                dec     AX                      ; down 1 to get zero base
005E  49                                dec     CX
005F  65: 67| 8B 3C46                   mov     DI,GS:[ESI+EAX*2]       ; Get the value from AX's
0064  65: 67| 87 3C4E                   xchg    DI,GS:[ESI+ECX*2]       ; exchange with CX's location
0069  65: 67| 89 3C46                   mov     GS:[ESI+EAX*2],DI       ; and complete the exchange
006E  40                                inc     AX
006F  41                                inc     CX                      ; and back up
0070                          order1:
0070  4A                                dec     DX                      ; See if we had a length of 2.
0071  74 D3                             jz      unstack                 ; We did - our 2 sort did it.
0073  8B D1                             mov     DX,CX                   ; Save right pointer.
0075  03 C8                             add     CX,AX                   ; point to center element.
0077  D1 E9                             shr     CX,1
0079  E8 013E R                         call    compare                 ; check a(l) to a(c)
007C  0F 86 0093 R                      jna     order2                  ; In order leaves 1 pair
0080  48                                dec     AX                      ; down 1 to get zero base
```

```
0081  49                            dec     CX
0082  65: 67| 8B 3C46               mov     DI,GS:[ESI+EAX*2]   ; Get the value
0087  65: 67| 87 3C4E               xchg    DI,GS:[ESI+ECX*2]   ; into CX's location
008C  65: 67| 89 3C46               mov     GS:[ESI+EAX*2],DI   ; and complete the exchange
0091  40                            inc     AX
0092  41                            inc     CX                  ; and back up
                    ;
                    ; We have the lowest in the first element now.  We may have to
                    ; reverse the second and third before we are done.
                    ;
0093                order2:
0093  92                            xchg    AX,DX               ; Save left pointer and get rt
0094  91                            xchg    AX,CX               ; point to second element.
0095  E8 013E R                     call    compare             ; check a(c) to a(r)
0098  0F 86 00AF R                  jna     order3              ; If in order - OK as is.
009C  48                            dec     AX                  ; down 1 to get zero base
009D  49                            dec     CX
009E  65: 67| 8B 3C46               mov     DI,GS:[ESI+EAX*2]   ; Get the value
00A3  65: 67| 87 3C4E               xchg    DI,GS:[ESI+ECX*2]   ; into CX's location
00A8  65: 67| 89 3C46               mov     GS:[ESI+EAX*2],DI   ; and complete the exchange
00AD  40                            inc     AX
00AE  41                            inc     CX                  ; and back up
                    ;
                    ; If our partition was of size 3, it is now sorted.
                    ; If more, we have the left, center, and right in order.
                    ;
00AF                order3:
00AF  92                            xchg    AX,DX               ; Get left in AX, center DX.
00B0  2B C8                         sub     CX,AX               ; Get count between l and r.
00B2  83 F9 02                      cmp     CX,2                ; Is partition in order?
00B5  74 8F                         je      unstack             ; If size is 3, it is.
00B7  03 C8                         add     CX,AX               ; Get right pointer back.
                    ;
                    ; We have a partition of 4 or more elements.  We choose the median
                    ; of the left, center or right elements as our pivot point.  Since
                    ; we have them sorted, the center is the median.
                    ;
                    ; Our pivot element is pointed to by DX.
                    ;
00B9  4A                            dec     DX                  ; down 1 to get zero base
                    ;
                    ; Now set the pivot element as our comparand in ES,DI.
                    ;
00BA  50                            push    AX                  ; Save registers used
00BB  56                            push    SI
00BC  65: 67| 8B 0456               mov     AX,GS:[ESI+EDX*2]   ; Get the element's pointer
00C1  E8 017F R                     call    arrandxp            ; Get pivot set into
00C4  8E C0                         mov     ES,AX
00C6  8B FE                         mov     DI,SI               ; ES:DI for all pivot compares
00C8  5E                            pop     SI
00C9  58                            pop     AX                  ; Restore the registers
                    ;
                    ; We have set a pivot point and fixed it in ES:DI.
                    ;
00CA  89 46 FF                      mov     left,AX             ; Save left and
00CD  89 4E FD                      mov     right,CX            ; right beginning pointers.
                    ;
                    ; Partition for higher elements
                    ;
00D0                nextright:
00D0  91                            xchg    AX,CX               ; Get working right in AX
00D1                workright:
```

```
00D1  48                        dec    AX                  ; step down 1
00D2  E8 0165 R                 call   pivotc              ; compare a(SI(AX)):pivot
00D5  77 FA                     ja     workright           ; if above - loop
                        ;
                        ; We have come down until we got an element <= to our pivot.
                        ;
                        ; Now go up from the left until we get an element >= to our pivot.
                        ;
00D7  91                        xchg   AX,CX               ; Get working left in AX
00D8                    workleft:
00D8  40                        inc    AX                  ; step it by one
00D9  E8 0165 R                 call   pivotc              ; compare a(SI(AX)):pivot
00DC  72 FA                     jb     workleft            ; if under - loop
                        ;
                        ; If our pointers have crossed, we are done.  Otherwise we swap
                        ; our out of order items and continue.
                        ;
00DE  3B C1                     cmp    AX,CX               ; check if we crossed
00E0  0F 87 00FB R              ja     crossed             ; if we did - partition done
00E4  74 EA                     je     nextright           ; If equal don't exchange
00E6  48                        dec    AX                  ; down 1 to get zero base
00E7  49                        dec    CX
00E8  65: 67| 8B 1446           mov    DX,GS:[ESI+EAX*2]   ; Get the value
00ED  65: 67| 87 144E           xchg   DX,GS:[ESI+ECX*2]   ; into CX's location
00F2  65: 67| 89 1446           mov    GS:[ESI+EAX*2],DX   ; and complete the exchange
00F7  40                        inc    AX
00F8  41                        inc    CX                  ; and back up
00F9  EB D5                     jmp    nextright           ; and continue
                        ;
                        ; We have two partitions, left to AX and CX to right.
                        ;
                        ; We stack the largest partition and sort the smallest.
                        ;
00FB                    crossed:
00FB  41                        inc    CX                  ; up for right and
00FC  48                        dec    AX                  ; down for left
00FD  50                        push   AX                  ; Save left
00FE  8B 56 FD                  mov    DX,right            ; Get right boundary
0101  2B D1                     sub    DX,CX               ; And the size of the part
0103  2B 46 FF                  sub    AX,left             ; get the size of the left
0106  3B C2                     cmp    AX,DX               ; check relative sizes
0108  0F 82 011A R              jb     bigright            ; Right is larger
                        ;
                        ; The left partition is larger than the right - We stack the left
                        ; then sort the right.  This minimizes the size of the stack.
                        ;
010C  8B 46 FF                  mov    AX,left             ; Get left index
010F  5A                        pop    DX                  ; Get the right index
0110  50                        push   AX                  ; Stack left index then
0111  52                        push   DX                  ; the right (we pop rt,lft)
0112  8B C1                     mov    AX,CX               ; CX becomes the new left
0114  8B 4E FD                  mov    CX,right            ; with old right the right.
0117  E9 0048 R                 jmp    qbegin              ; Go back and repartition
                        ;
                        ; The right partition is larger than the left - We stack the right
                        ; then sort the left.
                        ;
011A                    bigright:
011A  58                        pop    AX                  ; Get left off the stack
011B  51                        push   CX                  ; CX is the left
011C  FF 76 FD                  push   right               ; and right is still right
011F  8B C8                     mov    CX,AX               ; New partition is left
```

```
0121  8B 46 FF                 mov    AX,left              ; to AX.
0124  E9 0048 R                jmp    qbegin               ; Go back and repartition.
0127                   alldone:
0127  C9                       leave
0128  8C E8                    mov    AX,GS                ; Restore normal DS
012A  8E D8                    mov    DS,AX
012C  0F A9                    pop    GS                   ; and the entry registers.
012E  0F A1                    pop    FS
0130  07                       pop    ES
0131  66| 5F                   pop    EDI
0133  66| 5E                   pop    ESI
0135  66| 58                   pop    EAX
0137  66| 5B                   pop    EBX
0139  66| 59                   pop    ECX
013B  66| 5A                   pop    EDX
013D  C3                       ret                         ; and return.
                       ;
                       ; Compare routine: (Replace with whatever is needed for your sort).
                       ;               Compares the key in the record at SI(AX) to the key
                       ;               in the record at SI(CX) key(SI(AX)) - key(SI(CX)).
                       ;               It returns with the flags set.  The usage is such
                       ;               that a call to compare is followed by a conditional
                       ;               jump using the flag settings.
                       ;               The key as used in the demo program is a Social
                       ;               Security number with dashes, 000-00-0000 for
                       ;               instance. The key is the first field in the record.
013E                   Compare  PROC
013E  60                       pusha                       ; Save the registers
013F  56                       push   SI                   ; We need SI later
0140  48                       dec    AX                   ; Get indices on zero base.
0141  65: 67| 8B 0446          mov    AX,GS:[ESI+EAX*2]    ; Get indirect index for AX
0146  E8 017F R                call   arrandxp             ; Get the record location AX
0149  8E D8                    mov    DS,AX                ; Set the base
014B  8B FE                    mov    DI,SI                ; and index
014D  5E                       pop    SI                   ; For the indirect index load
014E  8B C1                    mov    AX,CX                ; Set the next record
0150  48                       dec    AX                   ; Zero base
0151  65: 67| 8B 0446          mov    AX,GS:[ESI+EAX*2]    ; Get indirect index for CX
0156  E8 017F R                call   arrandxp             ; and the record location.
0159  87 FE                    xchg   DI,SI                ; Fix indices
015B  8E C0                    mov    ES,AX                ; and get next base
015D  B9 000B                  mov    CX,11                ; Set count to compare
0160  FC                       cld                         ; and direction to up
0161  F3/ A6                   repz cmpsb                  ; Compare,
0163  61                       popa                        ; restore registers,
0164  C3                       ret                         ; and return.
0165                   Compare  ENDP
                       ;
                       ; Compare to pivot element.  Similar to the above but assumes that
                       ; the segment and offset for the pivot are set in ES:DI.  Thus
                       ; the comparison is always A(SI(AX)):pivot.
                       ;
0165                   Pivotc   PROC
0165  57                       push   DI                   ; Save registers used
0166  56                       push   SI
0167  50                       push   AX
0168  51                       push   CX
0169  48                       dec    AX                   ; Get indices on zero base.
016A  65: 67| 8B 0446          mov    AX,GS:[ESI+EAX*2]    ; Get indirect index for AX
016F  E8 017F R                call   arrandxp             ; Get the record location AX
0172  8E D8                    mov    DS,AX                ; Set the base
0174  B9 000B                  mov    CX,11                ; Set count to compare
```

```
0177  FC                    cld                           ; and direction to up
0178  F3/ A6                repz cmpsb                    ; Compare,
017A  59                    pop     CX                    ; restore registers,
017B  58                    pop     AX
017C  5E                    pop     SI
017D  5F                    pop     DI
017E  C3                    ret                           ; and return.
017F             Pivotc     ENDP
                 ;
                 ;
                 ; Purpose: The following procedure provides a method for computing
                 ;          a usable array element address.  This is required for
                 ;          accessing elements of large arrays (over 64k bytes in
                 ;          size) in a USE16 task.  It is a modification of the full
                 ;          routine.
                 ;
                 ; Inputs:  AX has the index of the array element (1 .. LAST) desired.
                 ;          BX has the segment array pointer.
                 ;
                 ;          The DS array is assumed to be of the form built by the
                 ;          ARRABLDP.ASM routine.
                 ;
                 ; Process: AX is decremented to get a zero base and DX is zeroed.
                 ;          DX-AX is divided by the number of elements per segment.
                 ;          The quotient is multiplied by 2 and used to select the
                 ;          ES value.  The remainder multiplied by the element size
                 ;          becomes the SI value.
                 ;
                 ; Output:  SI has the displacement to the record.  AX has the segment
                 ;          register value.
                 ;
017F             Arrandxp   PROC
017F  52                    push    DX                    ; Save entry registers
0180  51                    push    CX
0181  53                    push    BX
0182  48                    dec     AX                    ; Get index based on zero
0183  2B D2                 sub     DX,DX                 ; Clear upper word of dividend
0185  65: F7 77 04          div     GS:[BX].elepseg       ; Divide by elements / segment
0189  8B C8                 mov     CX,AX                 ; Save the quotient
018B  8B C2                 mov     AX,DX                 ; Position the remainder
018D  65: F7 67 02          mul     GS:[BX].elesize       ; Get the element's offset
0191  8B F0                 mov     SI,AX                 ; Into SI
0193  03 D9                 add     BX,CX                 ; Add the quotient to BX
0195  03 D9                 add     BX,CX                 ; twice to get the displacement
0197  65: 8B 47 06          mov     AX,GS:[BX].elesegs    ; of the descriptor.
019B  5B                    pop     BX                    ; Restore the entry registers
019C  59                    pop     CX
019D  5A                    pop     DX
019E  C3                    ret                           ; and return.
019F             Arrandxp   ENDP

019F             Qsort      ENDP
019F             code       ENDS
                            END
```

Program 9-9: ARRADRV

Microsoft (R) Macro Assembler Version 5.00

```
                                        PAGE    55,132
                                        .386
                              ;
                              ; Name:    ARRADRV
                              ;
                              ; Purpose: This program tests the array building and indexing
                              ;          procedures.
                              ;
                              ; Inputs:  The user is prompted for an element size and a number of
                              ;          elements.
                              ;
                              ; Process: The program gets the element size and the number of
                              ;          elements to build.  It then calls Arrabldp to get the
                              ;          memory and fill in the arradesc structure.  The structure
                              ;          is displayed in hex.  The program then prompts for element
                              ;          numbers to locate and displays the resulting segment and
                              ;          displacement in hex.  (The tester then hand verifies the
                              ;          result.)
                              ;
                              ; Outputs: The desired output is the confidence that the build and
                              ;          index routines are correct.
                              ;
                              ;
                              ;
                              ; Note:    Under MS-DOS using the Microsoft linker you must link
                              ;          with the option /CP:nnnn. This option overrides the default
                              ;          memory allocation which allocates all free memory to your
                              ;          program.  nnnn is the maximum number of paragraphs to be
                              ;          allocated to your program.  If it is less than the size of
                              ;          the program the program size is used.
                              ;
                              ;
                              ;
                              ;
                              ;
                              ; Declare the common structure
                              ;
                              arradesc  STRUC
0000  0000                    ndxmax    dw      0               ; Maximum element index
0002  0000                    elesize   dw      0               ; Size of an element
0004  0000                    elepseg   dw      0               ; Elements per segment
0006  0000                    elesegs   dw      0               ; First element of the DS
                              ;                                   array.  Further elements
                              ;                                   are assumed to follow
                              ;                                   sequentially.
0008                          arradesc  ENDS

                                        EXTRN   ARRABLDP:PROC
                                        EXTRN   ARRANDXP:PROC

                                        EXTRN   CODEASB:PROC
                                        EXTRN   CODEBTHX:PROC
                                        EXTRN   CODEBAS:PROC

0000                          stack     SEGMENT para 'STACK' STACK
0000  0100[                             dq      256 DUP(?)
         ??????????????
```

```
          ?
                         ]

0800                        stack      ENDS
0000                        data       SEGMENT para
0000  0100[                 string     db       256 DUP(?)          ; String scratch area
           ??
                         ]

0100  0A 0D 45 6E 74 65 72  query1     db       10,13,"Enter the size of an element: $"
      20 74 68 65 20 73 69
      7A 65 20 6F 66 20 61
      6E 20 65 6C 65 6D 65
      6E 74 3A 20 24
0121  0A 0D 45 6E 74 65 72  query2     db       10,13,"Enter the number of elements: $"
      20 74 68 65 20 6E 75
      6D 62 65 72 20 6F 66
      20 65 6C 65 6D 65 6E
      74 73 3A 20 24
0142  0A 0D 45 6E 74 65 72  query3     db       10,13,"Enter an index to locate: $"
      20 61 6E 20 69 6E 64
      65 78 20 74 6F 20 6C
      6F 63 61 74 65 3A 20
      24
015F  0A 0D 41 72 72 61 79  deschead   db       10,13,"Array descriptor: $"
      20 64 65 73 63 72 69
      70 74 6F 72 3A 20 24
0174  0A 0D 49 6E 64 65 78  indxhead   db       10,13,"Index gives       $"
      20 67 69 76 65 73 20
      20 20 20 20 20 20 24
                            ;
                            ;
                            ;
0189  90 90 90                         ALIGN    4
018C  0000                  desc       arradesc <>                  ; Build the descriptor
018E  0000
0190  0000
0192  0000

0194  0014[                            dw       20 DUP(0)           ; Save room for segment values
            0000
                         ]

01BC                        data       ENDS

0000                        code       SEGMENT para 'CODE' USE16 PUBLIC
                                       ASSUME   CS:code, DS:data
                            ;
                            ; Set up the environment
                            ;
0000                        Begin:
0000  B8 ---- R                        mov      AX,data             ; Get data segment pointer
0003  8E D8                            mov      DS,AX               ; into DS,
0005  8E C0                            mov      ES,AX               ; and ES.
0007  2B F6                            sub      SI,SI               ; Clear indices
0009  2B FF                            sub      DI,DI
000B                        getsize:
000B  8D 16 0100 R                     lea      DX,query1           ; Get the size
000F  E8 0107 R                        call     getinp
0012  E3 7F                            jcxz     exit                ; Quit if null
0014  E8 00E9 R                        call     getnbr              ; convert the number
0017  72 F2                            jc       getsize             ; an error goes back
```

```
0019  A3 018E R                  mov     desc.elesize,AX      ; set the size
001C                   getcount:
001C  8D 16 0121 R               lea     DX,query2            ; Prompt for number to build
0020  E8 0107 R                  call    getinp
0023  E3 F7                      jcxz    getcount             ; must have an input
0025  E8 00E9 R                  call    getnbr               ; convert the number
0028  72 F2                      jc      getcount             ; again if bad
002A  A3 018C R                  mov     desc.ndxmax,AX       ; Set the maximum
002D  8D 1E 018C R               lea     BX,desc              ; Point to array descriptor
0031  E8 0000 E                  call    Arrabldp             ; and fill it in
0034  72 D5                      jc      getsize              ; If an error - try again
                       ;
                       ; Dump the array descriptor just built.
                       ;
0036  8D 16 015F R               lea     DX,deschead          ; Point to header
003A  B4 09                      mov     AH,9
003C  CD 21                      int     21h                  ; and put it out
003E  A1 018C R                  mov     AX,desc.ndxmax       ; Get number
0041  8B D0                      mov     DX,AX                ; Save it
0043  E8 0099 R                  call    prtax                ; and print it
0046  A1 018E R                  mov     AX,desc.elesize      ; size
0049  E8 0099 R                  call    prtax                ; prints too
004C  A1 0190 R                  mov     AX,desc.elepseg      ; elements/segment
004F  8B C8                      mov     CX,AX                ; Save it too
0051  E8 0099 R                  call    prtax                ; Print as well
0054  8D 1E 0192 R               lea     BX,desc.elesegs      ; Point to segment list
0058                   nextseg:
0058  8B 07                      mov     AX,WORD PTR [BX]     ; Get the next segment
005A  E8 00BC R                  call    prtaxhx              ; Dump it
005D  83 C3 02                   add     BX,2                 ; step pointer
0060  2B D1                      sub     DX,CX                ; count out this group
0062  0F 84 0068 R               jz      nextindex            ; Ended even
0066  79 F0                      jns     nextseg              ; loop till all out
0068                   nextindex:
0068  8D 16 0142 R               lea     DX,query3            ; get an index value
006C  E8 0107 R                  call    getinp               ; and get it
006F  E3 9A                      jcxz    getsize              ; go try a new config
0071  E8 00E9 R                  call    getnbr               ; convert the index
0074  72 F2                      jc      nextindex            ; loop if bad
0076  8D 16 0174 R               lea     DX,indxhead          ; point to header
007A  50                         push    AX                   ; save number
007B  B4 09                      mov     AH,9
007D  CD 21                      int     21h
007F  58                         pop     AX
0080  8D 1E 018C R               lea     BX,desc              ; point to descriptor
0084  E8 0000 E                  call    Arrandxp             ; Get the seg:offset
0087  72 DF                      jc      nextindex            ; loop if bad
0089  E8 00BC R                  call    prtaxhx              ; Do the segment value
008C  8B C6                      mov     AX,SI                ; Get displacement
008E  E8 00BC R                  call    prtaxhx              ; and print it
0091  EB D5                      jmp     nextindex            ; loop on index gets

0093                   Exit:
0093  B0 00                      mov     AL,0                 ; Set return code
0095  B4 4C                      mov     AH,04ch              ; Set good-by
0097  CD 21                      int     21h                  ; Return to the system
                       ;
                       ; Print the number in AX
                       ;
0099                   prtax     PROC
0099  60                         pusha                        ; save everything
009A  66| 98                     cwde                         ; As a 32 bit integer
```

```
009C  8D 3E 0000 R                  lea     DI,string           ; Point to output area
00A0  E8 0000 E                     call    Codebas             ; Convert it
00A3  B4 02                         mov     AH,2
00A5                        numbout:
00A5  8A 15                         mov     DL,BYTE PTR [DI]    ; Get a byte
00A7  0A D2                         or      DL,DL               ; at end?
00A9  0F 84 00B2 R                  jz      numbout0            ; Yes
00AD  CD 21                         int     21h                 ; print it
00AF  47                            inc     DI                  ; point to next
00B0  EB F3                         jmp     numbout             ; and loop
00B2                        numbout0:
00B2  B2 2C                         mov     DL,','              ; follow with comma
00B4  CD 21                         int     21h
00B6  B2 20                         mov     DL,' '              ; and a space
00B8  CD 21                         int     21h
00BA  61                            popa                        ; restore
00BB  C3                            ret
00BC                        prtax   ENDP
                            ;
                            ; Print the number in AX in hex.
                            ;
00BC                        prtaxhx PROC
00BC  60                            pusha
00BD  50                            push    AX                  ; save the number
00BE  8A C4                         mov     AL,AH               ; Position high byte
00C0  E8 0000 E                     call    Codebthx            ; and convert it
00C3  8A D4                         mov     DL,AH               ; Set high byte
00C5  8A C8                         mov     CL,AL               ; save low
00C7  B4 02                         mov     AH,2
00C9  CD 21                         int     21h                 ; Put it out
00CB  8A D1                         mov     DL,CL               ; and low byte
00CD  CD 21                         int     21h
00CF  58                            pop     AX                  ; Get low byte
00D0  E8 0000 E                     call    Codebthx            ; Hex it
00D3  8A D4                         mov     DL,AH
00D5  8A C8                         mov     CL,AL               ; save low
00D7  B4 02                         mov     AH,2
00D9  CD 21                         int     21h                 ; print it
00DB  8A D1                         mov     DL,CL               ; and low byte
00DD  CD 21                         int     21h
00DF  B2 3A                         mov     DL,':'              ; follow with colon
00E1  CD 21                         int     21h
00E3  B2 20                         mov     DL,' '              ; and a space
00E5  CD 21                         int     21h
00E7  61                            popa
00E8  C3                            ret
00E9                        prtaxhx ENDP
                            ;
                            ; Convert the number just obtained
                            ;
00E9                        getnbr  PROC
00E9  8B F3                         mov     SI,BX               ; set input pointer
00EB  E8 0000 E                     call    codeasb             ; Convert to binary
00EE  0F 82 0105 R                  jc      badnbr              ; Overflow is too much
00F2  66| 0B C0                     or      EAX,EAX             ; check for a zero size
00F5  0F 84 0105 R                  jz      badnbr              ; that is bad too
00F9  66| 3D 00008000               cmp     EAX,08000h          ; Over 32K in size
00FF  0F 83 0105 R                  jnb     badnbr              ; if so - too big
0103  F8                            clc
0104  C3                            ret                         ; return ok
0105                        badnbr:
0105  F9                            stc                         ; flag error
```

```
0106  C3                            ret
0107                     getnbr     ENDP
                         ;
                         ; Read a string in response to a prompt
                         ; The prompt must be in DX.  The string will be returned in string.
                         ;
0107                     getinp     PROC
0107  50                            push    AX                  ; Save registers
0108  56                            push    SI
0109  B4 09                         mov     AH,9                ; and dos request
010B  CD 21                         int     21h                 ; put out the string
010D  8D 16 0000 R                  lea     DX,string           ; point to input area
0111  C6 06 0000 R FE               mov     string,254          ; Set max length in
0116  B4 0A                         mov     AH,10               ; Ask for read of string
0118  CD 21                         int     21h                 ; from DOS.
011A  8D 1E 0002 R                  lea     BX,string+2         ; Point to just read data
011E  8A 0E 0001 R                  mov     CL,string+1         ; Get length read
0122  B5 00                         mov     CH,0                ; as a word.
0124  8B F1                         mov     SI,CX               ; Set length
0126  C6 84 0002 R 00               mov     string+2[SI],0      ; and make an ASCIIZ string.
012B  5E                            pop     SI
012C  58                            pop     AX                  ; Restore registers
012D  C3                            ret                         ; and return.
012E                     getinp     ENDP

012E                     code       ENDS
                                    END     Begin
```

Program 9-10: ARRABLDP

```
                                  PAGE      55,132
                                  .386
0000                     code     SEGMENT   para 'CODE' PUBLIC USE16
                                  ASSUME    CS:code, DS:code, SS:code

                         ;
                         ; Name:     ARRABLDP
                         ;
                         ; Purpose:  The following procedure provides the means to build an
                         ;           array which exceeds the size of a single segment (64K).
                         ;           This is needed for MS-DOS and OS/2 even on the 80386.
                         ;
                         ;
                         ; Inputs:   BX points to the structure ARRADESC with the fields
                         ;           ndxmax and elesize set.
                         ;
                         ; Process:  First, the maximum number of elements per segment is
                         ;           computed.
                         ;
                         ;           The size to get is computed (the MS-DOS Allocate memory
                         ;           call is used as an example so the size is rounded up to
                         ;           the nearest paragraph).
                         ;
                         ;           The number of segments to get is computed and we loop
                         ;           getting them until we either have them all or an error
                         ;           is returned.
                         ;
                         ;           We set our return conditions and return.
                         ;
                         ; Output:   The field elepseg is set and the DS array is filled in
```

```
                              ;           with segment descriptors for each section of the array
                              ;           if no error occurred - in this case carry is reset on
                              ;           return.
                              ;
                              ;           If an error occurs we return all sections which we were
                              ;           successful in obtaining.  The return will have carry set.
                              ;
                              ;
                              ; Note:     Under MS-DOS using the Microsoft linker you must link
                              ;           with the option /CP:nnnn. This option overrides the default
                              ;           memory allocation which allocates all free memory to your
                              ;           program.  nnnn is the maximum number of paragraphs to be
                              ;           allocated to your program.  If it is less than the size of
                              ;           the program the program size is used.
                              ;
                              ;
                              ;
                              arradesc    STRUC
0000  0000                    ndxmax      dw      0                 ; Maximum element index
0002  0000                    elesize     dw      0                 ; Size of an element
0004  0000                    elepseg     dw      0                 ; Elements per segment
0006  0000                    elesegs     dw      0                 ; First element of the DS
                              ;                                       array.  Further elements
                              ;                                       follow sequentially.
0008                          arradesc    ENDS
                              ;
                              ;
                                          PUBLIC  Arrabldp
                              ;
0000                          Arrabldp    PROC
0000  52                                  push    DX                ; Save entry registers
0001  51                                  push    CX
0002  56                                  push    SI
0003  50                                  push    AX
0004  2B C0                               sub     AX,AX             ; Prepare low part of dividend
0006  BA 0001                             mov     DX,1              ; and get double word 64K
0009  F7 77 02                            div     [BX].elesize      ; Divide by element size
000C  89 47 04                            mov     [BX].elepseg,AX   ; Set the number in a segment
                              ;                                       (except the last)
000F  F7 67 02                            mul     [BX].elesize      ; Get the size to ask for
0012  05 000F                             add     AX,15             ; Round up to paragraph bound
0015  83 D2 00                            adc     DX,0              ; Propagate carry if any
0018  0F AC D0 04                         shrd    AX,DX,4           ; and divide by 16 (para size)
001C  8B C8                               mov     CX,AX             ; Set size for loop
001E  8B 07                               mov     AX,[BX].ndxmax    ; Get count of elements.
0020  2B D2                               sub     DX,DX             ; Clear upper word.
0022  03 47 04                            add     AX,[BX].elepseg   ; round up to get enough
0025  48                                  dec     AX                ; but not one too many.
0026  F7 77 04                            div     [BX].elepseg      ; AX now has count for loop.
0029  91                                  xchg    AX,CX             ; Flip size and count.
                              ;
                              ; We now loop ndmax/elepseg times getting AX paragraphs at a time.
                              ;
002A  8B F3                               mov     SI,BX             ; copy working pointer
002C  53                                  push    BX                ; and save it too.
002D                          memget:
002D  50                                  push    AX                ; save size (used by call)
002E  8B D8                               mov     BX,AX             ; Set paragraph count to get.
0030  B4 48                               mov     AH,048h           ; Set MS-DOS request code.
0032  CD 21                               int     21h               ; Try to get memory.
0034  0F 82 0048 R                        jc      memerror          ; MS-DOS returned an error.
0038  89 44 06                            mov     [SI].elesegs,AX   ; Save the new segment.
```

```
003B  83 C6 02                  add     SI,2              ; and step to next
003E  58                        pop     AX                ; Get our size back
003F  E2 EC                     loop    memget            ; and get as many as we need.
0041  5B                        pop     BX                ; clear stack
0042  F8                        clc                       ; and carry.
0043                    memexit:
0043  58                        pop     AX                ; Restore the entry registers
0044  5E                        pop     SI
0045  59                        pop     CX
0046  5A                        pop     DX
0047  C3                        ret                       ; and return.
                        ;
                        ; An error was returned by MS-DOS on our memory request!
                        ; If it is an out of memory condition, we will return all that we
                        ; got prior to returning with carry set.
                        ;
0048                    memerror:
0048  3C 08                     cmp     AL,8              ; Is it an out condition
004A  58                        pop     AX                ; Clean stack
004B  5B                        pop     BX                ; Get back the base
004C  0F 85 0064 R              jne     nogive            ; No - don't try returns.

0050                    giveloop:
0050  3B DE                     cmp     BX,SI             ; Are we at the base?
0052  0F 84 0064 R              je      nogive            ; Yes - we are done.
0056  83 EE 02                  sub     SI,2              ; Back down one segment.
0059  8B 44 06                  mov     AX,[SI].elesegs   ; Get the segment address
005C  8E C0                     mov     ES,AX             ; positioned for MS-DOS.
005E  B4 49                     mov     AH,049h           ; Set code for return.
0060  CD 21                     int     21h               ; and return it.
0062  73 EC                     jnc     giveloop          ; If we fouled up - quit.
0064                    nogive:
0064  F9                        stc                       ; set carry for exit
0065  EB DC                     jmp     memexit           ; and do it


0067                    Arrabldp        ENDP
0067                    code            ENDS
                                        END
```

Program 9-11: ARRANDXP

```
Microsoft (R) Macro Assembler Version 5.00


                                        PAGE      55,132
                                        .386
 0000                           code    SEGMENT   para 'CODE' PUBLIC USE16
                                        ASSUME    CS:code, DS:code, SS:code
                                ; Name:    ARRANDXP
                                ;
                                ;
                                ; Purpose: The following procedure provides a method for computing
                                ;          a usable array element address.  This is useful for
                                ;          accessing elements of large arrays (over 64k bytes in
                                ;          size).  This is an 80286 protected mode routine.  It is
                                ;          also usable in real mode on all 8086 family processors.
                                ;          It is usable on the 80386 in protected mode for 'Use 16'
                                ;          tasks ('Use 32'tasks, with 32 bit displacements available
                                ;          would normally get a segment of the array size and index
                                ;          it directly.)
                                ;
                                ;
                                ;
                                ; Inputs:  AX has the index of the array element (1 .. LAST) desired.
                                ;          BX has the DS array pointer.
                                ;
                                ;          The DS array is assumed to be of the form built by the
                                ;          ARRABLDP.ASM routine.  (See the structure arradesc below.)
                                ;
                                ; Process: The value in AX is checked against the maximum index value
                                ;          and carry is returned if AX is bad.
                                ;          AX is decremented to get a zero base and DX is zeroed.
                                ;          DX-AX is divided by the number of elements per segment.
                                ;          The quotient is multiplied by 2 and used to select the
                                ;          ES value.  The remainder multiplied by the element size
                                ;          becomes the SI value.
                                ;          Carry is reset and we return.
                                ;
                                ; Output:  The ES - SI registers will address the desired element if
                                ;          carry is reset (AX was ok).  AX has the segment value.
                                ;          ES - SI are unchanged if carry is set (AX was out of
                                ;          bounds).
                                ;
                                ;
                                ;
                                arradesc  STRUC
 0000  0000                     ndxmax    dw      0                  ; Maximum element index
 0002  0000                     elesize   dw      0                  ; Size of an element
 0004  0000                     elepseg   dw      0                  ; Elements per segment
 0006  0000                     elesegs   dw      0                  ; First element of the DS
                                ;                                      array.  Further elements
                                ;                                      are assumed to follow
                                ;                                      sequentially.
 0008                           arradesc  ENDS
                                ;
                                ;
                                          PUBLIC  Arrandxp
                                ;
 0000                           Arrandxp  PROC
 0000  3D 0001                            cmp     AX,1               ; Check low bound for AX
 0003  0F 8C 000D R                       jl      axisbad            ; If low to 1 it's bad
```

```
0007  3B 07                        cmp     AX,[BX].ndxmax      ; Check validity of index
0009  0F 8E 000F R                 jng     axisok              ; If index is ok continue
000D                       axisbad:
000D  F9                           stc                         ; Signal the error AX too big
000E  C3                           ret                         ; Return with carry set
000F                       axisok:
000F  52                           push    DX                  ; Save entry registers
0010  51                           push    CX
0011  53                           push    BX
0012  48                           dec     AX                  ; Get index based on zero
0013  2B D2                        sub     DX,DX               ; Clear upper word of dividend
0015  F7 77 04                     div     [BX].elepseg        ; Divide by elements / segment
0018  8B C8                        mov     CX,AX               ; Save the quotient
001A  8B C2                        mov     AX,DX               ; Position the remainder
001C  F7 67 02                     mul     [BX].elesize        ; Get the element's offset
001F  8B F0                        mov     SI,AX               ; Into SI
0021  03 D9                        add     BX,CX               ; Add the quotient to BX
0023  03 D9                        add     BX,CX               ; twice to get the displacement
0025  8B 47 06                     mov     AX,[BX].elesegs     ; of the descriptor.
0028  8E C0                        mov     ES,AX               ; We need to set it.
002A  F8                           clc                         ; Clear the carry
002B  5B                           pop     BX                  ; Restore the entry registers
002C  59                           pop     CX
002D  5A                           pop     DX
002E  C3                           ret                         ; and return.
002F                       Arrandxp ENDP
002F                       code     ENDS
                                    END
```

Program 9-12: ARRANDXR

```
                                PAGE      55,132
                                .386
0000                    code    SEGMENT   para 'CODE' PUBLIC USE16
                                ASSUME    CS:code, DS:code, SS:code

                        ; Name:     ARRANDXR
                        ;
                        ;
                        ;
                        ; Purpose: The following procedure provides a method for computing a
                        ;          usable array element address. This is useful for accessing
                        ;          elements of large arrays (over 64k bytes in size).
                        ;          This is an 8088/8086 (or real mode 80286/80386) routine.
                        ;
                        ;
                        ; Inputs:  AX has the index of the array element (1 .. LAST).
                        ;          BX has the DS value for element 1.
                        ;          CX has the element size in bytes.
                        ;          DX has the offset of element 1.
                        ;
                        ; Process: The element index is converted into a byte offset into the
                        ;          array [(index-1)*size]. The array offset is added to the
                        ;          result and the carry (if any) is propagated to DX. This
                        ;          gives us the byte offset from the array's segment
                        ;          descriptor. The low 4 bits of the result form the
                        ;          element's offset in SI. The total offset divided by 16
                        ;          is added to the segment's descriptor to form the
                        ;          descriptor for ES. Shifts were used instead of a divide
                        ;          for speed (about 1/3 the time).
```

```
                           ;
                           ; Output:  ES will have a segment descriptor and SI will contain
                           ;          an offset of 0-15 addressing the desired element.
                           ;
                           ;
                           ;
                                      PUBLIC  Arrandxr
                           ;
0000                       Arrandxr   PROC
0000  52                              push    DX              ; Save entry registers
0001  51                              push    CX
0002  53                              push    BX
0003  50                              push    AX
0004  8B F2                           mov     SI,DX           ; Position the offset
0006  48                              dec     AX              ; Get index based on zero
0007  F7 E1                           mul     CX              ; Get the offset increment
0009  03 C6                           add     AX,SI           ; Then the total increment
000B  0F 83 0010 R                    jnc     Ncfirst         ; If no carry - skip
000F  42                              inc     DX              ; passing the carry into DX
0010                       Ncfirst:
0010  8B F0                           mov     SI,AX           ; Set the offset in SI and
0012  83 E6 0F                        and     SI,000Fh        ; leave only the low 4 bits.
0015  B9 0004                         mov     CX,4            ; Get the shift count.
0018  D2 E2                           shl     DL,CL           ; Get overflow into top nibble.
001A  D3 E8                           shr     AX,CL           ; Get segment value in AX.
001C  02 E2                           add     AH,DL           ; With the top 4 bits from DX
001E  03 C3                           add     AX,BX           ; Add the segment value.
0020  8E C0                           mov     ES,AX           ; Place the value in ES.
0022  58                              pop     AX              ; Restore the entry registers
0023  5B                              pop     BX
0024  59                              pop     CX
0025  5A                              pop     DX
0026  C3                              ret                     ; and return.
0027                       Arrandxr   ENDP
0027                       code       ENDS
                                      END
```

Program 9-13: FIND_CFG

```
Microsoft (R) Macro Assembler Version 5.00


                                        PAGE     55,132
                                        .386
                                        .287
                                        EXTRN    CODEBAS:PROC
0000                            STACK   SEGMENT 'STACK' STACK
0000  00C8[                             DW       200 DUP(?)
          ????
                      ]

0190                            STACK   ENDS
0000                            CODE    SEGMENT para 'CODE' PUBLIC USE16
                                        ASSUME   CS:CODE, DS:CODE, SS:STACK
                                ;
                                ; Name:          FIND_CFG
                                ;
                                ; Purpose:       This program does several things:
                                ;                1.  Shows how to get the date and print it, calling
                                ;                        CODEBAS to turn the binary return from INT 21
                                ;                        Function 2A into printable ASCII.
                                ;                2.  Finds and prints the system configuration, using
                                ;                        INT 11.
                                ;                3.  Shows the default drive, using INT 21 Function 19.
                                ;                4.  Shows how to index into a fixed-length array to
                                ;                        find a message to print.
                                ;
                                ; Inputs:        None
                                ;
                                ; Process:       Use INT 11 which moves 16 bits into AX.  (Those
                                ;                bits are defined in Chapter 14, and Appendix
                                ;                6.)  "0D" is a carriage return. "0A" is a line
                                ;                feed.  Note that all character strings that print
                                ;                using function 9 of INT 21 must end with a "$".
                                ;                Note the character strings that have sub-divisions
                                ;                below them.  The sub-divisions are built all the same
                                ;                length so that the values in AX will act as indices
                                ;                into character string arrays.
                                ;
                                ; Outputs:       AX register holds the configuration data
                                ;                There will also be printed output, depending on what
                                ;                system configuration is used.  The date will print, as
                                ;                does the default drive.
                                ;
                                ; NOTE:          Some ROM BIOSs return nothing on an Interrupt 11.  Be
                                ;                sure to check register AX after INT 11 to see what your
                                ;                system returns.  When you purchase your system, you
                                ;                should get material that describes supported BIOS
                                ;                calls.
                                ;
0000                            FIND_CFG:
0000  8C C8                              MOV      AX,CS           ; Prepare to set DS
0002  8E D8                              MOV      DS,AX           ;   and set it.
0004  8E C0                              MOV      ES,AX
0006  E9 0230 R                          JMP      BEGINHERE

0009  0A 0D 54 68 69 73 20      HEADING  DB       0Ah,0Dh,'This system has the following: $'
      73 79 73 74 65 6D 20
```

```
      68 61 73 20 74 68 65
      20 66 6F 6C 6C 6F 77
      69 6E 67 3A 20 24
002B  0A 0D 20 4E 6F 74 20   VIDEO        DB  0Ah,0Dh,' Not Used-Video    $'
      55 73 65 64 2D 56 69
      64 65 6F 20 20 20 20
      24
0041  0A 0D 20 34 30 20 78                DB  0Ah,0Dh,' 40 x 25 Color Card$'
      20 32 35 20 43 6F 6C
      6F 72 20 43 61 72 64
      24
0057  0A 0D 20 38 30 20 78                DB  0Ah,0Dh,' 80 x 25 Color Card$'
      20 32 35 20 43 6F 6C
      6F 72 20 43 61 72 64
      24
006D  0A 0D 20 38 30 20 78                DB  0Ah,0Dh,' 80 x 25 Monochrome$'
      20 32 35 20 4D 6F 6E
      6F 63 68 72 6F 6D 65
      24
0083  0A 0D 20 4F 6E 65 20   DRIVES       DB  0Ah,0Dh,' One drive   $'
      64 72 69 76 65 20 20
      20 24
0093  0A 0D 20 54 77 6F 20                DB  0Ah,0Dh,' Two drives  $'
      64 72 69 76 65 73 20
      20 24
00A3  0A 0D 20 54 68 72 65                DB  0Ah,0Dh,' Three drives$'
      65 20 64 72 69 76 65
      73 24
00B3  0A 0D 20 46 6F 75 72                DB  0Ah,0Dh,' Four drives $'
      20 64 72 69 76 65 73
      20 24
00C3  20 52 53 32 33 32 20   RS232        DB  ' RS232 Cards$'
      43 61 72 64 73 24
00D0  0A 0D 20 41 6E 20 49   YESMODEM     DB  0Ah,0Dh,' An Internal Modem$'
      6E 74 65 72 6E 61 6C
      20 4D 6F 64 65 6D 24
00E5  0A 0D 20 4E 6F 20 49   NOMODEM      DB  0Ah,0Dh,' No Internal Modem$'
      6E 74 65 72 6E 61 6C
      20 4D 6F 64 65 6D 24
00FA  20 50 72 69 6E 74 65   PRINTERS     DB  ' Printers $'
      72 73 20 24
0105  20 24                  BLANK        DB  ' $'
0107  0A 0D 24               CR_LF        DB  0Ah,0Dh,'$'
010A  0A 0D 20 54 68 65 72   NO_PROCESSR  DB  0Ah,0Dh,' There is no Coprocessor installed',0Ah,0Dh,'$'
      65 20 69 73 20 6E 6F
      20 43 6F 70 72 6F 63
      65 73 73 6F 72 20 69
      6E 73 74 61 6C 6C 65
      64 0A 0D 24
0131  0A 0D 20 54 68 65 72   YES_PROCESR  DB  0Ah,0Dh,' There is a Coprocessor installed',0Ah,0Dh,'$'
      65 20 69 73 20 61 20
      43 6F 70 72 6F 63 65
      73 73 6F 72 20 69 6E
      73 74 61 6C 6C 65 64
      0A 0D 24
0157  0A 0D 20 41 6E 20 49   IPLYES       DB  10,13,' An IPL diskette is installed.$'
      50 4C 20 64 69 73 6B
      65 74 74 65 20 69 73
      20 69 6E 73 74 61 6C
      6C 65 64 2E 24
0178  0A 0D 20 41 6E 20 49   IPLNO        DB  10,13,' An IPL diskette is not installed.$'
      50 4C 20 64 69 73 6B
```

```
        65 74 74 65 20 69 73
        20 6E 6F 74 20 69 6E
        73 74 61 6C 6C 65 64
        2E 24
019D    0A 0D 44 61 74 65 20    DATE            DB      0Ah,0Dh,'Date = $'
        3D 20 24
01A7    000A[                   DATE1           DB      10 DUP (?)
            ??
                          ]

01B1    0000                    CWORD           DW      0
01B3    0A 0D 20 54 68 65 20    DEFAULT         DB      0Ah,0Dh,' The default drive is A     $'
        64 65 66 61 75 6C 74
        20 64 72 69 76 65 20
        69 73 20 41 20 20 20
        20 20 24
01D2    0A 0D 20 54 68 65 20                    DB      0Ah,0Dh,' The default drive is B     $'
        64 65 66 61 75 6C 74
        20 64 72 69 76 65 20
        69 73 20 42 20 20 20
        20 20 24
01F1    0A 0D 20 54 68 65 20                    DB      0Ah,0Dh,' The default drive is C     $'
        64 65 66 61 75 6C 74
        20 64 72 69 76 65 20
        69 73 20 43 20 20 20
        20 20 24
0210    0A 0D 20 54 68 65 20                    DB      0Ah,0Dh,' The default is not A,B, or C$'
        64 65 66 61 75 6C 74
        20 69 73 20 6E 6F 74
        20 41 2C 42 2C 20 6F
        72 20 43 24
                                ;
0230                            BEGINHERE:
                                ;       Date = CX=Year, DH=Month Number, DL=Day of Month,
0230    8D 16 019D R                            LEA     DX,DATE         ; Date header
0234    B4 09                                   MOV     AH,9
0236    CD 21                                   INT     21h
0238    B4 2A                                   MOV     AH,2Ah          ; Get date
023A    CD 21                                   INT     21h
023C    8B EA                                   MOV     BP,DX           ; Save month/day
                                ;
                                ;       CODEBAS
                                ;               EAX - Contains the word to be converted
                                ;               DI - Contains the pointer to converted data, on return
                                ;
023E    8D 3E 01A7 R                            LEA     DI,DATE1        ; String for converted data
0242    66| 2B C0                               SUB     EAX,EAX
0245    8A C6                                   MOV     AL,DH           ; Month
0247    E8 0000 E                               CALL    CODEBAS
                                ;
024A                            MONTH:
024A    8A 15                                   MOV     DL,BYTE PTR [DI]
024C    0A D2                                   OR      DL,DL
024E    0F 84 0259 R                            JE      SLASHO          ; Done with string?
0252    B4 02                                   MOV     AH,2            ; Print Month
0254    CD 21                                   INT     21h
0256    47                                      INC     DI              ; Go to next byte
0257    EB F1                                   JMP     MONTH
                                ;
0259                            SLASHO:
0259    2B D2                                   SUB     DX,DX
025B    B2 2F                                   MOV     DL,2Fh          ; Slash (/)
```

```
025D  B4 02                        MOV     AH,2
025F  CD 21                        INT     21h
                           ;
0261  66| 2B C0                    SUB     EAX,EAX         ; Zero out EAX
0264  8D 3E 01A7 R                 LEA     DI,DATE1
0268  8B D5                        MOV     DX,BP           ; Restore Month/Day
026A  8A C2                        MOV     AL,DL           ; Day
026C  E8 0000 E                    CALL    CODEBAS
                           ;
026F                       DAY:
026F  8A 15                        MOV     DL,BYTE PTR [DI]
0271  0A D2                        OR      DL,DL
0273  0F 84 027E R                 JE      SLASH1
0277  B4 02                        MOV     AH,2            ; Print Day
0279  CD 21                        INT     21h
027B  47                           INC     DI              ; Go to next byte
027C  EB F1                        JMP     DAY
                           ;
027E                       SLASH1:
027E  B2 2F                        MOV     DL,2Fh          ; Slash (/)
0280  B4 02                        MOV     AH,2
0282  CD 21                        INT     21h
                           ;
0284  8D 3E 01A7 R                 LEA     DI,DATE1
0288  8B C1                        MOV     AX,CX           ; Year
028A  E8 0000 E                    CALL    CODEBAS
028D  83 C7 02                     ADD     DI,2            ; Skip first two digits
0290                       YEAR:
0290  8A 15                        MOV     DL,BYTE PTR [DI]
0292  0A D2                        OR      DL,DL
0294  0F 84 029F R                 JE      SYSTEM
0298  B4 02                        MOV     AH,2
029A  CD 21                        INT     21h
029C  47                           INC     DI              ; Go to next digit
029D  EB F1                        JMP     YEAR
                           ;
029F                       SYSTEM:
029F  8D 16 0009 R                 LEA     DX,HEADING      ; Print the Heading
02A3  B4 09                        MOV     AH,9h
02A5  CD 21                        INT     21h
02A7  CD 11                        INT     11h             ; Get equipment information
02A9  50                           PUSH    AX              ; Save the info
02AA  2B D2                        SUB     DX,DX
                           ;
                           ; Do number of installed Drives
                           ;
02AC  C0 E8 06                     SHR     AL,6            ; Leave only # of drives
02AF  8D 16 0083 R                 LEA     DX,DRIVES       ; The beginning of this array
02B3  B1 10                        MOV     CL,16           ; Each array element is 16 bytes
02B5  F6 E1                        MUL     CL              ; This multiplies AL by 16
02B7  03 D0                        ADD     DX,AX           ; Now has the array start point
02B9  B4 09                        MOV     AH,9h           ; Ready to print drives
02BB  CD 21                        INT     21h
                           ;
                           ; Now do Video Mode
                           ;
02BD  2B D2                        SUB     DX,DX
02BF  58                           POP     AX              ; Retrieve the original info
02C0  50                           PUSH    AX              ; Keep info unchanged
02C1  8D 16 002B R                 LEA     DX,VIDEO        ; Beginning array point
02C5  C0 EC 02                     SHL     AL,2            ; Get rid of top 2 bits
02C8  C0 E8 06                     SHR     AL,6            ; Now Video mode=AL
02CB  B1 16                        MOV     CL,22           ; Each entry 22 bytes long
```

```
02CD  F6 E1                         MUL     CL              ; Multiply value in AL by 22
02CF  03 D0                         ADD     DX,AX           ; Point at right array element
02D1  B4 09                         MOV     AH,9h           ; Print
02D3  CD 21                         INT     21h

                    ;
                    ; Number of RS232 Cards
                    ;
02D5  8D 16 0107 R                  LEA     DX,CR_LF
02D9  B4 09                         MOV     AH,9h
02DB  CD 21                         INT     21h
02DD  8D 16 0105 R                  LEA     DX,BLANK        ; Print a blank, to line up output
02E1  B4 09                         MOV     AH,9h
02E3  CD 21                         INT     21h
02E5  58                            POP     AX              ; Go get that info again
02E6  50                            PUSH    AX              ; Save info
02E7  C0 E4 04                      SHL     AH,4            ; Get rid of top 4 bits
02EA  C0 EC 05                      SHR     AH,5
02ED  80 C4 30                      ADD     AH,30h          ; Make it printable
02F0  8A D4                         MOV     DL,AH           ; Put it where INT knows to print
02F2  B4 02                         MOV     AH,2h           ; Get ready to print RS232 #
02F4  CD 21                         INT     21h
02F6  8D 16 00C3 R                  LEA     DX,RS232        ; Print 'RS232'
02FA  B4 09                         MOV     AH,9h
02FC  CD 21                         INT     21h
                    ;
                    ; Internal Modem present?
                    ;
02FE  58                            POP     AX              ; Go retrieve info
02FF  50                            PUSH    AX              ; Save one more time
0300  A9 2000                       TEST    AX,0010000000000000B ; Is there an internal?
0303  0F 84 030E R                  JE      NONE
0307  8D 16 00D0 R                  LEA     DX,YESMODEM     ; Print that there IS a modem
030B  EB 05 90                      JMP     NEXTOPTN
030E                NONE:
030E  8D 16 00E5 R                  LEA     DX,NOMODEM      ; Print that there is NOT
0312                NEXTOPTN:
0312  B4 09                         MOV     AH,9h
0314  CD 21                         INT     21h
                    ;
                    ; Number of Printers Attached
                    ;
0316  8D 16 0107 R                  LEA     DX,CR_LF
031A  B4 09                         MOV     AH,9
031C  CD 21                         INT     21h
031E  8D 16 0105 R                  LEA     DX,BLANK        ; Print a blank, to line up output
0322  B4 09                         MOV     AH,9h
0324  CD 21                         INT     21h
0326  58                            POP     AX              ; Get info again.
0327  50                            PUSH    AX
0328  C0 EC 06                      SHR     AH,6            ; Printers in last two bits
032B  80 C4 30                      ADD     AH,30h          ; Make it printable
032E  8A D4                         MOV     DL,AH
0330  B4 02                         MOV     AH,2h           ; Print # of printers
0332  CD 21                         INT     21h
0334  8D 16 00FA R                  LEA     DX,PRINTERS     ; Now print 'Printers'
0338  B4 09                         MOV     AH,9h
033A  CD 21                         INT     21h
                    ;
                    ; Now see if there is a math coprocessor
                    ;
033C  58                            POP     AX
033D  50                            PUSH    AX
```

```
033E  A9 0002                         TEST    AX,0000000000000010B ;Is there one?
0341  0F 84 034C R                    JZ      NO_PROC          ; No
                        ;
0345                    INSTALLED:
0345  8D 16 0131 R                    LEA     DX,YES_PROCESR   ; Load offset to Message
0349  EB 05 90                        JMP     PRNTMSG          ; Exit this procedure
034C                    NO_PROC:
034C  8D 16 010A R                    LEA     DX,NO_PROCESSR   ; Load offset to Message
0350                    PRNTMSG:
0350  B4 09                           MOV     AH,9h            ; Get ready to print msg
0352  CD 21                           INT     21h              ; Print message

                        ;
                        ; Find default drive
                        ;       After INT 2  Function 19, AL holds the current disk, where
                        ;       0=A, 1=B, 2=C, and so on.
                        ;
0354  B4 19                           MOV     AH,19h
0356  CD 21                           INT     21h
0358  B1 1F                           MOV     CL,31            ; Each array element 31 bytes
035A  F6 E1                           MUL     CL               ; Multiply value in AL by 21
035C  8D 16 01B3 R                    LEA     DX,DEFAULT
0360  03 D0                           ADD     DX,AX            ; Point at right array element
0362  B4 09                           MOV     AH,9h            ; Get ready to print RAM #
0364  CD 21                           INT     21h
                        ;
                        ; Default disk the IPL disk?
                        ;
0366  58                              POP     AX               ; Retrieve again
0367  A9 0001                         TEST    AX,0000000000000001B ; Check the bit
036A  8D 16 0157 R                    LEA     DX,IPLYES        ; assume it is on
036E  0F 85 0376 R                    JNZ     GOODGUESS        ; It was
0372  8D 16 0178 R                    LEA     DX,IPLNO         ; oh well,
0376                    GOODGUESS:
0376  B4 09                           MOV     AH,9h            ; Get ready to print MSG
0378  CD 21                           INT     21h
                        ;
                        ; End of Program - Wrap-Up
                        ;
037A                    ENDHERE:
037A  B4 4C                           MOV     AH,4Ch           ; Standard Ending
037C  CD 21                           INT     21h
037E                    CODE          ENDS
                                      END     FIND_CFG
```

Program 9-14: GET_FREE

```
Microsoft (R) Macro Assembler Version 5.00


                                            PAGE    55,132
                                            .386
                                            EXTRN   CODEASB:PROC
                                            EXTRN   CODEBAS:PROC
 0000                               STACK   SEGMENT 'STACK' STACK
 0000   0064[                               DW      100 DUP(?)
            ????
                         ]

 00C8                               STACK   ENDS
 0000                               CODE    SEGMENT para 'CODE' PUBLIC USE16
                                            ASSUME  CS:CODE, DS:CODE, SS:STACK
                                    ;
                                    ; Name:             GET_FREE
                                    ;
                                    ; Purpose:          This program checks whichever disk number is
                                    ;                   entered and checks how many free bytes are
                                    ;                   available.
                                    ;
                                    ; Inputs:           Disk drive number, per menu.
                                    ;
                                    ; Process:
                                    ;
                                    ; Outputs:          A message with the number of free bytes.
                                    ;
 0000                               GET_FREE:
 0000   8C C8                                   MOV     AX,CS           ; Prepare to set DS
 0002   8E D8                                   MOV     DS,AX           ;   and set it.
 0004   8E C0                                   MOV     ES,AX
 0006   E9 00B3 R                               JMP     BEGINHERE
                                    ;
 0009   0A 0D 44 72 69 76 65        DRIVE_ERR   DB      0Ah,0Dh,'Drive is invalid.$'
        20 69 73 20 69 6E 76
        61 6C 69 64 2E 24
 001D   0A 0D 59 6F 75 72 20        DRIVE_MENU  DB      0Ah,0Dh,'Your choices are:'
        63 68 6F 69 63 65 73
        20 61 72 65 3A
 0030   0A 0D 20 20 30 20 3D                    DB      0Ah,0Dh,'  0 = Default'
        20 44 65 66 61 75 6C
        74
 003F   0A 0D 20 20 31 20 3D                    DB      0Ah,0Dh,'  1 = A'
        20 41
 0048   0A 0D 20 20 32 20 3D                    DB      0Ah,0Dh,'  2 = B'
        20 42
 0051   0A 0D 20 20 33 20 3D                    DB      0Ah,0Dh,'  3 = C'
        20 43
 005A   0A 0D 20 20 34 20 3D                    DB      0Ah,0Dh,'  4 = D'
        20 44
 0063   0A 0D 45 6E 74 65 72                    DB      0Ah,0Dh,'Enter Drive (0, - 4) > $'
        20 44 72 69 76 65 20
        28 30 2C 20 2D 20 34
        29 20 3E 20 24
 007D   0004[                       DRIVE_NO    DB      4 DUP(?)
            ??
                         ]
```

```
0081  0A 0D 54 68 65 20 64  FREE_SPACE   DB    0Ah,0Dh,'The drive has $'
      72 69 76 65 20 68 61
      73 20 24
0092  20 62 79 74 65 73 20  BYTE_FREE    DB    ' bytes free.$'
      66 72 65 65 2E 24
009F  0014[                 NO_BYTES     DB    20 DUP(?)
           ??
                       ]

                            ;
00B3                        BEGINHERE:
00B3  C6 06 007D R 04                    MOV   DRIVE_NO,4       ; Max one character entered
00B8  8D 16 001D R                       LEA   DX,DRIVE_MENU    ; First print choices header
00BC  B4 09                              MOV   AH,9
00BE  CD 21                              INT   21h
                            ;
00C0  8D 16 007D R                       LEA   DX,DRIVE_NO      ; Now get choice number
00C4  B4 0A                              MOV   AH,0Ah
00C6  CD 21                              INT   21h
                            ;
                            ; CODEASB:
                            ;       SI = String to be converted
                            ;       CX = Count of digits to be converted
                            ;       If Carry Flag = 0, successful
                            ;               AX contains the result
                            ;       If Carry Flag = 1, unsuccessful
                            ;               AX is 0
                            ;
00C8  8D 36 007D R                       LEA   SI,DRIVE_NO      ; Load input buffer into SI
00CC  83 C6 02                           ADD   SI,2             ; Skip the first two bytes
00CF  2B C9                              SUB   CX,CX
00D1  8A 0E 007E R                       MOV   CL,DRIVE_NO[1]   ; Count actually entered
00D5  E8 0000 E                          CALL  CODEASB
00D8  0F 82 00F0 R                       JC    ERROR0           ; Is Carry Flag set?
00DC  3D 0005                            CMP   AX,5             ; Too high a number?
00DF  0F 8D 00F0 R                       JGE   ERROR0
                            ;
00E3                        GETSPACE:
00E3  8A D0                              MOV   DL,AL            ; Drive Number (0,1,2,3,4)
00E5  B4 36                              MOV   AH,36h           ; Free disk space
00E7  CD 21                              INT   21h
                            ;
                            ; AX = FFFF if drive number is invalid
                            ;    = Number of sectors per cluster
                            ; BX = Number of available clusters
                            ; CX = Bytes per sector
                            ;
00E9  3D 0FFF                            CMP   AX,0FFFh         ; Was drive invalid?
00EC  0F 85 00FB R                       JNE   FREE0            ; No, go calculate
00F0                        ERROR0:
00F0  8D 16 0009 R                       LEA   DX,DRIVE_ERR     ; Entry error
00F4  B4 09                              MOV   AH,9
00F6  CD 21                              INT   21h
00F8  EB 41 90                           JMP   ENDHERE
                            ;
00FB                        FREE0:
00FB  66| 25 0000FFFF                    AND   EAX,0000FFFFh    ; Ensure top half is clear
0101  66| 81 E3 0000FFFF                 AND   EBX,0000FFFFh
0108  66| 81 E1 0000FFFF                 AND   ECX,0000FFFFh
010F  66| F7 E1                          MUL   ECX              ; Mul bytes x sectors=bytes/cluster
0112  66| F7 E3                          MUL   EBX              ; Mul by avail clusters
                            ;
```

```
                                ; CODEBAS
                                ;       AX = Number to be converted
                                ;       DI = Pointer to char string returned
                                ;
0115  8D 3E 009F R                          LEA     DI,NO_BYTES     ; Space for returned char str
0119  E8 0000 E                             CALL    CODEBAS
011C  8D 16 0081 R                          LEA     DX,FREE_SPACE   ; Print Header
0120  B4 09                                 MOV     AH,9
0122  CD 21                                 INT     21H
0124                            FREE1:
0124  8A 15                                 MOV     DL,BYTE PTR [DI]
0126  0A D2                                 OR      DL,DL
0128  0F 84 0133 R                          JE      LASTMSG
012C  B4 02                                 MOV     AH,2
012E  CD 21                                 INT     21h
0130  47                                    INC     DI
0131  EB F1                                 JMP     FREE1
                                ;
0133                            LASTMSG:
0133  8D 16 0092 R                          LEA     DX,BYTE_FREE    ; Print last word.
0137  B4 09                                 MOV     AH,9
0139  CD 21                                 INT     21h
013B                            ENDHERE:
013B  B4 4C                                 MOV     AH,4Ch          ; Standard Ending
013D  CD 21                                 INT     21h
013F                            CODE        ENDS
                                            END     GET_FREE
```

Program 9-15: FIND_COP

```
                                        PAGE     55,132
                                        .386
0000                            STACK   SEGMENT 'STACK' STACK
0000  0064[                             DW       100 DUP(?)
          ????
                       ]

00C8                            STACK   ENDS
0000                            CODE    SEGMENT para 'CODE' PUBLIC USE16
                                        ASSUME   CS:CODE, DS:CODE, SS:STACK
                                ;
                                ; Purpose:      This macro finds out whether or not the
                                ;               numeric coprocessor is installed.
                                ;
                                ;
                                ; Inputs:       Move 14h into Register AL
                                ;
                                ; Process:      Function 14h determines if the numeric
                                ;               coprocessor is installed.  Move 14h into
                                ;               AL and test if AL=10B.
                                ;
                                ;
                                ; Outputs:      A message whether or not a coprocessor is
                                ;               installed
                                ;
0000                            FIND_COP:
0000  8C C8                             MOV     AX,CS           ; Prepare to set DS
0002  8E D8                             MOV     DS,AX           ;   and set it.
0004  EB 48 90                          JMP     BEGINHERE
0007  54 68 65 72 65 20 69      NO_PROCESSR     DB      'There is no coprocessor installed',0Ah,0Dh,'$'
      73 20 6E 6F 20 63 6F
      70 72 6F 63 65 73 73
```

```
      6F 72 20 69 6E 73 74
      61 6C 6C 65 64 0A 0D
      24
002B  54 68 65 72 65 20 69    YES_PROCESR    DB      'There is a coprocessor installed',0Ah,0Dh,'$'
      73 20 61 20 63 6F 70
      72 6F 63 65 73 73 6F
      72 20 69 6E 73 74 61
      6C 6C 65 64 0A 0D 24
004E                          BEGINHERE:
004E  B0 14                                  MOV     AL,14h           ; Move function 14h into AL
0050  E6 70                                  OUT     70h,AL           ; Send the register request
0052  E4 71                                  IN      AL,71h           ; Read the register
0054  A8 02                                  TEST    AL,10b           ; Is bit 1 set?
0056  0F 84 0061 R                           JZ      NO_PROC          ; Send message if not installed
005A                          INSTALLED:
005A  8D 16 002B R                           LEA     DX,YES_PROCESR   ; Load offset to Message
005E  EB 06 90                               JMP     PRNTMSG          ; Exit this procedure
0061                          NO_PROC:
0061  50                                     PUSH    AX
0062  8D 16 0007 R                           LEA     DX,NO_PROCESSR   ; Load offset to Message
0066                          PRNTMSG:
0066  B4 09                                  MOV     AH,9h            ; Get ready to print msg
0068  CD 21                                  INT     21h              ; Print message
006A  58                                     POP     AX
006B                          EXITHERE:
006B  B4 4C                                  MOV     AH,4Ch           ; Standard Ending
006D  CD 21                                  INT     21h
006F                          CODE           ENDS
                                             END     FIND_COP
```

Program 9-16: FIND_VER

```
Microsoft (R) Macro Assembler Version 5.00


                                       PAGE     55,132
                                       .386
0000                           STACK   SEGMENT 'STACK' STACK
0000  0064[                            DW       100 DUP(?)
          ????
                      ]

00C8                           STACK   ENDS
0000                           CODE    SEGMENT para 'CODE' PUBLIC USE16
                                       ASSUME  CS:CODE, DS:CODE, SS:STACK
                               ;
                               ; Purpose:     This program finds which version of DOS
                               ;              is installed on a computer.
                               ;
                               ; Inputs:      Move 30h into AH
                               ;
                               ; Process:     Function 30h of INT 21 returns the DOS number.
                               ;              The major version number (for example, the "3"
                               ;              of 3.10) returns in AL.  The minor version number
                               ;              (the ".10" of 3.10) returns in AH.  Interrupt 21
                               ;              destroys registers BX and CS.
                               ;
                               ; Outputs:     Major version in AL, minor in AH.
                               ;
0000                           FIND_VER:
0000  8C C8                            MOV     AX,CS           ; Prepare to set DS
0002  8E D8                            MOV     DS,AX           ;   and set it.
0004  EB 18 90                         JMP     BEGINHERE
0007  59 6F 75 72 20 44 4F     Version_no      DB      'Your DOS version is $'
      53 20 76 65 72 73 69
      6F 6E 20 69 73 20 24

001C  2E 24                    Period          DB      '.$'
001E                           BEGINHERE:
001E  8D 16 0007 R                     LEA     DX,Version_no   ; Load offset to message
0022  B4 09                            MOV     AH,9h           ; Get ready to print the string
0024  CD 21                            INT     21h             ; Print it
0026  B4 30                            MOV     AH,30h          ; Move function 30 into AH
0028  CD 21                            INT     21h             ; This gets the DOS version
002A  50                               PUSH    AX              ; Save Version Number
002B  8A D0                            MOV     DL,AL           ; Move Major Version Number
002D  80 C2 30                         ADD     DL,30h          ; Make high order 0011/0100
0030  B4 02                            MOV     AH,2h           ; Get ready to print version
0032  CD 21                            INT     21h             ; Print major version
0034  8D 16 001C R                     LEA     DX,Period       ; Now print the "."
0038  B4 09                            MOV     AH,9h
003A  CD 21                            INT     21h
003C  58                               POP     AX              ; Retrieve the Major/Minor
003D  C1 E8 08                         SHR     AX,8            ; Move minor version
0040  50                               PUSH    AX              ;   and save it
0041  8B D0                            MOV     DX,AX           ; Save only minor version now
0043  80 C2 10                         ADD     DL,16
0046  C0 EA 04                         SHR     DL,4            ; Want high-order of two digits
0049  80 C2 30                         ADD     DL,30h          ; Make it printable
004C  B4 02                            MOV     AH,2h
004E  CD 21                            INT     21h
0050  58                               POP     AX              ; Now get low order number
```

```
0051  8B D0                          MOV     DX,AX
0053  C0 E2 07                       SHL     DL,7
0056  C0 EA 07                       SHR     DL,7
0059  80 C2 30                       ADD     DL,30h          ; Make it printable
005C  B4 02                          MOV     AH,2h
005E  CD 21                          INT     21h
0060                      ENDHERE:
0060  B4 4C                          MOV     AH,4Ch          ; Standard Ending
0062  CD 21                          INT     21h
0064                      CODE       ENDS
                                     END     FIND_VER
```

Program 9-17: PAUSE

```
                                  PAGE      55,132
                                  .386
0000                      code    SEGMENT   para 'CODE' USE16 PUBLIC
                                  ASSUME    CS:code, DS:code, SS:code
                          ;
                          ; Name;     PAUSE
                          ;
                          ; Purpose: The following procedure provides a means of pausing
                          ;          for a time span of from .02 seconds to 59.99 seconds.
                          ;          The clock does not increment smoothly so the granularity
                          ;          is not to the hundredth.
                          ;
                          ;
                          ; Inputs:  DH should contain the number of seconds to delay.
                          ;          DL should contain the number of hundredths to delay.
                          ;
                          ; Process: The seconds and hundredths are edited for conformance
                          ;          with their value range. (DH 0-59, DL 0-99 and DX >1)
                          ;          If invalid, carry is set and the procedure returns.
                          ;          The target time is computed as current time + ss.hh.
                          ;          We then loop, getting and checking the current time
                          ;          until we get a time greater than our target.
                          ;
                          ; Output:  The output is simply the delay in time.  Carry is set
                          ;          if the input values were bad and reset otherwise.
                          ;
                          ; Note:    The complete time is compared because the clock does
                          ;          not update 'smoothly' (which would allow us to check
                          ;          only the seconds and hundredths).
                          ;
                          ;
                                   PUBLIC  Pause              ; Make the name usable
0000                      Pause    PROC
0000  52                           push    DX                 ; Save entry registers
0001  51                           push    CX
0002  53                           push    BX
0003  50                           push    AX
0004  56                           push    SI
0005  83 FA 02                     cmp     DX,2               ; Check for minimum wait
0008  0F 82 0098 R                 jb      badwait            ; If < 2 it is bad
000C  80 FA 64                     cmp     DL,100             ; Is hundredths 0-99
000F  0F 83 0098 R                 jnb     badwait            ; If not - bad
0013  80 FE 3C                     cmp     DH,60              ; Is seconds 0-59
0016  0F 83 0098 R                 jnb     badwait            ; If not - bad
001A  8B DA                        mov     BX,DX              ; Save for computation
                          ;
```

```
                                ; Pause procedure, first compute the time to stop the loop.
                                ;
001C  B4 2C                             mov     AH,2ch          ; Get the Time of Day
001E  CD 21                             int     21h
0020  02 DA                             add     BL,DL           ; Add the current time (.01s)
0022  80 FB 64                          cmp     BL,100          ; Flow over the max hundredths?
0025  0F 82 002E R                      jb      notover         ; No overflow
0029  80 EB 64                          sub     BL,100          ; Get back to less than a sec
002C  FE C7                             inc     BH              ; Step the seconds figure
002E                            notover:
002E  02 FE                             add     BH,DH           ; add current seconds
0030  80 FF 3C                          cmp     BH,60           ; Flow over a minute?
0033  0F 82 0051 R                      jb      notovers        ; No
0037  80 EF 3C                          sub     BH,60           ; If so, bring down to range.
003A  FE C1                             inc     CL              ; add to minutes
003C  80 F9 3C                          cmp     CL,60           ; Overflow into hours?
003F  0F 82 0051 R                      jb      notovers        ; No - don't change
0043  80 E9 3C                          sub     CL,60           ; Back to minutes
0046  FE C5                             inc     CH              ; Roll to the hour
0048  80 FD 18                          cmp     CH,24
004B  0F 82 0051 R                      jb      notovers        ; Not across midnight
004F  2A ED                             sub     CH,CH           ; We are at hour zero
0051                            notovers:
0051  8B F3                             mov     SI,BX           ; Save low order times
0053  8B D9                             mov     BX,CX           ; Get target time hh:mm
0055                            gethour:
0055  CD 21                             int     21h             ; get next time
0057  3A FD                             cmp     BH,CH           ; check the hour
0059  0F 84 007B R                      je      getmin          ; we are there.
005D  0F 82 006D R                      jb      chkmid          ; If hour is high loop
                                ;
                                ; New hour is < target - if 0:23 we rolled over midnight
                                ;
0061  80 FF 17                          cmp     BH,23           ; Is target 2300
0064  75 EF                             jne     gethour         ; If not - not there yet
0066  0A ED                             or      CH,CH           ; Is new 0000 (2200)
0068  75 EB                             jne     gethour         ; No - let hour roll over
006A  EB 25 90                          jmp     passed          ; Yes - we went across
                                ;
                                ; Target hour is < new hour - if 0:23 wait for midnight
                                ;
006D                            chkmid:
006D  0A FF                             or      BH,BH           ; Across midnight
006F  0F 85 0091 R                      jnz     passed          ; if not - time is expired.
0073  80 FD 17                          cmp     CH,23           ; Waiting for midnight?
0076  74 DD                             je      gethour         ; Yes - delay some more.
0078  EB 17 90                          jmp     passed          ; No ( 0:1) time expired
                                ;
                                ; The hour is equal
                                ;
007B                            getmin:
007B  3A D9                             cmp     BL,CL           ; Check for minute
007D  0F 82 0091 R                      jb      passed          ; If target is low - done
0081  77 D2                             ja      gethour         ; If not there - loop
0083  8B CE                             mov     CX,SI           ; Get low order times
0085  3A EE                             cmp     CH,DH           ; At a second yet?
0087  77 CC                             ja      gethour         ; No - get another time
0089  0F 82 0091 R                      jb      passed          ; beyond - we get out.
008D  3A CA                             cmp     CL,DL           ; Check hundredths
008F  77 C4                             ja      gethour         ; If low, branch
0091                            passed:
0091  F8                                clc                     ; reset carry
```

```
0092                  exit:
0092  5E                      pop    SI
0093  58                      pop    AX              ; Restore the entry registers
0094  5B                      pop    BX
0095  59                      pop    CX
0096  5A                      pop    DX
0097  C3                      ret                    ; and return
0098                  badwait:
0098  F9                      stc                    ; set carry
0099  EB F7                   jmp    exit            ; and return
009B                  Pause   ENDP
009B                  code    ENDS
                              END
```

Program 9-18: CHKPAUSE

```
                                   .386
                           ; Name:     CHKPAUSE
                           ;
                           ; Purpose: This program provides a simple visual check of the pause
                           ;           routine.
                           ;
                           ; Inputs:   Nothing.
                           ;
                           ; Process: Display tick, call pause for .5 sec delay then flip to
                           ;           tock.  Repeat 200 times.
                           ;
                           ; Outputs: A tick TOCK display for 100 seconds.
                           ;
                           ; Declare the routines we are going to use
                                   EXTRN   Pause:PROC
                           ;
0000                       stack   SEGMENT para 'STACK' STACK
0000  0100[                        dq      256 DUP(?)
        ???????????????
        ?
                    ]

0800                       stack   ENDS
0000                       data    SEGMENT para
0000  0D 74 69 63 6B 24    tick    db      13,"tick$"
0006  0D 54 4F 43 4B 24    tock    db      13,"TOCK$"
000C                       data    ENDS
0000                       code    SEGMENT para 'CODE' USE16 PUBLIC
                                   ASSUME  CS:code, DS:data
                           ;
                           ; Set up the environment
                           ;
0000                       Begin:
0000  B8 ---- R                    mov     AX,data         ; Get data segment pointer
0003  8E D8                        mov     DS,AX           ; into DS,
0005  8E C0                        mov     ES,AX           ; and ES.
0007  2B F6                        sub     SI,SI           ; Clear indices
0009  2B FF                        sub     DI,DI
000B  8D 3E 0000 R                 lea     DI,tick
000F  8D 36 0006 R                 lea     SI,tock
0013  B9 00C8                      mov     CX,200
0016                       looph:
0016  87 F7                        xchg    SI,DI           ; Flip them
0018  8B D6                        mov     DX,SI
001A  B4 09                        mov     AH,9
001C  CD 21                        int     21h             ; display tick or TOCK
001E  BA 0032                      mov     DX,50           ; Set half second
0021  E8 0000 E                    call    Pause           ; Wait .5 seconds
0024  E2 F0                        loop    looph           ; Do it again
0026  B0 00                        mov     AL,0            ; Set return code
0028  B4 4C                        mov     AH,04ch         ; Set good-by
002A  CD 21                        int     21h             ; Return to the system
002C                       code    ENDS
                                   END     begin
```

Program 9-19: PCNAME

```
Microsoft (R) Macro Assembler Version 5.00


                                        PAGE     55,132
                                        .386
 0000                           STACK   SEGMENT 'STACK' STACK
 0000   0064[                           DW       100 DUP(?)
            ????
                        ]

 00C8                           STACK   ENDS
 0000                           CODE    SEGMENT para 'CODE' PUBLIC USE16
                                        ASSUME   CS:CODE, DS:CODE, SS:STACK
                                ;
                                ; Name:          PCNAME
                                ;
                                ; Purpose:       For most PCs currently in the market, this will get
                                ;                the "name" of the PC.  PCs often identify themselves
                                ;                in a one-byte ID in F000:FFFE, the next to the last
                                ;                location in regular memory.
                                ;
                                ; Inputs:        Nothing
                                ;
                                ; Process:       When the program assembles, the data segment is set.
                                ;                Then the location 0F000h is moved into BX and from
                                ;                there into DS, changing the pointer of the data
                                ;                segment to F000.  Then the offset is loaded into BX
                                ;                and the contents of that address moved into AL.
                                ;
                                ; Outputs:       Message with the name of the computer.
                                ;
                                ; Note:          FF - Original PC
                                ;                FE - PC XT
                                ;                FD - PC Jr
                                ;                FC - PC AT
                                ;
 0000                           PCNAME:
 0000   8C C8                                    MOV     AX,CS           ; Prepare to set DS
 0002   8E D8                                    MOV     DS,AX           ;   and set it.
 0004   EB 54 90                                 JMP     BEGINHERE
                                ;
 0007   0A 0D 20 43 6F 6D 70    HEADER           DB      0Ah,0Dh,' Computer:  $'
        75 74 65 72 3A 20 20
        24
 0016   20 20 20 20 20 20 20    PCTYPE           DB      '            $'
        20 20 20 20 20 24
 0023   20 50 43 20 41 54 20                     DB      ' PC AT      $'
        20 20 20 20 20 24
 0030   20 50 43 20 4A 72 20                     DB      ' PC Jr      $'
        20 20 20 20 20 24
 003D   20 50 43 20 58 54 20                     DB      ' PC XT      $'
        20 20 20 20 20 24
 004A   20 4F 72 69 67 69 6E                     DB      ' Original PC$'
        61 6C 20 50 43 24
 0057   0D 0A 24                CR_LF            DB      0Dh,0Ah,'$'
                                ;
 005A                           BEGINHERE:
 005A   BB F000                                  MOV     BX,0F000h
 005D   8E DB                                    MOV     DS,BX
```

```
005F  BB FFFE                             MOV     BX,0FFFEh
0062  8A 07                               MOV     AL,[BX]
                          ;
0064  8C CA                               MOV     DX,CS          ; Restore data segment
0066  8E DA                               MOV     DS,DX
0068  8B F0                               MOV     SI,AX          ; Save AL value
006A  8D 16 0007 R                        LEA     DX,HEADER      ; Print header
006E  B4 09                               MOV     AH,9
0070  CD 21                               INT     21h
0072  8D 16 0016 R                        LEA     DX,PCTYPE      ; Print header
0076  8B C6                               MOV     AX,SI          ; Restore value into AX
0078  B4 00                               MOV     AH,0           ; Clear AH
007A  2C F0                               SUB     AL,0F0h        ; Remove top nibble
007C  2C 0B                               SUB     AL,11          ; Make answer 1,2,3 or 4
007E  2B C9                               SUB     CX,CX
0080  B1 0D                               MOV     CL,13
0082  F6 E1                               MUL     CL             ; Each string is 13 bytes
0084  02 D0                               ADD     DL,AL          ; Index into PCTYPE array
0086  B4 09                               MOV     AH,9
0088  CD 21                               INT     21h
008A  8D 16 0057 R                        LEA     DX,CR_LF       ; Space up a line
008E  B4 09                               MOV     AH,9
0090  CD 21                               INT     21h
0092                      ENDHERE:
0092  B4 4C                               MOV     AH,4Ch         ; Standard Ending
0094  CD 21                               INT     21h
0096                      CODE            ENDS
                                          END     PCNAME
```

Program 9-20: RANDNUM

```
Microsoft (R) Macro Assembler Version 5.00


                                        PAGE    55,132
                                        .386
                                        EXTRN   CODEBAS:PROC
0000                            STACK   SEGMENT 'STACK' STACK
0000  0064[                             DW      100 DUP(?)
          ????
                         ]

00C8                            STACK   ENDS
0000                            CODE    SEGMENT para 'CODE' PUBLIC USE16
                                        ASSUME  CS:CODE, DS:CODE, SS:STACK
                                ;
                                ; Name:       RANDNUM
                                ;
                                ; Purpose:    This program generates pseudo-random numbers.  The
                                ;             assumed decimal point is on the left of the answer.
                                ;
                                ; Inputs:     None
                                ;
                                ; Process:    The program gets the time of day and uses the
                                ;             hundredths of a second as a key.  It then rotates
                                ;             the answer three times (arbitrary number).  Then it
                                ;             calls CODEBAS to turn the resultant binary into a
                                ;             printable ASCII.

                                ;
                                ; Outputs:    A message with the generated number.  When it is printed,
                                ;             a decimal point is printed first, to "force" the answer to
                                ;             be between 0 and 1.
                                ;
0000                            RANDNUM:
0000  8C C8                                   MOV     AX,CS           ; Prepare to set DS
0002  8E D8                                   MOV     DS,AX           ;   and set it.
0004  8E C0                                   MOV     ES,AX
0006  EB 3E 90                                JMP     BEGINHERE
                                ;
0009  0A 0D 20 59 6F 75 72      RANDOM        DB      0Ah,0Dh,' Your random number is > $'
      20 72 61 6E 64 6F 6D
      20 6E 75 6D 62 65 72
      20 69 73 20 3E 20 24
0025  000A[                     OUTPUT_ST     DB      10 DUP (?)
          ??
                         ]

002F  0A 0D 20 45 72 72 6F      CODE_ERR      DB      0Ah,0Dh,' Error in number.$'
      72 20 69 6E 20 6E 75
      6D 62 65 72 2E 24
0043  0A 0D 24                  CR_LF         DB      0Ah,0Dh,'$'
                                ;
0046                            BEGINHERE:
0046  2B C9                                   SUB     CX,CX           ; Empty CX
0048  B4 2C                                   MOV     AH,2Ch          ; Get time
004A  CD 21                                   INT     21h
                                ;
                                ; DL now has hundredths of a second
                                ;
```

```
004C  8A CA                                    MOV     CL,DL
004E  C1 C9 03                                 ROR     CX,3
                        ;
                        ; Convert result to printable ASCII with CODEBAS
                        ;       AX = Word to be converted
                        ;       DI = Points to char string for converted returned value
                        ;       If successful, Carry Flag = 0
                        ;       If not, Carry Flag = 1
                        ;
0051  8D 3E 0025 R                             LEA     DI,OUTPUT_ST
0055  66| 2B C0                                SUB     EAX,EAX
0058  8A C1                                    MOV     AL,CL           ; Move random number into DL
005A  E8 0000 E                                CALL    CODEBAS
005D  0F 83 006C R                             JNC     PRINTO
                        ;
                        ; Error in CODEBAS result
                        ;
0061  8D 16 002F R                             LEA     DX,CODE_ERR
0065  B4 09                                    MOV     AH,9
0067  CD 21                                    INT     21h
0069  EB 1E 90                                 JMP     ENDHERE
                        ;
                        ;
                        ; Print answer
                        ;
006C                    PRINTO:
006C  8D 16 0009 R                             LEA     DX,RANDOM       ; Print the header
0070  B4 09                                    MOV     AH,9
0072  CD 21                                    INT     21h
0074  BA 002E                                  MOV     DX,2Eh          ; Decimal point (period)
0077  B4 02                                    MOV     AH,2            ; Print the decimal point
0079  CD 21                                    INT     21h
007B  2B D2                                    SUB     DX,DX           ; Clear out DX
007D  8A 15                                    MOV     DL,BYTE PTR [DI] ; Move the byte into DL
007F  0A D2                                    OR      DL,DL           ; Is it hex 00 ?
0081  0F 84 0089 R                             JE      ENDHERE         ; Yes, go end
0085  B4 02                                    MOV     AH,2            ; Print a single character
0087  CD 21                                    INT     21h
                        ;
0089                    ENDHERE:
0089  8D 16 0043 R                             LEA     DX,CR_LF        ; Space down one space
008D  B4 09                                    MOV     AH,9
008F  CD 21                                    INT     21h
                        ;
0091  B4 4C                                    MOV     AH,4Ch          ; Standard Ending
0093  CD 21                                    INT     21h
0095                    CODE                   ENDS
                                               END     RANDNUM
```

Program 9-21: SQRT

```
Microsoft (R) Macro Assembler Version 5.00


                                        PAGE    55,132
                                        .386

                               ; Name:          SQRT
                               ;
                               ; Purpose:        This procedure finds the square root of integers of
                               ;                 up to five digits.
                               ;
                               ; Inputs:         The original number is requested to be input from
                               ;                 the keyboard.
                               ;
                               ; Process:        The procedure calculates the square root by
                               ;                 following Newton's Method, which says that if A
                               ;                 is an approximation for the square root of a
                               ;                 number N, then A1=(N/a + A)2 is a better
                               ;                 approximation.  To get to the first approximation,
                               ;                 the routine uses (N/200)+2 (where N is the contents
                               ;                 of DX:AX and the value 200 is arbitrary.  To get the
                               ;                 next approximation, it divides N by the first and
                               ;                 averages the two.  For the third, it divides N by
                               ;                 the second approximation and averages again.  It
                               ;                 repeats until it finds two approximations that are
                               ;                 identical (or differ only by 1, whether positive or
                               ;                 negative).
                               ;
                               ; Outputs:        Register BX holds the square root.
                               ;
                                        EXTRN   CODEASB:PROC
                                        EXTRN   CODEBAS:PROC
                                        EXTRN   STRZLNG:PROC
0000                           STACK    SEGMENT 'STACK' STACK
0000  0064[                             DW      100 DUP(?)
          ????
                         ]

00C8                           STACK    ENDS
0000                           DATA     SEGMENT para
                               ;
0000  0014[                    INPUT_STR        DB      20 DUP (?)
          ??
                         ]

0014  0014[                    OUTPUT_ST        DB      20 DUP (?)
          ??
                         ]

0028  0A 0D 20 49 6E 70 75     PROMPT           DB      0Ah,0Dh,' Input an integer (0 to end) > $'
      74 20 61 6E 20 69 6E
      74 65 67 65 72 20 28
      30 20 74 6F 20 65 6E
      64 29 20 3E 20 24
004A  0A 0D 20 54 68 65 20     HEADER           DB      0Ah,0Dh,' The answer (to one decimal) > $'
      61 6E 73 77 65 72 20
      28 74 6F 20 6F 6E 65
      20 64 65 63 69 6D 61
```

```
     6C 29 20 3E 20 24
006C 0A 0D 20 49 6E 63 6F       BADNUM          DB      0Ah,0Dh,' Incorrect number.  Re-enter.$'
     72 72 65 63 74 20 6E
     75 6D 62 65 72 2E 20
     20 52 65 2D 65 6E 74
     65 72 2E 24
008C 0A 0D 20 53 51 52 54       BADRTN          DB      0Ah,0Dh,' SQRT number incorrect.$'
     20 6E 75 6D 62 65 72
     20 69 6E 63 6F 72 72
     65 63 74 2E 24
00A6 20 24                      BLANK           DB      ' $'
00A8 0A 0D 24                   CR_LF           DB      0Ah,0Dh,'$'
00AB                            DATA    ENDS
0000                            CODE    SEGMENT para 'CODE' PUBLIC
                                        ASSUME  CS:CODE, DS:DATA, SS:STACK
0000                            DO_SQRT:
0000 66| B8 ---- R                              MOV     AX,DATA         ; Prepare to set DS
0004 66| 8E D8                                  MOV     DS,AX           ;   and set it.
0007 66| 8E C0                                  MOV     ES,AX
                                ;
                                ; Get the input number
                                ;
000A                            BEGINHERE:
000A 8D 15 00000028 R                           LEA     DX,PROMPT       ; Print the prompt
0010 B4 09                                      MOV     AH,9h
0012 CD 21                                      INT     21h
0014 C6 05 00000000 R 08                        MOV     INPUT_STR,8     ; Max 8 characters
001B 8D 15 00000000 R                           LEA     DX,INPUT_STR    ; Point at buffer
0021 B4 0A                                      MOV     AH,0Ah          ; Buffered keyboard input
0023 CD 21                                      INT     21h
                                ;
                                ; Allow only ten digits input
                                ;
0025 8A 0D 00000001 R                           MOV     CL,BYTE PTR INPUT_STR[1]
002B 80 F9 0A                                   CMP     CL,10
002E 0F 8F 0000004E R                           JG      ERR0
                                ;
                                ; Now convert the ASCII input to a binary number by calling
                                ;       CODEASB.  For CODEASB,
                                ;       SI points to the string to be converted
                                ;       CX is the count of characters
                                ;       If successful, Carry Flag = 0, AX holds returned number
                                ;       If not, Carry Flag = 1
                                ;
0034                            CONVERT:
0034 66| 2B C9                                  SUB     CX,CX           ; Be sure CX is empty
0037 8D 35 00000002 R                           LEA     SI,INPUT_STR+2  ; This holds the input number
003D 8A 0D 00000001 R                           MOV     CL,INPUT_STR[1] ; Count of bytes
0043 E8 00000000 E                              CALL    CODEASB         ; Convert to binary
0048 0F 83 0000006F R                           JNC     BEGIN
                                ;
                                ; Error - bad number
                                ;
004E                            ERR0:
004E 8D 15 0000006C R                           LEA     DX,BADNUM       ; Print error
0054 EB 09 90 90 90                             JMP     ERR2
0059                            ERR1:
0059 8D 15 0000008C R                           LEA     DX,BADRTN
005F                            ERR2:
005F B4 09                                      MOV     AH,9
0061 CD 21                                      INT     21h
0063 8D 15 000000A8 R                           LEA     DX,CR_LF        ; Go get next number
0069 B4 09                                      MOV     AH,9h
```

```
006B  CD 21                              INT     21h
006D  EB 9B                              JMP     BEGINHERE
                         ;
006F                     BEGIN:
006F  0B C0                              OR      EAX,EAX        ; Any number?
0071  0F 84 000000FE R                   JZ      ENDHERE        ; Yes, go end the program
                         ;
0077  B9 00000064                        MOV     ECX,100        ; Multiply by 100 for greater
007C  F7 E1                              MUL     ECX            ;   precision
                         ;
007E                     NEXTNUM:
007E  52                                 PUSH    EDX            ; Save the number
007F  50                                 PUSH    EAX
0080  66| 8B EC                          MOV     BP,SP          ; Point to it in stack
0083  BB 000000C8                        MOV     EBX,200        ; First approximation
0088  F7 F3                              DIV     EBX            ; Divide source by 200
008A  83 C0 02                           ADD     EAX,2
008D                     AGAIN:
008D  8B D8                              MOV     EBX,EAX        ; Save this guess/approximation
008F  67| 8B 56 04                       MOV     EDX,[BP+4]     ; Get source number again
0093  67| 8B 46 00                       MOV     EAX,[BP]
0097  F7 F3                              DIV     EBX            ; Divide by last approx.
0099  66| 2B D2                          SUB     DX,DX          ; First could need DX because
                                                                ; of scaling by 100.
009C  03 C3                              ADD     EAX,EBX        ; Average last two approx
009E  D1 E8                              SHR     EAX,1

                         ;
00A0  2B D8                              SUB     EBX,EAX        ; Check for difference of 1
00A2  0F 84 000000B3 R                   JE      FINISHED       ; Zero, go exit
00A8  0F 89 000000B0 R                   JNS     FINISHEDQ
00AE  F7 DB                              NEG     EBX            ; Get absolute value
00B0                     FINISHEDQ:
00B0  4B                                 DEC     EBX            ; Was diff 1?
00B1  75 DA                              JNZ     AGAIN
                         ;
                         ;       When finished, convert the binary back to ASCII by calling
                         ;       CODEBAS.  CODEBAS requires:
                         ;       EAX = the word to be converted (it holds square root now)
                         ;       DI points to the character string to store the answer
                         ;       If successful, Carry Flag = 0
                         ;       If not, Carry Flag = 1
                         ;
00B3                     FINISHED:
00B3  5B                                 POP     EBX            ; Clear the stack.
00B4  5B                                 POP     EBX
00B5  8D 3D 00000014 R                   LEA     DI,OUTPUT_ST
00BB  E8 00000000 E                      CALL    CODEBAS
00C0  72 8C                              JC      ERRO
                         ;
                         ; Print the result
                         ;       To decide where to put decimal on output, find the length
                         ;       of the answer, call STRZLNG
                         ;       STRZLNG: ES:DI - Address of ASCIIZ string
                         ;               Note: in this case DI already holds the correct start
                         ;                       of the string, so do not reset it.
                         ;               CX - Maximum length to examine
                         ;               If successful, Carry Flag=0, AX = count of bytes in
                         ;                       the string excluding the terminating null
                         ;               If not, Carry Flag = 1, AX returned equal to CX
                         ;
00C2  66| B9 000A                        MOV     CX,10          ; Max length of string
```

```
00C6  E8 00000000 E                 CALL   STRZLNG          ; Find length of the string
00CB  0F 83 000000D3 R              JNC    PRNT0
00D1  EB 86                         JMP    ERR1
00D3                   PRNT0:
00D3  66| 8B F0                     MOV    SI,AX            ; Save the length
00D6  8D 15 0000004A R              LEA    DX,HEADER
00DC  B4 09                         MOV    AH,9h
00DE  CD 21                         INT    21h
00E0  66| 2B D2                     SUB    DX,DX
00E3  66| 8B CE                     MOV    CX,SI            ; Put length in loop register
00E6  66| 49                        DEC    CX               ; Back up 1 count, then loop
00E8  B4 02                         MOV    AH,2             ; Print a character
00EA                   PRNT1:
00EA  67| 8A 15                     MOV    DL,BYTE PTR [DI] ; Print each digit
00ED  CD 21                         INT    21h
00EF  66| 47                        INC    DI
00F1  E2 F7                         LOOP   PRNT1
                       ;
00F3  B2 2E                         MOV    DL,2Eh           ; Decimal point
00F5  B4 02                         MOV    AH,2
00F7  CD 21                         INT    21h
00F9  67| 8A 15                     MOV    DL,BYTE PTR [DI] ; Now print last digit
00FC  CD 21                         INT    21h
                       ;
00FE                   ENDHERE:
00FE  8D 15 000000A8 R              LEA    DX,CR_LF         ; Space up one line
0104  B4 09                         MOV    AH,9
0106  CD 21                         INT    21h
                       ;
0108  B4 4C                         MOV    AH,4Ch           ; Standard Ending
010A  CD 21                         INT    21h
010C                   CODE         ENDS
                                    END    DO_SQRT
```

10

Graphics

Graphics have been going through major changes. A graphics color standard is emerging around the IBM-compatible Enhanced Graphics Adapter (EGA), which provides for 16 simultaneous colors from a 64-color palette. IBM's recent graphics innovation is the Video Graphics Array (VGA). It works in the IBM Personal System/2 models 50, 60, and 80 to improve text display and expand color options up to 256 colors. The VGA supports 640 × 480 for 16 colors in graphics mode and 720 × 400 for 15 colors in text mode.

Monochrome Mode

In monochrome mode, the Hercules monochrome adapter card is becoming a widely accepted standard. A *monochrome adapter card* is a printed circuit board installed inside the main computer cabinet and it works in conjunction with the monochrome display unit. Most monochrome adapters produce a textual display of 80 characters horizontally and 25 lines vertically, for a total of 2000 characters. The screen requires 4000 bytes (since two bytes are required for each character), so most monochrome adapter cards contain 4K (4096) bytes of memory. Figure 10-1 gives an overview of the specifics of monochrome adapters. The graphics tools in this chapter are designed for a monochrome monitor, using a Hercules (or compatible) graphics card.

Of the two bytes reserved for each character, each 16-bit location in screen memory uses the first byte (the even address) for the character to be displayed.

Mode	Text/ Graphics	Horizontal Resolution	Vertical Resolution	Char Per Row	Number of Rows
Low-resolution Text	Text	40	25	40	25
High-resolution Text	Text	80	25	80	25
Medium-resolution Text	Graphics	320	200	40	25
High-resolution	Graphics	640	200	80	25

Fig. 10-1. CGA graphics adapter overview.

The second byte (the odd address) describes the attribute of the character. There are four attributes, i.e., ways a character can be displayed: normal, bright, reverse-video (a dark character on a lighted background), and bright on a reverse-video field. You can make characters blink or not and you can underline them, blinking or not.

The lowest three bits of the attribute byte turn on the foreground. The next bit controls brightness. The next three control the background. The high-order bit controls blinking. Figure 10-2 shows the breakdown of the bits and a binary breakdown of how they work.

The Character Matrix

Each of the characters on the video display is formed within a matrix, often 9 dots wide by 14 dots tall, although most characters do not use the entire 9 × 14 matrix. For example, a capital letter may occupy a 7 × 9 matrix that sits inside the total matrix; this keeps space between the characters when they are printed, so they don't run into each other. The smaller 7 × 9 matrix does not include the leftmost and rightmost columns of the larger matrix. It also does not include the upper two rows and the bottom three rows of the larger matrix. This means there will be at least two dot positions horizontally and five dot positions vertically between capital letters.

Most of the lowercase characters fit with the 7 × 9 matrix also. Characters with descenders (like "g" and "q") drop two rows below, reaching the next-to-bottom row of the full matrix.

There are some symbols, like the caret (^), that reach the top row. There also are some special symbols for drawing single and double lines and corners, as shown in Fig. 10-3, and detailed in Appendix E. Some of the special characters reach the bottom row, the top, the leftmost column, or the rightmost. There are also block characters that fill the entire matrix.

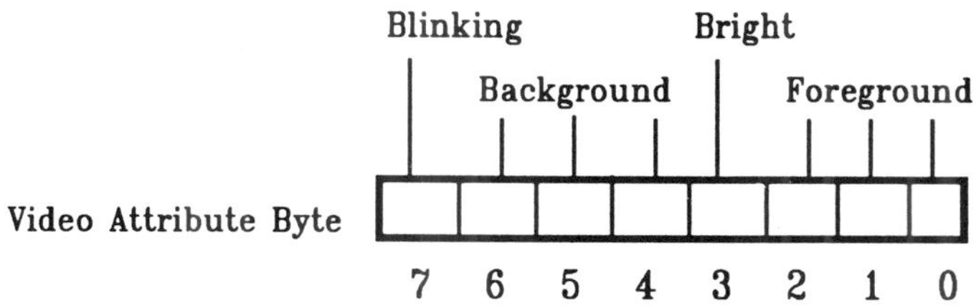

Type	Bit Pattern								Hex
Normal Character	0	0	0	0	0	1	1	1	7
Bright, Normal Char	0	0	0	0	1	1	1	1	F
Reverse Video Char	0	1	1	1	0	0	0	0	70
Bright Character, Reverse Video Background	0	1	1	1	1	0	0	0	78
No Character	0	0	0	0	0	0	0	0	0

Foreground	Background	Normal	Underline	Blinking	Blinking Underline
Normal	Dark	7	1	87	81
Bright	Dark	F	9	8F	89
Dark	Normal	70		F0	
Bright	Normal	78		F8	
Dark	Dark	0			

Fig. 10-2. Video attribute bytes.

The symbols in Fig. 10-3 are ASCII-format codes in the range from 179 to 218 and were designed for the extended character set, used on IBM's and compatibles. They do not appear in numeric order; they are grouped "logically" for easy use and lookup. You can produce these symbols directly on your screen: press the Alt key and type the corresponding three-digit ASCII code.

The special characters were designed to fit together to make larger figures, such as frames, underlines, and boxes. For each symbol, the patterns are set up within their matrix and all protruding lines extend all the way to the edges (using all the columns). This allows continuity of lines from one character to the next.

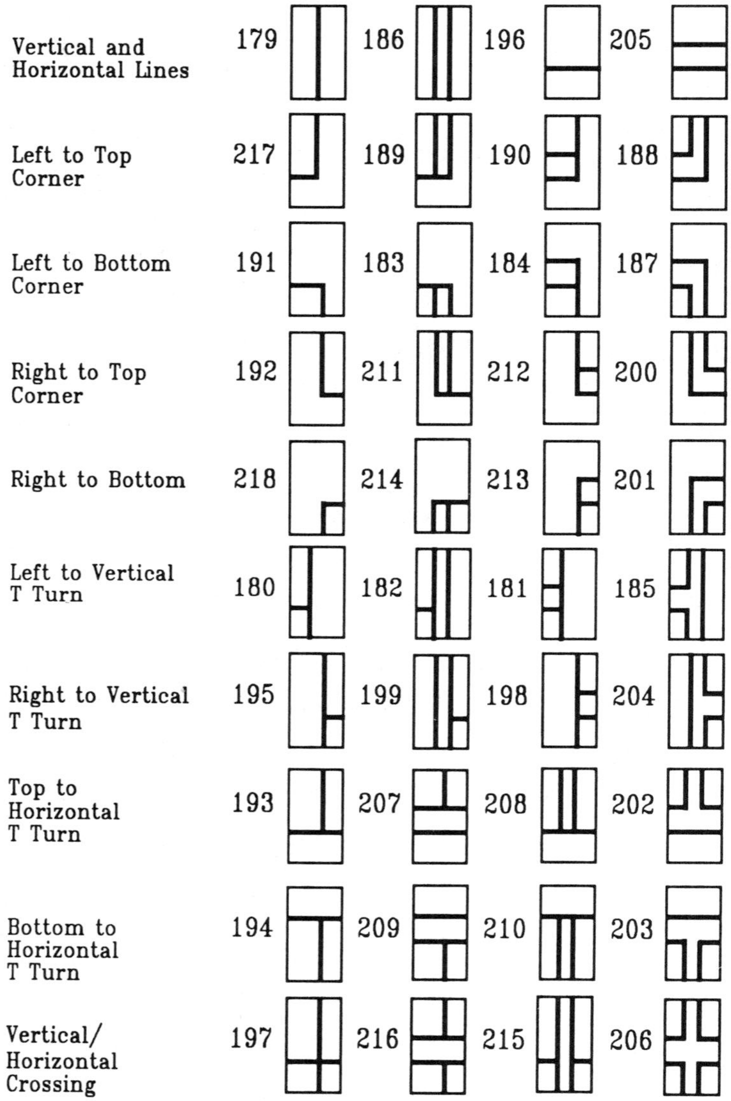

Fig. 10-3. Extended ASCII line and corner symbols.

Bit Shifting

Understanding bit shifting for graphics requires some thought. Many devices, such as display devices, fetch from memory a byte at a time. To do animation, you may wish to shift data in consecutive memory locations, but the hardware

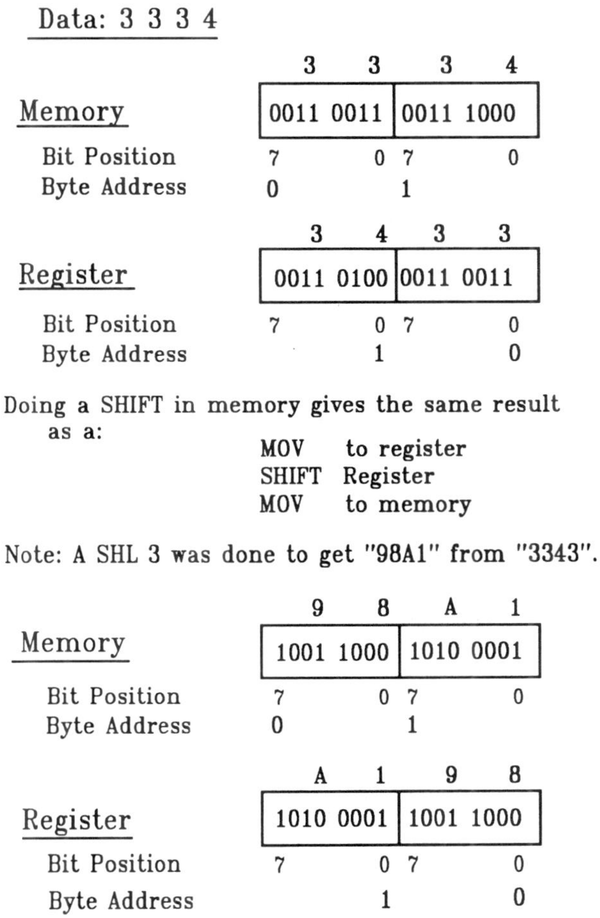

Fig. 10-4. Examples of SHIFT on memory and register.

doesn't allow you to do it as you might think. Figure 10-4 shows how bytes are stored in a register and in memory. (Note that the bytes are reversed.) If you do a shift left (SHL) of three bits, note what happens.

Pixels that appear adjacent on a screen are *not* adjacent in memory. If you want bit 7 of byte 1 to shift to bit 0 of byte 0, you are forced to use bit shifts into and out of the CF (Carry Flag). You can't do it as a word shift. In a register, bit 0 of byte 1 actually is adjacent to bit 7 of byte 0 because of how the 80386 treats words. They are stored in reverse by registers. (This can't be said too often, because it is one of the most confusing things about the 80386.)

ROM BIOS Video Services

Interrupt 10 (See Appendix G) performs a variety of operations that can be selected through a function number; Fig. 10-5 summarizes the functions. Select the function by placing the number in the AH register. When you want to "address" any row or column of the screen, remember that the top row is row 0 and that the left column is column 0. Rows run from 0 to 24; columns run from 0 to 79 for the 80-column mode, and from 0 to 39 for the 40-column mode. In the following function descriptions, remember that the function numbers are in hex.

Function 0: Set Video Mode. Most computer systems can use both monochrome and graphic screens. Since we're concentrating in this book on monochrome examples, the video mode always will be 7. If you have a graphics screen, you can switch to any of the seven graphics modes (0–6). To change from one mode to another, place the new mode in register AL and function number 0 in register AH. Then issue Interrupt 10. This clears the screen, even if the new video mode is the same as the previous.

Function 1: Change Cursor Size. The cursor shows where the next character will appear. Characters use a dot matrix (8 × 13 for monochrome and 5 × 7 for graphics). Initially, the cursor is formed from the bottom two rows of the matrix, rows 11 and 12 for the monochrome screen and rows 6 and 7 for the graphics screen.

To change the cursor, put the starting row in register CH and the ending row in register CL. Set register AH to 1 and issue Interrupt 10.

Function 2: Change Cursor Position. You can change the cursor position by putting the page number (monochrome has one page, graphics has four) in the BH register, the new row number in the DH register, and the new column number in the DL register. Then place function number 2 in the AH register and issue Interrupt 10.

Function 3: Find Cursor Position. To find where your cursor is, put the page number in the BH register, function number 3 in the AH register, and issue Interrupt 10. On return, the DH register has the row and the DL register has the column of the cursor position. Also, the cursor shape is identified; the CH register has the beginning row and CL has the ending row.

Function 5: Select Video Page. The monochrome monitor only has one page, so normally the page number is 0. If you have a graphics monitor, you can have four pages in the 80-column mode and eight in the 40-column mode. If you want to change pages, put the page number in AL, function number 5 in AH, and then issue Interrupt 10.

Function 6: Scroll Up. You can scroll either the entire screen or only a portion of it. To scroll up, place the number of lines to scroll (0 to 24) in the AL register, the left column number in CL, the upper row in CH, the right column in DL, and the lower row number in DH. If you want to clear the entire screen, place a 0 in AL. Also, as the text scrolls up, blank lines fill in below. The video attribute

Register AH	Function	Input	Output
0	Set Video Mode	AL = Mode	
1	Change Cursor Size	CH = Starting Scan Line CL = Ending Scan Line	
2	Change Cursor Position	BH = Page DH = Row DL = Column	
3	Find Cursor Position	BH = Page	BH = Page DH = Row DL = Column CH = Cursor Start Scan Line CL = Cursor Stop Scan Line
5	Select Video Page	AL = Page Number	
6	Scroll Up	AL = Lines Up CL = Left Column CH = Top Row DL = Right Column DH = Bottom Row BH = VIdeo Attribute	
7	Scroll Down	AL = Lines Down CL = Left Column CH = Top Row DL = Right Column DH = Bottom Row BH = VIdeo Attribute	
8	Read Character and Attribute	BH = Page	AL = Character AH = Attribute
9	Write Character and Attribute	AL = Character BL = Attribute BH = Page CX = Copies to Write	
A	Write Character	AL = Character BL = Attribute BH = Page CX = Copies to Write	
F	Find Video Mode		AL = Mode AH = Screen Width BH = Page

Fig. 10-5. ROM BIOS video services.

for the blank lines is placed in BH: 0 for blanks and 70 for reverse video. Set AH to 6 and issue Interrupt 10.

Function 7: Scroll Down. Scroll down is the opposite of scroll up. The only difference is what you see on the monitor. With this function, the lines go downward instead of upward.

Function 8: Read Character and Attribute. If you want to know what attribute a character has (at the cursor position), set BH to the display page (0 for monochrome, 0–4 for 80-column graphics, 0–7 in 40-column), AH to 8, and issue Interrupt 10. The character value in ASCII returns in AL and its attribute in AH.

Function 9: Write Character and Attribute. Place the character you want to write in the AL register and its desired attribute in BL. The page number is placed in BH and the number of characters to write goes in CX. Set AH to 9 and issue Interrupt 10. Since the cursor does not move after the character is written, you must move it with Function 2 after each write operation.

Function 0A: Write Character. Function 0A is like Function 9, except that you do not also write the character attribute. Set the AH register to 0A and issue Interrupt 10.

Function 0F: Find Video Mode. To find out what video mode you have, set the AH register to 0F and issue Interrupt 10. The video mode is returned in register AL, the video page in BH, and the screen width (40 or 80) in AH.

Elementary Graphics Routines

Many of the elementary text mode graphics routines have been combined into one program. Examples of clearing the screen, locating the cursor at a specific spot, drawing a line (vertical and horizontal) and scrolling are all in GRAPH_IT.

A Text-Mode Graphics Program

GRAPH_IT (Program 10-1) performs several functions. First, it draws horizontal and vertical lines to divide the full screen into four sections. A point at the line crossing is plotted and a graphic (+) is printed there. The line-drawing functions are procedures within the program; parameters of beginning locations, width, and depth are passed.

Second, GRAPH_IT uses a box-drawing procedure (also coded inside GRAPH_IT) to draw individual boxes (windows) within the four squares of the screen. Inside each of those four windows, additional features are shown. Figure 10-6 shows what the final screen looks like.

In window 1, five smaller boxes are drawn and then filled in. The fill-in procedure shows you how to fill a rectangular area on the screen. In window 2, horizontal and vertical lines are drawn, using the same procedure that drew the original lines dividing the full screen. Window 3 shows how to draw a checkerboard pattern. That section of GRAPH_IT code illustrates how to swap beginning columns

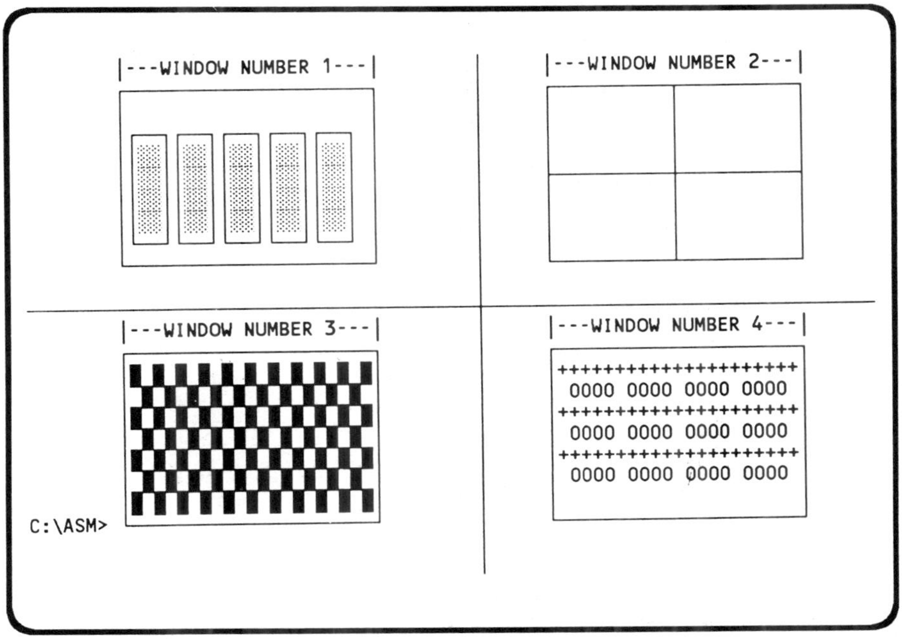

Fig. 10-6. GRAPH_IT example.

for printing alternating patterns. Window 4 displays scrolling within a smaller window (instead of the entire screen).

A Graphics-Mode Driver

GRAFDRV (Program 10-2) exercises 16 graphics routines that work in graphics mode. The graphics package is a good start for learning to program for Hercules and Hercules-compatible monochrome graphics cards. The package uses direct I/O to the 6845 controller chip. The chip only accepts 8-bit wide I/O, so the routines do not demonstrate the full power of the 80386.

The package consists of a driver (which exercises and tests the package routines) and a set of routines which are outlined below. One comment: This set of packages is almost impossible to "step through" with a debug package because the debug packages make assumptions about the state of the screen which this package invalidates. This caused us some extra work during debugging, as it will you when you begin to explore the graphics mode.

GRAFCLS: Clear the Screen. No input is required. The state of the graphics adapter is tested to determine the clearing size and value. The buffer is cleared. The output is a clear buffer.

GRAFOFF: Leave Graphics Mode. The page is cleared with a STOSD, which is twice as fast as an 80286 could do it. If the adapter is in text mode, nothing is done. If it is in graphics mode, here's what happens: The display is turned off, the 6845 controller is loaded with the text mode parameters, the screen is cleared, and the display is turned back on. The mode flag is set to text.

GRAFON: Enter Graphics Mode and Clear First Page. Again this is done twice as fast as you could do it on an 80286, because of the 32-bit STOSD instruction.

GRAFBXY: Locate a Dot. This procedure returns the byte offset and the bit mask for the bit X,Y. BX holds the horizontal displacement of the bit (0–719) X. AX had the vertical displacement of the bit (0–347) Y. The procedure computes the proper byte displacement for a Hercules compatible monochrome graphics adapter. The buffer displacement is:

```
8192h*(Y MOD 4) + 90*INT(Y/4) + INT(X/8)
```

Bit number is 7 – (X MOD 8). BX has the displacement into the graphics page (0000–7FFF). AH has the mask for setting the bit off (AND), AL has the mask for setting the bit on (OR). Carry will be reset (set to 0) if X,Y was valid for conversion. If an invalid X,Y coordinate is detected, Carry is set and the return is immediate; no registers are changed in this case.

GRAFSET: Set a Dot. This procedure sets the screen bit for the pixel given in BX and AX. BX has the horizontal displacement of the bit (0–719) X, and AX has the vertical displacement of the bit (0–347) Y. GRAFSET uses GRAFBXY to locate the bit to set, and then sets it. If the location is valid, the bit is set to 1 and Carry is reset (CF = 0) on return. The location (GRAFXVAL,GRAFYVAL) will set in this case. If the position is invalid, CF = 1 on return.

GRAFRSET: Reset a Dot. GRAFRSET resets the screen bit for the pixel given in BX and AX. It uses GRAFBXY to locate the bit to reset and resets it. BX has the horizontal displacement of the bit (0–719) X and AX has the vertical displacement of the bit (0–347) Y. If the location is valid, the bit is set to 0 and Carry is reset (CF = 0) on return. The location (GRAFXVAL,GRAFYVAL) will set in this case. If the position is invalid, CF = 1 on return.

GRAFLINE: Draw a Line. GRAFLINE draws or erases a line between the (GRAFXVAL,GRAFYVAL) point and the (BX,AX) point. BX has the horizontal displacement of the bit (0–719) X, and AX has the vertical displacement of the bit (0–347) Y. CL is zero for an erase and non-zero for a draw. GRAFLINE computes the factors for forming the line in terms of a step value for X and Y (+ – 1) and a direction. The line is either drawn or erased and Carry is reset (CF = 0) if the endpoints are valid. The point (GRAFXVAL, GRAFYVAL) will be set to the (BX,AX) values at the end. If the endpoint is invalid, return is made with CF = 1 and no changes made.

GRAFLOC: Return Location of Last Dot. GRAFLOC returns the location of the last pixel modified. The procedure loads the values of GRAFXVAL and GRAFYVAL into BX and AX. BX has the horizontal displacement of the bit (0–719) X, and AX has the vertical displacement of the bit (0–347) Y.

GRAFCLOC: Return Last Character's Location. GRAFCLOC returns the values MONOROW in BH, and MONOCOL in BL.

GRAFBIT: Return State of Pixel. GRAFBIT sets the condition code to the pixel given in BX and AX. BX has the horizontal displacement of the bit (0–719) X and AX has the vertical displacement of the bit (0–347) Y. The procedure uses GRAFBXY to locate the bit and copies it into the condition code.

GRAFTXT: Mimic Interrupt 21 Function 9. GRAFTXT displays text until it encounters an embedded "$" character. It honors backspace, line feed, and carriage returns. DX points to the text location.

GRAFDRV Memory Locations. Listed below are several labeled memory locations used by GRAFDRV:

GRAFMODE: A byte flag 00 = OFF, 01 = ON
GRAFXVAL: A word which has the last X
GRAFYVAL: A word which has the last Y
MONOROW: A word which has the last row
MONOCOL: A word which has the last column

Character Output in Graphics Mode

GRAFCHR (Program 10-3) provides a character output in graphics mode. The upper left graphic point of the character is computed (note that Hercules graphics font characters are 9 horizontal and 14 vertical positions in size, i.e., 80 by 24 with 12 positions vertical unused at the bottom of the screen). The character set resides in the font table portion of the program; the set we created is similar to the IBM standard font, but is not exactly the same. The 14 lines of the character are placed into the graphics buffer. The registers are restored and the Carry Flag is set if there's a problem. If set, no change in the display is made.

To save a lot of space, only a representative sample of the characters is included to illustrate the definition technique; you should define at least the lower 128 characters in ascending numerical order from 0 through 7Fh. In the listing area which defines the character set, you'll notice the character "C" to the right of the byte location and to the left of the DW. That indicates that this file/procedure/code was included during assembly from a separate .ASM file. (Our complete GRAFDRV font is available on the optional diskette for this book.)

Program 10-1: GRAPH_IT

```
Microsoft (R) Macro Assembler Version 5.00


                                        PAGE     55,132
                                        .386
                                        EXTRN    PAUSE:PROC
 0000                           STACK   SEGMENT 'STACK' STACK
 0000  0064[                            DW       100 DUP(?)
           ????
                        ]

 00C8                           STACK   ENDS
 0000                           CODE    SEGMENT para 'CODE' PUBLIC USE16
                                        ASSUME   CS:CODE, DS:CODE, SS:STACK
                                ;
                                ; Name:          GRAPH_IT
                                ;
                                ; Purpose:       This program does some simple graphics as a
                                ;                demonstration of screen handling, scrolling,
                                ;                line drawing, cursor positioning, and waiting for
                                ;                a while (pausing).
                                ;
                                ;                We wanted to slow the graphics down so each action is
                                ;                visible.  A procedure called PAUSE pauses for a time
                                ;                span from .02 seconds to 59.99 seconds.  PAUSE is
                                ;                described in Chapter 9 of "80386 Assembly Language
                                ;                Toolkit."
                                ;
                                ; Inputs:        ASCII strings are input with DB statements.
                                ;
                                ; Process:       The screen is cleared, lines are drawn vertically
                                ;                and horizontally, and then graphics are drawn in
                                ;                each section of the screen.  The pause was decided to
                                ;                be 1 second.  1 is stored in BH, 0 in BL for the call
                                ;                to PAUSE.  BX is then PUSHed and POPed when needed.
                                ;
                                ; Outputs:       Screen images.
                                ;
                                ; NOTE:          Parameters to be passed are kept in memory variables
                                ;                for easier code reading.  But in loops, the memory
                                ;                variables are moved into registers to keep from
                                ;                making multiple memory references.
                                ;
 0000                           GRAPH_IT:
 0000  8C C8                                     MOV      AX,CS            ; Prepare to set DS
 0002  8E D8                                     MOV      DS,AX            ;   and set it.
 0004  E9 00B1 R                                 JMP      BEGINHERE
 0007  2B 2B 2B 2B 2B 2B 2B     PLUS             DB       '++++++++++++++++++++$'
       2B 2B 2B 2B 2B 2B 2B
       2B 2B 2B 2B 2B 2B 2B
       24
 001D  20 30 30 30 30 20 30     ZEROS            DB       ' 0000 0000 0000 0000 $'
       30 30 30 20 30 30 30
       30 20 30 30 30 30 20
       24
 0033  B3 24                    VERT_LINE        DB       '│$'
 0035  C4 24                    HORIZ_LINE       DB       '─$'
 0037  C5 24                    CROSS            DB       '┼$'
 0039  7C 2D 2D 2D 57 49 4E     LABEL_1          DB       '|---WINDOW NUMBER 1---|$'
```

```
      44 4F 57 20 4E 55 4D
      42 45 52 20 31 2D 2D
      2D 7C 24
0051  7C 2D 2D 2D 57 49 4E      LABEL_2         DB      '|---WINDOW NUMBER 2---|$'
      44 4F 57 20 4E 55 4D
      42 45 52 20 32 2D 2D
      2D 7C 24
0069  7C 2D 2D 2D 57 49 4E      LABEL_3         DB      '|---WINDOW NUMBER 3---|$'
      44 4F 57 20 4E 55 4D
      42 45 52 20 33 2D 2D
      2D 7C 24
0081  7C 2D 2D 2D 57 49 4E      LABEL_4         DB      '|---WINDOW NUMBER 4---|$'
      44 4F 57 20 4E 55 4D
      42 45 52 20 34 2D 2D
      2D 7C 24
0099  BF 24                     RT_CORNER       DB      '┐$'
009B  D9 24                     RB_CORNER       DB      '┘$'
009D  DA 24                     LT_CORNER       DB      '┌$'
009F  C0 24                     LB_CORNER       DB      '└$'
00A1  C3 24                     LEFT_CONNECT    DB      '├$'
00A3  B4 24                     RIGHT_CONNECT   DB      '┤$'
00A5  C2 24                     TOP_CONNECT     DB      '┬$'
00A7  C1 24                     BOTTOM_CONNECT  DB      '┴$'
00A9  B1 24                     SHADE           DB      '▒$'
                                ;
                                ; Parameters to pass to box drawing procedure
                                ;
00AB  00                        LT_ROW          DB      0
00AC  00                        L_COLUMN        DB      0
00AD  00                        R_COLUMN        DB      0
00AE  00                        LB_ROW          DB      0
00AF  00                        WIDE            DB      0
00B0  00                        HEIGHT          DB      0
                                ;
                                ; This first routine clears the screen
                                ;
00B1                            BEGINHERE:
00B1  B4 0F                                     MOV     AH,15           ; Read the video mode
00B3  CD 10                                     INT     10h
00B5  B4 00                                     MOV     AH,0            ; Set the mode
00B7  CD 10                                     INT     10h
00B9  B6 01                                     MOV     DH,1            ; 1 second wait
00BB  B2 00                                     MOV     DL,0            ; No hundredths
00BD  52                                        PUSH    DX              ; Save DX on the stack
                                ;
                                ; Draw a horizontal line
                                ;
00BE  5A                                        POP     DX              ; Retrieve DX
00BF  E8 0000 E                                 CALL    PAUSE           ; Wait
00C2  52                                        PUSH    DX              ; Save it again
00C3  C6 06 00AB R 0B                           MOV     LT_ROW,11       ; Define on which row to draw
00C8  C6 06 00AC R 00                           MOV     L_COLUMN,0      ; Where to start
00CD  C6 06 00AF R 4F                           MOV     WIDE,79         ; How long to draw it
00D2  E8 043A R                                 CALL    DRAW_HORIZ
                                ;
                                ; Now draw a vertical line
                                ;
00D5  5A                                        POP     DX              ; Retrieve DX
00D6  E8 0000 E                                 CALL    PAUSE           ; Wait
00D9  52                                        PUSH    DX              ; Save it again
00DA  C6 06 00AB R 00                           MOV     LT_ROW,0        ; Start at top of screen
00DF  C6 06 00AC R 27                           MOV     L_COLUMN,39     ; Draw in middle
00E4  C6 06 00B0 R 18                           MOV     HEIGHT,24
```

```
00E9  E8 045F R                            CALL    DRAW_VERT
                            ;
                            ; Put a "+" where the lines cross
                            ;
00EC  5A                                   POP     DX            ; Retrieve DX
00ED  E8 0000 E                            CALL    PAUSE         ; Wait
00F0  52                                   PUSH    DX            ; Save it again
00F1  B6 0B                                MOV     DH,11         ; Move cursor to row 12
00F3  B2 27                                MOV     DL,39         ; Column 0
00F5  B4 02                                MOV     AH,2          ; Position the cursor
00F7  CD 10                                INT     10h
00F9  8D 16 0037 R                         LEA     DX,CROSS      ; Print the "+"
00FD  B4 09                                MOV     AH,9
00FF  CD 21                                INT     21h
                            ;
                            ; Draw a box in window 1
                            ;
0101  5A                                   POP     DX            ; Retrieve DX
0102  E8 0000 E                            CALL    PAUSE         ; Wait
0105  52                                   PUSH    DX            ; Save it again
0106  C6 06 00AB R 01                      MOV     LT_ROW,1      ; Left,top row is 2
010B  C6 06 00AC R 08                      MOV     L_COLUMN,8    ; Left column = 9
0110  C6 06 00AD R 1E                      MOV     R_COLUMN,30   ; Right column = 31
0115  C6 06 00AF R 15                      MOV     WIDE,21
011A  C6 06 00B0 R 07                      MOV     HEIGHT,7
011F  E8 048A R                            CALL    DRAW_BOX
                            ;
                            ; Labeling Window 1
                            ;
0122  5A                                   POP     DX            ; Retrieve DX
0123  E8 0000 E                            CALL    PAUSE         ; Wait
0126  52                                   PUSH    DX            ; Save it again
0127  C6 06 00AB R 00                      MOV     LT_ROW,0      ; Move cursor to row 1
012C  C6 06 00AC R 08                      MOV     L_COLUMN,8    ; Column 9
0131  8D 0E 0039 R                         LEA     CX,LABEL_1    ; Address of Label
0135  E8 0523 R                            CALL    DRAW_LABEL
                            ;
                            ; Draw Cards inside Window 1
                            ;
0138  5A                                   POP     DX            ; Retrieve DX
0139  E8 0000 E                            CALL    PAUSE         ; Wait
013C  52                                   PUSH    DX            ; Save it again
013D  C6 06 00AB R 03                      MOV     LT_ROW,3      ; Card 1
0142  C6 06 00AC R 09                      MOV     L_COLUMN,9
0147  C6 06 00AD R 0C                      MOV     R_COLUMN,12
014C  C6 06 00AF R 02                      MOV     WIDE,2
0151  C6 06 00B0 R 04                      MOV     HEIGHT,4
0156  E8 048A R                            CALL    DRAW_BOX
                            ;
0159  5A                                   POP     DX            ; Retrieve DX
015A  E8 0000 E                            CALL    PAUSE         ; Wait
015D  52                                   PUSH    DX            ; Save it again
015E  C6 06 00AB R 03                      MOV     LT_ROW,3      ; Card 2
0163  C6 06 00AC R 0D                      MOV     L_COLUMN,13
0168  C6 06 00AD R 10                      MOV     R_COLUMN,16
016D  C6 06 00AF R 02                      MOV     WIDE,2
0172  C6 06 00B0 R 04                      MOV     HEIGHT,4
0177  E8 048A R                            CALL    DRAW_BOX
                            ;
017A  5A                                   POP     DX            ; Retrieve DX
017B  E8 0000 E                            CALL    PAUSE         ; Wait
017E  52                                   PUSH    DX            ; Save it again
```

```
017F  C6 06 00AB R 03                   MOV    LT_ROW,3        ; Card 3
0184  C6 06 00AC R 11                   MOV    L_COLUMN,17
0189  C6 06 00AD R 14                   MOV    R_COLUMN,20
018E  C6 06 00AF R 02                   MOV    WIDE,2
0193  C6 06 00B0 R 04                   MOV    HEIGHT,4
0198  E8 048A R                         CALL   DRAW_BOX
                            ;
019B  5A                                POP    DX              ; Retrieve DX
019C  E8 0000 E                         CALL   PAUSE           ; Wait
019F  52                                PUSH   DX              ; Save it again
01A0  C6 06 00AB R 03                   MOV    LT_ROW,3        ; Card 4
01A5  C6 06 00AC R 15                   MOV    L_COLUMN,21
01AA  C6 06 00AD R 18                   MOV    R_COLUMN,24
01AF  C6 06 00AF R 02                   MOV    WIDE,2
01B4  C6 06 00B0 R 04                   MOV    HEIGHT,4
01B9  E8 048A R                         CALL   DRAW_BOX
                            ;
01BC  5A                                POP    DX              ; Retrieve DX
01BD  E8 0000 E                         CALL   PAUSE           ; Wait
01C0  52                                PUSH   DX              ; Save it again
01C1  C6 06 00AB R 03                   MOV    LT_ROW,3        ; Card 5
01C6  C6 06 00AC R 19                   MOV    L_COLUMN,25
01CB  C6 06 00AD R 1C                   MOV    R_COLUMN,28
01D0  C6 06 00AF R 02                   MOV    WIDE,2
01D5  C6 06 00B0 R 04                   MOV    HEIGHT,4
01DA  E8 048A R                         CALL   DRAW_BOX
                            ;
                            ; Shade in the boxes
                            ;
01DD  5A                                POP    DX              ; Retrieve DX
01DE  E8 0000 E                         CALL   PAUSE           ; Wait
01E1  52                                PUSH   DX              ; Save it again
01E2  C6 06 00AB R 04                   MOV    LT_ROW,4        ; Card 1
01E7  C6 06 00AC R 0A                   MOV    L_COLUMN,10
01EC  C6 06 00AF R 02                   MOV    WIDE,2
01F1  C6 06 00B0 R 04                   MOV    HEIGHT,4
01F6  8D 0E 00A9 R                      LEA    CX,SHADE
01FA  E8 0538 R                         CALL   FILL_REC
                            ;
01FD  5A                                POP    DX              ; Retrieve DX
01FE  E8 0000 E                         CALL   PAUSE           ; Wait
0201  52                                PUSH   DX              ; Save it again
0202  C6 06 00AB R 04                   MOV    LT_ROW,4        ; Card 2
0207  C6 06 00AC R 0E                   MOV    L_COLUMN,14
020C  C6 06 00AF R 02                   MOV    WIDE,2
0211  C6 06 00B0 R 04                   MOV    HEIGHT,4
0216  8D 0E 00A9 R                      LEA    CX,SHADE
021A  E8 0538 R                         CALL   FILL_REC
                            ;
021D  5A                                POP    DX              ; Retrieve DX
021E  E8 0000 E                         CALL   PAUSE           ; Wait
0221  52                                PUSH   DX              ; Save it again
0222  C6 06 00AB R 04                   MOV    LT_ROW,4        ; Card 3
0227  C6 06 00AC R 12                   MOV    L_COLUMN,18
022C  C6 06 00AF R 02                   MOV    WIDE,2
0231  C6 06 00B0 R 04                   MOV    HEIGHT,4
0236  8D 0E 00A9 R                      LEA    CX,SHADE
023A  E8 0538 R                         CALL   FILL_REC
                            ;
023D  5A                                POP    DX              ; Retrieve DX
023E  E8 0000 E                         CALL   PAUSE           ; Wait
0241  52                                PUSH   DX              ; Save it again
```

```
0242  C6 06 00AB R 04              MOV     LT_ROW,4            ; Card 4
0247  C6 06 00AC R 16              MOV     L_COLUMN,22
024C  C6 06 00AF R 02              MOV     WIDE,2
0251  C6 06 00B0 R 04              MOV     HEIGHT,4
0256  8D 0E 00A9 R                 LEA     CX,SHADE
025A  E8 0538 R                    CALL    FILL_REC
                          ;
025D  5A                           POP     DX                  ; Retrieve DX
025E  E8 0000 E                    CALL    PAUSE               ; Wait
0261  52                           PUSH    DX                  ; Save it again
0262  C6 06 00AB R 04              MOV     LT_ROW,4            ; Card 5
0267  C6 06 00AC R 1A              MOV     L_COLUMN,26
026C  C6 06 00AF R 02              MOV     WIDE,2
0271  C6 06 00B0 R 04              MOV     HEIGHT,4
0276  8D 0E 00A9 R                 LEA     CX,SHADE
027A  E8 0538 R                    CALL    FILL_REC
                          ;
                          ;
                          ; Draw a box in window 2
                          ;
027D  5A                           POP     DX                  ; Retrieve DX
027E  E8 0000 E                    CALL    PAUSE               ; Wait
0281  52                           PUSH    DX                  ; Save it again
0282  C6 06 00AB R 01              MOV     LT_ROW,1            ; Left,top row is 2
0287  C6 06 00AC R 2D              MOV     L_COLUMN,45         ; Left column = 46
028C  C6 06 00AD R 43              MOV     R_COLUMN,67         ; Right column = 68
0291  C6 06 00AF R 15              MOV     WIDE,21
0296  C6 06 00B0 R 07              MOV     HEIGHT,7
029B  E8 048A R                    CALL    DRAW_BOX
                          ;
                          ; Divide Window 2 into 4 boxes
                          ;
029E  5A                           POP     DX                  ; Retrieve DX
029F  E8 0000 E                    CALL    PAUSE               ; Wait
02A2  52                           PUSH    DX                  ; Save it again
02A3  B6 05                        MOV     DH,5                ; Row 6
02A5  B2 2D                        MOV     DL,45               ; Column 45
02A7  B4 02                        MOV     AH,2                ; Position cursor
02A9  CD 10                        INT     10h
02AB  8D 16 00A1 R                 LEA     DX,LEFT_CONNECT ; Print the left-side connector
02AF  B4 09                        MOV     AH,9
02B1  CD 21                        INT     21h
                          ;        Draw horizontal line in window 2
02B3  5A                           POP     DX                  ; Retrieve DX
02B4  E8 0000 E                    CALL    PAUSE               ; Wait
02B7  52                           PUSH    DX                  ; Save it again
02B8  C6 06 00AB R 05              MOV     LT_ROW,5            ; Row 6
02BD  C6 06 00AC R 2E              MOV     L_COLUMN,46         ; Column 47
02C2  C6 06 00AF R 15              MOV     WIDE,21
02C7  E8 043A R                    CALL    DRAW_HORIZ
                          ;
02CA  5A                           POP     DX                  ; Retrieve DX
02CB  E8 0000 E                    CALL    PAUSE               ; Wait
02CE  52                           PUSH    DX                  ; Save it again
02CF  8D 16 00A3 R                 LEA     DX,RIGHT_CONNECT ; Print the right-side connector
02D3  B4 09                        MOV     AH,9
02D5  CD 21                        INT     21h
                          ;         Draw vertical line in window 2
02D7  5A                           POP     DX                  ; Retrieve DX
02D8  E8 0000 E                    CALL    PAUSE               ; Wait
02DB  52                           PUSH    DX                  ; Save it again
02DC  B6 01                        MOV     DH,1                ; Draw top connector
02DE  B2 38                        MOV     DL,56
```

```
02E0  B4 02                 MOV   AH,2
02E2  CD 10                 INT   10h
02E4  8D 16 00A5 R          LEA   DX,TOP_CONNECT
02E8  B4 09                 MOV   AH,9
02EA  CD 21                 INT   21H
                      ;
02EC  5A                    POP   DX              ; Retrieve DX
02ED  E8 0000 E             CALL  PAUSE           ; Wait
02F0  52                    PUSH  DX              ; Save it again
02F1  C6 06 00AB R 02       MOV   LT_ROW,2        ; Start at row 2 for vert line
02F6  C6 06 00AC R 38       MOV   L_COLUMN,56     ; Draw at column 56
02FB  C6 06 00B0 R 07       MOV   HEIGHT,7
0300  E8 045F R             CALL  DRAW_VERT
                      ;
0303  5A                    POP   DX              ; Retrieve DX
0304  E8 0000 E             CALL  PAUSE           ; Wait
0307  52                    PUSH  DX              ; Save it again
0308  8A 16 00AC R          MOV   DL,L_COLUMN     ; Position cursor at bottom of box
030C  B6 09                 MOV   DH,9
030E  B4 02                 MOV   AH,2
0310  CD 10                 INT   10h
0312  8D 16 00A7 R          LEA   DX,BOTTOM_CONNECT ; Draw the bottom connector
0316  B4 09                 MOV   AH,9
0318  CD 21                 INT   21h
                      ;
                      ; Put a "+" where the lines cross
                      ;
031A  5A                    POP   DX              ; Retrieve DX
031B  E8 0000 E             CALL  PAUSE           ; Wait
031E  52                    PUSH  DX              ; Save it again
031F  B6 05                 MOV   DH,5            ; Move cursor to row 6
0321  B2 38                 MOV   DL,56           ; Column 56
0323  B4 02                 MOV   AH,2            ; Position the cursor
0325  CD 10                 INT   10h
0327  8D 16 0037 R          LEA   DX,CROSS        ; Print the "+"
032B  B4 09                 MOV   AH,9
032D  CD 21                 INT   21h
                      ;
                      ; Label Window 2
                      ;
032F  5A                    POP   DX              ; Retrieve DX
0330  E8 0000 E             CALL  PAUSE           ; Wait
0333  52                    PUSH  DX              ; Save it again
0334  C6 06 00AB R 00       MOV   LT_ROW,0        ; Row 1
0339  C6 06 00AC R 2D       MOV   L_COLUMN,45     ; Column 46
033E  8D 0E 0051 R          LEA   CX,LABEL_2
0342  E8 0523 R             CALL  DRAW_LABEL
                      ;
                      ;
                      ; Draw a box in window 3
                      ;
0345  5A                    POP   DX              ; Retrieve DX
0346  E8 0000 E             CALL  PAUSE           ; Wait
0349  52                    PUSH  DX              ; Save it again
034A  C6 06 00AB R 0D       MOV   LT_ROW,13       ; Left,top row is 14
034F  C6 06 00AC R 08       MOV   L_COLUMN,8      ; Left column = 9
0354  C6 06 00AD R 1E       MOV   R_COLUMN,30     ; Right column = 31
0359  C6 06 00AF R 15       MOV   WIDE,21
035E  C6 06 00B0 R 07       MOV   HEIGHT,7
0363  E8 048A R             CALL  DRAW_BOX
                      ;
                      ; Labeling Window 3
                      ;
```

```
0366  5A                                 POP     DX              ; Retrieve DX
0367  E8 0000 E                          CALL    PAUSE           ; Wait
036A  52                                 PUSH    DX              ; Save it again
036B  C6 06 00AB R 0C                    MOV     LT_ROW,12       ; Move cursor to row 13
0370  C6 06 00AC R 08                    MOV     L_COLUMN,8      ; Column 9
0375  8D 0E 0069 R                       LEA     CX,LABEL_3      ; Address of Label
0379  E8 0523 R                          CALL    DRAW_LABEL
                            ;
                            ;       Now draw a checkerboard in Window 3
                            ;
                            ;               The ASCII character is from the IBM-US Extended
                            ;               ASCII.
                            ;
                            ;               DX = Row/column for cursor positioning
                            ;               SI = Hex ASCII character
                            ;               BP = Even row column starting position
                            ;               DI = Odd row column starting position
                            ;
037C  5A                                 POP     DX              ; Retrieve DX
037D  E8 0000 E                          CALL    PAUSE           ; Wait
0380  52                                 PUSH    DX              ; Save it again
0381  2B ED                              SUB     BP,BP           ; Zero BP
0383  2B FF                              SUB     DI,DI           ; Zero DI
0385  BE 00DB                            MOV     SI,219          ; Blackouts (in hex=DB)
0388  B1 0A                              MOV     CL,10
038A  8B E9                              MOV     BP,CX           ; column 10
038C  B1 09                              MOV     CL,9
038E  8B F9                              MOV     DI,CX           ; column 9,10
0390  2B DB                              SUB     BX,BX           ; Make sure this is zero
0392  B6 0E                              MOV     DH,14           ; Row 15
0394                        CHECKER0:
0394  8B CF                              MOV     CX,DI           ; First time 9, second 10
0396  8A D1                              MOV     DL,CL           ; Column to begin in
0398  B4 02                              MOV     AH,2            ; Position cursor
039A  CD 10                              INT     10h
                            ;
039C                        CHECKER1:
039C  87 D6                              XCHG    DX,SI           ; Swap row/col with char string
039E  B4 02                              MOV     AH,2
03A0  CD 21                              INT     21H
03A2  87 F2                              XCHG    SI,DX           ; Swap back, now row/col in DX
03A4  80 C2 02                           ADD     DL,2            ; Skip a space & position cursor
03A7  CD 10                              INT     10h
03A9  80 FA 1E                           CMP     DL,30           ; All the way across?
03AC  7C EE                              JL      CHECKER1
                            ;
03AE  8B C2                              MOV     AX,DX           ; Save row/column
03B0  5A                                 POP     DX              ; Get time to pause
03B1  E8 0000 E                          CALL    PAUSE
03B4  52                                 PUSH    DX              ; Save time again
03B5  8B D0                              MOV     DX,AX           ; Retrieve row/column
03B7  87 EF                              XCHG    BP,DI           ; Swap which col to start on
03B9  FE C6                              INC     DH              ; Go to next row
03BB  80 FE 15                           CMP     DH,21           ; Done?
03BE  75 D4                              JNE     CHECKER0
                            ;
                            ;
                            ; Draw a box in window 4
                            ;
03C0  5A                                 POP     DX              ; Retrieve DX
03C1  E8 0000 E                          CALL    PAUSE           ; Wait
03C4  52                                 PUSH    DX              ; Save it again
```

```
03C5  C6 06 00AB R 0D                 MOV     LT_ROW,13        ; Left,top row is 14
03CA  C6 06 00AC R 2D                 MOV     L_COLUMN,45      ; Left column = 46
03CF  C6 06 00AD R 43                 MOV     R_COLUMN,67      ; Right column = 68
03D4  C6 06 00AF R 15                 MOV     WIDE,21
03D9  C6 06 00B0 R 07                 MOV     HEIGHT,7
03DE  E8 048A R                       CALL    DRAW_BOX
                          ;
                          ; Labeling Window 4
                          ;
03E1  5A                              POP     DX               ; Retrieve DX
03E2  E8 0000 E                       CALL    PAUSE            ; Wait
03E5  52                              PUSH    DX               ; Save it again
03E6  C6 06 00AB R 0C                 MOV     LT_ROW,12        ; Move cursor to row 13
03EB  C6 06 00AC R 2D                 MOV     L_COLUMN,45      ; Column 46
03F0  8D 0E 0081 R                    LEA     CX,LABEL_4       ; Address of Label
03F4  E8 0523 R                       CALL    DRAW_LABEL
                          ;
                          ; Scroll in window 4
                          ;
                          ;           AL = Number of lines blanked at bottom
                          ;           CH,CL = Upper left row/column of area to scroll
                          ;           DH,DL = Lower right row/column of area to scroll
                          ;           BH = Attribute used on blank line
                          ;           BP = Number of times to loop through scroll routine
                          ;
                          ;           Position cursor first, with DH,DL being position
                          ;           Then write a line of characters
                          ;
03F7  5A                              POP     DX               ; Retrieve DX
03F8  E8 0000 E                       CALL    PAUSE            ; Wait
03FB  52                              PUSH    DX               ; Save it again
03FC  8D 36 0007 R                    LEA     SI,PLUS          ; Address of Plus char string
0400  8D 3E 001D R                    LEA     DI,ZEROS         ; Address of Zero char string
0404  BD 0008                         MOV     BP,8             ; Number of times to loop
0407  2B DB                           SUB     BX,BX            ; Make sure this is zero
0409                      SCROLLO:
0409  B6 14                           MOV     DH,20            ; Position of bottom left corner
040B  B2 2E                           MOV     DL,46            ;    of window 4
040D  B4 02                           MOV     AH,2             ; Set cursor position
040F  CD 10                           INT     10h
                          ;
0411  87 D6                           XCHG    DX,SI            ; Swap row/col with char str addr
0413  B4 09                           MOV     AH,9
0415  CD 21                           INT     21h              ; Print char string
0417  87 D6                           XCHG    DX,SI            ; Swap back
0419  87 F7                           XCHG    SI,DI            ; This will print other string next
                          ;
041B  5A                              POP     DX               ; Retrieve DX
041C  E8 0000 E                       CALL    PAUSE            ; Wait
041F  52                              PUSH    DX               ; Save it again
0420  B5 0E                           MOV     CH,14            ; Row 15 - Top row of scroll
0422  B1 2E                           MOV     CL,46            ; Column 46 - Top column
0424  B6 14                           MOV     DH,20            ; Row 21 - Bottom row of scroll
0426  B2 42                           MOV     DL,66            ; Column 66 - Bottom column
0428  BB 0000                         MOV     BX,0
                          ;
042B  B4 06                           MOV     AH,6             ; Now scroll
042D  B0 01                           MOV     AL,1             ; Scroll 1 line
042F  CD 10                           INT     10h
0431  4D                              DEC     BP
0432  83 FD 00                        CMP     BP,0             ; Through with this?
0435  75 D2                           JNE     SCROLLO
```

```
                              ;
0437  E9 0572 R                             JMP     ENDHERE         ; Go around PAUSE code
                              ;
                              ; Draw a horizontal line
                              ;
                              ;             DX - Row/column to move cursor
                              ;                     Also for address of horizontal line character
                              ;             DI - Width
                              ;
043A                          DRAW_HORIZ    PROC
043A  60                                    PUSHA                   ; Save all registers
043B  B6 00                                 MOV     DH,0
043D  8A 16 00AF R                          MOV     DL,WIDE         ; Move memory reference to reg
0441  8B FA                                 MOV     DI,DX           ; Save width in DX
                              ;
0443  8A 36 00AB R                          MOV     DH,LT_ROW       ; Move cursor to row
0447  8A 16 00AC R                          MOV     DL,L_COLUMN     ; Column to begin drawing
044B  B4 02                                 MOV     AH,2            ; Position the cursor
044D  CD 10                                 INT     10h
                              ;
044F  8D 16 0035 R                          LEA     DX,HORIZ_LINE
0453  B4 09                                 MOV     AH,9            ; Get ready to print
0455                          LINE:
0455  CD 21                                 INT     21h
0457  4F                                    DEC     DI
0458  83 FF 00                              CMP     DI,0            ; Print it enough times?
045B  75 F8                                 JNE     LINE
                              ;
045D  61                                    POPA
045E  C3                                    RET
045F                          DRAW_HORIZ    ENDP
                              ;
                              ;
                              ; Draw a Vertical Line Procedure
                              ;
                              ;             SI - Address of vertical line character
                              ;             DI - Height
                              ;             DX - Row/column to move cursor
                              ;
045F                          DRAW_VERT     PROC
045F  60                                    PUSHA                   ; Save all registers
                              ;
0460  8D 36 0033 R                          LEA     SI,VERT_LINE    ; Save address of char string
0464  8A 16 00B0 R                          MOV     DL,HEIGHT
0468  B6 00                                 MOV     DH,0
046A  8B FA                                 MOV     DI,DX           ; Save height
046C  8A 36 00AB R                          MOV     DH,LT_ROW       ; Beginning row
0470  8A 16 00AC R                          MOV     DL,L_COLUMN
                              ;
0474                          LINE2:
0474  B4 02                                 MOV     AH,2
0476  CD 10                                 INT     10h             ; Position the cursor
0478  87 D6                                 XCHG    DX,SI           ; Swap row/col with char addr
047A  B4 09                                 MOV     AH,9            ; Get ready to print '|'
047C  CD 21                                 INT     21h
047E  87 D6                                 XCHG    DX,SI           ; Swap them back
                              ;
0480  FE C6                                 INC     DH              ; Increment row number
0482  4F                                    DEC     DI              ; Printed it enough times?
0483  83 FF 00                              CMP     DI,0            ; The right number of times?
0486  75 EC                                 JNE     LINE2
0488  61                                    POPA                    ; Retrieve all registers
```

```
0489  C3                                    RET
048A                      DRAW_VERT         ENDP
                          ;
                          ;
                          ;
                          ; Draw a box procedure
                          ;
                          ;                 DX - Row/column to move cursor
                          ;                      Also used for address of characters
                          ;                 CX - Width (CL) for drawing top
                          ;
048A                      DRAW_BOX                  PROC
048A  60                                            PUSHA            ; Save entry registers
                          ;
048B  8A 36 00AB R                          MOV     DH,LT_ROW        ; Move cursor to top row
048F  8A 16 00AC R                          MOV     DL,L_COLUMN      ; Left Column
0493  B4 02                                 MOV     AH,2
0495  CD 10                                 INT     10h
                          ;
0497  8D 16 009D R                          LEA     DX,LT_CORNER     ; Print top/left corner
049B  B4 09                                 MOV     AH,9
049D  CD 21                                 INT     21h
049F  8A 0E 00AF R                          MOV     CL,WIDE          ; However wide box is
04A3  8D 16 0035 R                          LEA     DX,HORIZ_LINE    ; Addr of horiz line character
04A7  B4 09                                 MOV     AH,9
04A9                      BOX_TOP:
04A9  CD 21                                 INT     21h
04AB  FE C9                                 DEC     CL
04AD  80 F9 00                              CMP     CL,0
04B0  75 F7                                 JNE     BOX_TOP
                          ;
04B2  8D 16 0099 R                          LEA     DX,RT_CORNER     ; Print right/top corner
04B6  B4 09                                 MOV     AH,9
04B8  CD 21                                 INT     21H
                          ;
                          ; Draw both sides at once
                          ;
                          ;                 CX - Left column(CH), Right column (CL)
                          ;                 SI - Address of vertical line character
                          ;                 DI - Height
                          ;
04BA  8D 36 0033 R                          LEA     SI,VERT_LINE     ; Addr of vertical line char
04BE  8A 2E 00AC R                          MOV     CH,L_COLUMN
04C2  8A 0E 00AD R                          MOV     CL,R_COLUMN
04C6  B6 00                                 MOV     DH,0             ; Save height
04C8  8A 16 00B0 R                          MOV     DL,HEIGHT
04CC  8B FA                                 MOV     DI,DX
04CE  8A 36 00AB R                          MOV     DH,LT_ROW        ; Move cursor to left top row
04D2  FE C6                                 INC     DH               ; Go to next row
04D4                      SIDE:
04D4  8A D5                                 MOV     DL,CH            ; Adjust to left column
04D6  B4 02                                 MOV     AH,2             ; Position cursor
04D8  CD 10                                 INT     10h
04DA  87 F2                                 XCHG    SI,DX            ; Swap row/col with char str addr
04DC  B4 09                                 MOV     AH,9             ; Draw left side
04DE  CD 21                                 INT     21h
04E0  87 F2                                 XCHG    SI,DX            ; Swap back
                          ;
04E2  8A D1                                 MOV     DL,CL            ; Right Column, Same Row
04E4  B4 02                                 MOV     AH,2             ; Position cursor
04E6  CD 10                                 INT     10h
04E8  87 F2                                 XCHG    SI,DX            ; Swap row/col & char addr string
04EA  B4 09                                 MOV     AH,9             ; Draw right side
04EC  CD 21                                 INT     21h
```

```
04EE  87 F2
04F0  FE C6                  XCHG    SI,DX             ; Swap back
04F2  4F                     INC     DH                ; New row
04F3  83 FF 00               DEC     DI
04F6  75 DC                  CMP     DI,0              ; Is it the right height?
                             JNE     SIDE              ; No, go draw another line

04F8  8A D5
04FA  B4 02                  MOV     DL,CH             ; Now have row/column of bottom
04FC  CD 10                  MOV     AH,2              ; Position cursor
04FE  8D 16 009F R           INT     10h
0502  B4 09                  LEA     DX,LB_CORNER      ; Print left/bottom corner
0504  CD 21                  MOV     AH,9
                             INT     21h

0506  8A 0E 00AF R      ;
050A  8D 16 0035 R           MOV     CL,WIDE
050E  B4 09                  LEA     DX,HORIZ_LINE     ; Now draw the bottom line
0510                         MOV     AH,9
0510  CD 21             BOX_BOTTOM:
0512  FE C9                  INT     21h
0514  80 F9 00               DEC     CL
0517  75 F7                  CMP     CL,0
                             JNE     BOX_BOTTOM

0519  8D 16 009B R      ;
051D  B4 09                  LEA     DX,RB_CORNER      ; Print right/bottom corner
051F  CD 21                  MOV     AH,9
0521  61                     INT     21h
0522  C3                     POPA                      ; Retrieve all registers
0523                         RET
                        DRAW_BOX        ENDP
                        ;
                        ;
                        ; Position Cursor and Draw a Label
                        ;
                        ;            DX - Row/column to move cursor
                        ;            CX - Address of label
                        ;
0523                    DRAW_LABEL   PROC
0523  60                             PUSHA             ; Save registers

0524  8A 36 00AB R      ;
0528  8A 16 00AC R           MOV     DH,LT_ROW         ; Row
052C  B4 02                  MOV     DL,L_COLUMN       ; Column
052E  CD 10                  MOV     AH,2
                             INT     10h

0530  8B D1             ;
0532  B4 09                  MOV     DX,CX             ; Address of label
0534  CD 21                  MOV     AH,9
                             INT     21h

0536  61                ;
0537  C3                     POPA                      ; Retrieve registers
0538                         RET
                        DRAW_LABEL   ENDP
                        ;
                        ;
                        ;  Fill a rectangular space
                        ;            SI - Fill character address
                        ;            DI - Height
                        ;            BP - Width
                        ;            CX - Brings in fill char address, used in PROC
                        ;                 as a counter
                        ;            DX - Row/column to move cursor
                        ;
0538                    FILL_REC     PROC
0538  60                             PUSHA             ; Save entry registers
                        ;
```

```
0539  8B F1                                 MOV     SI,CX           ; Addr of Fill character
053B  2B C9                                 SUB     CX,CX           ; Zero CX
053D  8A 0E 00B0 R                          MOV     CL,HEIGHT       ; Save height
0541  8B F9                                 MOV     DI,CX
0543  8A 0E 00AF R                          MOV     CL,WIDE         ; Save width
0547  8B E9                                 MOV     BP,CX
0549  8A 36 00AB R                          MOV     DH,LT_ROW       ; Row to begin fill
054D  8A 16 00AC R                          MOV     DL,L_COLUMN     ; Column to begin fill
0551                    FILL0:
0551  B4 02                                 MOV     AH,2            ; Position cursor
0553  CD 10                                 INT     10h
                        ;
0555  87 F2                                 XCHG    SI,DX           ; Swap row/col with fill char addr
0557  8B CD                                 MOV     CX,BP           ; Save width
0559  B4 09                                 MOV     AH,9
055B                    FILL1:
055B  CD 21                                 INT     21h
055D  FE C9                                 DEC     CL
055F  80 F9 00                              CMP     CL,0
0562  75 F7                                 JNE     FILL1
                                  ; Now go to next row
0564  87 F2                                 XCHG    SI,DX           ; Swap back
0566  8B CD                                 MOV     CX,BP           ; Restore width
0568  FE C6                                 INC     DH              ; Go to next row
056A  4F                                    DEC     DI              ; Printed enough?
056B  83 FF 00                              CMP     DI,0
056E  75 E1                                 JNE     FILL0
                        ;
0570  61                                    POPA                    ; Restore registers
0571  C3                                    RET
0572                    FILL_REC            ENDP
                        ;
                        ;
0572                    ENDHERE:
0572  B4 4C                                 MOV     AH,4Ch          ; Standard ending
0574  CD 21                                 INT     21h
0576                    CODE                ENDS
                                            END     GRAPH_IT
```

Program 10-2: GRAFDRV

Microsoft (R) Macro Assembler Version 5.00

```
                                         PAGE    55,132
                                         .386
                               ;
                               ; Name:   GRAFDRV
                               ;
                               ; Purpose: This program exercises the graphics package.
                               ;
                               ; Inputs:  Permission to start is prompted for, as is permission to
                               ;          end.  Anything entered is ok.
                               ;
                               ; Process: This driver prompts, then enters graphics mode.  The
                               ;          supplied font is displayed and the program pauses for 5
                               ;          seconds.  A diagonal line is drawn bit by bit and the
                               ;          program pauses.  A horizontal line is drawn, a pause,
                               ;          and the rest of a box is formed.  The box is erased in
                               ;          the same manner.  We then test an on and off pixel and
                               ;          use the text display to print the result.
                               ;          We then exit the graphic mode and prompt for permission
                               ;          to quit.
                               ;
                               ; Outputs: All output is displayed.
                               ;
                               ; Note:    This is a difficult package to debug.  The error routine
                               ;          must exit graphic mode in order to permit a debug package
                               ;          an intelligible display.  Individual routines were tested
                               ;          with graphics mode off to eliminate stack problems which
                               ;          cause entry into never never land.
                               ;
                               ; Declare the routines we are going to use
                               ;
                                         EXTRN   PAUSE:PROC
                                         EXTRN   GRAFON:PROC
                                         EXTRN   GRAFOFF:PROC
                                         EXTRN   GRAFCHR:PROC
                                         EXTRN   GRAFCLS:PROC
                                         EXTRN   GRAFSET:PROC
                                         EXTRN   GRAFRSET:PROC
                                         EXTRN   GRAFLINE:PROC
                                         EXTRN   GRAFBIT:PROC
                                         EXTRN   GRAFLOC:PROC
                                         EXTRN   GRAFCLOC:PROC
                                         EXTRN   GRAFTXT:PROC
                                         EXTRN   CODEBAS:PROC

0000                           stack     SEGMENT para 'STACK' STACK
0000  0100[                              dq      256 DUP(?)
        ???????????????
        ?
                  ]

0800                           stack     ENDS
0000                           data      SEGMENT para
0000  0100[                    string    db      256 DUP(?)          ; String scratch area
         ??
                  ]
```

```
0100 0A 0A 0D 45 6E 74 65      queryb    db      10,10,13,"Enter anything to begin: $"
     72 20 61 6E 79 74 68
     69 6E 67 20 74 6F 20
     62 65 67 69 6E 3A 20
     24
011D 0A 0A 0D 45 6E 74 65      querye    db      10,10,13,"Enter anything to end: $"
     72 20 61 6E 79 74 68
     69 6E 67 20 74 6F 20
     65 6E 64 3A 20 24
0138 0A 0A 0A 0D 4F 6E 20      bitonms   db      10,10,10,13,"On test ok.  $"
     74 65 73 74 20 6F 6B
     2E 20 20 24
014A 4F 66 66 20 74 65 73      bitoffms  db      "Off test ok.  $"
     74 20 6F 6B 2E 20 20
     24
0159 0A 0D 45 6E 64 65 64      errmsg    db      10,13,"Ended with error! $"
     20 77 69 74 68 20 65
     72 72 6F 72 21 20 24
016E                           data      ENDS
0000                           code      SEGMENT para 'CODE' USE16 PUBLIC
                                         ASSUME  CS:code, DS:data
                               ;
                               ; Set up the environment
                               ;
0000                           Begin:
0000 B8 ---- R                           mov     AX,data             ; Get data segment pointer
0003 8E D8                               mov     DS,AX               ; into DS,
0005 8E C0                               mov     ES,AX               ; and ES.
0007 2B F6                               sub     SI,SI               ; Clear indices
0009 2B FF                               sub     DI,DI
000B 8D 16 0100 R                        lea     DX,queryb           ; Put out start msg
000F E8 0102 R                           call    getinp
                               ;
                               ; set graphic mode on
                               ;
0012 E8 0000 E                           call    Grafon              ; Set it on
0015 B9 0050                             mov     CX,80               ; Prepare char set line 1
0018 2A C0                               sub     AL,AL               ; starting character
001A 2B DB                               sub     BX,BX               ; Col 0 row 0
001C                           first80:
001C E8 0000 E                           call    grafchr             ; put out a char
001F 0F 82 00F2 R                        jc      charerr             ; error routine if bad
0023 FE C7                               inc     BH
0025 FE C0                               inc     AL
0027 E2 F3                               loop    first80             ; Do 0-79
0029 FE C3                               inc     BL                  ; next row
002B B9 0050                             mov     CX,80               ; all of it
002E 2A FF                               sub     BH,BH               ; With col 0 as start
0030                           second80:
0030 E8 0000 E                           call    grafchr             ; Put character out
0033 0F 82 00F2 R                        jc      charerr             ; If error - quit
0037 FE C7                               inc     BH                  ; Step horizontal loc
0039 FE C0                               inc     AL                  ; and character
003B E2 F3                               loop    second80            ; do 80-159 (check folding)
003D BA 0500                             mov     DX,500h             ; Delay five seconds
0040 E8 0000 E                           call    pause
                               ;
                               ; The character set is now displayed - set some points below it
                               ;
0043 2B DB                               sub     BX,BX               ; start at left margin
0045 B8 0046                             mov     AX,70               ; and fifth char row
0048 B9 0032                             mov     CX,50
```

```
004B                    points1:
004B  E8 0000 E                  call   grafset         ; Set the point
004E  0F 82 00F2 R               jc     pointerr        ; If error - quit
0052  40                         inc    AX
0053  43                         inc    BX              ; diag.
0054  E2 F5                      loop   points1
0056  BA 0500                    mov    DX,500h         ; wait for half a sec
0059  E8 0000 E                  call   pause
005C  48                         dec    AX              ; to draw a line horizontal
005D  81 C3 012C                 add    BX,300          ; to the last bit set
0061  B1 01                      mov    CL,1            ; set to draw
0063  E8 0000 E                  call   grafline        ;
0066  BA 0500                    mov    DX,500h         ; wait half a second
0069  E8 0000 E                  call   pause

006C  05 00C8                    add    AX,200          ; Go down
006F  E8 0000 E                  call   grafline        ;
0072  81 EB 012C                 sub    BX,300          ; to the left
0076  E8 0000 E                  call   grafline
0079  2D 00C8                    sub    AX,200          ; and join the box
007C  E8 0000 E                  call   grafline
007F  BA 0500                    mov    DX,500h         ; Wait 5 seconds
0082  E8 0000 E                  call   pause

0085  81 C3 012C                 add    BX,300          ; to the last bit set
0089  B1 00                      mov    CL,0            ; set to erase
008B  E8 0000 E                  call   grafline        ;
008E  BA 0500                    mov    DX,500h         ; wait half a second
0091  E8 0000 E                  call   pause
0094  05 00C8                    add    AX,200          ; Go down
0097  E8 0000 E                  call   grafline        ;
009A  81 EB 012C                 sub    BX,300          ; to the left
009E  E8 0000 E                  call   grafline
00A1  2D 00C8                    sub    AX,200          ; and join the box
00A4  E8 0000 E                  call   grafline
00A7  BA 0500                    mov    DX,500h         ; Wait 5 seconds
00AA  E8 0000 E                  call   pause

00AD  B8 0046                    mov    AX,70           ; To first bit vert
00B0  2B DB                      sub    BX,BX           ; Horizontal at left margin
00B2  E8 0000 E                  call   grafbit
00B5  0F 82 00F2 R               jc     charerr         ; Can't be bad!
00B9  0F 84 00F2 R               jz     charerr         ; This should not be
00BD  8D 16 0138 R               lea    DX,bitonms      ; point to message
00C1  E8 0000 E                  call   Graftxt         ; and display it
00C4  B8 0046                    mov    AX,70           ;
00C7  BB 0001                    mov    BX,1            ; One to the right
00CA  E8 0000 E                  call   grafbit         ; test it
00CD  0F 82 00F2 R               jc     charerr         ; Location is ok
00D1  0F 85 00F2 R               jnz    charerr         ; Error if not off
00D5  8D 16 014A R               lea    DX,bitoffms     ; Point to message
00D9  E8 0000 E                  call   graftxt         ; and write it
00DC  BA 0500                    mov    DX,500h         ; wait 5 seconds
00DF  E8 0000 E                  call   pause           ;


00E2  E8 0000 E                  call   grafoff         ; Back into char mode
00E5  8D 16 011D R               lea    DX,querye       ; Ask permission
00E9  E8 0102 R                  call   getinp          ; to quit
00EC                    Exit:
00EC  B0 00                      mov    AL,0            ; Set return code
```

```
00EE  B4 4C                         mov     AH,04ch             ; Set good-by
00F0  CD 21                         int     21h                 ; Return to the system
00F2                        charerr:
00F2                        pointerr:
00F2  60                            pusha                       ; save on the stack all
00F3  0E                            push    CS
00F4  1E                            push    DS
00F5  06                            push    ES
00F6  E8 0000 E                     call    Grafoff
00F9  8D 16 0159 R                  lea     DX,errmsg           ; indicate error
00FD  E8 0102 R                     call    getinp
0100  EB EA                         jmp     exit                ; breakpoint here
                            ;
                            ; Read a string in response to a prompt
                            ; The prompt must be in DX.  The string will be returned in string.
                            ;
0102                        getinp  PROC
0102  50                            push    AX                  ; Save registers
0103  56                            push    SI
0104  B4 09                         mov     AH,9                ; and dos request
0106  CD 21                         int     21h                 ; put out the string
0108  8D 16 0000 R                  lea     DX,string           ; point to input area
010C  C6 06 0000 R FE               mov     string,254          ; Set max length in
0111  B4 0A                         mov     AH,10               ; Ask for read of string
0113  CD 21                         int     21h                 ; from DOS.
0115  8D 1E 0002 R                  lea     BX,string+2         ; Point to just read data
0119  8A 0E 0001 R                  mov     CL,string+1         ; Get length read
011D  B5 00                         mov     CH,0                ; as a word.
011F  8B F1                         mov     SI,CX               ; Set length
0121  C6 84 0002 R 00               mov     string+2[SI],0      ; and make an asciiz string.
0126  5E                            pop     SI
0127  58                            pop     AX                  ; Restore registers
0128  C3                            ret                         ; and return.
0129                        getinp  ENDP

0129                        code    ENDS
                                    END     Begin
```

```
                                PAGE    55,132
                                .386
0000                    code    SEGMENT para 'CODE' PUBLIC USE16
                                ASSUME  CS:code, DS:code, SS:code

                        ; Name:     GRAFON
                        ;
                        ; Purpose:  The following procedure sets the graphic adapter into
                        ;           graphic mode and clears the screen.
                        ;
                        ; Inputs:   No input is required.
                        ;
                        ; Process:  Nothing is done if the adapter is in graphic mode.  If it
                        ;           is in text mode, the display is turned off, the graphic
                        ;           controller is loaded with the parameters for graphic display
                        ;           mode, the screen is cleared, and graphic mode is set.
                        ;
                        ; Output:   The mode is changed and the screen is cleared.
                        ;

                                PUBLIC  Grafcls             ; A procedure to clear the scr
```

```
                                PUBLIC  Grafoff      ; A procedure to leave graphic
                                PUBLIC  Grafon       ; A procedure to enter graphic
                                PUBLIC  Grafbxy      ; A procedure to locate a dot
                                PUBLIC  Grafset      ; A procedure to set a dot
                                PUBLIC  Grafrset     ; A procedure to reset a dot
                                PUBLIC  Grafline     ; A procedure to draw a line
                                PUBLIC  Grafloc      ; A procedure to return last
                                                     ;   dot's location
                                PUBLIC  Grafcloc     ; A procedure to return last
                                                     ;   character's location
                                PUBLIC  Grafbit      ; A procedure to return the
                                                     ;   state of the pixel.
                                PUBLIC  Graftxt      ; A procedure which mimics
                                                     ;   code 9, int 21h. without
                                                     ;   scrolling.  (it wraps)

                                PUBLIC  Grafmode     ; A byte flag 00h=off, 01h=on
                                PUBLIC  Grafxval     ; A word which has the last x
                                PUBLIC  Grafyval     ; A word which has the last y
                                PUBLIC  Monorow      ; A word which has the last row
                                PUBLIC  Monocol      ; A word which has the last col

 = 03B4           indexpt   EQU     03b4h        ; I/O port which indexes the
                                                 ; data register selected.
 = 03B5           datapt    EQU     03b5h        ; I/O port for data register
                                                 ; load after selection.
 = 03BF           configpt  EQU     03bfh        ; I/O port which selects the
                                                 ; video ram configuration.
                                                 ; 0 = non-graphic,
                                                 ; 1 = graphic 32K at 0b0000h

                                                 ; 3 = graphic 2x32K (page
                                                 ;     selected by bit 7 3b8)
 = 03B8           modept    EQU     03b8h        ; I/O port which sets the mode
                                                 ;     of the display.
                                                 ; bit  if zero     non zero
                                                 ; 0    unused
                                                 ; 1    text        graphics
                                                 ; 2    unused
                                                 ; 3    blank scr   display scr
                                                 ; 4    unused
                                                 ; 5    no blink    char blink
                                                 ; 6    unused
                                                 ; 7    page 0      page 1 b8000
 = B000           Grafpg0   EQU     0b000h       ; Segment value of page 0
 = B800           Grafpg1   EQU     0b800h       ; Segment value of page 1
                                                 ;
                  ;
                  ; Position and mode information.
                  ;
 0000  0000       Grafxval  dw      0            ; Dot's row position 0-719
 0002  0000       Grafyval  dw      0            ; Dot's column position 0-347
 0004  0000       Monorow   dw      0            ; Char's row (vertical) 0-23
 0006  0000       Monocol   dw      0            ; Char's column (horizontal)
                                                 ;        1-79

 0008  00         Grafmode  db      0            ; Initial mode is off (text)
 0009  00                   db      0            ;
                  ;
                  ; line routine 's work area
                  ;
 000A  0000       linertnx  dw      0            ; Ending X value
 000C  0000       linertny  dw      0            ; Ending Y value
```

```
                          ;
                          ; Values for loading the monochrome registers
                          ;
000E  61                  Monoregs   db      98-1             ; Reg 0 chars + sync -1 per row
000F  50                             db      80               ; Reg 1 visible chars per row
0010  52                             db      83-1             ; Reg 2 pos of first char
                                                              ;       during sync -1.
0011  0F                             db      16-1             ; Reg 3 Chars during sync -1
0012  19                             db      26-1             ; Reg 4 Rows + retrace -1
0013  06                             db      6                ; Reg 5 Row fractions
0014  19                             db      25               ; Reg 6 number of visible rows
0015  19                             db      26-1             ; Reg 7 row starting retrace -1
0016  02                             db      2                ; Reg 8 Constant for 6845
0017  0D                             db      14-1             ; Reg 9 Scans per row -1
0018  0B                             db      11               ; Reg 10 top cursor line
0019  0C                             db      12               ; Reg 11 bottom cursor line
= 000C                    Regcount   EQU     $-Monoregs
                          ;
                          ; Values for loading the graphics registers
                          ;
001A  35                  Grafregs   db      54-1             ; Reg 0 Chars + sync -1
001B  2D                             db      45               ; Reg 1 visible chars per row
001C  2E                             db      47-1             ; Reg 2 first char pos -1
001D  07                             db      8-1              ; Reg 3 Chars during sync -1
001E  5B                             db      92-1             ; Reg 4 Rows + retrace -1
001F  02                             db      2                ; Reg 5 row fractions
0020  58                             db      88               ; Reg 6 number of visible rows
0021  58                             db      88               ; Reg 7 row starting retrace -1
0022  02                             db      2                ; Reg 8 Constant
0023  03                             db      4-1              ; Reg 9 Scans per row -1
0024  00                             db      0                ; Reg 10 top cursor line
0025  00                             db      0                ; Reg 11 bottom cursor line
                          ;
                          ;
                          ;
= 0002                    grafctl1   EQU     2                ; page 0, no vid, graphic ena.
= 000A                    grafctl2   EQU     2+8              ; Graphctl1 with video on.
= 0020                    monoctl1   EQU     20h              ; page 0, no vid, no graph
= 0028                    monoctl2   EQU     20h+8            ; video on

                                     EXTRN   Grafchr:PROC
                          ;
0026                      Grafon     PROC
0026  52                             push    DX               ; Save entry registers
0027  51                             push    CX
0028  56                             push    SI
0029  66| 57                         push    EDI
002B  66| 50                         push    EAX
002D  1E                             push    DS
002E  06                             push    ES
002F  8C C8                          mov     AX,CS            ; Set local DS and ES
0031  8E D8                          mov     DS,AX
0033  B8 B000                        mov     AX,Grafpg0       ; Display page
0036  8E C0                          mov     ES,AX
0038  F6 06 0008 R 01                test    Grafmode,01h     ; Are we in graphic mode
003D  0F 85 0083 R                   jnz     exiton           ; If so - Get out.
0041  FC                             cld                      ; Set direction up
0042  2A E4                          sub     AH,AH            ; Clear register index
0044  8D 36 001A R                   lea     SI,Grafregs      ; Point to register values
0048  B9 000C                        mov     CX,Regcount      ; Set count
004B  B0 01                          mov     AL,1
004D  BA 03BF                        mov     DX,configpt
```

```
0050  EE                        out     DX,AL
0051  BA 03B8                   mov     DX,Modept          ; Prepare to shut vid down
0054  B0 02                     mov     AL,grafctl1        ; Set for graphic with blank
0056  EE                        out     DX,AL              ; write to controller
0057  BA 03B4                   mov     DX,indexpt         ; Set index port
005A                   nexton:
005A  8A C4                     mov     AL,AH              ; Set register number
005C  EE                        out     DX,AL              ; Select register
005D  FE C4                     inc     AH                 ; next register
005F  42                        inc     DX                 ; and data load
0060  6E                        outsb                      ; write data
0061  4A                        dec     DX                 ; get reg select
0062  E2 F6                     loop    nexton             ; load all registers
0064  66| 2B C0                 sub     EAX,EAX            ; Clear to zeros
0067  66| 8B F8                 mov     EDI,EAX            ; index too
006A  B9 2000                   mov     CX,2000h           ; Number of dwords to clear.
006D  F3/ 66| AB                rep stosd                  ; Clear them
0070  66| A3 0000 R             mov     DWORD PTR Grafxval,EAX ; Clear dot location
0074  66| A3 0004 R             mov     DWORD PTR Monorow,EAX ; and the text location.
0078  BA 03B8                   mov     DX,modept          ; Change the mode to
007B  B0 0A                     mov     AL,grafctl2        ; video on
007D  EE                        out     DX,AL              ; Do it.
007E  C6 06 0008 R 01           mov     grafmode,1         ; Set graphics on flag.

0083                   exiton:
0083  07                        pop     ES                 ; Restore the entry registers
0084  1F                        pop     DS
0085  66| 58                    pop     EAX
0087  66| 5F                    pop     EDI
0089  5E                        pop     SI
008A  59                        pop     CX
008B  5A                        pop     DX
008C  C3                        ret                        ; and return.
008D                   Grafon   ENDP



                       ;

                       ; Name:    GRAFOFF
                       ;
                       ; Purpose: The following procedure sets the graphic adapter into
                       ;          text mode and clears the text screen.
                       ;
                       ;
                       ; Inputs:  No input is required.
                       ;
                       ; Process: If the adapter is in text mode, nothing is done.  If it
                       ;          is in graphic mode: the display is turned off,  the 6845
                       ;          controller is loaded with the text mode parameters, the
                       ;          screen is cleared, and the display is turned back on in
                       ;          text mode.  The mode flag is set to text.
                       ;
                       ;
                       ; Output:  The screen is cleared and the mode is changed to text.
                       ;
008D                   Grafoff  PROC
008D  52                        push    DX                 ; Save entry registers
008E  51                        push    CX
008F  56                        push    SI
0090  66| 57                    push    EDI
0092  66| 50                    push    EAX
0094  1E                        push    DS
```

```
0095  06                         push   ES
0096  8C C8                      mov    AX,CS                 ; Set local DS and ES
0098  8E D8                      mov    DS,AX
009A  B8 B000                    mov    AX,Grafpg0            ; Display page
009D  8E C0                      mov    ES,AX
009F  F6 06 0008 R 01            test   Grafmode,01h          ; Are we in graphic mode
00A4  0F 84 00EA R               jz     exitoff               ; If not - Get out.
00A8  FC                         cld                          ; Set direction up
00A9  2A E4                      sub    AH,AH                 ; Clear register index
00AB  8D 36 000E R               lea    SI,monoregs           ; Point to register values
00AF  B9 000C                    mov    CX,Regcount           ; Set count
00B2  BA 03B8                    mov    DX,Modept             ; Prepare to shut vid down
00B5  B0 20                      mov    AL,monoctl1           ; Set for monochrome with blank
00B7  EE                         out    DX,AL                 ; write to controller
00B8  BA 03B4                    mov    DX,indexpt            ; Set index port
00BB                       nextoff:
00BB  8A C4                      mov    AL,AH                 ; Set register number
00BD  EE                         out    DX,AL                 ; Select register
00BE  FE C4                      inc    AH                    ; next register
00C0  42                         inc    DX                    ; and data load
00C1  6E                         outsb                        ; write data
00C2  4A                         dec    DX                    ; get reg select
00C3  E2 F6                      loop   nextoff               ; load all registers
00C5  66| B8 07200720            mov    EAX,07200720h         ; Clear to blanks attr 7
00CB  66| 2B FF                  sub    EDI,EDI               ; Clear index
00CE  B9 03E8                    mov    CX,1000               ; Number of dwords to clear.
00D1  F3/ 66| AB                 rep stosd                    ; Clear them
00D4  66| 2B C0                  sub    EAX,EAX               ; Get double word of zeros.
00D7  66| A3 0000 R              mov    DWORD PTR Grafxval,EAX ; Clear dot location
00DB  66| A3 0004 R              mov    DWORD PTR Monorow,EAX ; and the text location.
00DF  BA 03B8                    mov    DX,modept             ; Change the mode to
00E2  B0 28                      mov    AL,monoctl2           ; video on
00E4  EE                         out    DX,AL                 ; Do it.
00E5  C6 06 0008 R 00            mov    Grafmode,0            ; Set it off

00EA                       exitoff:
00EA  07                         pop    ES                    ; Restore the entry registers
00EB  1F                         pop    DS
00EC  66| 58                     pop    EAX
00EE  66| 5F                     pop    EDI
00F0  5E                         pop    SI
00F1  59                         pop    CX
00F2  5A                         pop    DX
00F3  C3                         ret                          ; and return.
00F4                       Grafoff  ENDP
                           ; Name:     GRAFCLS
                           ;
                           ; Purpose: The following procedure clears either type of screen,
                           ;          graphic or text.
                           ;
                           ; Inputs:  No input is required.
                           ;
                           ; Process: The state of the graphic adapter is tested to determine
                           ;          the clearing size and value.  The buffer is cleared.
                           ;
                           ; Output:  The output is a clear buffer.
                           ;
00F4                       Grafcls  PROC
00F4  52                         push   DX                    ; Save entry registers
00F5  51                         push   CX
00F6  56                         push   SI
00F7  66| 57                     push   EDI
```

```
00F9  66| 50                     push    EAX
00FB  1E                         push    DS
00FC  06                         push    ES
00FD  8C C8                      mov     AX,CS                ; Set local DS and ES
00FF  8E D8                      mov     DS,AX
0101  B8 B000                    mov     AX,Grafpg0           ; Display page
0104  8E C0                      mov     ES,AX
0106  FC                         cld                          ; Set direction up
0107  66| 2B C0                  sub     EAX,EAX              ; Clear to zeros
010A  66| A3 0000 R              mov     DWORD PTR Grafxval,EAX ; Clear dot location
010E  66| A3 0004 R              mov     DWORD PTR Monorow,EAX ; and the text location.
0112  B9 2000                    mov     CX,2000h             ; for 32k
0115  F6 06 0008 R 01            test    Grafmode,01h         ; Are we in graphic mode
011A  0F 84 0127 R               jz      zeros                ; If so we are set
011E  66| B8 07200720            mov     EAX,07200720h        ; Clear to blanks attr 7
0124  B9 03E8                    mov     CX,1000              ; Number of dwords to clear.
0127                     zeros:
0127  66| 8B FF                  mov     EDI,EDI              ; Clear index
012A  F3/ 66| AB                 rep stosd                    ; Clear them
012D  07                         pop     ES                   ; Restore the entry registers
012E  1F                         pop     DS
012F  66| 58                     pop     EAX
0131  66| 5F                     pop     EDI
0133  5E                         pop     SI
0134  59                         pop     CX
0135  5A                         pop     DX
0136  C3                         ret                          ; and return.
0137                     Grafcls ENDP
                         ;
                         ; Name:    GRAFBXY
                         ;
                         ; Purpose: The following procedure returns the byte offset and
                         ;          the bit mask for the bit X,Y.
                         ;
                         ;
                         ;
                         ;
                         ; Inputs:  BX has the horizontal displacement of the bit (0-719) X.
                         ;          AX has the vertical displacement of the bit (0-347) Y.
                         ;
                         ; Process: The procedure computes the proper byte displacement for
                         ;          a HERCULES (tm) compatible monochrome graphics adapter.
                         ;          Buffer displacement is
                         ;                8192h*(Y MOD 4)+90*INT(Y/4)+INT(X/8).
                         ;          Bit number is 7-(X MOD 8).
                         ;
                         ; Output:  BX has the displacement into the graphics page (0000-7FFF).
                         ;          ES has the segment value for the graphics page (B000).
                         ;          AH has the mask for setting the bit off (and), AL has the
                         ;          mask for setting the bit on (or).  Carry will be reset if
                         ;          X,Y was valid for conversion.
                         ;          If an invalid X,Y coordinate is detected, carry is set and
                         ;          return is immediate - no registers are changed in this
                         ;          case.
                         ;
                         ;
                         ;
0137                     Grafbxy PROC
0137  81 FB 02CF                 cmp     BX,719               ; Check X
013B  0F 8F 0177 R               jg      error                ; Out if bad
013F  3D 015B                    cmp     AX,347               ; Check Y
0142  0F 8F 0177 R               jg      error                ; Out if bad
0146  52                         push    DX                   ; Save entry registers
0147  51                         push    CX
```

```
0148  8B CB                      mov      CX,BX
014A  8B D0                      mov      DX,AX
014C  C1 E8 02                   shr      AX,2               ; Get INT(Y/4)
014F  B1 5A                      mov      CL,90              ; set multiplier
0151  F6 E1                      mul      CL                 ; and multiply by 90
0153  80 E2 03                   and      DL,3               ; Get (Y MOD 4)
                        ;
                        ;  The algorithm calls for 2000h * (Y MOD 4). This can be a left
                        ;      shift of (Y MOD 4) of 13.  The following shifts 5 and adds
                        ;      the result to the high byte of AX thus getting a left shift
                        ;      of 8 for free.  (No gain on the 386 but 8 clocks for a 286.)
                        ;
0156  C0 E2 05                   shl      DL,5               ; Shift for 5
0159  02 E2                      add      AH,DL              ; Add to high byte 8+5=13.
015B  8B D3                      mov      DX,BX              ; Copy X
015D  C1 EA 03                   shr      DX,3               ; for INT(X/8)
0160  03 D0                      add      DX,AX              ; We have byte displacement in DX
0162  83 E3 07                   and      BX,7               ; Get X MOD 8
0165  03 DB                      add      BX,BX              ; times 2
0167  2E: 8B 87 0179 R           mov      AX,CS:masks[BX]    ; load masks
016C  8B DA                      mov      BX,DX              ; position byte displacement
016E  BA B000                    mov      DX,Grafpg0         ; Set segment value
0171  8E C2                      mov      ES,DX              ; into ES.
0173  F8                         clc                         ; ensure carry is off
0174  59                         pop      CX                 ; Restore registers
0175  5A                         pop      DX
0176  C3                         ret                         ; and return.
0177                    error:
0177  F9                         stc                         ; Flag the error
0178  C3                         ret                         ; and return.
                        ;                 AH AL
                        ;                 offon              (X MOD 8)  BIT # (7-(X MOD 8))
0179  7F80              masks    dw       07F80h           ;     0          7
017B  BF40                       dw       0BF40h           ;     1          6
017D  DF20                       dw       0DF20h           ;     2          5
017F  EF10                       dw       0EF10h           ;     3          4
0181  F708                       dw       0F708h           ;     4          3
0183  FB04                       dw       0FB04h           ;     5          2
0185  FD02                       dw       0FD02h           ;     6          1
0187  FE01                       dw       0FE01h           ;     7          0
0189                    Grafbxy  ENDP



                        ;
                        ; Name:     GRAFRSET
                        ;
                        ; Purpose: The following procedure resets the screen bit for the
                        ;           pixel given in BX and AX.
                        ;
                        ; Inputs:   BX has the horizontal displacement of the bit (0-719) X.
                        ;           AX has the vertical displacement of the bit (0-347) Y.
                        ;
                        ; Process: The procedure uses Grafbxy to locate the bit to reset and
                        ;           resets it.
                        ;
                        ; Output:   If the location is valid, the bit is set to 0 and carry
                        ;           is reset on return.  The location (Grafxval,Grafyval) will
                        ;           set in this case.
                        ;           If the location is invalid,n carry is set on return.
                        ;
```

```
0189                            Grafrset  PROC
0189  06                                  push    ES                  ; Save the registers
018A  53                                  push    BX
018B  50                                  push    AX
018C  E8 0137 R                           call    Grafbxy             ; compute the location
018F  0F 82 01A7 R                        jc      rsetexit            ; If error - just leave
0193  26: 20 27                           and     ES:[BX],AH          ; Reset the bit
0196  8C C8                               mov     AX,CS               ; Get Segment value
0198  8E C0                               mov     ES,AX               ; into ES
019A  58                                  pop     AX                  ; Get the Y value
019B  5B                                  pop     BX                  ; Get the X value
019C  26: 89 1E 0000 R                    mov     ES:Grafxval,BX      ; Into common loc
01A1  26: A3 0002 R                       mov     ES:Grafyval,AX      ; for Y too
01A5  07                                  pop     ES                  ; Register ES back
01A6  C3                                  ret                         ; and exit
                                ;
                                ; Error exit
                                ;
01A7                            rsetexit:
01A7  58                                  pop     AX                  ; Restore the registers
01A8  5B                                  pop     BX
01A9  07                                  pop     ES
01AA  C3                                  ret
01AB                            Grafrset  ENDP



                                ;
                                ; Name:     GRAFSET
                                ;
                                ; Purpose:  The following procedure sets the screen bit for the
                                ;           pixel given in BX and AX.
                                ;
                                ; Inputs:   BX has the horizontal displacement of the bit (0-719) X.
                                ;           AX has the vertical displacement of the bit (0-347) Y.
                                ;
                                ; Process:  The procedure uses Grafbxy to locate the bit to set and
                                ;           sets it.
                                ;
                                ; Output:   If the location is valid, the bit is set to 1 and carry
                                ;           is reset on return.  The location (Grafxval,Grafyval) will
                                ;           set in this case.
                                ;           If the location is invalid carry is set on return.
                                ;
01AB                            Grafset   PROC
01AB  06                                  push    ES                  ; Save the registers
01AC  53                                  push    BX
01AD  50                                  push    AX
01AE  E8 0137 R                           call    Grafbxy             ; compute the location
01B1  0F 82 01C9 R                        jc      setexit             ; If error - just leave
01B5  26: 08 07                           or      ES:[BX],AL          ; Set the bit
01B8  8C C8                               mov     AX,CS               ; Get Segment value
01BA  8E C0                               mov     ES,AX               ; into ES
01BC  58                                  pop     AX                  ; Get the Y value
01BD  5B                                  pop     BX                  ; Get the X value
01BE  26: 89 1E 0000 R                    mov     ES:Grafxval,BX      ; Into common loc
01C3  26: A3 0002 R                       mov     ES:Grafyval,AX      ; for Y too
01C7  07                                  pop     ES                  ; Register ES back
01C8  C3                                  ret                         ; and exit
                                ;
                                ; Error exit
```

```
                                  ;
01C9                              setexit:
01C9  58                                    pop     AX                 ; Restore the registers
01CA  5B                                    pop     BX
01CB  07                                    pop     ES
01CC  C3                                    ret
01CD                              Grafset   ENDP



                                  ;
                                  ; Name:     GRAFBIT
                                  ;
                                  ; Purpose: The following procedure sets the condition code to the
                                  ;          pixel given in BX and AX.
                                  ;
                                  ; Inputs:  BX has the horizontal displacement of the bit (0-719) X.
                                  ;          AX has the vertical displacement of the bit (0-347) Y.
                                  ;
                                  ; Process: The procedure uses Grafbxy to locate the bit and copies
                                  ;          it into the condition code.
                                  ;
                                  ; Output:  If the location is valid, the zero flag will reflect the
                                  ;          state of the pixel.  i.e. it is set if the bit is zero and
                                  ;          reset otherwise.   Carry is reset.
                                  ;          If the location is invalid carry is set on return and the
                                  ;          state of the zero flag is undefined.
01CD                              Grafbit   PROC
01CD  06                                    push    ES                 ; Save the registers
01CE  53                                    push    BX
01CF  50                                    push    AX
01D0  E8 0137 R                             call    Grafbxy            ; compute the location
01D3  0F 82 01EB R                          jc      bitexit            ; If error - just leave
01D7  26: 22 07                             and     AL,ES:[BX]         ; Set the zero flag.
01DA  8C C8                                 mov     AX,CS              ; Get Segment value
01DC  8E C0                                 mov     ES,AX              ; into ES
01DE  58                                    pop     AX                 ; Get the Y value
01DF  5B                                    pop     BX                 ; Get the X value
01E0  26: 89 1E 0000 R                      mov     ES:Grafxval,BX     ; Into common loc
01E5  26: A3 0002 R                         mov     ES:Grafyval,AX     ; for Y too
01E9  07                                    pop     ES                 ; Register ES back
01EA  C3                                    ret                        ; and exit
                                  ;
                                  ; Error exit
                                  ;
01EB                              bitexit:
01EB  58                                    pop     AX                 ; Restore the registers
01EC  5B                                    pop     BX
01ED  07                                    pop     ES
01EE  C3                                    ret
01EF                              Grafbit   ENDP



                                  ;
                                  ; Name:     GRAFCLOC
                                  ;
                                  ; Purpose: The following procedure returns the location of the next
                                  ;          character set on the screen.
                                  ;
```

```
                                ; Inputs:  No input is needed.
                                ;
                                ; Process: The procedure returns Monorow and Monocol.
                                ;
                                ; Output:  BH contains the horizontal position Monocol.
                                ;          BL contains the vertical position Monorow.
                                ;
01EF                            Grafcloc   PROC
01EF  50                                   push   AX                    ; Save a work register.
01F0  2E: 8B 1E 0004 R                     mov    BX,CS:Monorow         ; Get the row in BL
01F5  2E: A1 0006 R                        mov    AX,CS:Monocol         ; and the col in
01F9  8A F8                                mov    BH,AL                 ; BH
01FB  58                                   pop    AX                    ; Restore work register
01FC  C3                                   ret                          ; and exit
01FD                            Grafcloc   ENDP


                                ;
                                ; Name:    GRAFCSET
                                ;
                                ; Purpose: The following procedure sets the location of the next
                                ;          character to be set on the screen.
                                ;
                                ; Inputs:  BH contains the horizontal position for Monocol.
                                ;          BL contains the vertical position for Monorow.
                                ;
                                ; Process: The procedure edits and sets Monorow and Monocol.
                                ;
                                ; Outputs: The next position is set if the input was valid.
                                ;          In this case carry is reset.  If an error was detected,
                                ;          carry will be set and nothing changed.
                                ;
01FD                            Grafcset   PROC
01FD  80 FF 50                             cmp    BH,80
0200  0F 83 0217 R                         jnb    cseterr               ; too big a line
0204  80 FB 18                             cmp    BL,24
0207  0F 83 0217 R                         jnb    cseterr               ; too many lines
020B  2E: 88 1E 0004 R                     mov    BYTE PTR CS:Monorow,BL ; Get the row from BL
0210  2E: 88 3E 0006 R                     mov    BYTE PTR CS:Monocol,BH ; and the col too
0215  F8                                   clc
0216  C3                                   ret                          ; and exit
0217                            cseterr:
0217  F9                                   stc                          ; Set carry
0218  C3                                   ret                          ; and exit

0219                            Grafcset   ENDP


                                ;
                                ; Name:    GRAFTXT
                                ;
                                ; Purpose: The following procedure displays text until it encounters
                                ;          an embedded $.  It honors backspace, linefeed, and carriage
                                ;          returns.
                                ;
                                ; Inputs:  DX points to the text location.
                                ;
                                ; Process: The procedure displays text until a $ is encountered.
                                ;          Backspace is causes a wrapping erase action in addition
```

```
                                    ;          to reducing the 'cursor' position.
                                    ;          Linefeed causes the vertical position to be increased with
                                    ;          wrapping from 23 to zero.
                                    ;          Carriage return resets the horizontal position to zero.
                                    ;
                                    ; Output:  The data is displayed on the graphic screen.
                                    ;          No registers are changed.
                                    ;
0219                                Graftxt    PROC
0219  50                                       push    AX                  ; Save work registers
021A  53                                       push    BX
021B  51                                       push    CX
021C  52                                       push    DX
021D  56                                       push    SI
021E  06                                       push    ES
021F  8C C8                                    mov     AX,CS
0221  8E C0                                    mov     ES,AX               ; Set data pointer
0223  8B F2                                    mov     SI,DX               ; copy text pointer
0225                                nexttxt:
0225  AC                                       lodsb                       ; get character
0226  3C 24                                    cmp     AL,'$'              ; stopper?
0228  0F 84 02BD R                             je      txtend              ; Yes - get out
022C  3C 0D                                    cmp     AL,13               ; Is it a carriage return
022E  0F 85 023A R                             jne     textlfq             ; no - check more
0232  2B C0                                    sub     AX,AX               ; Get zeros
0234  26: A3 0006 R                            mov     ES:Monocol,AX       ; for column position
0238  EB EB                                    jmp     nexttxt             ; get next
023A                                textlfq:
023A  3C 0A                                    cmp     AL,10               ; Is it a line feed?
023C  0F 85 0254 R                             jne     textbspq            ; No - maybe a backspace?
0240  26: A1 0004 R                            mov     AX,ES:Monorow       ; Get vertical (row) position
0244  40                                       inc     AX
0245  3D 0018                                  cmp     AX,24               ; At the roll point
0248  0F 82 024E R                             jb      textlfok
024C  2B C0                                    sub     AX,AX               ; roll to zero
024E                                textlfok:
024E  26: A3 0004 R                            mov     ES:Monorow,AX       ; set new row position.
0252  EB D1                                    jmp     nexttxt             ; then get next character.
0254                                textbspq:
0254  3C 08                                    cmp     AL,8                ; Is it a backspace?
0256  0F 85 0288 R                             jne     txtother            ; Not here
025A  26: A1 0006 R                            mov     AX,ES:Monocol       ; Get column
025E  48                                       dec     AX                  ; less one
025F  0F 89 0276 R                             jns     textbsp0            ; If it is good - set it
0263  26: A1 0004 R                            mov     AX,ES:Monorow       ; need to step row
0267  48                                       dec     AX                  ; Back up one
0268  0F 89 026F R                             jns     textbsp1            ; Ok as is
026C  B8 0017                                  mov     AX,23               ; bottom line
026F                                textbsp1:
026F  26: A3 0004 R                            mov     ES:Monorow,AX       ; Set row
0273  B8 004F                                  mov     AX,79               ; and ending col
0276                                textbsp0:
0276  26: 8B 1E 0004 R                         mov     BX,ES:Monorow       ; Get row
027B  8A F8                                    mov     BH,AL               ; And the column
027D  26: A3 0006 R                            mov     ES:Monocol,AX       ; We have next position
0281  B0 20                                    mov     AL,' '              ; Blank it out
0283  E8 0000 E                                call    grafchr             ;
0286  EB 9D                                    jmp     nexttxt             ; Try another char
0288                                txtother:
0288  26: 8B 1E 0004 R                         mov     BX,ES:Monorow       ; Get row
028D  26: 8B 0E 0006 R                         mov     CX,ES:Monocol       ; and col
0292  8A F9                                    mov     BH,CL               ; combine
```

```
0294  E8 0000 E                        call    grafchr             ; Put character out
0297  41                               inc     CX                  ; Step column
0298  83 F9 50                         cmp     CX,80               ; Need to wrap?
029B  0F 82 02B5 R                     jb      txtocok             ; No - store it
029F  26: 8B 1E 0004 R                 mov     BX,ES:Monorow       ; Get the row
02A4  43                               inc     BX                  ; Plus 1
02A5  83 FB 18                         cmp     BX,24               ; Need to wrap to top?
02A8  0F 82 02AE R                     jb      txtorok             ; No - OK as is
02AC  2B DB                            sub     BX,BX               ; Wrap to top
02AE                           txtorok:
02AE  26: 89 1E 0004 R                 mov     ES:Monorow,BX
02B3  2B C9                            sub     CX,CX               ; Wrap to start of line
02B5                           txtocok:
02B5  26: 89 0E 0006 R                 mov     ES:Monocol,CX       ; Set next column
02BA  E9 0225 R                        jmp     nexttxt
02BD                           txtend:
02BD  07                               pop     ES                  ; Restore work registers
02BE  5E                               pop     SI
02BF  5A                               pop     DX
02C0  59                               pop     CX
02C1  5B                               pop     BX
02C2  58                               pop     AX
02C3  C3                               ret                         ; and exit
02C4                           Graftxt ENDP



                               ;
                               ; Name:     GRAFLOC
                               ;
                               ; Purpose:  The following procedure returns the location of the last
                               ;           pixel modified.
                               ;
                               ; Inputs:   No input is required.
                               ;
                               ; Process:  The procedure loads the values of Grafxval and Grafyval
                               ;           into BX and AX.
                               ;
                               ; Outputs:  BX has the horizontal displacement of the bit (0-719) X.
                               ;           AX has the vertical displacement of the bit (0-347) Y.
                               ;
                               ;
02C4                           Grafloc PROC
02C4  2E: A1 0002 R                    mov     AX,CS:Grafyval      ; Get y loc
02C8  2E: 8B 1E 0000 R                 mov     BX,CS:Grafxval      ; x loc
02CD  C3                               ret                         ; and exit
02CE                           Grafloc ENDP



                               ;
                               ; Name:     GRAFLINE
                               ;
                               ; Purpose:  The following procedure draws or erases a line between the
                               ;           (Grafxval, Grafyval) point and the (BX, AX) point.
                               ;
                               ; Inputs:   BX has the horizontal displacement of the bit (0-719) X.
                               ;           AX has the vertical displacement of the bit (0-347) Y.
                               ;           CL is zero for an erase, non-zero for a draw.
```

```
                         ;
                         ; Process: The procedure computes the factors for forming the line
                         ;          in terms of a step value for X and Y, (+ - 1) and a
                         ;          direction.
                         ;
                         ;
                         ;
                         ;
                         ;
                         ;
                         ; Output:  The line is either drawn or erased and carry is reset if
                         ;          the endpoints are valid.  (Grafxval, Grafyval) will be
                         ;          set to the BX, AX values at the end.
                         ;          If the end point is invalid, return is made with carry set
                         ;          and no changes made.
                         ;
02CE                     Grafline   PROC
02CE  3D 015B                       cmp     AX,347          ; Is Y valid?
02D1  0F 87 02DD R                  ja      lnexit          ; If not - exit with carry
02D5  81 FB 02CF                    cmp     BX,719          ; Is X valid?
02D9  0F 86 02DF R                  jna     lnvalid         ; Yes - draw the line.
02DD                     lnexit:
02DD  F9                            stc                     ; Set carry
02DE  C3                            ret                     ; and exit in error
02DF                     lnvalid:
02DF  60                            pusha                   ; Save all registers
02E0  1E                            push    DS
02E1  06                            push    ES
02E2  8C CA                         mov     DX,CS           ; Get local data segment
02E4  8E DA                         mov     DS,DX
02E6  89 1E 000A R                  mov     linertnx,BX     ; Save ending X
02EA  A3 000C R                     mov     linertny,AX     ; and Y
02ED  BA 0101                       mov     DX,0101h        ; Set Y (DH) and X (DL) steps
02F0  8B 36 0002 R                  mov     SI,Grafyval     ; Prepare to compute del y
02F4  3B F0                         cmp     SI,AX           ; Check if start > end
02F6  0F 8E 02FC R                  jng     ynotgreat       ; Leave DH as positive if not
02FA  B6 FF                         mov     DH,-1           ; Set it negative
02FC                     ynotgreat:
02FC  2B F0                         sub     SI,AX           ; del Y as Grafyval-AX
02FE  0F 89 0304 R                  jns     delyset         ; Value is positive or zero
0302  F7 DE                         neg     SI              ; Get absolute value
0304                     delyset:
0304  8B 3E 0000 R                  mov     DI,Grafxval     ; Prepare to compute del X
0308  3B FB                         cmp     DI,BX           ; Check if start > end
030A  0F 8E 0310 R                  jng     xnotgreat       ; Leave DL as positive if not
030E  B2 FF                         mov     DL,-1           ; Set it negative
0310                     xnotgreat:
0310  2B FB                         sub     DI,BX           ; del X as Grafxval-BX
0312  0F 89 0318 R                  jns     delxset         ; Value is positive or zero
0316  F7 DF                         neg     DI              ; Get absolute value
0318                     delxset:
0318  BD 0000                       mov     BP,0            ; Assume positive
031B  0F 85 0320 R                  jnz     notvertic       ; Vertical line if delta X = 0
031F  4D                            dec     BP              ; set direction to -1
0320                     notvertic:
0320  A1 0002 R                     mov     AX,Grafyval     ; Get starting Y
0323  8B 1E 0000 R                  mov     BX,Grafxval     ; and X
0327                     linedoneq:
0327  3B 1E 000A R                  cmp     BX,linertnx     ; Is X done?
032B  0F 85 0337 R                  jne     linenext        ; No - go do it
032F  3B 06 000C R                  cmp     AX,linertny     ; Is Y done too
0333  0F 84 0368 R                  jz      linedone        ; Yes - get out
0337                     linenext:
0337  0A C9                         or      CL,CL           ; Set or Reset?
```

```
0339  0F 85 0343 R              jnz     lineset          ; non zero is set/draw
033D  E8 0189 R                 call    grafrset         ; Reset the dot
0340  EB 04 90                  jmp     chkldir          ;
0343                    lineset:
0343  E8 01AB R                 call    Grafset          ; Set it on
0346                    chkldir:
0346  0B ED                     or      BP,BP            ; Check direction
0348  0F 88 035A R              js      linedoy          ; Go step Y.
034C  2B EE                     sub     BP,SI            ; Sub del Y from direction
034E  0A D2                     or      DL,DL            ; Up or down step
0350  0F 88 0357 R              js      decrx            ; Down one
0354  43                        inc     BX               ; Up one
0355  EB D0                     jmp     linedoneq        ; done yet?
0357                    decrx:
0357  4B                        dec     BX               ; Go down
0358  EB CD                     jmp     linedoneq        ; check if done
035A                    linedoy:
035A  03 EF                     add     BP,DI            ; Add del X to direction
035C  0A F6                     or      DH,DH            ; Up or down step
035E  0F 88 0365 R              js      decry            ; Down one
0362  40                        inc     AX               ; Up one
0363  EB C2                     jmp     linedoneq        ; done yet?
0365                    decry:
0365  48                        dec     AX               ; Go down
0366  EB BF                     jmp     linedoneq        ; check if done
                        ;
                        ; Do last point of the line
                        ;
0368                    linedone:
0368  0A C9                     or      CL,CL            ; Set or Reset?
036A  0F 85 0374 R              jnz     linesetd         ; non zero is set/draw
036E  E8 0189 R                 call    grafrset         ; Reset the dot
0371  EB 04 90                  jmp     nowdone          ;
0374                    linesetd:
0374  E8 01AB R                 call    Grafset          ; Set it on
0377                    nowdone:
0377  07                        pop     ES               ; Restore the registers,
0378  1F                        pop     DS
0379  61                        popa
037A  F8                        clc                      ; clear the carry,
037B  C3                        ret                      ; and return
037C                    Grafline ENDP

037C                    code    ENDS
                                END
```

Program 10-3: GRAFCHR

```
                                        PAGE    55,132
                                        .386
0000                            code    SEGMENT para 'CODE' PUBLIC USE16
                                        ASSUME  CS:code, DS:code, SS:code

                                ;
                                ; Name:     GRAFCHR
                                ;
                                ; Purpose: The following procedure provides a character output in
                                ;          graphics mode.
                                ;
                                ;
                                ;
                                ; Inputs:   AL contains the character to put out.
                                ;           BH contains the horizontal position (0-79).
                                ;           BL contains the vertical position (0-23).
                                ;
                                ; Process:  The position is checked and if invalid, return is made
                                ;           with carry set.
                                ;           The upper left graphic point of the character is computed.
                                ;           (Characters are 9 horizontal and 14 vertical positions in
                                ;            size.  i.e. 80 x 24 with 12 positions vertical unused at
                                ;            the bottom of the screen.)
                                ;           The character is located in the font table and the 14
                                ;           lines of the character are placed into the graphics
                                ;           buffer.  The registers are restored, carry is reset and we
                                ;           return.
                                ;
                                ; Output:   The carry flag indicates the result - if set, no change to
                                ;           the display was made.  If reset, the character is set in
                                ;           the display buffer.
                                ;
                                ;
                                ;
                                          PUBLIC Grafchr
                                          EXTRN  Grafbxy:PROC

0000                            Grafchr   PROC
0000  24 7F                               and     AL,127          ; Force into our 128 cset.
0002  80 FB 17                            cmp     BL,23           ; Check the vertical position.
0005  0F 8F 0010 R                        jg      error           ; If over - out with carry
0009  80 FF 4F                            cmp     BH,79           ; Check the horizontal position
000C  0F 8E 0012 R                        jng     posok           ; We are go!
0010                            error:
0010  F9                                  stc                     ; signal the error
0011  C3                                  ret                     ; and go back
0012                            posok:
0012  57                                  push    DI              ; Save entry registers
0013  56                                  push    SI
0014  55                                  push    BP
0015  52                                  push    DX
0016  51                                  push    CX
0017  53                                  push    BX
0018  50                                  push    AX
0019  06                                  push    ES
001A  B1 1C                               mov     CL,28           ; char * 2 * 14
001C  F6 E1                               mul     CL              ; for font index.
001E  8D 36 00B2 R                        lea     SI,CS:font      ; Font address plus
0022  03 F0                               add     SI,AX           ; index gives source.
0024  B0 0E                               mov     AL,14           ; Get multiplier of 14
```

```
0026  F6 E3                  mul     BL                ; Times bit's vertical
0028  8B D0                  mov     DX,AX             ; Save for Grafbxy call

002A  8D 2E 008A R           lea     BP,CS:stepyv      ; Get offset of y step value
002E  25 0003                and     AX,3              ; Bit position (Y) mod 4
0031  03 E8                  add     BP,AX             ; Added to y step value
0033  03 E8                  add     BP,AX             ; twice for word index.

0035  B0 09                  mov     AL,9              ; Get horizontal as position
0037  F6 E7                  mul     BH                ; times 9
0039  8B D8                  mov     BX,AX             ; to get horizontal displ.
003B  8A C8                  mov     CL,AL             ; Save the bit number
003D  8B C2                  mov     AX,DX             ; Set vertical

003F  E8 0000 E              call    Grafbxy           ; Get the starting bit's byte
                     ;                                   (Ignore the bit masks)
0042  B5 0E                  mov     CH,14             ; Get the repeat count
0044  80 E1 07               and     CL,7              ; Get Herc style bit number
0047  F6 D9                  neg     CL                ; as negative then
0049  80 C1 07               add     CL,7              ; convert to rotate count
004C  BA 03BA                mov     DX,03bah          ; Get vid status I/O address
004F                 nexty:
004F  26: 8B 07              mov     AX,ES:[BX]        ; Grab a word
0052  86 E0                  xchg    AH,AL             ; Get positioned as in memory
0054  D3 C8                  ror     AX,CL             ; Position in bits 8-0.
0056  25 FE00                and     AX,0FE00h         ; Set all to zeros
0059  2E: 0B 04              or      AX,CS:[SI]        ; Set on a font row
005C  83 C6 02               add     SI,2              ; Step to next row
005F  D3 C0                  rol     AX,CL             ; Get bits repositioned
0061  86 E0                  xchg    AH,AL             ; Position for their return.
0063  51                     push    CX                ; Save a work register
0064  8B C8                  mov     CX,AX             ; because I/O uses AL.
                     ;
                     ; First we wait for a non vertical retrace state.  When we get one,
                     ; we then wait for a change back to vertical retrace.  This allows
                     ; us to store into video memory without conflicting with video fetch
                     ; (which causes 'snow').
                     ;
0066                 waitnon:
0066  EC                     in      AL,DX             ; Get status from adapter
0067  24 01                  and     AL,1              ; and check if in vertical retrace.
0069  75 FB                  jnz     waitnon           ; it is on - so loop
006B                 waiton:
006B  EC                     in      AL,DX             ; Check status
006C  24 01                  and     AL,1              ; for retrace bit
006E  74 FB                  jz      waiton            ; Wait for it to reappear

0070  26: 89 0F              mov     ES:[BX],CX        ; return to vid buffer
0073  59                     pop     CX                ; restore our work register

0074  83 C5 02               add     BP,2              ; Step to next value
0077  2E: 03 5E 00           add     BX,CS:[BP]        ; for Y.
007B  FE CD                  dec     CH                ; count how many rows
007D  75 D0                  jnz     nexty             ; if not done, do another
007F  07                     pop     ES
0080  58                     pop     AX                ; Restore the entry registers
0081  5B                     pop     BX
0082  59                     pop     CX
0083  5A                     pop     DX
0084  5D                     pop     BP
0085  5E                     pop     SI
0086  5F                     pop     DI
```

```
0087  F8                            clc                       ; indicate no error
0088  C3                            ret                       ; and return.
                           ;
                           ; Stepping values for the 14 rows
0089  90                            EVEN
008A  0005[                stepyv   dw     5 dup(-24486,8192,8192,8192)
          A05A
          2000
          2000
          2000
                   ]

                           ;
                                    EVEN                      ; Get word alignment
                                    INCLUDE grafont0.asm      ; Bring the font in
                         C ;
                         C ; Here begins the character font definition table.
                         C ; Only a selected sampling is shown, to illustrate the technique.
                         C ; Set to 1 those bits corresponding to the pixels you want lighted
                         C ; within the 9 x 14 character cell.
                         C ;
00B2  0000               C font     dw     000000000b         ; First line of each cell
00B4  0000               C          dw     000000000b         ; is normally zero.
00B6  0000               C          dw     000000000b         ; First char is ASCII 0 (NUL).
00B8  0000               C          dw     000000000b         ;
00BA  0000               C          dw     000000000b         ;
00BC  0000               C          dw     000000000b         ;
00BE  0000               C          dw     000000000b         ;
00C0  0000               C          dw     000000000b         ;
00C2  0000               C          dw     000000000b         ;
00C4  0000               C          dw     000000000b         ;
00C6  0000               C          dw     000000000b         ;
00C8  0000               C          dw     000000000b         ;
00CA  0000               C          dw     000000000b         ;
00CC  0000               C          dw     000000000b         ;
                         C ;
00CE  0000               C          dw     000000000b         ; The character ☺ (01h)
00D0  0000               C          dw     000000000b         ;
00D2  0000               C          dw     000000000b         ;
00D4  007C               C          dw     001111100b         ;
00D6  0082               C          dw     010000010b         ;
00D8  0082               C          dw     010000010b         ;
00DA  00AA               C          dw     010101010b         ;
00DC  0092               C          dw     010010010b         ;
00DE  0082               C          dw     010000010b         ;
00E0  007C               C          dw     001111100b         ;
00E2  0000               C          dw     000000000b         ;
00E4  0000               C          dw     000000000b         ;
00E6  0000               C          dw     000000000b         ;
00E8  0000               C          dw     000000000b         ;
                         C ;
00EA  0000               C          dw     000000000b         ; The character ● (02h)
00EC  0000               C          dw     000000000b         ;
00EE  0000               C          dw     000000000b         ;
00F0  007C               C          dw     001111100b         ;
00F2  00FE               C          dw     011111110b         ;
00F4  00FE               C          dw     011111110b         ;
00F6  00FE               C          dw     011111110b         ;
00F8  00D6               C          dw     011010110b         ;
00FA  00EE               C          dw     011101110b         ;
00FC  007C               C          dw     001111100b         ;
00FE  0000               C          dw     000000000b         ;
```

```
0100  0000          C                dw      000000000b      ;
0102  0000          C                dw      000000000b      ;
0104  0000          C                dw      000000000b      ;
                    C  ;
0106  0000          C                dw      000000000b      ; The character ♥ (03h)
0108  0000          C                dw      000000000b      ;
010A  0000          C                dw      000000000b      ;
010C  006C          C                dw      001101100b      ;
010E  00FE          C                dw      011111110b      ;
0110  00FE          C                dw      011111110b      ;
0112  007C          C                dw      001111100b      ;
0114  0038          C                dw      000111000b      ;
0116  0010          C                dw      000010000b      ;
0118  0000          C                dw      000000000b      ;
011A  0000          C                dw      000000000b      ;
011C  0000          C                dw      000000000b      ;
011E  0000          C                dw      000000000b      ;
0120  0000          C                dw      000000000b      ;

                                            .
                                            .
                                            .
                    C  ; Beginning of standard set of printable characters
                    C  ;
0432  0000          C                dw      000000000b      ; The space character (20h)
0434  0000          C                dw      000000000b      ;
0436  0000          C                dw      000000000b      ;
0438  0000          C                dw      000000000b      ;
043A  0000          C                dw      000000000b      ;
043C  0000          C                dw      000000000b      ;
043E  0000          C                dw      000000000b      ;
0440  0000          C                dw      000000000b      ;
0442  0000          C                dw      000000000b      ;
0444  0000          C                dw      000000000b      ;
0446  0000          C                dw      000000000b      ;
0448  0000          C                dw      000000000b      ;
044A  0000          C                dw      000000000b      ;
044C  0000          C                dw      000000000b      ;
                    C  ;
044E  0000          C                dw      000000000b      ; The character ! (21h)
0450  0018          C                dw      000011000b      ;
0452  003C          C                dw      000111100b      ;
0454  003C          C                dw      000111100b      ;
0456  003C          C                dw      000111100b      ;
0458  003C          C                dw      000111100b      ;
045A  0018          C                dw      000011000b      ;
045C  0000          C                dw      000000000b      ;
045E  0018          C                dw      000011000b      ;
0460  0018          C                dw      000011000b      ;
0462  0000          C                dw      000000000b      ;
0464  0000          C                dw      000000000b      ;
0466  0000          C                dw      000000000b      ;
0468  0000          C                dw      000000000b      ;

                                            .
                                            .
                                            .
                    C  ; Beginning of numeric characters 0-9
                    C  ;
05F2  0000          C                dw      000000000b      ; The character 0 (30h)
05F4  007C          C                dw      001111100b      ;
05F6  0082          C                dw      010000010b      ;
05F8  0086          C                dw      010000110b      ;
```

```
05FA  008A        C              dw      010001010b        ;
05FC  0092        C              dw      010010010b        ;
05FE  00A2        C              dw      010100010b        ;
0600  00C2        C              dw      011000010b        ;
0602  0082        C              dw      010000010b        ;
0604  007C        C              dw      001111100b        ;
0606  0000        C              dw      000000000b        ;
0608  0000        C              dw      000000000b        ;
060A  0000        C              dw      000000000b        ;
060C  0000        C              dw      000000000b        ;
                  C  ;
060E  0000        C              dw      000000000b        ; The character 1 (31h)
0610  0010        C              dw      000010000b        ;
0612  0030        C              dw      000110000b        ;
0614  0050        C              dw      001010000b        ;
0616  0010        C              dw      000010000b        ;
0618  0010        C              dw      000010000b        ;
061A  0010        C              dw      000010000b        ;
061C  0010        C              dw      000010000b        ;
061E  0010        C              dw      000010000b        ;
0620  007C        C              dw      001111100b        ;
0622  0000        C              dw      000000000b        ;
0624  0000        C              dw      000000000b        ;
0626  0000        C              dw      000000000b        ;
0628  0000        C              dw      000000000b        ;
                                      .
                                      .
                                      .
                  C  ; Beginning of uppercase alphabetic characters
                  C  ;
07CE  0000        C              dw      000000000b        ; The character A (41h)
07D0  0000        C              dw      000000000b        ;
07D2  0010        C              dw      000010000b        ;
07D4  0028        C              dw      000101000b        ;
07D6  0044        C              dw      001000100b        ;
07D8  0082        C              dw      010000010b        ;
07DA  0082        C              dw      010000010b        ;
07DC  00FE        C              dw      011111110b        ;
07DE  0082        C              dw      010000010b        ;
07E0  0082        C              dw      010000010b        ;
07E2  0082        C              dw      010000010b        ;
07E4  0000        C              dw      000000000b        ;
07E6  0000        C              dw      000000000b        ;
07E8  0000        C              dw      000000000b        ;
                  C  ;
07EA  0000        C              dw      000000000b        ; The character B (42h)
07EC  0000        C              dw      000000000b        ;
07EE  00FC        C              dw      011111100b        ;
07F0  0042        C              dw      001000010b        ;
07F2  0042        C              dw      001000010b        ;
07F4  0042        C              dw      001000010b        ;
07F6  007C        C              dw      001111100b        ;
07F8  0042        C              dw      001000010b        ;
07FA  0042        C              dw      001000010b        ;
07FC  0042        C              dw      001000010b        ;
07FE  00FC        C              dw      011111100b        ;
0800  0000        C              dw      000000000b        ;
0802  0000        C              dw      000000000b        ;
0804  0000        C              dw      000000000b        ;
                                      .
                                      .
                                      .
```

```
                    C  ; Beginning of lowercase alphabetics
                    C  ;
0B4E   0000         C           dw      000000000b      ; The character a (61h)
0B50   0000         C           dw      000000000b      ;
0B52   0000         C           dw      000000000b      ;
0B54   0000         C           dw      000000000b      ;
0B56   0000         C           dw      000000000b      ;
0B58   0038         C           dw      000111000b      ;
0B5A   0004         C           dw      000000100b      ;
0B5C   003C         C           dw      000111100b      ;
0B5E   0044         C           dw      001000100b      ;
0B60   0044         C           dw      001000100b      ;
0B62   001A         C           dw      000011010b      ;
0B64   0000         C           dw      000000000b      ;
0B66   0000         C           dw      000000000b      ;
0B68   0000         C           dw      000000000b      ;
                    C  ;
0B6A   0000         C           dw      000000000b      ; The character b (62h)
0B6C   0000         C           dw      000000000b      ;
0B6E   0060         C           dw      001100000b      ;
0B70   0020         C           dw      000100000b      ;
0B72   0020         C           dw      000100000b      ;
0B74   0020         C           dw      000100000b      ;
0B76   0030         C           dw      000110000b      ;
0B78   002C         C           dw      000101100b      ;
0B7A   0022         C           dw      000100010b      ;
0B7C   0022         C           dw      000100010b      ;
0B7E   006C         C           dw      001101100b      ;
0B80   0000         C           dw      000000000b      ;
0B82   0000         C           dw      000000000b      ;
0B84   0000         C           dw      000000000b      ;

                                    .
                                    .
                                    .

0DD2   0000         C           dw      000000000b      ; The character x (78h)
0DD4   0000         C           dw      000000000b      ;
0DD6   0000         C           dw      000000000b      ;
0DD8   0000         C           dw      000000000b      ;
0DDA   0000         C           dw      000000000b      ;
0DDC   0042         C           dw      001000010b      ;
0DDE   0024         C           dw      000100100b      ;
0DE0   0018         C           dw      000011000b      ;
0DE2   0018         C           dw      000011000b      ;
0DE4   0024         C           dw      000100100b      ;
0DE6   0042         C           dw      001000010b      ;
0DE8   0000         C           dw      000000000b      ;
0DEA   0000         C           dw      000000000b      ;
0DEC   0000         C           dw      000000000b      ;
                    C  ;
0DEE   0000         C           dw      000000000b      ; The character y (79h)
0DF0   0000         C           dw      000000000b      ;
0DF2   0000         C           dw      000000000b      ;
0DF4   0000         C           dw      000000000b      ;
0DF6   0000         C           dw      000000000b      ;
0DF8   0044         C           dw      001000100b      ;
0DFA   0044         C           dw      001000100b      ;
0DFC   0044         C           dw      001000100b      ;
0DFE   0044         C           dw      001000100b      ;
```

```
0E00  003C        C           dw     000111100b       ;
0E02  0004        C           dw     000000100b       ;
0E04  0008        C           dw     000001000b       ;
0E06  0030        C           dw     000110000b       ;
0E08  0000        C           dw     000000000b       ;
                  C  ;
0E0A  0000        C           dw     000000000b       ; The character z (7Ah)
0E0C  0000        C           dw     000000000b       ;
0E0E  0000        C           dw     000000000b       ;
0E10  0000        C           dw     000000000b       ;
0E12  0000        C           dw     000000000b       ;
0E14  0000        C           dw     000000000b       ;
0E16  007C        C           dw     001111100b       ;
0E18  0044        C           dw     001000100b       ;
0E1A  0008        C           dw     000001000b       ;
0E1C  0010        C           dw     000010000b       ;
0E1E  0024        C           dw     000100100b       ;
0E20  007C        C           dw     001111100b       ;
0E22  0000        C           dw     000000000b       ;
0E24  0000        C           dw     000000000b       ;
                  C  ;
0E26  0000        C           dw     000000000b       ; The character { (7Bh)
0E28  0000        C           dw     000000000b       ;
0E2A  0030        C           dw     000110000b       ;
0E2C  0040        C           dw     001000000b       ;
0E2E  0040        C           dw     001000000b       ;
0E30  0040        C           dw     001000000b       ;
0E32  0080        C           dw     010000000b       ;
0E34  0040        C           dw     001000000b       ;
0E36  0040        C           dw     001000000b       ;
0E38  0040        C           dw     001000000b       ;
0E3A  0030        C           dw     000110000b       ;
0E3C  0000        C           dw     000000000b       ;
0E3E  0000        C           dw     000000000b       ;
0E40  0000        C           dw     000000000b       ;
                  C  ;
0E42  0000        C           dw     000000000b       ; The character | (7Ch)
0E44  0000        C           dw     000000000b       ;
0E46  0010        C           dw     000010000b       ;
0E48  0010        C           dw     000010000b       ;
0E4A  0010        C           dw     000010000b       ;
0E4C  0010        C           dw     000010000b       ;
0E4E  0000        C           dw     000000000b       ;
0E50  0010        C           dw     000010000b       ;
0E52  0010        C           dw     000010000b       ;
0E54  0010        C           dw     000010000b       ;
0E56  0010        C           dw     000010000b       ;
0E58  0000        C           dw     000000000b       ;
0E5A  0000        C           dw     000000000b       ;
0E5C  0000        C           dw     000000000b       ;
                  C  ;
0E5E  0000        C           dw     000000000b       ; The character } (7Dh)
0E60  0000        C           dw     000000000b       ;
0E62  0018        C           dw     000011000b       ;
0E64  0004        C           dw     000000100b       ;
0E66  0004        C           dw     000000100b       ;
0E68  0004        C           dw     000000100b       ;
0E6A  0002        C           dw     000000010b       ;
0E6C  0004        C           dw     000000100b       ;
0E6E  0004        C           dw     000000100b       ;
0E70  0004        C           dw     000000100b       ;
0E72  0018        C           dw     000011000b       ;
```

```
0E74  0000        C          dw     000000000b       ;
0E76  0000        C          dw     000000000b       ;
0E78  0000        C          dw     000000000b       ;
                  C   ;
0E7A  0000        C          dw     000000000b       ; The character ~ (7Eh)
0E7C  0000        C          dw     000000000b       ;
0E7E  0014        C          dw     000010100b       ;
0E80  0028        C          dw     000101000b       ;
0E82  0000        C          dw     000000000b       ;
0E84  0000        C          dw     000000000b       ;
0E86  0000        C          dw     000000000b       ;
0E88  0000        C          dw     000000000b       ;
0E8A  0000        C          dw     000000000b       ;
0E8C  0000        C          dw     000000000b       ;
0E8E  0000        C          dw     000000000b       ;
0E90  0000        C          dw     000000000b       ;
0E92  0000        C          dw     000000000b       ;
0E94  0000        C          dw     000000000b       ;
                  C   ;
0E96  0000        C          dw     000000000b       ; The character ■ (7Fh)
0E98  0000        C          dw     000000000b       ;
0E9A  00FE        C          dw     011111110b       ;
0E9C  00FE        C          dw     011111110b       ;
0E9E  00FE        C          dw     011111110b       ;
0EA0  00FE        C          dw     011111110b       ;
0EA2  00FE        C          dw     011111110b       ;
0EA4  00FE        C          dw     011111110b       ;
0EA6  00FE        C          dw     011111110b       ;
0EA8  00FE        C          dw     011111110b       ;
0EAA  00FE        C          dw     011111110b       ;
0EAC  0000        C          dw     000000000b       ;
0EAE  0000        C          dw     000000000b       ;
0EB0  0000        C          dw     000000000b       ;
                  C

                      ;
0EB2                  Grafchr    ENDP
0EB2                  code       ENDS
                                 END
```

Appendix A

80386 Architecture Overview

The 80386 features multitasking, on-chip memory management, virtual memory with paging, software protection, and large address space. Compatibility with earlier Intel chips (8086 through 80286) is preserved through the instruction set, register handling, and bus sizing. This appendix gives an overview of the 80386 architecture; for more complete information, see *80386: A Programming and Design Handbook*.

The 80386 is designed for applications needing high performance and is optimized for multitasking. The 32-bit registers support 32-bit addresses and data types. Instruction pipelining and on-chip address translation ensure execution at sustained rates of between 3 and 4 million instructions per second (MIPS).

The 80386 consists of six elements: an execution unit, a segment unit, a paging unit, an instruction decode unit, a code prefetch unit, and a bus interface unit (BIU). See Fig. A-1 for a graphic view of the six units of the 80386. The BIU unit provides the interface between the 80386 and its environment, accepting internal requests for code fetches (from the code prefetch unit) and data transfers (from the execution unit). The code prefetch unit implements the program lookahead function of the 80386. When the BIU is not performing bus cycles to execute instructions, the code prefetch unit uses the BIU to fetch sequentially along the instruction byte stream. These prefetched instructions are stored in the 16-byte code queue to wait processing by the instruction decode unit.

The instruction decode unit takes instruction bytes from the prefetch queue and translates them into microcode. The decoded instructions are then stored in

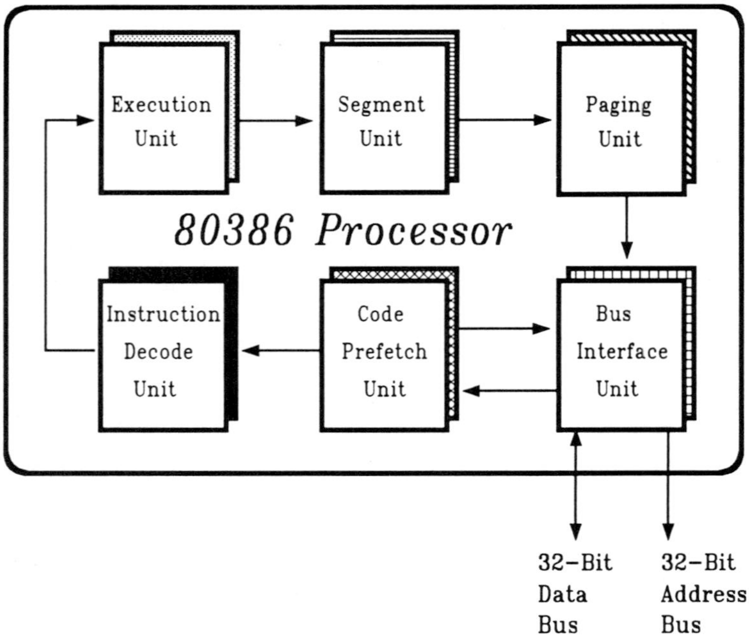

Fig. A-1. Six basic units of the 80386.

a three-deep instruction queue on a first-in first-out basis, to await processing by the execution unit. Immediate data and opcode offsets are taken from the prefetch queue.

Definitions

Listed below are definitions for terms you will need to know for this architecture overview. For other terms, see the glossary.

segment—Beginning with the 8086, Intel introduced the concept of segments, which were defined as units of contiguous (adjacent) address space. In the 8086, this space had a maximum of 64K or 65536 bytes. In the 80386, that limitation no longer applies and programmers can now view segments as one-dimensional subspaces, each with some specified length up to 4 gigabytes.

gates—A gate is a logic design that allows only certain processes to pass through it. The 80386 provides protection for control transfers among executable segments at differing privilege levels by use of gate descriptors. There are four: Call gates, Trap gates, Interrupt gates, and Task gates.

descriptor—A descriptor is a specific data structure used to define the characteristics of a program element. For example, descriptors describe a data record, a segment, or a task.

table—A table is a collection or ordering of data laid out in rows and columns for reference or stored as an array. Elements of a table can be obtained by direct calculation from a known selector or base address.

linear address space—An address indicates the location of a register, a particular place in storage, or some other data source or destination. In the 80386, the memory's linear address space runs from byte 0 to 4 gigabytes. A linear address points to a particular byte within this space. Figure A-2 outlines the linear address translation process.

logical address—First, there is no conceptual parallel from linear address space to the space used by logical addressing. A logical address consists of a selector and offset. The selector points to some segment descriptor (part of which is that segment's linear base address). The offset tells how far into the segment the required byte is. Figure A-3 depicts physical address translation.

physical address—The address which actually selects the memory where a required byte is located. In the 80386, linear and physical addresses differ only when paging is in effect (See Fig. A-4).

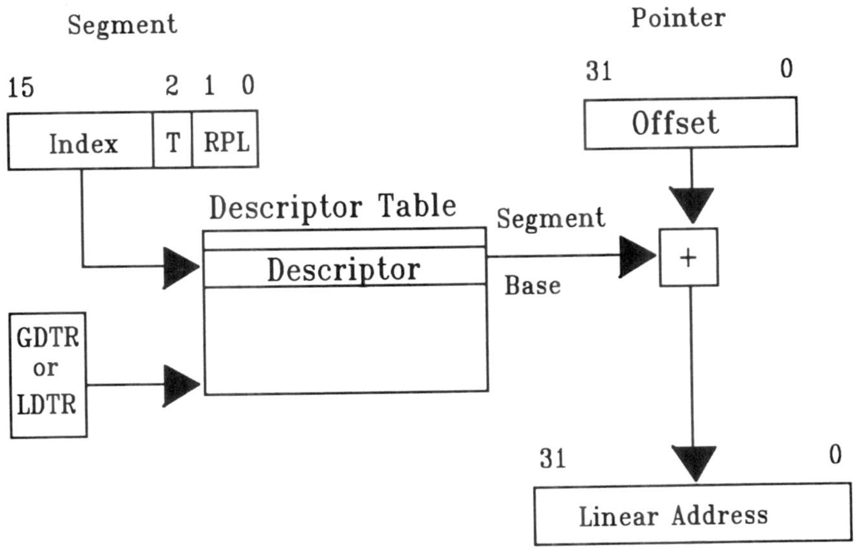

Fig. A-2. Linear address translation.

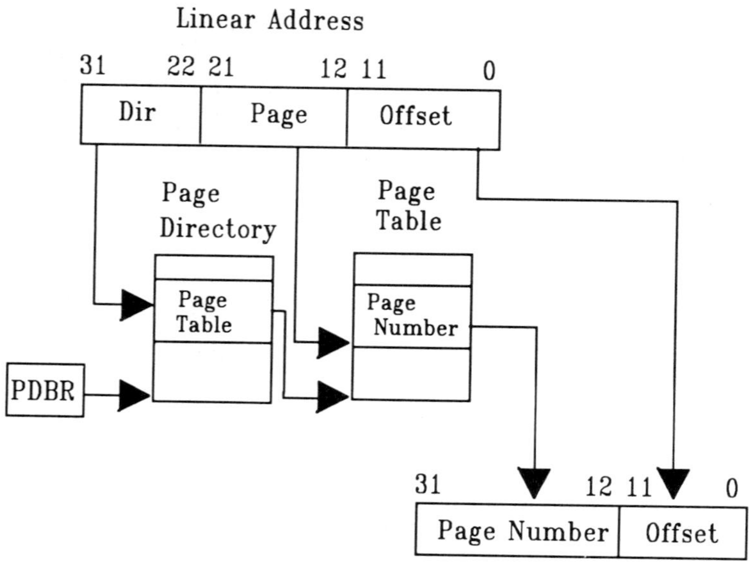

Fig. A-3. Physical address translation.

task—A task is a basic, unique function of a program or system. It can be one instance of the execution of a program. Tasks are also referred to as processes.

Task State Segment (TSS)—A TSS is a data structure delineated and pointed to by a descriptor, wherein the (interrupted) state of a task is stored. Systems software creates the TSSs and places the initial information in them, such as correct stack pointers for interrupt handlers.

microcode—A list of small program steps; also a set of control functions performed by the instruction decoding and executing logic of a computer system. It is code that lies "below" the level of assembly language.

paging—Paging refers to a procedure which transmits the consecutive bytes called a *page* between locations, such as between disk storage and memory. A paging function simplifies the operating system swap-

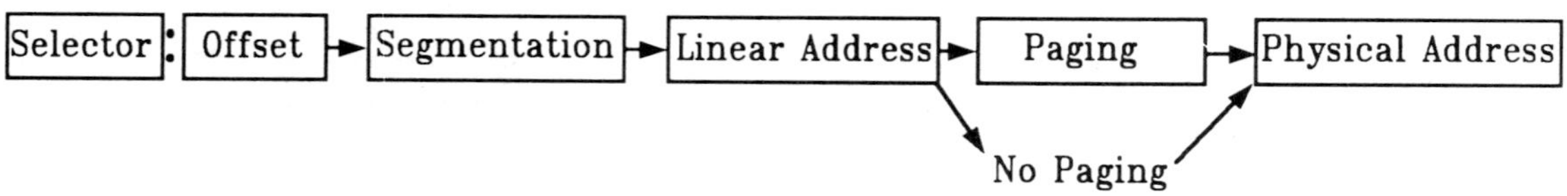

Fig. A-4. Control Register formats. (Zero entries indicate Intel reserved bits; do not define.)

ping algorithms because it provides a uniform mechanism for managing the physical structure of memory.

flag—A flag is an indicator whose state is used to inform a later section of a program that a condition has occurred. The condition is identified with the flag and designated by the state of the flag; that is, the flag is either set or not set.

Real- and Protected-Mode Architecture

The 80386 has two modes of operation: real address mode, called *real mode*, and *protected mode*. Real mode is required primarily to set up the processor for protected-mode operation and to allow execution of software for previous chip generations. Protected mode provides access to the advanced paging, memory management, and privilege capabilities of the 80386. These design features allow object-code compatibility with previous Intel chip generations.

Real Mode

When the processor is reset or powered up, it initializes in real mode. In this mode, the 80386 operates as a very fast 8086, but with 32-bit extensions if the programmer desires. Real mode has the same base architecture as the 8086, but also allows access to the 32-bit register set of the 80386. The 8086 addressing mechanism, memory size, and interrupt handling (and their consequent limitations) are all identical to the real mode on the 80386.

Like protected mode, real mode uses two components to form the logical address. A 16-bit selector is used to determine the linear base address of a segment. The base address is then used as the 32-bit physical address. The difference between the two modes lies in how the base address is calculated.

Relocatability is a property of programs or data such that they may be located in different places in memory at different times without requiring modification to system or application software. Segment relocation is done in the 80386 real mode as it is in the 8086. The 16-bit value in a segment selector is shifted left by four bits (multiplied by 16) to form the 20-bit base address of a segment. The effective address is extended with four high-order zeros (to give a 20-bit value) and added to the base to form a linear address. This linear address is equivalent to the physical address because paging is not used in real-address mode.

Interrupts and exceptions are breaks in the normal flow of a system or routine. Interrupts and exceptions in 80386 real-address mode work exactly as they do on the 8086. (See Chapter 9 for a list of the interrupts recognized by the 80386.) In real mode, the Interrupt Descriptor Table (IDT) is an 8086 real interrupt vector table, starting at real zero and extending through real 1024 (4 bytes per interrupt with 256 possible entries).

The only way to leave real-address mode is to switch explicitly to protected mode. The 80386 enters the protected mode when a MOV to CR0 (Move to Control Register Zero) instruction sets the protection enable (PE) bit in CR0. For compatibility with the 80286, the LMSW (Load Machine Status Word) instruction may also be used to set the PE bit.

The processor reenters real-address mode if software clears the PE bit in CR0 with a MOV to CR0 instruction.

Protected Mode

The complete capabilities of the 80386 are available when it operates in protected mode. Software can perform a task switch to enter tasks designated as virtual 8086 mode tasks. Each such task behaves with 8086 semantics (the relationship between symbols and their intended meanings independent of their interpretation devices). This allows 8086 software—an application program or an entire operating system—to execute on the 80386. At the same time, the virtual 8086 tasks are isolated and protected from one another and from the host 80386 operating system.

In protected mode, the 16-bit selector is used to specify an index into an operating system-defined table that contains the 32-bit base address of a given segment. The physical address is formed by adding the base address obtained from the table to the offset.

In general, programs designed for the 80286 will execute without modification on the 80386. Also, the 80386 supports the descriptors used by the 80286 as long as the Intel-reserved word (the last word) of the 80286 descriptor is zero. See Chapter 3 for additional tips to keep in mind when programming on the 80386.

Registers

The 80386 registers are a superset of the previous 8086, 80186, and 80286 registers. All the previous generations' 8- and 16-bit registers are contained within the 32-bit architecture. Register contents (flags and bits) are shown in Appendix C.

General Registers

The eight general-purpose registers are 32 bits long and hold addresses or data. They support data operands of 1, 8, 16, 32, and 64 bits (which require two registers) and bit fields of 1 to 32 bits, in addition to address operands of 16 and 32 bits. The 32-bit registers are named EAX, EBX, ECX, EDX, ESI, EDI, EBP, and ESP.

The least significant 16 bits of the registers are separately accessible. This is done by using the 16-bit names of the registers: AX, BX, CX, DX, SI, DI, BP, and SP. 8-bit operations can individually access the low byte (bits 0-7) and the high byte (bits 8-15) of the general registers AX, BX, CX, and DX. The low bytes are named AL, BL, CL, and DL, respectively, while the high bytes are named AH,

BH, CH, and DH. Again, this selection is done by using the register names. If one of the 8-bit registers is accessed, the contents of the remaining 24 bits are undisturbed.

Segment Registers

The 80386 architecture includes six directly accessible segment selector registers, which contain values that point to the segments. These selector values can be loaded as a program executes and also are task-specific, which means that the segment registers are automatically reloaded upon a task switch operation. Six 16-bit segment registers hold the segment selector values that identify the currently addressable memory segments. The registers are:

Code Segment (CS) Register. The CS points to the segment which contains the currently executing sequence of instructions. The 80386 fetches all instructions from this segment, using as an offset the contents of the instruction pointer. CS is changed as the result of intersegment control-transfer instructions, interrupts and exceptions. The CS cannot be explicitly loaded. See the programs in this book. Values are loaded into a general register and then the contents of that register can be MOVed to CS.

Stack Segment (SS) Register. Subroutine calls, parameters, and procedure activation records usually require a region of memory that is allocated for a stack. All stack operations use SS to locate that stack. Unlike the CS register, the SS register can be loaded explicitly by program instructions.

Data Segment Registers (DS, ES, FS, GS). The next four registers are data segment registers, each of which is addressable by the currently executing program. Having access to four separate data areas aids program efficiency by allowing them to access different types of data structures. These four registers can be changed under program control.

To use the data segment registers, the 80386 associates a base address with each segment selected. To address a data unit within a segment, a 32-bit offset is added to the segment's base address. Once a segment is selected (by loading the segment selector into a segment register), a data manipulation instruction needs only to specify the offset.

Segmented Memory Management Registers

These registers are also known as *System Address Registers*. Four registers locate the data structures that control segmented memory management. These registers are defined to reference the tables or segments supported by the 80286/80386 protection model.

The addresses of these tables and segments are stored in special System Address and System Segment Registers.

Global Descriptor Table Register (GDTR). The GDTR holds the 32-bit linear base address and the 16-bit limit of the Global Descriptor Table.

Local Descriptor Table Register (LDTR). This register holds the 16-bit selector for the Local Descriptor Table. Since the LDT is a task-specific segment, it's defined by selector values stored in the system segment registers.

Interrupt Descriptor Table Register (IDTR). The IDTR points to a table of entry points for interrupt handlers (the IDT). The register holds the 32-bit linear base address and the 16-bit limit of the Interrupt Descriptor Table.

Task Register (TR). This register points to the information needed by the processor to define the current task. The register holds the 16-bit selector for the Task State Segment descriptor. Since the TSS segment is task-specific, it is defined by selector values stored in the system segment registers. Figure A-7 shows how TR assists in linking TSSs.

Processor Control Registers

Two registers control the operation of the 80386 processor: EFLAGS, the processor status and control flags register, and EIP, the instruction-pointer register.

System Flags Register (EFLAGS). The EFLAGS register controls I/O, maskable interrupts, debugging, task switching, and enabling of virtual 8086 execution in a protected, multitasking environment; it does all this, in addition to providing status flags which represent the result of instruction execution. The low 16 bits (0-15) of EFLAGS contain the 80286 16-bit status or flag register named FLAGS, which is most useful when executing 8086 and 80286 code. See Appendix B for a detailed format of the EFLAGS register.

Instruction Pointer Register (EIP). The Extended Instruction Pointer (EIP) is a 32-bit register. EIP contains the offset address of the next sequential instruction to be executed. This offset is relative to the start (or base address) of the current code segment. The EIP is not directly visible to programmers, but is controlled explicitly by control-transfer instructions, interrupts, and exceptions.

The low-order 16 bits of EIP are named IP and can be used by the processor as a unit. This feature is useful when executing instructions designed for the 8086 and 80286 processors, which only have an IP.

Control Registers

The 80386 has three 32-bit control registers: CR0, CR2, and CR3 (CR1 is reserved by Intel). These hold machine states or global statuses. A global status is one that can be accessed by (or that controls) any of the logical units of the system. Along with the System Address Registers, these registers hold machine state information that affects all tasks in the system. Load and store instructions have been defined to access the control registers. Figure A-5 shows Control Register formats.

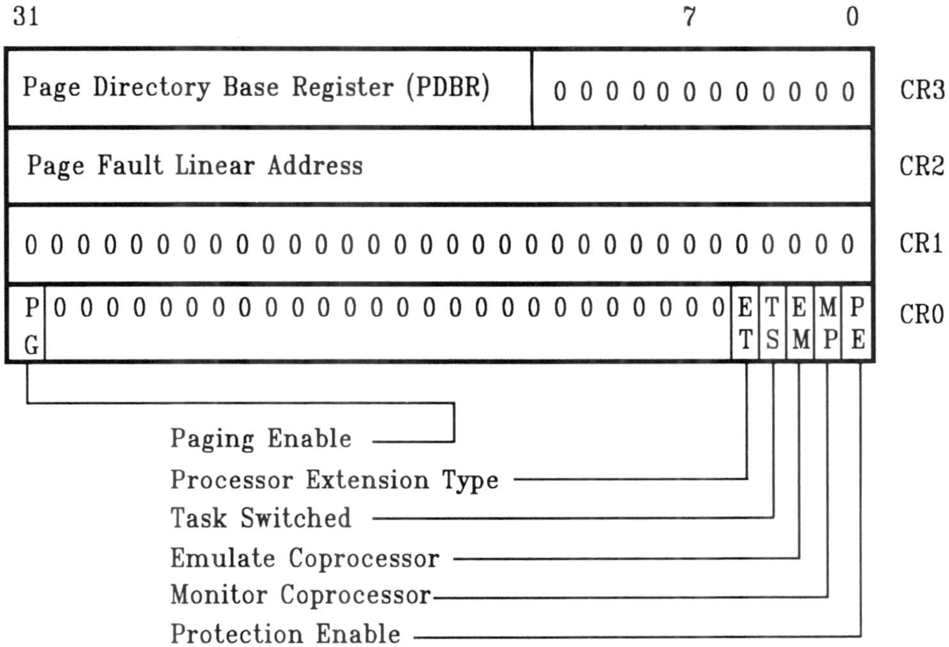

Fig. A-5. Virtual-to-physical address translation.

Control registers are accessible to systems programmers only via variants of the MOV instruction, which allows them to be loaded from or stored in general registers.

CR0. This register contains flags which control or indicate conditions that apply to the system as a whole, not to an individual task. The low-order 15 bits of this register is the Machine Status Word (MSW), bits 0-15, for compatibility with 80286 protected mode.

CR1. As noted earlier, this register is reserved for future Intel processors.

CR2. The CR2 register is used for handling page faults when the PG bit in CR0 is set. The 80386 stores in CR2 the linear address that triggers the fault. The error code pushed onto the page fault handler's stack when it is invoked provides additional status information on this page fault.

CR3. This register is used when PG (Paging) is set in CR0. CR3 enables the processor to locate the page table directory for the current task. This register contains the physical base address of the page directory table. The 80386 page directory table is always page-aligned (4 Kbyte-aligned). The lowest 12 bits of CR3 are ignored when written and they store as undefined. A task switch through a TSS that changes the value in CR3 (or as an explicit load to CR3) invalidates all cached page table entries in the paging unit cache. Note that if the value in CR3 does not change during the task switch, the cached page table entries are not flushed.

Debug Registers

A breakpoint allows you to set a specific condition at a particular linear address that causes program execution to jump into the exception handler. The 80386 supports four simultaneous breakpoint conditions, which allows you to set up to four locations in a program for which the 80386 will jump to the exception handler. To support the four breakpoints, additional registers are added to the 80386. These registers can only be read or written at privilege level 0; any attempted access at other levels raises an invalid opcode exception.

These six programmer-accessible debug registers (DR0–DR3 and DR6–DR7) bring advanced debugging abilities to the 80386, including data breakpoints and the ability to set instruction breakpoints without modifying code segments. Debug Registers DR0–DR3 specify the four linear breakpoints. DR4 and DR5 are reserved by Intel for future development. DR6 displays the current state of the breakpoints. DR7 is used to set the breakpoints.

Test Registers

Two test registers are used to control the testing of the RAM/CAM (Content Addressable Memories) in the translation lookaside buffer (TLB), the cache used for storing information from page tables. TR6 is the command test register and TR7 is the data register which contains the data of the TLB test. (TR0 through TR5 do not exist.) See Appendix B for a detailed format of the test registers.

These registers are accessed by variants of the MOV instruction, which is defined in both real-address mode and protected mode. In the protected mode, the MOV instruction that accesses them can be executed only at privilege level 0. Any attempt to read from or write to either of the test registers when executing in any other privilege level causes a general protection exception.

Translation Lookaside Buffer (TLB)

The Translation Lookaside Buffer (TLB) is a cache used for translating linear addresses to physical addresses. *Warning:* The TLB testing mechanism is unique to the 80386 and may not be continued in the same way in future processors. Software that uses this mechanism as it currently is may be incompatible with future processors.

The TLB is a four-way, set-associative memory. A set is a collection of elements that have some feature in common or which bear a certain relation to one another. In the TLB, there are:

- ☐ Content-addressable Memory (CAM). CAM holds 32 linear addresses and associated tag bits, which are used for data protection and cache implementation.

- ☐ Random Access Memory (RAM). RAM holds the upper 20 bits of the 32 physical addresses that correspond to the linear addresses in the CAM.
- ☐ Logic implements the four-way cache and includes a 2-bit replacement pointer that decides which of the four sets into which a new entry is directed during a write to the TLB.

Addresses and commands are written to the TLB through the command register, while data is read from or written to the TLB through the data register. Test Register Six (TR6) is the command register for TLB accesses while Test Register Seven (TR7) is used as the data register.

Segmentation

Segmentation organizes virtual memory as a collection of variable-sized units, called *segments*. The 80386 supports a wide range of segmentation strategies; each uses a two-part virtual address: a segment part and an offset part. Segments form the basis of the virtual-to-linear address translation mechanism. Each segment is defined by three parameters, two of which relate virtual addresses given by offsets within the segment to linear addresses. Those three parameters are:

base address—This is the starting address of the segment in the linear address space. The base address is the linear address corresponding to the virtual address at offset 0 within the segment.

limit—This is the largest offset that can be used with the segment in a virtual address and defines the size of the segment.

attributes—These indicate segment characteristics such as whether the segment can be read from, written to, or executed as a program, the privilege level of the segment, and so on.

Address space comes as one or more segments, any size from 1 byte to 4 gigabytes (four billion bytes). Each segment can be protected individually by privilege levels and selectively shared between tasks.

Segment Descriptor Tables

The *Global Descriptor Table* (GDT) and the *Local Descriptor Table* (LDT) are special segments that contain the segment descriptor tables. The hardware maintains the descriptor tables and references them by memory-management mechanisms. These segments should be stored in protected memory accessible only by operating system software, to prevent application software from modifying the address translation information.

The virtual address space divides into two equal halves, one half mapped by the GDT and the other half by the LDT. The total virtual address space consists of 2^{14} segments. A segment descriptor is located by indicating a descriptor table (either the GDT or the LDT) along with a descriptor number within the indicated table.

Segment Selectors

Segment selectors identify a segment and can be thought of as the name of the segment. A selector is a 16-bit pointer that, when loaded into a register or used with certain instructions, selects certain descriptors. That is, a selector names a segment by locating the descriptor for the segment. In a logical address, the selector portion identifies an individual descriptor by first specifying the descriptor table and then indexing to the descriptor within that table.

Segment Descriptors

Descriptors are those objects to which the segment selector point. They are 8-byte quantities which contain attributes about a given linear address space (that is, about a segment). These attributes include the segment 32-bit base linear address; the segment's 30-bit length and granularity, the protection level; read, write, or execute privileges; the default size of the operands (16- or 32-bit); and the type of segment.

All descriptor attribute information is contained in 12 bits of the segment descriptor. All segments on the 80386 have three attribute fields in common: the *P* (Present) bit, the *DPL* (Descriptor Privilege Level) bits, and the *S* (Segment Descriptor) bit.

Segment descriptors are stored in either a Global Descriptor Table (GDT) or Local Descriptor Table (LDT). These descriptor tables are stored in special segments maintained by the operating system and referenced by memory management hardware. The 80386 locates the GDT and the current LDT in protected memory by means of the GDTR and LDTR registers.

A segment descriptor provides the 80386 with the data it needs to map a logical address into a linear address. These descriptors are not created by programs, but by compilers, linkers, loaders, or the operating system.

Interrupts and Exceptions

Both hardware- and software-generated interrupts alter the programmed execution of the 80386. (A description of the 80386 interrupts is given in Chapter 5.) A hardware-generated interrupt occurs in response to an active input on one of two 80386 interrupt inputs: NMI, which is non-maskable, or INTR, which is maskable.

The NMI input signals a catastrophic event such as an imminent power loss, a memory error, or a bus parity error. The NMI causes the 80386 to execute the service routine that corresponds to location 2 in the IDT. The processor does not service subsequent NMI requests until the current one has been serviced.

Entry point descriptors to the service routines or the interrupt tasks are stored in memory in the Interrupt Descriptor Table (IDT). The IDT associates each interrupt or exception identifier with a descriptor for the instructions that service the associated event. The IDT is an array of 8-byte descriptors and can hold up to 256 identifiers. To locate the correct descriptor, the processor multiplies the identifier by eight.

Exceptions are classified as faults, aborts, or traps, depending on the way they are reported and also whether restart of the instruction that caused the exception is supported. Aborts are used to report severe errors such as illegal, inconsistent values in system tables, or hardware errors. An abort allows neither the restart of the program that caused the exception nor the identification of the precise location of the instruction causing the exception. Faults are exceptions that are either detected before the instruction begins to execute or during execution. A trap is reported at the instruction boundary immediately after the instruction in which the exception was detected.

Memory Organization

Segmentation is the division of memory into logical blocks for use by a computer. In the 80386, memory is organized into one or more variable-length segments, from one byte up to four gigabytes in size. Every task in the 80386 can have up to 16,381 segments (each up to 4 gigabytes in length), which provides 64 terabytes of virtual memory. Any given location of the linear address space (a segment of the physical memory) has several attributes associated with it: size, location, type (stack, code, or data), and protection characteristics.

80386 physical memory organizes into a sequence of 8-bit bytes. Each byte has a unique address that ranges from zero to $2^{32} - 1$, or 4 gigabytes. The three distinct address spaces are: physical, logical, and linear.

Physical addresses are the actual addresses used to select the physical memory chips which contain the data. A logical address consists of a segment selector and an offset into that segment. A linear address is the address formed by adding the offset to the base address of the segment.

Paging

Paging is a type of memory management useful in multitasking operating systems. Paging operates "underneath" segmentation to complete the virtual-to-physical address translation process. Segmentation translates virtual addresses to linear address. Paging translates the linear address put out by segmentation to physical addresses.

In the 80386, paging operates only in protected mode and provides a means of managing the very large segments that the 80386 supports. Paging divides programs into uniformly sized pages—unlike segmentation, which modularizes programs and data into variable-length segments. In a real sense, paging operates beneath segmentation; that is, the paging mechanism translates the protected linear address, which comes from the segmentation unit, into a physical address.

The paging mechanism is enabled by the PG bit in CR0. IF PG = 1, paging is enabled and linear addresses are translated to physical addresses. If PG = 0, paging is disabled and the linear addresses generated by the segmentation mechanism are used directly as physical addresses (see Fig. A-4).

The paging translation function is described by a memory-resident table called the *page table*. This page table is stored in the physical address space and can be thought of as a simple array of 2^{30} physical addresses. The linear-to-physical mapping function is simply an array lookup. Each page table entry is 32 bits in size.

80386 Cache Memory

Cache memory is a mechanism interposed in the memory hierarchy between main memory and the processor to improve effective memory transfer rates and to raise processor speeds. The cache anticipates the likely use of the CPU of data in main storage by organizing a copy of it in cache memory. The cache also includes data in adjacent blocks to the actual data needed; it is likely that the adjacent data will be requested next. This principle is called *locality of reference*.

The 80386 prototype cache is a 64K, direct-mapped cache, organized as 16,384 entries. Each entry contains 32 bits of data along with 16 bits of tag information. The line size (the unit of transfer) between the cache and Dynamic Random Access Memory (DRAM) is 32 bits. Together, the tag and index fields uniquely identify a doubleword location in main memory.

Privilege and Protection

The concept of privilege is central to the 80386. As applied to procedures, privilege is the degree to which the procedure can be "trusted" not to make a mistake that might affect other procedures or data. Applied to data, privilege is the degree of protection that a data structure should have from less trusted procedures. Privilege is implemented by assigning a value (from zero to three) to key objects which are recognized by the processor. This value is called the *privilege level*. The value zero is the greatest privilege, while the value three is the least privileged.

There are two broad classes of protection supported by the 80386. The first is the ability to separate tasks completely by giving each task a different virtual address space; this is accomplished by giving each task a different virtual-to-physical address translation map. The other protection mechanism operates within a task to protect operating system memory segments and special processor registers from access by application programs. The key items the processor recognizes are:

Descriptor Privilege Level (DPL). Descriptors contain a field called the DPL. This is the least privilege that a task must have to access the descriptor.

Requester's Privilege Level (RPL). The RPL represents the privilege level requested by the procedure that originate a selector.

Current Privilege Level (CPL). The CPL is equal to the segment DPL of the code segment which the processor is currently executing. CPL changes when control transfers to segments with differing DPLs.

Multitasking

To switch tasks efficiently, the 80386 uses special high-speed hardware. Only a single instruction or interrupt keys the processor to do a switch. Running at 16 MHz, the 80386 can save the state of one task (all registers), load the state of another task, and resume execution in less than 16 microseconds. The 80386 uses no special instructions to control multitasking. Instead, it interprets ordinary control-transfer instructions when they refer to the special data structures.

Task State Segment (TSS)

A TSS is a data structure (a special segment) that holds the state of a task's virtual processor. The TSS for the active task is addressed by the TR register. The 80386 schedules and executes tasks based on a priority set by the operating system. To switch tasks, the operating system issues a Jump (JMP) or Call (CALL) instruction whose operand is a selector for the TSS or the task gate of the new task. Figure A-6 shows the Task State Segment (TSS).

To resume execution of the old task, the operating system issues a JMP instruction to the old task's TSS. The privilege level at which execution restarts in the incoming task is not restricted by the privilege level of the outgoing task. The tasks are isolated by their separate address spaces and TSSs and privilege access rules are used to prevent improper access to a TSS.

The TSS link field is at offset 0 in the TSS and it is a 32-bit field with a selector in the low-order 16 bits. This link field is used in conjunction with the NT bit in the EFLAGS register to link the TSSs for task suspended by CALL instructions or interrupts. Figure A-7 shows how TSSs are linked.

Also in the TSS is an I/O Permission Bitmap which defines what addresses in the 64K I/O space can be accessed by programs executing at any privilege level. A 64K bit string is stored in the current TSS, each bit corresponding to a single,

<table>
<tr><th>31 23 16</th><th>15 7 0</th><th></th></tr>
<tr><td>I/O Permission Bitmap Base</td><td>0 0 0 0 0 0 0 0 0 0 0 0 0 0 0 | T</td><td>64</td></tr>
<tr><td>0 0 0 0 0 0 0 0 0 0 0 0 0 0 0 0</td><td>Local Descriptor Table (LDT)</td><td></td></tr>
<tr><td>0 0 0 0 0 0 0 0 0 0 0 0 0 0 0 0</td><td>GS</td><td></td></tr>
<tr><td>0 0 0 0 0 0 0 0 0 0 0 0 0 0 0 0</td><td>FS</td><td></td></tr>
<tr><td>0 0 0 0 0 0 0 0 0 0 0 0 0 0 0 0</td><td>DS</td><td></td></tr>
<tr><td>0 0 0 0 0 0 0 0 0 0 0 0 0 0 0 0</td><td>SS</td><td></td></tr>
<tr><td>0 0 0 0 0 0 0 0 0 0 0 0 0 0 0 0</td><td>CS</td><td></td></tr>
<tr><td>0 0 0 0 0 0 0 0 0 0 0 0 0 0 0 0</td><td>ES</td><td>48</td></tr>
<tr><td colspan="2">EDI</td><td></td></tr>
<tr><td colspan="2">ESI</td><td></td></tr>
<tr><td colspan="2">EBP</td><td></td></tr>
<tr><td colspan="2">ESP</td><td></td></tr>
<tr><td colspan="2">EBX</td><td></td></tr>
<tr><td colspan="2">EDX</td><td></td></tr>
<tr><td colspan="2">ECX</td><td>2C</td></tr>
<tr><td colspan="2">EAX</td><td></td></tr>
<tr><td colspan="2">EFLAGS</td><td></td></tr>
<tr><td colspan="2">EIP</td><td></td></tr>
<tr><td colspan="2">CR3 (PDBR)</td><td></td></tr>
<tr><td>0 0 0 0 0 0 0 0 0 0 0 0 0 0 0 0</td><td>SS2</td><td>18</td></tr>
<tr><td colspan="2">ESP2</td><td></td></tr>
<tr><td>0 0 0 0 0 0 0 0 0 0 0 0 0 0 0 0</td><td>SS1</td><td></td></tr>
<tr><td colspan="2">ESP1</td><td>0C</td></tr>
<tr><td>0 0 0 0 0 0 0 0 0 0 0 0 0 0 0 0</td><td>SS0</td><td></td></tr>
<tr><td colspan="2">ESP0</td><td></td></tr>
<tr><td>0 0 0 0 0 0 0 0 0 0 0 0 0 0 0 0</td><td>Back Link to Previous TSS</td><td>0</td></tr>
</table>

Fig. A-6. Task State Segment (TSS). (Zero entries indicate Intel reserved bits; do not define.)

byte-wide I/O address. Bit 0 corresponds to I/O address 0, bit 1 to I/O address 1, and so on. A zero stored in the bitmap indicates that the corresponding I/O address is accessible to programs at any privilege level. A 1 indicates that the I/O address is only accessible to programs at IOPL, or an inner level. An exception is raised if a program attempts to access an I/O address corresponding to a 1 in the bitmap while executing at an outer level relative to IOPL.

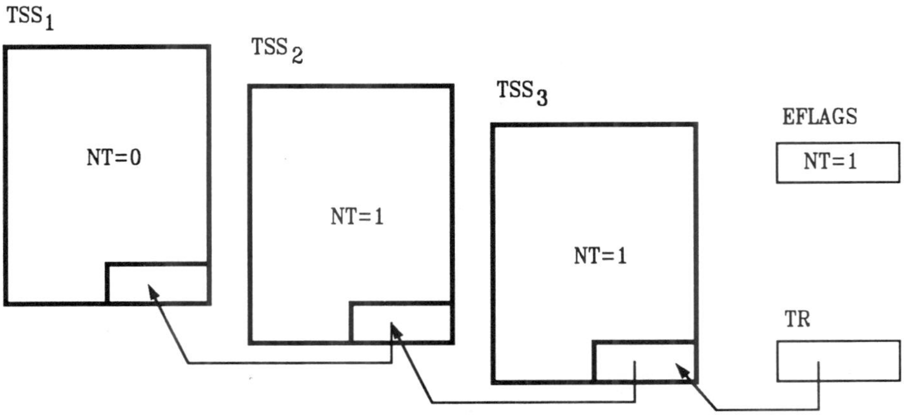

Fig. A-7. Linked TSS's.

The T bit in the TSS causes the debug handler to be invoked whenever a task switch through this TSS occurs. This provides a convenient way for the debugger to monitor the activities of certain tasks. The BT bit of DR6 notes that this condition was detected. There is no specific enable bit for this condition in DR7.

Bus Interfacing

The 80386 features 32-bit wide internal and external data paths and eight general-purpose 32-bit registers. The processor communicates with external memory, I/O, and other devices through a parallel bus interface. This interface consists of a bidirectional data bus, a separate address bus, five bus status pins, and three bus control pins.

The 80386 uses a double-frequency clock (CLK2) that generates the 80386's internal processor clock signal (CLK). This internal clock matches the external Clock Generator (82384) CLK.

Each bus cycle is made up of at least two states. Each of the states in turn is comprised of two CLK2 cycles. The maximum data transfer rate for a bus operation is determined by the 80386 internal clock, and is 32 bits for every two CLK cycles. That works out to 32 megabytes per second, when CLK2 = 32 MHz and the internal CLK = 16 MHz.

The 80386 offers both pipelined and nonpipelined bus cycles. When pipelining is selected, the 80386 overlaps bus cycles which allows longer access times. Since cache memory can be accessed without wait states, nonpipelined cycles are often preferred. Using nonpipelined cycles minimizes latency between the processor requesting information from the outside world and data becoming available at the 80386 pins.

Appendix B

80386 Registers, Flags, and Bits

The register set available to programmers consists of eight 32-bit general purpose registers (EAX, EBX, ECX, EDX, ESP, EBP, ESI, and EDI); 32-bit status registers (EIP and EFLAGS); 16-bit segment pointer registers (ES, CS, SS, DS, FS, and GS); 32-bit test registers (TR6 and TR7); and the 32-bit debug registers (DR0, DR1, DR2, DR3, DR6 and DR7). Not discussed below are the general registers (whose contents depend on program need) and the EIP (since the contents of an instruction pointer depend on the location of the next line of code).

The first section of this appendix shows the location of the flags in the various registers which contain flags and bits that control your use of the 80386. The second section alphabetically lists the 80386 registers. The third section gives an alphabetical list of all flags used in and with the 80386. In the following descriptions, the term "set" means "set to 1," and "reset" means "clear to zero."

System Flags Register (EFLAGS)

The 32-bit EFLAGS register contains status flag and control flag bits. Your program sets the control bits to control the operation of certain functions of the 80386. The 80386 sets the status bits, which are then tested by the program after arithmetic operations to check for special conditions. Bits 31 through 18, 15, 5, 3 and 1 are Intel reserved.

VM (Virtual 8086 Mode) Bit 17. The VM bit provides Virtual 8086 Mode within the protected mode. If set while the processor is in protected mode, the 80386

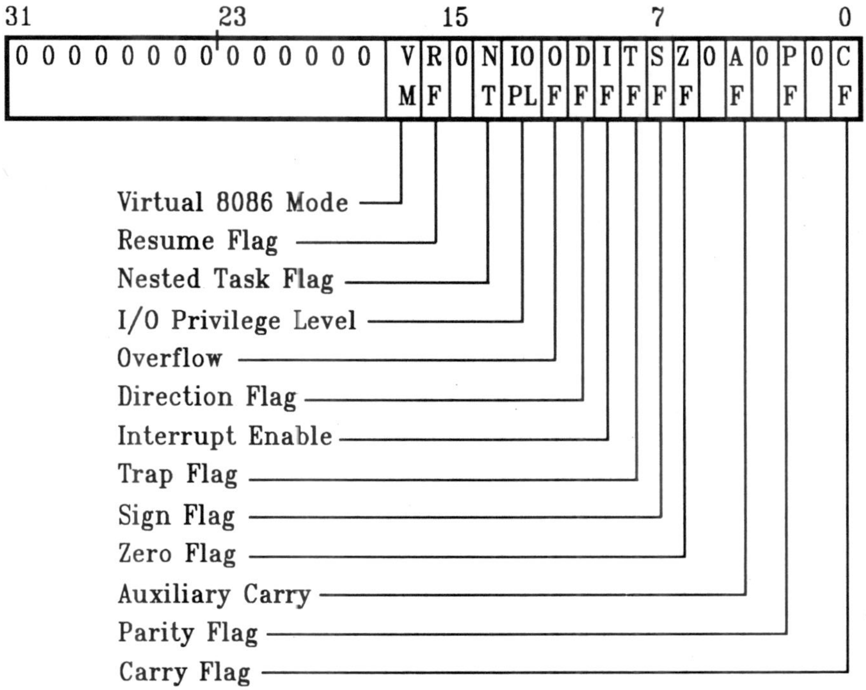

Fig. B-1. EFLAGS register. (Zero entries indicate Intel reserved bits; do not define.)

switches to Virtual 8086 operation. The VM flag can be set *only* two ways: in protected mode by the IRET instruction and only if Current Privilege Level is zero; and by task switches at any privilege level.

RF (Resume Flag) Bit 16. This flag temporarily disables debug exceptions (breaks to normal program flow) so that an instruction can be restarted after a debug exception without immediately causing another debug exception.

NT (Nested Task) Bit 14. The 80386 uses this flag to control chaining of interrupted and CALLed tasks. A CALL transfers the program execution sequence on a temporary basis to a subroutine or subprogram. On termination of that subroutine, execution is resumed at the instruction following the CALL. NT influences the operation of the IRET instruction.

IOPL (Input/Output Privilege Level) Bits 13-12. This two-bit field applies to protected mode. IOPL shows the highest current privilege level (CPL) value permitted to execute I/O instructions without generating an exception 13 fault or consulting the I/O Permission Bitmap. It also shows the highest CPL value that allows change of the IF (INTR Enable Flag) bit when new values are popped into the EFLAGS register.

OF (Overflow Flag) Bit 11. OF is set if the operation resulted in carry/borrow into the sign bit (high-order bit) of the result but did not result in a carry/borrow out of the high-order bit, or vice versa.

DF (Direction Flag) Bit 10. DF defines whether the ESI and/or EDI registers are to decrement or increment during string operations. If DF = 0, the registers increment; if DF = 1, they decrement.

IF (Interrupt-Enable) Bit 9. Setting IF allows the CPU to recognize external (maskable) interrupt requests. Clearing this bit disables these interrupts. IF has no effect on either non-maskable external interrupts or exceptions.

TF (Trap Flag) Bit 8. Setting TF puts the processor into single-step mode for debugging. The CPU automatically generates an Exception 1 after each instruction, which allows a program to be inspected as it executes each instruction. When TF is reset, Exception 1 traps occur only as a function of the breakpoint addresses loaded into debug registers DR0–DR3. Further information is given in an upcoming discussion of the debug registers.

SF (Sign Flag) Bit 7. SF is set if the high-order bit of the result is set; otherwise it is reset. For 8-, 16-, and 32-bit operations, SF reflects the state of bit 7, 15, and 31, respectively.

ZF (Zero Flag) Bit 6. ZF is set if all bits of the result are 0. Otherwise, it is reset.

AF (Auxiliary Carry Flag) Bit 4. This flag is used to simplify the addition and subtraction of packed BCD quantities. Regardless of the operand length (8, 16, or 32 bits), AF is set if the operation resulted in a borrow into bit 3 (which is a subtraction) or a carry out of bit 3 (which is an addition). Otherwise, AF is reset. Remember that BCD uses bits 0 through 3 to represent decimal digits.

PF (Parity Flag) Bit 2. PF is set if the low-order eight bits of the operation contains an even number of "1's" (even parity). PF is reset if the low-order eight bits have odd parity. PF is a function of only the low-order bits, regardless of operand size.

CF (Carry Flag) Bit 0. CF is set if the operation resulted in a carry out of the high-order bit (an addition), or a borrow into the high-order bit (a subtraction). Otherwise CF is reset. For 8-, 16-, or 32-bit operations, CF is set according to the carry/borrow at bit 7, 15, or 31, respectively.

Control Register Flags

There are four 32-bit control registers: CR0, CR1, CR2 and CR3. CR1 is reserved for future processors and is undefined for the 80386. If you use an instruction that codes CR1 as the register, you'll get an invalid opcode exception. These control registers can be loaded and stored only by programs executing at privilege level 0, by using special forms of the MOV instructions.

Control Register CR0

CR0 contains bits that enable and disable paging and protection, and bits that control the operation of the floating-point coprocessor. Bits 30 through 5 are re-

Fig. B-2. Processor modes with PG and PE.

PG	PE	Execution Mode
0	0	Real mode
0	1	Protected mode, paging disabled
1	0	Illegal combination, do not use
1	1	Protected mode, paging enabled

served and must be loaded with zeros. The PE bit (bit 0) and the PG bit (bit 31) control the operation of the segmentation and paging mechanisms. Figure B-2 shows processor modes with PG and PE, and Fig. B-3 shows control register formats.

PG (Paging) Bit 31. PG indicates whether the 80386 uses page tables to translate linear addresses into physical addresses. If PG = 1, paging is enabled; if PG = 0, paging is disabled and the linear addresses produced by the segmentation mechanism are passed through as physical addresses.

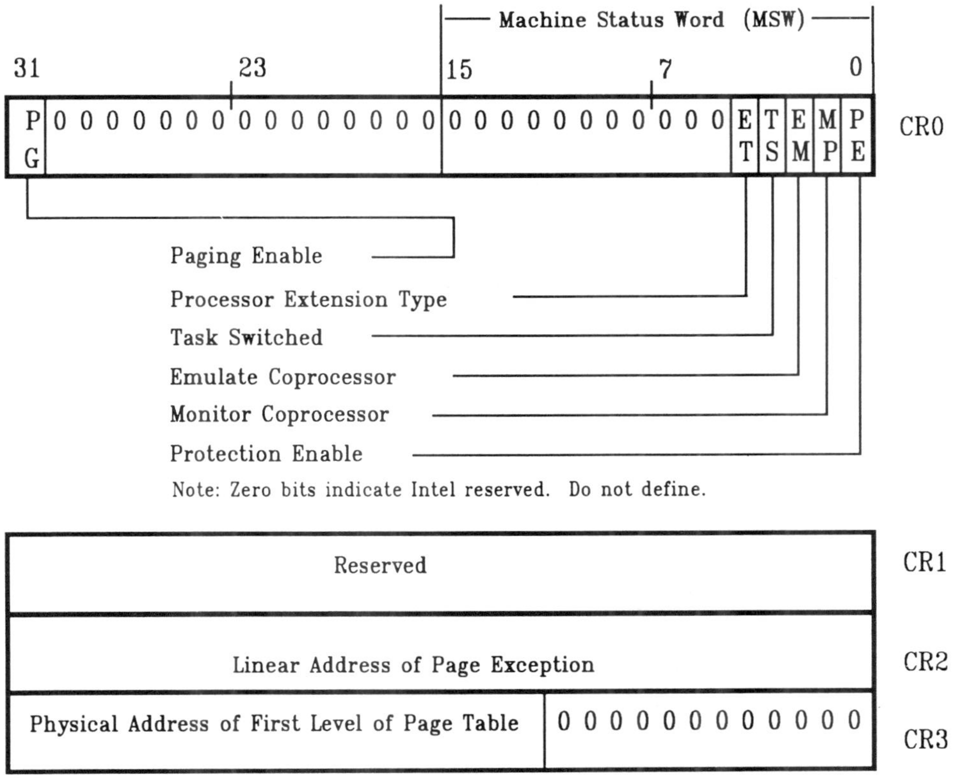

Fig. B-3. Control Register formats.

ET (Extension Type) Bit 4. ET indicates the type of coprocessor present in the system, either an 80287 or 80387.

TS (Task Switched) Bit 3. The processor sets TS with every task switch. It also tests TS when it interprets coprocessor instructions because the only time the coprocessor status needs to be saved is when a new task requires the coprocessor. Loading into the CR0 register can reset TS. Also the CLTS instruction specifically resets the TS.

EM (Emulation) Bit 2. EM indicates whether coprocessor functions are to be emulated. Emulation is designed to imitate one system or process with another so that the imitating system accepts the same data, executes the same programs, and achieves the same results as the imitated system or function. Setting EM often occurs when there is no coprocessor present.

MP (Math Present) Bit 1. MP controls the function of the WAIT instruction, which is used to coordinate a coprocessor.

PE (Protection Enable) Bit 0. If PE = 1, the 80386 operates with segmentation mechanism enabled. When PE = 1, the 80386 is said to be operating in protected mode. If PE = 0, segmentation is turned off and the processor operates in real mode as an 8086.

Control Registers CR2 and CR3

CR2 and CR3 are used by the paging mechanism. Bits 11 through 0 of CR3 are reserved and must be loaded with zeros. CR2 is used to report error information when a page exception is raised. The 80386 stores the linear address that caused the exception into CR2 when reporting a page exception. CR3 contains the physical address of the page containing the first level of the page table, the directory. The directory is page-aligned, so only the top 20 bits are significant. The bottom 1 bits are reserved for use in future processors. Be sure to load zeros into them when loading a new value into CR3.

Test Registers TR6 and TR7

Two test registers, TR6 and TR7, control the testing of the RAM/CAM (content addressable memory) in the translation lookaside buffer (TLB), the cache used for storing information from page tables. TR6 is the command test register and TR7 is the data register which contains the data of the TLB test. These two registers are diagrammed in Fig. B-4. (Note also that TR0 through TR5 do not exist.)

C Bit 0. TR6 contains a command and an address tag. To cause an immediate TLB lookup, move a doubleword into TR6 that contains a 1 in this bit. To cause an immediate write to the TLB, move a doubleword that has a 0 in this bit.

Linear Address Bits 12–31. On a TLB write, a TLB entry is allocated to this linear address. The rest of the TLB entry is set depending on the value of TR7 and the value just written into TR6. On a TLB lookup, the TLB is

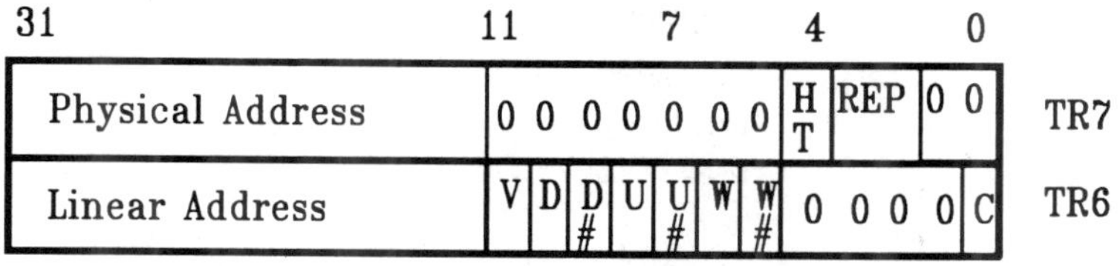

TR7	HT	= Lookup was a HIT=1, MISS=0
	REP	= Block where tag was found, if HT=1, Undefined if HT=0.
TR6	V	= Valid bit
	D/D#	= Dirty bit
	U/U#	= User bit
	W/W#	= Read/Write bit
	C	= Command bit

Fig. B-4. Test Registers TR6 and TR7. (Zero entries indicate Intel reserved bits; do not define.)

per this value. If one and only one TLB entry matches, the rest of the fields of TR6 and TR7 are set from the matching TLB entry.

V Bit 11. This is the valid bit. The TLB uses it to identify entries that contain valid data. Valid means a successful translation has been made. Entries in the TLB that have not been assigned values have zero in the valid bit. All valid bits can be cleared by writing to Control Register 3 (CR3).

D, D# Bits 10 and 9. Bit 10 is the dirty bit (the entry has been changed) and bit 9 is its complement for/from the TLB entry.

U, U# Bits 8 and 7. Bit 8 is the U/S (User accessible) bit and bit 7 is its complement for/from the TLB entry.

W, W# Bits 6 and 5. Bit 6 is the R/W (Writeable) bit and bit 5 is its complement for/from the TLB entry.

Physical Address Bits 31–12. This is the data field of the TLB. On a write to TLB, the TLB entry allocated to the linear address in TR6 is set to this value. On a TLB lookup, if HT is set, the data field (physical address) from the TLB is read out to this field. If HT bit is not set, this field is undefined.

HT Bit 4. For a TLB write, HT must be set to 1. For a TLB lookup, the HT bit indicates whether the lookup was a hit (HT = 1) or a miss (HT = 0).

REP Bits 3 and 2. For a TLB write, one of four associative blocks of the TLB is to be written. These bits indicate which. For a TLB read, if HT is set, REP shows in which of the four associative blocks the tag was found. If HT is not set on a TLB read, REP is undefined.

Debug Registers

The six programmer-accessible debug registers (DR0–DR3, DR6 and DR7) bring advanced debugging to the 80386, including breakpoints and the ability to set instruction breakpoints without modifying code segments. Registers DR0 through DR3 specify the four linear breakpoints. DR4 and DR5 are reserved for future Intel developments. DR6 displays the current state of the breakpoints and DR7 is used to set the breakpoints. Figure B-5 shows the debug register formats.

Debug Register DR6

The bit assignments for debug register DR6 are described below.

BT Bit 15. The BT bit indicates that the cause for the debug exception was a task switch into a task where the debug trap bit in the TSS is enabled.

BS Bit 14. This bit is set if a single-step exception occurs. The single-step condition is enabled by the TF bit in the EFLAGS register. The BS bit is set only if a single-step trap actually occurs, not if a single-step condition (enabled or not) was detected.

BD Bit 13. The BD bit is set at an instruction boundary if the next instruction reads or writes to one of the eight debug registers (debug register protection). BD is set whenever a read or write to the debug registers is about to occur. The condition does not need to be enabled by the GD bit of DR7.

B0, B1, B2, and B3 Bits 3–0. These bits indicate that the breakpoint condition specified by the corresponding breakpoint linear address register was detected.

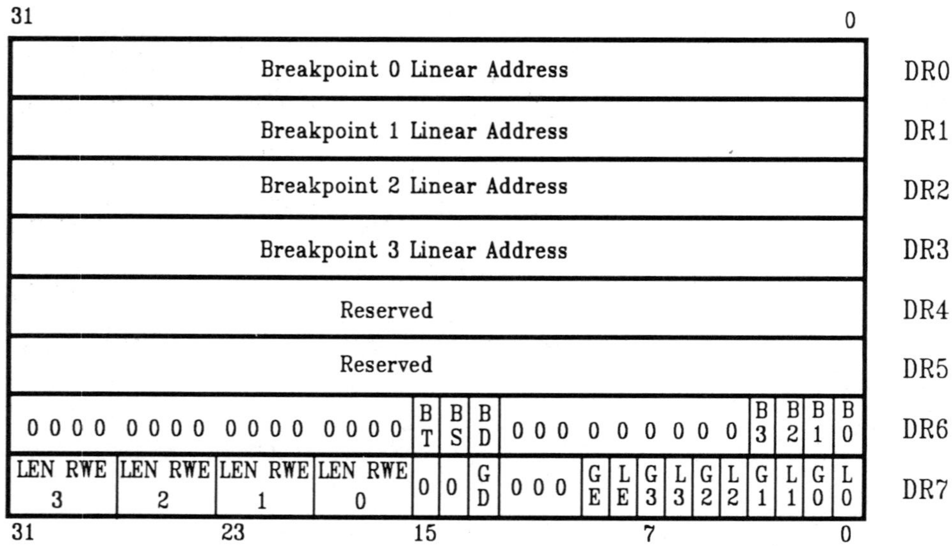

Fig. B-5. Debug Register formats.

Debug Register DR7

LEN. The four 2-bit LEN fields indicate the length of the breakpoint for each of the four breakpoint registers. The encoding is:

00 One-byte length
01 Two-byte length
10 Reserved
11 Four-byte length

RWE. The four 2-bit RWE fields indicate the type of access that causes a breakpoint exception to be raised. The encoding is:

00 Instruction execution only
01 Data writes only
10 Reserved
11 Data reads or writes

GD Bit 13. The GD bit enables the debug register protection condition that is flagged by BD of DR6. GD is cleared at entry to the debug exception handler by the processor which allows the handler free access to the debug registers.

GE/LE. These bits indicate the exact data breakpoints (global and local, respectively). If GE or LE is set, the 80386 slows execution such that data breakpoints are reported on exactly the instruction that causes them. If these bits are not set, the 80386 may get slightly ahead of the reporting of the breakpoint conditions on instructions that perform data writes near the end of their execution.

L0–L3 and G0–G3 Bits 7–0. The L0 through L3 and G0 through G3 bits are the local and global enable signals for the four debug breakpoint registers. If either the local or global enable is set, the breakpoint specified by the corresponding breakpoint register DRn is enabled.

Selector Flags

Figure B-6 shows the Selector format. In a general selector, the fields are as described below.

Index. These bits (15–3) select one of up to 8192 descriptors in a descriptor table. The 80386 multiplies this index value by eight (the length of a descriptor) and then adds the result to the base address of the descriptor table. This accesses the correct entry in the table.

Table Indicator (TI). This bit specifies the descriptor table to which the selector refers: a zero points to the GDT (Global Descriptor Table) and a one indicates the current LDT (Local Descriptor Table).

Requested Privilege Level (RPL). Bits 1 and 0 are used by the system protection mechanism. See Chapter 6 for more on protection and privilege.

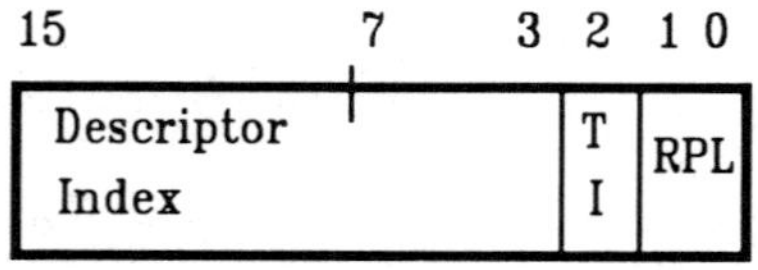

Fig. B-6. Selector format.

RPL = Requestor Privilege Level

TI = Identifies the Descriptor Table which contains the descriptor of the segment

TI = 0, Descriptor is in the GDT

TI = 1, Descriptor is in the LDT

Descriptor Index = The index within the GDT or LDT where the segment descriptor is

Segment Descriptor Flags/Fields

Shown in Fig. B-7, Descriptor Format, these fields are:

BASE. This defines the location of the segment within the 4-gigabyte linear address space. The 80386 concatenates the three fragments of the base address to form a single 32-bit value.

LIMIT. This field defines the size of the segment. The 80386 links the two parts of the LIMIT field, to form a 20-bit result. The processor then interprets the LIMIT field in one of two ways, depending on the setting of the Granularity Bit:

1. In units of one byte, to define a LIMIT of up to 1 megabyte.
2. In units of 4 Kilobytes (one page), to define a LIMIT of up to 4 gigabytes. The LIMIT is shifted left by 12 bits when loaded, and low-order one-bits are inserted.

Granularity Bit. This bit specifies the units with which the LIMIT field is interpreted. When G = 0, LIMIT is interpreted as units of one byte. If G = 1, LIMIT is interpreted in units of 4 kilobytes.

S Bit. The Segment bit determines if a given segment is a system segment (S = 0), or a code or data segment (S = 1).

TYPE. This differentiates between various kinds of descriptors. Code and data descriptors split TYPE into a 3-bit TYPE and 1-bit of Accessed Flag. System segments use the following set of values in TYPE:

0 = Invalid
1 = Available 286 TSS
2 = LDT
3 = Busy 286 TSS

4 = 286 Call Gate
5 = Task Gate (286 or 386)
6 = 286 Interrupt Gate
7 = 286 Trap Gate

Data Segment Descriptor

31 23 15 7 0

Base 31..24	G	B	0	AVL	Limit 19..16	P	DPL	TYPE 1 0 E W A	Base 23..16
Segment Base 15..0						Segment Limit 15..0			

Executable Segment Descriptor

31 23 15 7 0

Base 31..24	G	D	0	AVL	Limit 19..16	P	DPL	TYPE 1 1 C R A	Base 23..16
Segment Base 15..0						Segment Limit 15..0			

System Segment Descriptor

31 23 15 7 0

Base 31..24	G	X	0	AVL	Limit 19..16	P	DPL	0	TYPE	Base 23..16
Segment Base 15..0						Segment Limit 15..0				

- A Accessed
- AVL Available
- B Big
- C Conforming
- D Default
- DPL Descriptor Privilege Level
- E Expand Down
- G Granularity
- P Segment Present
- R Readable
- W Writeable

Fig. B-7. Descriptor format.

8 = Invalid	C = 386 Call Gate
9 = Available 386 TSS	D = Intel Reserved
A = Intel Reserved	E = 386 Interrupt Gate
B = Busy 386 TSS	F = 386 Trap Gate

DPL (Descriptor Privilege Level). This is used by the protection mechanism.

Segment-Present Bit. If this bit holds a zero value, the descriptor is not valid for use in address translation. The 80386 signals an exception when a selector for the descriptor is loaded into a segment register.

Accessed Bit. The 80386 sets this bit when the segment is accessed in data and code descriptors. Operating systems that implement virtual memory at the segment level may monitor the frequency of segment usage by periodically testing and clearing this bit.

Alphabetic Listing of Registers

The registers described in preceding sections are listed below in alphabetical order.

AH	High-order byte of AX Register
AL	Low-order byte of AX Register
AX	16-bit Register, part of EAX
BH	High-order byte of BX Register
BL	Low-order byte of BX Register
BP	16-bit Register, part of EBP
BX	16-bit Register, part of EBX
CH	High-order byte of CX Register
CL	Low-order byte of CX Register
CR0	Control Register, low order 16 bits is MSW
CR1	Control Register, Reserved
CR2	Page Fault Linear Address Register
CR3	Page Directory Base Address
CX	16-bit Register, part of ECX
DH	High-order byte of DX Register
DI	16-bit Register, part of EDI
DL	Low-order byte of DX Register
DR0	Debug Register, Linear Breakpoint Address 0
DR1	Debug Register, Linear Breakpoint

	Address 1
DR2	Debug Register, Linear Breakpoint Address 2
DR3	Debug Register, Linear Breakpoint Address 3
DR4	Debug Register, Intel Reserved
DR5	Debug Register, Intel Reserved
DR6	Debug Register, Breakpoint Status
DR7	Debug Register, Breakpoint Control
DS	Data Segment Register
DX	16-bit Register, part of EDX
EAX	General 32-bit Register
EBP	General 32-bit Register, Stack-Frame Base Pointer
EBX	General 32-bit Register
ECX	General 32-bit Register
EDI	General 32-bit Register
EDX	General 32-bit Register
EFLAGS	Flags Register
EIP	Instruction Pointer
ES	Data Segment Register
ESI	General 32-bit Register
ESP	Stack Pointer Register
FLAGS	The low-order 16 bits of EFLAGS
FS	Data Segment Register
GDT	Global Descriptor Table
GS	Data Segment Register
IDT	Interrupt Descriptor Table
IP	Instruction Pointer, low-order 16 bits of EIP.
LDT	Local Descriptor Table
SI	16-bit Register, part of ESI
SP	16-bit Register, part of ESP
SS	Stack Segment Register
TR6	Test Register for Page Cache, Test Control
TR7	Test Register for Page Cache, Test Status
TSS	Task State Segment

Alphabetic Listing of Flags and Bits

The following is a list of the flags used in the 80386 and its environs, along with which register they're in. Note that if the bit is in the EFLAGS register, it is commonly called a "flag"; otherwise it's called a "bit."

Bit/Flag	*Location*	*Description*
A	Bit 5 of Page Table Entry	Accessed
AF	Bit 4 of EFLAGS	Auxiliary Carry
B0–B3	Bits 0 to 3 of DR6	Breakpoint Conditions detected
BD	Bit 13 of DR6	If instruction reads or writes to debug registers
BS	Bit 14 of DR6	Single-step exception
BT	Bit 15 of DR6	Cause for debug exception
CF	Bit 0 of EFLAGS	Carry Flag
D	Bit 6 of Page Table Entry	Dirty
DF	Bit 10 of EFLAGS	Direction Flag
EM	Bit 2 of CR0	Emulate Coprocessor
ET	Bit 4 of CR0	Processor Extension Type
GD	Bit 13 of DR7	Enable debug register protection
GE/LE	Bits 0 to 7 of DR7	Global or Local Data breakpoints
IF	Bit 9 of EFLAGS	Interrupt Enable
IOPL	Bit 13/12 of EFLAGS	I/O Privilege Level
L0–L3/G0–G3	Bits 0 through 7 of DR7	Local or Global enable signals
MP	Bit 1 of CR0	Monitor Coprocessor
NT	Bit 14 of EFLAGS	Nested Task Flag
OF	Bit 11 of EFLAGS	Overflow
P	Bit 0 of Page Table Entry	Present
PE	Bit 0 of CR0	Protection Enable
PF	Bit 2 of EFLAGS	Parity Flag
PG	Bit 31 of CR0	Paging Enable
R/W	Bit 1 of Page Table Entry	Read/Write
RF	Bit 16 of EFLAGS	Resume Flag

SF	Bit 7 of EFLAGS	Sign Flag
TF	Bit 8 of EFLAGS	Trap Flag
TS	Bit 3 of CR0	Task Switched
U/S	Bit 2 of Page Table Entry	User/Supervisor
VM	Bit 17 of EFLAGS	Virtual 8086 Mode
ZF	Bit 6 of EFLAGS	Zero Flag

Appendix C

The 80386 Instruction Set

The 80386 instruction set is a superset of previous generations' instructions, with additional instructions for specific 80386 uses. The instruction set is listed in this appendix in alphabetic order by mnemonic. Along with each instruction, the forms are given for each operand combination, including the object code which is produced, the operands required, and a description of the instruction.

There are 14 new instructions on the 80386. They are: BSF, BSR, BT, BTC, BTR, BTS, MOVSX, MOVZX, SET*cc*, SHLD, SHRD, LSS, LFS, and LGS.

Appendix D gives an overview of the 80386/80387 coprocessor floating-point instructions.

Instruction Format

80386 instructions are made up of various elements and have various formats. Of the elements described below, only one (the opcode) is always present in each individual instruction. The others may or may not be present, depending on the operation involved and on the location and type of the operands.

Instructions are made up of optional instruction prefixes, one or two primary opcode bytes, possibly an address specifier which consists of the Mod R/M byte and the Scale Index Base byte, a displacement (if required), and an immediate data field (if required). All the instruction encodings are subsets of the general instruction format shown in Fig. C-1.

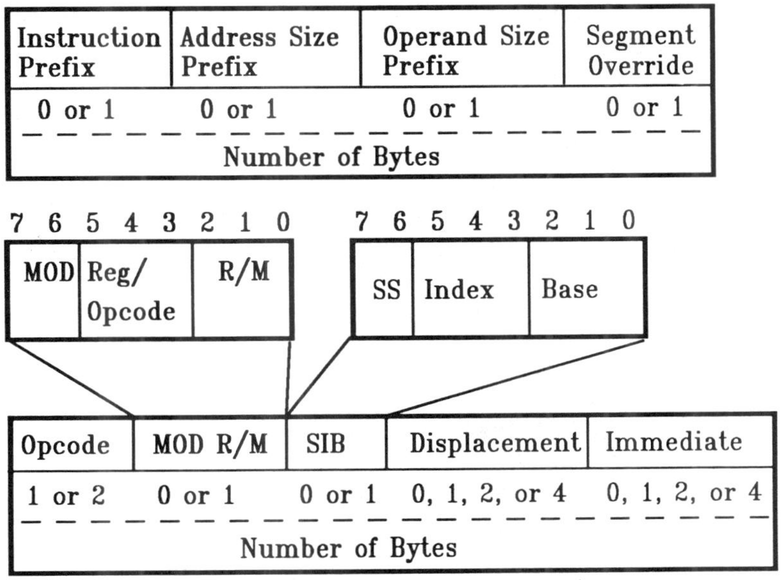

Fig. C-1. General instruction format.

The elements of an instruction, in their order of occurrence are as follows:

Prefixes. A prefix consists of one or more bytes preceding an instruction that modify the operation of that instruction. There are four types of prefixes:

- **Repeat** is used with a string instruction to cause the instruction to act on each element of the string.
- **Operand Size** switches between 32-bit and 16-bit operands.
- **Address Size** switches between 32-bit and 16-bit address generation.
- **Segment Override** explicitly specifies which segment register an instruction should use. This overrides the default segment-register selection generally used by the 80386 for that instruction.

Opcode. This specifies the operation performed by the instruction. Some operations have several different opcodes. Each specifies a different variant of the operation.

Register Specifier. The instruction may specify one or two register operands. Register specifiers may occur in either the same byte as the opcode, or in the same byte as the addressing-mode specifier.

Addressing-Mode Specifier. When present, this element specifies whether an operand is a register or a memory location. If it's in memory, this specifies whether a displacement, an index register, a base register, and scaling is to be used.

MOD R/M and SIB (Scale Index Base) Bytes. Most instructions that can refer to an operand in memory have an addressing-form byte following the primary opcode byte(s). This byte specifies the address form to be used. Some encodings of the MOD R/M byte indicate a second addressing byte, the Scale Index Base (SIB) byte.

The MOD R/M and SIB bytes contain the following information:

1. The indexing type or register number to be used in the instructions.
2. The register to be used, or more information to select the instruction.
3. The base, index, and scale information.

The MOD R/M byte contains these three fields:

MOD (bits 7 and 6) occupies the two most significant bits of the byte. They combine with the R/M field to form 32 possible values: eight registers and 24 indexing modes.

REG (bits 5, 4, and 3) specify either a register number or three more bits of opcode information. The meaning of REG is specified by the first (opcode) byte of the instruction.

R/M (bits 2, 1, and 0) can specify a register as the location of an operand, or it can form part of the addressing-mode encoding in combination with the MOD field as described above.

The SIB byte includes these three fields:

SS (bits 7 and 6) specifies the scale factor.

INDEX (bits 5, 4, and 3) specifies the register number of the index register.

BASE (bits 2, 1, and 0) specifies the register number of the base register.

Encoding of 32-bit Address Mode. Register modifiers for address computation are all 32-bit registers (EAX, for example). Address computation without Scale Index Base (SIB) byte includes the following: a MOD of 00, which specifies address computation of DS:[*r/m*], which specifies a register as follows:

000	DS:[EAX]
001	DS:[ECX]
010	DS:[EDX]
011	DS:[EBX]
100	SIB Present
101	DS:*32-bit displacement*
110	DS:[ESI]
111	DS:[EDI]

Thus, the effective address is DS:*32-bit modifier* from register or memory.

A MOD of 01 adds an 8-bit displacement to the above, so that these *r/m* values are of the following form:

000 DS:[EAX + *8-bit displacement*]
100 SIB Present
101 SS:[EBP + *8-bit displacement*]

A MOD of 10 adds a 32-bit displacement. An *r/m* of 000 is DS:[EAX + *displacement*]:

000 DS:[EAX + *32-bit displacement*]
100 SIB Present
101 SS:[EBP + *32-bit displacement*]

A MOD of 11 specifies a register in the *r/m* with the following equivalences:

000 AL or EAX
001 CL or ECX
010 DL or EDX
011 BL or EBX
100 AH or ESP
101 CH or EBP
110 DH or ESI
111 BH or EDI

The register selected depends on whether an 8-bit operation or a 32-bit operation is specified in the W bit.

The MOD value indicates the length of the displacement field to address:

00 No displacement, except for base 101
01 8-bit displacement
10 32-bit displacement

Therefore the SIB modifies the computed address:

DS:[*base* + *scaled index* + *displacement*]

except for the base where the base is ESP or EBP and then the logical substitution of SS: is made for the segment, instead of DS:.

Where an SIB is present, *r/m* = 100 for MOD = 00, 01, or 10. The address computation is done using a combination of the following:

- ☐ A 32-bit scaled index value is computed as index $* \ 2^{scale}$ where *scale* is the first two bits of the SIB byte and specified by its binary value. The index register is specified as an index of:

000 EAX
001 ECX
010 EDX
011 EBX
100 no index value, scale must be 0
101 EBP
110 ESI
111 EDI

- ☐ If the byte is laid out, the bits appear as SSIIIBBB, where SS is the scale, III is the index and BBB is the base. The base is selected as follows:

000 EAX
001 ECX
010 EDX
011 EBX
100 ESP
101 Special (a 32-bit displacement if MOD is 00 and the EBP register otherwise)
110 ESI
111 EDI

Displacement. When the addressing-mode specifier indicates that a displacement will be used to compute the address of an operand, the displacement is encoded in the instruction. A displacement is a signed integer of 8, 16, or 32 bits. The 8-bit form is used in the common case when the displacement is sufficiently small.

Immediate Operand. When present, this element provides the value of an operand of the instruction. Immediate operands may be 8, 16, or 32 bits wide. In cases where an 8-bit immediate operand is combined in some way with a 16- or 32-bit operand, the processor automatically extends the size of the 8-bit operand, taking into account the sign.

Description Notations

The following explains the notational conventions used and abbreviations used when illustrating the instruction set.

+rb, +rw, +rd — A register code, 0 through 7, which is added to the hexadecimal byte given at the left of the plus sign, in order to form a single opcode byte. The codes are:

rb	*rw*	*rd*
AL = 0	AX = 0	EAX = 0
CL = 1	CX = 1	ECX = 1
DL = 2	DX = 2	EDX = 2
BL = 3	BX = 3	EBX = 3
AH = 4	SP = 4	ESP = 4
CH = 5	BP = 5	EBP = 5
DH = 6	SI = 6	ESI = 6
BH = 7	DI = 7	EDI = 7

/digit — The digit is generally between 0 and 7. It indicates that the MOD R/M byte of the instruction uses only the register or memory (*r/m*) operand. The *reg* field contains the digit that provides an extension to the instruction's opcode.

/r — This shows that the instruction's MOD R/M byte contains both a register operand *and* an *r/m* operand.

cb, cw, cd, cp — A 1-byte (*cb*), 2-byte (*cw*), 4-byte (*cd*), or a 6-byte (*cp*) value that follows the opcode is used to specify a code offset and possibly a new value for the code segment register.

ib, iw, id — A 1-byte (*ib*), 2-byte (*iw*), or 4-byte (*id*) immediate operand to the instruction that follows the opcode, MOD R/M bytes or scale-indexing bytes. The opcode determines if the operand is a signed value. Note that all words and doublewords are given with the low-order byte first.

imm8 — An immediate byte value. *imm8* is a signed number between −128 and +127, inclusive. For those instructions where *imm8* combines with a word or doubleword operand, the immediate value is sign-extended to form a word or doubleword. The upper byte of the word/doubleword is filled with the topmost bit of the immediate value.

imm16 — An immediate word value. It is used for instructions whose operand-size attribute is 16 bits. Inclusive, this number runs from −32768 to +32767.

imm32	An immediate doubleword. The *imm32* abbreviation is used for instructions whose operand-size attribute is 32 bits. The range of numbers is, inclusive, from −2147483648 to +2147483647.
m8	A memory byte. It is addressed by DS:SI or ES:DI.
m16	A memory word. It is addressed by DS:SI or ES:DI.
m32	A memory doubleword. It is addressed by DS:SI or ES:DI.
moffs8, moffs16, moff232	A memory offset. A simple memory variable of type BYTE, WORD, or DWORD, used by some variants of the MOV instruction. The actual address is given by a simple offset relative to the segment base. The number shows with the *moffs* indicates its size, which is determined by the address-size attribute of the instruction. No MOD R/M byte is used in the instruction.
ptr16:16, ptr16:32	FAR pointer. Typically it is in a code segment different from that of the instruction. The notation 16:16 shows that the pointer value has two parts. The value to the left of the colon is the offset within the destination segment. The value to the right of the colon is a 16-bit selector or value destined for the code segment register. When the instruction's operand has a size attribute of 16, use 16:16. For the 32-bit attribute, use 16:32.
r8	One of the byte registers: AL, CL, DL, BL, AH, CH, DH, or BH.
r16	One of the word registers: AX, CS, DX, BX, SP, BP, SI, or DI.
r32	One of the doubleword registers: EAX, ECX, EDX, EBX, ESP, EBP, ESI, or EDI.
rel8	A relative address in the range from 128 bytes before

the end of the instruction to 127 bytes after the instruction's end.

rel16, rel32 — A relative address within the same code segment as the instruction assembled: *rel16* is applied to instructions whose operand-size attribute is 16 bits, while *rel32* is applied to the instructions with a 32-bit operand-size attribute.

r/m8 — A one-byte operand. It is either the contents of a byte from memory or from a byte register—AL, BL, CL, DL, AH, BH, CH, or DH.

r/m16 — A word register or memory operand. It is used for instructions whose operand-size attribute is 16 bits. The contents of memory are found at the address provided by the effective address computation. The word registers are: AX, BX, CX, DX, SP, BP, SI, and DI.

r/m32 — A doubleword register or memory operand. It is used for instructions whose operand-size attribute is 32 bits. The contents of memory are found at the address provided by the effective address computation. The doubleword registers are: EAX, EBX, ECX, EDX, ESP, EBP, ESI, and EDI.

rrr — When *rrr* appears in the binary equivalent column, it appears as the last three digits of the binary figure and indicates a particular register is referenced. The *rrr* translates to the following:

000	=	AX/EAX	100	=	SP/ESP
001	=	CX/ECX	101	=	BP/EBP
010	=	DX/EDX	110	=	SI/ESI
011	=	BX/EBX	111	=	DI/EDI

Sreg — A segment register. The segment register bit assignments are ES = 0, CS = 1, SS = 2, DS = 3, FS = 4, and GS = 5.

Description of Modifiers and Specifications

In the figures that illustrate each instruction, there are some extension that show modifiers, register specifications and register/memory specifications. The notation "*mm* 00 *r/m*" specifies memory and "*mm* 11 *r/m*" specifies *rrr*. A further explanation of how those interact with the opcode follows, *disp8* is an 8-byte displacement, *disp16* is a 16-byte displacement, and *disp32* is a 32-byte displacement.

8-Bit Modifiers

rrr	8-Bit Registers	16- or 32-Bit
000	AL	AX, EAX
001	CL	CX, ECX
010	DL	DX, EDX
011	BL	BX, EBX
100	AH	SP, ESP
101	CH	BC, EBP
110	DH	SI, ESI
111	BH	DI, EDI

16-Bit Modifiers

r/m or *mm*	00	01	10	11
000	[BX + SI]	+ *disp8*	+ disp16	rrr
001	[BX + DI]			
010	[BP + SI]			
011	[BP + DI]			
100	[SI]			
101	[DI]			
110	*disp16*	[BP] + *disp8*	[BP] + *disp16*	[BP] + *disp16*
111	[BX]	+ *disp8*	+ *disp16*	

32-Bit Modifiers

r/m and *mm*	00	01	10	11
000	[EAX]	+ *disp8*	+ *disp32*	*rrr*
001	[ECX]	+ *disp8*		
010	[EDX]	+ *disp8*		
011	[EBX]	+ *disp8*		
100	SIB Follows			
101	disp32	[EBC] + *disp8*	[EBP] + *disp32*	
110	[ESI]	[EBC] + *disp8*		
111	[EDI]			

Scaled Index Byte (SIB)

In the coding scheme below, SS = the scale factor.

SS		
	00	Times 1
	01	Times 2
	10	Times 4
	11	Times 8

Index	Base
000 EAX	000 EAX
001 ECX	001 ECX
010 EDX	010 EDX
011 EBX	011 EBX
100 None	100 ESP
101 EBP	101 Special
110 ESI	110 ESI
111 EDI	111 EDI

AAA ASCII Adjust after Addition

INSTRUCTION	OPCODE	BINARY
AAA	37	00110111

Purpose: AAA changes the contents of register AL to a valid unpacked decimal number and zeros the top 4 bits. AAA follows the addition of two unpacked decimal operands in AL, but it can be used for other BCD conversions also. If a decimal carry results from the addition, or the contents of the lower nibble of AL are greater than 9, then AL is incremented by 6, AH incremented by 1, and CF and AF set to 1. If no decimal carry occurred, AH is unchanged, CF and AF set to 0, and the lower 4 bits of AL are unchanged. Whether or not a decimal carry occurred, the upper 4 bits of AL are cleared.

AAD ASCII Adjust Register AX before Division

INSTRUCTION	OPCODE	BINARY
AAD	D5 0A	11010101 00001010

Purpose: AAD modifies the numerator in AH and AL, to prepare for the division of two valid unpacked decimal operands so that the quotient produced by the division will be a valid unpacked decimal number. AH should contain the high-order digit and AL the low-order digit. AAD adjusts the value and places the result in AL. AH will contain zero.

AAM ASCII Adjust AX Register after Multiplication

INSTRUCTION	OPCODE	BINARY
AAM	D4 0A	11010100 00001010

Purpose: Two BCD digits multiplied together *may* produce an invalid BCD result. AAM corrects the result of a multiplication of two valid unpacked decimal numbers back into a pair of digits in AH and AL. AAM follows the multiplication of two decimal numbers to produce a valid result. The high-order digit is left in AH, the low-order in AL.

AAS ASCII Adjust AL Register after Subtraction

INSTRUCTION	OPCODE	BINARY
AAS	3F	00111111

Purpose: AAS changes the contents of register AL to a valid unpacked decimal number and zeros the top 4 bits. AAS follows the subtraction of one unpacked decimal operand from another in AL. If a decimal borrow results from the subtraction, then AL is decremented by 6, AH is decremented by 1, and the CF and AF flags are set. If no decimal carry occurred, AH is unchanged, CF and AF are set to 0, and the lower 4 bits of AL are unchanged. Whether a decimal carry occurred or not, the upper 4 bits of AL are cleared.

ADC Add Integers with Carry

INSTRUCTION	OPCODE	BINARY
ADC AL,*imm8*	14 *ib*	00010100
ADC AX,*imm16*	15 *iw*	00010100
ADC EAX,*imm32*	15 *id*	00010101
ADC *r/m8,imm8*	90 /2 *ib*	10010000 *mm* 010 *r/m*
ADC r/m16,imm16	90 /2 *lw*	10010000 *mm* 010 *r/m*
ADC *r/m32,imm32*	91 /2 *id*	10010001 *mm* 010 *r/m*
ADC *r/m16,imm8*	93 /2 *ib*	10010011 *mm rrr r/m*
ADC *r/m32,imm8*	93 /2 *ib*	10010011 *mm rrr r/m*
ADC *r/m8,r8*	10 /*r*	00010000 *mm rrr r/m*
ADC *r/m16,r16*	11 /*r*	00010001 *mm rrr r/m*
ADC *r/m32,r32*	11 /*r*	00010001 *mm rrr r/m*
ADC *r8,r/m8*	12 /*r*	00010010 *mm rrr r/m*
ADC *r16,r/m16*	13 /*r*	00010011 *mm rrr r/m*
ADC *r32,r/m32*	13 /*r*	00010011 *mm rrr r/m*

Purpose: ADC sums the operands, adds one if CF is set and replaces the destination operand with the result. If CF is cleared, ADC does the same operation as the ADD instruction. An ADD followed by multiple ADC instructions can be used to add numbers longer than 32 bits.

ADD Add Integers

INSTRUCTION	OPCODE	BINARY
ADD AL,*imm8*	04 *ib*	00000100
ADD AX,*imm16*	05 *iw*	00000101
ADD EAX,*imm32*	05 *id*	00000101
ADD *r/m8,imm8*	80 /0 *ib*	10000000 *mm* 000 *r/m*
ADD *r/m16,imm16*	81 /0 *iw*	10000001 *mm* 000 *r/m*
ADD *r/m32,imm32*	81 /0 *id*	10000001 *mm* 000 *r/m*
ADD *r/m16,imm8*	83 /0 *ib*	10000011 *mm* 000 *r/m*
ADD *r/m32,imm8*	83 /0 *ib*	10000011 *mm* 000 *r/m*
ADD *r/m8,r8*	00 /r	00000000 *mm rrr r/m*
ADD *r/m16,r16*	01 /r	00000001 *mm rrr r/m*
ADD *r/m32,r32*	01 /r	00000001 *mm rrr r/m*
ADD *r8,r/m8*	02 /r	00000010 *mm rrr r/m*
ADD *r16,r/m16* 03 /r	00000011 *mm rrr r/m*	
ADD *r32,r/m32*	03 /r	00000011 *mm rrr r/m*

Purpose: ADD replaces the destination operation with the sum of the source and destination operands. It sets CF if there is an overflow.

AND Logical AND

INSTRUCTION	OPCODE	BINARY
AND AL,*imm8*	24 *ib*	00100100
AND AX,*imm16*	25 *iw*	00100101
AND EAX,*imm32*	25 *id*	00100101
AND *r/m8,imm8*	A0 /4 *ib*	10100000 *mm* 100 *r/m*
AND *r/m16,imm16*	A1 /4 *iw*	10100001 *mm* 100 *r/m*
AND *r/m32,imm32*	A1 /4 *ib*	10100001 *mm* 100 *r/m*
AND *r/m16,imm8*	A3 /4 *ib*	10100011 *mm* 100 *r/m*
AND *r/m32,imm8*	A3 /4 *ib*	10100011 *mm* 100 *r/m*

INSTRUCTION	OPCODE	BINARY
AND *r/m8,r8*	20 /*r*	00100000 *mm rrr r/m*
AND *r/m16,r16*	21 /*r*	00100001 *mm rrr r/m*
AND *r/m32,r32*	21 /*r*	00100001 *mm rrr r/m*
AND *r8,r/m8*	22 /*r*	00100010 *mm rrr r/m*
AND *r16,r/m16*	23 /*r*	00100011 *mm rrr r/m*
AND *r32,r/m32*	23 /*r*	00100011 *mm rrr r/m*

Purpose: AND is used to ensure that user-specified bits are off, e.g. the parity bit in an ASCII input stream from a terminal. When AND is used in conjunction with a compare, AND makes certain that the specified bits are on. In use, AND is executed prior to the compare. Both AND and the compare use known masks.

ARPL   Adjust Requester Privilege Level of Selector

INSTRUCTION	OPCODE	BINARY
ARPL *r/m16,r16*	63 /*r*	01100011 *mm rrr r/m*

Purpose: ARPL is used by systems software to guarantee that selector parameters to a subroutine do not request more privilege than allowed to the caller. ARPL has two operands. The first, a 16-bit word register or memory variable that contains the value of the selector. The second operand is generally a register that contains the caller's CS selector value.

ARPL checks that the requested privilege level (RPL) of the first operand against the RPL of the second. The RPL is specified in the least significant bits of each operand. If RPL of the first operand is less than that of the second, the Zero Flag (ZF) is set to 1.

BOUND   Check Array Index against Bounds

INSTRUCTION	OPCODE	BINARY
BOUND *r16,m16&16*	62 /*r*	01100010 *mm rrr r/m*
BOUND *r32,m32&32*	62 /*r*	01100010 *mm rrr r/m*

Purpose: BOUND verifies that the signed value contained in the specified register lies within specified limits. Interrupt 5 occurs if the value in the register is less than the lower bound or greater than the upper bound. The upper and lower limit values may each be a word or a doubleword.

The block of memory that specifies the lower and upper limits of an array may typically reside just before the array itself. This makes the array bounds accessible at a constant offset from the beginning of the array. Because the address of the array is already present in a register, this avoids extra calculations to obtain the effective address of the array bounds.

BOUND includes two operands. The first specifies the register being tested. The second contains the effective address of the two signed BOUND limit values. BOUND assumes that the upper limit and the lower limit are in adjacent memory locations. These limit values *cannot* be register operands. If they are, an invalid opcode exception occurs.

BSF Bit Scan Forward

INSTRUCTION	OPCODE	BINARY
BSF *r16,r/m16*	0F BC	00001111 10111100 *mm rrr r/m*
BSF *r32,r/m32*	0F BC	00001111 10111100 *mm rrr r/m*

Purpose: This instruction scans a word or doubleword (from the least significant bit to the most significant bit) for a one-bit and stores the number of the first set bit into a register. The bit string being scanned may be either in a register or in memory. ZF is set if the entire word is zero; that is, no set bits are found. ZF is cleared if a one-bit is found. Note: If no set bit is found, the value of the destination register is undefined.

This instruction is new with the 80386. It is useful for scanning allocation bitmaps for an allocatable or free bit. Returning the number of the bit provides the relative number of the item within the word being examined.

BSR Bit Scan Reverse

INSTRUCTION	OPCODE	BINARY
BSR *r16,r/m16*	0F BD	00001111 10111101 *mm rrr r/m*
BSR *r32,r/m32*	0F BD	00001111 10111101 *mm rrr r/m*

Purpose: This instruction scans a word or doubleword (from the most significant bit to the least significant bit) for a one-bit and stores the index of the first set bit into a register. The bit string being scanned may be either in a register or in memory. ZF is set if the entire word is zero; that is, no set bits are found. ZF is cleared if a one-bit is found. This is a new instruction with the 80386.

Note: If no set bit is found, the value of the destination register is undefined.

BT Bit Test

INSTRUCTION	OPCODE	BINARY
BT *r/m16,r16*	0F A3	00001111 10100011 *mm rrr r/m*
BT *r/m32,r32*	0F A3	00001111 10100011 *mm rrr r/m*
BT *r/m16,imm8*	0F BA */r ib*	00001111 10111010 *mm 100 r/m*
BT *r/m32,imm8*	0F BA */r ib*	00001111 10111010 *mm 100 r/m*

Purpose: BT is a means of determining if a bit in a bitmap is set or not. BT sets CF to the same value as the bit being tested. This instruction is new with the 80386. It is recommended not to use BT to reference memory-mapped I/O registers directly. Use MOV to load from or store to the memory-mapped device registers and then use the register form of BT.

BTC Bit Test and Complement

INSTRUCTION	OPCODE	BINARY
BTC *r/m16,r16*	0F BB	00001111 10111011 *mm rrr r/m*
BTC *r/m32,r32*	0F BB	00001111 10111011 *mm rrr r/m*
BTC *r/m16,imm8*	0F BA /7 *ib*	00001111 10111010 *mm 111 r/m*
BTC *r/m32,imm8*	0F BA /7 *ib*	00001111 10111010 *mm 111 r/m*

Purpose: BTC tests a specific bit, copies that bit to CF, and inverts the original bit (e.g., if the bit was a 1 it's changed to a 0, and CF set to 1). This instruction is new with the 80386. It is recommended not to use BTC to reference memory-mapped I/O registers directly. Use MOV to load from or store to the memory-mapped device registers and then use the register form of BTC.

BTS Bit Test and Set

INSTRUCTION	OPCODE	BINARY
BTS *r/m16,r16*	0F AB	00001111 10101011 *mm rrr r/m*

INSTRUCTION	OPCODE	BINARY
BTS *r/m32,r32*	0F AB	00001111 10101011 *mm rrr r/m*
BTS *r/m16,imm8*	0F BA /5 *ib*	00001111 10111010 *mm 101 r/m*
BTS *r/m32,imm8*	0F BA /5 *ib*	00001111 10111010 *mm 101 r/m*

Purpose: BTS tests a specific bit, copies that bit to CF, and sets the original bit to 1. This instruction is new with the 80386. It is recommended not to use BTC to reference memory-mapped I/O registers directly. Use MOV to load from or store to the memory-mapped device registers and then use the register form of BTS.

CALL — Call a Procedure

INSTRUCTION	OPCODE	BINARY
CALL *rel16*	E8 *cw*	11101000
CALL *r/m16*	FF /2	11111111 *mm* 010 *r/m*
CALL *ptr16:16*	9A *cd*	10011010
CALL *m16:16*	FF /3	11111111 *mm* 011 *r/m*
CALL *rel32*	E8 *cd*	11101000
CALL *r/m32*	FF /2	11111111 *mm* 010 *r/m*
CALL *ptr16:32*	9A *cp*	10011010
CALL *ptr32:32*	9A *cp*	10011010
CALL *m16:32*	FF /3	11111111 *mm* 011 *r/m*

Purpose: CALL transfers control from one code segment location to another. These locations can be within the same code segment (*near*) or in different ones (*far*). Prior to actual transfer, CALL saves on the stack the address of the instruction following the CALL and the current value of EIP.

CALL instructions have relative, direct, and indirect versions. Indirect instructions specify an absolute address in one of two ways: (1) the 80386 can obtain the destination address from a memory operand specified in the instruction; or (2) the program CALLs a location specified by a general register (EAX, EDX, ECX, EBX, EBP, ESI, or EDI).

CBW — Convert Byte to Word
CWDE — Convert Word to Doubleword

INSTRUCTION	OPCODE	BINARY
CBW	98	10011000

INSTRUCTION	OPCODE	BINARY
CWDE	99	10011001

Purpose: These instructions extend the sign bit into the top portion of the larger register so that arithmetic operations can occur with correct results. The value of bit 7 of AX or bit 15 of EAX is placed in every bit of AH or the upper 16 bits of EAX.

CLC Clear Carry Flag (CF)

INSTRUCTION	OPCODE	BINARY
CLC	F8	11111000

Purpose: This instruction sets the CF to zero. No other flags are affected.

CLD Clear Direction Flag (DF)

INSTRUCTION	OPCODE	BINARY
CLD	FC	11111100

Purpose: CLD sets DF to zero. No other flags are affected. By setting DF to zero, DF now signals the automatic indexing feature to increment the index registers ESI and EDI. Automatic indexing is used by string instructions.

CLI Clear Interrupt Flag (IF)

INSTRUCTION	OPCODE	BINARY
CLI	FA	11111010

Purpose: If the current privilege level is at least as privileged as the IOPL, CLI sets the interrupt flag (IF) to zero. No other flags are affected. An exception is raised if the program does not have the correct I/O privilege.

Note: External interrupts are ignored at the end of CLI until the interrupt flag is set.

CLTS Clear Task-Switched Flag in CR0

INSTRUCTION	OPCODE	BINARY
CLTS	0F 06	00001111 00000110

Purpose: CLTS sets the Task Switched (TS bit in CR0) to zero. TS is set to 1 by the 80386 at each occurrence of a task switch. If a task switch has occurred and the new task attempts to use the 80387 coprocessor, a fault occurs. The fault handler must save the context of the 80387 and execute a CLTS instruction. The new task can then use the 80387 without destroying any of the previous task's data. This way, only tasks which use the 80387 incur the overhead of saving the prior state of the 80387.

Note: CLTS is used in systems programming. It is a privileged instruction, running at privilege level zero only.

CMC Complement Carry Flag (CF)

INSTRUCTION	OPCODE	BINARY
CMC	F5	11110101

Purpose: CMC reverses the value of the carry flag, e.g., CF becomes a zero if it was a one. No other flags are affected.

CMP Compare

INSTRUCTION	OPCODE	BINARY
CMP AL,*imm8*	3C *ib*	00111100
CMP AX,*imm16*	3D *iw*	00111101
CMP EAX,*imm32*	3D *id*	00111101
CMP *r/m8,imm8*	80 /7 *ib*	10000000 *mm* 111 *r/m*

INSTRUCTION	OPCODE	BINARY
CMP *r/m16,imm16*	81 /7 *iw*	10000001 *mm* 111 *r/m*
CMP *r/m32,imm32*	81 /7 *id*	10000001 *mm* 111 *r/m*
CMP *r/m16,imm8*	83 /7 *ib*	10000011 *mm* 111 *r/m*
CMP *r/m32,imm8*	83 /7 *ib*	10000011 *mm* 111 *r/m*
CMP *r/m8,r8*	38 /*r*	00111000 *mm rrr r/m*
CMP *r/m16,r16*	39 /*r*	00111001 *mm rrr r/m*
CMP *r/m32,r32*	39 /*r*	00111001 *mm rrr r/m*
CMP *r8,m8*	3A /*r*	00111010 *mm rrr r/m*
CMP *r16,r/m16*	3B /*r*	00111011 *mm rrr r/m*
CMP *r32,r/m32*	3B /*r*	00111011 *mm rrr r/m*

Purpose: CMP subtracts the source operand from the destination operand but does not store the result. Only the flags are changed. That is, CMP updates OF, SF, ZF, AF, PF, and CF, but does not alter the source and destination operands.

CMPS Compare String Operands
CMPSB Compare String Byte
CMPSW Compare String Word
CMPSD Compare String Doubleword

INSTRUCTION	OPCODE	BINARY
CMPS *m8,m8*	A6	10100110
CMPS *m16,m16*	A7	10100111
CMPS *m32,m32*	A7	10100111

Note: CMPSB is a common assembler mnemonic for CMPS *m8,m8*.
CMPSW is a common mnemonic for CMPS *m16,m16*.
CMPSD is a common mnemonic for CMPS *m32,m32*.

Purpose: These instructions operate on strings rather than on logical or numeric values. They operate on one element of a string, which may be a byte, a word, or a doubleword. The string elements are addressed by the registers ESI and EDI. After each string operation, ESI and/or EDI are automatically updated to point to the next element of the string. If DF = 0, the index registers are incremented. If DF = 1, they are decremented. The amount incremented or decremented is 1, 2, or 4, depending on the size of the string element.

CMPS subtracts the destination string element (at ES:EDI) from the source string element (at DS:ESI). It then updates the flags AF, SF, PF, CF, and OF. If the string elements are equal, ZF = 1. Otherwise, ZF = 0. If DF = 0, the 80386 increments the memory pointers ESI and EDI for two strings. The segment register used for the source address can be changed with a segment register override prefix. The destination segment register *cannot* be overridden.

The assembler always translates CMPS into one of the other types. CMPSB compares bytes. CMPSW compares words. CMPSD compares doublewords.

If the REPE or REPNE prefix modifies this instruction, the 80386 compares the value of the destination string element to the value of the source string element, stepping SI and DI in the direction indicated by the DF (direction flag), by the indicated size, until either the REPE/REPNE condition is false or ECX counts to zero.

CWD Convert Word to Doubleword
CDQ Convert Doubleword to Quadword
CWDE Convert Word to Doubleword Extended

INSTRUCTION	OPCODE	BINARY
CWD	99	10011001
CDQ	99	10011001

Note: CDQ is for 32-bit mode.

Purpose: CWD doubles the size of the source operand. CWD extends the sign of the word in register AX throughout register DX. CWD can be used to produce a doubleword dividend from a word before a word division.

CWDE extends the sign of the word in register AX throughout EAX. CDQ extends the sign of the doubleword in EAX throughout EDX. CDQ can be used to produce a quadword dividend from a doubleword before doubleword division.

DAA Decimal Adjust AL Register After Addition

INSTRUCTION	OPCODE	BINARY
DAA	27	00100111

Purpose: DAA adjusts the result of adding two valid packed decimal operands in AL. DAA must always follow the addition of two pairs of packed decimal numbers (one digit in each half-byte) to obtain a pair of valid packed decimal digits as results.

If the low nibble of AL is greater than 9, AF is set and 6 added to AL. Otherwise, AF is reset. If the high nibble is greater than 9h or the CF flag is set, then add 60h to AL and set CF. Otherwise, CF is reset.

DAS Decimal Adjust AL Register After Subtraction

INSTRUCTION	OPCODE	BINARY
DAS	2F	00101111

Purpose: DAS adjusts the result of subtracting two valid packed decimal operands in AL. DAS follows subtraction of one pair of packed decimal numbers (one digit in each half-byte) from another to obtain a pair of valid packed decimal digits as results. If the low nibble of AL is greater than 9 or if AF is set, then AL has 6 subtracted from it and AF is set. Otherwise, AF is reset. If the high nibble of AL is greater than 9h or the CF bit is set, then AL has 60h subtracted from it and CF is set. Otherwise, CF is reset.

DEC Decrement by 1

INSTRUCTION	OPCODE	BINARY
DEC *r/m8*	FE /1	11111110 *mm* 001 *r/m*
DEC *r/m16*	FF /1	11111111 *mm* 001 *r/m*
DEC *r/m32*	FF /1	11111111 *mm* 001 *r/m*
DEC *r16*	48 + *rw*	01001*rrr*
DEC *r32*	48 + *rw*	01001*rrr*

Purpose: DEC subtracts 1 from the destination operand and replaces the result into the destination operand. DEC does *not* update CF. Use SUB with an operand of 1 if a Carry Flag update is desired.

DIV Unsigned Integer Divide

INSTRUCTION	OPCODE	BINARY
DIV AL,*r/m8*	F6 /6	11110110 *mm* 110 *r/m*
DIV AX,*r/m16*	F7 /6	11110111 *mm* 110 *r/m*
DIV EAX,*r/m32*	F7 /6	11110111 *mm* 110 *r/m*

Length of Operand 1	Dividend	Divisor	Quotient	Remainder
8	AX	Operand 1	AL	AH
16	DS:AX	Operand 1	AX	DX
32	EDX:EAX	Operand 1	EAX	EDX

Fig. C-2. Summary of registers and operands for DIV.

Purpose: DIV divides an unsigned number in the accumulator by the source operand. The dividend (which is the accumulator) is twice the size of the divisor (which is the source operand); the dividend is AX, DX:AX, or EDX:EAX, for divisors of 8, 16, or 32 bits. The quotient and the remainder have the same size as the divisor. The quotient is placed in AL, AX, or EAX for 8-, 16-, or 32-bit operands, respectively. The remainder is in AH, DX, or EDX. Registers and operands of DIV are summarized in Fig. C-2.

A divisor of zero or a quotient too large for the designated register causes an 80386 interrupt zero (0).

Note: Non-integer quotients are truncated to integers. The remainder is always less than the divisor. For unsigned byte division, the largest quotient is 255. For unsigned word division, the largest quotient is 65,535. For unsigned doubleword division, the largest quotient is $2^{32} - 1$.

ENTER Make Stack Frame for Procedure Parameter

INSTRUCTION	OPCODE	BINARY
ENTER *imm16*,0	C8 *iw* 00	11001000
ENTER *imm16*,1	C8 /2 *01*	11001000
ENTER *imm16,imm8*	C8 *iw ib*	11001000

Purpose: ENTER creates a stack frame that can be used to implement the rules of block-structured high-level languages. A LEAVE instruction at the end of the procedure complements the ENTER.

ENTER has two parameters. The first specifies the number of bytes of dynamic storage to be allocated on the stack for the routine being entered. The second parameter corresponds to the lexical nesting level of the routine: 0 to 31. This level determines how many sets of stack frame pointers the CPU copies into the new stack frame from the proceeding frame. This list of stack frames is often called the *display*. Lexical level has *no* relationship to either the protection levels or to the I/O privilege level.

ENTER creates the new display for a procedure. Then it allocates the dynamic storage space for that procedure by decrementing ESP by the number of bytes specified in the first parameter. This new value of ESP serves as the starting point for all PUSH and POP operations within that procedure.

ENTER can be used either nested or non-nested. If the lexical level is zero, the non-nested form is used. The main procedure operates at the highest logical level, level 1. The first procedure it calls operates at the next deeper level, level 2. And so on. A level 2 procedure can access the variables in the main program because a program operating at a higher logical level (calling a program at a lower level) requires that the called procedure have access to the variables of the calling program.

A procedure calling another procedure at the *same* level implies that they are parallel procedures and should *not* have access to the variables of the calling program. The new stack frame does not include the pointer for addressing the calling procedure's stack frame. ENTER treats a re-entrant procedure as a procedure calling another procedure at the same level.

HLT Halt

INSTRUCTION	OPCODE	BINARY
HLT	F4	11110100

Purpose: HALT stops the execution of all instructions and places the 80386 in a HALT state. An NMI, reset, or an enabled interrupt will resume execution. A HLT would normally be the last instruction in a sequence which shuts down the system, i.e., for a checkpoint after a power failure is detected.

IDIV Signed Divide

INSTRUCTION	OPCODE	BINARY
IDIV *r/m8*	F6 /7	11110110 *mm* 111 *r/m*
IDIV AX,*r/m16*	F7 /7	11110111 *mm* 111 *r/m*
IDIV EAX,*r/m32*	F7 /7	11110111 *mm* 111 *r/m*

Purpose: IDIV does signed division. The dividend, quotient, and remainder are implicitly allocated to fixed registers (see Fig.C-3), while only the divisor is

Size	Divisor	Quotient	Remainder	Dividend
Byte	r/m 8	AL	AH	AX
Word	r/m 16	AX	DX	DX:AX
Dword	r/m 32	EAX	EDX	EDX:EAX

Fig. C-3. Registers to use for IDIV.

given as an explicit *r/m* (register or memory) operand. The divisor determines which registers are to be used. Figure C-3 shows which registers to use for IDIV. Nonintegral quotients are truncated toward zero. Remainders are always the same sign as the dividend and always have less magnitude than the divisor.

An 80386 interrupt zero (0) is taken if a zero divisor or a quotient too large for the destination register is generated. If a divide by zero occurs, the quotient and remainder are undefined.

IMUL Signed Integer Multiply

INSTRUCTION	OPCODE	BINARY
IMUL *r/m8*	F6 /5	11110110 *mm* 101 *r/m*
IMUL *r/m16*	F7 /5	11110111 *mm* 101 *r/m*
IMUL *r/m32*	F7 /5	11110111 *mm* 101 *r/m*
IMUL *r16,r/m16*	0F AF /*r*	00001111 10101111 *mm rrr r/m*
IMUL *r32,r/m32*	0F AF /*r*	00001111 10101111 *mm rrr r/m*
IMUL *r16,r/m16,imm8*	6B /*r ib*	01101011 *mm rrr r/m*
IMUL *r32,r/m32,imm8*	6B /*r ib*	01101011 *mm rrr r/m*
IMUL *r16,imm8*	6B /*r ib*	01101011 *mm rrr r/m*
IMUL *r32,imm8*	6B /*r ib*	01101011 *mm rrr r/m*
IMUL *r16,r/m16,imm16*	69 /*r iw*	01101001 *mm rrr r/m*
IMUL *r32,r/m32,imm32*	69 /*r id*	01101001 *mm rrr r/m*
IMUL *r16,imm16*	69 /*r iw*	01101001 *mm rrr r/m*
IMUL *r32,imm32*	69 /*r id*	01101001 *mm rrr r/m*

Purpose: IMUL performs a signed multiplication operation. This instruction has three variations. In the one-operand form, the operand may be a byte, word or doubleword located in memory or in a general register. IMUL uses EAX and EDX as implicit operands in the same way that MUL does.

In a two-operand form, one of the source operands may be in any general register while the other may be either in memory or in a general register. The product replaces the general-register operand. If the result is within the range of the first operand, CF and OF are zero. Otherwise, CF and OF are set to 1.

In a three-operand form, two operands are source and one is destination. One of the source operands is an immediate value stored in the instruction. The second may be in memory or in any general register. The product may be stored in any general register. The immediate operand is treated as signed. If the immediate operand is a byte, the processor automatically sign-extends it to the size of the second operand before doing the multiplication. If the result is within the range of the first operand, CF and OF are zero. Otherwise, CF and OF are set to 1.

IN Input From Port

INSTRUCTION	OPCODE	BINARY
IN AL,*imm8*	E4 *ib*	11100100
IN AX,*imm8*	E5 *ib*	11100101
IN EAX,*imm8*	E5 *ib*	11100101
IN AL,DX	EC	11101100
IN AX,DX	ED	11101101
IN EAX,DX	ED	11101101

Purpose: IN brings a byte, word, or dword from a specified port and stores it in a register AL, AX, or EAX, respectively. The port is specified by the second operand and is in the range of 0 to 64K-1. The port is accessed by using an immediate operand or by placing its number into the DX register and using an IN instruction with DX as the second parameter. The immediate byte allows ports 0 to 255 to be accessed, in which case the upper bits of the port are always zero. The register form (DX) allows for the full range to be used. An exception occurs if the current task has insufficient privilege for the I/O.

INC Increment by 1

INSTRUCTION	OPCODE	BINARY
INC *r/m8*	FE /0	11111110 *mm* 000 *r/m*
INC *r/m16*	FF /0	11111111 *mm* 000 *r/m*
INC *r/m32*	FF /0	11111111 *mm* 000 *r/m*
INC *r16*	40 + rw	01000*rrr*
INC *r32*	40 + *rd*	01000*rrr*

Purpose: INC adds one to the destination operand, but (unlike ADD) INC does not affect CF. Other flags are set according to the result. Use ADD with an operand of 1 if the Carry Flag update is desired.

INS	**Input String from Port**
INSB	**Input Byte**
INSW	**Input Word**
INSD	**Input Doubleword**

INSTRUCTION	OPCODE	BINARY
INS *r/m8*,DX	6C	01101100
INS *r/m16*,DX	6D	01101101
INS *r/m32*,DX	6D	01101101

Note: INSB is a common assembler mnemonic for INS *r/m8*,DX
INSW is a common assembler mnemonic for INS *r/m16*,DX
INSD is a common assembler mnemonic for INS *r/m32*,DX

Purpose: These instructions allow a read from a specified device into memory (ES:EDI), the input device being specified in the DX register. After the transfer is made, EDI is updated to point to the next string location, depending on how DF (the Direction Flag) is set. If DF = 0, EDI increments by 1, 2, or 4. If DF = 1, EDI is decremented by −1, −2, or −4. The data is read into the segment specified by ES and no segment override is possible. INS does *not* allow port number specification as an immediate value. The port must be addressed through DX.

These instructions normally use a REP prefix, to indicate the reading of the number of bytes as specified in CX. An exception is raised if the current task has insufficient privilege to perform I/O.

INT	**Call to Interrupt Procedure**
INTO	**Interrupt on Overflow**

INSTRUCTION	OPCODE	BINARY
INT 3	CC	11001100
INT *imm8*	CD *ib*	11001101
INTO	CE	11001110

Purpose: INT transfers control from one code segment location to another. These locations can be within the same code segment (*near*) or in different code segments (*far*). INT is a software-generated interrupt that allows a programmer to transfer control to an interrupt service routine from within a program.

When any of the INTs are used, the flags register, the code segment register, and the instruction pointer are pushed onto the stack. When CS is PUSHed onto the stack, a full 32-bit word is PUSHed. This keeps the stack aligned which improves the 80386 performance.

INT *n* activates the interrupt service that corresponds to the number coded in the instruction. INT may specify any interrupt type. Note that Interrupts 0–31 are reserved by Intel. INT *n* returns control at the end of the service routine with an IRET.

INTO invokes Interrupt 4 if the Overflow Flag (OF) is set and Interrupt 4 is reserved for this purpose. OF is set by several arithmetic, logical, and string instructions.

INT 3 is a single-byte form (the breakpoint instruction), which is useful for debugging.

IRET — Return from Interrupt
IRETD — Return from Interrupt (32-bit mode)

INSTRUCTION	OPCODE	BINARY
IRET	CF	11001111
IRETD	CF	11001111

Purpose: IRET returns control to an interrupted procedure. IRET differs from RET in that it also POPs the flags register, the code segment register, and the instruction pointer from the stack. The registers are PUSHed onto the stack by the interrupt mechanism. When CS is popped, the full 32-bit word is popped for stack alignment and the upper 16 bits are discarded. Stack alignment improves 80386 performance.

Note: In the case of IRET, the flags register is Flags. If IRETD is used, then it's the EFLAGS register.

JMP — Jump
Jcc — Jump on Condition Code

INSTRUCTION	OPCODE	BINARY
JA *rel8*	77 *cb*	01110111
JAE *rel8*	73 *cb*	01110011

JB *rel8*	72 *cb*	01110010
JBE *rel8*	76 *cb*	01110110
JC *rel8*	72 *cb*	01110010
JCXZ *rel8*	E3 *cb*	11100011
JECXZ *rel8*	E3 *cb*	11100011
JE *rel8*	74 *cb*	01110100
JZ *rel8*	74 *cb*	01110100
JG *rel8*	7F *cb*	01111111
JGE *rel8*	7D *cb*	01111101
JL *rel8*	7C *cb*	01111100
JLE *rel8*	7E *cb*	01111110
JNA *rel8*	76 *cb*	01110110
JNAE *rel8*	72 *cb*	01110010
JNB *rel8*	73 *cb*	01110011
JNBE *rel8*	77 *cb*	01110111
JNC *rel8*	73 *cb*	01110011
JNE *rel8*	75 *cb*	01110101
JNG *rel8*	7E *cb*	01111110
JNGE *rel8*	7C *cb*	01111100
JNL *rel8*	7D *cb*	01111101
JNLE *rel8*	7F *cb*	01111111
JNO *rel8*	71 *cb*	01110001
JNP *rel8*	7B *cb*	01111011
JNS *rel8*	79 *cb*	01111001
JNZ *rel8*	75 *cb*	01110101
JO *rel8*	70 *cb*	01110000
JP *rel8*	7A *cb*	01111010
JPE *rel8*	7A *cb*	01111010
JPO *rel8*	7B *cb*	01111011
JS *rel8*	78 *cb*	01111000
JZ *rel8*	74 *cb*	01110100
JA *rel16/32*	0F 87 *cw/cd*	00001111 10000111
JAE *rel16/32*	0F 83 *cw/cd*	00001111 10000011
JB *rel16/32*	0F 82 *cw/cd*	00001111 10000010
JBE *rel16/32*	0F 86 *cw/cd*	00001111 10000110
JC *rel16/32*	0F 82 *cw/cd*	00001111 10000010
JE *rel16/32*	0F 84 *cw/cd*	00001111 10000100
JZ *rel16/32*	0F 84 *cw/cd*	00001111 10000100
JG *rel16/32*	0F 8F *cw/cd*	00001111 10001111
JGE *rel16/32*	0F 8D *cw/cd*	00001111 10001101
JL *rel16/32*	0F 8C *cw/cd*	00001111 10001100
JLE *rel16/32*	0F 8E *cw/cd*	00001111 10001110
JNA *rel16/32*	0F 86 *cw/cd*	00001111 10000110
JNAE *rel16/32*	0F 82 *cw/cd*	00001111 10000010

JNB *rel16/32*	0F 83 *cw/cd*	00001111 10000011
JNBE *rel16/32*	0F 87 *cw/cd*	00001111 10000111
JNC *rel16/32*	0F 83 *cw/cd*	00001111 10000011
JNE *rel16/32*	0F 85 *cw/cd*	00001111 10000101
JNG *rel16/32*	0F 8E *cw/cd*	00001111 10001110
JNGE *rel16/32*	0F 8C *cw/cd*	00001111 10001100
JNL *rel16/32*	0F 8D *cw/cd*	00001111 10001101
JNLE *rel16/32*	0F 8F *cw/cd*	00001111 10001111
JNO *rel16/32*	0F 81 *cw/cd*	00001111 10000001
JNP *rel16/32*	0F 8B *cw/cd*	00001111 10001011
JNS *rel16/32*	0F 89 *cw/cd*	00001111 10001001
JNZ *rel16/32*	0F 85 *cw/cd*	00001111 10000101
JO *rel16/32*	0F 80 *cw/cd*	00001111 10000000
JP *rel16/32*	0F 8A *cw/cd*	00001111 10001010
JPE *rel16/32*	0F 8A *cw/cd*	00001111 10001010
JPO *rel16/32*	0F 8B *cw/cd*	00001111 10001011
JS *rel16/32*	0F 88 *cw/cd*	00001111 10001000
JZ *rel16/32*	0F 84 *cw/cd*	00001111 10000100

Purpose: JMP transfers control from one code segment location to another. The J*cc* jumps depend on the flags, as shown below. These locations can be within the same code segment (*near*) or in different code segments (*far*). JMP unconditionally transfers control to the target location and is a one-way transfer. JMP does *not* save a return address on the stack as CALL does.

JMP's implementation varies depending on whether the address is directly specified within the instruction or indirectly through a register or memory. A direct JMP includes the destination address as part of the instruction. An indirect JMP gets the destination address through a register or a pointer variable. An indirect JMP specifies an absolute address by one of the following ways: (1) a register modifies the address of the memory pointer to select a destination address; (2) the program can JMP to a location specified by a general register (EAX, EDX, ECX, EBX, EBP, ESI, or EDI)—the 80386 moves this 32-bit value into EIP and resumes execution; or (3) the 80386 obtains the destination address from a memory operand specified in the instruction.

The following J*cc* conditional transfer instructions may or may not transfer control, depending on the state of the flags when the instruction executes. The flags are assumed to have been set in some meaningful way by preceding instruction(s).

JA/JNBE	Above, not below nor equal	CF = 0, ZF = 0
JAE/JNB	Above or equal, not below	CF = 0
JB/JNAE	Below, not above nor equal	CF = 1

JBE/JNA	Below or equal, not above	CF = 1, ZF = 1
JC	Carry	CF = 1
JE/JZ	Equal, zero	ZF = 1
JNC	Not carry	CF = 0
JNE/JNZ	Not equal, not zero	ZF = 0
JNP/JPO	Not parity, parity odd	PF = 0
JP/JPE	Parity, parity even	PF = 1

The following *Jcc* instructions are signed control transfers:

JG/JNLE	Greater, not less nor equal	ZF = 0, SF = OF
JGE/JNL	Greater or equal, not less	SF = OF
JL/JNGE	Less, not greater nor equal	SF = OF
JLE/JNG	Less or equal, not greater	SF = OF, ZF = 1
JNO	Not overflow	OF = 0
JNS	Not sign	SF = 0
JO	Overflow	OF = 1
JS	Sign (negative)	SF = 1

JCXZ (Jump if ECX is zero) branches to the label specified in the instruction if it finds a value of zero in the ECX register. JCXZ is useful in that sometimes it is desirable to design a loop that executes zero times if the count variable in ECX is initialized to zero. When used with repeated string scan and compare instructions, JCXZ determines whether the repetitions ended due to a zero in ECX or to satisfaction of the scan or compare conditions.

LAHF Load Flags into AH Register

INSTRUCTION	OPCODE	BINARY
LAHF	9F	10011111

Purpose: Though specific instructions exist to alter CF and DF, there is no direct way of altering the other applications-oriented flags. The flag transfer instructions (LAHF and SAHF) allow a program to alter the other flag bits with the bit manipulation instructions after transferring these flags to the stack or the AH register.

LAHF copies SF, ZF, AF, PF, and CF to AH bits 7, 6, 4, 2, and 0, respectively. The contents of the remaining bits (5, 3, and 1) are undefined. The flags remain unaffected (see Fig. C-4).

7	6	5	4	3	2	1	0
S	Z		A		P		C
F	F	0	F	0	F	1	F

Fig. C-4. Low byte of the Flags register.

LAR — Load Access Rights Byte

INSTRUCTION	OPCODE	BINARY
LAR *r16,r/m16*	0F 02 /*r*	00001111 00000010 *mm rrr r/m*
LAR *r32,r/m32*	0F 02 /*r*	00001111 00000010 *mm rrr r/m*

Purpose: LAR reads a segment descriptor and puts the Granularity (bit 23), Programmer Available (bit 20), Present (bit 15), DPL (bit 14), Type (bit 9-11), and Accessed (bit 8) into a 32-bit register, the first operand. If you specify a 16-bit register as the first operand, the Granularity, and Programmer Available bits are not moved.

The segment attribute field is simply the high-order four bytes of the descriptor ANDed with 00FxFF00h, where x indicates that bits 16 through 19 are undefined in the value loaded by LAR.

Note: The only valid special segment and gate descriptor types are shown in Fig. C-5. The descriptor specified by the selector in the first operand must be within the descriptor table limits, have a valid Type field, and be accessible at both CPL and RPL of the selector in the second operand compared to DPL. If so, ZF is set to 1 and the segment attributes are loaded to operand 1. If not, ZF is set to zero and the first operand is unmodified.

LEA — Load Effective Address

INSTRUCTION	OPCODE	BINARY
LEA *r16,m*	8D /*r*	10001101 *mm rrr r/m*
LEA *r32,m*	8D /*r*	10001101 *mm rrr r/m*

Purpose: LEA transfers the offset of the source operand, rather than its value, to the destination operand. The source operand must be a memory operand. The destination operand must be a general register. LEA is particularly useful for initializing registers before the execution of the string primitives or the XLAT.

Type	Name
0	Undefined, invalid
1	Available 80286 TSS
2	Local Descriptor Table
3	Busy 80286 TSS
4	80286 Call Gate
5	80286/80386 Task Gate
6	80286 Interrupt Gate
7	80286 Trap Gate
8	Undefined, invalid
9	Available 80386 TSS
A	Undefined, invalid
B	Busy 80386 TSS
C	80386 Call Gate
D	Undefined, invalid
E	80386 Interrupt Gate
F	80386 Trap Gate

Fig. C-5. Valid Special Segment and Gate Descriptor types.

LEAVE High-Level Procedure Exit

INSTRUCTION	OPCODE	BINARY
LEAVE	C9	11001001

Purpose: LEAVE reverses the action of a previous ENTER. LEAVE does not use any operands. LEAVE copies EBP to ESP to release all stack space allocated to the procedure by the most recent ENTER. Then LEAVE POPs the old value of EBP from the stack. A subsequent RET can then remove any arguments that were pushed on the stack by the calling program for use by the called procedure.

LGDT Load Global Descriptor Table Register
LIDT Load Interrupt Descriptor Table Register

INSTRUCTION	OPCODE	BINARY
LGDT *m16&32*	0F 01 /2	00001111 00000001 *mm* 010 *r/m*
LIDT *m16&32*	0F 01 /3	00001111 00000001 *mm* 011 *r/m*

Purpose: LGDT loads the global descriptor table (GDT) register. LGDT loads the global descriptor table (GDTR) from the 48-bit pseudo-descriptor given in the instruction. This 48-bit group has two components: the limit and base. The 16-bit limit is stored at the low word and the 32-bit base at the high dword.

LIDT tells the hardware where to go in case of interrupts. LIDT loads the interrupt descriptor table (IDTR) from the 48-bit pseudo-descriptor given in the instruction. This 48-bits has two components: the limit and base. The 16-bit limit is stored at the low word and the 32-bit base at the high dword.

Both GDT and IDT are loaded at system reset (initialization of the operating system). This generally happens at the beginning of the work session.

LGS Load Full Pointer
LSS Load Pointer Using SS
LDS Load Pointer Using DS
LES Load Pointer Using ES
LFS Load Pointer Using FS

INSTRUCTION	OPCODE	BINARY
LDS *r16,m16:16*	C5 */r*	11000101 *mm rrr r/m*
LDS *r32,m16:32*	C5 */r*	11000101 *mm rrr r/m*
LSS *r16,m16:16*	0F B2 */r*	00001111 10110010 *mm rrr r/m*
LSS *r32,m16:32*	0F B2 */r*	00001111 10110010 *mm rrr r/m*
LES *r16,m16:16*	C4 */r*	11000100 *mm rrr r/m*
LES *r32,m16:32*	C4 */r*	11000100 *mm rrr r/m*
LFS *r16,m16:16*	0F B4 */r*	00001111 10110100 *mm rrr r/m*
LFS *r32,m16:32*	0F B4 */r*	00001111 10110100 *mm rrr r/m*
LGS *r16,m16:16*	0F B5 */r*	00001111 10110101 *mm rrr r/m*
LGS *r32,m16:32*	0F B5 */r*	00001111 10110101 *mm rrr r/m*

Purpose: The data pointer instructions load a pointer which consists of a segment selector and an offset into a segment register and a general register.

LDS transfers a pointer variable from the source operand to DS and the destination register. The source operand must be a memory operand. The destination operand must be a general register. DS receives the segment-selector of the pointer. The destination register receives the offset part of the pointer, which points to a specific location within the segment. The other instructions use the various registers, as noted in the instruction mnemonic.

LSS is particularly important because it allows the two registers that identify the stack (SS:ESP) to be changed in one uninterruptible operation.

LLDT — Load Local Descriptor Table Register

INSTRUCTION	OPCODE	BINARY
LLDT *r/m16*	0F 00 /2	00001111 00000000 *mm* 010 *r/m*

Purpose: The Local Descriptor Table is loaded whenever a task or major subsystem gains or regains control of the system. LLDT loads the Local Descriptor Table Register (LDTR). The operand (memory or register) should hold a selector to the GDT. The descriptor registers are not affected and the LDT field in the task state segment does not change. The first operand may be a null selector, which causes the LDT to be marked invalid. Loading a selector naming an LDT segment raises a segment load exception if LDTR contains a null selector.

LMSW — Load Machine Status Word

INSTRUCTION	OPCODE	BINARY
LMSW *r/m16*	0F 01 /6	00001111 00000001 *mm* 110 *r/m*

Purpose: LMSW loads the machine status word (MSW) into CR0 from the source as specified in the first operand. LMSW can be used to switch to Protected Mode, by setting the PE bit to 1. If so, the instruction queue must be flushed and LMSW followed by an intrasegment jump instruction. LMSW will *not* switch back to Real Address Mode; that is, you cannot alter the PE bit to zero with an LMSW.

For compatibility with the 80286, the ET bit of MSW is not altered by the LMSW instruction. ET is the processor Extension Type.

LOCK — Assert LOCK# Signal Prefix

INSTRUCTION	OPCODE	BINARY
LOCK	F0	11110000

Purpose: LOCK asserts a hold on shared memory so that the 80386 has exclusive use of it during the instruction which immediately follows the LOCK. LOCK's integrity is not affected by memory field alignment. LOCK will only work with:

BT, BTS, BTR, BTC	*memory, reg/imm*
ADD, OR, ADC, SBB, AND, SUB, XOR	*memory, reg/imm*
NOT, NEG, INC, DEC	*memory*
XCHG	*reg, memory* or *memory, reg*

An undefined opcode trap is generated if LOCK is used with any instruction not listed here. Note that XCHG always asserts LOCK# whether or not it has the LOCK prefix.

Note: LOCK is *not* assured if another 80386 is concurrently executing an instruction that has any of the following characteristics:

1. If it is not one of the instructions in the list above.
2. If it is not preceded by a LOCK prefix.
3. If it specifies a memory operand that does not *exactly* overlap the destination operand. LOCK is not guaranteed for partial overlap, even if one memory is contained wholly within the other.

LODS Load String Operand
LODSB Load Byte
LODSW Load Word
LODSD Load Doubleword

INSTRUCTION	OPCODE	BINARY
LODS *m8*	AC	10101100
LODS *m16*	AD	10101101
LODS *m32*	AD	10101101

Purpose: These instructions operate on strings rather than on logical or numeric values. They operate on one element of a string, which may be a byte, a word, or a doubleword. The string elements are addressed by the DS (default) and ESI registers. After each string operation, ESI is automatically updated to point to the next element of the string. If DF = 0, the index register is incremented. If DF = 1, it is decremented. The amount incremented or decremented is 1, 2, or 4, depending on the size of the string element.

LODS places the source string element at ESI into AL for byte strings, AX for word strings, and in EAX for doubleword strings. LODS increments or decrements ESI according to DF.

The operand specifies the length of the operand, e.g., AH specifies 8 bits, AX 16, and EAX 32. The actual transfer is always done with the address specified in ESI. A segment override prefix can be specified in the operand, which is applied to [ESI].

LOOP	**Loop Control while ECX Counter Not Zero**
LOOP*cond*	
LOOPE	**Loop while Equal**
LOOPZ	**Loop while Zero**
LOOPNE	**Loop while Not Equal**
LOOPNZ	**Loop while Not Zero**

INSTRUCTION	OPCODE	BINARY
LOOP *rel8*	E2 *cb*	11100010
LOOPE *rel8*	E1 *cb*	11100001
LOOPNE *rel8*	E1 *cb*	11100001

Note: LOOPZ is an alternate mnemonic for LOOPE rel8
LOOPNZ is an alternate mnemonic for LOOPNE rel8

Purpose: The LOOP instructions are conditional jumps that use a value stored in ECX to specify the number of times a section of software will loop to a label. All LOOPs automatically decrement ECX and terminate when ECX = 0. LOOP is placed at the bottom of the loop and the label at the top.

LOOP first decrements ECX before testing ECX for the branch condition. If ECX is not zero, the program branches to the target label specified in the instruction. If ECX = 0, control transfers to the instruction immediately following the LOOP. ECX is decremented without affecting any of the flags.

LOOPE and LOOPZ are synonymously the same instruction. These instructions decrement ECX before testing ECX and ZF for branch condition. If ECX is non-zero and ZF = 1, the program branches to the target label as specified in the instruction. If LOOPE or LOOPZ finds ECX = 0 *or* ZF = 0, control transfers to the instruction immediately following the LOOPE or LOOPZ.

LOOPNE and LOOPNZ are synonymously the same instruction. These instructions decrement ECX before testing ECX or ZF for branch conditions. If ECX is non-zero and ZF = 0, the program branches to the target label specified by the instruction. If ECX = 0 *or* ZF = 1, control transfers to the instruction immediately following LOOPNE or LOOPNZ.

LSL Load Segment Limit

INSTRUCTION	OPCODE	BINARY
LSL *r16,r/m16*	0F 03 /*r*	00001111 00000011 *mm rrr r/m*
LSL *r32,r/m32*	0F 03 /*r*	00001111 00000011 *mm rrr r/m*

Purpose: LSL loads a user-specified register with a segment limit from the descriptor for the segment specified by the selector in the second operand. If the source selector is visible at the CPL and the descriptor is a type accepted by LSL (See Fig. C-6), LSL sets ZF to 1. Otherwise, LSL sets ZF to 0 and keeps the destination register unchanged. The 32-bit forms of LSL store the 32-bit granular limit in the 16-bit destination register.

Note that this segment limit is a byte granular value. If the descriptor uses a page granular (the G bit = 1) segment limit, LSL translates that value to a byte limit (shifts it left 12 bits and fills the low 12 bits with 1s) and then loads it into the destination register.

Fig. C-6. Valid system segments and gates for LSL.

Type	Name
0	Undefined, invalid
1	Available 80286 TSS
2	Local Descriptor Table
3	Busy 80286 TSS
4	80286 Call Gate
5	80286/80386 Task Gate
6	80286 Interrupt Gate
7	80286 Trap Gate
8	Undefined, invalid
9	Available 80386 TSS
A	Undefined, invalid
B	Busy 80386 TSS
C	80386 Call Gate
D	Undefined, invalid
E	80386 Interrupt Gate
F	80386 Trap Gate

LTR Load Task Register

INSTRUCTION	OPCODE	BINARY
LTR *r/m16*	0F 00 /3	00001111 00000000 *mm* 011 *r/m*

Purpose: The first operand of LTR specifies the source register or memory location which contains information for the task register. LTR loads data from that location into the task register. The loaded TSS is marked busy; however, a task switch does *not* occur. The given selector must point to a global descriptor table (GDT) entry that is of the descriptor type TSS. If this is the case, the Task Register is loaded.

MOV Move Data

INSTRUCTION	OPCODE	BINARY
MOV *r/m8,r8*	88 /*r*	10001000 *mm rrr r/m*
MOV *r/m16,r16*	89 /*r*	10001001 *mm rrr r/m*
MOV *r/m32,r32*	89 /*r*	10001001 *mm rrr r/m*
MOV *r8,r/m8*	8A /*r*	10001010 *mm rrr r/m*
MOV *r16,r/m16*	8B /*r*	10001011 *mm rrr r/m*
MOV *r32,r/m32*	8B /*r*	10001011 *mm rrr r/m*
MOV *r/m16,sreg*	8C /*r*	10001100 *mm rrr r/m*
MOV *Sreg,r/m16*	8D /*r*	10001101 *mm rrr r/m*
MOV AL,*moffs8*	A0	10100000
MOV AX,*moffs16*	A1	10100001
MOV EAX,*moffs32*	A1	10100001
MOV *moffs8*,AL	A2	10100010
MOV *moffs16*,AX	A3	10100011
MOV *moffs32*,EAX	A3	10100011
MOV *reg8,imm8*	B0 + *rb*	10110*rrr*
MOV *reg16,imm16*	B8 + *rw*	10111*rrr*
MOV *reg32,imm32*	B8 + *rd*	10111*rrr*
MOV *r/m8,imm8*	C6	11000110 *mm rrr r/m*
MOV *r/m16,imm16*	C7	11000111 *mm rrr r/m*
MOV *r/m32,imm32*	C7	11000111 *mm rrr r/m*

Purpose: MOV transfers a byte, word, or doubleword from the source operand to the destination operand. MOV is useful for transferring data along these paths:

- ☐ Immediate data to a memory location
- ☐ Immediate data to a register
- ☐ Between general registers
- ☐ To a register from memory
- ☐ To memory from a register

There are some variations of MOV that operate on segment registers, which is how the segment registers are initialized in programs in this book.

Note: MOV cannot move from memory to memory or from segment register to segment register. Memory to memory can be done with the string move instruction MOVS.

MOV — Move To/From Special Registers

INSTRUCTION	OPCODE	BINARY
MOV *r32*,CR0/CR2/CR3	0F 20 /r	00001111 00100000 *mm ccc r/m*
MOV CR0/CR2/CR3,*r32*	0F 22 /r	00001111 00100010 *mm ccc r/m*
MOV *r32*,TR6/TR7	0F 24 /r	00001111 00100100 *mm + + + r/m*
MOV TR6/TR7,*r32*	0F 26 /r	00001111 00100110 *mm + + + r/m*
MOV *r32*,DR0-3/6/7	0F 21 /r	00001111 00100001 *mm ddd r/m*
MOV DR0–3/6/7,*r32*	0F 23 /r	00001111 00100011

Purpose: These forms of MOV load or store special registers or from a general register. They are particularly designed for the Control Registers (CR0, CR2, CR3), Test Registers (TR6 and TR7), and the Debug Registers (DR0, DR1, DR2, DR3, DR6, and DR7).

MOVS — Move Data from String to String
MOVSB — Move String Byte
MOVSW — Move String Word
MOVSD — Move String Doubleword

INSTRUCTION	OPCODE	BINARY
MOVS *m8,m8*	A4	10100100
MOVS *m16,m16*	A5	10100101
MOVS *m32,m32*	A5	10100101

Note: MOVSB is a common assembler mnemonic for MOVS *m8,m8*
MOVSW is a common assembler mnemonic for MOVS *m16,m16*
MOVSD is a common assembler mnemonic for MOVS *m32,m32*

Purpose: These instructions operate on strings rather than on logical or numeric values. They operate on one element of a string addressed by [ESI] (which may be a byte, a word, or a doubleword) and move it to the area addressed by ES:[EDI]. After each string operation, ESI and/or EDI are automatically updated to point to the next element of the string. If the direction (DF) is 0, the index registers are incremented. If DF = 1, they are decremented. The amount incremented or decremented is 1, 2, or 4, depending on the size of the string element.

When prefixed by REP, MOVS operates as a memory-to-memory block transfer and repeats for the number of times of the value stored in ECX. To set this up, the program must first initialize ECX and the register pairs ESI and EDI. ECX specifies the number of bytes, words or doublewords in the block. If the direction flag (DF) is 0, the program must point ESI to the first element of the source string and point EDI to the destination address for the first element. If DF = 1, the program points these two registers to the last element of the source string and to the destination address for the last element, respectively.

MOVSX Move with Sign Extension

INSTRUCTION	OPCODE	BINARY
MOVSX *r16,r/m8*	0F BE /*r*	00001111 10111110 *mm rrr r/m*
MOVSX *r32,r/m8*	0F BE /*r*	00001111 10111110 *mm rrr r/m*
MOVSX *r32,r/m16*	0F BF /*r*	00001111 10111111 *mm rrr r/m*

Purpose: MOVSX sign-extends an 8-bit value to a 16-bit value and an 8-bit or 16-bit value to 32-bit value. If both operands are words, a normal move occurs. This instruction is new to the 80386.

MOVZX Move with Zero Extension

INSTRUCTION	OPCODE	BINARY
MOVZX *r16,r/m8*	0F B6 /*r*	00001111 10110110 *mm rrr r/m*
MOVZX *r32,r/m8*	0F B6 /*r*	00001111 10110110 *mm rrr r/m*
MOVZX *r32,r/m16*	0F B7 /*r*	00001111 10110111 *mm rrr r/m*

Purpose: MOVZX extends an 8-bit value to a 16-bit value and an 8- or 16-bit value to 32-bit value by padding with high-order zeros. If both operands are words, a normal move occurs. This instruction is new to the 80386.

MUL Unsigned Integer Multiply of AL, AX, or EAX

INSTRUCTION	OPCODE	BINARY
MUL AL,*r/m8*	F6 /4	11110110 *mm* 100 *r/m*
MUL AX,*r/m16*	F7 /4	11110111 *mm* 100 *r/m*
MUL EAX,*r/m32*	F7 /4	11110111 *mm* 100 *r/m*

Purpose: MUL multiplies the numbers in the source operand and the accumulator. If the source is a byte, the 80386 multiplies it by the contents of AL and returns the double-length result in AH and AL. If the source operand is a word, the 80386 multiplies it by the contents of AX and returns the double-length result to DX and AX. If the source is a doubleword, the processor multiplies it by the contents of EAX and returns the 64-bit result in EDX and EAX. MUL sets CF and OF to zero, if AH, DX, or EDX is all zeros for 8-, 16-, or 32-bit operations. Otherwise CF and OF are set to 1.

NEG Negate (Two's Complement)

INSTRUCTION	OPCODE	BINARY
NEG *r/m8*	F6 /3	11110110 *mm* 011 *r/m*
NEG *r/m16*	F7 /3	11110111 *mm* 011 *r/m*
NEG *r/m32*	F7 /3	11110111 *mm* 011 *r/m*

Purpose: NEG subtracts a signed integer operand from zero. Its effect is to make a positive into a negative or vice versa. That is, NEG forms a two's complement of a given operand, which is subtracted from zero. The result is placed in the operand. The Carry Flag (CF) is set to 1, except when the operand prior to the NEG was zero.

NOP No Operation

INSTRUCTION	OPCODE	BINARY
NOP	90	10010000

Purpose: NOP occupies a byte of storage. It affects nothing but the instruction pointer, EIP. NOP is useful for providing space in "fixing up" branch addresses, i.e., the address may require an 8- or 16-bit displacement—if 16 bits are reserved, an 8-bit displacement and a NOP can be used to fill the 16 bits.

NOT Negate (One's Complement)

INSTRUCTION	OPCODE	BINARY
NOT *r/m8*	F6 /2	11110110 *mm* 010 *r/m*
NOT *r/m16*	F7 /2	11110111 *mm* 010 *r/m*
NOT *r/m32*	F7 /2	11110111 *mm* 010 *r/m*

Purpose: NOT inverts the bits in the specified operand to form a one's complement of the operand. NOT is a unary operation (refers to an arithmetic operator having only one term) that uses a single operand in a register or memory. The result is stored in the operand. NOT has no effect on flags.

OR Logical Inclusive OR

INSTRUCTION	OPCODE	BINARY
OR AL,*imm8*	0C *ib*	00001100
OR AX,*imm16*	0D *iw*	00001101
OR EAX,*imm32*	0D *id*	00001101
OR *r/m8,imm8*	80 /1 *ib*	10000000 *mm* 001 *r/m*
OR *r/m16,imm16*	81 /1 *iw*	10000001 *mm* 001 *r/m*
OR *r/m32,imm32*	81 /1 *id*	10000001 *mm* 001 *r/m*
OR *r/m16,imm8*	83 /1 *ib*	10000011 *mm* 001 *r/m*
OR *r/m32,imm8*	83 /1 *ib*	10000011 *mm* 001 *r/m*
OR *r/m8,r8*	08 /*r*	00001000 *mm* 001 *r/m*
OR *r/m16,r16*	09 /*r*	00001001 *mm* 001 *r/m*
OR *r/m32,r32*	09 /*r*	00001001 *mm* 001 *r/m*
OR *r8,r/m8*	0A /*r*	00001010 *mm rrr r/m*
OR *r16,r/m16*	0B /*r*	00001011 *mm rrr r/m*
OR *r32,r/m32*	0B /*r*	00001011 *mm rrr r/m*

Purpose: OR compares its two operands and computes the following: if each corresponding bit in the operands are zeros, the result is a zero; otherwise, the result is a 1.

Operand 1	0 0 1 1
Operand 2	0 1 1 0
Result	0 1 1 1

The result is stored in the operand.

OUT — Output To Port

INSTRUCTION	OPCODE	BINARY
OUT *imm8*,AL	E6 *ib*	11100110
OUT *imm8*,AX	E7 *ib*	11100111
OUT *imm8*,EAX	E7 *ib*	11100111
OUT DX,AL	EE	11101110
OUT DX,AX	EF	11101111
OUT DX,EAX	EF	11101111

Purpose: OUT transfers data from a register to an output port. The source is a register (AL, AX, or EAX) and is given as the second operand. The output port is specified in the first operand. To output data to any port from 0 to 65536, the port number is placed in the DX register. OUT is then used with DX as the first operand. If the instruction contains an 8-bit port ID, the value is zero-extended to 16 bits in DX. If the immediate 8 is used, only ports from 0 to 255 are valid. In this case, the upper bits of the port address are zero.

Note: I/O ports 00F8 through 00FF are reserved by Intel.

OUTS — Output String to Port
OUTSB — Output Byte
OUTSW — Output Word
OUTSD — Output Doubleword

INSTRUCTION	OPCODE	BINARY
OUTS DX,*r/m8*	6E	01101110
OUTS DX,*r/m16*	6F	01101111
OUTS DX,*r/m32*	6F	01101111

Note: OUTSB is a common assembler mnemonic for OUTS DX,*r/m8*
OUTSW is a common assembler mnemonic for OUTS DX,*r/m16*
OUTSD is a common assembler mnemonic for OUTS DX,*r/m32*

Purpose: OUTS operates much like OUT, in that it transfers data (memory byte, word, or doubleword) at the source- index register to the output port addressed by the DX register. After the data transfer, the source-index register (SI or ESI, see below) is advanced; that is, it is either incremented or decremented. If the DF is 0 (CLD was executed), the index is incremented. If DF is 1 (STD was executed), it is decremented. The amount it is changed depends on the size of the output: a 1 if it is a byte, a 2 if a word, or 4 if a doubleword.

The source data address is determined by the contents of a source-index register. The correct index value must be loaded into either SI or ESI prior to executing these instructions. SI is used for the source-index register if the address size attribute for these instructions is 16 bits. Otherwise, ESI is used and the address size attribute is 32 bits.

The port must be addressed through the DX register value. OUTS does *not* allow specification of the port number as an immediate value.

OUTS can be preceded by the REP prefix. In this case, ECX bytes, words, or dwords are transferred.

POP   Pop a Word from the Stack

INSTRUCTION	OPCODE	BINARY
POP *m16*	8F /0	10001111 *mm* 000 *r/m*
POP *m32*	8F /0	10111111 *mm* 000 *r/m*
POP *r16*	58 + *rw*	01011*rrr*
POP *r32*	58 + *rd*	01011*rrr*
POP DS	1F	00011111
POP ES	07	00000111
POP SS	17	00010111
POP FS	0F A1	00001111 10100001
POP GS	0F A9	00001111 10101001

Purpose: POP transfers the word or doubleword at the current top of stack (indicated by SS:ESP) to the destination operand. It then increments SS:ESP to point to the new top of stack. Care should be taken when popping 16-bit operands, to avoid misaligning the stack, which causes performance degradation.

POPA   POP All Registers
POPAD   POP All Registers (32-Bit Mode)

INSTRUCTION	OPCODE	BINARY
POPA	61	01100001
POPAD	61	01100001

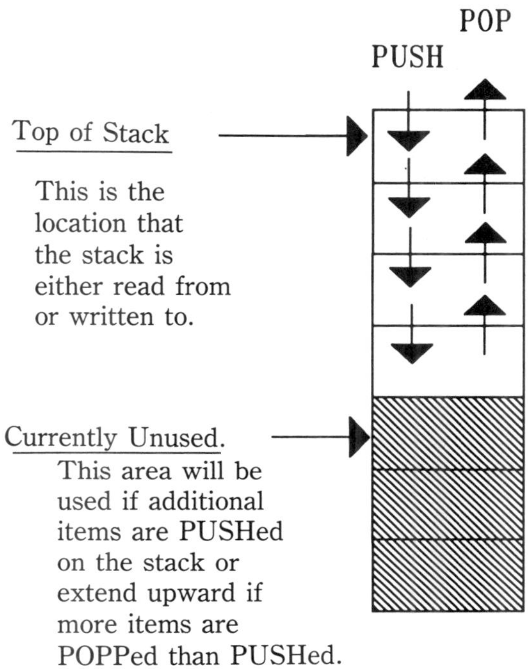

Fig. C-7. Representation of stack processing.

Purpose: POPA restores the eight general-purpose registers saved on the stack by PUSHA. It discards the saved value of ESP. The order the registers are popped is: DI, SI, BP, SP, BX, DX, CX, and AX for POPA, or EDI, ESI, EBP, ESP, EBX, EDX, ECX, and EAX for POPAD.

POPF — POP Stack into FLAGS or EFLAGS
POPFD — POP Stack (32-bit Mode)

INSTRUCTION	OPCODE	BINARY
POPF	9D	10011101
POPFD	9D	10011101

Purpose: POPF transfers specific bits from the word at the top of stack into the low-order byte of EFLAGS. Then POPF increments ESP by two. POPFD transfers the 16 or 32 bits and increments ESP by four. The RF and VM flags are not changed by either POPF or POPFD.

PUSHF and POPF are useful for storing the flags in memory where they can be examined and modified. They are useful also for preserving the state of the flags register while executing a procedure.

The IOPL (I/O Privilege Level) flag will only be altered if the Current Privilege Level (CPL) is 0. If not 0, IOPL is not altered and no exception results. If CPL is as privileged or more privileged than the current IOPL, the interrupt enable flag (IF) is altered. If not, IF is unchanged and no exception results.

PUSH — Push Operand To the Stack

INSTRUCTION	OPCODE	BINARY
PUSH *m16*	FF /6	11111111 *mm* 110 *r/m*
PUSH *m32*	FF /6	11111111 *mm* 110 *r/m*
PUSH *r16*	50 + /*r*	01010rrr
PUSH *r32*	50 + /*r*	01010rrr
PUSH *imm8*	6A	01101010
PUSH *imm16*	68	01101000
PUSH *imm32*	68	01101000
PUSH CS	0E	00001110
PUSH SS	16	00010110
PUSH DS	1E	00011110
PUSH ES	06	00000110
PUSH FS	0F A0	00001111 10100000
PUSH GS	0F A8	00001111 10101000

Purpose: PUSH decrements the stack pointer (ESP) then transfers the source operand to the top of stack (TOS) indicated by ESP. PUSH is often used to place parameters on the stack before calling a procedure. It is also the means of storing temporary variables on the stack. PUSH operates on memory operands, register operands (including segment registers) and immediate operands.

Immediate data is always considered to be 32 bits in size, although it may be encoded in the instruction as an 8-bit immediate.

Be careful when pushing 16-bit operands to avoid misaligning the stack, which causes performance degradation.

PUSHA PUSHAD — Push All General Registers

INSTRUCTION	OPCODE	BINARY
PUSHA	60	01100000
PUSHAD	60	01100000

Purpose: PUSHA saves the contents of the eight general purpose registers on the stack. PUSHA eliminates the need for eight consecutive PUSH instructions. The order of the registers PUSHed is: AX, CX, DX, BX, SP, BP, SI and DI for word, or EAX, ECX, EDX, EBX, ESP, EBP, ESI and EDI for dword. Note that the value PUSHed for SP or ESP is the original value. The order of the registers PUSHed is correct for a subsequent POPA.

PUSHF / PUSHFD — Push Flags Register EFLAGS onto the Stack

INSTRUCTION	OPCODE	BINARY
PUSHF	9C	10011100
PUSHFD	9C	10011100

Purpose: PUSHF decrements ESP (Stack Pointer) by two and then transfers the low-order word of EFLAGS to the word at the top of stack pointed to by ESP. PUSHFD decrements ESP by four then transfers both words of the EFLAGS to the top of stack pointed to by ESP. Note the VM and RF flags are not moved.

PUSHF and POPF are useful for storing the flags in memory, where they can be examined and modified. They are useful also for preserving the state of the flags register while executing a procedure.

RCL / RCR / ROL / ROR

RCL — **Rotate Left through Carry (Uses CF)**
RCR — **Rotate Right through Carry (Uses CF)**
ROL — **Rotate Left (Wrap Bits Around)**
ROR — **Rotate Right (Wrap Bits Around)**

INSTRUCTION	OPCODE	BINARY
RCL *r/m8*,1	D0 /2	11010000 *mm* 010 *r/m*
RCL *r/m8*,CL	D2 /2	11010010 *mm* 010 *r/m*
RCL *r/m8,imm8*	C0 /2 *ib*	11000000 *mm* 010 *r/m*
RCL *r/m16*,1	D1 /2	11010001 *mm* 010 *r/m*
RCL *r/m16*,CL	D3 /2	11010011 *mm* 010 *r/m*
RCL *r/m16,imm8*	C1 /2 *ib*	11000001 *mm* 010 *r/m*
RCL *r/m32*,1	D1 /2	11010001 *mm* 010 *r/m*
RCL *r/m32*,CL	D3 /2	11010011 *mm* 010 *r/m*
RCL *r/m32,imm8*	C1 /2 *ib*	11000001 *mm* 010 *r/m*
RCR *r/m8*,1	D0 /3	11010000 *mm* 011 *r/m*

INSTRUCTION	OPCODE	BINARY
RCR *r/m8*,CL	D2 /3	11010010 *mm* 011 *r/m*
RCR *r/m8,imm8*	C0 /3 *ib*	11000000 *mm* 011 *r/m*
RCR *r/m16*,1	D1 /3	11010001 *mm* 011 *r/m*
RCR *r/m16*,CL	D3 /3	11010011 *mm* 011 *r/m*
RCR *r/m16,imm8*	C1 /3 *ib*	11000001 *mm* 011 *r/m*
RCR *r/m32*,1	D1 /3	11010001 *mm* 011 *r/m*
RCR *r/m32*,CL	D3 /3	11010011 *mm* 011 *r/m*
RCR *r/m32,imm8*	C1 /3 *ib*	11000001 *mm* 011 *r/m*
ROL *r/m8*,1	D0 /0	11010000 *mm* 000 *r/m*
ROL *r/m8*,CL	D2 /0	11010010 *mm* 000 *r/m*
ROL *r/m8,imm8*	C0 /0 *ib*	11000000 *mm* 000 *r/m*
ROL *r/m16,*1	D1 /0	11010001 *mm* 000 *r/m*
ROL *r/m16*,CL	D3 /0	11010011 *mm* 000 *r/m*
ROL *r/m16,imm8*	C1 /0 *ib*	11000001 *mm* 000 *r/m*
ROL *r/m32*,1	D1 /0	11010001 *mm* 000 *r/m*
ROL *r/m32,*CL	D3 /0	11010011 *mm* 000 *r/m*
ROL *r/m32,imm8*	C1 /0 *ib*	11000001 *mm* 000 *r/m*
ROR *r/m8*,1	C0 /1	11000000 *mm* 001 *r/m*
ROR *r/m8*,CL	D2 /1	11010010 *mm* 001 *r/m*
ROR *r/m8,imm8*	C0 /1 *ib*	11000000 *mm* 001 *r/m*
ROR *r/m16*,1	D1 /1	11010001 *mm* 001 *r/m*
ROR *r/m16*,CL	D3 /1	11010011 *mm* 001 *r/m*
ROR *r/m16,imm8*	C1 /1 *ib*	11000001 *mm* 001 *r/m*
ROR *r/m32*,1	D1 /1	11010001 *mm* 001 *r/m*
ROR *r/m32*,CL	D3 /1	11010011 *mm* 001 *r/m*
ROR *r/m32,imm8*	C1 /1 *ib*	11000001 *mm* 001 *r/m*

Purpose: Rotate instructions allow bits in bytes, words and doublewords to be rotated. Bits rotated out of an operand are not lost as in a shift but are "circled back" into the other "end" of the operand. Rotates affect only the carry and overflow flags. CF may act as an extension of the operand in two of the rotate instructions. This allows a bit to be isolated and then tested by a conditional jump instruction (JC or JNC). CF always contains the value of the last bit rotated out, even if the instruction does not use this bit as an extension of the rotated operand.

In single-bit rotates, OF is set if the operation changes the high-order (sign) bit of the destination operand. If the sign bit retains its original value, OF is cleared. On multibit rotates, the value of OF is *always* undefined.

RCL rotates bits in the byte, word, or doubleword destination operand *left* by one or by the number of bits specified in the count operand. RCL differs from ROL in that it treats CF as a high-order one-bit extension of the destination operand. Each high-order bit that exits from the left side of the operand moves to CF before it returns to the operand as the low-order bit on the next rotation cycle.

RCR rotates bits in the byte, word, or doubleword destination *right* by one or by the number of bits specified in the count operand. RCR differs from ROR in that it treats CF as a low-order one-bit extension of the destination operand. Each low-order bit that exits from the right side of the operand moves to CF before it returns to the operand as the high-order bit on the next rotation cycle.

ROL rotates the byte, word, or doubleword destination operand *left* by one or by the number of bits specified in the count operand, ECX. For each rotation specified, the high-order bit that exits from the left of the operand returns at the right to become the new low-order bit of the operand. If the ROL count is 1, the overflow flag (OF) is set to 0 if the Carry Flag (after the ROL) equals the high bit of the resultant operand. Otherwise, OF is set to 1. If ROL is not 1, OF is undefined. ROL with a 0 count does not affect OF or CF.

ROR rotates the byte, word, or doubleword destination operand *right* by one or by the number of bits specified in the count operand. For each rotation, the low-order bit that exits from the right of the operand returns at the left to become the new high-order bit of the operand. If the ROR count is 1, the overflow flag (OF) is set to 0 if the top two bits of the resultant operand are equal. Otherwise, OF = 1. If the ROR count is not 1, OF is undefined. Rotates with a zero count do not alter OF or CF.

Note: Rotates with a count equal to 0 do not alter the Carry Flag. Also, RCL or RCR of 32 or 33 bits (for dwords) cannot be done, since only a count of 0 to 31 are valid.

REP — Repeat Following String Operation
REPE — Repeat while Equal
REPZ — Repeat while Zero
REPNE — Repeat while Not Equal
REPNZ — Repeat while Not Zero

INSTRUCTION	OPCODE	BINARY
REP INS *r/m8*,DX	F3 6C	11110011 01101100
REP INS *r/m16*,DX	F3 6D	11110011 01101101
REP INS *r/m32*,DX	F3 6D	11110011 01101101
REP MOVS *m8,m8*	F3 A4	11110011 10100100
REP MOVS *m16,m16*	F3 A5	11110011 10100101
REP MOVS *m32,m32*	F3 A5	11110011 10100101
REP OUTS DX,*r/m8*	F3 6E	11110011 01101110
REP OUTS DX,*r/m16*	F3 6F	11110011 01101111
REP OUTS DX,*r/m32*	F3 6F	11110011 01101111
REP STOS *m8*	F3 AA	11110011 10101010
REP STOS *m16*	F3 AB	11110011 10101011

REP STOS *m32*	F3 AB	11110011 10101011
REPE CMPS *m8,m8*	F3 A6	11110011 10100110
REPE CMPS *m16,m16*	F3 A7	11110011 10100111
REPE CMPS *m32,m32*	F3 A7	11110011 10100111
REPE SCAS *m8*	F3 AE	11110011 10101110
REPE SCAS *m16*	F3 AF	11110011 10101111
REPE SCAS *m32*	F3 AF	11110011 10101111
REPNE CMPS *m8,m8*	F2 A6	11110010 10100110
REPNE CMPS *m16,m16*	F2 A7	11110010 10100111
REPNE CMPS *m32,m32*	F2 A7	11110010 10100111
REPNE SCAS *m8*	F2 AE	11110010 10101110
REPNE SCAS *m16*	F2 AF	11110010 10101111
REPNE SCAS *m32*	F2 AF	11110010 10101111

Purpose: The REP prefixes specify repeated operation of a string, which enables the 80386 to process strings much faster than with a regular software loop. When a string operation has one of these repeat prefixes, the operation is executed repeatedly for ECX times. Each time, the operation uses a different element of the string. The repetition ends when one of the conditions specified by the prefix is satisfied.

At the repetition of the instruction, the string operation can be suspended temporarily to handle an external interrupt or exception. After that interrupt has been handled, the string operation begins where it left off.

REPE repeats ECX times or until Zero Flag (ZF) becomes zero. REPZ is synonymous with REPE. REPNE repeats ECX times, or until ZF becomes 1. REPNZ is synonymous with REPNE.

RET Return from Procedure

INSTRUCTION	OPCODE	BINARY
RET	C3	11000011
RET *imm16*	CA /*w*	11001010

Purpose: RET ends the execution of a CALLed procedure and transfers control through the back-link on the top of the stack, which is the EIP value. The back-link points to the program that originally invoked the procedure. RET restores the value of EIP (instruction pointer) that was saved on the stack by the previous CALL instruction.

RET can optionally specify an immediate operand. By adding this constant to the new top-of-stack pointer, RET removes any arguments that the CALLing program pushed onto the stack before the CALL executed.

SAHF — Store AH into Flags Register

INSTRUCTION	OPCODE	BINARY
SAHF	9E	10011110

Purpose: Though specific instructions exist to alter CF and DF, there is no direct way of altering the other applications-oriented flags. The flag transfer instructions (LAHF and SAHF) allow a program to alter the other flag bits with the bit manipulation instructions after transferring these flags to the stack or the AH register. Then SAHF stores the contents of AH to the low byte of EFLAGS.

SAL SAR SHL SHR — Shift Instructions

INSTRUCTION	OPCODE	BINARY
SAL *r/m8*,1	D0 /4	11010000 *mm* 100 *r/m*
SAL *r/m8*,CL	D2 /4	11010010 *mm* 100 *r/m*
SAL *r/m8,imm8*	C0 /4 *ib*	11000000 *mm* 100 *r/m*
SAL *r/m16*,1	D1 /4	11010001 *mm* 100 *r/m*
SAL *r/m16*,CL	D3 /4	11010011 *mm* 100 *r/m*
SAL *r/m16,imm8*	C1 /4 *ib*	11000001 *mm* 100 *r/m*
SAL *r/m32*,1	D1 /4	11000001 *mm* 100 *r/m*
SAL *r/m32*,CL	D3 /4	11010011 *mm* 100 *r/m*
SAL *r/m32,imm8*	C1 /4 *ib*	11000001 *mm* 100 *r/m*
SAR *r/m8*,1	D0 /7	11010000 *mm* 111 *r/m*
SAR *r/m8*,CL	D2 /7	11000010 *mm* 111 *r/m*
SAR *r/m8,imm8*	C0 /7 *ib*	11000000 *mm* 111 *r/m*
SAR *r/m16*,1	C1 /7	11000001 *mm* 111 *r/m*
SAR *r/m16*,CL	D3 /7	11010011 *mm* 111 *r/m*
SAR *r/m16,imm8*	C1 /7 *ib*	11000001 *mm* 111 *r/m*
SAR *r/m32*,1	D1 /7	11010001 *mm* 111 *r/m*
SAR *r/m32*,CL	D3 /7	11010011 *mm* 111 *r/m*
SAR *r/m32,imm8*	C1 /7 *ib*	11000001 *mm* 111 *r/m*
SHR *r/m8*,1	D0 /5	11010000 *mm* 101 *r/m*
SHR *r/m8*,CL	C2 /5	11000010 *mm* 101 *r/m*

SHR *r/m8,imm8*	C0 /5 *ib*	11000000 *mm* 101 *r/m*
SHR *r/m16*,1	D1 /5	11010001 *mm* 101 *r/m*
SHR *r/m16*,CL	D3 /5	11010011 *mm* 101 *r/m*
SHR *r/m16,imm8*	C1 /5 *ib*	11000001 *mm* 101 *r/m*
SHR *r/m32*,1	D1 /5	11010001 *mm* 101 *r/m*
SHR *r/m32*,CL	D3 /5	11010011 *mm* 101 *r/m*
SHR *r/m32,imm8*	C1 /5 *ib*	11000001 *mm* 101 *r/m*

Note: SHL is an alternate assembler opcode for SAL.

Purpose: The bits in bytes, words and doublewords can be shifted logically or arithmetically. Bits can be shifted up to 31 places, depending on a specified count in ECX. Shift instructions specify the count in one of three ways: (1) implicitly by specifying the count as a single shift; (2) specifying the count as an immediate value; or (3) specifying the count as the value contained in ECX. The result is stored back into the first operand.

The shift instructions provide a convenient way to do multiplication or division by binary. The division of signed numbers by shifting right is *not* the same kind of division performed by IDIV.

CF always contains the value of the last bit shifted out of the destination operand. In a single-bit shift, OF is set if the value of the high-order (sign) bit was changed by the operation. If the sign bit was not changed, OF is cleared. After a multibit shift, the contents of OF is *always* undefined.

SAL shifts the destination byte, word, or doubleword operand left by one or by the number of bits specified in the count register. The processor shifts zeros in from the right (low-order) side of the operand as bits exit from the left (high-order) side. If the shift count is 1, the overflow flag (OF) is set to 0 if the Carry Flag (CF) after the shift equals the high bit of the first operand. Otherwise, OF = 1. If the shift count is not 1, OF is undefined.

SAR shifts the destination byte, word, or doubleword operand to the right by one or by the number of bits specified in the count operand. The processor preserves the sign of the operand by shifting in zeros on the left (high-order) side if the value is positive or by shifting by ones if the value is negative. If the shift count is 1, OF is set to 0. Otherwise, it is unchanged. Another way to think of SAR is that operand 1 is being divided by 2, *shift-count* times.The divide rounds to negative infinity (which is different than IDIV) for negative numbers. Shifts of zero do not alter any flags.

SHL is a synonym for SAL.

SHR shifts the destination byte, word, or doubleword operand right by one or by the number of bits specified in the count operand. The processor shifts zeros in from the left (high-order) side of the operand as bits exit from the right (low-order) side.

SBB Subtract Integers with Borrow

INSTRUCTION	OPCODE	BINARY
SBB AL,*imm8*	1C *ib*	00011100
SBB AX,*imm16*	1D *iw*	00011101
SBB EAX,*imm32*	1D *id*	00011101
SBB *r/m8,imm8*	80 /3 *ib*	10000000 *mm* 011 *r/m*
SBB *r/m16,imm16*	81 /3 *iw*	10000001 *mm* 011 *r/m*
SBB *r/m32,imm32*	81 /3 *id*	10000001 *mm* 011 *r/m*
SBB *r/m16,imm8*	83 /3 *ib*	10000011 *mm* 011 *r/m*
SBB *r/m32,imm8*	83 /3 *ib*	10000011 *mm* 011 *r/m*
SBB *r/m8,r8*	18 /*r*	00011000 *mm rrr r/m*
SBB *r/m16,r16*	19 /*r*	00011001 *mm rrr r/m*
SBB *r/m32,r32*	19 /*r*	00011001 *mm rrr r/m*
SBB *r8,r/m8*	1A /*r*	00011010 *mm rrr r/m*
SBB *r16,r/m16*	1B /*r*	00011011 *mm rrr r/m*
SBB *r32,r/m32*	1B /*r*	00011011 *mm rrr r/m*

Purpose: SBB subtracts the source operand from the destination operand and then returns the results to the destination operand. It subtracts 1 if CF is set. If CF is cleared, SBB performs the same operation as does SUB. SUB followed by multiple SBB instructions may be used to subtract numbers longer than 32 bits.

SCAS Compare String Data
SCASB Compare Byte
SCASW Compare Word
SCASD Compare Doubleword

INSTRUCTION	OPCODE	BINARY
SCAS *m8*	AE	10101110
SCAS *m16*	AF	10101111
SCAS *m32*	AF	10101111

Note: SCASB is a common assembler mnemonic for SCAS *m8*
SCASW is a common assembler mnemonic for SCAS *m16*
SCASD is a common assembler mnemonic for SCAS *m32*

Purpose: These instructions operate on strings rather than on logical or numeric values. They operate on one element of a string, which may be a byte, a word, or a doubleword. SCAS subtracts ES:[EDI] from AL, AX, or EAX (for byte, word, or dword) operations. The result of the subtraction is not stored; only the flags are changed. After each string operation, EDI is updated to point to the next element of the string. If the Direction Flag (DF) is 0, the index register is incremented. If DF = 1, it is decremented. The amount incremented or decremented is 1, 2, or 4, depending on the size of the string element.

If the values are equal, the Zero Flag (ZF) is set to 1. Otherwise, ZF = 0. If DF = 0, the 80386 increments the memory pointer (EDI) for the string. The destination segment register (ES) cannot be overridden.

SCAS may be preceded by REPE (REPZ) or REPNE (REPNZ). If preceded by REPE<, SCAS is repeated while ECX is not 0 and the string elements are equal to AL, AX, or EAX (ZF = 1). If preceded by REPNE, SCAS is repeated while ECX is not 0 and the string element is not equal to AL, AX, or EAX (ZF = 0). In this way, SCAS is useful to find the first mismatch (REPE) or match (REPNE) to AL, AX or EAX in the string if they exist.

The specification of mem is used by the assembler to determine the length of the operation only. The string is always taken from ES:[EDI]. No segment override is possible for SCAS.

SET*cc* Set Byte on Condition Code

INSTRUCTION	OPCODE	BINARY
SETA *r/m8*	0F 97	00001111 10010111 *mm rrr r/m*
SETAE *r/m8*	0F 93	00001111 10010011 *mm rrr r/m*
SETB *r/m8*	0F 92	00001111 10010010 *mm rrr r/m*
SETBE *r/m8*	0F 96	00001111 10010110 *mm rrr r/m*
SETC *r/m8*	0F 92	00001111 10010010 *mm rrr r/m*
SETE *r/m8*	0F 94	00001111 10010100 *mm rrr r/m*
SETG *r/m8*	0F 9F	00001111 10011111 *mm rrr r/m*
SETGE *r/m8*	0F 9D	00001111 10011101 *mm rrr r/m*
SETL *r/m8*	0F 9C	00001111 10011100 *mm rrr r/m*
SETLE *r/m8*	0F 9E	00001111 10011110 *mm rrr r/m*
SETNA *r/m8*	0F 96	00001111 10010110 *mm rrr r/m*
SETNAE *r/m8*	0F 92	00001111 10010010 *mm rrr r/m*
SETNB *r/m8*	0F 93	00001111 10010011 *mm rrr r/m*
SETNBE *r/m8*	0F 97	00001111 10010111 *mm rrr r/m*
SETNC *r/m8*	0F 93	00001111 10010011 *mm rrr r/m*
SETNE *r/m8*	0F 95	00001111 10010101 *mm rrr r/m*
SETNG *r/m8*	0F 9E	00001111 10011110 *mm rrr r/m*
SETNGE *r/m8*	0F 9C	00001111 10011100 *mm rrr r/m*
SETNL *r/m8*	0F 9D	00001111 10011101 *mm rrr r/m*

INSTRUCTION	OPCODE	BINARY
SETNLE *r/m8*	0F 9F	00001111 10011111 *mm rrr r/m*
SETNO *r/m8*	0F 91	00001111 10010001 *mm rrr r/m*
SETNP *r/m8*	0F 9B	00001111 10011011 *mm rrr r/m*
SETNS *r/m8*	0F 99	00001111 10011001 *mm rrr r/m*
SETNZ *r/m8*	0F 95	00001111 10010101 *mm rrr r/m*
SETO *r/m8*	0F 90	00001111 10010000 *mm rrr r/m*
SETP *r/m8*	0F 9A	00001111 10011010 *mm rrr r/m*
SETPE *r/m8*	0F 9A	00001111 10011010 *mm rrr r/m*
SETPO *r/m8*	0F 9B	00001111 10011011 *mm rrr r/m*
SETS *r/m8*	0F 98	00001111 10011000 *mm rrr r/m*
SETZ *r/m8*	0F 94	00001111 10010100 *mm rrr r/m*

Purpose: New to the 80386, SET*cc* sets a byte to zero or one depending on any of the conditions defined by the status flags, and shown below. The byte may be in memory or may be a one-byte general register. SET*cc* sets the byte to one if the condition *cc* is true; otherwise, it sets the byte to zero. The condition codes are:

SETB/SETNAE/SETC	CF = 1
SETBE/SETNA	CF = 1, ZF = 1
SETE/SETZ	ZF = 1
SETL/SETNGE	SF = OF
SETLE/SETNG	SF = OF, ZF = 1
SETNB/SETAE/SETNC	CF = 0
SETNBE/SETA	CF = 0, ZF = 1
SETNE/SETNZ	ZF = 0
SETNL/SETGE	SF = OF
SETNLE/SETG	ZF = 0, SF = OF
SETNO	OF = 0
SETNP/SETPO	PF = 0
SETNS	SF = 0
SETO	OF = 1
SETP/SETPE	PF = 1
SETS	SF = 1

SGDT Store Global Descriptor Table
SIDT Store Interrupt Descriptor Table

INSTRUCTION	OPCODE	BINARY
SGDT *m*	0F 01 /0	00001111 00000001 *mm* 000 *r/m*
SIDT *m*	0F 01 /1	00001111 00000001 *mm* 001 *r/m*

Purpose: These instructions copy the contents of the Global Descriptor Table (GDT) register or the Interrupt Descriptor table (IDT) register the 6 bytes (48 bits) indicated by the operand. The 16-bit forms of the SGDT/SIDT instructions are compatible with the 80286, but only if the value in the upper 8 bits is not referenced. The 80286 stores "1's" in these bits while the 80386 stores "0's".

The 16-bit Limit is stored in the low word and the 32-bit Base is stored in the high dword.

SHLD Double Precision Shift Left
SHRD Double Precision Shift Right

INSTRUCTION	OPCODE	BINARY
SHLD *r/m16,r16,imm8*	0F A4	00001111 10100100 *mm rrr r/m*
SHLD *r/m32,r32,imm8*	0F A4	00001111 10100100 *mm rrr r/m*
SHLD *r/m16,r16*,CL	0F A5	00001111 10100101 *mm rrr r/m*
SHLD *r/m32,r32*,CL	0F A5	00001111 10100101 *mm rrr r/m*
SHRD *r/m16,r16,imm8*	0F AC	00001111 10101100 *mm rrr r/m*
SHRD *r/m32,r32,imm8*	0F AC	00001111 10101100 *mm rrr r/m*
SHRD *r/m16,r16*,CL	0F AD	00001111 10101101 *mm rrr r/m*
SHRD *r/m32,r32*,CL	0F AD	00001111 10101101 *mm rrr r/m*

Purpose: New to the 80386, SHLD and SHRD provide the basic operations needed to implement operations on long unaligned bit strings. The double shifts either (1) take two word operands as input producing a one-word output, or (2) take two doubleword operands as input and producing a doubleword output. The result is stored back in the first operand.

One of the two input operands may either be in a general register or in memory; the other may only be in a general register. The results replace the memory or register operand. The number of bits to be shifted is specified either in the CL register or in an immediate byte of the instruction. This count is masked to 5 bits; thus, shifts of 0 to 31 bits are performed. CF is set to the value of the last bit shifted out of the destination operand. SF, ZF, and PF are set according to the value of the result. OF and AF are left undefined.

If the count is zero, the instructions are equivalent to a NOP and do not alter the flags. If the shift count is greater than the operand length, the flags and the result in the first operand are undefined.

SLDT Store Local Descriptor Table Register

INSTRUCTION	OPCODE	BINARY
SLDT *r/m16*	OF 00 /0	00001111 00000000 *mm* 000 *r/m*

Purpose: The LDT is pointed to by a selector that resides in the LDT Register. SLDT stores the LDTR in the register or memory location indicated by the effective address operand.

Note: The operand-size attribute has no effect on the operation of SLDT.

SMSW Store Machine Status Word

INSTRUCTION	OPCODE	BINARY
SMSW *r/m16*	0F 01 /4	00001111 00000001 *mm* 100 *r/m*

Purpose: The Machine Status Word is part of Control Register Zero (CR0). SMSW stores this word in the 2-byte register or memory location indicated by the effective address operand. SMSW provides compatibility with the 80286. 80386 programs should use MOV CR0.

STC Set Carry Flag (CF)

INSTRUCTION	OPCODE	BINARY
STC	F9	11111001

Purpose: STC sets the Carry Flag (CF) to 1.

STD Set Direction Flag (DF)

INSTRUCTION	OPCODE	BINARY
STD	FD	11111101

Purpose: STD sets the Direction Flag (DF) to 1. This causes all subsequent string operations to decrement the index register(s) SI (or ESI), DI (or EDI).

STI — Set Interrupt Flag (IF)

INSTRUCTION	OPCODE	BINARY
STI	FB	11111011

Purpose: STI sets the Interrupt Flag (IF) to 1. After executing the next operation, the 80386 responds to external interrupts—if the next instruction allows the interrupt flag to remain enabled. However, if external interrupts are disabled, code STI, RET (like at the end of a subroutine) and RET is allowed to execute before external interrupts are recognized. Also, if external interrupts are disabled, and STI, CLI are coded, the interrupts *are not* recognized because CLI clears the interrupt flag during its execution.

If the current task has insufficient privilege to alter IF, an undefined opcode fault is generated.

STOS — Store String Data
STOSB — Store Byte
STOSW — Store Word
STOSD — Store Doubleword

INSTRUCTION	OPCODE	BINARY
STOS *m8*	AA	10101010
STOS *m16*	AB	10101011
STOS *m32*	AB	10101011

Purpose: These instructions operate on strings rather than on logical or numeric values. They operate on one element of a string, which may be a byte, a word, or a doubleword. The string elements are transferred from AL, AX, or EAX into ES:[EDI]. After each string operation, EDI is automatically updated to point to the next element of the string. If DF = 0, the index registers are incremented. If DF = 1, they are decremented. The amount incremented or decremented is 1, 2, or 4, depending on the size of the string element.

STOS can be preceded by a REP prefix. This allows a string to be filled with the contents of AL, AX or EAX.

STR — Store Task Register

INSTRUCTION	OPCODE	BINARY
STR *r/m16*	0F 00 /1	00001111 00000000 *mm* 001 *r/m*

Purpose: STR copies the contents of the Task Register to the 2-byte register or memory location specified in the first operand. The operand-size attribute has no effect on STR.

SUB — Subtract Integers

INSTRUCTION	OPCODE	BINARY
SUB AL,*imm8*	2C *ib*	00101100
SUB AX,*imm16*	2D *iw*	00101101
SUB EAX,*imm32*	2D *id*	00101101
SUB *r/m8,imm8*	80 /5 *ib*	10000000 *mm* 101 *r/m*
SUB *r/m16,imm16*	81 /5 *iw*	10000001 *mm* 101 *r/m*
SUB *r/m32,imm32*	81 /5 *id*	10000001 *mm* 101 *r/m*
SUB *r/m16,imm8*	83 /5 *ib*	10000011 *mm* 101 *r/m*
SUB *r/m32,imm8*	83 /5 *ib*	10000011 *mm* 101 *r/m*
SUB *r/m8,r8*	28 /*r*	00101000 *mm rrr r/m*
SUB *r/m16,r16*	29 /*r*	00101001 *mm rrr r/m*
SUB *r/m32,r32*	29 /*r*	00101001 *mm rrr r/m*
SUB *r8,r/m8*	2A /*r*	00101010 *mm rrr r/m*
SUB *r16,r/m16*	2B /*r*	00101011 *mm rrr r/m*
SUB *r32,r/m32*	2B /*r*	00101011 *mm rrr r/m*

Purpose: SUB subtracts the source operand from the destination operand and then replaces the destination operand with the result. If a borrow is required, CF is set. The operands may be signed or unsigned bytes, words, or doublewords.

TEST — Logical Compare

INSTRUCTION	OPCODE	BINARY
TEST AL,*imm8*	A8 *ib*	10101000
TEST AX,*imm16*	A9 *iw*	10101001

TEST EAX,*imm32*	A9 *id*	10101001
TEST *r/m8,imm8*	F6 /0 *ib*	11110110 *mm* 000 *r/m*
TEST *r/m16,imm16*	F7 /0 *iw*	11110111 *mm* 000 *r/m*
TEST *r/m32,imm32*	F7 /0 *id*	11110111 *mm* 000 *r/m*
TEST *r/m8,r8*	84 /*r*	10000100 *mm rrr r/m*
TEST *r/m16,r16*	85 /*r*	10000101 *mm rrr r/m*
TEST *r/m32,r32*	85 /*r*	10000101 *mm rrr r/m*

Purpose: TEST "ANDs" two operands. It then clears OF and CF, leaves AF undefined and updates SF, ZF, and PF.The flags can be tested by conditional control transfer instructions or by the byte-set-on-condition instructions.

The difference between TEST and AND is that TEST does *not* store the result in the first operand. TEST differs from BT (Bit Test) in that TEST tests the value of multiple bits in one operation, while BT tests a single bit.

VERR Verify a Segment for Reading
VERW Verify a Segment for Writing

INSTRUCTION	OPCODE	BINARY
VERR *r/m16*	0F 00 /4	00001111 00000000 *mm* 100 *r/m*
VERW *r/m16*	0F 00 /5	00001111 00000000 *mm* 101 *r/m*

Purpose: These instructions verify whether a segment noted by the selector is reachable with the current privilege level and if the segment is readable. If the segment is accessible, the Zero Flag (ZF) is set to 1. If not, ZF is set to 0. The validation done is the same as if the segment were loaded into DS, ES, FS or GS and the indicated read was performed.

Since ZF receives the result of the validation, the selector's value does not result in a protection exception. This allows software to anticipate possible segment access problems.

XCHG Exchange Register/Memory with Register

INSTRUCTION	OPCODE	BINARY
XCHG AX,*r16*	90 + *r*	10010*rrr*
XCHG *r16*,AX	90 + *r*	10010*rrr*
XCHG EAX,*r32*	90 + *r*	10010*rrr*
XCHG *r32*,EAX	90 + *r*	10010*rrr*

XCHG *r/m8,r8*	86 /*r*	10000110 *mm rrr r/m*
XCHG *r8,r/m8*	86 /*r*	10000110 *mm rrr r/m*
XCHG *r/m16,r16*	87 /*r*	10000111 *mm rrr r/m*
XCHG *r16,r/m16*	87 /*r*	10000111 *mm rrr r/m*
XCHG *r/m32,r32*	87 /*r*	10000111 *mm rrr r/m*
XCHG *r32,r/m32*	87 /*r*	10000111 *mm rrr r/m*

Note that "XCHG, AX,AX" is a NOP.

Purpose: XCHG swaps the contents of two operands and takes the place of three MOV instructions. It does not require a temporary location to save the contents of one operand while loading the other. XCHG is useful for implementing semaphores or similar data structures for process synchronization.

If one of the operands is memory, the bus transfer is always performed as if a LOCK prefix is given, even if LOCK was not specified.

XLAT XLATB — Table Lookup-Translation

INSTRUCTION	OPCODE	BINARY
XLAT m8	D7	11010111

Purpose: XLAT is useful for translating from one coding system to another, such as from EBCDIC to ASCII. The translate table can be up to 256 bytes long. The value placed in AL serves as an index to the location of the corresponding translation value.

XLAT replaces a byte in AL with a byte from a user-coded translation table at [EBX + AL]. AL is always an unsigned value. When XLAT is executed, AL should have the unsigned index to the table addressed by EBX. XLAT changes the contents of AL from the table index to the table entry. EBX is unchanged.

The table is always based at [EBX], regardless of the *m8*. However, *m8* does allow a segment override to be specified rather than the default DS:[EBX].

XOR — Logical, Exclusive OR

INSTRUCTION	OPCODE	BINARY
XOR AL,*imm8*	34 *ib*	00110100
XOR AX,*imm16*	35 *iw*	00110101
XOR EAX,*imm32*	35 *id*	00110101

XOR *r/m8,imm8*	80 /6 *ib*	10000000 *mm* 110 *r/m*
XOR *r/m16,imm16*	81 /6 *iw*	10000001 *mm* 110 *r/m*
XOR *r/m32,imm32*	81 /6 *id*	10000001 *mm* 110 *r/m*
XOR *r/m16,imm8*	83 /6 *ib*	10000011 *mm* 110 *r/m*
XOR *r/m32,imm8*	83 /6 *ib*	10000011 *mm* 110 *r/m*
XOR *r/m8,r8*	30 /*r*	00110000 *mm rrr r/m*
XOR *r/m16,r16*	31 /*r*	00110001 *mm rrr r/m*
XOR *r/m32,r32*	31 /*r*	00110001 *mm rrr r/m*
XOR *r8,r/m8*	32 /*r*	00110010 *mm rrr r/m*
XOR *r16,r/m16*	33 /*r*	00110011 *mm rrr r/m*
XOR *r32,r/m32*	33 /*r*	00110011 *mm rrr r/m*

Purpose: XOR compares the bits in its two operands and stores the result into the first operand. Each bit of the result is 1 if the corresponding bits in the operands are *different*. Each bit is 0 if the corresponding bits are the same. The result replaces the first operand.

Operand 1	110001
Operand 2	001101
Result	111100

Appendix D

The 80387 Coprocessor Instruction Set

This appendix gives the complete set of floating-point instructions available in an 80386/80387 system, along with the two instructions that access the 80387: ESC and WAIT. Some of the syntax for the floating-point instructions is different from that used for the 80386, so that is discussed and the examples of operands is kept more simple. (For instance, there is no binary shown.) There is a Control Word register, Tag-Word register, and Status Word register that control the operation of the floating-point instructions and provide status information. Those registers are discussed first.

80387 Registers

The 80387 is used with the 80386 for high-performance operations on data. When used with the 80386, the numeric coprocessor adds three sets of registers to support floating-point calculations. Those registers are: (1) four 32-bit error pointer registers to identify the instruction and memory operand causing an exception: FOS, FOO, FCS, and FIP; (2) three 16-bit status and control registers: one for a status word, one for a control word, and one for a tag word; and (3) a stack of eight 80-bit accumulators to hold up to eight floating-point operands.

Floating-Point Accumulator Stack

The accumulator stack is an array of eight physical registers, with a separate 3-bit field that identifies the current stack top, as shown in Fig. D-1. A 3-bit field

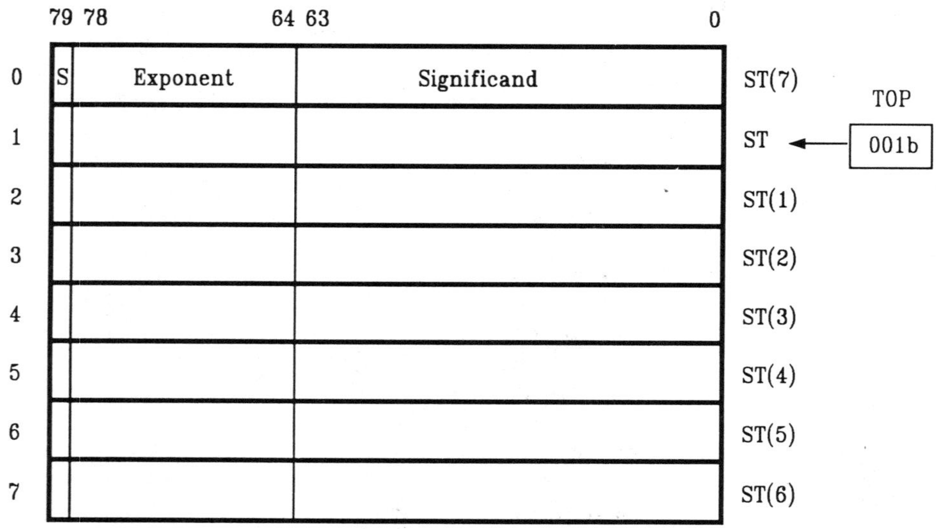

If TOP (in the Status Word) = 001b, then ST is at the second register, or register 1. After a PUSH, TOP increments by 1 and all the registers have their values incremented also. The increments and decrements ignore wrap-around. If TOP = 000b, a PUSH decrements TOP to 111b and stores the new value in register 7.

Fig. D-1. 80387 accumulator stack registers.

(named TOP) in the status word contains the absolute register number of the current top of the accumulator stack, ST. After a PUSH, the previous ST becomes ST(1), and all the stacked accumulators have their ST-relative names incremented by 1.

Tag-Word Register

The 16-bit Tag-Word Register, as shown in Fig. D-2, contains eight 2-bit fields, one for each of the eight floating-point registers. The TAG fields indicate whether the corresponding register holds a valid, zero, special floating-point number, or is empty. To avoid the need to rotate the tag word as the accumulator stack is pushed and popped, the fields in the TAG word correspond to the physical registers, rather than being relative to the stack top.

Control Word Register

The Control Word register contains three fields, all under program control:

Bits 0 to 5 contain the exception masks for the conditions that occur in the 80387.

	15 14	13 12	11 10	9 8	7 6	5 4	3 2	1 0
TW (Tag Word)	TAG7	TAG6	TAG5	TAG4	TAG3	TAG2	TAG1	TAG0

Tag Field Encoding

TAG	Meaning
00	Valid
01	Zero
10	Special – Infinity, NaN, Denormal
11	Empty

Fig. D-2. Tag Word register.

Bits 8 to 9 specify Precision Control, PC. The results of floating-point arithmetic are rounded to one of the precisions as shown in Fig. D-3, before they are stored in the destination.

Bits 10 to 11 are for Rounding Control, RC. There are four rounding modes, as shown in Fig. D-3.

Status Word Register

The 80387 sets certain bits in the Status Word register and these bits can be tested under program control. Figure D-4 shows the format of the Status Word register. The fields are:

Bits 0 to 5 are set if an exception is detected and are "sticky" bits. That is, the 80387 sets them and they must be explicitly reset under program control.

Bit 6, Stack Fault (SF) is a flag that is set if an invalid operation exception is due to over- or underflow of the accumulator stack. Otherwise, it is reset.

Bit 7 and Bit 15 are set to 1 if any unmasked exception is indicated by the exception bits in the lower 6 bits of the Status Word, as masked by the exception mask in the lower 6 bits of the Control Word. Otherwise, bit 7 and 15 are set to 0.

Bits 8 (C0), 9 (C1), 10 (C2), and 14 (C3) are Condition Code flags. These flags are set depending on the floating-point operations. They can be moved to the lower 8 bits of the 80386 EFLAGS register.

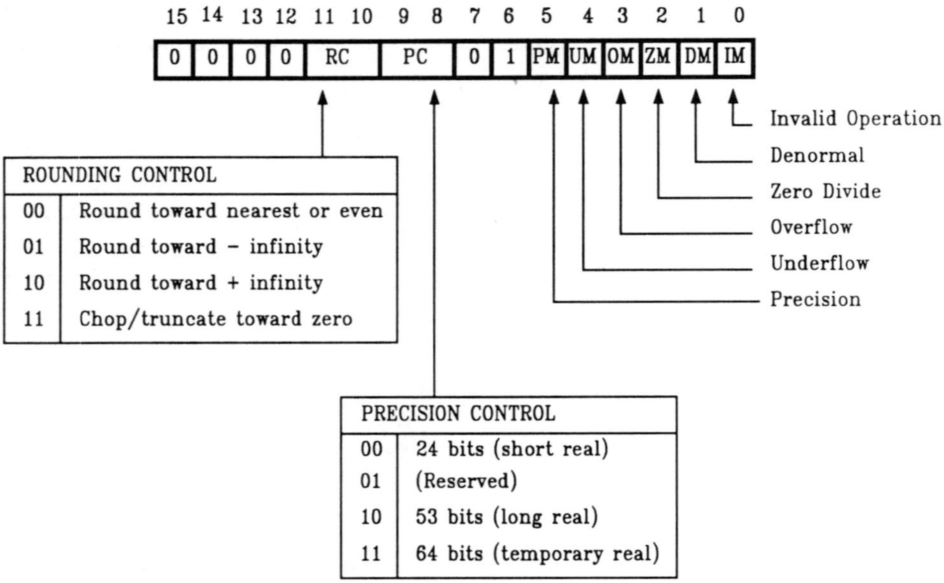

Fig. D-3. Control Word register.

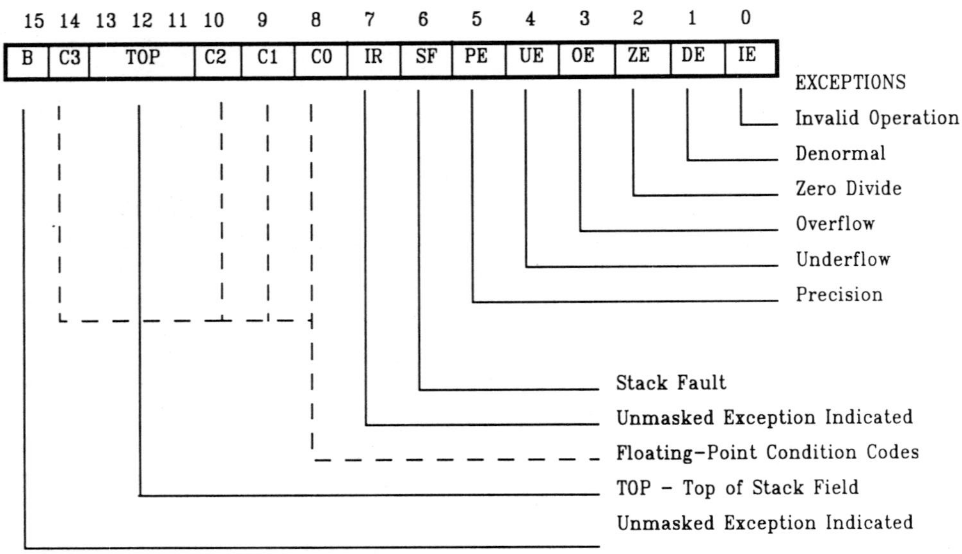

Fig. D-4. Status Word register.

Bit 11 to 13, TOP. This field indicates which of the seven accumulator registers is the top of the stack.

Error Pointer Registers

There are four 32-bit registers which hold pointers to the last 80387 instruction executed and that instruction's data, as shown in Fig. D-5. These four registers are useful in analyzing and reporting exceptions that occur during floating-point instruction execution. You need these registers, since the 80386 and 80387 can operate in parallel and you could lose the error if the registers weren't present.

FIP and FCS point to the 80387 instruction, along with the first two opcode bytes of that instruction, ignoring prefixes. FCS holds the selector and opcode and FIP holds the offset. The opcode field is formed by combining the low-order 3 bits of the first instruction byte with the second instruction byte. The two bytes selected

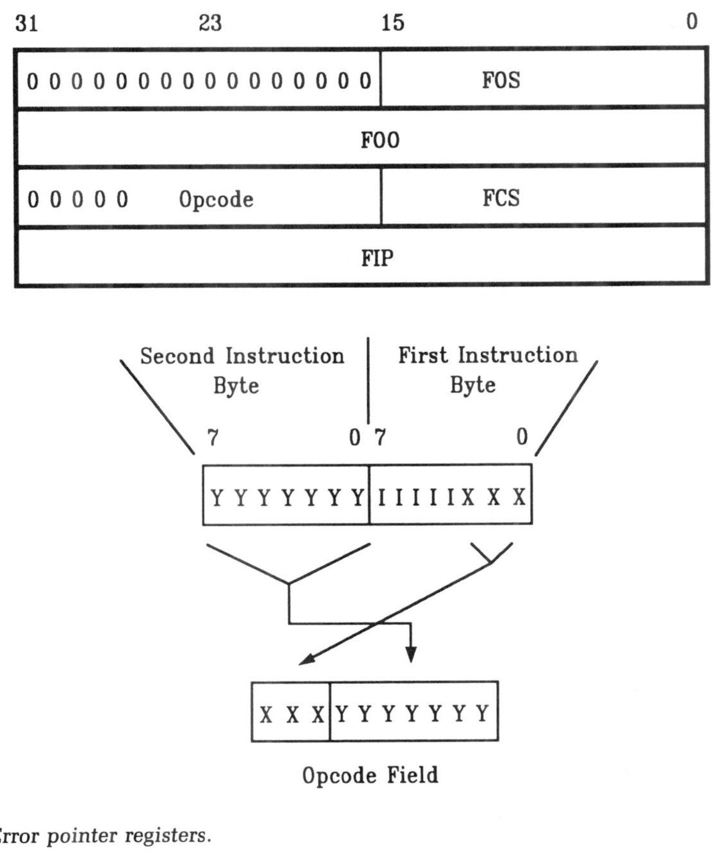

Fig. D-5. Error pointer registers.

come after any prefixes, which means they contain the opcode field and the first byte of the MODRM field.

FOO and FOS, the second pair of registers, point to the memory operand of the last instruction. FOS holds the selector and FOO holds the offset. Note that if the last instruction did not have a memory operand, FOO and FOS are undefined.

80387 Instructions

The assembler mnemonics follow a standard notation. That is:

F	All floating-point instructions begin with F. No other 80386 instructions do.
FB	The instructions that operate on BCD data types begin with FB.
FI	The instructions that operate upon integer data begin with FI.
FNxx	Instructions (except for those that begin with FN) check for unmasked numeric exceptions prior to execution. The FN*xx* instructions do not.
FxxP	Instructions that cause the stack to be popped once end with P.
FxxPP	Instructions that cause the stack to be popped twice end in PP.

The 80387 uses an accumulator stack and almost all operations must have the stack top (referred to as ST) as one operand. The other accumulators are referenced in relation to ST, using the notation ST(*n*), which indicates the *n*th stack element beneath the current top of stack.

ESC Escape

INSTRUCTION	OPCODE	BINARY
ESC	D8 + *TTT*	11011*TTT mod LLL r/m* where TTT and LLL are opcode information for the coprocessor

Purpose: A numeric coprocessor provides an extension to the instruction set of the 80386. The coprocessor supports high-precision integer and floating-point calculations, in addition to containing a set of useful constants to enhance the speed of numeric calculations. The coprocessor operates in parallel with the CPU to provide maximum instruction throughput.

A program contains coprocessor instructions in the same instruction stream with the 80386 instructions. The system executes the coprocessor set in the same order as they appear in the stream.

ESC is a 5-bit sequence that begins with the opcodes that identify floating-point numeric instructions. This sequence is "11011B." This pattern tells the 80386 to send the opcode and addresses of operands to the numerics coprocessor.

F2XM1 $2^x - 1$

INSTRUCTION	OPERANDS
F2XM1	

Purpose: The item in the top of stack is ST in the computation of $2^{ST} - 1$. The result of this computation replaces the initial ST. The input operand range is bounded by -0.5 and 0.5. If the operand is out of this range, the results are undefined.

FABS Absolute Value

INSTRUCTION	OPERANDS
FABS	

Purpose: The top stack element is changed to its absolute value. The top stack element is always positive, following the FABS instruction execution.

FADD Real Addition
FIADD Integer Addition
FADDP Real Addition and POP

INSTRUCTION	OPERANDS
FADD	*Operand1* ST(*n*) *m32* *m64* *Operand1,Operand2*

Instruction	Operands
	ST,ST(*n*)
	ST(*n*),ST
FIADD	*Operand1*
	m16
	m32
FADDP	*Operand1,Operand2*
	ST,ST(*n*)
	ST(*n*),ST

Purpose: The explicitly defined or implicitly specified floating-point operands are added, with the result being stored in the first operand. The destination (or first) operand in all cases is the stack top, except the two-operand form where the destination can be ST(*n*), where *n* is the accumulator in the stack with reference to the top of stack.

If the first operand is a memory operand, it is automatically converted to temporary real (which is the 80387 internal format) before any operations are performed on it.

Note: An FADDP or FADD without operands causes the stack to be popped. Thus FADD with no operands is synonymous with FADDP ST(1),ST.

FBLD BCD Load

Instruction	Operands
FBLD	*m80*

Purpose: The ten-byte packed BCD memory operand pointed to by *m80* is converted to a temporary real value and PUSHed onto the top of the stack. The conversion is always exact. The BCD digits are assumed to be in the range 0h to 9h. An attempt to load invalid BCD digits puts an undefined temporary real value into ST.

FBSTP BCD Store and POP

Instruction	Operands
FBSTP	*m80*

Purpose: The stack top is converted to an 18-digit BCD number, which is then stored into the ten-byte location pointed to by *m80*, and then the stack is popped. ST is rounded to an integer. This instruction is very slow and may cause an interrupt latency problem. ST for FBSTP can be a denormal (it could not be for an 80287). If ST is a quiet NaN, an invalid operation will be generated. Operations with quiet NaNs do not usually generate exceptions.

FCHS Change Sign

INSTRUCTION	OPERANDS
FCHS	

Purpose: The sign of the top of stack element is complemented. If the stack top was +0.9, it is changed to −0.09 by FCHS.

FCLEX FNCLEX Clear Exceptions

INSTRUCTION	OPERANDS
FCLEX	
FNCLEX	

Purpose: These instructions cause the 80387 to clear all exceptions and the busy bit of the status-word register. FCLEX checks for unmasked numeric exceptions, while FNCLEX does not.

FCOM Compare
FCOMP Compare and POP
FCOMPP Compare and POP Twice

INSTRUCTION	OPERANDS
FCOM	*Operand1*
	m32
	m64
	ST(*i*)

INSTRUCTION	OPERANDS
FCOMP	*Operand1*
	m32
	m64
	ST(*i*)
FCOMPP	

Purpose: The given operand is numerically compared with the top of stack. The condition codes are set according to the table shown in Fig. D-6.

If the opcode was FCOMPP, the operand compared against the top of stack is ST(1)—the first below the top of stack. If the operand was FCOMP, the stack is popped once after comparison. Unordered comparison occurs if either of the two operands are NaNs. The sign of zero is ignored in comparisons.

FCOM generates an invalid operation exception if either operand is a quiet NaN. Usually, operations with quiet NaNs do not cause operation exceptions.

Fig. D-6. Compare condition codes. (See the section on the Status Word register for locations of C0, C2, and C3.)

Operation	C3	C2	C0
ST > Operand 1	0	0	0
ST < Operand 1	0	0	1
ST = Operand 1	1	0	0
Unordered	1	1	1

FCOS Cosine

INSTRUCTION	OPERANDS
FCOS	

Purpose: New to the 80387, the cosine of ST (top of stack) is computed. After the computation, the stack top is set to the cosine of ST and 1.0 is PUSHed onto the stack. The input operand to FCOS must be in the range of 0 to PI$*2^{62}$. If the source operand is within this range, C2 is set to 0 (See the section on the Status Word for the location of C2). Otherwise, C2 is set to 1, ST is left intact, and the stack-top pointer is unchanged.

FDECSTP Decrement Stack Pointer

INSTRUCTION	OPERANDS
FDECSTP	

Purpose: One is subtracted from the stack-top pointer TOP in the status word. See the section on the Status Word for the location of TOP. This instruction allows direct control of the stack pointer, which can be useful if a "virtual" accumulator stack that is larger than the eight hardware accumulators provided on the 80387 is needed. The virtual stack registers would reside in memory and software would manage this stack when stack invalid operation exceptions are detected.

Using FDECSTP, the tag word or the stack top itself is not updated. If an FDECSTP is executed when TOP is 0, ST becomes 7. Pushing a new element onto the stack causes the stack pointer to be decremented, as does FDECSTP.

FDIV Real Division
FIDIV Integer Divide
FDIVP Real Divide and POP

INSTRUCTION	OPERANDS
FDIV	*Operand1* ST(*n*) *m32* *m64* *Operand1,Operand2* ST,ST(*n*) ST(*n*),ST
FIDIV	*Operand1* *m16* *m32*
FDIVP	*Operand1,Operand2* ST,ST(*n*) ST(*n*),ST

Purpose: The explicitly or implicitly specified floating-point operands are divided, with the result being placed back into the first operand, the destination. The destination is the stack top in all cases except the two-operand form, where the destination can be ST(*n*). If operand 1 is a memory operand, it is automatically converted to temporary real (the internal 80387 format) before any operations are performed with it.

An FDIV without operands causes the stack to be popped. FDIV with no operands is synonymous with FDIVP ST(1),ST.

FDIVR Division Reverse
FIDIVR Integer Divide Reverse
FDIVRP Real Divide Reverse and POP

INSTRUCTION	OPERANDS
FDIVR	*Operand1*
	ST(*n*)
	m32
	m64
	Operand1,Operand2
	ST,ST(*n*)
	ST(*n*),ST
FIDIVR	*Operand1*
	m16
	m32
FDIVRP	*Operand1,Operand2*
	ST,ST(*n*)
	ST(*n*),ST

Purpose: The explicitly or implicitly specified operands are divided with the result being stored into the first operand, the destination. The destination is the stack top in all cases except the two-operand form where the destination can be ST(*n*). These operations are equivalent to FDIV/FIDIV/FDIVP, except numerator and divisor are reversed.

If Operand1 is a memory operand, it is automatically converted to temporary (the 80387 internal format) before any operations are performed on it. An FDIVR without operands causes the stack to be popped, which makes it synonymous with FDIVRP ST(1),ST.

FFREE Free Register

INSTRUCTION	OPERANDS
FFREE	ST(*n*)

Purpose: The tag-word bits associated with the specified register are set to 11b, which indicates that the specified stack element is changed to empty. Neither the floating-point stack nor the floating-point stack pointer is modified. The tag word describes the physical stack registers and FFREE gives an accumulator stack reference that is relative to the stack top.

FICOM Integer Compare
FICOMP Integer Compare and POP

INSTRUCTION	OPERANDS
FICOM	*Operand1*
	m16
	m32
FICOMP	*Operand1*
	m16
	m32

Purpose: The given operand is converted from word or short integer into temporary real and numerically compared against the top of stack. The condition codes are set according to the table shown in Fig. D-7.

Unordered comparison occurs if the stack top is a NaN. The sign of zero is ignored in comparisons. If the operand is FICOMP, the stack is popped.

Operation	C3	C2	C0
ST > Operand 1	0	0	0
ST < Operand 1	0	0	1
ST = Operand 1	1	0	0
Unordered	1	1	1

Fig. D-7. Integer compare condition codes. (See the section on the Status Word register for locations of C0, C2, and C3.)

FILD Integer Load

INSTRUCTION	OPERANDS
FILD	*Operand1*
	m16
	m32
	m64

Purpose: The memory word, short, or long integer specified by the first operand is read from memory and converted into temporary real (the 80387 internal format). The stack is pushed and the temporary real is placed in the new top of stack.

FINCSTP Increment Stack Pointer

INSTRUCTION	OPERANDS
FINCSTP	

Purpose: This instruction allows direct control of the stack pointer. One is added to the stack pointer in the Status Word (see the section on the Status Word Register for the location of the pointer). The tag word (TW) and the contents of the floating-point stack are not updated. If FINCSTP is executed when the stack-top pointer (TOP) is 7, ST becomes 0. Popping an element off the stack causes the stack pointer to be incremented.

FINIT FNINIT Initialize Processor

INSTRUCTION	OPERANDS
FINIT FNINIT	

Purpose: These two instructions set all the control-word, status-word, and tag-word registers to their default values. After execution, the machine rounding control is set to round to nearest, all exceptions masked, precision set to 64 bits, the status word (SW) cleared except for the four condition code bits (which are undefined), and all floating-point stack registers (TW) are set to empty. FINIT checks for unmasked numeric exceptions, while FNINIT does not.

FIST Integer Store

INSTRUCTION	OPERANDS
FIST	*Operand1* *m16* *m32*

Purpose: The stack top is rounded to an integer whose length matches that of the first operand. The rounding is as specified by the round control (RC) bits of the control word (CW). The integer is then stored into the first operand. Negative zero is converted to two's complement positive zero before storing. FIST cannot store a long integer. If ST is a quiet NaN, an invalid operation exception is generated.

FISTP Integer Store and POP

INSTRUCTION	OPERANDS
FISTP	*Operand1* *m16* *m32* *m64*

Purpose: The stack top is rounded to an integer, whose length matches that of the first operand. The rounding is as specified by RC in the Control Word register. The integer is then stored into the first operand. FISTP can store a long integer, where FIST cannot. Negative zero is converted to two's complement positive zero. The stack is popped.

FLD Real Load

INSTRUCTION	OPERANDS
FLD	*Operand1* *m32* *m64* *m80* ST(*i*) where *i* is any position on the stack

Purpose: The operand specified in *Operand1* is pushed onto the top of the stack. If the operand is a short or long real, the operand is converted to a temporary real (the 80387 internal format) prior to being pushed onto the stack.

FLD*con* Load Constant

INSTRUCTION	OPERANDS
FLD1	
FLDL2E	
FLDL2T	
FLDLG2	
FLDLN2	
FLDPI	
FLDZ	

Purpose: The constant value that is specified by the instruction itself is pushed onto the stack and becomes the new top of stack. FLD is 1.0. FLDL2E is $\log_2 e$. FLDL2T is $\log_2 10$. FLDLG2 is $\log_{10} 2$. FLDLN2 is $\log_e 2$. FLDPI is the value of π. FLDZ is 0.0.

FLDCW Load Control Word

INSTRUCTION	OPERANDS
FLDCW	*m16*

Purpose: This instruction loads the Control Word (CW) with the value found in *m16*. An exception is flagged if any of the exception flags in SW (the Status Word) are unmasked by the new Control Word.

FLDENV Load Environment

INSTRUCTION	OPERANDS
FLDENV	*m*

Purpose: This instruction loads the machine environment from the given memory area. This environment consists of the tag-word register, the status-word register, and the control word register, along with the error-pointer registers of the most recent floating-point instruction executed. Note that the error-pointer registers contain information on the most recent opcode and the data referenced.

FMUL Real Multiply
FIMUL Integer Multiply
FMULP Real Multiply and POP

INSTRUCTION	OPERANDS
FMUL	*Operand1*
	ST(*n*)
	m32
	m64
	Operand1,Operand2
	ST,ST(*n*)
	ST(*n*),ST
FIMUL	*Operand1*
	m16
	m32
FMULP	*Operand1,Operand2*
	ST,ST(*n*)
	ST(*n*),ST

Purpose: The specified operands are multiplied, with the result being stored in the first operand, the destination. The destination is the top of stack in all cases except the two-operand form where the destination can be ST(*n*).

If the first operand is a memory operand, it is automatically converted to temporary real (the 80387 internal format) before any operations are performed on it. An FMUL without operands causes the stack to be popped, which makes it synonymous with FMULP ST(1),ST.

FNOP No Operation

INSTRUCTION	OPERANDS
FNOP	

Purpose: FNOP stores the stack to the stack top, which is effectively a NOP.

FPATAN Partial Arctangent

INSTRUCTION	OPERANDS
FPATAN	

Purpose: The arctangent of ST(1)/ST is computed. After the computation, the stack is popped once and the result placed in the new top of stack.

FPREM Partial Remainder

INSTRUCTION	OPERANDS
FPREM	

Purpose: FPREM computes the partial remainder of ST/ST(1). The remainder is computed by a series of successive scaled subtractions, so the remainder produced is exact with no precision error possible. If the operands differ greatly in magnitude, this series of subtractions can take a very long time. To prevent severe performance degradation, the instruction only partially computes the remainder and a software loop is required to complete the reduction.

FPREM reduces a magnitude difference up to 2^{64} in one execution. If the reduction is complete, condition code 2 is set to 0 and condition code 0, 3, and 1 (in that order) reflect the least significant 3 bits of the quotient. If the reduction was incomplete, condition code 2 is set to 1. See the section on the Control Word to find the location of the condition codes. The result follows the relation:

REM = ST − ST(1) * *Quotient*

where the remainder always has the sign of the original ST.

FPREM1 Partial Remainder (IEEE)

INSTRUCTION	OPERANDS
FPREM1	

Purpose: New with the 80387, this instruction computes the partial remainder of ST/ST(1). It is for the purpose of IEEE compatibility.

The remainder is computed by a series of successive scaled subtractions, so the remainder is exact with no precision error. When the operands differ greatly in magnitude, these subtractions can take a very long time. To prevent severe degradation of interrupt latency, the instruction only partially computes the remainder. A software loop is required to complete the reduction.

FPREM1 reduces a magnitude difference up to 2^{64} in one execution. If the reduction is complete, condition code 2 is set to 0 and condition codes 0, 3, and

1 (in that order) reflect the three least significant bits of the quotient. If the reduction is incomplete, condition code 2 is set to 1. (See the section on the Control Word for the location of the condition codes.) The result obeys the relation:

REM = ST − ST(1) * *Quotient*

where the quotient is the integer nearest to the exact value of ST/ST(1). Rounding mode and precision control do not affect the results except when ST(1) exactly divides into ST. In this case, the result is plus zero for rounding control of nearest, up, or chop and minus zero for down. If ST(1) was initially infinity, ST is unchanged and the quotient (condition codes) is set to zero.

FPTAN Partial Tangent

INSTRUCTION	OPERANDS
FPTAN	

Purpose: The tangent of ST is computed. After the computation, the stack top is set to the tangent of ST and 1.0 PUSHed onto the stack. Thus:

ST(1)/ST = tan(ST′)

where ST′ is the stack top prior to the tangent instruction. ST is always 1.0 and ST(1) is the tangent of ST′.

FRNDINT Round To Integer

INSTRUCTION	OPERANDS
FRNDINT	

Purpose: FRNDINT rounds the top of stack element to an integer. The rounding obeys the RC (rounding control) setting found in the Control Word (See the section on the Control Word for the location of RC). The four rounding modes are: 00 = nearest, 01 = minus infinity, 10 = plus infinity, and 11 = chop.

FRSTOR Restore State

INSTRUCTION	OPERANDS
FRSTOR	*m*

Purpose: This instruction reloads the complete state of the 80387 from a 108-byte location given by *m*. The format of the load memory is identical with that of the FSAVE instruction. Included in the restore is the 80387 environment and the eight 80-bit floating-point stack registers. Any exception is possible, if the combination of the status word and the control word are in an exception condition.

FSAVE FNSAVE — Save State

INSTRUCTION	OPERANDS
FSAVE	*m*
FNSAVE	*m*

Purpose: These instructions store the complete state of the 80387 into the memory location *m*. This environment consists of the Control-Word register, the Status-Word register, and the Tag-Word registers, the error-pointer registers, and the complete floating-point stack (eight 80-bit registers). See the section at the beginning of this appendix for the formats of these registers.

After storing the 80387 state, FSAVE initializes the 80387 in the same way the FINIT instruction does. FSAVE checks for unmasked numeric exceptions, while FNSAVE does not.

FSCALE — Power of Two Scaling

INSTRUCTION	OPERANDS
FSCALE	

Purpose: FSCALE scales the top of stack by the power of two given in ST(1). This ST(1) value is treated as an integer (chopped) and is added to the exponent of ST, which is useful as a quick way of multiplying by powers of two. Operands that cause overflow or underflow signal exceptions.

FSIN — Sine

INSTRUCTION	OPERANDS
FSIN	

Purpose: New with the 80387, FSIN computes the sine of ST. After the computation, the stack top is set to the sine of ST and 1.0 is pushed onto the stack. Thus:

ST(1)/ST = sin(ST′)

where ST′ is the stack top prior to the sine operation. ST is always 1.0 and ST(1) is the sine of ST′. The input operand to FSIN must be in the range of 0 to PI$*2^{62}$. If the source operand is in this range, C2 is set to 0; otherwise, C2 is set to 1 and ST and TOP are unchanged. See the section at the beginning of this appendix for the locations of C2 and TOP.

FSINCOS Sine and Cosine

INSTRUCTION	OPERANDS
FSINCOS	

Purpose: New with the 80387, this instruction computes both the sine and cosine of ST. After the computation is complete, the stack top is set to the sine of ST and then the cosine is pushed onto the stack. Thus, at the end of the execution:

ST(1) = sin(ST′)

and

ST = cos(ST′)

where ST′ is the stack top prior to FSINCOS. The input operand to this instruction must be in the range of 0 to PI$*2^{62}$. If it is, C2 is set to 0. Otherwise, C2 is set to 1 and ST and TOP are unchanged. See the section at the beginning of this appendix for the locations of the condition codes and TOP.

FSQRT Square Root

INSTRUCTION	OPERANDS
FSQRT	

Purpose: The top of the stack is replaced with the square root of the top of the stack. The following conditions hold true:

FSQRT(−0) = −0
FSQRT(+ infinity) = plus infinity
FSQRT(− infinity) is invalid

FST Real Store

INSTRUCTION	OPERANDS
FST	*Operand1*
	m32
	m64
	ST(*i*), where i is any position in the stack

Purpose: The top of stack is stored in *Operand1*. If it is a short or long real, the top of stack is first converted to the type according to RC (round control) in the Control Word—see the section at the beginning of this appendix for the location and meaning of the round control. If the top of stack is a NaN or an infinity, the stack-top exponent and significand are chopped rather than rounded to fit the destination sizes.

FST cannot store a temporary real operand to memory, where FSTP can.

FNSTCW Store Control Word

INSTRUCTION	OPERANDS
FSTCW	*m16*
FNSTCW	*m16*

Purpose: These instructions store the Control Word into *m16*. FSTCW checks for unmasked numeric exceptions, while FNSTCW does not.

FSTENV FNSTENV Store Environment

INSTRUCTION	OPERANDS
FSTENV	*m*
FNSTENV	*m*

Purpose: These instructions store the machine environment to the given memory location. This environment consists of the Control-Word register, the Status-Word register, and the Tag-Word register, and the error pointers of the most recent floating-point instruction executed. See the beginning of this appendix for the formats of the registers. FSTENV checks for unmasked numeric exceptions, while FNSTENV does not.

FSTP Real Store and POP

INSTRUCTION	OPERANDS
FSTP	*Operand1*
	m32
	m64
	m80
	ST(*i*), where (*i*) is any position on the stack

Purpose: The top of stack is stored into the first operand. If it's a short or long real, the top of stack is first converted as specified by RC (rounding control)—see the section at the beginning of this appendix for the location and meaning of RC. If the top of stack is a NaN or infinity, the stack-top exponent and the significand are chopped rather than rounded to fit the destination sizes. FSTP can store a temporary real number to memory, where FST cannot.

FSTSW FNSTSW Store Status Word

INSTRUCTION	OPERANDS
FSTSW	*m16*
FNSTSW	*m16*

Purpose: These instructions store the current Status Word into m16. FSTSW checks for unmasked numeric exceptions, while FNSTSW does not.

FSTSW AX FNSTSW AX Store Status Word into AX

INSTRUCTION	OPERANDS
FSTSW	AX
FNSTSW	AX

Purpose: These instructions store the current Status Word into the 80386 AX register. FSTSW checks for unmasked numeric exceptions, while FNSTSW does not. These instructions are useful for control-flow changes based on the condition flag settings of the 80387.

FSUB — **Real Subtraction**
FISUB — **Integer Subtraction**
FSUBP — **Real Subtraction and POP**

INSTRUCTION	OPERANDS
FSUB	*Operand1*
	ST(*n*)
	m32
	m64
	Operand1,Operand2
	ST,ST(*n*)
	ST(*n*),ST
FISUB	*Operand1*
	m16
	m32
FSUBP	*Operand1,Operand2*
	ST,ST(*n*)
	ST(*n*),ST

Purpose: The operands are subtracted with the result being stored in the first operand, the destination. The destination is the stack top in all cases, except the two-operand form where the destination can be ST(n). If the first operand is a memory operand, it is automatically converted to temporary real (the 80387 internal format) before any operations are performed with it. An FSUB without operands causes the stack to be popped, which makes it synonymous with FSUBP ST(1),ST.

FSUBR — **Real Subtraction Reverse**
FISUBR — **Integer Subtraction Reverse**
FSUBRP — **Real Subtraction Reverse with POP**

INSTRUCTION	OPERANDS
FSUBR	*Operand1*
	ST(*n*)
	m32

	m64
	Operand1,Operand2
	ST,ST(*n*)
	ST(*n*),ST
FISUBR	*Operand1*
	m16
	m32
FSUBRP	*Operand1,Operand2*
	ST,ST(*n*)
	ST(*n*),ST

Purpose: The operands are subtracted, with the result being placed in the first operand, the destination. The destination is the stack top in all cases except the two-operand form where the destination can be ST(n). If the first operand is a memory operand, it is automatically converted to temporary real (the 80387 internal format) before any operations are performed with it. An FSUBR without operands causes the stack to be popped, which makes it synonymous with FSUBRP ST(1),ST.

FTST Test

INSTRUCTION	OPERANDS
FTST	

Purpose: The stack top is numerically compared against 0. The condition code bits in the Status Word are set according to the table shown in Fig. D-8.

See the section at the beginning of this appendix for the location of the condition codes. Unordered comparison occurs if ST is a NaN. The sign of zero is ignored in comparisons.

Operation	C3	C2	C0
ST > 0.0	0	0	0
ST < 0.0	0	0	1
ST = 0.0	1	0	0
Unordered	1	1	1

Fig. D-8. Test condition codes. (See the section on the Status Word register for locations of C0, C2, and C3.)

FUCOM Unordered Compare
FUCOMP Unordered Compare with POP
FUCOMPP Unordered Compare and POP Twice

INSTRUCTION	OPERANDS
FUCOM	*Operand1* *m32* *m64* ST(*i*) where (i) is any position on the stack
FUCOMP	*Operand1* *m32* *m64* ST(*i*), where (i) is any position on the stack
FUCOMPP	

Purpose: The operand is numerically compared with the top of the stack. The condition codes are set according to the table shown in Fig. D-9. See the beginning of this appendix for the location of the condition codes. If the opcode was FUCOMPP, the operand compared against the top of stack is ST(1) and the stack popped twice. If the operand was FUCOMP, the stack is popped once. Unordered comparison occurs if either the operands is a NaN. The sign of zero is ignored in the comparisons.

Operation	C3	C2	C0
ST > Operand 1	0	0	0
ST < Operand 1	0	0	1
ST = Operand 1	1	0	0
Unordered	1	1	1

Fig. D-9. Unordered compare condition codes. (See the section on the Status Word register for locations of C0, C2, and C3.)

FXAM Examine

INSTRUCTION	OPERANDS
FXAM	

Purpose: The stack top is examined. The condition codes of the Status Word are modified according to the table in Fig. D-10. See the section at the beginning of this appendix for the location of the condition codes in the Status Word. The unsupported entry in the table refers to any pseudo-NaN, pseudo-infinity, or pseudo-zero.

ST Value	C3	C2	C1	C0
+ Unsupported	0	0	0	0
+ NaN	0	0	0	1
− Unsupported	0	0	1	0
− NaN	0	0	1	1
+ Normal	0	1	0	0
+ Infinity	0	1	0	1
− Normal	0	1	1	0
− Infinity	0	1	1	1
+ 0	1	0	0	0
+ Empty	1	0	0	1
− 0	1	0	1	0
− Empty	1	0	1	1
+ Denormal	1	1	0	0
+ Empty	1	1	0	1
− Denormal	1	1	1	0
− Empty	1	1	1	1

Fig. D-10. Examine compare condition codes. (See the section on the Status Word register for locations of C0, C2, and C3.)

FXCH Exchange Registers

INSTRUCTION	OPERANDS
FXCH	*Operand1*
	ST(*n*)

Purpose: The contents of the first operand are exchanged with the contents of the top of stack. This provides a convenient way to use the various 80387 instructions that operate only on the top of stack, such as FSQRT and FSIN.

FXTRACT Extract Exponent and Significand

INSTRUCTION	OPERANDS
FXTRACT	

Purpose: The unbiased exponent of the original stack top is placed on the stack top as a real number. The significand and sign are pushed onto the stack, as the new top of stack. Thus, the original stack top is decomposed into a true exponent, ST(1), and a significand, ST, portion. The significand has an exponent of zero.

If the operand is zero, ST(1)—the exponent—is set to negative infinity and ST—the significand—is set to 0 with the same sign as the original stack top. This differs from the 80287. If the operand was infinity, the ST(1) exponent is positive infinity and the ST significand is infinity with the sign of the original stack top.

FYL2X $Y * \log_2 X$

INSTRUCTION	OPERANDS
FYL2X	

Purpose: The top two stack elements are used in the comparison of the function:

$$ST(1) * \log_2 ST$$

The stack is popped and the new stack top is replaced with the result of the computation. ST must be in the range of 0 to positive infinity. The ST(1) operand can be minus infinity to plus infinity. If the operands are not in this range, the instruction produces an undefined result and no exception will be detected.

FYL2XP1 Y * $\log_2$ (X + 1)

INSTRUCTION	OPERANDS
FYL2XP1	

Purpose: The top two stack elements are used in the computation:

$$ST(1) * \log_2(ST + 1.0)$$

The stack is popped and the new stack top is replaced with the result of the computation. ST must be in this range:

$$-(1 - \sqrt{2/2}) \text{ to } 1 + (1 - \sqrt{2/2})$$

ST(1) can be in the range of minus infinity to plus infinity. If the operands are not in this range, the instruction will produce an undefined result and no exception will be detected.

WAIT Wait until BUSY# Pin Is Inactive (High)

INSTRUCTION	OPCODE	BINARY
WAIT	9B	10011011

Purpose: A numeric coprocessor provides an extension to the instruction set of the 80386. The coprocessor supports high-precision integer and floating-point calculations, in addition to containing a set of useful constants to enhance the speed of numeric calculations. The coprocessor operates in parallel with the CPU to provide maximum instruction throughput.

A program contains coprocessor instructions in the same instruction stream with the 80386 instructions. The system executes the coprocessor set in the same order as they appear in the stream.

WAIT suspends 80386 program execution until the 80386 CPU detects that the BUSY pin is inactive. This indicates that the coprocessor has completed its processing task and that the CPU can now obtain the results.

Appendix E

ASCII Characters and Keyboard Codes

There are certain conventions in the use of keyboard keys that should be followed to make software more user-friendly. That is, users could move from software package to package without having to relearn some basic conventions. While recognizing that even the biggest companies violate the conventions, those recommended conventions are:

Backspace	Removes the character to the left of the cursor, moves the cursor to that position, and shifts left all that follows.
Shift-Tab	Jumps the cursor left when struck.
Ctrl-Tab	Moves the cursor left or right by one word. Alternatively, scrolls the screen horizontally one tab-width to the left or right.
Ctrl-End	Deletes all text from the cursor to the end of the line.
Ctrl-Home	Clears the screen and positions the cursor at the top left.
Ctrl-PgDn	Deletes all text from the cursor to the bottom of the screen.
Del	Removes the character under the cursor and moves all that follows one space left.

End	Moves the cursor to the end of the line, or alternatively, to the end of the document.
Esc	Exits from a program or program routine.
Home	In text, moves the cursor to the start of a line, or alternatively, to the start of the document. In menus, switches to the topmost menu.
Ins	Toggles in and out of a mode where text is inserted in the midst of other text.
PgUp	Scrolls backward one screen, less 1 line.
PgDn	Scrolls forward one screen, less 1 line.
Scroll Lock	Toggles the cursor keys in and out of a state where they scroll the screen rather than move the cursor.
Tab	Jumps the cursor right when the Tab key is struck.

Low 4 Bits	High 3 Bits							
	000	001	010	011	100	101	110	111
0000	NUL	DLE	SP	0	@	P	`	p
0001	SOH	DC1	!	1	A	Q	a	q
0010	STX	DC2	"	2	B	R	b	r
0011	ETX	DC3	#	3	C	S	c	s
0100	EOT	DC4	$	4	D	T	d	t
0101	ENQ	NAK	%	5	E	U	e	u
0110	ACK	SYN	&	6	F	V	f	v
0111	BEL	ETB	'	7	G	W	g	w
1000	BS	CAN	(	8	H	X	h	x
1001	HT	EM	)	9	I	Y	i	y
1010	LF	SUB	*	:	J	Z	j	z
1011	VT	ESC	+	;	K	[	k	{
1100	FF	FS	,	<	L	\	l	|
1101	CR	GS	-	=	M	]	m	}
1110	SO	RS	.	>	N	^	n	~
1111	SI	US	/	?	O	—	o	DEL

Fig. E-1. Standard ASCII codes.

Where:

NUL	Null	DLE	Data Link Escape
SOH	Start of Heading	DC1	Device Control 1
STX	Start of Text	DC2	Device Control 2
ETX	End of Text	DC3	Device Control 3
EOT	End of Transmission	DC4	Device Control 4
ENQ	Enquiry	NAK	Negative Acknowledge
ACK	Acknowledge	SYN	Synchronous Idle
BEL	Audible Bell	ETB	End of Transmission Block
BS	Backspace	EM	End of Medium
HT	Horizontal Tab	SUB	Substitute
LF	Line Feed	ESC	Escape
VT	Vertical Tab	FS	File Separator
FF	Form Feed	GS	Group Separator
CR	Carriage Return	RS	Record Separator
SO	Shift Out	US	Unit Separator
SI	Shift In	DEL	Delete

(Fig. E-1 ends.)

In addition to the 128 standard ASCII codes shown in Fig. E-1, there are codes which are called "box graphic" codes. You can access them by giving your program the hex number associated with the graphic. As shown in Fig. E-2, these codes are easy to use to draw a series of complex boxes or other maze-type figures.

IBM PC Keyboard Scan Codes

The keys on the IBM PC keyboard have assigned numbers, called *scan codes*. These codes run 1 to 83. When you press a key, the system converts these codes to ASCII (if it can) and sends the results to the keyboard buffer. However, certain keystrokes and combinations cannot be represented in ASCII. For these keys, two bytes are sent. The first byte is a zero and the second is the extended code shown in Fig. E-3.

IBM PC AT Keyboard Scan Codes

The 80286 PC AT keyboard has a range of keyboard scan numbers that goes from 1 to A6. The numbers begin with the numeric and alphabetic characters, go

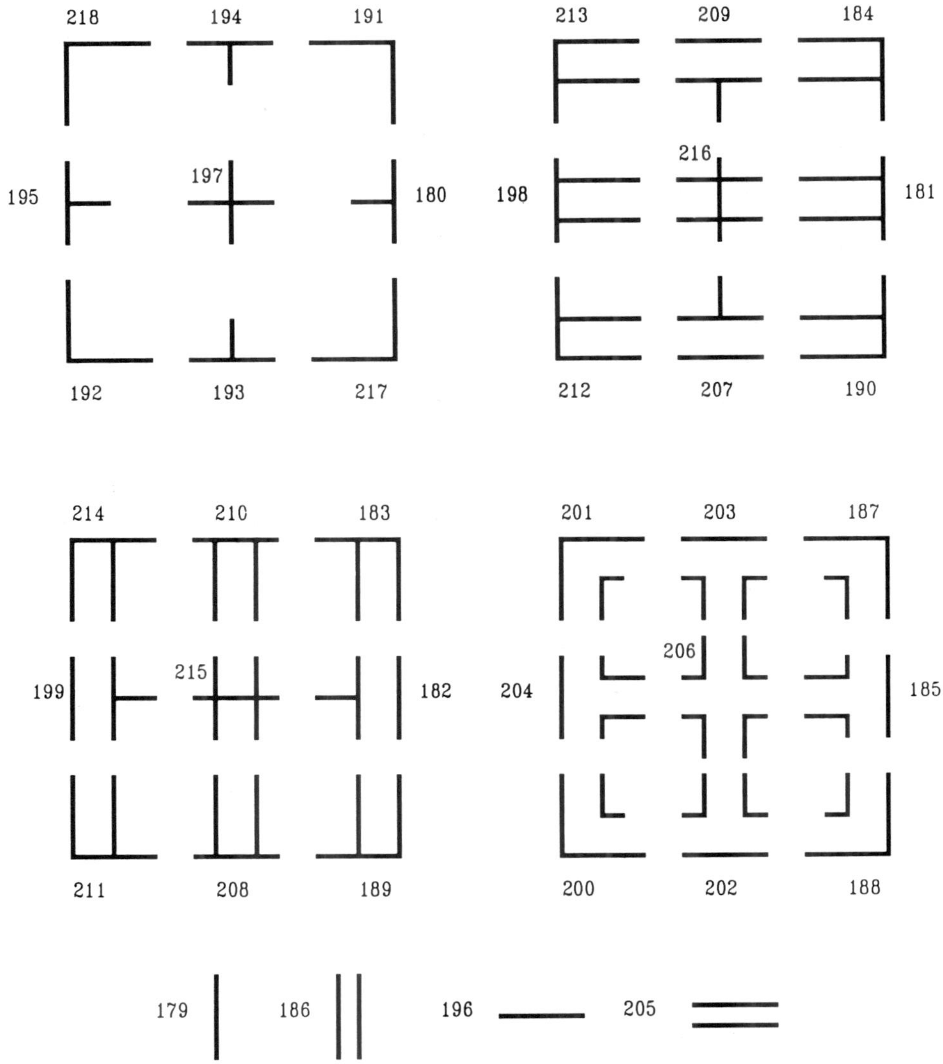

Fig. E-2. Overview of box graphic characters.

on with functions keys, and finish with cursor keys. When you press one of the keys, the keyboard sends the scan code to the computer (the "make" code). When a key is released, the scan code + 80 is sent (the "break" code). The scan codes are shown in Fig. E-3.

Normally BIOS translations of the keyboard scan codes are sufficient. If you intercept Interrupt 9h, however, you will need to handle the "make" and "break" interrupts, and translate scan codes as your application requires.

Hex	Decimal	PC Key	PC AT Key
1	1	ESC	Tilde ~
2-B	2-11	1-9, 0	1-9, 0
C	12	Minus, Underline	Minus, Underline
D	13	Equal, Plus	Equal, Plus
E	14	Backspace	Blackslash \, Vertical Bar |
F	15	Tab	Backspace
10	16	ALT Q	Tab
11	17	ALT W	ALT Q
12	18	ALT E	ALT W
13	19	ALT R	ALT E
14	20	ALT T	ALT R
15	21	ALT Y	ALT T
16	22	ALT U	ALT Y
17	23	ALT I	ALT U
18	24	ALT O	ALT I
19	25	ALT P	ALT O
1A	26	[	ALT P
1B	27	]	[
1C	28	ENTER	]
1D	29	CTRL	
1E	30	ALT A	CTRL
1F	31	ALT S	ALT A
20	32	ALT D	ALT S
21	33	ALT F	ALT D
22	34	ALT G	ALT F
23	35	ALT H	ALT G
24	36	ALT J	ALT H
25	37	ALT K	ALT H
26	38	ALT L	ALT J
27	39	Semicolon, Colon	ALT L
28	40	Quote	Semicolon, Colon
29	41	Tilde ~	Quote
2A	42	Left Shift	
2B	43	Blackslash \, Vertical Bar |	ENTER

Fig. E-3. IBM PC and PC AT keyboard scan codes.

Hex	Decimal	PC Key	PC AT Key
2D	45	ALT X	
2E	46	ALT C	ALT Z
2F	47	ALT V	ALT X
30	48	ALT B	ALT C
31	49	ALT N	ALT V
32	50	ALT M	ALT B
33	51	Comma	ALT N
34	52	Period	ALT M
35	53	Slash /, Question Mark ?	Comma
36	54	Right Shift	Period
37	55	Asterisk *, PrtSc	Slash /, Question Mark ?
38	56	ALT	
39	57	Space Bar	Right Shift
3A	58	Caps Lock	ALT
3B	59	F1	
3C	60	F2	
3D	61	F3	Space Bar
3E	62	F4	
3F	63	F5	
40	64	F6	Caps Lock
41	65	F7	F2
42	66	F8	F4
43	67	F9	F6
44	68	F10	F8
45	69	Num Lock	F10
46	70	Scroll Lock, BREAK	F1
47	71	Home	F3
48	72	Up Arrow	F5
49	73	PgUp	F7
4A	74	Minus (Far Left)	F9
4B	75	Left Arrow	
4C	76	Keypad 5	
4D	77	Right Arrow	

(Fig. E-3 continues.)

Hex	Decimal	PC Key	PC AT Key
4E	78		
4F	79	End	
50	80	Down Arrow	
51	81	PgDn	
52	82	Insert	
53	83	Delete	
5A	90		Escape
5B	91		Home
5C	92		Left Arrow
5D	93		End
5F	95		Num Lock
60	96		Up Arrow
61	97		Keypad 5
62	98		Down Arrow
63	99		Insert
64	100		Scroll Lock
65	101		PgUp
66	102		Right Arrow
67	103		PgDn
68	104		Delete
69	105		Sys
6A	106		Asterisk, PrSc
6B	107		Minus
6C	108		Plus

(Fig. E-3 ends.)

Appendix F

An Overview of OS/2

IBM recently announced their Personal System/2 (PS/2) line of computers—Figure F-1 gives an overview of those systems. The new line has, as its top end, a system based on Intel's 80386 microprocessor. For the remainder of the PS/2 systems, IBM adapted the existing PC hardware, while maintaining functional compatibility with the old line. The top three models support an advanced graphics standard, video graphics array (VGA), the new Micro Channel bus, 1.44 M disks, and an 80286 or 80386 microprocessor. Model 50 and 60 use the 80286 with a faster 10MHz clock and no wait states; the Model 80 uses the 80386 with a 16MHz clock.

For users, PS/2 translates to greater integration with the IBM family of computers, better performance, and easier installation. For users with a current installed base of IBM or IBM-clone systems, PS/2 offers upgradability: software that runs on PS/2 computers runs on existing PC-class clones. You can choose how to move programs and data between the 5.25-inch and the 3.5-inch drives.

Operating System/2

IBM announced the Operating System/2 at the same time as the PS/2, but did not deliver OS/2. The early version of OS/2, called the "Standard Edition," is a joint Microsoft/IBM product. It runs on PS/2 systems, PC/ATs and clones that duplicate those systems. The Extended Edition will be available some time later and will include all the features of the Standard Edition.

System	CPU/ System Speed	Standard RAM	Maximum RAM	Standard Drive	Expansion Slots	Operating System(s)
Model 30	8086 8MHz	640K	N/A	Two 3.5-inch, 720K floppy drives	3	PC-DOS 3.3 MS-DOS 3.3
Model 50	80286 10 MHz	1Mb	7Mb	one 1.44M, 3.5-inch floppy drive and a 20Mb hard disk	3	PC-DOS 3.3 MS-DOS 3.3 OS/2
Model 60	80286 10MHz	1Mb	15Mb	one 1.44Mb 3.5-inch floppy drive and a 44Mb hard disk	7	PC-DOS 3.3 MS-DOS 3.3 OS/2
Model 80	80386 16MHz-20MHz	1Mb-2Mb	16Mb	one 1.44Mb, 3.5-inch floppy drive and a 44Mb hard disk	7 3 32-bit 4 16-bit	PC-DOS 3.3 MS-DOS 3.3 OS/2

Fig. F-1. Overview of IBM Personal Systems/2.

The largest benefit of an operating system with a large set of features is the convenience of a single environment. This allows software people to develop only one version of their applications. Support in the operating system for so many functions also allows you to concentrate on the application instead of extensions to the system to facilitate the application. Thus, you become more efficient.

An OS/2 Glossary

OS/2 introduces some new terms and reintroduces some old ones. Here are a few of them, with their definitions.

anonymous pipe—A data storage buffer that OS/2 maintains in RAM, used for inter-process communications.

Applications Program Interface—API, the set of calls a program uses to obtain services from the operating system. API denotes a service interface, whatever its form.

background category—A classification of processes that consists of those associated with a screen group not currently being displayed.

captive thread—A thread (see below) that has been created by a dynlink package and that stays within the dynlink code, never transferring back to the client process's code. Also a thread that is used to call a service entry point and that will never return or that will return only if some specific event occurs.

child process—A process created by another process (its parent process).

closed system—hardware or software design that cannot be enhanced in the field by third-party suppliers.

command subtree—A process and all its descendants.

cooked mode—A mode established by programs for keyboard input. In cooked mode, OS/2 handles the line-editing characters such as back space.

dynamic link—dynlink. A method of postponing the resolution of external references until loadtime or runtime. A dynamic link allows the called subroutines to be packaged, distributed, and maintained independently of their callers. OS/2 extends dynlink mechanisms to serve as the primary method by which all system and nonsystem services are obtained.

dynlink—See *dynamic link*.

exitlist—A list of subroutines that OS/2 calls when a process has terminated. The exitlist is executed after process termination but before the process is actually destroyed.

Family Applications Program Interface—Family API. A standard execution environment under MS-DOS versions 2.*x* and 3.*x* and OS/2. Programmers can use the Family API to create an application that uses a subset of OS/2 functions (but a superset of MS-DOS 3.*x* functions) that runs in a binary-compatible fashion under MS-DOS versions 2.*x* and 3.*x* and OS/2.

general priority category—The OS/2 classification of threads that consists of three subcategories: background, foreground, and interactive.

handle—An arbitrary integer value that OS/2 returns to a process so that the process can return it to OS/2 on subsequent calls, known to OS/2 designers as a *magic cookie*.

interprocess communications (IPC)—The ability of processes and threads to transfer data and messages among themselves, used to offer services to and receive services from other programs.

KBD—An abbreviated name for the dynlink package that manages the keyboard device.

kernel—The central part of OS/2. It resides permanently in fixed memory locations and executes in the privileged ring 0 state (see below).

magic cookie—See *handle*.

named pipe—A data storage buffer that OS/2 maintains in RAM, used for interprocess communication.

parent process—A process that creates another process, which is called the *child process*.

PID—Process Identification Number, a unique code that OS/2 assigns to a process when the process is created.

Presentation Manager—The graphic-to-user interface for OS/2.

raw mode—A mode established by programs for keyboard mode. In raw mode, OS/2 passes to the caller each character typed immediately as it is typed. The caller is responsible for handling line-editing characters such as the back space.

ring 0—A special execution mode (privilege mode) supported by the 80286/80386 hardware. Code executing in this mode can execute restricted instructions that are used to manipulate key system structures and tables. Only the OS/2 kernel and device drivers run in this mode (see Fig. F-2).

ring 3—The privilege level that is used to run applications. Code that executes at this level cannot modify critical system structures.

scheduler—The part of OS/2 that decides which thread to run and how long to run it before assigning the CPU to another thread. Also, the part of OS/2 that determines the priority value for each thread.

System File Table—SFT, an internal OS/2 table that contains an entry for every file currently open.

thread—The OS/2 mechanism that allows more than one path of execution through the same instance of an application program.

VIO—An abbreviated name of the dynlink package that manages the display device.

3x box—The OS/2 environment that emulates an 8086-based PC running MS-DOS versions 2.*x* and 3.*x*.

OS/2 Features

OS/2 features include database and communications programs; network, minicomputer and mainframe links; and software development tools. The Standard

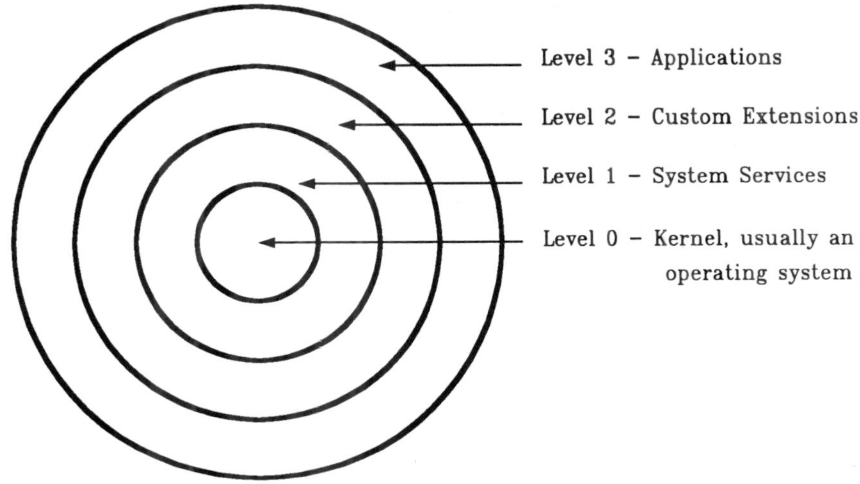

Fig. F-2. Privilege levels represented as rings.

Edition, according to Microsoft, is based around windows; in fact, it's almost impossible to use without windows. These windows, by the way, are overlapped instead of tiled. The Presentation Manager runs with windows and icons. (You move the cursor to the icons with a mouse or by using pop-up menus.) The number of windows you can use depends on the amount of memory your system has.

OS/2 uses a Session Manager that you call at any point to review active applications or invoke new ones. To start a new application, select *Start New Programs* which takes you to an MS-DOS prompt, from which you load the program. The first thing you'll notice is the default prompt. It changes from the standard "C:>" to "C:\". The Session Manager starts as a small box and expands as you add applications.

OS/2 is built to be extendible. If the system doesn't support what your application needs, you can add it yourself. These additions to the system become an integral part of it, indistinguishable from the operating system. This extendibility is how Microsoft and IBM will integrate products such as the LAN Manager and the Presentation Manager.

DOS error messages have been replaced with specific and helpful messages. For instance, "Not ready reading Drive A. Abort, Retry, Ignore?" has changed to "The diskette is not compatible with the drive," or "The diskette is not properly inserted into drive A."

Both the Standard and Extended versions of OS/2 require a lot of memory; the minimum requirements are 1.5Mb of RAM and a hard disk. Both levels of OS/2 can address up to 16Mb of RAM. If you want to run both OS/2 and MS-DOS, you will need another megabyte of memory to run your MS-DOS applications in real mode, with OS/2's "compatibility box." (The Compatibility box is Microsoft's way of maintaining upward compatibility. The Session Manager tells you that you're running in real mode by prefixing your program name with an "R").

Real-Time Processing

Efficient real-time systems are usually memory-resident, or at least allow more direct control of virtual memory or overlays. OS/2 supports time-critical tasks and eliminates the use of virtual memory. This makes OS/2 ideal for "less strenuous" real-time tasks, such as controlling point-of-sale devices. (A strenuous task would be like running the Airline Ticketing System.) A significant advantage of OS/2 is that it runs standard real-time applications.

Multitasking

OS/2 allows more than one program to run at one time. It does this in two ways. First, more than one program can be loaded and executed. You can write or alter code while the compiler processes previously edited code in the background, using the large number of CPU cycles that exist between your keystrokes, cycles that otherwise would not be used.

Second, a program (which OS/2 refers to as a *process*) kicks off its own set of tasks (OS/2 calls them *threads*) to perform a set of concurrent operations. OS/2 is optimized to support the process/thread multitasking model, rather than provide efficient multi-user operation. Microsoft defined OS/2 as a single-user, multitask system, with emphasis on one user.

A benefit of this task-oriented system is that it does not require an interactive user. OS/2 performs as a network server and has the added advantage of being able to execute programs on the server that previously could run only on a workstation. Further, since multitasking requires that tasks be able to pass data or instructions between themselves, OS/2 provides facilities for this task-to-task passing. The facilities allow all the traditional information such as semaphores, shared memory, signals, pipes and queues.

OS/2 offers an extension of the pipe feature, called *named pipes*. This allows a pipe to exist not just between two tasks in the same machine but between two tasks on different machines. For instance, a work station program could command a program to load and run on a server. The named pipe provides a private communications link from the workstation to the server program.

Differences from MS-DOS

There are many differences between MS-DOS and OS/2. Here, we'll discuss a few. The first is BIOS interfaces. Avoid BIOS interrupt interfaces except for Interrupt 10 (the screen display functions) and Interrupt 16 (the keyboard functions).

Interrupt 10 functions are contained in the OS/2 VIO package and Interrupt 16 functions are in the OS/2 KBD package. Other BIOS interrupts provide functions that are available under OS/2 only in considerably modified forms.

MS-DOS versions 2 and 3 silently truncate a file name that is longer than eight characters or an extension that is longer than three characters. MS-DOS generates no error messages when performing this task. In real mode, OS/2 also silently truncates a file name or extension that exceeds the maximum length. In protected mode, however, it does not. Therefore, a real mode application program needs to perform this truncation. The program should check file name length and refuse names that are longer than the eight-character maximum. This prevents improperly formatted names from becoming embedded in data and control files, which could cause a protected mode version of the application to fail when it presents that invalid name to the operating system. When you convert programs to protected mode API, remove the length-checking code. OS/2 checks the length and returns an error code as appropriate.

Files are truncated by means of a zero-length write under MS-DOS versions 2 and 3. Under OS/2 in protected mode, files are truncated with a special API. File truncation operations should be encapsulated in a special routine to facilitate conversion to OS/2 protected mode or the Family API.

MS-DOS versions 2 and 3 never close file-system searches (Find First File/Find Next File). The returned search contains the information necessary for MS-DOS to continue the search later and no harm is done if the search is never continued. OS/2, however, retains the necessary search continuation information in an internal structure of limited size. For this reason, your program should not depend on more than about 10 simultaneous searches and it should close each search when it is done. OS/2 further provides a Find Close function that releases the internal search information. Protected mode programs should use this call at the end of every search sequence.

FCBs are not supported in OS/2 protected mode. Use handle-based calls instead.

MS-DOS versions 2 and 3 use an interrupt-based interface. OS/2 protected mode uses a procedure-call interface. Write your code to accommodate this difference by encapsulating the interrupt-based interfaces into individual subroutines that can then easily be modified to use the OS/2 procedure-call interface. OS/2 procedure-call interface preserves all registers except AX and FLAGS. Write your program to assume that the contents of AX and the contents of any register modified by MS-DOS version 2 and 3 interrupt interfaces are destroyed at each system call, regardless of the success or failure of that call.

Seeks to negative offsets and to devices also create compatibility issues. Your programs should not attempt to seek to a negative file location. A negative seek offset is permissible as long as the sum of the seek offset and the current file position is positive. MS-DOS versions 2 and 3 allow seeking to a negative offset as long as you do not attempt to read or write the file at that offset. OS/2 returns an error code for negative net offsets.

Because multiple programs can run under OS/2 simultaneously and because the system can be networked, conflicts can occur when two programs try to access the same file. OS/2 handles this situation with special file-sharing support. Although programs ignorant of file-sharing rules can run in real mode, you should explicitly specify file-sharing rules in your program. This reduces the number of file-access conflicts your user will encounter.

Summary

OS/2 benefits the end user because of its more efficient use of computing resources and its ability to improve throughput. In addition, OS/2 can load many programs at the same time, programs that no longer conflict with one another the way so many did with MS-DOS or PC-DOS. OS/2 should reduce complexity for the end-user and support groups. Its automatic installation procedures are much easier and the use of applications within the environment is more consistent.

Appendix G

Overview of BIOS/MS-DOS Interrupts and Calls

A full list of BIOS and MS-DOS interrupts is described later in this appendix. First, since you often need to find a function because of a task you need to program, a useful way to get an overview of the very useful Interrupt 21 is to look at a list of the INT 21 functions by grouping them into the type of task they perform.

Interrupt 21 Function Summary

Character Input

01 Character input with echo
03 Auxiliary input
06 Direct console I/O
07 Unfiltered character input without echo
08 Character input without echo
0A Buffered keyboard input
0B Check keyboard status
0C Flush buffer, read keyboard

Character Output

02 Character output
04 Auxiliary output
05 Print character
05 Direct console I/O

09 Display string (which ends with "$")

Disk Management

0D Disk reset
0E Select disk
19 Get current disk
1B Get default drive data
1C Get drive data
2E Set/Reset verify flag
36 Get disk free space
54 Get verify flag

File Management

0F Open file with FCB
10 Close file with FCB
11 Find first file
12 Find next file
13 Delete file
16 Create file with FCB
17 Rename file
1A Get DTA address
23 Get file size
2F Get DTA address
3C Create file with handle
3D Open file with handle
3E Close file
41 Delete file
43 Get/Set file attributes
45 Duplicate file handle
46 Force duplicate file handle
4E Find first file
4F Find next file
56 Rename file
57 Get/Set Date/Time of file
5A Create temporary file
5B Create new file
5C Lock/Unlock file region

Information Management

14 Sequential read

15 Sequential write
21 Random read
22 Random write
24 Set relative record
27 Random block read
28 Random block write
3F Read file or device
40 Write file or device
42 Move file pointer

Directory Management

39 Create directory
3A Remove directory
3B Change current directory
47 Get current directory

Process Management

00 Terminate process
31 Terminate and stay resident
4B Load and execute program (EXEC)
4C Terminate process with return code
4D Get return code of child process
59 Get extended error information

Memory Management

48 Allocate memory block
49 Free memory block
4A Resize memory block
58 Get/Set allocation strategy

Miscellaneous System Management

25 Set interrupt vector
26 Create new program segment prefix
29 Parse file name
2A Get date
2B Set date
2C Get time
2D Set time

30 Get MS-DOS version number
33 Get/Set Ctrl-C check flag
35 Get interrupt vector
38 Get/Set current country
44 IOCTL
5E Network Machine Name/Printer setup
5F Get/Make assign list entry
62 Get program segment prefix address

General BIOS Interrupts

BIOS means *Basic I/O System*. It does just what the name implies—handles the system's I/O while keeping track of equipment connected to the system.

BIOS updates appear as often (or perhaps more so) than DOS. This means that some of the information in this appendix will change at some point in time. However, MS-DOS and BIOS designers seem to be keeping the basic user interfaces the same, which is good news, even if the underlying code changes.

Interrupt 0: Divide by Zero

If the processor executes a divide by zero, INT 0 is called. Generally, this stops program execution.

Interrupt 1: Single Step

INT 1 single steps through code, a necessity for program debug. There is a call to INT 1 in between each line of program code.

Interrupt 2: Non-Maskable Interrupt (NMI)

INT 2 is a hardware interrupt that cannot be blocked off by using either STI or CLI. INT 2 executes when called.

Interrupt 3: Breakpoint

INT 3 is another important debug interrupt. In fact, the programs DEBUG and SYMDEB use INT 3 with the GO command. For instance, if you want to execute code to a particular address and then stop, DEBUG and SYMDEB insert INT 3 into the code at that point and give control to the program. When the INT 3 is reached, the debugger takes control again.

Interrupt 4: Overflow

If there is an overflow condition, INT 4 is called. Generally, no action is called for and BIOS returns.

Interrupt 5: Print Screen

The PrtSc key uses INT 5 to print the screen. Your program can do the same by simply calling this interrupt.

Interrupt 6 and 7: Reserved

As with undefined bits in registers, you *can* use these interrupts for your own uses, but it's highly recommended that you do not because future development will cause you to go back and reprogram.

Interrupt 8: Time of Day

INT 8 updates the computer's internal time of day. It does this however many times a second your internal clock runs. This interrupt calls INT 1C (Timer Tick Interrupt). We recommend that you actually use INT 1C if you need to write a handler that interacts with the clock.

Interrupt 9: Keyboard Input

Each time you press a keyboard key, INT 9 is generated. The waiting keystroke is read from the keyboard port, processed, and stored in the keyboard buffer (if required). INT 9 does a lot of work, so we recommend that you allow INT 9 to do its job and read from the keyboard buffer (if anything is stored there).

Interrupt 0A: Reserved

The same caveat is stressed here. You can use this if you are willing to invest the future time to go back and rewrite when BIOS finally uses this interrupt.

Interrupts 0B through 0F: End-of-Interrupt Routines

These interrupts point to the BIOS routine End-of-Interrupt (D_EOI) routine. D_EOI simply resets the interrupt handler at port 20h and return.

BIOS Interrupt 10: Screen/Character Handling

BIOS INT 10 includes a whole collection of routines that use AH as input with with various quantities as output. Each of the functions have an Input and Output notation. Input values are always in AH. In the notation below, "B&W" means black and white on a graphics screen and does not refer to a monochrome screen.

INT 10 Function 00: Set Screen Mode

This function of INT 10 establishes the video operating mode of the computer.

Input: AH = 00
AL = mode:

00	16-shade gray text, 40 × 25 EGA: 64-color
01	16/8-color text, 40 × 25 EGA: 64-color
02	16-shade gray text, 80 × 25 EGA: 64-color
03	16/8-color text, 80 × 25 EGA: 64-color
04	4-color graphics, 320 × 200
05	4-shade gray graphics, 320 × 200
06	2-shade gray graphics, 640 × 200
07	monochrome text, 80 × 25
08	16-color graphics, 160 × 200
09	16-color graphics, 320 × 200
0A	4-color graphics, 640 × 200
0B	Reserved
0C	Reserved
0D	16-color graphics, 320 × 200
0E	16-color graphics, 640 × 200
0F	monochrome graphics, 640 × 350
10	16/64-color graphics, 640 × 350

INT 10 Function 01: Set Cursor Type

INT 10 Function 1 allows you to change how your cursor looks. The cursor on a monochrome screen is 14 lines tall (0–13) and on a graphics screen is 8 (0–7) lines tall. You put the starting line of the cursor matrix in CH and the end in CL. For instance, if you want the cursor to be only one line tall, store 0C in CH and 0D in CL before you issue INT 10. If you wanted the cursor to be at both the top and bottom, use the wrap-around feature: store 0D in CH and 00 in CL. You can't stop the cursor from blinking—that's set in hardware—but you can redesign or eliminate it.

Input: AH = 01
CH = Starting scan line
CL = Ending scan line

Note: CH<CL gives normal one-part cursor, CH>CL gives two-part cursor, and CH=20 gives no cursor.

INT 10 Function 02: Set Cursor Position

This function changes the position of the cursor. Store the row number in DH and the column in DL, remembering that 0,0 is the upper left of your screen. If you're using a graphics screen with a possibility of 4 pages, put the page number in BH. If you're using a monochrome display, store a 0 in BH.

Input: AH = 02
BH = Display Page Number (0 in graphics)
DH = Row Number
DL = Column Number

INT 10 Function 03: Find Cursor Position

This function allows you to find where your cursor is, remembering that 0,0 is the upper left of the screen. If you're using a graphics screen with 4 pages, put the page number into BH. If you're using monochrome, store a 0 in BH. Function 3 of INT 10 returns the row number in DH, the column number in DL, the cursor mode in CH,CL (where the matrix starting line is in CL and the ending line is in CH).

Input: AH = 03
BH = Display Page Number

Output: CH = Matrix Ending Line
CL = Matrix Starting Line
DH = Row Number
DL = Column Number

INT 10 Function 04: Read Light Pen Position

This function returns the light pen position. (Remember that 0,0 is the upper left corner of the screen.)

Input: AH = 04

Output: AH = 00 Light pen switch not set.
AL = 01 then:
DH = Row of Light Pen Position
DL = Column of Light Pen Position
CH = Pixel line (vertical row) 0-199
CX = Pixel line number (for some EGA modes)
BX = Pixel column (horizontal column) 0-319,639

INT 10 Function 05: Set Active Display Page

By using INT 10 Function 05, you can move between the various pages in text mode on graphics monitors. Note that if you are doing graphics on the graphics monitor, only one page (page 0) is available for your use. On monochrome monitors, you only have page 0.

Input: AH = 05
AL = Page number:
0–7 Screen modes 0 and 1 = 40-column text modes
0–3 Screen modes 2 and 3 = 80-column text modes

Note: Each page = 2K in 40-column text mode, 4K in 80-column text mode.

Int 10 Function 06: Scroll Active Page Up

INT 10 Function 06 is useful when you have "fill in the blank" types of applications when you selectively clear parts of the screen (see Fig. G-1). It's also useful for scrolling windows.

Input: AH = 06
AL = Number of lines blanked at bottom of the screen (00 blanks entire screen)
BH = Display attribute used on blank lines
CH = Upper left row of area to scroll

Fig. G-1. Example of scrolling selectively.

CL = Upper left column of area to scroll
DH = Lower right row of area to scroll
DL = Lower right column of area to scroll

INT 10 Function 07: Scroll Active Page Down

This function is the "inverse" of Function 06.

Input: AH = 07
AL = Number of lines blanked at top of screen (00 blanks entire screen)
BH = Display attribute used on blank lines
CH = Upper left row of area to scroll
CL = Upper left column of area to scroll
DH = Lower right row of area to scroll
DL = Lower right column of area to scroll

INT 10 Function 08: Read Attribute and Character at Cursor Position

This function returns the character byte and the following attribute byte for the current cursor position.

Input: AH = 08
BH = Display page number (for text mode only)

Output: If text mode:
AL = Character read (in ASCII)
AH = Attribute of character (alphanumerics only)
If graphics mode:
AL = ASCII character (00 if unmatched)

INT 10 Function 09: Write Attribute and Character at Cursor Position

This function of INT 10 is the same as Function 8, except that it's a write operation.

Input: AH = 09
AL = ASCII Character to write
BH = Display page Number (Graphics 1–4, Monochrome = 0)
BL = Text attribute (Alpha Mode)
= Color of foreground (Graphics Mode)
CX = Number of times to write characters (must be > 0)

Note: Function 09 modifies AL, even though this is undocumented. AL returns with the last character in the character string, hex 24, a "$."

INT 10 Function 0A: Write Character Only at Cursor Position

This function writes only the specified character, which assumes whatever attribute happens to be current.

Input: AH = 0A
AL = ASCII Character to write
BH = Display page Number (Graphics 1–4, Monochrome = 0)
BL = Graphics foreground color (unused in text modes)
CX = Number of times to write character (must be > 0)

INT 10 Function 0B: Select Color Palette

This function selects one of two color palettes.

Input: AH = 0B

BH = Palette Color ID
BL = Background Color (if BH = 0)
   = Palette Number (if BH = 1)
      0 - Green/Red/Yellow
      1 - Cyan/Magenta/White

INT 10 Function 0C: Write Dot

Note that in this function, the column number is in CX, instead of using DX for row/column.

Input: AH = 0C
AL = Color attribute of pixel (0–3)
CX = Pixel column number (0–319,639)
DX = Pixel raster line number (0–199)

INT 10 Function 0D: Read Pixel Dot

In this function, if bit 7 of AL is set 1, then the color value is XORed with the current value of the dot. Position 0,0 is the upper left of the screen.

Input: AH = 0D

Output: AL = Pixel color attribute
DX = Pixel row number (0–199)
CX = Pixel column number (0–319,639)

INT 10 Function 0E: Teletype Write to Active Page

The cursor position is advanced. Beep, backspace, linefeed, and carriage return are active; all other characters are displayed.

Input: AH = 0E
AL = ASCII character
BH = Display page number
BL = Foreground Color (Graphics Mode) (unused in text mode)

INT 10 Function 0F: Return Video State

This function returns the current values of the video state.

Input: AH = 0F

Output: AH = Characters per line (20, 40, 80)
AL = Current video mode

00	16-shade gray text, 40 × 25 EGA: 64-color
01	16/8-color text, 40 × 25 EGA: 64-color
02	16-shade gray text, 80 × 25 EGA: 64-color
03	16/8-color text, 80 × 25 EGA: 64-color
04	4-color graphics, 320 × 200
05	4-shade gray graphics, 320 × 200
06	2-shade gray graphics, 640 × 200
07	monochrome text, 80 × 25
08	16-color graphics, 160 × 200
09	16-color graphics, 320 × 200
0A	4-color graphics, 640 × 200
0B	Reserved
0C	Reserved
0D	16-color graphics, 320 × 200
0E	16-color graphics, 640 × 200
0F	monochrome graphics, 640 × 350
10	16/64-color graphics, 640 × 350

BH = Active display page

INT 10 Function 13: Write Character String

This function contains an implicit loop that iterates the same number of times as there are characters in the string.

Input: AH = 13
AL = Subfunction Number
00 String shares attribute in BL, cursor unchanged
01 String shares attribute in BL, cursor advanced
02 Each character has attribute, cursor unchanged
03 Each character has attribute, cursor advanced
BH = Active display page
BL = String attribute (for AL = 00 or 01 only)

CX = Length of character string
DH = Starting row number
DL = Starting column number
ES:BP = Address of string to be displayed

Note: For AL = 00 or 01, string = (*char,char,* . . .)
For AL = 02 or 03, string = (*char,attr,char,attr,* . . .)
For AL = 01 or 03, cursor position set to location following last character output.

BIOS Interrupt 11: Equipment Determination

This interrupt tells most of the equipment that is installed in/on your computer. Look at the program FIND_CFG in Chapter 9 to see how INT 11 can be used.

Input: AH = 11

Output: AX Bits =

- 0 = 1 if IPL diskette installed
- 1 = 1 if numerics coprocessor here
- 2,3 = Unused
- 4,5 = Video Mode
  - 00 = Reserved
  - 01 = 40 × 25 Color Card
  - 10 = 80 × 25 Color Card
  - 11 = 80 × 25 Monochrome
- 6,7 = Number of Diskette Drives
  - 00 = 1
  - 01 = 2
  - 10 = 3
  - 11 = 4
- 8 = Unused
- 9,10,11 = Number of RS-232 Cards
- 12 = Unused
- 13 = If internal modem installed
- 14,15 = Number of Printers Attached

Interrupt 12: Determine Memory Size

INT 12 checks the size of installed memory, as shown by the internal DIP switches.

Input: AH = 12

Output: AX = Number of contiguous 1K memory blocks

BIOS Interrupt 13: Disk I/O

INT 13 is used as the fundamental channel to most disk activities in most IBM PCs and clones. INT 13 works for both hard disk drives and floppy disk drives. Different drive numbers are used to distinguish between the two. For floppy drives, the numbers 0–3 are used. For hard disks, use 80 to 87 (remember all numbers are hex, unless stated specifically that they are not). Note that floppy disks only support functions 00 through 05 of INT 13. Hard drives support all INT 13 functions.

INT 13 Function 00: Reset Disk

INT 13, Function 00, is a hard reset to the disk controller to restore things to the boot status. If there is an error using this function, CF (the Carry Flag) is set and AH will contain the error code. The disk error codes are shown in Fig. G-2.

Input: AH = 00
AL = Drive number
00–07 Floppy disk
80–FF Fixed disk
Output: Carry Flag = 0 (AL = 0) success
Carry Flag = 1 (AL = Error Code)

INT 13 Function 01: Read Status of Last Operation

If the function does not go to correct completion, an error code is stored into AL. See Fig. G-2 for a list of error codes and their meanings.

Input: AH = 01

Output: AH = Disk Status (00 if successful)

INT 13 Function 02: Read Sectors into Memory

As with function 00 and 01, if this function is not successful, AH contains an error code. See Fig. G-2 for a list of the error codes and their meanings. For hard disks, the drive number (in DL) can range from 80 to 87.

Input: AH = 02
AL = Number of Sectors to Read
Floppies 1–8
Hard Disk 1–80
Hard Disk Read/Write Long 1–79

Input	
AH = Function Number of INT 13	
Output	
AL = Disk Error Code	
00	No error
01	Bad command passed to controller
02	Address mark not found
03	Diskette is write-protected
04	Sector not found
05	Reset failed
06	Floppy Disk Removed
07	Drive parameters wrong
08	DMA Overflow
09	DMA across segment end
0A	Bad sector flag
0B	Bad track flag seen
10	Data error
11	Data is error-corrected
20	Controller failure
40	Seek operation failed
80	No response from disk , Time out
AA	Drive not ready
BB	Undefined error
E0	Status Error
0FF	Sense operation failed

Fig. G-2. Disk error codes. (All codes are in hexadecimal.)

CH = Cylinder or Track (Floppy disk) Number
CL = Sector Number
DH = Head Number
DL = Drive Number
ES:BX = Buffer address

Output: Carry Flag = 0 (AL = 0) Successful
Carry Flag = 1 (AL contains error code)

INT 13 Function 03: Write Sectors to Disk

As with functions 00 through 02, if this function is not successful, AH contains an error code. See Fig. G-2 for a list of the error codes and their meanings. For hard disks, the drive number (in DL) can range from 80 to 87.

Input:

AH = 03
AL = Number of Sectors to Write
  Floppy diskettes = 1–8
  Hard Disks = 1–80
  Hard Disks Read/Write long = 1–79
CH = Cylinder or Track (floppy) Number
CL = Sector Number
DH = Head Number
DL = Drive Number
ES:BX = Address of buffer for reads/writes

Output:

Carry Flag = 0 (AL = 00) Successful
Carry Flag = 1 (AL has error code)

INT 13 Function 04: Verify Sectors

As with functions 00 through 03, if this function is not successful, AH contains an error code. See Fig. G-2 for a list of the error codes and their meanings. For hard disks, the drive number (in DL) can range from 80 to 87.

Input:

AH = 04
AL = Number of Sectors to Verify
  Floppy diskettes = 1–8
  Hard Disks = 1–80
  Hard Disks Read/Write long = 1–79
CH = Cylinder (hard drive) or Track (floppy) Number
CL = Sector Number
DH = Head Number
DL = Drive Number

Output:

Carry Flag = 0 (AL = 00) Successful
Carry Flag = 1 (AL has error code)

INT 13 Functions 05, 06, and 07: Formatting

Function 05 is supported only by floppy diskettes. Functions 06 and 07 work only on hard disks. As with functions 00 through 04, if this function is not successful,

AH contains an error code. See Fig. G-2 for a list of the error codes and their meanings. For hard disks, the drive number (in DL) can range from 80 to 87.

Input:

- AH = 05 Format desired track
- AH = 06 Format desired track and set bad sector flags
- AH = 07 Format the desired disk starting at the indicated track
- CH = Cylinder (hard drive) or Track (floppy) Number
- DH = Head Number
- DL = Drive Number (80–87 only allowed for hard disks)
- ES:BX = 4-byte address field entries, 1 per sector
  - byte 0: Cylinder number
  - byte 1: Head number
  - byte 2: Sector number
  - byte 3: Sector-size code
    - 00 - 128 bytes/sector
    - 01 - 256 bytes/sector
    - 02 - 512 bytes/sector
    - 03 - 1024 bytes/sector

INT 13 Function 08: Return Drive Parameters

Function 08 of INT 13 only works on hard disks.

Input:

- AH = 08
- DL = Drive number

Output:

- AH = 00
- BH = 00
- BL = Drive type
- CH = Low-order 8 bits of 10-bit maximum number of cylinders
- CL = Bits 7 and 6 - High-order 2 bits of 10-bit maximum number of cylinders
  Bits 5-0 - Maximum number of sectors/track
- DH = Maximum value for head number
- DL = Number of drives attached to the controller
- ES:DI = Address of floppy-disk drive parameter table

INT 13 Function 09: Initialize Drive

Function 09 is used by BIOS to initialize the drive and to point INT 41 to the drive's parameter block.

Input: AH = 09

INT 13 Functions 0A and 0B: Read/Write Long Sectors

As with most INT 13 functions, if function 0A/0B is not successful, AL will contain an error code. See Fig. G-2 for a list of the error codes and their meanings. For hard disks, the drive number (in DL) can range from 80 to 87. Function 0A is for Read and 0B is for Write. This function is only for hard disks.

Input:
AH = 0A,0B
AL = Number of Sectors to Read
Floppies 1–8
Hard Disk 1–80
Hard Disk Read/Write long 1–79
CH = Cylinder or Track (Floppy disk) Number
CL = Sector Number
DH = Head Number
DL = Drive Number
ES:BX = Buffer address

Output:
Carry Flag = 0 (AL = 0) Successful
Carry Flag = 1 (AL has error code)

INT 13 Function 0C: Seek

As with most INT 13 functions, if function 0C is not successful, AL will contain an error code. See Fig. G-2 for a list of the error codes and their meanings. This function is only for hard disks, and the drive number (in DL) can range from 80 to 87.

Input:
AH = 0C
AL = Number of Sectors to Read
Floppies 1–8
Hard Disk 1–80
Hard Disk Read/Write Long 1–79
CH = Cylinder or Track (Floppy disk) Number
CL = Sector Number
DH = Head Number
DL = Drive Number
ES:BX = Buffer address

Output:
Carry Flag = 0 (AL = 0) Successful
Carry Flag = 1 (AL has error code)

INT 13 Function 0D: Alternate Disk Reset

This alternate disk reset is used only for hard disk drives. Function 0 also works to reset diskettes as well.

Input: AH = 0D
DL = Drive number

INT 13 Function 0E and 0F: Read/Write Sector Buffer

As with most INT 13 functions, if function 0D is not successful, AH contains an error code. See Fig. G-2 for a list of the error codes and their meanings. For hard disks, the drive number (in DL) can range from 80 to 87. Function 0E is for Read and 0F is for Write. This function is only for hard disks.

Input: AH = 0E,0F
DH = Head Number
DL = Drive Number (80–87 allowed)
CH = Cylinder Number
CL = Sector Number
ES:BX = Address of buffer for Reads/Writes

Output: Carry Flag = 0 (AL = 0) Successful
Carry Flag = 1 (AL has error code)

INT 13 Function 10: Test Drive Ready

Function 10 of INT 13 tests whether or not a hard disk is ready for a read or write.

INT 13 Function 11: Recalibrate Hard Drive

As with most INT 13 functions, if Function 11 is not successful, AH contains an error code. See Fig. G-2 for a list of the error codes and their meanings. For hard disks, the drive number (in DL) can range from 80 to 87. This function is only for hard disks.

Input: AH = 11
DL = Drive Number (80–87 allowed)

Output: Carry Flag = 0 (AL = 0) Successful
Carry Flag = 1 (AL has error code)

INT 13 Function 12 and 13: Diagnostic Services

As with most INT 13 functions, if Function 13 is not successful, AH contains an error code. See Fig. G-2 for a list of the error codes and their meanings. For hard disks, the drive number (in DL) can range from 80 to 87. This function is only for hard disks.

Input: AH = 12 RAM Diagnostics
AH = 13 Drive Diagnostics
AH = 14 Controller Diagnostics
DL = Drive Number (80-87 allowed)

Output: Carry Flag = 0 (AL = 0) Successful
Carry Flag = 1 (AL has error code)

INT 13 Function 14: Controller Diagnostic

As with other INT 13 functions, if Function 14 is not successful, AH contains an error code. See Fig. G-2 for a list of status codes and their meanings.

Input: AH = 14

Output: AH = Status

INT 13 Function 15: Get Disk Type

As with other INT 13 functions, if Function 15 is not successful, AH contains an error code. See Fig. G-2 for a list of status codes and their meanings.

Input: AH = 15
DL = Drive number

Output: AH = Disk drive code:
00 - No drive present
01 - Cannot sense when floppy is changed
02 - Can sense when floppy is changed
03 - Fixed disk, also CX:DX = Number of sectors

INT 13 Function 16: Check for Change of Floppy Disk Status

As with other INT 13 functions, if Function 16 is not successful, AH contains an error code. See Fig. G-2 for a list of status codes and their meanings.

Input: AH = 16

DL = Number of drive to check

Output: AH = 00 - No change
06 - Floppy disk change

INT 13 Function 17: Set Disk Type

As with other INT 13 functions, if Function 17 is not successful, AH contains an error code. See Fig. G-2 for a list of status codes and their meanings.

Input: AH = 17
AL = Floppy-disk type code
DL = Drive number

Interrupt 14: Port Usage

INT 14's various functions initialize RS-232C ports, send characters to them, receive characters from them, or return the status of the port.

INT 14 Function 00: Initialize RS-232 Port

This function configures the RS-232 port for one of eight baud rates and sets up the other parameters necessary for correct transmission of data. There must be an installed RS-232 card in your system before this function works.

Input: AH = 00
AL =

Bits 0,1 = Character length
- 00 = Unused
- 01 = Unused
- 10 = 7 bits
- 11 = 8 bits

2 = Stop Bits
- 0 = 1 stop bit
- 1 = 2 stop bits

3,4 = Parity
- 00 = None
- 01 = Odd
- 10 = None
- 11 = Even

5,6,7 = Baud Rate

000 = 110 Baud
001 = 150 Baud
010 = 300 Baud
011 = 600 Baud
100 = 1200 Baud
101 = 2400 Baud
110 = 4800 Baud
111 = 9600 Baud

DX = Serial port number (0 = first port)

INT 14 Function 01: Send One Character

INT 14 Function 01 allows you to send data over your system's serial port. You load the character to send in AL, store 1 in AH, and call INT 14. AH holds the status on return. See Fig. G-3 for a list of the status and error codes and their meanings.

Return Value	Meaning
8000	Time out
4000	Transfer shift register empty
2000	Transfer holding register empty
1000	Break detect
0800	Framing error
0400	Parity error
0200	Overrun error
0100	Data ready
0080	Received line signal detect
0040	Ring indicator
0020	Data set ready
0010	Clear to send
0008	Delta receive line signal detect
0004	Trailing edge ring detector
0002	Delta data set ready
0001	Delta clear to send

Fig. G-3. RS-232 status and error codes.

Input: AH = 01
AL = Character to send
DX = Serial port number (0 = first port)

Output: AX = Status (See Fig. G-3)

INT 14 Function 02: Receive Character

Function 02 allows you to read a character from the RS-232 port. AH holds the status on return. See Fig. G-3 for a list of the status and error codes and their meanings.

Input: AH = 02
DX = Serial port number (0 = first)

Output: AH = Status (See Fig. G-3)
If successful, AL holds the character

INT 14 Function 03: Return Status

Function 03 gives you the status of an RS-232 port. The status returns in AH. For a list of the status and error codes, see Fig. G-3.

Input: AH = 03
DX = Serial port number (0 = first)

Output: AH = Status

Interrupt 15: Cassette I/O

INT 15 is the only BIOS support for cassettes, since they are rarely used. They can supply a large amount of storage and accurate, rapid backups are coming into the market.

Input: AH = 00 Turn cassette motor on
= 01 Turn cassette motor off
= 02Read one or more 256 byte blocks. Store data at ES:BX.
CX = Count of bytes to read
On return, DX holds number of bytes read.
ES:BX points to one byte past the last read
= 03 Write one or more 256 byte blocks from ES:BX.
CX = Count of bytes to write
On return, CX = 00 ES:BX points to location following last byte written

Output: DX = Number of bytes actually read
Carry Flag = 1, if error
If set, AH = 01 CRC
= 02 Data transitions lost
= 03 No Data found

Interrupt 16: Keyboard Services

INT 16 handles keyboard input. AL will contain the ASCII code on return. However, if the key pressed was in the extended code, AH will contain the scan code.

INT 16 Function 00: Read Key from Keyboard

Function 00 waits until a character is read; it then removes the character from the keyboard buffer.

Input: AH = 00

Output: If standard ASCII:
AH = Standard keyboard scan code
AL = ASCII code

If extended (ASCII):
AH = Extended ASCII code
AL = 00

INT 16 Function 01: Check If Key Ready to Be Read

This function returns immediately and does not remove the character from the keyboard buffer.

Input: AH = 01

Output: Zero Flag (ZF) = 0
Zero Flag (ZF) = 1 Buffer is empty

If standard ASCII:
AH = Standard keyboard scan code
AL = ASCII Code

If extended ASCII:
AH = Extended ASCII code
AL = 00

INT 16 Function 02: Get Shift Status

This function returns the status of the various shift keys. There can be multiple shifts active at the same time.

Input: AH = 02

Output: AL = Shift Status

01 - Right shift active
02 - Left shift active
04 - Ctrl active
08 - Alt active
10 - Scroll Lock active
20 - Num Lock active
40 - Caps Lock active
80 - Insert state active

Interrupt 17: Printer Services

INT 17 Function 00: Send Byte to Printer

INT 17 Function 00 is how BIOS talks to your printer. Set DX to the printer number you will print on (numbers range from 0–2 and correspond to printer cards). Generally you'll choose 0. To print a character, store it in AL, set AH to 0, and issue INT 17.

Input: AH = 00
AL = Character to be printed
DX = Printer number (0, 1, 2)

Output: AH = Printer Status (See Fig. G-4)

INT 17 Function 01: Initialize Printer Port

INT 17 Function 01 resets the printer and prepares it for output. On return, AH holds the printer's status as shown in Fig. G-4. If you select a printer you don't have, you get a time-out for status.

Input: AH = 01
DX = Printer number (0, 1, 2)

Output: AH = Printer Status

Return Value	Meaning
80	Printer not busy
40	Printer Acknowledgement
20	Out of paper
10	Printer selected
08	I/O Error
04	Unused
02	Unused
01	Time out

Fig. G-4. Printer status codes. (Multiple states can be active simultaneously.)

INT 17 Function 02: Read Printer Status into AH

In case your program seems to be having problems getting information out to the printer, you can check on its status. See Fig. G-4 for a list of the status codes that will return in AH.

Input: AH = 02
DX = Printer number (0, 1, 2)

Output: AH = Status

Interrupt 18: Resident BASIC

INT 18 starts ROM-resident BASIC.

Interrupt 19: Bootstrap (Warm Start)

INT 19 loads the boot record from disk, if there is one. If not, ROM-resident BASIC gets executed.

Interrupt 1A: Time of Day

Your system's clock increments at a vast rate, depending on the megahertz rate of its clock. The functions of INT 1A work with that timer.

INT 1A Function 00: Read Time of Day

Function 00 of Interrupt 1A reads the time of day from the system clock.

Input:	AH	= 00
Output:	AL	= 0 if timer has not passed 24 hours since last read
	CX	= High word of timer count
	DX	= Low word of timer count

INT 1A Function 01: Set Time of Day

Function 01 sets the time of day.

Input:	AH	= 01
	CX	= High word of timer count
	DX	= Low word of timer count

INT 1A Function 02: Read Real-Time Clock

Function 02 returns the number of hours, minutes, and seconds since the last system reset.

Input:	AH	= 02
Output:	CF	= 0 Clock running
		= 1 Clock stopped
	CH	= Hours in BCD
	CL	= Minutes in BCD
	DH	= Seconds in BCD

Note: See the procedures in Chapter 4 (BCDUNPK) to get digits into AH,AL.

INT 1A Function 03: Set Real-Time Clock

See procedures in Chapter 4 on how to pack BCD values before calling this function.

Input:	AH	= 03
	CH	= Hours in BCD
	CL	= Minutes in BCD
	DH	= Seconds in BCD

DL = 00 Standard Time
01 Daylight saving time

INT 1A Function 04: Read Date from Real-Time Clock

See procedures in Chapter 4 on how to unpack BCD.

Input: AH = 04

Output: CF = 0 Clock running
1 Clock stopped
CH = Century in BCD
CL = Year in BCD
DH = Month in BCD
DL = Day in BCD

INT 1A Function 05: Set Date in Real-Time Clock

Before calling this function, see procedures in Chapter 4 on how to pack BCD.

Input: AH = 05
CH = Century in BCD
CL = Year in BCD
DH = Month in BCD
DL = Day in BCD

INT 1A Function 06: Set Alarm

See procedures in Chapter 4 on how to pack BCD.

Input: AH = 06
CH = Hours in BCD
CL = Minutes in BCD
DH = Seconds in BCD

Output: CF = 0 Operation successful
= 1 Alarm already set or clock stopped

INT 1A Function 07: Reset Alarm (Turn Alarm Off)

This function cancels the activity of Function 6.

Input: AH = 07

Other BIOS Interrupts

Interrupt 1B: Keyboard Break Address

INT 1B holds the address that control will be transferred to if your program is broken with a Break. You can write your own Break handler by intercepting and redirecting this interrupt. This is useful if/when you don't want your user to interrupt the run of your program.

Interrupt 1C: Timer Tick Interrupt

INT 1C is called by INT 8. Originally, INT 1C points only to an IRET instruction. You can redirect it where you wish.

Interrupt 1D: Video Parameter Tables

INT 1D points to the address of the video controller parameter tables.

Interrupt 1E: Diskette Parameters

INT 1E is like INT 1D, in that it points to a parameter table, the Diskette Base Table, 11 bytes long. Since it's in ROM, you can't change it. However, DOS also

DOS Memory 0000:0078	
Byte 0,1	Contain step rate time and head load/unload times
2	The time it takes diskette motors to turn off after an operation
3	Number of bytes per sector
4	Number of sectors per track
5,6,7	These bytes are concerned with the layout of the disk sectors
8	Fill byte - The byte used to fill newly formatted disk sectors
9	Head settle time - the time given for the diskette head to come to rest after it has shot into position over the track
10	Diskette motor start and warm-up time.

Fig. G-5. Diskette base table. (It is recommended that you do not change these values.)

stores it in low memory, at 0000:0078, which you *can* change. See Fig. G-5 for the table format. It is recommended, however, that you do not change the values.

Interrupt 1F: Graphics Character Definitions

INT 1F points to a table in memory that allows you to define the top 128 ASCII characters in high-resolution graphics mode—for graphics screens only. The table is a list of 128 characters, with eight bytes each, for 1,024 total bytes.

About MS-DOS Interrupts

Many operating systems are disk-based and offer interactive operation to users. MS-DOS offers many special features in tightly coded system interrupts. These interrupts allow multitasking and pipeline processing, both of which keep a processor busy instead of waiting for work. This busyness allows more processes to flow through a computer, which means that more tasks are accomplished in a shorter period of time.

The MS-DOS interrupts, 20–F0, are usable by systems programmers.

Interrupt 20: Terminate

At the end of user programs, INT 20 terminates the program and gives control back to MS-DOS.

Interrupt 21: Service Interrupts

INT 21 is a power-packed interrupt, with a great number of subfunctions. To call one of its functions, load the function number into AH (and any other register values as shown in each of the functions) and issue INT 21. As throughout this book, all numbers are hexadecimal unless specifically stated otherwise.

INT 21 Function 0: Program Terminate

This function of INT 21 is exactly the same as INT 20. It ends your program and returns control to MS-DOS.

Input: AH = 0

INT 21 Function 1: Keyboard Input

With this function, any key you press (that has a graphic) is echoed to the display screen. When you use Function 1, processing stops until a key is pressed; that is, it waits for input. If the corresponding character is ASCII, it prints it on the screen. The tab character is automatically expanded to the end of the next eight-column field by adding spaces. Holding the Ctrl key and pressing Break terminates operation.

If the pressed key corresponds to an extended code, the AL register contains a value of zero. Then you must execute this function again to get the code. If the second value is less than 84, it represents the scan code of the pressed key. For example, a value of 30 says that the Alt key and the letter A were pressed. Values above 83 are more difficult to decode but are shown in Appendix E. Input can be read from another device or disk file by redirection of the standard input.

Input: AH = 1

Output: AL = ASCII code of struck key

INT 21 Function 2: Character Output on Screen

This function displays the character contained in the DL register onto the screen. It is useful for writing a single character (use Function 9 for a string). Function 2 is useful for displaying the dollar sign ($), since Function 9 uses the $ as the end-of-string character. The Backspace key moves the cursor to the left, but does not erase the character printed there. The output can be sent to another device or disk file by redirecting the standard output.

Input: AH = 2
DL = ASCII character

INT 21 Function 3: Standard Auxiliary Device Input

This function reads a character from the standard auxiliary device, generally the serial port, defined as AUX or COM1. However, you can change the standard auxiliary port to COM2. Function 3 waits until a byte is available.

Input: AH = 3

Output: Character in AL

INT 21 Function 4: Standard Auxiliary Device Output

Function 4 sends the byte in register DL to the auxiliary port AUX or COM1.

Input: AH = 4
DL = The character to output

INT 21 Function 5: Printer Output

This function sends the character in register DL to the standard printer port, PRN or LPT1. As with Function 4, the byte to be written to the printer is passed in DL. You could also use INT 17 for this purpose.

Input: AH = 5
DL = The character to output

INT 21 Function 6: Console Input/Output

Function 6 can do both input and output; it can also determine the input status. It does *not* wait for input. Also, the input character is *not* automatically displayed and Ctrl-Break does not terminate the operation.

Input: AH = 6

Output: If DL = FF AL holds the character if one is ready
DL < FF Type ASCII code in DL out

INT 21 Function 7: Console Input without Echo

INT 21 Function 7, like Function 1, waits for keyboard entry. If an ASCII character is entered, the ASCII value is returned in the AL register. The IBM graphics characters can be entered by holding the Alt key and typing the decimal value with the keypad numbers. If an extended character (such as a function key) is entered, a 0 is stored in AL. This function must then be called a second time to determine the character. Unlike Function 1, Function 7 does *not* display the input character. Also, Ctrl-Break does not terminate the process.

Input: AH = 7

Output: AL = ASCII code of struck key

INT 21 Function 8: Console Input without Echo, but with Break Check

Function 8 waits for a character and terminates when Ctrl-Break is pressed. The input character is not displayed and tab characters are not expanded.

Input: AH = 8

Output: AL = ASCII code of struck key

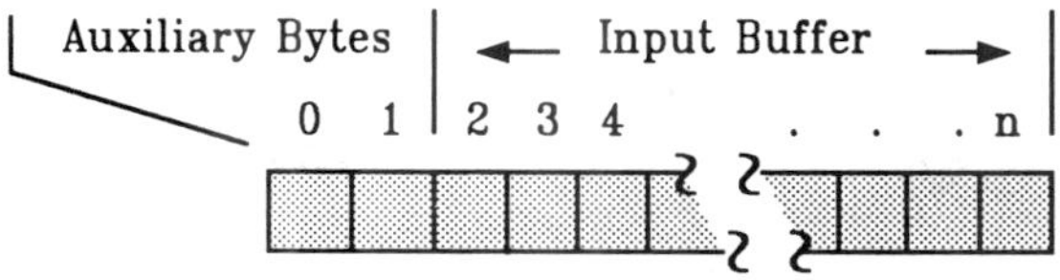

Aux byte 0 = The maximum length of the input (set by user)
1 = The number of bytes actually entered (set by DOS)
This count does NOT include the carriage return
that DOS adds to the end of the string.

Fig. G-6. Input buffer format.

INT 21 Function 9: String Print

INT 21 Function 9 is useful for printing a string of characters on the screen. Function 9 is easy to use. To do so, place the string somewhere in memory and terminate it with a dollar sign ($), which means that you cannot include a dollar sign as part of the string (use Function 2 to print a $). The address of the string is placed in the DS:DX registers.

Input: AH = 9
DS:DX = Address of the string that ends in "$"

INT 21 Function 0A: String Input

All characters typed by the user are entered into the keyboard buffer. When the Return key is pressed, the line is stored into the input buffer.

Before you use this function, set up a buffer in memory. Remember that there are two auxiliary bytes located at the beginning of the buffer, as shown in Fig. G-6. The first byte defines the maximum length of text that can be stored in the buffer. The second byte gives the number of characters that were entered by the user. You set the value of the first byte. MS-DOS fills in the second byte after the buffer has been read. MS-DOS also adds a carriage return to the end of the input string. However, this carriage return is not included in the count that MS-DOS enters in the second byte. So, you should set the maximum size of the buffer to be one byte larger than you need.

Input: AH = 0A
[DS:DX] = Length of buffer

Output: Buffer at DS:DX filled
Echoes the typed keys

INT 21 Function 0B: Check Input Status

This function is useful for checking to see if there is any keyboard input waiting, which avoids having a program wait for something if there's no need to. On return from this function, AL contains a zero if no key has been pressed. Any other AL value indicates a character is waiting to be read—although this function does *not* read the character.

Input: AH = 0B

Output: AL = FF if a character is ready
AL = 0 if nothing is there to be read in

INT 21 Function 0C: Clear Buffer and Invoke Service

INT 21 Function 0C clears the keyboard buffer before it invokes a keyboard function (1, 6, 7, 8, or 0A). This is important when your user may be "typing ahead" (because of familiarity with your software, the user "knows" what question comes next and will type an answer before the question hits the screen). If your program finds an error (such as an *Abort, Retry, Ignore?*), you must have a correct answer to that prompt before you can allow your normal software to go on. So you flush the keyboard buffer and wait for that answer to be entered. INT 21 Function 0C also checks for Break.

Input: AH = 0C
AL = Keyboard function number

INT 21 Function 0D: Disk Reset

This function serves the same purpose as BIOS Interrupt 13 Function 00.

Input: AH = 0D

INT 21 Function 0E: Select Disk

INT 21 Function 0E is how MS-DOS selects your default disk. Whenever you type "C:" at a prompt, INT 21 Function 0E is called. This was one of the early MS-DOS interrupts. INT 21 Function 3B is more comprehensive; it allows you to change the current directory, including the default drives.

Input: AH = 0E
DL = Drive number

INT 21 Function 0F: Open Pre-existing File

This function opens a file that you created some time in the past (it can be just before you used this function), but the file already exists. It does not create the file for you. It uses file control blocks (FCBs). FCBs are supported under all MS-DOS versions, although it's recommended now to use file handles, because FCB do not allow you to specify subdirectories. See Fig. G-7 for the format of an opened FCB.

There is no space in the "normal" FCB for either the file's creation time or its attribute. You can add the attribute by using an extended FCB. The extended FCB looks the same as the FCB, with an added seven bytes at the beginning: a byte of FF, five bytes of zeros, and the attribute byte. See Fig. G-8 for a list of file attributes and their meaning.

Using the FCBs (instead of file handles) is somewhat awkward, so instead of continuing, we're recommending that you study your MS-DOS manual carefully. There are two ways to read files, sequential and random. Sequential files need a marker between records (since MS-DOS knows that the records may be of differing lengths). If you use MS-DOS sequential read/writing functions, MS-DOS takes care of worrying about the markers. Random files, on the other hand, need records of the same size. MS-DOS defaults to a size of 128 bytes. If your record size is different, you must modify the record size in the FCB after a successful open.

Input: AH = 0F
DS:DX points to an FCB.

Output: AL = 0 if successful
AL = FF if unsuccessful

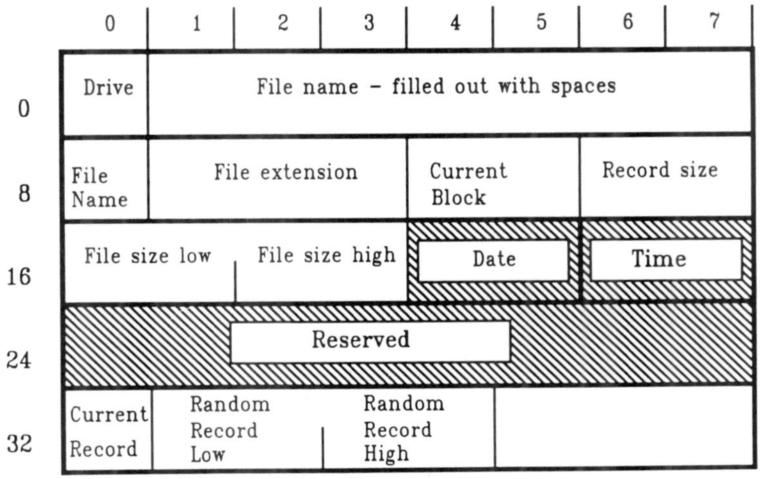

Fig. G-7. File Control Block (FCB) format for an opened file. (Shaded areas are reserved by MS-DOS.)

Attribute Bit	Meaning
0	Read-only
1	Hidden. Directory searches will not find.
2	System file, same attribute as IBMDOS.COM
3	Volume file, the eleven letters of the file name actually are the disk's label
4	Directory
5	Archive, this bit is checked by BACKUP to see if the file has been rewritten since last BACKUP run
6	Reserved
7	Reserved

Fig. G-8. File attribute byte for extended FCB.

INT 21 Function 10: Close File

To keep your data intact, be sure to close all files before you exit your program. INT 21 Function 10 reads what's in the FCB and writes it to the directory. Its major use is to give the file a non-zero size. MS-DOS usually keeps track of file size, but you can use this function to do so.

Input: AH = 10
DS:DX points to an FCB.

Output: AL = 0 if successful
AL = FF if unsuccessful

INT 21 Function 11: Search for First Matching File

MS-DOS itself uses INT 21 Function 11 to search the disk for files. Point DX:DX at an unopened FCB and call this function. The FCB can use a "?" wildcard (but not the "*," which file handle functions can). For example, if you want to find all the file names with a ".ASM" extension, you would have to fill the FCB file name with "????????" and the extension with ASM. The eight question marks will find any length file name, from a single character to eight. If the search finds a match, an unopened FCB (for the matching file) will be stored in the DTA. You can use this FCB for any use, just as you would any other FCB.

Input:	AH = 11 DX:DX points to an unopened FCB.
Output:	AL = 0 if successful AL = FF if unsuccessful DTA holds FCB for match

INT 21 Function 12: Search for Next Matching File

After you find the first matching file (using INT 21 Function 11), MS-DOS fills part of the reserved areas in the FCB. This function uses that information to find the next match in the directory.

Input:	AH = 12 DX:DX points to an unopened FCB.
Output:	AL = 0 if successful AL = FF if unsuccessful DTA holds FCB for match

INT 21 Function 13: Deletes Files

INT 21 Function 13 simply deletes files. All you have to do is to point DS:DX at an unopened FCB and issue this interrupt and function.

Input:	AH = 13 DTA holds FCB for match. DX:DX points to an unopened FCB.
Output:	AL = 0 if successful AL = FF if unsuccessful

INT 21 Function 14: Sequential Read

INT 21 Function 14 reads sequential records from an opened file. You set the current block field (bytes 0C–0D in the FCB) and the current record field from 0 to 127 in byte 1F. The data read is dumped in the DTA. If you change the record length from the default 128 bytes, you would get whatever your change in the DTA.

The record address increments with each read, which means that if the current record is 127 the next record will be 0.

Input: AH = 14
Current address is incremented, current block and record is set in FCB, and DX:DX points to an opened FCB.

Output: Requested record put in DTA
AL = 0 if successful
1 End of file, no data in record
2 DTA segment too small for record
3 end of file, record padded with 0's

INT 21 Function 15: Sequential Write

INT 21 Function 15 writes a record from the Disk Transfer Area—DTA (always used in FCB operations) to an open file. The record address increments. Note that if your record size is significantly smaller than a sector (512 bytes), MS-DOS buffers your data and only writes it when there is enough to write, or when you end the program. (Note this is one of the tasks that INT 20 or INT 27 takes care of for you.)

Input: AH = 15
Record address is incremented, current block and record is set in FCB, and DX:DX points to an opened FCB.

Output: One record read from DTA and written
AL = 0 if successful
1 Disk full
2 DTA segment too small for record

INT 21 Function 16: Create File

INT 21 Function 16 creates a file. If a file already exists with the same name (the one you put into the FCB), that file will be opened and set to zero length—which may destroy valid data you stored there earlier, if you overwrite it by accident. If there is no identical file, a directory entry is opened for this new one. If there is no space left on your diskette or hard disk, this function returns an FF and you have to free some space.

Input: AH = 16
DS:DX points to an unopened FCB.

Output: AL = 0 if successful
FF Directory full

INT 21 Function 17: Rename File

If you need to rename files, use this interrupt and function (it's the way MS-DOS does it). The FCB can use a "?" wildcard (but not the "*," which file handles functions can). For example, if you want to find all the file names with a ".ASM" extension, you would have to fill the FCB file name with "????????" and the extension with ASM. The eight question marks will find any length file name, from a single character to eight.

To use INT 21 Function 17, set up an unopened FCB for the file(s) you want to rename.

Input: AH = 17
DX:DX points to a modified FCB. For a modified FCB, the second file name starts six bytes after the end of the first file name at DS:DX + 11.

Output: AL = 0 if successful
FF Directory full

INT 21 Function 18: Internal to MS-DOS

This function is used only by MS-DOS. It is here so you can see that it is used and unavailable for your use.

INT 21 Function 19: Find Current Disk

INT 21 Function 19 is handy if you want to find out where you are.

Input: AH = 19

Output: AL = Current disk
0 = A
1 = B
2 = C
3 = D (and so on)

INT 21 Function 1A: Set Disk Transfer Area (DTA) Location

MS-DOS default DTA (Disk Transfer Area) and record size in the FCB are only 128 bytes, but you may need a larger size. One area you can use for more bytes is the end of your program in memory. Be careful not to overwrite the stack that MS-DOS supplies at the top of every .COM file's segment.

Input: AH = 1A
DS:DX points to new DTA address.

INT 21 Function 1B: File Allocation Table (FAT) Information

This function returns FAT information for the default drive.

Input: AH = 1B

Output: AL = Number of Sectors/Cluster
DS:BX points to the FAT byte
DX = Number of clusters
CX = Size of a sector (e.g., 512)

INT 21 Function 1C: File Allocation Table (FAT) Information for Specified Drive

After issuing this interrupt, DX holds the number of usable clusters. AL holds the number of sectors/cluster, while CX holds the size of a physical sector on the drive selected.

Input: AH = 1C

Output: AL = Number of Sectors/Cluster
DS:BX points to the FAT byte
DX = Number of clusters
CX = Size of a sector (e.g., 512)

INT 21 Function 1D through 20: Internal to MS-DOS

These functions are used only by MS-DOS. They're here so you can see that they are used and unavailable for your use.

INT 21 Function 21: Random Read

To write into the disk transfer area (DTA) from a random read, set the random record field in an opened File Control Block (FCB). DS:DX + 21 holds the low word of the random record number and DS:DX + 23 holds the high word. When you request the read, MS-DOS sets the current block and current record fields for you.

Input: AH = 21
DS:DX points to an opened FCB. Set FCB's Random Record field at DS:DX+21 and DS:DX+23.

Output: AL = 00 Successful
01 End of file, no more data
02 Not enough space in DTA segment
03 End of file, partial record padded with 0's

INT 21 Function 22: Random Write

To use INT 21 Function 22, fill the disk transfer area (DTA) with the record you want to write. Set the random record field in the file control block (FCB). It's recommended that you double-check your record field and record number. If you use an incorrect record field, you'll overwrite something you don't want destroyed. Also, if your record number is far in excess of what is currently in your file, MS-DOS will simply extend your file the "required" length to stick that record at the end and fill in the intervening space (if there was garbage in storage, that's what you get in the intervening space). MS-DOS sets the current block and current record fields for you.

Input: AH = 21
DS:DX points to an opened FCB. Set FCB's Random Record field at DS:DX+21 and DS:DX+23.

Output: AL = 00 Successful
01 Disk is full
02 Not enough space in DTA segment

INT 21 Function 23: File Size

If you want to know the size of a file (without having to bother opening it), use this function. You'll need an unopened FCB. Point DS:DX at the FCB and MS-DOS searches the current directory for a match to the file name. If it finds a match, the random record fields of the FCB will be set to the total length of the file in records—rounded up. If you set the record length to a value, the total bytes are divided by that number and the result rounded up. If you want the total size in bytes, set the record length to one byte. If MS-DOS does not find a match in the directory, AL returns FF.

Input: AH = 22
DS:DX points to an unopened FCB.

Output: AL = 00 Successful
FF = No file found that matched FCB
Random Record Field is set to file length in records, rounded up;

INT 21 Function 24: Set Random Record Field

Random Record Field is set to match Current Record and Current Block.

Input: AH = 24
DX:DX points to an opened FCB

INT 21 Function 25: Set Interrupt Vector

The value in DS:DX *is* the address. It is not a segment value (DS) and an offset (DX).

Input: AH = 25
AL = Interrupt number
DS:DX = New address

INT 21 Function 26: Create a New Program Segment

This is an old implementation of the operation needed for creating new segments. Use Function 4B instead.

INT 21 Function 27: Random Block Read

When you read in a random record, INT 21 Function 27 updates the random record field. When the function is finished, the random record field is set to the number of the *next*, unread record.

Input: AH = 27
DS:DX points to an opened FCB. Set FCB's Random Record field at DS:DX+21 and DS:DX+23.

Output: AL = 00 Successful
01 End of file, no more data
02 Not enough space in DTA segment
03 End of file, partial record padded with 0's
CX = Number of records read
Random Record Fields are set to access next record.

INT 21 Function 28: Random Block Write

If you set CX to 0 when you call this function, the fill will be set to the length given by the random record field. This may force the file to be truncated or enlarged. If it enlarges, it includes whatever garbage is in the free sectors on the disk.

Input: AH = 28
CX = Number of records to write.
0 - File is set to size indicated in Random Record field.
Random Record Fields set to access next record, DS:DX points to an opened FCB, and FCB's Random Record field is set at DS:DX + 21 and DS:DX + 23.

Output: AL = 00 Successful
01 Disk is full
02 Not enough space in DTA segment

INT 21 Function 29: Parse File Name

INT 21 Function 29 is useful in parsing file names from the command line. You give it the address of the command line. If it finds a file name, the function places an unopened FCB for the file at address ES:DI. If the command line does not contain a valid file name, ES:[DI + 1] will contain blanks.

Input: AH = 29
AL = Bit 0 = 1 Leading separators are scanned off command line
1 = 1 Drive ID in final FCB will be changed ONLY if a drive was specified
2 = 1 File name in FCB changed ONLY if command line includes file name
3 = 1 File name extension in FCB will be changed ONLY if command line contains a file name extension
DS:SI = Command line to parse
ES:DI = Address to put FCB

Output: DS:SI = First character after filename
ES:DI = Valid FCB

INT 21 Function 2A: Get Date

Input: AH = 2A

Output: CX = Year 1980 through 2099
DH = Month Number, where January = 1
DL = Day of the month

INT 21 Function 2B: Set Date

Input: AH = 2B
CX = Year - 1980
DH = Month number, where January = 1
DL = Day of the month

Output: AL = 0 if successful
AL = FF if date not valid

INT 21 Function 2C: Get Time

Input: AH = 2C

Output: CH = Hours (0–23)
CL = Minutes (0–59)
DH = Seconds (0–59)
DL = Hundredths of seconds (0–99)

INT 21 Function 2D: Set Time

Input: AH = 2D
CH = Hours (0–23)
CL = Minutes (0–59)
DH = Seconds (0–59)
DL = Hundredths of seconds (0–99)

Output: AL = 0 if successful
AL = FF if time is invalid

INT 21 Function 2E: Set or Reset Verify Switch

INT 21 Function 2E turns verification for disk writing on or off. This helps protect you against disk errors.

Input: AH = 2E
AL = 0 Turn verify off
1 Turn verify on
DL = 0

INT 21 Function 2F: Get Current DTA

This function is useful if you move the DTA location often and want to know where you are.

Input: AH = 2F

Output: ES:BX = Current DTA address

INT 21 Function 30: Get MS-DOS Version Number

This function lets you know what version of MS-DOS you're using. AL holds the major version, the "3" in MS-DOS 3.10. AH holds the minor version, the "10" of 3.10. If AL returns a 0, you're working with an early MS-DOS, before 2.0. Program FIND_VER shows a use of this function.

Input: AH = 30

Output: AL = Major version number
AH = Minor version number
BX = 0
CX = 0

INT 21 Function 31: Terminate Process and Stay Resident

This is the preferred method of installing a "TSR" routine. It is intended to supersede INT 27.

Input: AH = 31
AL = Binary Exit Code
DX = Size of memory request in paragraphs.

INT 21 Function 32: Internal to MS-DOS

This function is used only by MS-DOS. It's here so you can see that it is used and unavailable for your use.

INT 21 Function 33: Control Break Check

MS-DOS uses this function to check if a Break is pending each time a MS-DOS function is called. Otherwise, the user can wait a long time for a Break to be noticed and processed.

Input: AH = 33
AL = 0 to check the state of BREAK checking
1 to set the state of BREAK checking
DL = 0 to turn it off
1 to turn it on

Output: DL = 0 if Off
1 if On

INT 21 Function 34: Internal to MS-DOS

This function is used only by MS-DOS. It's here so you can see that it is used and unavailable for your use.

INT 21 Function 35: Get Interrupt Vector

This function works with Function 25, which sets vectors.

Input: AH = 35
AL = Interrupt number

Output: ES:BX = Interrupt vector

INT 21 Function 36: Get Free Disk Space

MS-DOS uses this function when it tells you how many free bytes are available on a disk. The smallest piece of the disk that is kept track of is the cluster, so the number of bytes in a cluster multiplied by cluster number gives the total number of bytes available. INT 21 Function 36 returns about the same information as INT 21 Function 1C, except that instead of pointing at the file allocation table (FAT) byte, BX holds the number of free clusters.

Input: AH = 36
DL = Drive Number
0 - Default
1 - A
2 - B, and so on

Output: AX = 0FFF - Drive number is invalid.
Number of sectors/clusters
BX = Number of available clusters
CX = Size of a sector
DX = Number of clusters

The 32–byte block format:	
0,1	Date/Time Format 0 = USA (H:M:S M/D/Y) 1 = Europe (H:M:S D/M/Y) 2 = Japan (H:M:S D:M:Y)
2	Currency symbol ASCII
3	Set to 0
4	Thousands separator ASCII
5	Set to 0
6	Decimal separator ASCII
7	Set to 0
8–31	Used internally, do not use

Fig. G-9. Country-dependent information.

INT 21 Function 37: Internal to MS-DOS

This function is used only by MS-DOS. It's here so you can see that it is used and unavailable for your use.

INT 21 Function 38: Return Country-Dependent Information

This function is valuable if you're writing or modifying international software. See Fig. G-9 for the formats of the various fields.

Input: AH = 38
AL = 0
DS:DX = Address of 32-byte block

Output: Filled-in 32-byte block (See Fig. G-9)

INT 21 Function 39: Create a Subdirectory

The MS-DOS command MKDIR uses this function to create a subdirectory. All you have to do to create a subdirectory is to point DX:DX to a string that has the disk, path, and subdirectory information. For example, use a line in your program like:

```
MK_SUB  DB  'C:\ASM',0
```

A subdirectory ASM will be created. If there's one already there, or some other problem is encountered, an error returns in AH.

Input: AH = 39
DS:DX points to ASCIIZ string with directory name.

Output: Carry Flag = 0 Successful
Carry Flag = 1 AH holds error value
= 3 Path not found
= 5 Access denied

INT 21 Function 3A: Delete a Subdirectory

INT 21 Function 3A is the companion of INT 21 Function 39. The MS-DOS command RMDIR uses this function to remove directories. Point DS:DX to a string with the disk, and path in it. Use a line in your program such as:

```
RM_DIR  DB  'C:\ASM',0
```

As with the MS-DOS command, the subdirectory must be empty before you can remove it. You can use INT 21 Function 41 to delete all the files in it. If you try and delete a subdirectory that still has files, AH will return with a 5.

Input: AH = 3A
DS:DX points to ASCIIZ string with directory name.

Output: Carry Flag = 0 Successful
Carry Flag = 1
AH holds error value
= 3 Path not found
= 5 Access denied

INT 21 Function 3B: Change a Current Directory

INT 21 Function 3B allows you to change the default directory. It's useful when you're searching for files and you're not certain in which subdirectory the file exists. MS-DOS uses this function for the CD command.

Input: AH = 3B
DS:DX points to ASCIIZ string with directory name.

Output: Carry Flag = 0 Successful
Carry Flag = 1
AH holds error value
= 3 Path not found

INT 21 Function 3C: Create a File

INT 21 Function 3C needs a string that gives drive, directories (and any subdirectories), and file name (with any extension). Point DS:DX at the character string. You might have a string definition in your program such as:

```
MY__FILE  DB  'C:\ASM\MACRO/SQRT.ASM',0
```

If that file already exists in that subdirectory, it is set to a 0 length. However, if that file exists and is marked "read only", error 5 returns in AL. If this function works correctly, a 16-bit file handle returns in AX. You can use this word to refer to the file from then on; it's the file handle.

Input: AH = 3C
CX = File attribute
DS:DX pointed to ASCIIZ string with directory name

Output: Carry Flag = 0 Successful
AH = File Handle
Carry Flag = 1
AL holds error value
= 3 Path not found
= 4 Too many files open
= 5 Directory full, or previous read-only file exists

INT 21 Function 3D: Open a File

This function uses the file handle (see INT 21 Function 3C as to how the handle can be created). You don't need to specify if you're opening the file for sequential or random access, or specify a record size. Just give this function an ASCIIZ string with the drive, path name, and a file name. Enter the access code in AL (0, 1, or 2) which specifies how you want to work with the file. Those codes are shown below. If the Carry Flag is set, there was an error, which returns in AL.

Input: AH = 3D
AL = Access code

0 File opened for reading
1 File opened for writing
2 Filed opened for reading and writing
DS:DX pointed to ASCIIZ string with directory name

Output: Carry Flag = 0 Successful
AH = File Handle
Carry Flag = 1
AL holds error value
= 3 Path not found
= 4 Too many files open
= 5 Directory full, or previous read-only file exists

INT 21 Function 3E: Close a File Handle

INT 21 Function 3E needs the file handle loaded into BX. If there was an error during the close, the Carry Flag is set.

Input: AH = 3E
BX = Valid file handle

Output: Carry Flag Set, AL = 6 Invalid file handle

INT 21 Function 3F: Read from a File or Device

This function reads bytes from your file, not records. However many bytes you want to read, you store in CX and this function returns them to whatever location you've specified in DS:DX (but not in the disk transfer area, DTA). AX returns the number of bytes read. Since MS-DOS won't read past the end of the file, check AX to see that you got the full number of bytes expected.

Input: AH = 3F
BX = File handle
CX = Number of bytes to read
DS:DX = Data buffer address

Output: Carry Flag = 0 Successful
AX = Number of bytes read
Carry Flag = 1
AL = 5 Access denied
= 6 Invalid handle

INT 21 Function 40: Write to a File or Device

To use this function, load the number of bytes you want to write into DX. AX returns the number of bytes actually written. If the numbers don't match, you have an error—most likely the disk is full. Note that INT 21 Function 40 does *not* consider a full disk an error. Redirecting output is easy, using file handles. To change output from the screen to the printer, change the handle number from 1 to 4. One caution: If you use the keyboard as an input file, you are limited to 80 bytes, no matter what limit you set.

Input: AH = 40
BX = File handle
CX = Number of bytes to write
DS:DX = Data buffer address

Output: Carry Flag = 0 Successful
AX = Number of bytes written
Carry Flag = 1
AL = 5 Access denied
= 6 Invalid handle

INT 21 Function 41: Delete a File

In this function, you cannot use wildcards in the file names and strings that identify drive, pathname and file name are limited to 63 characters. The string can look like:

```
DEL_FILE  DB    'C:\ASM\FILE.OBJ',0
```

Input: AH = 41
DX:DX = ASCIIZ file name

Output: Carry Flag = 0 Successful
Carry Flag = 1
AL = 2 File not found
= 5 Access denied

INT 21 Function 42: Move Read/Write Pointer

The read/write pointer is your position in a file. You can skip around in the file by moving the pointer.

Input: AH = 42

AL = Method value
0 Read/write pointer moved to CX:DX from the start of file
1 Pointer incremented CX:DX bytes
2 Pointer moved to end-of-file plus offset CX:DX
BX = File handle
CX:DX = Desired offset

Output: Carry Flag = 0
DX:AX = new pointer location
Carry Flag = 1
AL = 1 Illegal function number
= 6 Invalid handle

INT 21 Function 43: Change a File's Attribute

Figure G-8 lists the possible file attributes. To summarize: 0 is normal, 1 is read-only, 2 is hidden, 4 is a system file, 8 is a volume label, 10 a subdirectory, and 20 an archive. Use INT 21 Function 43 to change the attributes when you need to.

Input: AH = 43
AL = 0 File's current attribute returned in CX
1 File attribute changed, CX holds new attribute
DS:DX = ASCIIZ file string

Output: Carry Flag = 0 Successful
Carry Flag = 1
AL = 0, CX returns attribute
= 2 File not found
= 3 Path not found
= 5 Access denied

INT 21 Function 44: Input/Output Control

INT 21 Function 44 is used for I/O Control (IOCTL) when you set up and define your own devices. It has many, many options and cautions in its use. Because of its complexity, we recommend that you study your MS-DOS manual.

INT 21 Function 45: Duplicate a File Handle

Use this function if you want to refer to a file with more than one handle. This service duplicates the handle for you. When you move around in the file using one handle, the duplicate one moves, too.

Input: AH = 45
BX = File handle to duplicate

Output: Carry Flag = 0
AX = New, duplicated handle
Carry Flag = 1
AL = 4 Too many files open
= 6 Invalid file handle

INT 21 Function 46: Force Duplication of a File Handle

If you're locked into a particular file handle, this function can help. Note that handle 2 (standard error output) cannot be redirected and, if you try, your program will crash. The function does not return an error in that case.

Input: AH = 46
BS = File handle to duplicate
CX = Second file handle

Output: Carry Flag = 0 Handles refer to same stream
Carry Flag = 1
AL = 6 Invalid handle

INT 21 Function 47: Get Current Directory on Specified Drive

Note that in this function, the drive letter is *not* returned in the ASCIIZ string, only the directory. It returns the name of the current default directory at a location pointed to by DS:SI. To call INT 21 Function 47, point DS:SI at a 64-byte free region and store the drive number in DL.

Input: AH = 47
DL = Drive number
DS:SI Points to 64-byte buffer

Output: Carry Flag = 0 Successful, ASCIIZ at DS:SI
Carry Flag = 1
AH = 15 Invalid drive specified

INT 21 Function 48: Allocate Memory

When you load a .COM file, MS-DOS gives all memory to it. When you load an .EXE file, this isn't always the case (see program ARRADRV in Chapter 9). You can request more memory in your program by using this function. If you ask for too much, the maximum number you will be allowed returns in BX, the trick is to request a huge number and then use whatever returns in BX as your "real" request.

Input AH = 48
BX = Number of paragraphs requested

Output: Carry Flag = 0 Successful
AX:0000 Memory block address
Carry Flag = 1
AL = 7 Memory control blocks destroyed
AL = 8 Insufficient memory, BX contains max. allowed

INT 21 Function 49: Free Allocated Memory

This function frees memory that was allocated by Function 48. A program that loads and runs another program must first free the memory in which it is to load the second program. As a normal practice, it's not good for memory-resident programs to use these memory allocation functions, since you might just free memory that belongs to another program. MS-DOS would then crash.

Input AH = 49
ES = Segment of block being freed

Output: Carry Flag = 0 Successful
Carry Flag = 1
AL = 7 Memory control blocks destroyed
AL = 9 Incorrect memory block address

INT 21 Function 4A: Set Block

INT 21 Function 4A allows you to expand or shrink memory blocks. If you're expanding, ask for a huge amount, let it come back with an error and the actual maximum allowable in BX. Then issue this again, using BX as your "real" request.

Input AH = 4A
BX = Requested size in paragraphs
ES = Segment of block to modify

Output: Carry Flag = 0 Successful
Carry Flag = 1
AL = 7 Memory blocks destroyed
= 8 Insufficient memory, BX holds max. allowed
= 9 Invalid memory block address

INT 21 Function 4B: Load or Execute a Program (EXEC)

INT 21 Function 4B allows you to load another program and run it. The environment is a set of strings that indicate something about the PC's operating environment. For example, if you set VERIFY On, the environment will hold the string VERIFY + ON. Before loading another program into memory, you must free memory for it (with Function 4A). If you load another program and run it, control returns to the instruction after the INT 21 when the second program finishes.

Input: AH = 4B
AL = 0 Load and execute the program
Parameter block:
Segment address of environment (word)
Address of command to put at PSP + 80 (dword)
Address of default FCB to put at PSP + 5C (dword)
Address of second default FCB to put at PSP + 6C (dword)

AL = Load but create no PSP. Don't run (overlay).
Parameter block:
Segment address to load file at (word)
Relocation factor for image (word)

DS:DX = 3 ASCIIZ string with drive, path name, file name
ES:BX = Parameter Block Address for AL

Output: Carry Flag = 0 Successful
Carry Flag = 1
AL = 1 Invalid function number
= 2 File not found
= 5 Access denied
= 8 Insufficient memory
= 10 Invalid environment
= 11 Invalid format

INT 21 Function 4C: Exit with Return Code

Use INT 21 Function 4C to end your program if you want to communicate with a calling program. A program that was loaded and run can send a return code to the parent program if the parent program uses INT 21 Function 4D. So these two functions can work together.

Input: AH = 4C
AL = Binary return code

INT 21 Function 4D: Get Return Code of Subprocess

The binary return code loaded into AL (before issuing INT 21 Function 4C) can be retrieved with this call in the subprocess program. Also, AH tells you how the subprocess ended (normally, with a Break Error or with Function 31).

Input: AH = 4D

Output: AL = Binary return code from subprocess
AH = 0 if subprocess ended normally
1 if subprocess ended with Break
2 if subprocess ended with a critical device error
3 if subprocess ended with Function 31

INT 21 Function 4E: Find First Matching File

Point DS:DX at an ASCIIZ string that has the drive letter, path name, and wildcards. If MS-DOS finds the file(s), the disk transfer area (DTA) is filled with 43 bytes of information as shown in Fig. G-10.

Since the file name is returned without drive or path name, you'll have to construct your own if you want to do anything with the file.

Input: AH = 4E
CX = Attribute to match
DS:DX = ASCIIZ file string

Disk Transfer Area – First 43 bytes	
0–20	Reserved
21	Found Attribute
22–23	File's Time
24–25	File's Date
26–27	Size – Low word
28–29	Size – High word
30–42	Name and extension of found file in ASCIIZ form

Fig. G-10. DTA information from INT 21 Function 4E. Note that there is no path name or drive returned.

Output: Carry Flag = 0 DTA filled with:
21 reserved bytes
1 byte Found Attribute
2 bytes File's Time
2 bytes File's Date
2 bytes Low Word - Size
2 bytes High Word -Size
13 bytes Name and extension of found file in ASCIIZ form (no pathname)
Carry Flag = 1
AL = 2 No match found
18 No more files

INT 21 Function 4F: Find Next Matching File

Use INT 21 Function 4D before this function. This function finds all subsequent matches to a file name, but only after the first one has been found. The 21 reserved bytes (as shown in Fig. G-10) in the DTA that MS-DOS used contain information that this function requires.

Input: AH = 4F

Output: Carry Flag = 0 DTA filled with information - See Fig. G-10.
Carry Flag = 1
AL = 18 No more files

INT 21 Function 50-53: Internal to MS-DOS

These functions are used only by MS-DOS. They're listed here so you can see that they are used and unavailable for your use.

INT 21 Function 54: Get/Verify State

INT 21 Function 54 check to see if disk writes are being verified or not. If so, AL returns 1. If not, AL returns 0. Verify can be turned on and off with Function 2E.

Input: AH = T54

Output: AL = 0 Verify is Off
1 Verify is On

INT 21 Function 55: Internal to MS-DOS

This function is used only by MS-DOS. It's here so you can see that it is used and unavailable for your use.

INT 21 Function 56: Rename a File

When you use this function, remember that a file can *not* be sent to another drive.

Input:
AH = 56
DS:DX = ASCIIZ file string to be renamed
ES:DI = ASCIIZ file string that holds the new name

Output:
Carry Flag = 0 Successful
Carry Flag = 1
AL = 3 Path not found
= 5 Access denied
= 17 Not the same device

INT 21 Function 57: Get/Set a File's Date and Time

To use this function, the file must already be open. Store the file handle in BX and load AL with a 1 or 0, depending on what you want to do. If you want to set the date and time, store the values in DX and DX first.

Input:
AH = 57
AL = 0 Get Date and Time
AL = 1 Store Time as located in CX
Store Date as located in DX

Time: (2,045 × hours) + (32 × minutes) + (seconds/2)
Date: 512 × (Year – 1980) + (32 × Month number) + Day

Output:
Carry Flag = 0
CX returns Time
DX returns Date
Carry Flag = 1
AL = 1 Invalid function number
= 6 Invalid handle

INT 21 Function 58: Internal to MS-DOS

This function is used only by MS-DOS. It's here so you can see that it is used and unavailable for your use.

INT 21 Function 59: Get Extended Error

This function only works with MS-DOS releases newer than 3.0. When there was an error, this function returns an extended error code and tells you where the error was physically located, plus suggests corrective action. See program EXTERROR in Chapter 5.

Input: AH = 59

INT 21 Function 5A: Create Unique File

This function only works with MS-DOS releases newer than 3.0. This function creates a temporary file and returns a string with the file's name.

INT 21 Function 5B: Create a New File

This function only works with MS-DOS releases newer than 3.0. INT 21 Function 5B will *not* create a file with a name that already exists.

INT 21 Function 5C: Lock/Unlock Access to a File

This function only works with MS-DOS releases newer than 3.0. With a shared file, you can lock a certain number of bytes or a byte range.

INT 21 Function 5E00: Get Machine Name

This function only works with MS-DOS releases newer than 3.0. Note that with this function, you must load the full word into AX. MS-DOS uses the full word to distinguish between functions, such as between Function 5E00 and 5E02. INT 21 5E00 returns an ASCIIZ string filled with the computer's name—a 15-character string that can be set in PC networks.

INT 21 Function 5E02: Set Printer Setup

Note that with this function, you must load the full word into AX. This function only works with MS-DOS releases newer than 3.0.

INT 21 Function 5E03: Get Printer Setup

Note that with this function, you must load the full word into AX. This function only works with MS-DOS releases newer than 3.0.

INT 21 Function 5F02: Get Redirection List Entry

This function only works with MS-DOS releases newer than 3.0. Note that with this function, you must load the full word into AX.

INT 21 Function 5F03: Redirect Device

INT 21 Function 5F03 defines the current directories and redirects printer output in a PC network. Note that with this function, you must load the full word into AX. This function only works with MS-DOS releases newer than 3.0.

INT 21 Function 5F04: Cancel Redirection

This function cancels the action of Function 5F03. Note that with this function, you must load the full word into AX. This function only works with MS-DOS releases newer than 3.0.

INT 21 Function 62: Get PSP

INT 21 Function 62 returns the PSP of the currently executing process. This function only works with MS-DOS releases newer than 3.0.

Interrupt 22: Terminate Address

This interrupt stores the address to which control will be transferred when your program is done. It's recommended that you let MS-DOS functions use this terminate address and not call it yourself.

Interrupt 23: Control Break Exit Address

INT 23 stores the address to which control will be transferred when you type Break.

Interrupt 24: Critical Error Handler

INT 24 holds the address to which control transfers if there is a critical error, such as a seek error. You can intercept the INT 24 handler and install your own handler if you want. If the most significant bit of AH = 0, the error was a disk error; otherwise bit 7 = 1. Error codes are round in the lower four bits of DI and are shown in Fig. G-11. If you execute an IRET, MS-DOS takes an action based on the values in AL.

Interrupt 25: Absolute Disk Read

INT 25 destroys the contents of *all* registers. Also, flags are PUSHed onto the stack because this INT call is returned in current flags. Error type is returned in AH, as shown in Fig. G-12. After you check the current flags, be sure to POP the flags off the stack. The difference between this interrupt and the BIOS interrupts is that, here, you use the logical sector number. MS-DOS calculates the head number, cylinder, number, and so on (that BIOS needs) and passes the information to BIOS, which does the work.

DI – Lower Four Bits:		Meaning
0	0000	Diskette is write protected
1	0001	Unknown unit
2	0010	The requested drive is not ready
3	0011	Unknown Command
4	0100	Cyclic Redundancy Check error in the data
5	0101	Bad request structure length
6	0110	Seek error
7	0111	Media type unknown
8	1000	Sector not found
9	1001	Printer is out of paper
A	1010	Write fault
B	1011	Read fault
C	1100	General failure
D	1101	Not used
E	1110	Not used
F	1111	Invalid disk change

Fig. G-11. Critical Error Handler error codes.

If Carry Flag (CF) = 1, AH =	Meaning
80 10000000	Disk did not respond
40 01000000	Seek failed
20 00100000	Controller failure
10 00010000	Bad Cyclic Redundancy Check
08 00001000	DMA overrun
04 00000100	Sector not found
03 00000011	Write protect error
02 00000010	Address Mark missing
00 00000000	Bad command

Fig. G-12. Absolute disk read error flags.

A logical sector starts from 0 and runs (on a double-sided, nine-sectored diskette) up to:

2 (sides) × 40 (tracks) × 9 (sectors) − 1 = 719

BIOS does not start sectoring at 0, but at 1 (as far as we can see, the only time that counting begins at 1). For that reason, logical sector zero is track 0, head 0, sector 1. This continues until all sectors in the current track, and current head (side) are used. For example, logical sector 8 is track 0, head 0, sector 9. Which means that logical sector 9 is track 0, head 1, sector 1. The values change from right to left, which says that head changes before track does.

Input: AH = 25
AL = Drive number
CX = Number of sectors to read
DX = First logical sector
DS:BX = Buffer address

Output: Carry Flag = 0 Successful
Carry Flag = 1
AH = See Fig. G-12

Interrupt 26: Absolute Disk Write

INT 26 destroys the contents of *all* registers. Also, flags are PUSHed onto the stack because this INT call is returned in current flags. Error type is returned in AH, as shown in Fig. G-12. After you check the current flags, be sure to POP the flags off the stack. The difference between this interrupt and the BIOS interrupts is that, here, you use the logical sector number. MS-DOS calculates the head number, cylinder, number, and so on (that BIOS needs) and passes the information to BIOS, which does the work.

A logical sector starts from 0 and runs (on a double-sided, nine-sectored diskette) up to:

2 (sides) × 40 (tracks) × 9 (sectors) − 1 = 719

BIOS does not start sectoring at 0, but at 1 (as far as we can see, the only time that counting begins at 1). For that reason, logical sector zero is track 0, head 0, sector 1. This continues until all sectors in the current track, and current head (side) are used. For example, logical sector 8 is track 0, head 0, sector 9. Which means that logical sector 9 is track 0, head 1, sector 1. The values change from right to left, which says that head changes before track does.

Input: AH = 25
AL = Drive number
CX = Number of sectors to write
DX = First logical sector
DS:BX = Buffer address

Output: Carry Flag = 0 Successful
Carry Flag = 1
AH = See Fig. G-12

Interrupt 27: Terminate and Stay Resident

INT 27 makes .COM files code memory-resident, but not .EXE files. If you need additional memory space, use INT 21 Function 31. To use INT 27, set DS:DX to the address at which programs may be loaded; that is, set DS:DX to the end of the program you want to keep in memory and ADD 1 to DX.

Interrupts 28–2E: Internal to MS-DOS

These interrupts are used only by MS-DOS. They're here so you can see that they are used and unavailable for your use.

Interrupt 2F: Multiplex Interrupt

INT 2F sets up communication between two process. It can also create queues. This is a complex interrupt and it's recommended that you study your MS-DOS manual carefully before you use it.

Interrupts 30–3F: Internal to MS-DOS

These interrupts are used only by MS-DOS. They're here so you can see that they are used and unavailable for your use.

Interrupts 40–5F: Reserved

These interrupts are reserved for future use only by MS-DOS. They're here so you can see that they *could* be used but you'd better consider them unavailable.

Interrupts 60–67: Reserved for User Software

These are specifically set aside for your use. Your programs can use them without fear of overlapping current MS-DOS implementation.

Interrupts 68–7F: Not Used

To date, these interrupts have not been used by MS-DOS software.

Interrupts 80–85: Reserved by BASIC

BASIC compilers use these interrupts.

Interrupts 86–F0: Used by BASIC Interpreter

The interpreted BASIC uses these interrupts. You can consider them usable only if you *never* use BASIC.

Interrupts F1–FF: Not Used

To date, these interrupts have not been used by MS-DOS software.

Appendix H

Debugging Tools

Debugging tools help you troubleshoot your programs by allowing you to step through the instructions one at a time and by showing you how registers and (sometimes) variables change as your code uses them. The debugger described in this appendix, SYMDEB, happens to be by Microsoft Corporation, but others are available and are as good.

The overview descriptions below are not intended to be an exhaustive account of the package. They are included to show you some of its usefulness and, by extension, other debug packages. Each debug package comes with its own documentation, often with more detail than you really want, so we're not trying to duplicate it. We recommend that you read the documentation for details.

About SYMDEB

SYMDEB is a symbolic debug utility that helps you test executable files. You display and execute program code, set breakpoints that stop the execution at the points you wish, examine and change values in memory, and work with programs that use floating-point emulation conventions used by Microsoft languages. One handy aspect of SYMDEB is that you refer to data and instructions by name rather than address.

In addition to trouble-shooting assembly language, SYMDEB allows you to debug C, Pascal and Fortran programs at the source level as well as at the machine level. This appendix, however, only addresses assembly language aspects of SYMDEB.

```
C> SYMDEB [Options] [Symbol Files] [Executable File] [Arguments]
```

Fig. H-1. SYMDEB command line.

Starting SYMDEB

To start SYMDEB, enter the SYMDEB command line at the MS-DOS command prompt. There are several options you can include on the start line, as shown in Fig. H-1. The *Options* are one or more options as described in the SYMDEB manuals, such as setting a Break key. The *Symbol Files* are names of symbol files, other special-purpose debug aides. The *Executable File* is the name of a binary or executable file to be loaded by SYMDEB. The *Arguments* are parameters you may want to pass to the *Executable File*.

You tell SYMDEB to load an executable program (a program, for instance, with an .EXE extension, which was an output from your link editor) by including the name on the SYMDEB command line, as shown in Fig. H-2.

The *Executable File* is the only required entry on the command line. The example in Fig. H-3 shows the most simple way to get into SYMDEB and begin the debug process. Here, the program GRAPH_IT was used (see Chapter 10 for a complete listing of GRAPH_IT.) SYMDEB comes up and gives you a start-up message and tells you what processor is installed in your system. Finally, it prints the "-" (dash) where you enter SYMDEB commands.

When SYMDEB loads an executable file, it prepares a 256-byte program header in the lowest available segment in memory. It then copies the contents of the file to the free memory immediately following the header. SYMDEB copies the program size (in bytes) to the register pair BX:CX and adjusts the segment and other registers to the initial values defined in the file.

Once you've stepped through your program (a sample is shown in Fig. H-4), SYMDEB prints a termination message. If your program terminates correctly, you'll see "Program Terminated normally (0)." Then another dash prints. To actually quit SYMDEB, type in a "Q" (See a list of SYMDEB Commands in Fig. H-5).

```
C> SYMDEB GRAPH_IT.EXE
```

Fig. H-2. Simple use of SYMDEB.

```
C:\ASM>SYMDEB GRAPH_IT.EXE
Microsoft (R) Symbolic Debug Utility  Version 4.00
Copyright (C) Microsoft Corp 1984, 1985.  All rights reserved.

Processor is [80286]
```

Fig. H-3. SYMDEB start-up message, where GRAPH_IT.EXE is your executable file.

SYMDEB Options

There are five options that can be entered on the SYMDEB command line (see Fig. H-6). Enter any *Options* before the *Executable File* name so that SYMDEB does not interpret them as parameters, as shown in the SYMDEB command line in Fig. H-1. The *Option* designation can be either a slash (/) or dash (-) and the option letter

```
C:\ASM>SYMDEB GET_TIME.EXE
Microsoft (R) Symbolic Debug Utility  Version 4.00
Copyright (C) Microsoft Corp 1984, 1985.  All rights reserved.

Processor is [80286]
-T
AX=1744  BX=0000  CX=00DF  DX=0000  SP=00C8  BP=0000  SI=0000  DI=0000
DS=1727  ES=1727  SS=1737  CS=1744  IP=0002   NV UP EI PL NZ NA PO NC
1744:0002 8ED8          MOV     DS,AX
-T
AX=1744  BX=0000  CX=00DF  DX=0000  SP=00C8  BP=0000  SI=0000  DI=0000
DS=1744  ES=1727  SS=1737  CS=1744  IP=0004   NV UP EI PL NZ NA PO NC
1744:0004 EB01          JMP     0007
-T
AX=1744  BX=0000  CX=00DF  DX=0000  SP=00C8  BP=0000  SI=0000  DI=0000
DS=1744  ES=1727  SS=1737  CS=1744  IP=0007   NV UP EI PL NZ NA PO NC
1744:0007 B42C          MOV     AH,2C                          ;','
-T
AX=2C44  BX=0000  CX=00DF  DX=0000  SP=00C8  BP=0000  SI=0000  DI=0000
DS=1744  ES=1727  SS=1737  CS=1744  IP=0009   NV UP EI PL NZ NA PO NC
1744:0009 CD21          INT     21   ;Get Time
-
```

Fig. H-4. Stepping through a program with SYMDEB.

Command	Command Name	Command	Command Name
?	Display Values, Display Help	H	Hex
!	Shell Escape	I	Input
.	Source Line Display	K	Stack Trace
<{	Redirect Input	L	Load
}>	Redirect Output	M	Move
=~	Redirect Input and Output	N	Name
*	Comment	O	Output
A	Assemble	P	PTrace
BC	Breakpoint Clear	Q	Quit
BD	Breakpoint Disable(s)	R	Register
BE	Breakpoint Enable(s)	S	Search, Set Source Mode
BL	Breakpoint List	T	Trace
BP	Breakpoint Set	U	Unassemble
C	Compare	V	View
D	Dump	W	Write
E	Enter	X	Examine Symbol Map
F	Fill	XO	Open Symbol Map
G	Go	Z	Set Symbol Value

Fig. H-5. SYMDEB commands.

Command	Command Name
/IBM	Enable IBM–Compatible Mode
/K	Enable BREAK Key (SCROLL LOCK)
/N	Enable Non–masked Interrupt
/S	Enable Screen Flip
/"*Commands*"	Designates Start–up Commands

Fig. H-6. SYMDEB command-line options.

can be either upper- or lowercase letters. Because of the way SYMDEB uses dashes, files that contain a dash in the file name must be renamed before use with SYMDEB or SYMDEB interprets the dash as an option designator.

Useful is the /K which enables the Scroll Lock key on IBM and clone computers as an interactive breakpoint key. If the key is enabled, you can usually stop program execution by pressing it. For example, it's very handy when you're caught in an unending loop. The interactive Break does not work in certain situations, such as when interrupts are turned off. Also, if the program is waiting for input, press Ctrl-C rather than Break to interrupt program execution.

Also useful is the /S option, which allows you to flip back and forth between a screen showing the debugger and a screen showing the program being debugged. This feature is great for debugging graphic software (and any other) that continually sends changes to the screen. One note: The /S cannot be used with graphics modes that use more than 32K of memory.

SYMDEB Commands

When you enter SYMDEB commands, use any of the special editing keys. You can also press Ctrl-C to abort execution of a SYMDEB command or press Ctrl-S to suspend execution. Ctrl-C and Ctrl-S can abort or suspend execution of the Go command (G) if the program being debugged is engaged in input or output. If not, the only way to stop execution is with the Break key or if the /K option was used.

At their simplest, SYMDEB commands are one- or two-key commands. Figure H-5 gives a list of the commands and the command names.

The *Command name* is a one- or two-character name and many have parameters which are numbers, symbols, or expressions that represent values or addresses to be used by the command. You can use any combination of upper- and lowercase letters in the command. The number of parameters used with each command depends on the command. If the command takes two or more parameters, they're separated with commas.

An *address* is a combination of two 16-bit values, one which represents a segment address, the other a segment *offset*. When combined, the values specify a unique memory location. A full address has both a segment address and an offset, separated by a colon (:). Discussed below are a few of the more common, useful commands.

Assemble Command

The Assemble command assembles 8086-family (8086, 8087, 8088, 80186, 80287, and 80286-unprotected) instruction mnemonics and places the resulting instruction codes into memory at the specified address. If no address is specified, the assembly starts at the address specified by the current values of the CS and IP registers. One caution: Do not assemble 8087 or 80287 instructions if your system is not equipped with one of these numeric coprocessors. The WAIT instruction, for example, cause your system to hang if you try to execute it without the coprocessor.

The three-line program in Fig. H-7 assembles to a program that outputs a beep. At each line shown in the example, SYMDEB printed the addresses at the left and the actual instructions were typed in.

Breakpoint Commands

SYMDEB uses "sticky" breakpoints and has five commands to govern breakpoint manipulation. Sticky breakpoints stop program execution each time the program reaches the breakpoint address and cause SYMDEB to display the current values of all registers and flags in the Register (R) command format. Sticky breakpoints, unlike breakpoints created by the Go (G) command, remain in the program until removed using the Breakpoint Clear (BC) command, or temporarily disabled using the Breakpoint Disable (BD) command. The format of the Breakpoint commands is shown in Fig. H-8.

SYMDEB allows up to 10 sticky breakpoints (0 through 9). The number specifies which breakpoint is to be created. If no number is specified, the first available breakpoint number is used. The address can be any valid instruction address (that is, the first byte of an instruction opcode).

```
C:\ASM>SYMDEB
Microsoft (R) Symbolic Debug Utility  Version 4.00
Copyright (C) Microsoft Corp 1984, 1985.  All rights reserved.

Processor is [80286]
-A
15AF:0100 MOV   AH,2
15AF:0102 MOV   DL,7
15AF:0104 INT   21h
15AF:0106
-T
AX=0200  BX=0000  CX=0000  DX=0000  SP=E940  BP=0000  SI=0000  DI=0000
DS=15AF  ES=15AF  SS=15AF  CS=15AF  IP=0102   NV UP EI PL NZ NA PO NC
15AF:0102 B207          MOV    DL,07
-T
AX=0200  BX=0000  CX=0000  DX=0007  SP=E940  BP=0000  SI=0000  DI=0000
DS=15AF  ES=15AF  SS=15AF  CS=15AF  IP=0104   NV UP EI PL NZ NA PO NC
15AF:0104 CD21          INT    21  ;Display Character
-
```

Fig. H-7. Example of the Assemble command.

```
BP [Number] Address [Passcount] ["commands"]
```

Examples:

1. Set Breakpoint at Code Segment Address and skip it 16 times (10h)

   ```
   BP CS:0020 10
   ```

2. Clear Breakpoints 0, 2, and 5

   ```
   BC 0 2 5
   ```

3. Temporarily disable Breakpoint 4 (the Breakpoint is not deleted)

   ```
   BD 4
   ```

4. Temporarily disable all Breakpoints

   ```
   BD *
   ```

Fig. H-8. Breakpoint command format and examples.

Dump Commands

There are eight dump commands that allow you to dump ASCII, bytes, words, dwords, short reals, long reals, and ten-byte reals. The Dump command displays the contents of memory at the specified address or in the specified range of addresses. Dump uses the most recent dump command to dump data. For example, if you dump words (DW) and then dump a short real, Dump displays a word because the previous command was a DW.

Dump displays one or more lines, depending on the address or range specified. Each line displays the address of the first item displayed (See Fig. H-9). The command always displays at least one value. If a range is specified, SYMDEB displays all values in the range. If neither address nor range is specified, SYMDEB dumps memory starting at the byte after the last byte dumped by a previous dump command. If no previous dump command has been used, SYMDEB dumps data from the current location of the Instruction Pointer (IP). If no segment is specified in an initial dump command, SYMDEB uses the DS (data segment pointer) register value as the default segment.

Figure H-9 shows the use of Dump where program bytes in Code Segment address 1744 to 1800 are being dumped in hexadecimal and ASCII text format. The hex values are separated by spaces, except the eighth and ninth values, which are separated by a dash (-). ASCII values are printed without separation. Unprintable ASCII values (lower than 20 or higher than 7E) are displayed as dots (.).

```
D [Address | Range]
```

```
C:\ASM>SYMDEB GRAPH_IT.EXE
Microsoft (R) Symbolic Debug Utility  Version 4.00
Copyright (C) Microsoft Corp 1984, 1985.  All rights reserved.

Processor is [80286]
-DB CS:1744 1800
1744:1740                       0A 00 E8 98-65 C4 7E 06 06 57 E8 AD       ..h.eD~..Wh-
1744:1750  C7 B9 5D 00 E8 8A 65 C4-7E 06 06 B9 57 00 E8 E0   G9].h.eD~..9W.h`
1744:1760  64 E8 4B C8 C4 7E 06 06-57 8A 46 04 32 E4 5F 07   dhKHD~..W.F.2d_.
1744:1770  26 88 45 35 C4 7E 06 26-8A 05 32 E4 3D 07 00 74   &.E5D~.&..2d=..t
1744:1780  03 E9 58 00 C4 06 93 90-8C C2 89 46 FA 89 56 FC   .iX.D....B.Fz.V|
1744:1790  C4 46 FA 8C C2 52 50 33-C0 33 D2 5B 59 E8 AB 6B   DFz.BRP3@3R[Yh+k
1744:17A0  75 03 E9 37 00 C4 7E FA-26 8B 45 33 50 C4 7E 06   u.i7.D~z&.E3PD~.
1744:17B0  58 26 3B 45 33 74 03 E9-10 00 C4 7E FA 06 57 8A   X&;E3t.i..D~z.W.
1744:17C0  46 04 32 E4 5F 07 26 88-45 35 C4 7E FA 26 C4 45   F.2d_.&.E5D~z&DE
1744:17D0  4E 8C C2 89 46 FA 89 56-FC E9 B4 FF E9 00 00 8B   N.B.Fz.V|i4.i...
1744:17E0  E5 5D C2 06 00 55 8B EC-55 E9 00 00 83 EC 0E B8   e]B..U.lUi...l.8
1744:17F0  01 00 A2 C7 90 C4 7E 14-06 57 C4 7E EC 26 8A 05   .."G.D~..WD~l&..
1744:1800  32                                                2
-
```

Fig. H-9. Dump format and example.

One word of warning here: If you do a dump (or display) of memory and let the full eight lines of hex and ASCII print, the display shows the bytes as they are stored in memory. However, if you dump a byte, SYMDEB "helps" you and swaps how they're displayed (as if they're in a register). The differences are shown in Fig. H-10.

Go Command

The Go (G) command passes execution control to the program. The format is G [= *Start*][*Break*], where *Start* and *Break* are addresses expressed in hex. Control begins with the *Start* address and continues to the end of the program or until SYMDEB encounters the optional *Break* address. If no *Start* is specified, Go passes execution control to the address specified by the current values of the CS and IP registers. The equal sign (=) indicates that the value is a *Start* address. Any values specified without the equal sign are assumed to be *Break* addresses.

If you specify a *Break* address on which SYMDEB is to stop and display registers, you must use an instruction address; that is, the address must contain the first byte of an instruction opcode. That's easy. Just enter the address at the left of your assembled listing. Up to 10 addresses can be entered at any one time; if you enter more, SYMDEB displays an error message. You can enter the addresses in any order and SYMDEB sorts them. When your program reaches a breakpoint, SYMDEB displays the current values of all registers and flags. It also displays the next address to be executed.

```
C:\ASM>SYMDEB
Microsoft (R) Symbolic Debug Utility  Version 4.00
Copyright (C) Microsoft Corp 1984, 1985.  All rights reserved.

Processor is [80286]
-D 40:10
0040:0010  71 84 E0 80 02 00 00 40-00 00 1E 00 1E 00 0D 1C  q.`....@........
0040:0020  53 1F 59 15 4D 32 44 20-45 12 42 30 0D 1C 44 20  S.Y.M2D E.BO..D
0040:0030  20 39 34 05 30 0B 3A 27-31 02 30 0B 0D 1C 03 00   94.0.:'1.0.....
0040:0040  5E 00 08 03 00 4C 01 05-02 07 50 00 00 40 00 00  ^....L....P..@..
0040:0050  00 0B 00 00 00 00 00 00-00 00 00 00 00 00 00 00  ................
0040:0060  0C 0B 00 B4 03 29 30 03-00 00 C8 04 F7 43 12 00  ...4.)0...H.wC..
0040:0070  00 00 00 00 00 01 00 00-14 14 14 14 01 01 01 01  ................
0040:0080  1E 00 3E 00 18 00 00 00-00 00 00 88 00 00 00 44  ..>............D
-D 40:10 11
0040:0010  71 84                                            q.
-DW 40:10 11
0040:0010  8471
-Q

C:\ASM>
```

Fig. H-10. Differences in SYMDEB dump output.

Quit Command

The Quit (Q) command terminates SYMDEB execution and returns control to MS-DOS. This is the way to terminate the debug run.

Register Command

The Register (R) command displays the contents of the central processing unit (CPU) registers and allows the contents to be changed to new values. The R command and examples are shown in Fig. H-11. If no register name is specified, the command displays all registers, flags, and the instruction at the address pointed to by the current CS and IP register values, which is the next instruction in the instruction stream.

In Fig. H-11, the first "R" command displays the registers, the address of the next instruction and the instruction itself. The next example shows how you'd work with a particular register you're interested in, perhaps the AX register. If you wish to explore what would happen if AX contained another value (you're not certain which you should use), use "R" and the register name and press Enter. SYMDEB asks for input. In the example, the hex value 0200 was entered and SYMDEB stored that value in AX, as the next "R" shows. The run was ended with a "Q" command.

R [Register [=Value]]

```
C:\ASM>SYMDEB GRAPH_IT.EXE
Microsoft (R) Symbolic Debug Utility  Version 4.00
Copyright (C) Microsoft Corp 1984, 1985.  All rights reserved.

Processor is [80286]
-R
AX=0000  BX=0000  CX=028D  DX=0000  SP=00C8  BP=0000  SI=0000  DI=0000
DS=1727  ES=1727  SS=1737  CS=1744  IP=0000   NV UP EI PL NZ NA PO NC
1744:0000 8CC8            MOV     AX,CS
-R AX
AX 0000
:0200
-R
AX=0200  BX=0000  CX=028D  DX=0000  SP=00C8  BP=0000  SI=0000  DI=0000
DS=1727  ES=1727  SS=1737  CS=1744  IP=0000   NV UP EI PL NZ NA PO NC
1744:0000 8CC8            MOV     AX,CS
-Q

C:\ASM>
```

Fig. H-11. Register command format and examples.

Trace Command

This command allows you to specify a trace (by either entering a start address or allowing SYMDEB to start where the CS and IP registers indicate). You can also specify how many instructions Trace is to go through. Figure H-12 shows the Trace format and two examples. In the first, three instructions were traced at once, each printing their register contents. Then a single T was entered and one additional instruction was traced. An entry of "Q" ended the run. SYMDEB prints the registers in the R command format.

Use Trace if you want to trace through calls and interrupts. If you want to execute interrupts or calls without displaying them, use the Ptrace (P) command instead. Both Trace and Ptrace commands execute MS-DOS function calls (e.g., INT 21) without tracing through them.

Unassemble Command

The Unassemble (U) command displays the instructions and/or statements of

```
T [=Start address] [Count]
```

```
C:\ASM>SYMDEB GRAPH_IT.EXE
Microsoft (R) Symbolic Debug Utility  Version 4.00
Copyright (C) Microsoft Corp 1984, 1985.  All rights reserved.

Processor is [80286]
-T 3
AX=1741  BX=0000  CX=028D  DX=0000  SP=00C8  BP=0000  SI=0000  DI=0000
DS=1724  ES=1724  SS=1734  CS=1741  IP=0002   NV UP EI PL NZ NA PO NC
1741:0002 8ED8           MOV    DS,AX
AX=1741  BX=0000  CX=028D  DX=0000  SP=00C8  BP=0000  SI=0000  DI=0000
DS=1741  ES=1724  SS=1734  CS=1741  IP=0004   NV UP EI PL NZ NA PO NC
1741:0004 EB3C           JMP    0042
AX=1741  BX=0000  CX=028D  DX=0000  SP=00C8  BP=0000  SI=0000  DI=0000
DS=1741  ES=1724  SS=1734  CS=1741  IP=0042   NV UP EI PL NZ NA PO NC
1741:0042 B40F           MOV    AH,0F
-T
AX=0F41  BX=0000  CX=028D  DX=0000  SP=00C8  BP=0000  SI=0000  DI=0000
DS=1741  ES=1724  SS=1734  CS=1741  IP=0044   NV UP EI PL NZ NA PO NC
1741:0044 CD10           INT    10
-Q

C:\ASM>
```

Fig. H-12. Trace format and example.

the program being debugged, or the MS-DOS code as Fig. H-14 shows how to unassemble INT 10. The display format depends on the current display mode set by the Set Source Mode (S) command, and on whether the program was developed with a high-level language. Assembly language programs are translated from memory bytes.

Unassemble has one parameter, a range. If you specify *Range,* Unassemble displays instructions generated from code within the specified range. If you don't specify a *Range,* SYMDEB displays the instructions generated from the first eight lines of code at the current Unassemble address. The current Unassemble address is the address of the first byte (line) after the last byte (line) displayed by any previous Unassemble command.

SYMDEB displays both the hex and ASCII value of 8-bit immediate operands. The hex value is shown as part of the instruction, while the ASCII value is shown as a comment (following a semicolon) on the same display. Protected-mode 80286 mnemonics cannot be displayed.

In the example in Fig. H-13, we're interested in INT 10. Each INT vector uses 4 bytes in high memory, so we display memory, starting with byte 0. We find INT

```
C:\ASM>SYMDEB
Microsoft (R) Symbolic Debug Utility  Version 4.00
Copyright (C) Microsoft Corp 1984, 1985.  All rights reserved.

Processor is [80286]
-D 0000:0000
0000:0000  E8 4E 2E 01 F0 01 70 00-1B 2C 1E 0E F0 01 70 00  hN..p.p..,..p.p.
0000:0010  F0 01 70 00 54 FF 00 F0-6F EF 00 F0 6F EF 00 F0  p.p.T..poo.poo.p
0000:0020  A5 FE 00 F0 AD 2B 1E 0E-6F EF 00 F0 4F 09 A5 0C  %~.p-+..oo.pO.%.
0000:0030  6F EF 00 F0 BE 01 00 C8-57 EF 00 F0 F0 01 70 00  oo.p>..HWo.pp.p.
0000:0040  B8 0B A5 0C 4D F8 00 F0-41 F8 00 F0 AB 09 70 00  8.%.Mx.pAx.p+.p.
0000:0050  39 E7 00 F0 59 F8 00 F0-2E E8 00 F0 D2 EF 00 F0  9g.pYx.p.h.pRo.p
0000:0060  AD E3 00 F0 DD 0A 70 00-6E FE 00 F0 F2 00 E6 07  -c.p].p.n~.pr.f.
0000:0070  53 FF 00 F0 A4 F0 00 F0-22 05 00 00 00 00 00 00  S..p$p.p".......
-D 0:44
0000:0040              4D F8 00 F0-41 F8 00 F0 AB 09 70 00      Mx.pAx.p+.p.
0000:0050  39 E7 00 F0 59 F8 00 F0-2E E8 00 F0 D2 EF 00 F0  9g.pYx.p.h.pRo.p
0000:0060  AD E3 00 F0 DD 0A 70 00-6E FE 00 F0 F2 00 E6 07  -c.p].p.n~.pr.f.
0000:0070  53 FF 00 F0 A4 F0 00 F0-22 05 00 00 00 00 00 00  S..p$p.p".......
0000:0080  C3 12 2E 01 E4 12 2E 01-8E 09 1E 0E 2B 0A 1E 0E  C...d.......+...
0000:0090  56 09 1E 0E 5B 14 2E 01-9E 14 2E 01 4D 5B 2E 01  V...[.......M[..
0000:00A0  C9 12 2E 01 EF 02 E6 07-C9 12 2E 01 C9 12 2E 01  I...o.f.I...I...
0000:00B0  C9 12 2E 01 C9 12 2E 01-57 02 CD 0B AB 15 2E 01  I...I...W.M.+...
0000:00C0  EA CA 12 2E                                      jJ..
-
```

Fig. H-13. *Locating interrupt addresses in high memory.*

```
C:\ASM>SYMDEB
Microsoft (R) Symbolic Debug Utility  Version 4.00
Copyright (C) Microsoft Corp 1984, 1985.  All rights reserved.

Processor is [80286]
-U F000:F84D
F000:F84D 1E               PUSH   DS
F000:F84E B84000           MOV    AX,0040
F000:F851 8ED8             MOV    DS,AX
F000:F853 A11000           MOV    AX,[0010]
F000:F856 1F               POP    DS
F000:F857 CF               IRET
F000:F858 61               POPA
F000:F859 E91EC0           JMP    B87A
-U
F000:F85C 49               DEC    CX
F000:F85D 6E               OUTSB
F000:F85E 63               DB     63
F000:F85F 2E204177         AND    CS:[BX+DI+77],AL
F000:F863 61               POPA
F000:F864 7264             JB     F8CA
F000:F866 20536F           AND    [BP+DI+6F],DL
F000:F869 66               DB     66
-
```

Fig. H-14. *Unassembling INT 10.*

10 at displacement 44. The second D shows the four bytes of INT 10. We see that the code begins at F000 F84D (Remember that memory shows reverse of what a register would show.)

Next we want to see how INT 10 handles some of its code. So, as shown in Fig. H-14, we display location F000:F84D. Then with succeeding U commands (each of which displays 8 lines of code), we can track as far as we want.

Write Command

Write (W) copies the contents of a specified memory location to a named file, or to a specified logical record on disk. To write a file, set the file name with a Name command (N) and set BX:CX to the number of bytes to be written. If you do not specify an address, Write copies bytes starting from the address CS:100, where CS is the current value of the CS register. If you specify a starting address, Write copies bytes starting at that address.

Do not write data to an absolute disk sector, unless you are *sure* the sector is free. Write can destroy the contents of a file, or even the entire disk if you point it at the wrong place.

Write is useful if you're debugging a file. You can make changes to the program with SYMDEB and then write the new program to a file. When you load the file, the file length, starting address, and the file name will be set correctly for writing. Remember, though, if you use the Go, Ptrace, or Trace commands during debugging (or if you change the BX:CX registers), you must reset each of these conditions before writing the file to disk.

One note: You cannot use Write to write .EXE or .HEX files to disk. There are ways to modify and write them and we recommend that you study your SYMDEB documentation and experiment prior to doing this.

Glossary

access—To make use of a reference; that is, to execute the statement in which the reference is contained.

access byte—In 80386 terms, this is a field in a descriptor that contains protection information and identifies the descriptor's type.

access time—The interval between a request for data or information from the memory unit and its actual availability to the processing unit.

accumulator—A register used to hold sums during arithmetic operations. In 80386 terms, this is another name for the AX register.

address—Information used to identify individual storage locations or words in a memory unit.

address, absolute—The fully defined address by a memory address number.

address decoder—In 80386 terms, this is a circuit that converts the 80386 address into chip-select signals which are sent to the bus control logic.

address decoding—Condensing an address on the bus into a single signal, which then either selects or disables a particular device.

address latch—A circuit that maintains its contents for a specified period of time. Latches are used to maintain the I/O address for the duration of a bus cycle.

address, memory—Every word in memory has a unique address. A word may be defined as a set of bits comprising the largest addressable unit of information in a programmable memory.

address space—The total area accessible to a program.

address translation—In 80386 terms, this is the conversion of a selector and offset into a physical address.

addressability—The characteristic of certain storage devices in which each storage area or location has a unique address. This address is then usable by the programmer to access the information stored at that location.

addressing capacity—The programming addressing range determines how large a program can be written without resorting to special external hardware and internal software techniques.
adjacency—A term used to describe modules that execute one right after the other.
aggregate—A contiguous group of statements, bounded by boundary elements.
algorithm—A strategy or plan or series of steps for the solution of a problem.
aliases—Two or more descriptors referring to the same segment.
alternate returns—A module linkage convention that allows the subordinate to return to a location other than the normal return location.
ALU—See *Arithmetic Logic Unit.*
American Standard Code for Information Interchange (ASCII)—A binary encoding scheme using seven bits to represent characters, numbers, and special symbols. ASCII was originally designed for information interchange among data processing systems, data communication systems and associated equipment.
analog computer—A specialized computer that handles data coming from sensing devices rather than data in digital form. It is usually used in special scientific applications or as a process-control device.
anticipatory loading—An automatic storage management discipline that loads modules into memory before they are invoked, based on knowledge of the hierarchy of modules in the system.
applications software—Programs written to perform particular business functions, such as inventory, payroll, or accounts receivable, as opposed to systems software which operates a computer system.
architecture—An orderly organization of subsystems to satisfy overall system objectives.
Arithmetic Logic Unit (ALU)—A unit that performs all the arithmetic and logic operations in a microprocessor.
ASCII—See *American Standard Code for Information Interchange.*
assembler—A software program that translates assembly language into binary machine language.
assembly language—A symbolic notation for writing machine instructions. The language is at a high enough level to free the programmer from working directly in machine code.
auxiliary storage—A place for the long-term storage of data. Storage of this type usually is on magnetic media, such as diskette, and has the capability of storing millions or even billions of characters. Also known as secondary storage.

balanced systems—Systems that are not input-driven or output-driven. Such systems usually have a deep hierarchy of modules to obtain inputs and to deliver outputs.
bar—A sign that denotes the inverse, or complement, of a function. It is written as a line over the function or value.
base address—In 80386 terms, the physical address of the start of a segment.
base load—A set of modules activated by an unbroken chain of explicit commands.
BASIC—Beginner's All-purpose Symbolic Instruction Code, a programming language with a small repetoire of commands and a simple syntax.
baud—A unit of signaling speed equal to the number of discrete conditions or signal events per second.
BCD—See Binary Coded Decimal.
benchmark testing—The process of actually testing in terms of time, ease of operation, ability to perform the job as described and so on.

binary—A term used to describe the base-two number system.
binary coded decimal (BCD)—A coding scheme in which every decimal digit from 0 to 9 is represented by its equivalent four-bit binary number.
binary search—A method of searching an index in which the system first goes to the middle of the index to see which half of the index could contain the item wanted. Each succeeding test goes to the midpoint of the remaining part of the index that is being searched. The net effect is that a large index can be searched very quickly.
BIOS—Basic Input/Output System. The ROM-resident BIOS provides device level control of the major I/O devices in a microprocessor system unit.
bit—Binary digit, a single binary position that can exist in only one of two states: On (1) or Off (0).
bit field—A contiguous sequence of bits. A bit field may begin at any bit location of any byte and may contain up to 32 bits (in the 80386).
bit string—A contiguous sequence of bits. A bit string may begin at any bit position of any byte and (in the 80386) may contain up to 2^{32} - 1 bits.
black box—A system (or a component) with known inputs, known outputs, and generally a known transform, but with unknown (or irrelevant) contents.
bootstrap—A technique or device designed to bring itself into a desired state by means of its own action, e.g., a machine routine whose first few instructions are sufficient to bring the rest of itself into the computer from an input device.
bottom-up testing—A testing strategy in which bottom-level modules are tested first, and then are integrated into higher-level superordinates. Usually contrasted with top-down testing.
branch—The act of causing control to be shifted to another part of the program.
buffer—Storage elements such as registers or memory locations for the temporary storage of information prior to its use by the intended system, such as a peripheral device.
bus—A collection of signal transmission lines.
bus controller—A component which produces bus commands and other useful signals by monitoring the processor's status pins.
bus cycle—A single transfer of information on the bus.
bus pipelining—A timing trick that allows a device to take more time than a single bus cycle to carry out a bus transaction, without slowing down the bus.
byte—A collection of eight adjacent bits.

cache—A buffer type of high-speed memory that is filled at medium speed from main memory. Cache memory (especially in the 80386) is the fastest portion of the overall memory that stores only the data that the processor may need in the immediate future.
Cathode Ray Tube (CRT)—A display device such as a monochrome monitor.
Central Processing Unit (CPU)—The electronic device that controls all other parts of the computer system.
channel—Circuitry responsible for generating memory references for use in direct memory accessing (DMA).
character—This general term refers to all alphabetic characters, alphabetic punctuation marks, mathematical operators, and the coded representation of such symbols.
clear/reset—This process sets all relevant data to binary zero.
code—A set of unambiguous rules specifying the manner in which data may be represented in a discrete form. Also a computer program or part of a computer program.
coding—The process of writing the computer instructions after procedural design has been

carried out by a programmer, after structural design has been carried out by a designer, and after specifications have been developed by a systems analyst.

common-data environment—A means of describing data such that the data can be accessed by any module in a system.

communications channels—Paths over which data is moved. These paths or links are usually described in terms of their speed and capacity to carry information.

compiler—A software program that translates procedure-oriented or problem-oriented instructions into machine language.

complexity of interface—One of the factors influencing coupling between modules. The complexity of the interface is approximately equal to the number of different items being passed—the more items, the higher the coupling.

computer—A data processor that can perform substantial computation, including numerous arithmetic operations, or logic operations, without intervention by a human operator during the run.

conditioned transfer—A jump out from the current execution sequence with the condition that control eventually will be returned to the execution sequence from which the jump was made; for example, a subroutine call.

conforming—In 80386 terms, a property of a segment that indicates that each procedure in that segment will move outward to the ring of its caller when it is called.

constant—A value that does not change during the execution of a program. Compare with *variable*.

control register—In the 80386, these registers hold data of machine states of a global nature. They are called CR0, CR1, CR2, and CR3. The low-order 15 bits of CR0 are called the Machine Status Word (MSW) for 80286 compatibility with the 80386.

control structure—The structure of a program defined by references which represent transfers of control.

control transfers—In the 80386, transfer of control is done by use of exceptions, interrupts and by the instructions CALL, JMP, INT, IRET, and RET. A "near" transfer goes to a place within the current code segment. "Far" transfers go to other segments.

control unit—The electronic part of the central processing unit (CPU) that, under program direction, coordinates the action of the system hardware.

conversion—Changing from one method to another.

coprocessor—An auxiliary processor that operates in coordination with the CPU, allowing architectural capabilities which, in view of the limitations of contemporary technology, could not otherwise be provided. Coprocessors furnish the hardware to perform functions that would otherwise be performed in software. In addition, they extend the instruction set of the main processor.

counter—A programming device used to control the number of times a process is executed.

coupling—A measure of the strength of interconnection between one module and another.

CRT—See *Cathode Ray Tube.*

Current Privilege Level (CPL)—In the 80386, this is the privilege level of the program which currently is executing. In general, CPL can be determined by examining the lowest 2 bits of the Code Segment (CS) register.

cylinder—A group of disk tracks that are accessed at one time by a single set of read/write heads. A disk pack having 40 tracks on each disk surface would have 40 cylinders.

data—A representation of facts, concepts, or instructions in a formalized manner suitable for communication, interpretation, or processing by humans or automatic means. Also, any representations such as characters to which meaning is, or might be assigned.

database—An integrated source of data that is accessed by many users (or often by one user), and that is controlled by a database management system.

database management system (DBMS)—A package of programs designed to operate internally with a collection of computer-stored files.

data conversion—The act of changing data from one form to another.

data-coupling—A form of coupling caused by an intermodule connection that provides output from one module and that serves as input to another module.

data field—The column or consecutive columns used to store a particular piece of information.

data file—A collection of data records usually organized on a logical basis.

data item—The smallest accessible element in a database.

data record—A collection of data fields pertaining to a particular subject.

data-structure design—A type of design strategy that derives a structural design from consideration of the structure of data sets associated with the problem.

debug registers—In the 80386, there are six programmer-accessible registers: DR0–DR3 and DR6 and DR7. DR0–DR3 specify the four linear breakpoints. DR4 and DR5 are reserved by Intel for future implementation. DR6 displays the current state of the breakpoints, and DR7 is used to set the breakpoints.

debugger—A program that helps a programmer locate the source of problems found during run-time testing of a program.

debugging—The act of removing errors or bugs from a computer program.

decoupling—Any systematic method or technique by which modules can be made more independent.

descriptor—In the 80386, a descriptor is an 8-byte quantity specifying an independently protected object. The descriptor for an object specifies the object's base address or the address of its entry point, in addition to protection information.

Descriptor Privilege Level (DPL)—In the 80386, the DPL is a field in a descriptor that indicates how protected the descriptor is. The DPL is the least privileged level at which a task may access a particular descriptor and access the segment associated with that descriptor.

design principles—Very broad principles that generally work in the sense that they favor increasing quality for decreased development cost.

device driver—A program that transforms I/O requests made in a standard, device-independent fashion into the operations necessary to make a specific piece of hardware fulfill that request.

device monitor—A mechanism that allows processes to track and/or modify device data streams.

digital computer—A general-purpose computer that handles data in numerical or digital form.

DIP—Dual in-line package, a widely used container for an integrated circuit. DIP pins are usually in two parallel rows, are spaced on 1/10 inch intervals, and come in different configurations ranging from a 14-pin assembly to a 40-pin configuration.

direct addressing—Specifying a memory location by an address embedded in an instruction.

direct memory addressing (DMA)—This is a technique for transferring data in or out of memory without disturbing the program being executed by the processing unit.

disjoint LDT space—The LDT selectors reserved for memory objects that are shared or that may be shared among processes.

disk storage—A magnetic storage device that closely resembles a phonograph record. However, the tracks of data are in concentric rings instead of a single spiral that a phonograph record has.

diskette—Small, plastic disk platters used as auxiliary storage on many small computer systems.

displacement—In the 80386, this is a 16-bit value specified in an instruction and used for computing address offsets.

DMA—See *direct memory addressing.*

documentation—The sum total of the forms, flow charts, program listings, and so on, associated with a computer program.

driver—A primitive simulation of a superordinate module and used in the bottom-up testing of a subordinate module.

dump—Recording the system's memory contents on an external medium, such as magnetic tape or printer.

dynamic recursion—A form of recursion that exists wherever a module is shared by two or more tasks that can be among active jobs at the same time. For example, it is used by routines handling different interrupts.

E notation—Also known as scientific notation, E notation is a format for the representation of numbers that are larger than six digits. The notation consists of two parts: a mantissa and an exponent.

EBCDIC—Extended Binary Coded Decimal Interchange Code.

editing—As used by a programmer, editing instructions allow the programmer to add, replace and otherwise modify code. As done by a computer, editing allows human to modify storage.

Effective Privilege Level (EPL)—In the 80386, the EPL is the least privilege of the RPL and DPL.

EIP—See *Instruction Pointer.*

emulation—The act of executing a program written for one computer on a different computer.

encapsulation—The principle of hiding the internal implementation of a program, function, or service so that its clients can tell what it does but not how it does it.

ESC (escape) instruction—An instruction having an ESC opcode. Escape instructions are executed by the numeric (or mathematic) coprocessor, in concert with the main processor.

exception—A condition when an instruction violates the rules of normal operation. An exception generally causes an interrupt.

exclusion—A strategy for designing generalized systems in which the designer examines as many applications as possible, but excludes those aspects that make the application special or unique.

expand down—A property of a segment that causes the processor to check that, in all accesses to that segment, offsets are greater than the segment's limits.This is used for stack segments.

expand up—A property of a segment that causes the processor to check that all accesses to that segment are no greater than the segment's limit. Generally, all segments other than stack segments have this property.

exponent—The rightmost part of a number that has been converted into E notation. This position tells the power of 10 to which the original number had to be raised in order to generate a correct mantissa.

far pointer—In the 80386, a 48-bit logical address of two components: a 16-bit segment selector and a 32-bit offset.

feasibility study—A study, normally conducted at the beginning of a systems development project, to determine the likelihood that a system can, in fact, be built within the constraints of time, manpower, and budget.

field—One or more contiguous bits which represent a piece of a larger item of data.

file handle—A binary value that represents an open file, used in all file I/O calls.

firmware—Memory chips with the software programs already built in.

fixed-point arithmetic—Operations on numbers without decimal points.

flag—A field in the flags register. A flag indicates the status of a previously executed instruction or controls the operation of the processor.

flag bit—A single bit that indicates one of two mutually exclusive conditions or states.

flat memory organization—In the 80386, an address space that consists of a single array of up to 4 gigabytes. The 80386 maps the 4-gigabyte flat space onto the physical address space by address translation mechanisms.

flexibility—A measure of the degree to which a system, as is, can be used in a variety of ways.

floppy disk—See *diskette.*

flow charting—A representation of a data processing activity by the use of special graphic symbols.

font—A full assortment of one size and style of printing type.

function—In programming, a function is a prebuilt series of instructions that can be used or called by means of a single word or term. A typical function is SQRT to do square root.

function key—A specific key on a keyboard which, when operated, causes a receiving device to perform a certain mechanical function so that a message will be received in proper form. Also keys on keyboards which are used to query the system or have it perform certain operations.

function key, programmable—By changing the keyboard handling routine, the user can change the function of any key or symbol that will be displayed on the screen.

functional requirements—A precise description of the requirements of a computer system. They include a statement of the inputs to be supplied by the user, the outputs desired by the user, the algorithms involved in any computations desired by the user, and a description of such physical constraints as response time, volumes, and so on.

gate—The simplest logic circuit. In the 80386, there are four types of gates: a call gate, a trap gate, an interrupt gate, and a task gate.

GDT—See *Global Descriptor Table.*

GDTR—See *Global Descriptor Table Register.*

general register—In the 80386, one of the 16-bit registers: AX, BX, CX, or DX.

generality—A measure of the degree to which a system exhibits the properties of a general-purpose system.

generation—A differentiation of the ages to which computer equipment belongs. Considerable controversy exists as to what generation we are currently in. Generally, it is agreed that we are in the last of a fourth generation and entering a fifth.

giga—A prefix meaning one billion (10^9). Also, the power of 2 closest to 1 billion, 2^{30} = 1,073,741,824. This latter description is used when referring to computer memory (gigabyte, gigabit, and so on).

GIGO—A term standing for "garbage-in, garbage-out." It simply means that if incorrect data is fed into a computer, incorrect answers result.

giveaway shared memory—A shared memory mechanism in which a process that already has access to the segment can grant access to another process. Processes cannot obtain access for themselves; access must be granted by another process that already has access.

Global Descriptor Table (GDT)—In the 80386, a table in memory that contains descriptors for segments that are shared by all tasks.

Global Descriptor Table Register (GDTR)—In the 80386, this register holds the 32-bit linear base address and the 16-bit limit of the Global Descriptor Table.

graphic display—A communications terminal linked to a computer that displays data in shapes and drawings, usually a CRT.

graphics—Symbols produced by a process such as handwriting or printing, synonymous with graphic symbol.

hardware—The physical parts of a computer system, usually a printer, video screen device, circuit chips, and so on.

hashing routine—A mathematical formula that is applied to a key field to determine where the record is stored.

heuristic—A specific rule of thumb that usually works but is not guaranteed.

hexadecimal—A base-16 number system, most often called hex. The hex digits are 0, 1, 2, 3, 4, 5, 6, 7, 8, 9, A (=10), B (=11), C (=12), D (=13), E (=14), and F (=15).

high-order position—The leftmost position in a string of characters.

Hollerith card—The name given to the punched-card developed by Dr. Herman Hollerith. It is also commonly known as an IBM card.

identifier—The name, address, label, or distinguishing index of an object in a program.

IDT—See *Interrupt Descriptor Table.*

IDTR—See *Interrupt Descriptor Table Register.*

immediate operand—In the 80386, a constant contained in an instruction and used as an operand.

impact printer—Any printing mechanism that employs some hitting or striking mechanism to print.

incremental implementation—A testing/implementation strategy for adding a new (potentially error-prone) module to a tested collection of modules, and then testing the new combination.

index—A listing of the data records and the disk areas on which they are stored.

index register—In the 80386, one of the 16-bit registers: SI or DI. Generally, an index register holds an offset into the current data or extra segment.

indirect addressing—Accessing a memory location by first fetching the desired address from some other memory location or register.

initialize—A programming term that refers to the act of establishing fixed values in certain areas of memory. Generally, the term refers to all the housekeeping that must be completed before the main part of the program can be executed.

input—The general term used to describe the act of entering data into a data processing system, or the data being entered.

Input/Output (I/O)—Pertaining to a device or to a channel that may be involved in an input process and, at a different time, in an output process. Also pertaining to a device whose parts can be performing an input process and an output process at the same time.

Instruction Pointer (IP)—A register that contains the offset of the instruction currently being executed. A selector for the segment containing this instruction is stored in the CS register. In the 80386, the EIP (an extended instruction pointer) is a 32-bit register that contains the offset address of the next sequential instruction to be executed. The low-order 16 bits of the EIP are the IP.

instruction register—A register that stores the current instruction being executed.

instruction set—The set of all machine-language instructions which can be executed by a processor.

interactive program—A program whose function is to obey commands from a user, such as an editor or a spreadsheet program. Programs such as compilers may literally interact by asking for file names and compilation options, but they are considered noninteractive because their function is to compile a source program, not to provide answers to user-entered commands.

interface—A connecting point between two systems.

intermodular connection—A reference from one module to an identifier in a different module.

interpreter—A computer program used to interpret. Also synonymous with interpretive program.

interrupt—To suspend execution of the current program in order to service one or more peripheral devices. Also, a forced call, not appearing explicitly in a program, which is triggered by an exception, by a signal from a device external to the processor, or by a special interrupt instruction.

Interrupt Descriptor Table (IDT)—In the 80386, this is a table in memory which is indexed by interrupt number and which contains gates to the corresponding interrupt handlers.

Interrupt Descriptor Table Register (IDTR)—In the 80386, this register points to a table of entry points for interrupt handlers. The IDTR holds the 32-bit linear base address and the 16-bit limit of the IDT.

interrupt handler—A procedure or task which is called in response to an interrupt.

interrupt module—A module activated by an interrupt.

I/O Permissions Bit Map—The mechanism that allows the 80386 to selectively trap references to specific I/O addresses. The Permissions Bit Map resides in the Task State Segment (TSS). The map is a bit vector and its size and location in the TSS are variable. The 80386 locates the map by means of the I/O Map Base field in the fixed portion of the TSS.

IP—See *Instruction Pointer.*

jump—An instruction that causes a transfer of control from one part of the program to another.

K—Kilo, a prefix meaning one thousand (10^3). Also, the power of 2 closest to 1 thousand, namely $2^{10} = 1024$. This latter definition is used when referring to computer memory (kilobytes).

Kb—Kilobyte, a thousand bytes.

Khz—Kilohertz, a unit of frequency equal to 1000 hertz.

labels—Identifying statements or numbers used to describe locations. Also, a set of symbols used to identify or describe an item, record, message, or file.

LDT—See *Local Descriptor Table.*

LDTR—See *Local Descriptor Table Register.*

lexical—Of or pertaining to the program as written, as it appears in a program listing. Also, the order in which items appear.

light pen—A pen-like device used in interactive graphic units to communicate between the computer and the user.

linear address space—Address space that runs from 0 bytes to the maximum physical address that a processor can address. In the 80386, the linear address space runs up to 4 gigabytes.

local address space—In the 80386, this is the collection of segments accessible through a task's LDT.

Local Descriptor Table (LDT)—A table in memory that contains descriptors for segments which are private to a task.

Local Descriptor Table Register (LDTR)—In the 80386, this register holds the 16-bit selector for the Local Descriptor Table.

localization—A technique of decoupling affected by subdividing the data elements communicated through a common environment into a number of regions common to a smaller number of modules.

lock—In a multiple processor system, this is the signal from one processor which prevents the others from accessing memory. The processor has exclusive use of the memory until it stops sending the lock signal.

logic design—The design of the procedural logic within a single module.

logical address—In the 80386, a logical address consists of a selector and offset. The selector points to some segment's descriptor, which includes a segment's linear base address. The offset tells how far into the segment the required byte is.

logical device—A symbolic name for a device that the user can cause to be mapped to any physical (actual) device.

logical directory—A symbolic name for a directory that the user can cause to be mapped to any actual drive and directory.

low-order position—The rightmost position in a string of characters.

low priority category—A classification of processes that consists of processes that get CPU time only when no other thread in the other categories needs it. This category is lower in priority than the general priority category.

M—Mega is 1 million (10^6). Also, the power of 2 that is closest to 1 million, 2^{20} = 1,048,576. This latter definition is used when referring to computer memories (megabyte).

macro—A module whose body is effectively copied in-line during translation (compilation or assembly) as a result of being invoked by name.

machine cycle—A set period of time in which the computer can perform a specific machine operation.

machine language—A language that is used directly by a machine. Also, another term for computer instruction code. At this level, instructions are usually in the form of a string of digits that have particular meaning to the internal circuitry of the computer.

Machine Status Word (MSW)—A register that contains a bit for controlling the mode (real versus virtual) and bits which control the processor's execution of WAIT and ESC instructions. In the 80386, the low-order 15 bits of the Control Register Zero (CR0) are the MSW, for upward compatibility from the 80286.

macro instructions—Those instructions that are so complex that a single command generates several machine-language instructions.

maintainability—The extent to which a system can be easily corrected when errors are discovered during the system's productive lifetime.

mantissa—The leftmost part of a number that has been put into E notation. In the mantissa portion, all numbers are reduced to a single-digit whole number plus a decimal fraction.

mask bit—A bit used to cover up or disable some condition.

masking—A means of examining only certain bits in a word. This is usually done by ANDing the word with a mask containing 1's in the desired bit locations.

matrix printer—An output device that prints each character by means of a specially placed series of dots.

memory address—A value that selects one specific memory location.

memory map—The list of memory locations addressed directly by the computer.

memory-mapped input/output—A technique whereby a peripheral device masquerades as a memory location.

Mhz—Megahertz, a unit of frequency equal to one million hertz.

microprocessor—A central processing unit implemented on a single chip.

microsecond—One-millionth of a second.

millisecond—One-thousandth of a second.

mnemonic—Symbol or symbols used instead of terminology more difficult to remember. Usually a mnemonic has two or three letters.

mode—A method of operation, e.g., the binary mode.

modifiability—The ability of a system to be changed or enhanced to meet the needs of a user during the system's productive lifetime.

module—A contiguous sequence of program statements, bounded by boundary elements, having an aggregate identifier.

monitor—A device that observes and verifies the operation of a data processing system and indicates any specific departure from the norm. Also, a television type display such as a monochrome monitor.

MSW—See *Machine Status Word.*

nano—1 billionth (10^{-9}).

nanosecond—One-billionth of a second.

near pointer—In the 80386, this is a 32-bit logical address. A near pointer is an offset within a segment.

NMI—See *nonmaskable interrupt.*

nonmaskable interrupt (NMI)—A signal to the processor from an external device that indicates that a problem has arisen or is imminent.

not present—In a virtual memory, this describes a segment which is on disk but not in main memory.

null selector—A selector in which all bits are zero (0).

object program—The numeric, machine language output of an assembler.

offset—A quantity specifying the position of a byte within a segment.

opcode—The part of an instruction that specifies the operation to be performed, such as ADD, as opposed to the items upon which the operation is performed.

open system—Hardware or software design that allows third-party additions and upgrades in the field.

operand—Data operated on arithmetically or logically by a processor.

operating system—OS, the collection of programs for operating a computer.

output—Pertaining to a device, process, or channel involved in an output process, or to the data or states involved in an output process.

output-driven system—A system in which the top-level module produces the output of the system in elementary (or raw) form.

overflow—An exception which occurs when a number is too large in absolute value to be represented. Stack overflow is an exception which occurs when too much data is pushed onto a stack.

packaging—The assignment of the modules of a total system into sections handled as distinct physical units for execution on a computer.

packed BCD—A packed byte representation of two decimal digits, each in the range of 0 through 9. One digit is stored in each half-byte. The digit in the high-order half-byte is the most significant.

page—A set of consecutive bytes. In the 80386, pages begin on 4K byte boundaries. Paging divides programs into multiple uniform-sized pages which have no direct relationship to the logical structure of the program.

page fault—In the 80386, if the processor finds one of the two following conditions, it issues an Interrupt 14: (1) if the current procedure does not have enough privilege to access the indicated page; or (2) if the page-table entry or page-directory that is needed for the address translation has a zero in its P (present) bit. That is, the page is not currently loaded from auxiliary storage.

page frame—A 4K unit of contiguous addresses of a physical memory. The page frame address specifies the physical starting address of a page. The low-order 12 bits are always zero.

page table—In the 80386, this is an array of 32-bit page specifiers. The table itself is a page, containing pointers to 4 kilobytes of memory, or up to 1K 32-bit entries.

peripheral device—An electronic device connected to the processor. Peripheral devices communicate to the processor by means of input and output instructions, interrupts, or memory-mapped input/output.

personal computer—PC, a small home or business computer complete with a system unit, keyboard, and available with a variety of options such as monochrome monitor and dot matrix printer.

phased implementation—A form of testing/implementation in which several untested modules are combined together at once, and the collection tested for correctness.

physical address—A number transmitted to the memory hardware in order to specify the location of a memory access. Also, the mechanism which actually selects the memory where a required byte is located. In the 80386, the physical address differs from linear address only when paging is in effect.

pointer—An entity containing or having the value of an identifier. In the 80386, this also is an address which is used by software and consists of a selector and offset. In real mode, pointers are real addresses. In virtual mode, they are virtual addresses.

pointer register—In the 80386, one of the BP or BX registers. Generally, a pointer register holds an offset into the current stack segment.

port—A connection to an input/output (I/O) device which may be used by input and output instructions.

portability—A property of a program representing ease of movement among distinct solution environment.

prefix—A byte preceding the opcode of an instruction. It specifies that the instruction should be repeated, or locked, or that an alternate segment should be used.

priority—This is a precedence relationship applied to simultaneous occurrences.

privilege level—A number in a predetermined range that indicates the degree of protection or degree of privilege.

processing element—Any part of the task performed by a module—not only the processing accomplished by statements executed within that module, but also that which results from calls on subroutines.

program—A system composed of precise, ordered statements and aggregate. Also, a series of code designed to achieve a certain result.

program counter—A register in a processor that stores the address of the next instruction to be executed.

Program Status Word (PSW)—A special register used to keep track of the address of the next instruction to be executed; also, often other status flags are stored in the PSW.

programmer—An informal term used to describe the person who designs and writes the programming instructions to implement a module. Often, the programmer is also responsible for the structural design of the system.

protected virtual address mode—A mode of operation in which the processor offers multitasking, advanced protection facilities, and virtual memory.

PSW—See *Program Status Word.*

read/write head—A magnetic coil device that is capable of magnetizing or detecting magnetism on a tiny spot on the surface of a magnetic storage device.

real address—In the 80386, this is an address that consists of a selector and offset in real address mode.

real address mode—In the 80386, this is a mode of operation in which the processor closely mimics the behavior of a "lower-level" chip in the same chip family. For example, the 80386 mimics an 8086.

recursion—The act of invoking a module as a subroutine of itself.

re-entrant—A module is re-entrant if it can be activated correctly at any time, whether or not it has been suspended by a conditioned transfer or return.

register—Fast, temporary-storage locations, usually in the processor itself.

reliability—A measure of the quality of a program or system, sometimes expressed as mean time between failure (MTBF).

Requested Privilege Level (RPL)—In the 80386, this is a field in a selector which indicates the degree of "trust" or privilege a program has in the selector. RPL is determined by the least two significant bits of a selector.

RPL—See *Requested Privilege Level.*

scan code—The first byte of a two-byte extended ASCII code sent to a system, to indicate that the next byte is from the extended ASCII character set. The second byte is actually the character.

scatter read—Reading a block of data into noncontiguous locations in memory.

scope of control—The scope of control of a module consists of the module itself and all of its subordinates.

security kernel—That part of an operating system devoted to protection and security.

segment—A region of memory, in a range of 1 byte to the maximum that can be handled by the processor. Also, units of contiguous address space.

segment descriptor table—A memory array of 8-byte entries that contain descriptors. An 80386 descriptor table may contain up to 8192 descriptors.

segment register—In the 80386, one of the registers CS, DS, ES, or SS.

segmented memory organization—An address space that consists of up to 16,383 linear address spaces up to 4 gigabytes each. The total space, as viewed by a program in the 80386, can be as large as 2^{46} bytes (64 terabytes).

selector—In the 80386, this is a quantity that specifies a segment.

semaphore—A software flag or signal used to coordinate the activities of two or more threads, commonly used to protect a critical section.

serial printers—Devices that print one character at a time, such as a typewriter.

shared memory—A memory segment that can be accessed simultaneously by more than one process.

signals—Notification mechanisms implemented in software that operate in a fashion analogous to hardware interrupts.

single stepping—Executing a program one instruction at a time and pausing after each instruction. This is a means by which programmers determine the effect of a line of code.

software—The computer programs, procedures, rules, and possibly associated documentation concerned with the operation of a data processing system.

software reliability—A measure of the quality of a program or system, sometimes expressed as mean time between failures (MTBF).

source program—The original program submitted to the computer for translation or compiling.

stack—A buffer whose information is generally accessed in a last-in-first-out (LIFO) manner.

stack pointer—A register that stores the memory address of the top (last-in) element of a stack in memory.

statement—A line, sentence, or other similar well-defined construct of a programming language that defines, describes, or directs one step or part of the problem, or part of the solution of the problem.

string—A contiguous sequence of bytes, words, or double words. In the 80386, a string may contain from zero bytes through $2^{32} - 1$ bytes (or 4 gigabytes).

structural design—The design of the structure of a system, the specification of the pieces and the interconnection between the pieces.

structured design—A set of guidelines and techniques that assists a systems designer in determining which modules, interconnection in which way, will best solve a well-stated problem.

structured programming—A disciplined programming technique that ensures a single entry point and a single exit point from every processing module.

subroutine—A module activated at execution time by a conditioned transfer.

swapping—Moving a segment from disk to memory (swapping in) or from memory to disk (swapping out).

systems analyst—An informal term for a person whose job it is to analyze the user's needs, and to then derive the functional requirements of a system.

system clock—The fundamental time signal in a computer. The system clock runs at twice the frequency of the 80386.

task—A defined function that is unique within the computer.
task dispatching—Selecting a task which is not currently running and running it. This includes saving the status of the currently running task in its TSS.
Task Register (TR)—In the 80386, this register points to the information needed by the processor to define the current task.
Task State Segment (TSS)—In the 80386, a TSS is a segment which holds the contents of a task's registers when the processor is executing another task.
task switch—Switching from one task to another.
terminal failure—A software error that causes a system to completely stop functioning.
test registers—In the 80386, registers TR6 and TR7 are used to control testing of the CAM (Content Addressable Memory) in the Translation Lookaside Buffer (TLB).
testing—A process of demonstrating that a system carries out its functions as specified.
text—In ASCII and data communications, a sequence of characters treated as an entity.
text editing—The general term that covers any additions, changes, or deletions made to electronic stored material.
TLB—See *Translation Lookaside Buffer.*
top-down design—A design strategy in which the major functions of a system are identified, and their implementation expressed in terms of lower-level primitives. The design process is then repeated on the primitives until the designer has identified primitives of a sufficiently low level that their implementation can be expressed in terms of available program statements.
top-down testing—A testing/implementation strategy in which high-level modules are tested before low-level modules.
TR—See *Task Register.*
track—In reference to magnetic disk the term refers to the concentric rings on the disk surface on which data are recorded.
transaction—Any element of data, control, signal, event or change of state which causes, triggers, or initiates some action or sequence of actions.
transfer rate—In reference to magnetic tape or disk, this term indicates how much data can be moved from auxiliary storage to memory per second.
Translation Lookaside Buffer (TLB)—In the 80386, the TLB is a cache used for translating linear addresses to physical addresses. The TLB is a four-way, set-associative memory. The TLB testing mechanism is unique to the 80386, and may not be implemented in the same way in future Intel processors.
TSS—See *Task State Segment.*

unconditional transfer—A transfer of control from one module to another with no tacit condition of return.
underflow—A numeric underflow is an exception which occurs when a number is too small in absolute value to be represented as a normalized floating-point number. Stack underflow is an exception which occurs when an instruction attempts to *pop* more data off the stack than is currently on the stack.
unpacked BCD—A representation for integers in which each decimal digit is represented by 4 bits, and each byte contains only a single decimal digit.

user—A term describing the person, persons, or organizations that expects to benefit from the development of a computer hardware or software system.

variable—As opposed to a constant, a variable is a value that does change during the execution of a program.

vectored interrupt—A technique of interrupt processing in which each interrupt specifies the address of the first instruction of its service routine.

video—A computer display shown or displayed on a cathode ray tube monitor or display.

virtual address—An address that consists of selector and offset in protected virtual address mode.

virtual memory—A technique for running programs which are larger than the available physical memory. Pieces of the program are stored on disk and are moved into memory only as necessary. This movement is automatically performed by the operating system and is invisible to the program.

virtual mode—See *protected virtual address mode*.

virtual storage—A hardware/software technique that allows the programmer to write programs that are larger than main memory. The system automatically breaks the program into pages and brings the pages into memory when required.

virtualization—The general technique of hiding a complicated actual situation behind a simple, standard interface.

wait state—An extra processor cycle added to the bus cycle in order to allow for slower devices on the bus to respond.

word—A machine-dependent unit of storage that is generally the width of the data bus or internal registers. In the 80386, a word is 32 bits.

word processing—A system comprised of people, procedures, and automated electronic equipment to more effectively produce written communication.

writethrough—An option when a file write operation is performed which specifies that the normal caching mechanism is to be sidestepped and the data to be written through to the disk surface immediately.

zone punch—A punch in the 12, 11, or 0 row of the Hollerith card. The zone punches are usually combined with the digit punches to make alphabetic characters.

Bibliography

Brumm, Penn and Don Brumm, *80386—A Programming and Design Handbook*, TAB BOOKS Inc., Blue Ridge Summit, Pa., 1986.

Crawford, John H. and Patrick P. Gelsinger, *Programming the 80386*, Sybex, San Francisco, Calif., 1987.

Duncan, Ray, ed., *The MS-DOS Encyclopedia*, Microsoft Press, Redmond, Wash., 1988.

Microsoft Corporation, *Microsoft Macro Assembler*, Microsoft Corporation, Redmond, Wash., 1985.

Sedgewick, Robert, *Algorithms*, Addison-Wesley Publishing Company, Menlo Park, Calif., 1983.

Wirth, Niklaus, *Algorithms and Data Structures*, Prentice-Hall, Englewood Cliffs, N.J., 1986.

Yourdon, Edward, *Techniques of Program Structure and Design*, Prentice-Hall, Englewood Cliffs, N.J., 1975.

Index

Edited by Stephen Moore

80386 Assembly Language
A Complete Tutorial and Subroutine Library

If you are intrigued with the possibilities of the programs included in *80386 Assembly Language: A Complete Tutorial and Subroutine Library* (TAB Book No. 3047), you definitely should consider having them on disk. This disk contains not only the source code for all the programs, but also all the object code in easy-to-link LIB form. This software is guaranteed free from manufacturer's defects. (If you have any problems, simply return the disk within 30 days, and we'll send you a new one.) Not only will you save the time and tedium of typing in the code, the disk eliminates the possibility of errors that can prevent the programs from functioning. Interested?

Available at $29.95 on 2 double density or 1 high density disk for 80386-based computers (AT-style bus or PS/2 Micro Channel) running MS-DOS 3.*x* and Microsoft Macro Assembler 5.0 or later. Please include $1.50 per unit ordered for shipping and handling.

I'm interested. Send me:

__________ double density disk set (6665S)
__________ high density disk (6666S)
__________ TAB BOOKS catalog

Check/Money Order enclosed for $29.95 plus $1.50 shipping and handling for each unit ordered.

__________ VISA __________ MasterCard

Account No. ____________________ Expires ____________________

Name ____

Address ____

City ________________ State ________________ Zip __________

Signature ____

Mail To: **TAB BOOKS Inc.**
Blue Ridge Summit, PA 17294-0850

OR CALL TOLL-FREE TODAY: **1-800-233-1128**
IN PENNSYLVANIA AND ALASKA CALL: **717-794-2191.**

(Pa. add 6% sales tax. Orders outside U.S. must be prepaid with international money orders in U.S. dollars.)
*Prices subject to change without notice.

TAB 3047

See page 627 for a Special Companion Diskette Offer.

I'm interested. Send me:

______ double density disk for set (6665S)

______ High density disk (6666S)

______ TAB BOOKS catalog

Charge my credit card for ______ ($29.95 plus $1.50 shipping and handling for each disk ordered).

Check one: ☐ VISA ☐ MasterCard ☐ American Express

Account No. ______ Expires ______

Signature ______

Name ______

Address ______

City ______ State ______ Zip ______

OR CALL TOLL-FREE TODAY: **1-800-233-1128**

IN PENNSYLVANIA AND ALASKA, CALL: **717-794-2191**

*Prices subject to change without notice.

(Pa. residents add 6% sales tax. Orders outside U.S. must be prepaid with international money orders in U.S. dollars.)

TAB 3047

NO POSTAGE
NECESSARY
IF MAILED
IN THE
UNITED STATES

BUSINESS REPLY MAIL

FIRST CLASS PERMIT NO. 9 BLUE RIDGE SUMMIT, PA 17214

POSTAGE WILL BE PAID BY ADDRESSEE

TAB BOOKS Inc.
Blue Ridge Summit, PA 17214-9988

NO POSTAGE
NECESSARY
IF MAILED
IN THE
UNITED STATES

BUSINESS REPLY MAIL

FIRST CLASS PERMIT NO. 9 BLUE RIDGE SUMMIT, PA 17214

POSTAGE WILL BE PAID BY ADDRESSEE

TAB BOOKS Inc.
Blue Ridge Summit, PA 17214-9988